Frommer's
France

FrommerMedia LLC

Published by
FROMMER MEDIA LLC

ISBN 978-1-62887-152-4 (paper), 978-1-62887-153-1 (e-book)

Editorial Director: Pauline Frommer
Editor: Elizabeth Heath
Production Editor: Carol Pogoni
Cartographer: Liz Puhl
Photo Editor: Helen Stallion

For information on our other products or services, see www.frommers.com.

Frommer Media LLC also publishes its books in a variety of electronic formats. Some content that appears in print may not be available in electronic formats.

Manufactured in China

5 4 3 2 1

ABOUT THE AUTHORS

Lily Heise went to Paris as an exchange student in 2000 and fell in love with the country. She has extensive experience in the travel and culture sectors and contributes to various international and local publications, both in print and online. She lives in Montmartre and spends her free time exploring off-beat Paris, in addition to villages and vineyards around the country.

Mary Novakovich is an award-winning travel writer and journalist and a member of the British Guild of Travel Writers. She has been writing extensively about France and her other countries for 15 years for "The Independent," "The Guardian," "Sunday Times Travel Magazine," "The Daily Telegraph," the BBC, "France Magazine," and CNN, among others. She has also written guidebooks for Frommer's, Berlitz and Insight Guides, and is based in Hertfordshire, England.

Tristan Rutherford has been a freelance writer for over a decade. His lucky first assignment took him to Nice and he's been based there ever since. He has visited over 60 countries and written about 20 of them for "The Independent" and the "Sunday New York Times Travel Magazine." Tristan also lectures on travel journalism at London's Central Saint Martins. He lives in Nice, France.

Margie Rynn has been living and writing about France for over 13 years. The author of "Pauline Frommer's Paris," she has also written features for several travel magazines, as well as "Time Out New York" and "Yoga Journal." In a previous New York life, she acted in a Broadway play and performed her own one-woman show. Margie is married to a kind and understanding Frenchman and they have a lovely 11-year-old son. She lives in Paris, France.

Louise Simpson fell in love with all things French as a teenager on holidays to her family home in Dordogne and as a French student at Cambridge University. Since moving to Southern France in 2003, she has authored over 10 print and online travel guides to Southern and Central France and written for the "Financial Times Weekend," "Independent on Sunday," and "Timesonline" in the U.K., as well as Zagat and Google in the US. She also writes a regular food column for "Monaco Life." Louise lives in Nice, France.

Kathryn Tomasetti is US-born and Italian-raised. She writes travel and food features for a variety of publications including "The Guardian" and "The Times." Her library of holiday photos—snapped from as far afield as China, Albania and Chile—have been published by "National Geographic" and "Time Out." Kathryn's favorite places in Provence are the pavement cafes of Avignon and the art-filled city of Arles. She resides in Nice, France.

Victoria Trott is a British freelance travel and food journalist who specializes in France. She is the co-author of "Frommer's Provence." She lives in London.

CONTENTS

THE BEST OF FRANCE

By Tristan Rutherford and Kathryn Tomasetti

France presents visitors with an embarrassment of riches—you may find yourself overwhelmed by all the choices. We've tried to make the task easier by compiling a list of our favorite experiences and discoveries. In the following pages, you'll find the kind of candid travel advice we'd give our closest friends.

FRANCE'S best AUTHENTIC EXPERIENCES

o **Wine Tastings at a Burgundy Vineyard:** Where better to taste a Burgundy wine than in the vineyard where it was made? The average producer in this region manages just 20 acres of vines and many offer the opportunity to sample their nectar on site. Ask at the tourist office for details of visits for individuals—otherwise we recommend booking a trip with a specialist tour guide. See chapter 9.

o **Whiling Away an Afternoon in a Parisian Cafe:** There is something quintessentially Parisian about doing nothing in a public space, especially when that space is a cafe. You can read a book, look out the window, chat with a friend, sip some wine, or simply ponder the mysteries of life. Better still, no one will attempt to dislodge you from your cafe chair, even if you sit there for hours.

o **Breaking the Bank at Monte-Carlo:** The **Casino de Monte-Carlo** has been the most opulent place to have a flutter for over 150 years. Its creation by architect Charles Garnier (of Paris Opera House fame) in 1863 turned the tables for Monaco, transforming a provincial port into a world-class tourist

ABOVE: **An outdoor cafe at Place Colette, Paris**
PREVIOUS PAGE: **Eiffel Tower, Paris**

destination. Expect frescoed ceilings and wealthy, well-dressed clientele from as far afield as China, Russia, and the U.S. See p. 475.

o **Ogling the Pomp of the Pope's Medieval Party Pad:** Those medieval popes knew a thing or two about interior design. Avignon's **Palais des Papes,** or Pope's Palace, is a moneyed medley of Gothic architecture and vast banqueting halls. The Châteauneuf-du-Pape papal vineyards just north of Avignon still produce some of the most noted wine in France. See p. 368.

o **Eating** *Boeuf Bourgignon:* Burgundy is as well known for its gastronomy as its wine. One of its most famous dishes is *boeuf bourgignon,* ideally made with Charolais beef (from the famous white cows which originated in the Charolais area near Mâcon) slow cooked with onions and mushrooms in a regional red wine. See chapter 9.

Fresh bread at a French bakery

o **Buying Your Daily Bread:** That cute little boulangerie just down the street? Depending on where you are, there's likely to be another—or several—a short stroll away. The daily baguette run is a ritual for many French people. Get your coins ready (one euro, give or take 10 centimes) and join the queue. To really fit in, ask for your baguette chewy (*pas trop cuite*), or crusty (*bien cuite*).

o **Shopping at a Market:** Markets are one of the best ways to explore French towns like a local. We recommend the open-air market in **Arles,** one of Provence's most authentic destinations. A colorful line of vendors sells olives, fresh bread, cheese, and local ham underneath the city ramparts, a few blocks from the town's Roman amphitheater. Alternatively, French covered markets are time machines—visiting one is like taking a trip back through the centuries. Bordeaux's vast **Marché des Capucins** offers not just good things to take home, but great things to eat on site from various stands, including Chez Jean-Mi, where you can enjoy oysters straight out of nearby Arcachon Bay. See p. 489. And in the Rhône Valley, local gourmands crowd the covered market of Lyon's **Les Halles** to stock up on high-quality Lyonnaise specialties, from creamed fish *quenelles* to sweet *bugnes*—either round and doughnut-like, or flat and crunchy. See p. 346.

o **Sampling the Best of Chinon's Cellars:** Vines blanket the whole of the Loire, providing an excellent oenological break from castle touring. The area around Chinon is a treasure trove of welcoming vineyards where you can experience winemaking firsthand—and, of course, taste delicious *vins.* See p. 203.

o **Cycling among the Vines** (Rhône Valley): A novel way to tour the Northern Rhône vineyards is by motorized electric bicycle. Sommelier Fabien Louis will explain the vicissitudes of *terroir* as you pedal around the coveted appellations of Hermitage and Crozes-Hermitage. See p. 356.

A couple strolling along the Seine, Paris

o **Shucking Fresh Oysters:** The French adore oysters and there's no better place to get the freshest than in Cancale, Brittany. Today everyone has access to these jewels of the sea—once a favorite of King Louis XIV—perfectly paired with a crisp white wine down by the old port. See chapter 8.

o **Strolling along the Seine:** The lifeblood of the City of Light, the Seine is at the center of Paris's history, which becomes obvious when you stroll along its banks. Just about every major monument can be seen from here, including the **Eiffel Tower, Notre-Dame,** and the **Louvre.** And now that many of Seine's embankments have been restored and improved, promenading along them is a pedestrian delight.

o **Château-hopping through the Loire Valley:** An excursion to the châteaux dotting the valley's rich fields and forests will familiarize you with the French Renaissance's architectural aesthetics and the intrigues of the kings and their courts. Visit the main castles, such as **Chambord** or **Chenonceau,** and then stop in at some lesser-visited ones, like **Chaumont** or **Valençay.** See chapter 6.

o **Touring the Villages along France's Oldest "Wine Road"** (Alsace-Lorraine): More than 60 villages line the famous Alsatian wine road. Enjoy their medieval town squares and half-timbered houses while stopping in at the local vineyards. See chapter 10.

o **Taking a Trip on a Gabarre down the Dordogne River** (Bordeaux & Dordogne): *Gabarres* are traditional flat-bottomed boats that used to ply the shallow Dordogne, taking goods from one town to the next. Today they are used for guided river cruises, offering tourists a unique way to experience this unspoiled waterway. See p. 507.

secret **FRANCE**

o **Cycling in the Countryside:** The country that hosts the Tour de France offers thousands of options for bike trips, all of them ideal for leaving the crowds far behind. You're even welcome to take your bike aboard most trains in

France, free of charge. For cycling through Provence's vineyards and past pretty hilltop villages, check out **Vélo Loisir en Luberon**'s downloadable routes. See p. 376.

o **Hunting for Antiques:** The 18th- and 19th-century French aesthetic was gloriously different from that of England and North America. Many objects bear designs with mythological references to the French experience. France has some 13,000-plus antiques shops throughout the country. Stop where you see the sign antiquaire or brocante.

o **Traveling First Class:** France's TGV rail network is arguably the world's fastest. Yet these trains are not just high-speed. When routes are booked in advance, they're wallet-friendly, too. Throw in decor by Christian Lacroix and PlayStation Portables available to rent, and you're looking at the classiest public transport on the planet. See chapter 15.

o **Cruising France's Rivers:** Floating slowly down one of France's major rivers is a superb way to see hidden corners of the countryside. Most luxury barge cruises offer daily excursions, elegant dinners on deck, and bicycles for solitary exploration. See chapter 15.

o **Reveling in St-Etienne-du-Mont:** One of the prettiest in Paris, this stunning church that sits atop the highest point in the Latin Quarter is often left off the tourist itinerary. A delightful mix of late-Gothic and Renaissance styles, the church has a 16th-century chancel boasting the city's only rood screen, a magnificent work with decorations inspired by the Italian Renaissance. See p. 118.

o **Sipping Tea at the Mosquée de Paris:** A delicious fountain bubbles in the patio of this beautiful mosque tearoom, which serves mint-scented tea and Middle Eastern pastries in lovely mosaic-tiled surroundings. An ideal spot for relaxing after a long day of sightseeing.

Antiques market in Nice

Beach at Roquebrune-Cap-Martin in the French Riviera

o **Going Underground at Touraine's Troglodyte Caves:** Admire art, sample regional wine, and even stay the night underground in the Loire's Touraine region, home to France's largest concentration of Troglodyte caves. See p. 199.

o **Returning to the Time of the Crusades** (Loire): See the history behind the foolhardy Crusades at the 12th-century Abbey of Fontevraud. It's one of the largest medieval monasteries in Europe as well as the final resting place of most of the Plantagenets. See p. 205.

o **Peeking at Crypt Murals** Auxerre (Burgundy): The overused term 'hidden gems' is appropriate to describe Auxerre's two crypt murals because that is exactly what they are. Underneath the remains of the Abbaye Saint-Germain are a series of religious wall murals dating from the 9th century, the oldest so far found in France. Those at the nearby Cathédrale Saint-Etienne go back to the 11th century and are famous for depicting a rare image of Christ on a horse. See p. 282.

o **Discovering Secret Beaches between Monaco and Roquebrune-Cap-Martin** (Riviera): The Riviera's rippling coastal path turns up plenty of hidden surprises. Head east out of Monaco, passing the Monte-Carlo Beach Hotel. The trail then meanders along the Mediterranean shoreline. Aleppo pines and fig trees part to reveal the tiniest turquoise coves. Be sure to pack your swimming suit. See p. 477.

o **Tracking down Art Nouveau** (Lorraine): Nancy is one of Europe's Art Nouveau capitals. Start at the Ecole de Nancy museum located in a period house, then wander the city in search of its many architectural treasures of the era. See p. 322.

o **Tracing the Trenches:** While Normandy usually attracts most visitors interested in war history, the western front of World War I carved its way through Eastern France. Many moving battlefield sites and memorials are located near Verdun. See p. 325.

o **Escaping to an Island:** There are thousands of wild and inhabited islands off Brittany's rugged coastline. You'll be enchanted by the beauty and breathtaking sea views of **Ile de Bréhat** or **Belle-Ile-en-Mer.** See p. 255 and 263.

o **Marveling at France's "Stonehenge"** (Brittany): The seaside resort of Carnac is home to the largest megalithic site in the world. A visit might not answer how these massive stones got turned upright, but it will certainly leave you pondering the mysteries and theories surrounding this curious site. See p. 264.

o **Exploring the Glamorous Château des Millandes** (Dordogne): This splendid Renaissance castle was the former home of singer/dancer Josephine Baker. Learn about her fascinating life and visit rooms furnished as they were when she lived there, then take a stroll in the gardens. See p. 507.

o **Stepping Back into Medical History** (Rhône Valley): Concealed in Bourg-en-Bresse's Hôtel de Dieu hospital, nuns manufactured medicines in this 18th-century apothecary laboratory using ancient alembic distillers, wooden presses, and copper mortars. The adjoining wooden-paneled storeroom and shop are lined with pots—some of which still contain medicine such as licorice pills and even powdered deer antler. See p. 347.

o **Meandering through Traboules in Vieux Lyon** (Rhône Valley): Hidden behind brown-painted doorways lie flower-ringed courtyards and vaulted masonry ceilings. You'll discover many architectural gems on a 2-hour tour around Vieux Lyon's medieval *traboules*—corridors connecting two streets through a building or courtyard. See p. 342.

o **Enjoying a Semi-Private Beach on the Iles de Lérins** (Riviera): The Iles de Lérins may lie a 20-minute ferry ride from Cannes. Yet these two car-free islands attract just a fraction of the visitors. Take a picnic lunch and a good book, and get ready to leave the crowds back on the coast. See p. 427.

o **Rambling the Sentier des Ocres de Roussillon** (Provence): Located in the heart of the Luberon, Roussillon once possessed some of the world's most important ochre quarries. Today this landscape is just as brilliantly hued, and can be explored via a picturesque hiking trail. See p. 377.

o **Going Underground at Grotte de Rouffignac** (Bordeaux & Dordogne): Not as well-known as the other famous prehistorically decorated caves like Lascaux and Font-de-Gaume, it's easier to get tickets here. You'll hop on an electric train that will take you deep into the tunnels, where you will see enigmatic paintings of bison, rhinoceros, and lots of mammoths. See p. 505.

FRANCE'S best FOR FAMILIES

o **Climbing the Heights of Mont-St-Michel** (Normandy): Straddling the tidal flats between Normandy and Brittany, this Gothic marvel is the most spectacular fortress in northern Europe. Said to be protected by the archangel Michael, much of it stands as it did during the 1200s. As of 2014, however, a brand-new pedestrian path connects the visitor center to Mont-St-Michel itself. You can now stroll, bike, or trot (in a horse-drawn carriage) across to the fortress. See chapter 7.

o **Getting Medieval in the Hilltop Town of Les Baux** (Provence): The age-old hilltown of **Les Baux** commands views over hundreds of miles of Provençal countryside. The film-set location, including the hilltop ruins of its "ghost village," plus a volley of great restaurants, have made it a retreat for France's rich and famous. Kids will love its car-free medieval streets and awesome views, not to mention the daily display of a siege engine catapult. See chapter 12.

o **Making the Most of Modern Art in Antibes** (French Riviera): The **Musée Picasso** (Picasso Museum) in Antibes highlights some of the most accessible

Monumental Mont-St-Michel, Normandy

art in France. The Spanish painter set up shop in the atmospheric old quarter of Antibes's Château Grimaldi some 70 years ago. In such relaxed surroundings, children can appreciate the color, vibrancy, and playfulness that made Picasso one of the greats of the 20th century. The far-out sculptures and sunny views of the surrounding coastline will please non-art fans, too. See p. 438.

o **Joining the Cowboys in the Camargue** (Provence): Riding a sturdy Camarguais horse and with a local cowboy to guide you, make your way through the marshes of these beautiful, remote wetlands. Spot pink flamingos and watch the *gardians* with their large felt hats rounding up black bulls bred for the bullrings of the south. If the children don't ride, then slow boats, bicycles, and jeeps make great alternatives. See chapter 12.

o **Staying on a Working Farm** (Bordeaux & Dordogne): At the **Domaine de la Rhonie,** you can not only eat delicious meals and sleep in restored farm buildings, but your kids can also participate in nature workshops (in English), splash in the pool, or play in the game room. They can also watch the owners at work with their geese, sheep, and horses. See p. 509.

o **Sailing along a Canal** (Burgundy): Burgundy has France's largest network of waterways. As well as the navigable rivers of the Yonne, Saône, and Seille, seven canals were built between the 17th and 19th century to link the rivers Seine, Loire, and Rhône. Hire your own boat or take an organized trip passing châteaux and vineyards, going through tunnels, over aqueducts, and up or down staircase locks.

o **Adventuring around the World in Eighty Minutes** Nantes (Brittany): Delve into the magical world of writer Jules Verne at **Les Machines de l'Ile.** In between a small theme park and workshop, young and older spirits get their thrills on the 20,000 Leagues under the Sea carrousel. See p. 270.

o **Getting a Chocolate Education** (Rhône Valley): The trials of finding a museum suitable for children are solved upon discovering the cacao-infused wonders of La Cité du Chocolat. All five senses are used in the interactive exhibits that entertain little ones with the rich experience of chocolate making and tasting. See p. 356.

o **Exploring the Calanques** (Provence): The **Parc National des Calanques** became France's newest national park in 2012. This stunning series of limestone cliffs and tumbling fjords stretch along the coast for some 30km (18 miles) southeast of Marseille. Serious hikers can trek the Calanques' rocky promontories. Families with children can take in the coastline from aboard one of the many tour boats that depart from Marseille's port. See p. 406.

o **Walking through a Real Fairy Tale** (Loire): The whole region of the Loire offers kids the chance to live out their fairy-tale fantasies. Step right into a storybook at the **Château d'Ussé,** the inspiration for "Sleeping Beauty." See p. 203.

o **Remembering Fallen Heroes on Normandy's D-Day Beaches:** On June 6, 1944, the largest armada ever assembled departed on rough seas and in dense fog from southern England. For about a week, the future of the civilized world teetered between the Nazi and Allied armies. Today the entire family can immerse itself in the past with superb interactive exhibits, such as the personal tales detailed at the **Normandy American Visitor Center.** Kids can then run wild on the windswept sands below. See p. 236.

o **Playing in the Jardin des Plantes** (Paris): A splendid place for a picnic, this historic botanical garden is a quiet oasis in the Latin Quarter, where families can relax and tiny travelers can enjoy the playground, hothouses, and green spaces. When playtime is over, everyone can wander over to the small zoo or the adjoining natural-history museum. See p. 116.

o **Stargazing at Cité des Sciences et de l'Industrie** (Paris): Set amid the vast Parc de la Villette, this huge museum of science and industry includes a planetarium, an Imax theater, and even an authentic submarine that kids can climb into. But the biggest draw is the Cité des Enfants, a supremely kid-friendly collection of hands-on exhibits and displays. See p. 114.

The American Cemetery at Colleville-sur-Mer, Normandy

o **Hameau Duboeuf,** Romanèche-Thorins (Burgundy): To the south of Mâcon is the Beaujolais wine area and the "wine hamlet," created by wine merchant Georges Duboeuf, is the place to go for the whole family to learn about this particular drink from its origins to the present day. Kids will love "flying" over the Mâconnais countryside and playing crazy golf, while adults can enjoy a tasting or two. See p. 297.

o **Pioneering à la Francaise,** Ungersheim (Alsace): Enter a rebuilt historic Alsatian hamlet at the Ecomuseum near Colmar. Kids will adore the country-style houses. They may take in a horse-and-cart ride and observe the costumed "villagers" at work. See p. 325.

o **Being a Pirate on the Ramparts,** St-Malo (Brittany): Chase the spirits of *corsairs* along the city walls of St-Malo. This naval city was from where these daring privateers and New World explorer Jacques Cartier set sail. See p. 247.

o **Understanding Cavemen in the Ardèche** (Rhône Valley): This double attraction at Le Grand Site de L'Aven Orgnac fills wet days as the limestone cave is at its most beautiful when it rains. The neighboring archaeological museum re-opened in 2014 with child-friendly exhibits and 3D animations that will leave visitors of all ages with a palpable idea of how prehistoric humans lived. See p. 360.

o **Bicycling in the Dordogne:** The inclines are as gentle as the landscape in this lush countryside, where bikes and helmets can be easily rented and back roads are plentiful. See p. 502.

FRANCE'S best BEACHES

o **Plage de Deauville** (Normandy): Coco Chanel used the chic resort of Deauville to propel herself to stardom and then added greatly to the town's sense of glamour. Revel in the sun-kissed sense of style and nostalgia with a stroll along the elegant Les Planches boardwalk, which skirts the edge of Deauville's silky, sandy, parasol-dotted *plage* for 2km (1¼ miles). See p. 224.

o **Plage de Pampelonne** St-Tropez (French Riviera): Any blonde feels like Brigitte Bardot in sunny St-Tropez. And the scantily clad satyrs and nymphs splashing in the summertime surf at Plage de Pampelonne can perk up the most sluggish libido. The real miracle here is that the charm of this 5km (3-mile) crescent of white sand still manages to impress, despite its celebrity hype and hordes of A-list visitors. See p. 415.

o **Hi-Beach** Nice (French Riviera): A day along the Riviera seaside may be a little different from home: Most beaches here feature private clubs with mattresses, parasols, and chilled champagne on demand. Nice's Hi-Beach certainly offers all of the above. Yet its contemporary design, organic restaurant, and stellar cocktails set it apart from the crowd. See p. 456.

o **Paloma Plage** Cap Ferrat (French Riviera): Tucked into one of Cap Ferrat's sheltered bays, petite Paloma Plage is part chic beach club and part family-friendly stretch of pebbly shoreline. In the afternoon, fragrant Aleppo pines shade much of the beach. Brad and Angelina have been known to stop by for drinks. See p. 463.

o **Plage de Arromanches-les-Bains** (Normandy): This immense beach is dotted with the mammoth, otherworldly remains of Winston, a prefabricated port essential for the D-day landings. At low tide, the sandy expanse is firm

Villefranche-sur-Mer on the Cote d'Azur, French Riviera

(you can push a stroller or cycle along it!) and truly vast, rendering it ever-popular with families. See p. 237.

o **The Beaches of Juan-les-Pins** (French Riviera): In the resort that invented waterskiing, it's little surprise that all the summertime action centers around Juan-les-Pins' golden shores. Spread your towel on central **Plage de Juan-les-Pins** or follow the locals to the unnamed sandy suntrap of beach pinched between the Hôtel Belles-Rives and Port Gallice. See p. 434.

o **Calanque d'En Vau** (Provence): Nestled into the heart of Parc National des Calanques, Calanque d'En Vau wouldn't look out of place in the tropics: Imagine an ice-white pairing of pebbly sands and transparent turquoise waters. Sitting at the base of limestone cliffs, it's accessible only on foot (for experienced hikers) or by kayak or boat. See p. 406.

o **Plage des Marinières** Villefranche-sur-Mer (French Riviera): A seemingly endless sweep of honey-hued sand, this popular beach sits at the base of a giant sun-kissed bay. It's perfect for families, as the sea shelves slowly and waves are seldom seen. See p. 460.

o **Paris Plage** (Paris): The wildly popular initiative of Paris's former mayor, Bertrand Delanoë, has brought tons of sand, activities, and fun to the banks of the Seine. Every year from mid-July to mid-August, you can find a sandy beach with lounge chairs, snack stands, concerts, dances, and so forth along the edge of the Right Bank and on the Bassin de la Villette.

o **Plage de la Garoupe** Cap d'Antibes (French Riviera): The sun rises at dawn over the Cap d'Antibes' most mythical beach. Views pan out over Antibes to the Alps beyond; beach bars serve chilled rosé behind. And a coastal footpath around the secluded peninsula starts to your right. What more could you possibly want? See p. 434.

o **Plages de Dinard** (Brittany): The poshest *plage* along Brittany's Emerald coast, this historic seaside resort features 10 easy-access beaches, the best being la plage du Prieuré. See p. 251.

o **Plage des Grand-Sables** Belle-Ile-en-Mer (Brittany): The wild coast of Quiberon peninsula near Carnac is lined with gorgeous beaches. Take the ferry out to Belle-Ile and set your towel down on the nice sandy beach of Grand-Sables. The tropical waters will make you doubt you're in France. See p. 263.

FRANCE'S best FREE THINGS TO DO

o **Visiting a Municipal Museum:** There are 14 municipal museums in Paris and you won't pay a single centime to get into their permanent collections. This includes the Musée Carnavalet, the Petit Palais, the Maison de Victor Hugo, and the Musée Zadkine.

- o **Wandering through a Market:** If you want to get a sense of what Paris really is like, poke around one of the many *marches* that are sprinkled around the city. Not only does it make for great people-watching, but at many markets you can also find tempting morsels to eat on site.

- o **Taking in the Parisian Rooftops from the Top of the Printemps:** There's no charge for hanging out on a bench and enjoying the view on the huge rooftop terrace of this famous department store; just take the escalators up to the top floor and bring your camera.

- o **Getting Lost in Loches** (Loire): The medieval village of Loches is perfect for wandering around. Its tiny cobblestone lanes, arched bridges over the river, and scenic views of church and castle towers don't cost a cent. See p. 197.

- o **Reveling in the Tour de Normandie (Bernay to Bayeux)** (Normandy): Join the party for four days in June when this classic car race zooms through Normandy's historic towns. In the 150 or so municipalities along the route, each town will put on festivities, with the drivers themselves dressed up in the fashion of their vehicle's bygone era. See p. 232.

- o **Getting Festive at Medieval Fairs** (Normandy): The Middle Ages come to life in the summer as many of Normandy's picturesque towns put on lively medieval festivals. The biggest and most spectacular of the region's medieval fairs is in Bayeux every July. Costumed performers fill the streets alongside market stalls, medieval games for kids, and colorful jousters. See p. 232.

- o **Beachcombing in Brittany:** The whole of the Breton coastline makes for phenomenal touring. Hike, bike, or drive from the northern Emerald coast

The Royal Apartments in medieval Loches, Loire Valley

with its sparkling waters to the wilder western seaboard with its rocky bays and Atlantic waves.

○ **Counting Watchtowers** Dinan (Brittany): Amble amongst half-timbered house through the narrow streets of Dinan. A medieval walled city, it is encircled by 3.5km (2 miles) of ramparts interspersed with 14 imposing watchtowers. See p. 254.

○ **Admiring the *Hôtels Particuliers* in Dijon** (Burgundy): Dijon has more than 100 townhouses, which were built for wealthy families between the 15th and 18th centuries. Some of the finest examples can be seen on Rue des Forges including Hôtel Chambellan (No. 34) and the ornately decorated Maison Maillard (No. 38), both of whose courtyards can be visited for free (enter via the open passageways).

○ **Staring up at Sculptural Heavens** Strasbourg (Alsace): You'll be awe-struck at the facade of Strasbourg cathedral, the tallest Gothic building in Europe. Entrance is free. Though the cathedral's towers and astronomical clock come with a fee, these additional sites are gratis on the first Sunday of each month. See p. 305.

○ **Driving the La Route des Crêtes,** near Colmar (Alsace): The countryside of Alsace makes for beautiful driving. If you've done the wine road, head uphill along la Route des Crêtes for the best panoramic views of the valley and the Vosges mountains beyond. See p. 317.

○ **Ogling the Orchids in Lyon** (Rhône Valley): Housed within the grounds of France's largest city-based public park, Lyon's Botanical Garden is completely free. One may explore over 6,000 plants ranging from orchids to cacti and carnivorous flowers. You'll also find deer wandering freely around the surrounding Parc de la Tête d'Or with its broad tree-lined avenues and lakeside setting. See p. 345.

○ **Admiring the Rose Window in Lyon's Cathedral** (Rhône Valley): It's hard not to be moved by the multi-colored brilliance of Primatiale St-Jean's 14th-century rose window. Come before sunset as the light filters through the stained glass of this west-facing window to find the nave bathed in an ethereal white light. See p. 342.

○ **Photographing Provence's Fields of Lavender:** Sure, we've all seen those shots of iridescent Provençal hills cloaked with purple lavender. But it's another thing entirely to get out and snap these stunning—and fragrant—fields in person. Lavender's peak blooming season is usually between mid-June and mid-July; the area concentrated around Plateau de Valensole is particularly vibrant.

○ **Touring Marseille's Waterfront** (Provence): Following a prominent year as European Capital of Culture 2013, much of Marseille boasts an all-new appearance. Head down to the city's J4 Esplanade for unbeatable views over the Vieux Port, 12th-century Fort Saint-Jean, and Rudy Ricciotti's ultra-contemporary MuCEM. See p. 399.

○ **Hiking the Caps** (Riviera): The Riviera's *sentier du littoral* is an almost continuous coastal footpath that winds its way along the country's seductive southern shores. Leave the coastal hubbub behind and spend a day wandering between the wealthy private mansions and the sparkling sea on Cap Ferrat or Cap d'Antibes. See chapter 13.

o **Soaking up History and Culture in Nice** (Riviera): Nice boasts more museums than any city outside of Paris. Better yet, almost all of them are free. Revel in the 19th-century opulence of the Musée des Beaux-Arts, peek into the creative mind of an artistic genius at the Musée Matisse, or learn about Nice's time-honored multiculturalism at the Musée Masséna. See chapter 13.

o **Wandering the Streets of Sarlat-la-Canéda** (Bordeaux & Dordogne): A medieval jewel, this perfectly preserved town is a warren of pretty, narrow streets opening onto picturesque plazas, ideal for random explorations and discoveries. See p. 510.

o **Visiting a Wine Estate** (Bordeaux & Dordogne): While it's not always a cinch to find one that's open to visitors, when you do visit one of the Bordeaux area's thousands of wineries, chances are your tour and a tasting will be absolutely free. See p. 496.

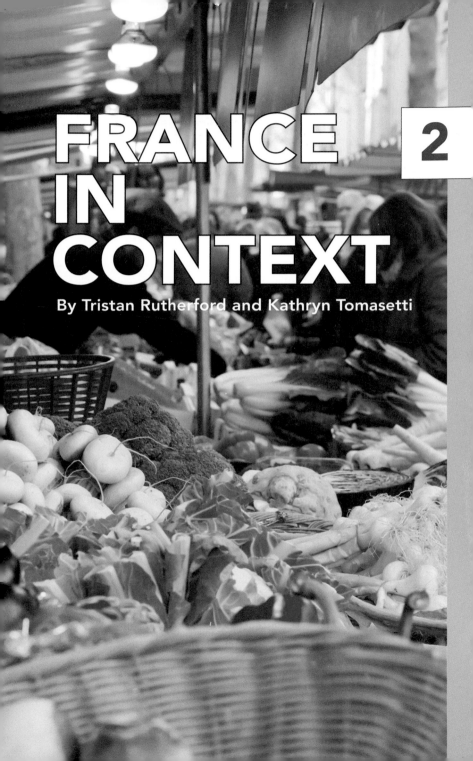

FRANCE IN CONTEXT

By Tristan Rutherford and Kathryn Tomasetti

The civilization and culture of France—not to mention the French way of life—makes the country easily the most visited in the world. The savoir-faire of its people lures travelers from across the globe to a country that covers an area smaller than Texas. Yet despite France's size, each region is so intriguing and varied that you may immerse yourself in one province so deeply that you'll never have time to see what's on the other side. You'd be surprised how many people do just that. Perhaps more than any other country in the world, France is a land to be savored. Ideally, France is discovered slowly by car or along the country's magnificent rail network, which lets you stop whenever and wherever you wish.

No European country, not even Britain, Italy, or Spain, can beat France in its pageantry of personalities. Its colorful characters range from Madame de Pompadour to Charles de Gaulle, from Jean-Luc Godard to Gustave Flaubert, from Catherine de Médici to Joan of Arc, from Emperor Napoleon to footballer Zinedine Zidane. You'll be introduced to some of these figures in the pages ahead. Seeing where they lived, worked, loved, and became legends is part of the experience of visiting France.

This guide is meant to help you decide where to go in France, but ultimately the most gratifying experience will be your own serendipitous discoveries—sunflowers, a picnic in a poppy field, an hour spent chatting with a small winemaker—whatever it is that stays in your memory for years to come.

FRANCE TODAY

France remains one of the world's most hyped and written-about destinations. It can inspire a masterpiece—and has on countless occasions. Even the cantankerous James McNeill Whistler would allow his masterpiece, a portrait of his mother, to hang in no other city save Paris.

Although not large by North American standards (about the size of Britain and Germany combined), France is densely packed with attractions, both cultural and recreational. Even better, it's permeated with cool and known for its *joie de vivre.*

As for style, it has always been foolhardy to try to compete with the French on their terms. The theatrical backdrops of the sometimes-silly Gallic monarchs have been interpreted by latter-day aesthetes as history's crowning achievement when it comes to conspicuous displays of wealth and prestige.

In politics and ideology, France has long been a leader and remains so today. Fueled by Enlightenment writings, whose most articulate voices were French, the 1789 Revolution toppled Europe's most deeply entrenched regime and cracked the foundations of dozens of other governments. In 1968 the revolutionaries were on the streets again: the original political spring.

PREVIOUS PAGE: **Boulevard Raspail farmer's market, Paris**

Newcomers have commented (often adversely) on the cultural arrogance of the French. But despite its linguistic and cultural rigidity, France has received more immigrants and political exiles than any other European country. Part of this derives from France's status as one of Europe's least densely populated nations per square mile, and part of it from the tendency of the French to let others be until their actions become dangerous or obnoxious, not necessarily in that order.

If you're a first-timer, everything in France, of course, is new. But if you've been away for a long time, expect changes. Taxi drivers in Paris may no longer correct your fractured French, but address you in English—and that's tantamount to a revolution. Part of this derives from the country's interest in music, culture, and films from foreign countries, and part from France's growing awareness of its role as a leader of a united Europe.

Yet France has never been more concerned about the loss of its unique identity within a landscape that has attracted an increasing number of immigrants from its former colonies. Many worry that France will continue to lose the battle to keep its language strong, distinct, and unadulterated by foreign slang or catchwords (and good luck with banning such terms as *l'email* and *le week-end*). But as the country moves deeper into the millennium, foreign tourists spending much-needed cash are no longer perceived as foes or antagonists. *Au contraire:* France welcomes the world to its palaces, parks, beaches, and UNESCO World Heritage sites. And if those tens of millions of guests spend a few euros—and soak up a little local culture while they're here—that's all to the good.

THE HISTORY OF FRANCE

EARLY GAUL   When the ancient Romans considered France part of their empire, their boundaries extended deep into the forests of the Paris basin and up to the edges of the Rhine. Part of Julius Caesar's early reputation came from his defeat of King Vercingetorix at Alésia in 52 b.c., a victory he was quick to publicize in one of the ancient world's literary masterpieces, "The Gallic Wars." In that year, the Roman colony of Lutetia (Paris) was established on an island in the Seine (Ile de la Cité).

The Roman Arena at Arles, Provence

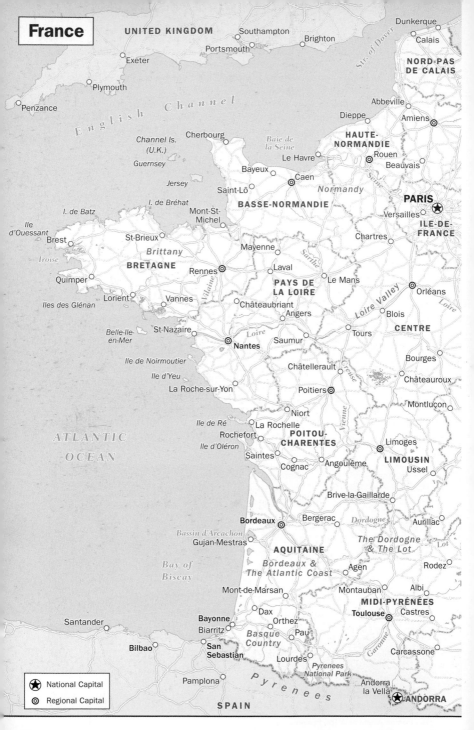

As the Roman Empire declined, its armies retreated to the flourishing colonies that had been established along a strip of the Mediterranean coast—among others, these included Orange, Arles, Antibes, and Marseille, which today retain some of the best Roman monuments in Europe.

As one of their legacies, the Roman armies left behind the Catholic Church, which, for all its abuses, was the only real guardian of civilization during the anarchy following the Roman decline. A form of low Latin was the common language. This slowly evolved into the archaic French that the more refined language is based upon today.

THE CAROLINGIANS   From the wreckage of the fall of the Roman Empire emerged a new dynasty: the Carolingians. One of their leaders, Charles Martel, halted a Muslim invasion of northern Europe at Tours in 743 and left a much-expanded kingdom to his son, Pepin. The Carolingian empire eventually stretched from the Pyrénées to a point deep in the German forests, encompassing much of modern France, Germany, and northern Italy. The heir to this vast land was Charlemagne. Crowned emperor in Rome on Christmas Day in 800, he returned to his capital at Aix-la-Chapelle (Aachen) and created the Holy Roman Empire. Charlemagne's rule saw a revived interest in scholarship, art, and classical texts, defined by scholars as the Carolingian Renaissance.

THE MIDDLE AGES   When the Carolingian dynasty died out in 987, the hectic, migratory Middle Ages officially began. Invasion by Hungarians, Vikings, and the English (who ruled half the country) lent France a cosmopolitan, if fractured, air. Politically driven marriages among the ruling families more than doubled the size of the territory controlled from Paris, a city that was increasingly recognized as the country's capital. Philippe II (reigned 1179–1223) infiltrated more prominent families with his genes than anyone else in France, successfully marrying members of his family into the Valois, Artois, and Vermandois. He also managed to win Normandy and Anjou back from the English. Louis IX (St. Louis) emerged as the 13th century's most memorable king, though he ceded most of the hard-earned military conquests of his predecessors back to the English.

The 14th century saw an increase in the wealth and power of the French kings, an increase in general prosperity, and a decrease in the power of the feudal lords. The death of Louis X without an heir in 1316 prompted more than a decade of scheming and plotting before the eventual emergence of the Valois dynasty.

France's burgeoning wealth and power was checked by the Black Death, which began in the summer of 1348. The rat-borne plague killed an estimated 33 percent of Europe's population, decimating the population of Paris and setting the stage for the exodus of the French monarchs to safer climes in such places as the Loire Valley. A financial crisis, coupled with a series of ruinous harvests, almost bankrupted the nation.

During the Hundred Years' War, the English made sweeping inroads into France in an attempt to grab the throne. At their most powerful, they controlled almost all of the north (Picardy and Normandy), Champagne, and parts of the Loire Valley. The peasant-born charismatic visionary Joan of Arc rallied the dispirited French troops as well as the timid *dauphin* (crown prince), whom she managed to have crowned as Charles VII. As threatening to the Catholic Church as she was to the English, she was declared a heretic and burned at the stake in Rouen in 1431. The place of her demise is now sited in the city's marketplace.

THE RISING POWER   By the early 17th century, France was a modern state. Few vestiges of feudalism remained. In 1624, Louis XIII appointed a Catholic cardinal, the duc de Richelieu, as his chief minister. Amassing enormous power,

Richelieu virtually ruled the country until his death in 1642. His sole objective was investing the monarchy with total power, and in trying to attain this goal he committed a series of truly horrible acts, paving the way for the eventual absolutism of a dynasty of future despotic rulers.

Although he ascended the throne when he was only 9, Louis XIV was the most powerful monarch Europe had seen since the Roman emperors. The estimated population of France at this time was 20 million, as opposed to 8 million in England and 6 million in Spain. French colonies in Canada, the West Indies, and America (Louisiana) were stronger than ever. The mercantilism that Louis's brilliant finance minister, Colbert, implemented was one of the era's most important fiscal policies, hugely increasing France's power and wealth. The arts flourished, as did a sense of aristocratic style that's remembered with a bittersweet nostalgia today. Louis's palace of Versailles is the perfect monument to the most flamboyantly consumptive era in French history.

Louis's territorial ambitions so deeply threatened the other nations of Europe that they united to hold him in check. France entered a series of expensive and demoralizing wars that, coupled with high taxes and bad harvests, stirred up much civil discontent. England was viewed as a threat both within Europe and in the global rush for lucrative colonies. The rise of Prussia as a militaristic neighbor posed an additional problem. Fresh political ideas from abroad unsteadied the status quo.

THE REVOLUTION & THE RISE OF NAPOLEON   Meanwhile, the Enlightenment was training a new generation of thinkers for the struggle against absolutism, religious fanaticism, and superstition. On August 10, 1792, troops from Marseille, aided by a Parisian mob, threw the dimwitted Louis XVI and his tactless Austrian-born queen, Marie Antoinette, into prison. After months of bloodshed and bickering among violently competing factions, the two thoroughly humiliated monarchs were executed.

France's problems got worse before they got better. In the ensuing bloodbaths, both moderates and radicals were guillotined in full view of a bloodthirsty crowd that included voyeurs like Dickens's Mme. Defarge, who brought her knitting every day to place de la Révolution (later renamed place de la Concorde) to watch the beheadings. Only the militaristic fervor of Napoleon Bonaparte could reunite France and bring an end to the revolutionary chaos. A political and military genius who appeared on the landscape at a time when the French were thoroughly sickened by the anarchy following their revolution, he restored a national pride that had been severely tarnished. He also established a bureaucracy and a code of law that has been emulated in other legal systems around the world. In 1799, at the age of 30, he entered Paris and was crowned

Chapel of Saint Louis des Invalides, Paris, site of Napoleon's tomb first consul and master of France. Soon after, a decisive victory in his northern Italian campaign solidified his power at home.

Alas, Napoleon's victories made him overconfident—and made the rest of Europe clamor for his demise. Just as he was poised on the verge of conquering the entire continent, Napoleon's famous retreat from Moscow during the winter of 1812 reduced his formerly invincible army to tatters. As a plaque in the Lithuanian town of Vilnius once told the tale: "napoleon bonaparte passed this way in 1812 with 400,000 men"—and on the other side are the words "napoleon bonaparte passed this way in 1812 with 9,000 men." Napoleon was then decisively beaten at Waterloo by the combined armies of the English, Dutch, and Prussians. Exiled to the British-held island of St. Helena in the South Atlantic, he died in 1821, probably the victim of a prison poisoner.

THE BOURBONS & THE SECOND EMPIRE   In 1814, following the destruction of Napoleon and his dream of Empire, the Congress of Vienna redefined the map of Europe. The Bourbon monarchy was reestablished, with reduced powers for Louis XVIII, an archconservative. After a few stable decades, Napoleon I's nephew, Napoleon III, was elected president in 1848. Appealing to the property-protecting instinct of a nation that hadn't forgotten the violent upheavals of less than a century before, he initiated a repressive right-wing government in which he was awarded the totalitarian status of emperor in 1851. Steel production was begun, and a railway system and Indochinese colonies were established. New technologies fostered new kinds of industry, and the bourgeoisie flourished. The baron Georges-Eugène Haussmann radically altered Paris by laying out the grand boulevards the world knows today.

As ever, intra-European conflict knocked France off its pedestal once again. In 1870, the Prussians—a rising power in the German east—defeated Napoleon III at Sedan and held him prisoner with 100,000 of his soldiers. Paris was besieged and occupied, an inglorious state for the world's greatest city. After the Prussians withdrew, a violent revolt ushered in the Third Republic and its elected president, Marshal MacMahon, in 1873. Peace and prosperity slowly returned, France regained its glamour, a mania of building occurred, the Impressionists made their visual statements, and writers like Flaubert redefined the French novel into what today is regarded as the most evocative in the world. As if as a symbol of this period, the Eiffel Tower was built as part of the 1889 Universal Exposition.

THE WORLD WARS   International rivalries, lost colonial ambitions, and conflicting alliances led to World War I, which, after decisive German victories for 2 years, degenerated into the mud-slogged horror of trench warfare. Mourning between 4 and 5 million casualties, Europe was inflicted with psychological scars that never healed. In 1917, the United States broke the European deadlock by entering the war.

After the Allied victory, grave economic problems, plus the demoralization stemming from years of fighting, encouraged the growth of socialism and communism. The French government demanded every centime of reparations it could wring from a crushed Germany, humiliating the country into a vengeful spiral that would have repercussions two decades later.

The worldwide Great Depression of 1929 devastated France. Poverty and widespread bankruptcies weakened the Third Republic to the point where successive coalition governments rose and fell (although a number of expatriate writers, among them Ernest Hemingway and F. Scott Fitzgerald, enjoyed the dollar exchange rate and relative freedoms while they could). The crises reached a

Impressions

François Hollande is an intelligent man. I do not have a problem with him. The only thing is, he has never held office at the state level. Honestly, can you imagine François Hollande as president of France?

—Nicolas Sarkozy,
former French President

crescendo on June 14, 1940, when Hitler's armies arrogantly marched down the Champs-Élysées, and newsreel cameras recorded French people openly weeping. Under the terms of the armistice, the north of France was occupied by the Nazis, and a puppet French government was established at Vichy under the authority of Marshal Pétain. The immediate collapse of the French army is viewed as one of the most significant humiliations in modern French history. In Europe, Britain was left to counter the Nazi threat alone.

Pétain and his regime cooperated with the Nazis in unbearably shameful ways. Not the least of their errors included the deportation of more than 75,000 French Jews to German work camps. Pockets of resistance fighters *(le maquis)* waged small-scale guerrilla attacks against the Nazis throughout the course of the war. Charles de Gaulle, the irascible giant who is forever associated with the politics of his era, established himself as the head of the French government-in-exile.

The scene was radically altered on June 6, 1944, when the largest armada in history—a combination of American, British, and Canadian troops—successfully established a beachhead on the shores of Normandy. Paris rose in rebellion even before the Allies arrived. On August 26, 1944, de Gaulle entered the capital as head of the government. The Fourth Republic was declared even as pockets of Nazi snipers continued to shoot from scattered rooftops throughout the city.

THE POSTWAR YEARS Plagued by the bitter residue of colonial policies that France had established during the 18th and 19th centuries, the Fourth Republic witnessed the rise and fall of 22 governments and 17 premiers. Many French soldiers died on foreign battlefields as once-profitable colonies in North Africa and Indochina rebelled. After suffering a bitter defeat in 1954, France ended its occupation of Vietnam and freed its former colony. It also granted internal self-rule to Tunisia and Morocco.

Algeria was to remain a greater problem. The advent of the 1958 Algerian revolution signaled the end of the much-maligned Fourth Republic. De Gaulle was called back from retirement to initiate a new constitution, the Fifth Republic, with a stronger set of executive controls. To nearly everyone's dissatisfaction, de Gaulle ended the Algerian war in 1962 by granting the country full independence. The sun had finally set on most of France's far-flung empire.

In 1968, major social unrest and a violent coalition hastily formed between the nation's students and blue-collar workers eventually led to the collapse of the government. De Gaulle resigned when his attempts to placate some of the marchers were defeated. The reins of power passed to his second-in-command, Georges Pompidou, and his successor, Valérie Giscard d'Estaing, both of whom continued de Gaulle's policies emphasizing economic development and protection of France as a cultural resource to the world.

In 1981, François Mitterrand was elected the first Socialist president of France since World War II (with a close vote of 51 percent). In almost immediate response, many wealthy French decided to transfer their assets out of the country, much to the delight of banks in Geneva, Monaco, and the Cayman Islands. Though reviled by the rich and ridiculed for personal mannerisms that often seemed inspired by Louis XIV, Mitterrand was reelected in 1988. During his two terms, he spent billions of francs on his *grands projets* (like the Louvre pyramid, Opéra Bastille, Cité de la Musique, and Grande Arche de La Défense), although unemployment and endemic corruption remained.

On his third try, on May 7, 1995, Jacques Chirac won the presidency with 52 percent of the vote and immediately declared war on unemployment. But his popularity soon faded in the wake of unrest caused by an 11.5 percent unemployment rate and a stressed economy struggling to meet entry requirements for the European Union that France had signed up for 3 years before.

Financial crisis or not, in May 1996 thousands of Parisian workers took to the streets, disrupting passenger train service to demand a workweek shorter than the usual 39 hours. Most French now work a 35-hour week and retire at 60 years old.

In 1999, France joined with other European countries in adopting the euro as its standard of currency. The new currency accelerated the creation of a single economy comprising over 500 million Europeans, although the ability of several fiscally wayward states to borrow at preferential rates has led to a sovereign debt crisis that remains today. Nonetheless, the European Union now boasts a combined gross national product approaching 17€ trillion ($23 million), a shade larger than that of the United States.

Although Chirac steadied the ship—and most French today think he ran a decent presidency—in 2005 a rotten core was exposed. Decades of pent-up resentment felt by the children of African immigrants exploded into an orgy of violence and vandalism. Riots began in the suburbs of Paris and spread around the country. Throughout France, gangs of youths battled the French police, torching schools, cars, and businesses. Rioting followed in such cities as Dijon, Marseille, and Rouen. Most of the rioters were the sons of Arab and black African immigrants, Muslims living in a mostly Catholic country. The reason for the protests? Leaders of the riots claimed they live "like second-class citizens," even though they are French citizens. Unemployment is 30 percent higher in the ethnic ghettos of France.

Against a backdrop of discontent regarding issues of unemployment, immigration, and healthcare, the charismatic Nicolas Sarkozy swept into the presidential office in May 2007. Sarkozy, the combative son of a Hungarian immigrant, promised to reinvigorate ties with France's traditional ally, the United States. He even made a summer vacation trip to New England directly after his election.

In the ensuing years, Sarkozy found time to divorce a wife and take a beautiful new bride. A glamorous model-turned-singer, Carla Bruni, became first lady of France in 2008. The tabloids had a field day with Bruni, whose former lovers include Mick Jagger, Eric Clapton, and Donald Trump.

Outside of politics, the French looked at Sarkozy's personal life with ridicule. His marriage to Bruni and his holidays with the rich and famous earned him the title of the "bling bling president." In a show of how divided France was over his administration, he lost the 2012 presidential election by a whisker to Socialist challenger François Hollande.

Hollande promised a government of hard-working technocrats. Alas, "Monsieur Normal" proved anything but. A series of gaffes—including employing a minister with a secret Swiss bank account to superintend France's endemic tax evasion—made him, in 2014, the least popular president since polling began, with a disapproval rating of 75 percent. Soaring unemployment hasn't helped either. Nor has his decision to raise taxes (in particular his infamous 75% tax rate

> ### Impressions
>
> *Above 1m euros ($1.3m), the tax rate should be 75 percent because it's not possible to have that level of income.*
>
> —François Hollande,
> current French President

for those who earn over a million) in order to boost the economy. The nail in Hollande's claim to run a scandal free administration came in early 2014. Here, the president's private life once again became front-page news. Not content with family ties to his first girlfriend, Ségolène Royale, or his now-former mistress-turned-First Lady, Valérie Trierweiler, he embarked on another relationship with actress Julie Gayet. His method of courting Miss Gayet (which essentially involved turning up to her apartment on the back of his bodyguard's scooter wearing a motorcycle helmet) was deemed tacky by the French press.

Politicians and public alike await the 2017 elections with bated breath.

ART

France's manifold art treasures range from Rodin's "The Thinker" to Monet's Impressionist "Water Lilies"; its architecture encompasses Roman ruins and Gothic cathedrals as well as Renaissance châteaux and postmodern buildings like the Centre Pompidou. This brief overview is designed to help you make sense of it all.

A fine place to start is Paris's **Louvre.** The world's greatest museum abounds with Renaissance works by Italian, Flemish, and German masters, including **Michelangelo** (1475–1564) and **Leonardo da Vinci** (1452–1519). Da Vinci's **"Mona Lisa"** (1503–05), the most famous painting on the planet, hangs here.

Back in the early 19th century, the **romantics** felt that both the ancients and the Renaissance had gotten it wrong and that the Middle Ages was the place to be. They idealized romantic tales of chivalry and the nobility of peasantry. Some great artists and movements of the era, all with examples in the **Louvre,** include **Theodore Géricault** (1791–1824), who painted "The Raft of the Medusa" (1819), which served as a model for the movement; and **Eugène Delacroix** (1798–1863), whose "Liberty Leading the People" (1830) was painted in the romantic style.

Decades later, the **Impressionists** adopted a free, open style, seeking to capture the *impression* light made as it reflected off objects. They painted deceptively loose compositions, using swift, visible brushwork and often light colors. For subject matter, they turned to landscapes and scenes of modern life. You'll find some of the best examples of their works in the **Musée d'Orsay.**

Impressionist greats include **Edouard Manet** (1832–83), whose groundbreaking "Luncheon on the Grass" (1863) and "Olympia" (1863) helped inspire the movement with their harsh realism, visible brush strokes, and thick outlines; **Claude Monet** (1840–1926), who launched the movement officially in an 1874 exhibition in which he exhibited his Turner-inspired "Impression, Sunrise" (1874), now in the **Musée Marmottan; Pierre-Auguste Renoir** (1841–1919), known for his figures' ivory skin and chubby pink cheeks; **Edgar Degas** (1834–1917), an accomplished painter, sculptor, and draftsman—his pastels of dancers and bathers are particularly memorable; and **Auguste Rodin** (1840–1917), the greatest Impressionist-era sculptor, who crafted remarkably expressive bronzes. The **Musée Rodin,** Rodin's former Paris studio, contains, among other works, his "Burghers of Calais" (1886), "The Kiss" (1886–98), and "The Thinker" (1880).

The smaller movements or styles of Impressionism are usually lumped together as "post-Impressionism." Again, the best examples of these turn-of-the-20th-century works are exhibited at the **Musée d'Orsay,** though you'll find pieces by Matisse, Chagall, and the cubists, including Picasso, in the **Centre Pompidou** and the key museums of Nice, Rouen, Avignon and Marseille. Important post-Impressionists include **Paul Cézanne** (1839–1906), who adopted the short brush strokes, love of landscape, and light color palette of his Impressionist friends; **Henri de Toulouse-Lautrec** (1864–1901), who created paintings and posters of wispy, fluid lines anticipating Art Nouveau and often depicting the bohemian life of Paris's dance halls and cafes; **Vincent van Gogh** (1853–90), who combined a touch of crazy Japanese influence with thick, short strokes; **Henri Matisse** (1869–1954), who created **fauvism** (a critic described those who used the style as *fauves,* meaning "wild beasts"); and **Pablo Picasso** (1881–1973), a Málaga-born artist who painted objects from all points of view at once, rather than using such optical tricks as perspective to fool viewers into seeing "cubist" three dimensions.

FRANCE IN POPULAR CULTURE
Books

For a taste of French culture before you travel, we recommend you load a half-dozen titles on your iPad or Kindle. Simon Schama's "Citizens" is the pick of the bunch for a history of the French Revolution. Moving into the 20th century, "Paris Was Yesterday, 1925–1939," is a fascinating collection of excerpts from Janet Flanner's "Letters from Paris" column in the *New Yorker*, while "On Paris" comprises a newly bound series of essays by Ernest Hemingway, written for the *Toronto Star* between 1920 and 1924. Two unusual approaches to French history are Rudolph Chleminski's "The French at Table," a funny and honest history of why the French know how to eat better than anyone and how they go about it; and "Parisians: An Adventure History of Paris" by Graham Robb, entertaining historical snippets that range from the French Revolution through the 1968 riots. More recently, "Chocolat" by Joanne Harris illustrates the tension between tradition and modernity in rural France by way of the nation's favorite treat.

And travel? Well, since 1323, some 10,000 books have been devoted to exploring Paris. One of the best is "Paris: Capital of the World," by Patrice Higonnet. This book takes a fresh social, cultural, and political look at the City of Light, exploring Paris as "the capital of sex" and, in contrast, the "capital of art." In "The Flâneur: A Stroll Through the Paradoxes of Paris," Edmund White wants the reader to experience Paris as Parisians do. Hard to translate exactly, a *flâneur* is someone who wanders, loafs, or idles. And for the frequent visitor, Jean-Christophe Napais's "Quiet Corners of Paris: Unexpected Hideaways, Secret Courtyards, Hidden Gardens" is sure to turn up plenty of undiscovered gems.

Representing the city's most fabulous era are "A Moveable Feast," Ernest Hemingway's recollections of Paris during the 1920s, and Morley Callaghan's "That Summer in Paris: Memories of Tangled Friendships with Hemingway, Fitzgerald and Some Others," an anecdotal account of the same period. Another great read is "The Autobiography of Alice B. Toklas," by Gertrude Stein.

For a fictional tour of the 19th century, pick up "Madame Bovary," by Gustave Flaubert. The carefully wrought characters, setting, and plot attest to Flaubert's genius in presenting the tragedy of Emma Bovary; Victor Hugo's "Les Misérables," a classic tale of social oppression and human courage set in the era of Napoleon I; and "Selected Stories," by the master of the genre, Guy de Maupassant.

Films

The world's first movie was shown in Paris on December 28, 1895. Its makers were the Lumière brothers, who scared an audience to death with images of a train moving towards the audience seats. Later, Charles Pathé and Léon Gaumont were the first to exploit filmmaking on a grand scale.

The golden age of the French silent screen on both sides of the Atlantic was 1927 to 1929. Actors were directed with more sophistication, and technical abilities reached an all-time high. The film "Hugo" (2011), directed by Martin Scorsese, is a heart-warming tale set against the film industry's transformation during this period. And despite its mind-numbing length, Abel Gance's masterpiece "Napoleon" (1927) is also sweepingly evocative. Its grisly battle scenes are easily as chilling as any war film made today.

In 1936, the Cinémathèque Française was established to find and preserve old (usually silent) French films. By that time, an average of 130 films a year was made in France, by (among others) Jean Renoir, Charles Spaak, and Marcel Carne. This era also brought such French luminaries as Claudette Colbert and Maurice Chevalier to Hollywood.

After World War II, two strong traditions—*film noir* and French comedy—offered viewers new kinds of genre, like Jacques Tati's sidesplitting "Les Vacances du Monsieur Hulot" ("Mr. Hulot's Holiday"). By the mid-1950s, French filmmaking ushered in the era of enormous budgets and the creation of such frothy potboilers as director Roger Vadim's "And God Created Woman," which helped make Brigitte Bardot a celebrity around the world, contributing greatly to the image in America of France as a kingdom of sexual liberation.

By the late 1950s, counterculture was flourishing on both sides of the Atlantic. François Truffaut, widely publicizing his auteur theories, rebelled with a series of short films (like "The 400 Blows" in 1959). Other contemporary directors included Jean-Luc Godard ("A Bout de Soufflé"), Alain Resnais ("Muriel"), Agnès Varda ("Le Bonheur"), Jacques Demy ("Les Parapluies de Cherbourg"), and Marguerite Duras ("Detruire, Dit-elle").

Many American films were filmed in Paris (or else used sets to simulate Paris). Notable ones have included the classic "An American in Paris," starring Gene Kelly, and "Moulin Rouge," starring Ewan McGregor as a Parisian artist. "Last Tango in Paris," with Marlon Brando, was one of the most controversial films set in Paris. Woody Allen's acclaimed "Midnight in Paris" was the most recent film to celebrate the City of Light. The film features beautiful shots of the city and includes cameos of iconic figures who lived in Paris in the 1920s. The big French movie of 2014 was another Allen number, "Magic in the Moonlight." This romantic comedy stars Colin Firth and Emma Stone against the sun-kissed backdrop of the French Riviera.

One French film that continues to enchant is Jean-Pierre Jeunet's "Amélie," with its beautiful scenes shot in Montmartre. More recently, "La Vie en Rose" earned Marion Cotillard an Oscar in 2008 for her performance as "The Little Sparrow," Edith Piaf.

Music

Music and France have gone together since the monks in the 12th century sang Gregorian chants in Notre-Dame. Troubadours with their ballads traveled all over France in the Middle Ages. In the Renaissance era, **Josquin des Prez** (c. 1440–1521) was the first master of the High Renaissance style of polyphonic vocal music. He became the greatest composer of his age, a magnificent virtuoso. **Jean-Baptiste Lully** (1632–87) entertained the decadent court of Versailles with his operas. During the reign of Robespierre, **Claude-Joseph Rouget de Lisle** (1760–1836) immortalized himself in 1792 when he wrote "La Marseillaise," the French national anthem. Regrettably, he died in poverty.

The rise of the middle class in the 1800s gave birth to both grand opera and opéra comique. Both styles merged into a kind of lyric opera, mixing soaring arias and tragedy in such widely popular hits as Bizet's "Carmen" in 1875 and St-Saën's "Samson et Dalila" in 1877.

During the romantic period of the 19th century, foreign composers moving to Paris often dominated the musical scene. **Frédéric Chopin** (1810–49) was half French, half Polish. He became the most influential composer for piano and even invented new musical forms such as the ballade. **Félix Mendelssohn** (1809–47) had to fight against anti-Semitism to establish himself with his symphonies, concerti, and chamber music.

At the dawn of the 20th century, music became more impressionistic, as evoked by **Claude Débussy** (1862–1918). In many ways, he helped launch modernist music. His "Prélude à L'Après-midi d'un Faune" in 1894 and "La Mer" in 1905 were performed all over Europe. From Russia came **Igor Stravinsky** (1882–1971), who made *Time* magazine's list of the 100 most influential people of the 20th century. He achieved fame as a pianist, conductor, and composer. His "Le sacre du printemps" (The Rite of Spring), with its pagan rituals, provoked a riot in Paris when it was first performed in 1913.

A revolutionary artist, **Yves Klein** (1928–62) was called a "neo-Dada." His 1960 "The Monotone Symphony" with three naked models became a notorious performance. For 20 minutes, he conducted an orchestra on one note. Dying of a heart attack at the age of 34, Klein is considered today an enigmatic postmodernist. **Pierre Boulez** (b. 1925) developed a technique known as integral serialism using a 12-tone system pioneered in the 1920s. As director of the IRCAM institute at the Centre Pompidou from 1970–92, he influenced young musicians around the world.

France took to American jazz like no other country. Louis Armstrong practically became a national hero to Parisians in the 1930s, and in 1949 Paris welcomed the arrival of Miles Davis. **Stéphane Grappelli** (1908–97), a French jazz violinist, founded the Quintette du Hot Club de France, the most famous of all-string jazz bands. **Django Reinhardt** (1910–53) became one of the most prominent jazz musicians of Europe, known for such works as "Belleville" and "My Sweet."

Some French singers went on to achieve world renown, notably **Edith Piaf** (1915–63), "The Little Sparrow" and France's greatest pop singer. Wherever you go in France, you will hear her "La Vie en Rose," which she first recorded in 1946. Born in 1924, **Charles Aznavour** remains an eternal favorite. He's known for his unique tenor voice with its gravelly and soulful low notes. **Jacques Brel** (1929–78), a singer-songwriter, saw his songs interpreted by everybody from Frank Sinatra to David Bowie. A popular chanson singer, **Juliette Gréco** (b. 1927) became known as "the High Priestess of Existentialism" on Paris's Left

Bank and was beloved by Jean-Paul Sartre. She dressed all in black and let her long, black hair hang free before coming to Hollywood and becoming the mistress of mogul Darryl Zanuck.

Among rock stars, the French consider **Johnny Halladay** (b. 1943) their equivalent of Elvis Presley. He has scored 18 platinum albums, selling more than 100 million records. Another pop icon is **Serge Gainsbourg** (1928–91). He was a master of everything from sexy rock to jazz and reggae. Upon his death, President François Mitterrand called him "our Baudelaire, our Apollinaire." In the late 1990s, a dreamy French house secured international notoriety with bands such as **Air** and **Daft Punk.** More recently, chart-topping indie band **The Dø** performed another first—headlining the French album charts with songs sung entirely in English.

Artists with immigrant backgrounds often are the major names in the vibrant French music scene of today, with influences from French Africa, the French Caribbean, and the Middle East. Along with rap and hip-hop, these sounds rule the nights in the boîtes of France's biggest cities. **Khaled** (b. 1960), from Algeria, has become known as the "King of Raï." The most influential French rapper today is **MC Solaar** (b. 1969); born in Senegal, he explores racism and ethnic identity in his wordplays.

EATING & DRINKING IN FRANCE

As any French person will attest, French food is the best in the world. That's as true today as it was during the 19th-century heyday of the master chef Escoffier. A demanding patriarch who codified the rules of French cooking, he ruled the kitchens of the Ritz in Paris, standardizing the complicated preparation and presentation of *haute cuisine.*

However, at the foundation of virtually every culinary theory ever developed in France is a deep-seated respect for the *cuisine des provinces* (also known as *cuisine campagnarde*). Ingredients usually included only what was produced locally, and the rich and hearty result was gradually developed over several

Dining and people-watching in Paris

generations of *mères cuisinières*. Springing from an agrarian society with a vivid sense of nature's cycles, the cuisine provided appropriate nourishment for bodies that had toiled through a day in the open air. The movement is alive and well today with a tradition for eating locally produced—or *zero km*—foods.

Despite the availability of top-quality ingredients across the country, regional cuisine is more sought after than ever before. Try salmon, lark pâté, goat's milk cheese, partridge, rillettes, herb-flavored black pudding, and fine white wines from the Loire Valley. Not forgetting sole, brill, mackerel, turbot, mussels, and big fat lobsters from the Normandy coast, often bathed in the region's rich butter sauce. Just don't forget the Camembert for dessert.

Gourmets, not just beach lovers, should go to the Riviera. Bouillabaisse, an exquisite fish soup said to have been invented by Venus, is Marseille's best-known dish. Riviera specialties include *daube* (slow-cooked beef stew), *soupe au pistou* (vegetable soup with basil); and *salade Niçoise* (traditionally made with tomatoes, olives, radishes, scallions, peppers, and tuna or anchovies). All are best served with a glass of ice-cold *rosé* in the afternoon sun.

And Paris? At the center of the country's gastronomic crossroads, it tops the lot. The city literally has thousands of restaurants to choose from. The best of them are listed in this book, or discussed on websites likes **Chowhound** (www.chow.com) and **Time Out** (www.timeout.fr). Beef from Lyon, lamb from the Auvergne, crêpes from Brittany, and *cassoulet* from southwest France are served up in abundance. This city of 10 million gastronomes has also become a mecca for creative foreign fare. Until you've eaten sashimi, bimimbap, ceviche, and gourmet burgers in Paris, you haven't lived.

To accompany such cuisine, let your own good taste—and your wallet—determine your choice of wine. Most wine stewards, called *sommeliers,* are there to help you in your choice, and only in the most dishonest of restaurants will they push you toward the most expensive selections. Of course, if you prefer only bottled water, or perhaps a beer, or even a cider in Normandy, then be firm and order your choice without embarrassment. Some restaurants include a beverage in their menu rates *(boisson compris)*, either as part of a set tasting menu in ritzy restaurants or as part of a fixed-price formula in cheaper establishments. Some of the most satisfying wines we've drunk in France came from unlabeled house bottles or carafes, called a *vin de la maison.* In general, unless you're a real connoisseur, don't worry about labels and vintages. When in doubt, you can rarely go wrong with a good burgundy or bordeaux. As a rule of thumb, expect to spend about one-third of the restaurant tab on wine.

WHEN TO GO

The best time to visit France is in the spring (Apr–June) or fall (Sept–Nov), when things are easier to come by, from Métro seats to good-tempered waiters. The weather is temperate year-round. July and August are the worst for crowds but best for beaches. That's when Parisians desert their city, leaving it to the tourists.

A Bastille Day (July 14) parade, Paris

France's weather varies from region to region. Despite its latitude, Paris never gets very cold. Normandy is a little fresher—and foggier—but the Mediterranean boasts one long summer, with the French Riviera soaking up 300 days of sun per year. Provence dreads *le mistral* (an unrelenting wind), which most often blows in the winter for bouts of a few days at a time, but can also last up to 2 weeks.

Paris's Average Daytime Temperature & Rainfall

	JAN	FEB	MAR	APR	MAY	JUNE	JULY	AUG	SEPT	OCT	NOV	DEC
Temp. °F	38	39	46	51	58	64	66	66	61	53	45	40
Temp. °C	3	4	8	11	14	18	19	19	16	12	7	4
Rainfall (in.)	3.2	2.9	2.4	2.7	3.2	3.5	3.3	3.7	3.3	3.0	3.5	3.1

France Calendar of Events

JANUARY

Monte Carlo Motor Rally (Le Rallye de Monte Carlo). The world's most venerable car race. Mid-January. www.acm.mc

FEBRUARY

Carnival of Nice. Parades, music, fireworks, and "Les Batailles des Fleurs" (Battles of the Flowers) are all part of this celebration. The climax is the burning of the Carnival king effigy. Late February to early March. www.nicecarnaval.com

MARCH

International Ready-to-Wear Fashion Shows (Le Salon International de Prêt-à-Porter). Tapis Rouge, 67 rue du Faubourg St-Martin, Paris. See what you'll be wearing next season. Early March; also

held late September. www.capsuleshow. com

APRIL

Foire du Trône, on the Reuilly Lawn of the Bois de Vincennes, 12e, Paris. This mammoth fun fair operates daily from noon to midnight. Early April to late May. www.foiredutrone.com

International Garden Festival, Château de Chaumont, Amboise (Loire). An international competition showcasing the best in garden design. Mid-April to mid-October. www.domaine-chaumont.fr

International Marathon of Paris. Runners from around the world compete along the Champs-Elysées. Early April. www. parismarathon.com

Vin'Estival, Mâcon. France's largest wine tourism festival allows visitors to learn about and taste the wines of the Mâconnais and Beaujolais regions. There is also a competition to find France's best Grand Vin. www.vinestival.com

MAY

Cannes Film Festival (Festival International du Film). Movie madness transforms this Mediterranean town into a media circus. Admission to films and parties is by invitation. Other films play 24 hours a day. Mid-May. www.festival-cannes.com

Normandy Impressionist Festival. New region-wide event that showcases the area's favorite painters (Monet, Manet, Signac) in museums across Normandy, held every 2 to 3 years. May to September. www.normandie-impressionniste.eu

Monaco Formula 1 Grand Prix. The world's most high-tech cars race through Monaco's narrow streets in a blizzard of hot metal and ritzy architecture. Late May. www.formula1.com

Coupes Moto Légende, Dijon. Thousands of motorcyclists, including well-known names, descend upon Dijon to race their vintage bikes around the Prenois track. Late May. www.coupes-moto-legende.fr

Festival de St-Denis. A celebration of music in the burial place of the French kings, a grim early Gothic monument in Paris's northern suburb of St-Denis. Late May to late June. www.festival-saint-denis.com

French Open Tennis Championship, Stade Roland-Garros, 16e, Paris. The French Open features 2 weeks of men's, women's, and doubles tennis on hot, red, dusty clay courts. Late May to early June. www.rolandgarros.com

JUNE

Prix du Jockey Club and Prix Diane-Longines, Hippodrome de Chantilly. Thoroughbreds from as far away as Kentucky and Dubai compete in this race. On race days, dozens of trains depart from Paris's Gare du Nord for Chantilly, where racegoers take free shuttle buses to the track. Early to mid-June. www.france-galop.com

Paris Air Show. France's military-industrial complex shows off its high-tech hardware. Fans, competitors, and industrial spies mob Le Bourget Airport. Next event mid-June 2015. www.paris-air-show.com

Catalpa Festival, Auxerre. This three-night world music festival takes place in various venues around town including the atmospheric surrounds of the cloister of the Abbaye Saint-Germain. www.lesilex.fr

Les 24 Heures du Mans Voitures. Racing cars blast around the clock at this venerable circuit. Also hosts the huge September motorcycle rally. Mid-June. www.24h-lemans.com

Festival Chopin, Paris. Everything you've ever wanted to hear by the Polish exile, who lived most of his life in Paris. Piano recitals take place in the Orangerie du Parc de Bagatelle, 16e. Mid-June to mid-July. www.frederic-chopin.com

Gay Pride Parade, place du 18 Juin 1940 to place de la Bastille, Paris. A week of expositions and parties climaxes in a parade patterned after those in New York and San Francisco. Late June. www.gaypride.fr

JULY

Les Chorégies d'Orange, Orange. One of southern France's most important lyric festivals presents oratorios, operas, and choral works in France's best-preserved Roman amphitheater. Early July to early August. www.choregies.fr

Les Nocturnes du Mont-St-Michel. This sound-and-light tour meanders through the stairways and corridors of one of Europe's most impressive medieval monuments. Early July to late August. www.ot-montsaintmichel.com

Colmar International Festival, Colmar. Classical concerts are held in public buildings of one of the most folkloric towns in Alsace. Early July. www.festival-colmar.com

Getting Tickets

Visitors can purchase tickets for almost every music festival, soccer game, or cultural event in France online. Try the official website first, or log onto **FNAC** (www.fnactickets.com), France's largest music chain, which offers both a digital reservation service as well as in-store ticket booths.

Tour de France. The world's most hotly contested bicycle race sends crews of wind-tunnel–tested athletes along an itinerary that detours deep into the Pyrenees, Alps, Provence, and Normandy. The finish line is on the Champs-Elysées. First 3 weeks of July. www.letour.fr

Festival d'Avignon. This world-class festival has a reputation for exposing new talent to critical scrutiny and acclaim. The focus is usually on avant-garde works in theater, dance, and music. Last 3 weeks of July. www.festival-avignon.com

Bastille Day. Celebrating the birth of modern-day France, the nation's festivities reach their peak with country-wide street fairs, fireworks, and feasts. In Paris, the day begins with a parade down the Champs-Elysées and ends with fireworks at Montmartre. July 14.

Paris Quartier d'Eté. For 4 weeks, music rules sounds around the city. Two-dozen French and international performances take place at unusual venues all over the city, like the Musée de Cluny, the Gare du Nord, and the Parc de Belleville. Mid-July to mid-August. www.quartierdete.com

Nice Jazz Festival. The most prestigious jazz festival in Europe. Concerts begin in the afternoon and go on until late at night (sometimes all night) in place Masséna and the Jardin Albert 1er, overlooking Nice's promenade des Anglais. Mid-July. www.nicejazzfestival.fr

Festival d'Aix-en-Provence. A musical event *par excellence,* with everything from Gregorian chants to operas composed on synthesizers. Recitals are in the medieval cloister of the Cathédrale St-Sauveur. Expect heat, crowds, and loud sounds. July. www.festival-aix.com

Réncontre d'Arles. The prettiest town in Provence hosts a city-wide photography festival. Prepare to be wowed. July to September. www.rencontres-arles.com

Festival de Cornouaille, Quimper. An annual weeklong celebration of Breton culture. The festivities include parades in traditional costume and Celtic and Breton concerts throughout the city. Late July. www.festival-cornouaille.com

AUGUST

Festival Interceltique de Lorient, Brittany. Celtic verse and lore are celebrated in the Celtic heart of France. The 150 concerts include classical and folkloric musicians, dancers, singers, and painters. Traditional Breton pardons (religious processions) take place in the once-independent maritime duchy. Early August. www.festival-interceltique.com

Musical Gatherings (Les Rencontres Musicales), Vézelay. Four days of classical music concerts held in several venues including the magnificent basilica. www.rencontresmusicalesdevezelay.com

SEPTEMBER

Deauville American Film Festival. The likes of Clooney, Pitt, and Travolta jet in for a yearly celebration of movies, glitz, and glamour. First week September. www.festival-deauville.com

La Villette Jazz Festival. Some 50 concerts are held in churches, auditoriums, and concert halls in the Paris suburb of La Villette. Past festivals have included Kenny Garrett, Jamie Callum, and other international artists. Early to mid-September. www.jazzalavillette.com

Festival d'Automne, Paris. One of France's most famous festivals is also one of its most eclectic, focusing mainly on modern music, ballet, theater, and art. Mid-September to mid-January. www.festival-automne.com

Festival de la Loire, Orléans (Loire). The Loire River and its banks come alive with sails, music, and food during the largest boat festival in Europe. Late September, every other year; next in 2015. www.orleans.fr

OCTOBER

Paris Auto Show, Parc des Expositions, Porte de Versailles, 15e, Paris. This biennial showcase for European car design comes complete with glitzy attendees, lots of hype, and the latest models. Mid-October; next in 2016. www.mondial-automobile.com

Prix de l'Arc de Triomphe, Hippodrome de Longchamp, 16e, Paris. France's answer to England's Ascot is the country's most prestigious horse race, culminating the equine season in Europe. Early October. www.prixarcdetriomphe.com

NOVEMBER

Armistice Day, nationwide. In Paris, the signing of the document that ended World War I is celebrated with a military parade from the Arc de Triomphe to the Hôtel des Invalides. November 11.

Dijon Gastronomy Fair (Foire gastronomique de Dijon). One of France's biggest food fairs attracts around 600 exhibitors and 200,000 visitors each year. www.dijon-congrexpo.com

Hospices de Beaune Wine Auction (Vente des vins des Hospices de Beaune). Three days of wine tastings, street entertainment and a half marathon culminating in the world-famous charity wine auction. www.beaune-tourisme.fr

DECEMBER

Boat Fair (Le Salon Nautique de Paris). Europe's major exposition of what's afloat, at Porte de Versailles. One week in early December. www.salonnautiqueparis.com

Fête de Lumières, Lyon. In honor of the Virgin Mary, lights are placed in windows throughout the city. Early December. www.fetedelumieres.lyon.fr

Fête de St-Sylvestre (New Year's Eve), nationwide. In Paris, this holiday is most boisterously celebrated in the Latin Quarter. At midnight, the city explodes. Strangers kiss, and boulevard St-Michel and the Champs-Elysées become virtual pedestrian malls. December 31.

RESPONSIBLE TRAVEL

From pioneering eco-friendly *autopartage* (car-sharing) programs to an unabashed enthusiasm for *biodynamique* wines, the French have embraced sustainability. In an age when environmental, ethical, and social concerns are becoming ever more important, France's focus on green principles—whether through traditional markets, carbon-neutral public transport, or all-natural outdoor adventure—offers visitors and residents alike plenty in the way of sustainable tourism.

In 2007, Paris mayor **Bertrand Delanoë** introduced the **Vélib'** scheme (www.velib.paris.fr), a public bicycle "sharing" program. With tens of thousands of bicycles and bike-rental stations spread throughout the city, it is a fast and inexpensive way to get around. Similar schemes are in place in many other major French cities, including Nice, Avignon, Aix-en-Provence, Rouen, Lyon, Bordeaux, and Marseille.

Also under Delanoë's guidance, a similar car-sharing program called the **Autolib'** (www.autolib.fr) was launched in Paris in 2011. More than 5,000 eco-friendly and exhaust-free public cars now slip silently around the Parisian streets; passes for their use can be purchased by the hour, day, month, or year. Nice followed suit in 2012 with **Auto Bleue** (www.auto-bleue.org). Nearly 200 electric cars with a range of 100km (62 miles) now ply the streets. More importantly, the scheme's 50 recharging points serve as charging depots for an increasing number of resident-owned electric cars. Similar systems now exist across France, like **AutoCool** (www.bordeaux.citiz.coop) in Bordeaux.

In order to crisscross France's vast countryside, many French ditch their cars and opt instead for travel on a **TGV** (www.tgv-europe.com). This network of high-speed trains is powered by SNCF, France's government-owned rail company, which is dedicated to becoming completely carbon-neutral. TGVs run from Paris's hub to cities throughout the country, including Nantes, Rouen, Lyon, Dijon, Rennes, Avignon, Aix-en-Provence, Nice, and Marseille.

Many hotels in France have undertaken measures to preserve the environment, and those that have are awarded with a green label. Look for hotels with the title of ***La Clef Verte*** (Green Key; www.laclefverte.org). The label rewards hotels that take a more environmental approach to water, energy, and waste, and help raise the awareness of their guests. Even if you don't stay at a green hotel, you can still do your bit: Turn off the air-conditioning when you leave the room, request that your sheets aren't changed every day, and use your towels more than once. Laundry makes up around 40 percent of an average hotel's energy use.

When planning your travels, it's equally important to consider the impact your visit will have on the environment. France's rippling vineyards, **Grande Randonnée (GR)** hiking trails, and pristine coastline all make for enchanting (and eco-friendly) escapes.

Responsible tourism also means leaving a place in the same condition you found it. You can do this by not dropping litter and respecting the color-coded garbage bin system. Support the local economy and culture by shopping in small neighborhood stores and at open-air markets that showcase the seasonal harvest of local, often organic (*bio*) producers. Look out for organic and *biodynamique* (biodynamic) wines, frequently sold at wine shops and farmers' markets, too. And given the myriad of tiny, family-run restaurants scattered throughout France's cities, towns, and countryside, it's all too easy to dig into a home-cooked meal.

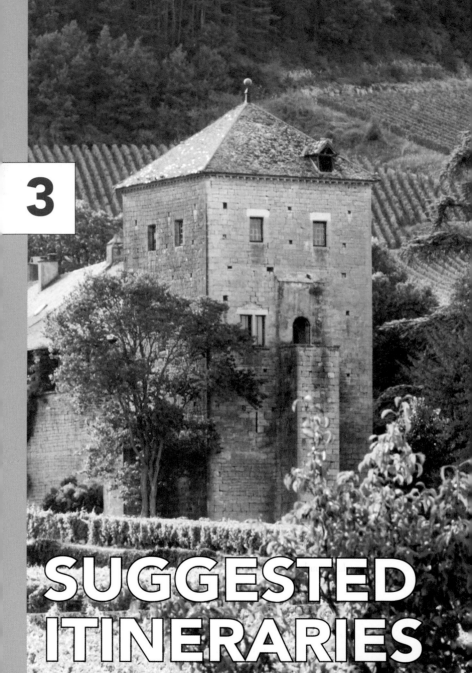

3

SUGGESTED ITINERARIES

By Tristan Rutherford and Kathryn Tomasetti

W hen the Frommer's guidebooks were first launched, founder Arthur Frommer cautioned his readers, "You can get lost in France." It's still an apt warning—and promise—today. For those with unlimited time, one of the world's great pleasures is getting "lost" in France, wandering at random, making new discoveries off the beaten path. Few of us have this luxury, however, and so here we present 1- and 2-week itineraries to help you make the most of your time.

France is so treasure-filled that you could barely do more than skim the surface in a week. So relax and savor Paris, Mont-St-Michel, Chardonnay, or Cannes—among other alluring destinations—saving the rest for another day. You might also review chapter 1, "The Best of France," to find out what experiences or sights have special appeal to us and then adjust your itineraries to suit your particular travel plans.

The itineraries that follow take you to some major attractions and some charming off-the-beaten-track towns. The pace may be a bit breathless for some visitors, so feel free to skip a town or sight if you'd like to give yourself some chill-out time. You're on vacation, after all. Of course, you may also use these itineraries merely as a jumping-off point to develop your own custom-made trip.

THE REGIONS IN BRIEF

Although France's 547,030 sq. km (211,209 sq. miles) make it slightly smaller than the American state of Texas, no other country has such a diversity of sights and scenery in such a compact area. A visitor can travel through the north's flat, fertile lands; the Loire Valley's green hills; the east's Alpine ranges; the Pyrénées; and the southeast's Mediterranean coast. Even more noteworthy are the cultural and historical differences of each region.

Destinations in France are within easy reach from Paris and each other. **French National Railroads (SNCF)** offers fast service to and from Paris. For example, the highlights of Normandy and the Loire Valley (the château country) are just 1 or 2 hours away from Paris by train. You can travel from Paris to Cannes on the Riviera in 5 hours—or fly down in 45 minutes.

You can motor along nearly 71,000km (about 44,020 miles) of French roads, including a good number of well-maintained superhighways. But do your best to drive the secondary roads too: Nearly all of France's scenic splendors are along these routes.

A "grand tour" of France is nearly impossible for the visitor who doesn't have a lifetime to explore. If you want to get to know a province, try to devote at least a week to a specific region. Note that you'll probably have a more rewarding trip if you concentrate on getting to know two or three areas at a leisurely pace rather than racing around trying to see everything! To help you decide where to spend your time, we've summarized the highlights of each region for you.

Château de Sully-sur-Loire, Loire Valley

PARIS & ILE DE FRANCE The Ile de France is an island only in the sense that rivers—with odd-sounding names such as Essonne, Epte, Aisne, Eure, and Ourcq—and a handful of canals delineate its boundaries (about an 81km/50-mile radius from the center of Paris). France was born in this temperate basin, where the attractions include Paris, Versailles, Fontainebleau, Notre-Dame de Chartres, and Giverny. Despite industrialization (and Disneyland Paris), many pockets of charm remain, including the forests of Rambouillet and Fontainebleau, and the artists' hamlet of Barbizon. For more information, see chapters 4 and 5.

THE LOIRE VALLEY This area includes two ancient provinces, Touraine (centered on **Tours**) and Anjou (centered on **Angers**). It was beloved by royalty and nobility, flourishing during the Renaissance until Henry IV moved his court to Paris. Head here to see the most magnificent castles in France. Irrigated by the Loire River and its many tributaries, the valley produces many superb wines. For more information, see chapter 6.

NORMANDY This region will forever be linked to the 1944 D-day invasion. Some readers consider a visit to the D-day beaches the most emotionally worthwhile part of their trip. Normandy boasts 599km (371 miles) of coastline and a maritime tradition. It's a popular weekend getaway from Paris, and many hotels and restaurants thrive here, especially around the casino town of **Deauville.** Normandy's great attractions include **Rouen**'s cathedral, medieval **Bayeux,** the fishing village of **Honfleur,** and the abbey at **Mont St-Michel.** For more information, see chapter 7.

BRITTANY Jutting into the Atlantic, the westernmost region of France is known for its rocky coastlines, Celtic roots, frequent rain, and ancient dialect, akin to the Gaelic tongues of Wales and Ireland. Many French vacationers love the seacoast (rivaled only by the Côte d'Azur) for its sandy beaches, cliffs, and relatively modest—by French standards—prices. **Quimper** is Brittany's cultural capital, whereas **Carnac** is home to ancient Celtic dolmens and burial mounds. For more information, see chapter 8.

BURGUNDY   Few trips will prove as rewarding as several leisurely days spent exploring Burgundy, with its splendid old cities such as **Dijon.** Besides its famous cuisine (*boeuf* and *escargots à la bourguignonne*), the district contains, along its Côte d'Or, hamlets whose names (Mercurey, Beaune, Puligny-Montrachet, Vougeot, and Nuits-St-Georges) are synonymous with great wine. For more information, see chapter 9.

ALSACE-LORRAINE & THE FRENCH ALPS   Between Germany and the forests of the Vosges is the most Teutonic of France's provinces: Alsace, with cosmopolitan **Strasbourg** as its capital. Celebrated for its cuisine, particularly its *foie gras* and *choucroute,* this area is home to villages with half-timbered designs and the oldest wine road in France. Lorraine, birthplace of Joan of Arc, witnessed many battles during the world wars, though its capital **Nancy,** remains elegant and holds the beautiful place Stanislas. The much-eroded peaks of the Vosges forest, the closest thing to a wilderness in France, offer lovely hiking while the French Alps offer amazing skiing in **Chamonix** and **Courchevel** and incredible scenery of snowcapped peaks, glaciers, and Alpine lakes. Don't miss **Annecy** for a picturesque sightseeing town or **Evian-les-Bains** for a relaxing break after all your touring. For more information, see chapter 10.

THE RHÔNE VALLEY   This fertile area in eastern France follows the curves of the River Rhône from Beaujolais wine country in the North towards the borders of Provence in the South. The district is thoroughly French, unflinchingly bourgeois, and dedicated to preserving the gastronomic and cultural traditions that have produced some of the most celebrated chefs in France. Only two hours by train from Paris, the region's cultural centerpiece, **Lyon,** is France's "second city." Wine lovers will enjoy contrasting the aromatic red wines of **Beaujolais** with the robust red wines of the Northern Rhône or mythical appellations such as Côte Rôtie and Hermitage. Gourmands should travel to **Valence** to dine with France's only Michelin-starred female chef or to Bresse's ancient capital, **Bourg-en-Bresse,** which produces the world's finest poultry. Try to visit the medieval

Village of Vergisson surrounded by vineyards, Burgundy

Mont Blanc reflected in Cheserys Lake, French Alps

villages of **Pérouges** and **Vienne,** 27km (17 miles) south of Lyon; the latter is known for its Roman ruins. For more information, see chapter 11.

PROVENCE   One of France's most popular destinations stretches from the southern Rhône River to the Italian border. Long frequented by starving artists, *la bourgeoisie,* and the downright rich and famous, its premier cities are **Aix-en-Provence,** associated with Cézanne; **Arles,** famous for bullfighting and Van Gogh; **Avignon,** the 14th-century capital of Christendom; and **Marseille,** a port city established by the Phoenicians that today is the melting pot of France. Quieter and more romantic are villages such as **St-Rémy-de-Provence, Les Baux,** and **Gordes.** To the west, the **Camargue** is the marshy delta formed by two arms of the Rhône River. Rich in bird life, it's famous for its grassy flats and such fortified medieval sites as **Aigues-Mortes.** For more information, see chapter 12.

THE FRENCH RIVIERA (CÔTE D'AZUR)   The resorts of the fabled Côte d'Azur (Azure Coast) still evoke glamour: **Cannes, St-Tropez, Cap d'Antibes,** and **Juan-les-Pins.** July and August are the most buzzing months, while spring and fall are still sunny but way more laid-back. **Nice** is the biggest city and most convenient base for exploring the area. The Principality of **Monaco** only occupies about 2 sq. km (¾ sq. mile) but has enough sights, restaurants, and opulence to go around. Along the coast are some sandy beaches, but many are pebbly. Topless bathing is common, especially in St-Tropez, and some of the restaurants are citadels of conspicuous consumption. Dozens of artists and their patrons have littered the landscape with world-class galleries and art museums. For more information, see chapter 13.

BORDEAUX & DORDOGNE   Frequently ignored by North Americans, this delicious and delightful region has long been discovered by the English, who have staged a post-modern invasion of their historic territory, Aquitaine. Bordeaux, the area's largest (and liveliest) city, is famed for its booming wine industry and its grand 18th century architecture. Nearby, the legendary vineyards of the Bordelais create wines like St-Emilion and Pauillac. The splendid Dordogne River valley has been a vacation spot since Cro-Magnon peoples were painting bison on cave walls in Lascaux. Today visitors flock to the valley to marvel at prehistoric sites, ramble through exquisite villages, and enjoy the gastronomic pleasures of Périgord (duck confit, foie gras, truffles…). For more information, see chapter 14.

FRANCE ITINERARIES
1 WEEK IN PARIS & NORMANDY

If you budget your days carefully, 1 week provides enough time to visit the major attractions of Paris, such as the **Musée du Louvre** (the world's greatest art gallery), the **Eiffel Tower,** and **Notre-Dame.** After 2 days in Paris, head for the former royal stamping grounds of **Versailles,** followed by Normandy (an easy commute from Paris), visiting such highlights as the **D-day beaches,** the cathedral city of **Rouen** (where Joan of Arc was burned at the stake), the tapestry of **Bayeux,** and the incredible monastery of **Mont-St-Michel.**

DAYS 1 & 2: arrive in Paris ★★★

Take a flight that arrives in Paris as early as possible on **DAY 1.** Check into your hotel and hit the nearest cafe for a pick-me-up café au lait and a croissant. Since you are probably still groggy with jet lag, limit intellectual activity and head to the **Eiffel Tower ★★★** for a literal overview of the city. After coming back to Earth, take the RER C to **place St-Michel** and find lunch in the **Latin Quarter ★★★.** If jet lag is a problem, now is the time to return to the hotel and take a nap. Continue, refreshed, to the **Ile de la Cité** and marvel at the stained glass of the **Ste-Chapelle ★★★** and the heavenly vaulted arches of the Cathedral of **Notre Dame ★★★.** Now take a break from cultural icons and enjoy some shopping or sit in a cafe and enjoy the sunset in the trendy—and beautiful—**Marais ★★★** neighborhood, before scouting out a restaurant for dinner (if you have the wherewithal you can visit one of the many small-ish museums in this area). Walk off your meal with a romantic stroll along the **quays of the Seine,** and enjoy the magical nighttime lighting of the various monuments along the river's banks.

On **DAY 2,** get an early start and head for the **Louvre ★★★.** Spend at least a couple hours soaking in its many artistic wonders (and don't forget to see the **Mona Lisa**). Recover with a stroll and a sit in the **Tuilleries Garden ★★★,** and perhaps a picnic. Continue strolling to the **place de la Concorde ★★★** and admire the Egyptian obelisk, then peer down the **Champs-Elysées ★★** and see the **Arc de Triomphe ★★★** in the distance. End the day poking around the delightful **St-Germain ★★★** neighborhood, where you can visit a church (St-Germain-des-Prés or St-Sulpice), check out famous cafes (Les Deux Magots, Café de Flore), or shop until you drop. Enjoy one of the many nearby restaurants and then scope out Parisian nightlife.

DAY 3: a day trip to Versailles ★★★

Bid *adieu* to Paris and take the RER Line C to the **Versailles/Rive Gauche station.** You can spend a full day at Versailles and see the château, meander in the gardens, and visit Marie Antoinette's domain. Or else just go for the palace highlights, which should take around 3 hours and, includes the Grands and Petits

Versailles

Appartements, the glittering Hall of Mirrors, Gabriel's Opera House, the Royal Chapel, and the gardens.

DAY 4: Normandy's capital of Rouen ★★

Take an early train to Rouen and check in to one of the city's great hotels. Spend at least 2 hours exploring the city's ancient core, especially its **Cathédrale Notre-Dame** (p. 215), immortalized in paintings by Monet. Stand at the **place du Vieux-Marché** (p. 214), where Joan of Arc was executed for heresy in 1431, and visit the **Eglise St-Maclou** (p. 216), a 1432 church in the Flamboyant Gothic style. After lunch, rent a car for the rest of your trip and drive to **Giverny**—it's only 60km (37 miles) southeast of Rouen. At Giverny, visit the **Claude Monet Foundation,** returning to your hotel in Rouen for the night.

DAY 5: Bayeux ★★ & Caen ★

Even after a leisurely breakfast, you can easily be in the city of Caen by late morning, with plenty of time to visit **Abbaye aux Hommes** (p. 230), founded by William the Conqueror. After a hearty Norman lunch in Caen, continue west to the city of **Bayeux** to view the celebrated **Musée de la Tapisserie de Bayeux** (p. 233). Stay overnight in Bayeux.

DAY 6: the D-Day beaches ★★★

Reserve this day for exploring the D-day beaches where Allied forces launched "the Longest Day," the mammoth invasion of Normandy in June, 1944 that signaled the beginning of the end of Hitler's Third Reich.

Your voyage of discovery can begin at the seaside resort of Arromanches-les-Bains, where you can visit the **Musée du Débarquement** (p. 237) before heading to **Omaha Beach** (p. 234), the moving **Normandy American Visitor Center** (p. 236), and the **Overlord Museum** (p. 237), with an easy roadside lunch en route.

That evening, drive to **Mont-St-Michel** (less than 2 hr. away) and overnight in the pedestrianized village on "the Rock," giving you plenty of time for an early-morning—and relatively tourist-free—visit to this popular UNESCO-protected attraction.

DAY 7: Mont-St-Michel ★★★

Allow around 3 hours to explore **Mont-St-Michel** (p. 240). Taking an English-language tour is one of the best ways to enjoy its great abbey, founded in 966. After lunch, return your car to Rouen, where you'll find frequent train service back to Paris and your flight home the following day.

A 1-WEEK EXTENSION TO THE LOIRE VALLEY & THE CÔTE D'AZUR

If you have 2 weeks to explore France, you'll have time to visit several regions—not only Paris, but also the best of the Loire Valley châteaux, the most history-rich town of Provence (Avignon), and several resorts on the Riviera, taking in the beaches, art galleries, and even the Principality of Monaco.

For days 1 through 7, follow the "1 Week in Paris & Normandy" itinerary, above.

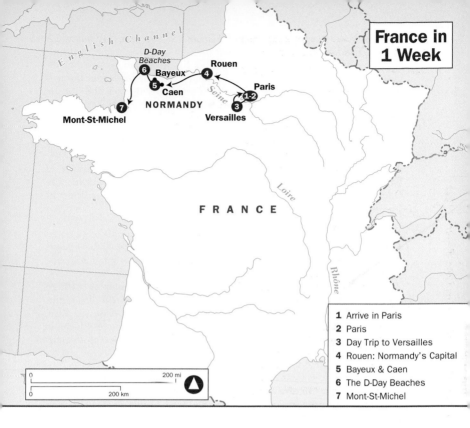

France in
1 Week

D-Day Beaches
Bayeux
Rouen
Caen
Paris
NORMANDY
Mont-St-Michel
Versailles

English Channel
Seine
Loire
Rhône

F R A N C E

0 — 200 mi
0 — 200 km

1 Arrive in Paris
2 Paris
3 Day Trip to Versailles
4 Rouen: Normandy's Capital
5 Bayeux & Caen
6 The D-Day Beaches
7 Mont-St-Michel

DAY 8: Orléans, gateway to the Loire Valley ★

Leave Paris on an early train to **Orléans** (trip time: 1 hr., 15 min.). Rent a car here and drive west to the **Château de Chambord** (p. 178), the largest château in the Loire Valley, representing the apogee of the French Renaissance architectural style. Allow 2 hours for a visit. Back on the road again, continue southwest to the **Château de Blois** (p. 177), called "the Versailles of the Renaissance" and a virtual illustrated storybook of French architecture. Stay overnight in Blois.

DAY 9: Amboise ★★ & Chenonceau ★★★

In the morning, continue southeast from Blois to **Amboise,** where you can check into a hotel for the night. Visit the 15th-century **Château d'Amboise** (p. 184), in the Italian Renaissance style, and also **Clos-Lucé** (p. 184), last residence of Leonardo da Vinci. In the afternoon, drive southeast to the **Château de Chenonceau** (p. 186), famous for the French dames who have occupied its precincts, including Diane de Poitiers (mistress of the king) and Catherine de Médicis (the jealous queen). You can spend a couple of hours at the château before driving back to Amboise for the night.

DAY 10: Avignon, gateway to Provence ★★★

From Amboise, get an early start and drive east to Orléans to return your rental car. Then take an early train from Orléans to Paris's Gare d'Austerlitz, then the Métro or a taxi to the Gare de Lyon, and hop on a TGV bound for Avignon (2½ hr.).

Check into a hotel in **Avignon,** one of Europe's most beautiful medieval cities. Before the day fades, you should have time to wander through the old city to get your bearings, shop for Provençal souvenirs, and see one of the smaller sights, such as the **Pont St-Bénézet.** See p. 367.

DAY 11: Avignon to St-Tropez ★★★

In the morning, spend 2 hours touring the **Palais des Papes** (p. 368), the capital of Christendom during the 14th century. After lunch in one of Avignon's cozy bistros or cobblestoned outdoor cafes, rent a car and drive to **St-Tropez** (p. 410). Spend a good part of the early evening in one of the cafes along the harbor, indulging in that favorite French pastime of people-watching.

DAY 12: chic Cannes ★★★

Before leaving St-Tropez in the morning, check out the Impressionist paintings at **Musée de l'Annonciade** (p. 415). Drive 50km (31 miles) east along the coast until you reach Cannes.

Assuming it's summer, get in some time at the beach, notably at **Plage de la Croisette** (p. 424), and feel free to wear your most revealing swimwear. In the afternoon, take the ferry to **Ile Ste-Marguerite** (p. 427), where the "Man in the Iron Mask" was imprisoned. You can visit his cell. That evening, you may want to flirt with Lady Luck at one of the plush **casinos** (p. 427).

DAY 13: Nice, capital of the Riviera ★★★

It's only a 32km (20-mile) drive east from Cannes to **Nice,** the Riviera's largest city. After checking in to a hotel (the most affordable along the Riviera), stroll through **Vieille Ville** (p. 453), the Old Town. Enjoy a snack of

The Mediterranean Sea at Nice, French Riviera

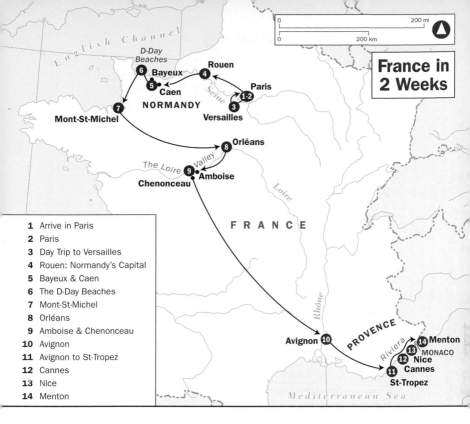

France in 2 Weeks

1 Arrive in Paris
2 Paris
3 Day Trip to Versailles
4 Rouen: Normandy's Capital
5 Bayeux & Caen
6 The D-Day Beaches
7 Mont-St-Michel
8 Orléans
9 Amboise & Chenonceau
10 Avignon
11 Avignon to St-Tropez
12 Cannes
13 Nice
14 Menton

socca, a round crepe made with chickpea flour that vendors sell steaming hot in the cours Saleya market. Then head for the **promenade des Anglais** (p. 452), the wide boulevard along the waterfront. In the afternoon, head for the famed hill town of **St-Paul-de-Vence,** only 20km (12 miles) to the north. You can wander its ramparts in about 30 minutes before descending to the greatest modern-art museum in the Riviera, the **Fondation Maeght** (p. 442).

Continue on to **Vence** (p. 443) for a visit to the great Henri Matisse's artistic masterpiece, **Chapelle du Rosaire** (p. 445). From there, it's just 24km (15 miles) southeast back to Nice, where you can enjoy dinner at a typical Niçois bistro.

DAY 14: Nice to Menton ★★

While still overnighting in Nice, head east for the most thrilling drive in all of France, a trip along the **Grande Corniche** highway, which stretches 31km (19 miles) east from Nice to the little resort of **Menton** (p. 476) near the Italian border. Allow 3 hours for this trip. Highlights along this road include **Roquebrune-Cap Martin** and **La Turbie** (p. 466 and p. 477). The greatest view along the Riviera is at the **Eze Belvedere,** at 1,200m (3,936 ft.). Return to Nice by dinnertime and prepare for your flight home in the morning.

FRANCE FOR FAMILIES

France offers many attractions for kids. Our suggestion is to limit the bustle of **Paris** to 2 days, and then spend a day wandering the spectacular grounds and glittering interiors of **Versailles,** 2 days in **Disneyland Paris,** and 2 days on the **Riviera.**

DAYS 1 & 2: Paris ★★★

On **DAY 1**, spend the morning at the **Luxembourg Gardens ★★★**, where your offspring can go wild at the huge playground, sail boats in the fountain, ride a pony, or just run around and have fun. Parents can take turns sneaking off to visit nearby attractions like the **Panthéon ★**, **Musée Zadkine ★★**, and **St-Etienne-du-Mont ★★**, or just find peace and quiet in a **Latin Quarter** cafe. Then walk down to **St-Germain-des-Près ★★** and visit the church before lunch. After settling your bill, duck into **St-Sulpice ★★** and then hop the #87 bus to the **Champs de Mars** and visit the **Eiffel Tower ★★★**. After that, everyone will probably be pooped and ready to relax with **a boat ride on the Seine,** which departs near the tower.

On **DAY 2,** start the day at the **Jardin des Plantes ★★**, where you can choose between the **Museum National d'Histoire Naturelle ★★**, the **Ménagerie ★** (a small zoo), and a playground. There's also a fun boxwood labyrinth at the top of the hill. Lunch at the tiled tearoom (with an enclosed patio) at the nearby **Mosquée de Paris.** Once stomachs are filled, head over to **Notre Dame ★★★**, and if your kids are old enough (and the line is not too long), climb the 255 steps to the first level of the cathedral's towers, where there is a beautiful view framed by a collection of photogenic gargoyles. Now take the metro #12 up to the **Butte Montmartre ★★★** to see the sunset from the esplanade in front of the **Basilique du Sacré-Coeur ★**. Even if your kids don't appreciate the view, they will enjoy the ride in the **funicular** that you take to get there. Up on the esplanade, there is plenty of room to run around, and lots of buskers for entertainment. If that doesn't work, there is always the merry-go-round at **place des Abbesses ★** when you head back down to your hotel.

DAY 3: Versailles ★★★

Tear yourself away from the glories of Paris for a day at the **Château de Versailles** (p. 145). Take the RER line C to the Versailles/Rive Gauche station. Hopefully, your kids will be old enough to appreciate that they are wandering around a royal palace and seeing where the king and queen slept. If not (or if they just don't care), they might enjoy running around or riding a bike through the park, or rowing a boat on the Grand Canal. You can buy a picnic lunch in Paris and enjoy it on the grounds, or else purchase a sandwich at one of the stands placed in discreet corners of the garden.

DAYS 4 & 5: Disneyland Paris ★★

Do it for the kids—they've put up with three days of grown-up stuff (or at least that's how they'll see it). Allow a full day to see the highlights of **Disneyland Paris,** plus part of another day to either absorb some secondary adventures, or take in **Walt Disney Studios.** You can probably see the main park, with all its classic areas (**Main Street, U.S.A., Frontierland, Tomorrowland,** and so on) on the first day, and visit **Walt Disney**

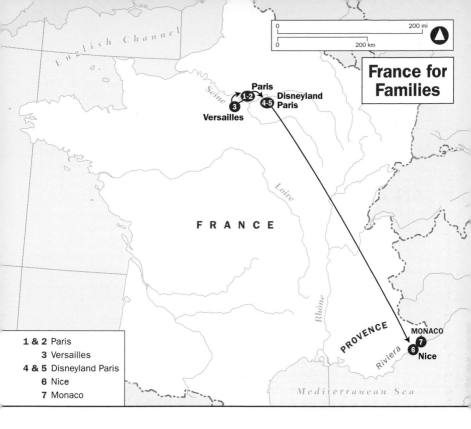

0   200 mi

0   200 km

France for Families

English Channel

Seine

Paris
1-2

Disneyland Paris
4-5

3
Versailles

Loire

F R A N C E

Rhône

Loire

PROVENCE

MONACO
7
6
Nice

Riviera

Mediterranean Sea

1 & 2	Paris
3	Versailles
4 & 5	Disneyland Paris
6	Nice
7	Monaco

Studios, the second day, leaving early enough to get back to Paris. Stay overnight in one of the many onsite hotels, which range from ridiculously expensive to only slightly so (there are oodles of attractive package deals). The RER commuter express train A takes you from Etoile in Paris to Marne-la-Vallée/Chessy in 45 minutes.

DAY 6: Nice ★★★

Fly to Nice, capital of the French Riviera. If you flew Air France transatlantic, Nice can often be attached as a low-cost extension of your round-trip fare.

In Nice, you can check into your hotel for 2 nights, as the city has the most affordable hotels on the coast. Set out to explore this old city. There's always a lot of free entertainment in summer along Nice's seafront boardwalk, the **promenade des Anglais** (p. 452), and the people-watching on the Riviera—particularly on the beach—is likely to leave your kids wide-eyed.

In the afternoon, journey to the evocative hill town of **St-Paul-de-Vence** (p. 440). Children delight in touring the ramparts, strolling along the pedestrian-only rue Grande, or exploring the sculpture garden at the **Fondation Maeght** (p. 442), one of France's greatest modern-art museums.

Return to Nice for the evening and take your kids for a stroll through the Old Town, dining as the sun dips over the Mediterranean.

DAY 7: Monaco ★★★

While still based in Nice, head for the tiny principality of Monaco, which lies only 18km (11 miles) east of Nice.

Children will enjoy the changing-of-the-guard ceremony at **Les Grands Appartements du Palais** (p. 473), where Prince Albert married South African swimmer Charlene Wittstock in 2011. But the best part of Monaco for kids is the **Musée Océanographique de Monaco** (p. 474), home to sharks and other exotic sea creatures.

Return to Nice that night and prepare for your flight home in the morning.

3 | AN ART LOVER'S TOUR OF FRANCE

From contemporary art in Paris to modern masters along the southern coast, France is a country infused with art. Aficionados can experience an unforgettable trip taking in Paris (2 days), Aix-en-Provence (1 day), and then the Riviera between St-Tropez and Nice (4 days). Museum visits can be interspersed with wonderful meals, sunbathing, and stops at the area's architectural and artistic highlights.

DAYS 1 & 2: Paris ★★★

Start your art tour of Paris with a quick check of what's currently on the city: The **Grand Palais ★★** (p. 106), **Musée de Luxembourg,** and the **Pinacothèque de Paris** all host excellent temporary exhibitions.

You can attend a show at any of these venues, or begin your day at the newly renovated **Musée de Montmartre ★★** (p. 112), formerly home to both Renoir and Utrillo. Then hop onto the Métro and head south to the **Jardin du Luxembourg ★★★**. After a nice stroll in the gardens, head over to tiny **Musée Zadkine ★★** dedicated to sculptor Ossip Zadkine and located in the artist's former house and atelier. Take a minute to rest in the pretty little garden. Enjoy a leisurely lunch at one of the neighborhood's many bistros. Round out the afternoon by taking in a cutting-edge contemporary exhibition at the wacky **Palais de Tokyo** (p. 109).

On **DAY 2,** spend the morning admiring the contemporary art on display at the **Centre Pompidou ★★**. After lunching at one of the many nearby restaurants, amble over to the **Marais** (p. 97), and either cruise the art galleries, or visit the newly re-opened **Musée Picasso ★★★**.

Mid-afternoon, jump aboard one of the many TGV trains heading south to Aix-en-Provence. The journey takes around 3 hours, leaving you plenty of time to enjoy a typical Provençal dinner upon arrival.

DAY 3: Aix-en-Provence ★★

Paul Cézanne is Aix's most celebrated son. Begin your day at his **Atelier** (p. 391), almost perfectly preserved as it was when the great

Clock tower at Aix-en-Provence

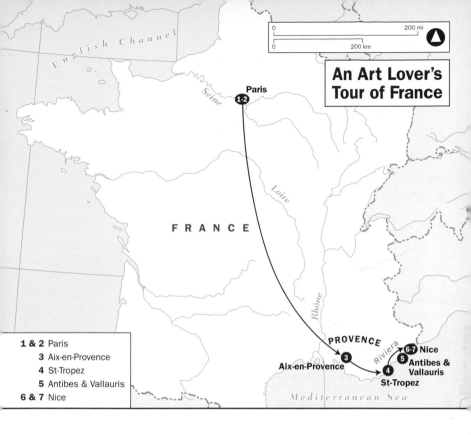

An Art Lover's Tour of France

English Channel

Seine

Paris **1-2**

FRANCE

Loire

Rhône

PROVENCE

3 Aix-en-Provence

Riviera

6-7 Nice

5 Antibes & Vallauris

4 St-Tropez

Mediterranean Sea

1 & 2 Paris
3 Aix-en-Provence
4 St-Tropez
5 Antibes & Vallauris
6 & 7 Nice

0   200 mi
0   200 km

artist worked here more than a century ago. There are regularly scheduled English-language tours of the site. Afterward, a visit to the city's famed **Musée Granet** (p. 392)—one of the region's most superb modern-art museums—is a must.

Aix's plane-tree-shaded **cours Mirabeau** is almost a work of art in itself. Be sure to drop into **Brasserie Les Deux Garçons** (p. 391), where Cézanne used to drink and debate with the famous French writer Emile Zola.

After lunch, rent a car and drive to **St-Tropez** (p. 410). Warm evenings are best enjoyed strolling the port's pretty quays or taking in the million-dollar panoramas from the hilltop **Citadelle** (p. 414).

DAY 4: St-Tropez ★★★

Since the 1890s, when painters Signac and Bonnard discovered St-Tropez, artists and their patrons have been drawn to the French Riviera. Spend the morning appreciating the **Musée de l'Annonciade**'s (p. 415) Impressionist paintings, many of them depicting St-Tropez and the surrounding coast.

After lunch in one of the town's sidewalk cafes, drive around 100km (62 miles) east along the coast until you reach Nice, where you'll base yourself for the next 3 nights. Return your rental car—traffic-heavy roads, combined with excellent public transportation, render your own vehicle unnecessary here.

DAY 5: Antibes & Vallauris ★★

Today you'll spend the day following in the footsteps of one of the 20th-century's modern masters: Pablo Picasso. Take one of the frequent trains from Nice to Antibes (20 min.). On the edge of the picturesque, pedestrian-friendly Old Town sits the 14th-century Grimaldi Château, now home to the **Musée Picasso** (p. 438). The Spanish artist lived and worked in this castle in 1946.

Stroll through Antibes' covered market, then—appetite piqued—stop into a small bistro, such as **Entre 2 Vins** (p. 437), for a light lunch. Next, make your way to Antibes' bus station, where frequent buses depart for Vallauris (35 min.). Picasso moved to this hilltop village during the 1950s, reviving the local ceramic-making industry and personally producing thousands of pieces of pottery. Visit Picasso's mammoth paintings in the **Musée National Picasso La Guerre et La Paix** (p. 429), the artist's tribute to pacifism.

Make your way back to Nice (it's quickest to simply reverse your route). Spend the evening strolling the promenade des Anglais or wandering the city's atmospheric Old Town.

DAYS 6 & 7: Nice ★★★

Outside of Paris, Nice is home to more museums than any other city in France. Begin your Day 6 citywide explorations in the neighborhood of Cimiez, where both the famed **Musée Matisse** (p. 454) and the **Musée National Message Biblique Marc Chagall** (p. 455) are located. It's possible to walk between the two (around 15 min.), but be sure to hit the Matisse Museum first—then it's downhill all the way to see Chagall's ethereal artworks.

If it's summertime, spend a couple of hours picnicking on the beach or relaxing with a glass of wine in one of the city's many sidewalk cafes. Mid-afternoon, make your way over the **Musée Masséna** (p. 454), where a combination of local art and history gives visitors a peek at the ritzy French Riviera of the past.

Use your final day to make a day trip to the hilltop village of **St-Paul-de-Vence** (p. 440), 20km (12 miles) to the north. Wander the St-Paul-de-Vence's ramparts for half an hour, before descending to the world-class modern art on display at the **Fondation Maeght** (p. 442). En route back to Nice, stop into the **Musée Renoir** in Cagnes-sur-Mer. The artist's former home and gardens were completely renovated in 2013. Note that you can either rent a car for the day or access both St-Paul-de-Vence and Cagnes-sur-Mer via frequent buses from Nice.

Spend your final night in Nice savoring a hearty Niçois dinner, paired with plenty of local wine.

PARIS

By Margie Rynn

4

Threw the word "Paris" conjures up such a potent brew of images and ideas that it's sometimes hard to find the meeting point between myth and reality. But the city's graceful streets, soaked in history, really are as elegant as they say, its monuments and museums as extraordinary; and a slightly world-weary, *fin-de-siècle* grandeur really is part of day-to-day existence. Paris is much more than a beautiful assemblage of buildings, however; it is the pulsing heart of the French nation.

Where to begin? With so many wonderful things to see, it's easy to get overwhelmed in the City of Light. If you are here for only a few days, you'll probably be spending most of your time in the city center, the nucleus of which is the Ile de la Cité. The **top neighborhoods** on most short-term visitors' hit parade are the 1st through 8th arrondissements (see "City Layout," below), which includes the Ile de la Cité, the Louvre area, the Champs Elysées, the Eiffel Tower, the Latin Quarter, the Marais, and St-Germain. **If you have a bit more time,** you should explore some of the outlying neighborhoods, like the funky and dynamic eastern areas of Mesnilmontant, Belleville, Canal St-Martin, and Bastille, or the elegant, museum-rich depths of the 16th arrondissement. Whether you're here for a few days or longer, this chapter is designed to give you the essential information you need to create a Paris itinerary that's just right for you.

ESSENTIALS & ORIENTATION
Arriving
BY PLANE

Paris has two international airports: **Aéroport d'Orly,** 18km (11 miles) south of the city (for both airports: www.aeroportsdeparis.fr; ☎ **00-33-1-70-36-39-50** from abroad, or **39-50** from France), and **Aéroport Roissy-Charles-de-Gaulle** (also known as CDG), 30km (19 miles) northeast. If you are taking Ryanair or another discount airline that arrives at **Beauvais** (www.aeroportbeauvais.com; ☎ **08-92-68-20-66**), be advised that that airport is located about 70km (40 miles) from Paris.

CHARLES DE GAULLE AIRPORT (ROISSY) **By commuter train:** The quickest way into central Paris is the **RER B** (www.ratp.fr), suburban trains that leave every 10 to 15 minutes between 5am and 10pm (midnight on weekends). It takes about 40 minutes to get to Paris, and RER B stops at several Métro stations including Châtelet-Les-Halles, Saint-Michel-Notre-Dame, and Luxembourg. A single ticket costs 9.50€ and you can buy it from the machines located in the stations at both terminals.

By bus: Air France operates two bus routes (**Les Cars Air France;** www.lescarsairfrance.com; ☎ **08-92-35-08-20**) from the airport to Port Maillot/Charles de Gaulle–Etoile and Gare de Lyon/Gare Montparnasse. Depending on the route, a one-way trip costs 15€ to 16€ adults and 7.50€ to 8€ children 2 to

11; both trips take about an hour, depending on traffic. Buses leave every 30 minutes between 6am and 9:30pm. The **Roissybus** (www.ratp.fr; ✆ **32-46** from France only) departs from the airport daily from 6am to 11pm and costs 10.50€ for the 60-minute ride. The bus leaves you in the center of Paris, at the corner of rue Scribe and rue Auber, near the Opera House.

By taxi: A taxi from Roissy into the city will cost at least 50€, not including 1€ per item of luggage, and the fare is 15 percent higher from 5pm to 10am, as well as on Sundays and bank holidays.

ORLY AIRPORT **By commuter train:** Take the 8-minute monorail **OrlyVal** to the station in the town of Anthony, and take the **RER B** into the center. Combined travel time is about 45 minutes. Trains run between 6am and 11pm, and the one-way fare for the OrlyVal plus the RER B is 11.45€ adults and 5.70€ children under 10. Alternatively, you can take the **"Paris par le Train" bus** (www. parisparletrain.fr) to the Pont de Rungis station and then get **RER C** to Paris. Buses leave every 15 minutes between 4:40am and 1am. Combined travel time is about 30 minutes, and the one-way fare for the Paris par le Train bus and the RER C is 6.60€.

By bus: Les Cars Air France (www.cars-airfrance.com; ✆ **08-92-35-08-20**) leaves every 20 minutes between 6am and 11:40pm, stopping at Gare Montparnasse, Invalides, and Charles de Gaulle–Etoile. The fare is 12.50€ one-way, 21€ round-trip, and 6.50€ children ages 2 to 11. Depending on the traffic, the journey takes about an hour.

By taxi: A taxi from Orly to central Paris will cost at least 50€, not including 1€ per item of luggage, and the fare is 15 percent higher from 5pm to 10am, as well as on Sundays and bank holidays.

BEAUVAIS AIRPORT Buses leave about 20 minutes after each flight has landed, and, depending on the traffic, take about 1 hour and 15 minutes to get to Paris. The bus drops you at Porte Maillot (Métro: Porte Maillot). To return to Beauvais, you need to be at the bus station at least 3 hours before the departure of your flight. A one-way ticket costs 16€.

BY TRAIN

Paris has six major train stations: **Gare d'Austerlitz** (13th arrond.), **Gare de Lyon** (12th arrond.), **Gare Montparnasse** (14th arrond.), **Gare St-Lazare** (8th arrond.), **Gare de l'Est** (10th arrond.), and **Gare du Nord** (10th arrond.). Each station can be reached by bus or Métro; details on each station can be found on the **SNCF** station site (www.gares-connexions.com/en). *Warning:* As in most major cities, the stations and surrounding areas are rather seedy and frequented by pickpockets. Be alert, especially at night.

BY BUS

Most long-haul buses arrive at the **Eurolines France** station on the eastern edge of the city, 23 av. du Général-de-Gaulle, Bagnolet (www.eurolines.fr; in France ✆ **08-92-89-90-91;** other countries **01-41-86-24-21;** Métro: Gallieni).

BY CAR

While I wouldn't recommend driving in Paris to my worst enemy, renting a car and driving around France before or after your Paris trip can be a lovely way to see the country. All of the major car-rental companies have offices here (see below), but you'll often get better deals if you reserve before you leave home. **AutoEurope** (www.autoeurope.com) is an excellent source for discounted rentals. Check its prices against **Avis** (www.avis.com; ✆ **08-21-23-07-60**); **Budget**

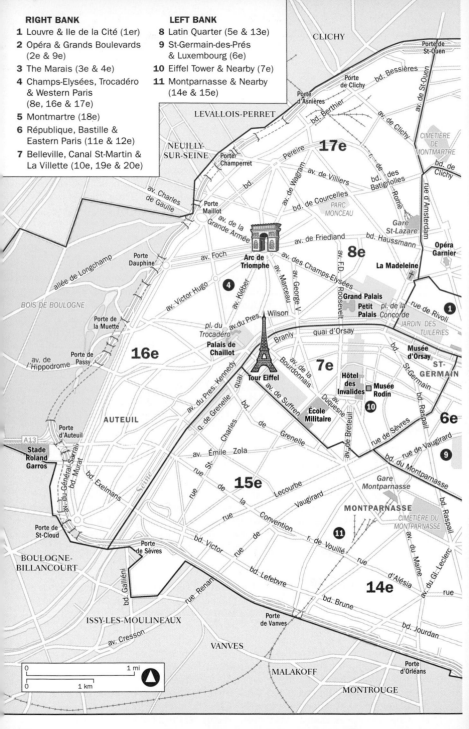

RIGHT BANK

1 Louvre & Ile de la Cité (1er)
2 Opéra & Grands Boulevards (2e & 9e)
3 The Marais (3e & 4e)
4 Champs-Elysées, Trocadéro & Western Paris (8e, 16e & 17e)
5 Montmartre (18e)
6 République, Bastille & Eastern Paris (11e & 12e)
7 Belleville, Canal St-Martin & La Villette (10e, 19e & 20e)

LEFT BANK

8 Latin Quarter (5e & 13e)
9 St-Germain-des-Prés & Luxembourg (6e)
10 Eiffel Tower & Nearby (7e)
11 Montparnasse & Nearby (14e & 15e)

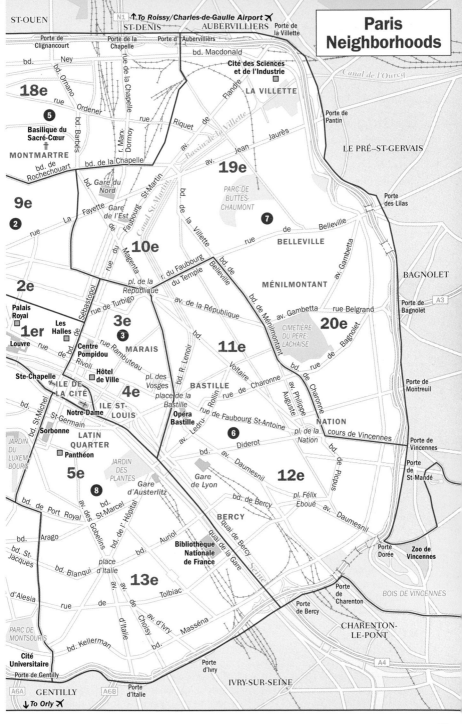

(www.budget.com; ✆ 08-25-00-35-64); **Europcar** (www.europcar.com; ✆ 08-25-35-83-58); **Hertz** (www.hertz.com; ✆ 08-25-86-18-61); **Rent-a-Car** (www.rentacar.fr; ✆ 08-91-70-02-00); or **Thrifty** (www.thrifty.com; ✆ 01-82-88-16-77).

Before you step on the gas, at the very least, try to get a hold of a list of international road signs; your rental agency should have one.

Getting Around Town

For everything you ever wanted to know about the city's public transport, visit the **RATP** (www.ratp.fr; ✆ 32-46 in France). Paris and its suburbs are divided into six travel zones, but you'll probably only be concerned with zones 1 and 2, which cover the city itself.

RATP tickets are valid on the Métro, bus, and RER. You can buy tickets over the counter (if you are lucky—ticket booths are an endangered species) or from machines at most Métro entrances. A **single ticket** costs 1.70€ and a *carnet* of 10 tickets costs 13.70€. Children 4 to 9 years old pay half price; kids under 4 ride free. Tourists can benefit from a **Paris Visite** pass, which offers unlimited travel in zones on bus, Métro, and RER, and discounts on some attractions. Think hard about how much you are going to use your pass however, as you'll probably end up walking a lot, and in the end a cheaper *carnet* of 10 tickets might do the trick. A 1-day Paris Visite adult pass for zones 1 to 3 costs 10.85€, a 2-day pass 17.65€, a 3-day pass 24.10€, and a 5-day pass 34.70€. Each day begins at midnight and finishes at midnight the following day. It is also possible to buy more expensive passes for zones 1 to 5, which will also get you to the airport. For a slightly cheaper 1-day pass, try a **Mobilis** ticket, which offers unlimited travel in zones 1 up to 5; a pass for zones 1 and 2 costs 6.80€. For travelers under 26, look for the **Ticket Jeunes,** a 1-day ticket that can be used on a Saturday, Sunday, or bank holiday and provides unlimited travel in zones 1 to 3 for 3.75€, or zones 1 to 5 for 8.10€.

BY MÉTRO OR RER (SUBWAY)

The city's first Métro, or subway, was at the apex of high tech when it was inaugurated on July 19, 1900. Today, more than a century later, it still functions very well. Aside from the occasional strike or work slowdown, the Métro is usually efficient and civilized, especially if you avoid rush hour (7:30–9:30am and 6–8pm). It's generally safe at night (although you might want to think twice about using it to get to more isolated parts of the city); the service shuts down between midnight and 1am weekdays, and at 2am on Friday, Saturday, and pre-holiday evenings. The suburban trains (the RER; see below) close down around the same time (without the weekend bonus hour). The **RER** (pronounced "ehr-euh-ehr") is the suburban train network that dashes through the city making limited stops. The downsides are: (a) They don't run as often as the Métro, and (b) they're hard to figure out since they run on a different track system and the same lines can have multiple final destinations. *Important:* Make sure to hold on to your ticket; you'll need it to get *out* of the turnstile on the way out.

BY BUS

Thanks to a rash of new dedicated bus lanes, the buses can be an efficient way to get around town, and you'll get a scenic tour to boot. The majority run from 6:30am to 9:30pm (a few operate until 12:30am), and service is reduced on Sundays and holidays. You can use Métro tickets on the buses or you can buy tickets directly from the driver (2€/$3). Tickets need to be validated in the machine next to the driver's cabin. Your regular Métro ticket gives you a free transfer, to be used within 1½ hours; if you buy your ticket on the bus there is no transfer included.

BY TRAM

Over the past few years, Paris has added three new tramway lines, with extensions and new lines in progress. They connect Paris with its suburbs; within Paris they run along the outer circle of boulevards that trace the city limits. Tickets are the same price as the Métro.

BY TAXI

This is the most expensive way to get around and not necessarily the most efficient. Merely hailing a cab can be an ordeal, since you'll have to find a taxi stand (in practice, you can hail them in the street, but not all will stop). Taxi stands resemble bus stops and sport a blue "taxi" sign. You can also call the dispatcher at ✆ 01-45-30-30-30.

Calculating fares is a complicated business. When you get in, the meter should read 2.50€. Then, the basic rates for Paris *intramuros* ranges from 1€–1.50€ per kilometer, depending on the day of the week and the hour. There's a minimum fare of 6.86€; if you have more than three people in your party, you'll also be charged 3€ for each additional passenger. You'll be charged 1€ for each suitcase you put in the trunk. The saving grace here is that the distances are usually not huge, and barring excessive traffic, your average cross-town fare should fall between 15€ and 20€ for two without baggage. Tipping is not obligatory, but a 1€ tip is customary for short trips; for longer hauls a 5 to 10 percent tip should do.

It's often easier to call a cab then to hail one on the street: contact **Les Taxis Bleus** (✆ 36-09, .15€ per min; www.taxis-bleus.com) or **Taxi G7** (✆ 36-07, .15€ per min; www.taxisg7.fr). Avoid minicabs or unlicensed taxis.

BY BICYCLE

Cycling in Paris has been revolutionized by the hugely successful **Vélib'** bike rental scheme (the name comes from *vélo* meaning bicycle and *liberté* meaning freedom) launched in 2007. It takes a little effort for a tourist to sign up, but it's worth it to see Paris from two wheels (see box, below).

Alternatively, you can rent a bike from **Paris à vélo, c'est sympa!,** 22 rue Alphonse Baudin (www.parisvelosympa.com; ✆ 01-48-87-60-01; Métro: St-Sébastien-Froissart or Richard Lenoir). Rentals cost 12€ for half a day and 15€ for a full day, but they do require 250€ or a passport as a deposit.

ON FOOT

If you have the time and the energy, the best mode of transport in this small and walkable city is your own two feet. You can cross the center of town (say from the Place St-Michel to Les Halles) in about 20 minutes. This is the best way to see and experience the city, and take in all the little details that make it all so wonderful.

BY CAR

Driving is *not* recommended in Paris, but the auto-adventurous may want to try tooling around in a small electric car through **Autolib'** (www.autolib.eu; ✆ 08-00-94-20-00), the recent outgrowth of the popular Velib' bicycle rental program (see above). A similar concept to its cycling cousin, the scheme involves short-term electric car rental. To register you can go to one of the Autolib' parking spaces or to the Autolib' information center (5 rue Edouard VII, 9th arrond.) with

Velib': A Great Way to Cycle Around Paris

Since July 2007, when the mayor's office inaugurated the **Velib'** (vel-*LEEB*) system of low-cost bike rentals, Parisians have been pedaling up a storm. Traffic be dammed: It's fun to ride around town, drop off your bike near your destination, and not have to worry about locking it up. The way it works is this: You buy a 1- or 7-day subscription (1.70€ or 8€/$2 or $11, respectively) from the machine at one of hundreds of bike stands, which gives you the right to as many half-hour rides as you'd like for 1 or 7 days. If you want to go over a half-hour, you pay 1€ for your extra half-hour, 2€ for the half-hour after that one and 4€ for the third half-hour on. Everything is meticulously explained, in English, on the website, www.velib.fr, and there's even a number you can call for English-speaking assistance (© **01-30-79-79-30**). There's one big catch, however—to use the machines you must have a credit or debit card with a chip in it. This can be a problem for North American tourists, so I advise either getting a TravelEx "cash passport" with money on it (www.travelex.com), or, even easier, just buy your subscription ahead of time online (make sure you have your secret code to punch in on the stand). Helmets are not provided, so if you're feeling queasy about launching into traffic, bring one along. There are few bike lanes so far, but success has been such that new ones are being added, and cyclists have the right to ride in the bus lanes. *One more tip:* Before you ride, get a map of the city that shows where the bike stands are so you don't waste precious time looking for a place to check in or check out.

your driving license, a valid form of ID, and a credit card, or you can simply register online. A 1-day subscription is free, but you pay 9€ per half hour. A 7-day subscription is 10€ plus 7€ per half hour, a month is 25€ plus 6.50€ per half-hour, and a year is 120€ plus 5.5€ per half hour. You are given a badge that you then pass over a sensor at a rental station to unlock the car. Unplug it from the charger and drive away. To return it, you must find a spot at an Autolib' station and plug in your car.

Visitor Information

A good place to start any information quest is at the Paris Tourist Office (25 rue des Pyramides, 1st arrond.; www.parisinfo.com; © **01-49-52-42-63;** Métro: Pyramides). There's always a multilingual person on the other end of the line when you call (if you'd prefer not to spring for an international call, surf to their comprehensive website). The Tourist Office has several branches sprinkled around the city; check the website for addresses and hours.

City Layout

One of the nice things about Paris is that it's relatively small. It's not a sprawling megalopolis like Tokyo or London; in fact, Paris *intramuros,* or inside the long-gone city walls, numbers a mere 2.27 million habitants, and, excluding the large exterior parks of Bois de Vincinnes and the Bois de Boulogne, measures about 87 sq. km (34 sq. miles). (The suburbs, on the other hand, are sprawling, but chances are you won't be spending much, if any, time there.) So getting around is not difficult, provided you have a general sense of where things are.

The city is vaguely egg shaped, with the Seine cutting a wide upside-down "U"-shaped arc through the middle. The northern half is known as the **Right Bank,** and the southern, the **Left Bank.** To the uninitiated, the only way to remember is to face west, or downstream, so that the Right Bank will be to your right, and the Left to your left.

If you can't get your banks straight, don't worry, because most Parisians don't talk in terms of Right or Left Bank, but in terms of ***arrondissements,*** or districts. The city is neatly split up into 20 official arrondissements, which spiral out from the center of the city. So the lower the number, the closer you'll be to the center, and as the numbers go up, you'll head toward the outer limits. Though their borders don't always correspond to historical neighborhoods, they do chop up the city into easily digestible chunks, so if you know what arrondissement your destination is in, your chances of finding it easily go way up. Your chances will be even better if you have a good map. Even if you're only in the city for a week, it's worthwhile to invest in a purse-size map book (ask for a "Paris par Arrondissement" at bookstores or larger newsstands), which costs around 8€. The book should include a street index and a detailed set of maps by arrondissement—one of the best is called "Le Petit Parisien," which includes separate Métro, bus, and street maps for each district. To get a general sense of where the arrondissements are, see the map on p. 54 and 55.

[FastFACTS] PARIS

ATMs/Banks   ATMs can be found all over the city. For currency exchange, look for **Travelex** (www.travelex.fr) counters at Paris airports and train stations. **American Express** still changes money and cashes travelers checks at its Kanoo Change (11 rue Scribe), but it no longer sells travelers checks in France.

Dentists & Doctors   To download a list of English-speaking dentists and doctors in Paris, visit the U.S. Citizens Services page on the U.S. Embassy website (http://france.usembassy.gov) and click on "Resources for U.S. Citizens." You can also reach U.S. Citizens Services by phone at ☏ **01-43-12-22-22.**

Hospitals   Paris has good public hospitals; visit www.aphp.fr for locations and details on specialties. Private hospitals with English-speaking staff: **American Hospital of Paris** (63 bd. Victor Hugo, 92200 Neuilly-sur-Seine; ☏ **01-46-41-25-25;** www.american-hospital.org) and **Institut Hospitalier Franco-Britannique** (3 rue Barbès or 4 rue Kleber, Levallois; ☏ **01-47-59-59-59;** www.ihfb.org/en).

Embassies   See planning chapter, p. 520.

Emergencies   For an ambulance, call ☏ **15.** Emergency services: ☏ **112.** You can also call the fire brigade (*Sapeurs-Pompiers;* ☏ **18**), who are trained to deal with all kinds of medical emergencies, not just fires. For the police, call ☏ **17.**

Lost & Found   **Bureau des Objets Trouvés** (36 rue des Morillons, 15e; ☏ **08-21-00-25-25,** .12€ per min). If you lose something in the Métro or on a train, contact the station on the line where you lost the object.

Mail & Postage   There are post offices (**La Poste,** ☏ **36-31;** www.laposte.fr) in every arrondissement. Most are open Mon–Fri 8:30am–8pm, Sat 8am–1pm; the main post office (52 rue du Louvre Métro: Louvre-Rivoli) is open Mon–Sat 7:30am–6am and Sunday 10am–6am. Stamps are also sold in *tabacs* (tobacconists).

Pharmacies There are pharmacies all over the city; look for the green neon cross above the door. Most are closed Sundays; both the **Pharmacie les Champs** (84 av. des Champs-Elysées, ✆ **01-45-62-02-41**) and the **Pharmacie Européene** (6 place de Clichy; ✆ **01-48-74-65-18**) are open 24 hours daily.

Safety In general, Paris is a safe city and it is safe to use the Métro at any time, though it's best to avoid the RER late at night. **Beware of pickpockets,** especially in tourist areas and the Louvre; organized gangs will even use children as decoys. Avoid walking around the less safe neighborhoods (Barbès-Rochechouart, Strasbourg St-Denis, Châtelet-Les-Halles) alone at night and never get into an unmarked taxi.

Toilets Paris is full of gray-colored, street toilet kiosks, which are a little daunting to the uninitiated, but free, and are automatically washed and disinfected after each use.

WHERE TO STAY

Paris has more than 1,500 hotels, from palaces fit for a pasha to tiny family-run operations whose best features are their warm welcome and personal touch. In theory, you should be able to find something in line with your budget, your time-frame, and your personal tastes. But even if you can't find the hotel of your dreams in the list below, don't despair—at the end of this section I list a few alternative lodging options, including bed-and-breakfasts and short-term apartment rentals.

The Right Bank

LOUVRE & ILE DE LA CITÉ (1ST ARRONDISSEMENT)

The area surrounding the Louvre is littered with hotels, most of which are dread-fully overpriced. Yes, if you only are in town for 1 or 2 days, a central locale is key, since time is of the essence. But if you have a little more time, you'll find much more comfortable lodgings, at the same or lower prices, a 10-minute walk away.

Expensive

Hotel Brighton ★★ Did someone say "view"? How about a panorama of the Louvre and the Tuileries gardens from your bed? While not every room in this gracious hotel has the jackpot view, those in the "deluxe" and "executive" catego-ries do, and all have a subdued, classic look with elegant fabrics draping windows and tasteful decorative touches. This classy establishment, under the arcades of the rue de Rivoli may not be not quite as grand as the Meurice, just down the block, but it is about one-third the price. Understandably, rooms with views book up early, so plan ahead.

218 rue de Rivoli, 1st arrond. ✆ **01-47-03-61-61.** www.paris-hotel-brighton.com. 61 units. 239€–450€ double; 399€–460€ suite. Métro: Tuileries. **Amenities:** Bar, concierge, laundry service, room service, tea room, free Wi-Fi.

Moderate

Hôtel Britannique ★★ When you step into the salon off the lobby here, you'll be tempted to immediately throw yourself into one of the plush armchairs and order a cup of tea. Decidedly British in décor and atmosphere, the immacu-late, soundproofed rooms are comfortably and conservatively furnished, with gentle swags of drapery hanging over the bed and windows. Rooms facing the street are the most pleasant, with large windows that offer views of the Théâtre du Châtelet across the street; rooms on the courtyard are larger though, and can be made into triples if needed. There are adjoining rooms for families and one suite that sleeps four. A good value, considering the quality of the lodgings and the central location.

20 av. Victoria, 1st arrond. ✆ **01-42-33-74-59.** www.hotel-britannique.fr. 39 units. 190€–266€ double; 335€–394€ for suite 2 to 4 people. Métro: Châtelet. **Amenities:** Bar, room service after 6pm, free Wi-Fi.

Hôtel du Cygne ★   Chock-full of exposed beams and stone walls, this 17th-century building has been carefully restored, and the simple lodgings receive ongoing tender-loving care. Most rooms are predictably small but cheerfully decorated, with fresh white walls, floral bedspreads, and the owner's personal touch. If you can handle the climb to the top floor, you'll be rewarded with a roomy suite that sleeps three. The hotel is located near Les Halles (a little seedy at night) and the Montorgueil neighborhood (very hip at night). There is no elevator.

3–5 rue du Cygne, 1st arrond. ✆ **01-42-60-14-16.** www.cygne-hotel-paris.com. 18 units. 100€–132€ double; 147€–167€ suite. Métro: Etienne Marcel. RER: Les Halles. **Amenities:** Free Wi-Fi.

Hôtel Thérèse ★★   Just a few steps from the Palais Royal and the Louvre, these recently overhauled lodgings combine old-fashioned Parisian charm with modern Parisian chic. Soft grey/teal blues highlight a creative decor that complements the building's age instead of fighting it. Comfy sofas invite you to relax in the lobby, whose stylish look includes mirrors, bookcases, and unique lighting fixtures. The comfort factor extends to the rooms, many of which have very high ceilings, interesting drapery fabrics, and upholstered headboards.

5–7 rue Thérèse, 1st arrond. ✆ **01-42-96-10-01.** www.hoteltherese.com. 40 units. 180€–390€ double. Métro: Palais-Royal or Pyramides. **Amenities:** Concierge, library/bar, free Wi-Fi.

LE MARAIS (3RD & 4TH ARRONDISSEMENTS)

Centuries ago, this neighborhood was a swamp *(marais)*, but now it's merely swamped with stylish boutiques, restaurants, and people who seem to have just stepped out of a hair salon. Stunning 16th- and 17th-century mansions house terrific museums; the narrow streets harbor clothing stores, cool bars, clubs, and the remnants of the city's historic Jewish quarter.

Expensive
Pavillon de la Reine ★★★   Just off the place des Vosges, the "Queen's Pavilion" harkens back to the days when the magnificent square was home to royalty. Set back from the hustle and bustle of the Marais, this heavenly hideaway feels intimate, like a lord's private hunting lodge in the country. The decor is a suave combination of subtle modern and antique: The dark period furniture blends with rich colors on the walls and beds; choice objects and historic details abound. Several deluxe duplexes have staircases leading to cozy sleeping lofts.

28 place des Vosges, 3rd arrond. ✆ **01-40-29-19-19.** www.pavillon-de-la-reine.com. 54 units. 385€–550€ double; 600€–1,200€ suite. Métro: Bastille. **Amenities:** Bar; concierge; fitness room, laundry service, room service, sauna, spa, free Wi-Fi.

Moderate
Hôtel de la Bretonnerie ★★   This popular and affordable hotel, located smack in the middle of the Marais, has a remarkably high charm factor. Rooms feature exposed beams, period prints, and high ceilings, as well as large windows that let in light from either the small street or the courtyard. Romantics on a budget will appreciate the rooms with four-poster beds; those who need to stretch out will enjoy the spacious junior suites and duplexes. The enthusiastic manager

is passionate about her work and the service is excellent. *Note:* The rooms are prettier than the photos on the website.

22 rue Sainte Croix de la Bretonnerie, 4th arrond. ✆ **01-48-87-77-63.** www.hotelbretonnerie. com. 29 units. 150€–185€ double; 210€–235€ junior suites and duplexes for up to 4 people. Métro: Hôtel de Ville. **Amenities:** Computer in lobby, free Wi-Fi.

Hôtel Caron de Beaumarchais ★★★   In the 18th century, Pierre Auguste Caron de Beaumarchais—author of "The Barber of Seville"—lived near here, and this small hotel celebrates both the playwright and the magnificent century he lived in. Delightful details give you a taste of what life was like back in the day: Walls are covered in high-quality reproductions of period fabrics; rooms are furnished with authentic antique writing tables; and period paintings and first-edition pages of "The Barber of Seville" hang on the walls. A pianoforte that dates from 1792 stands in the lobby, next to an antique card table set up for a game. You half expect Pierre Auguste himself to come prancing through the door.

12 rue Vieille-du-Temple, 4th arrond. ✆ **01-42-72-34-12.** www.carondebeaumarchais.com. 19 units. 145€–198€ double. Métro: St-Paul or Hôtel de Ville. **Amenities:** Free Wi-Fi.

Inexpensive
Hôtel Jeanne d'Arc le Marais ★★   With a prime location, comfortable rooms, and great prices, it's no wonder this hotel books up months in advance. It's located in the lower Marais, right next to the leafy place du Marché St-Catherine. While definitely not luxurious, the rooms are in excellent shape, decked out in warm colors and old-fashioned prints; several have been given a more modern makeover and new bathrooms. Families will be interested in the reasonably priced quads as well as the two adjoined rooms on the sixth floor. *Note:* There is another hotel with the same name in the 13th arrondissement—make sure you contact the right one when you reserve, or you'll be in for an unpleasant surprise.

3 rue de Jarente, 4th arrond. ✆ **01-48-87-62-11.** www.hoteljeannedarc.com. 35 units. 110€–150€ double; 180€ triple; 220€ quad. Métro: St-Paul. **Amenities:** Computer in lobby, free Wi-Fi.

CHAMPS-ELYSÉES, TROCADÉRO & WESTERN PARIS (8TH, 16TH & 17TH ARRONDISSEMENTS)
Affordable lodgings are scarce in this opulent environment, especially near the Champs and the Arc de Triomphe, where high prices often have more to do with location than the quality of the lodging. Ironically, the location is not particularly central; it's a good hike from here to Notre-Dame.

Expensive
Hôtel Balzac ★★★   Chandeliers and swags of rich fabric await you in the lobby of these luxurious lodgings, which were built for the director of the Paris Opéra in 1853. Just a few steps away from the Champs-Elysées, this classy townhouse features spacious rooms with huge beds, high thread-counts, and swags of chiffon and velour around the bed and windows. The ambiance is classic and very French, with reproduction antiques, high ceilings, and subtle colors. Visiting dignitaries can opt for a Royal or Presidential Suite with views of the Eiffel Tower; junior and "regular" suites feature separate sitting areas and dressing rooms. There's an interior courtyard where you can enjoy a drink on a plush sofa; if you're itching to get out, Louis Vuitton and Fouquet's are just around the corner. If you want luxury on a small, personal scale, this is an excellent choice; the service is impeccable and polite, and the hotel is small enough to still feel intimate. Pierre Gagnaire, a Michelin three-star gourmet pleasure palace, is in the same building.

6 rue Balzac, 8th arrond. ☎ **01-44-35-18-00.** www.hotelbalzac.com. 69 units. 320€–600€ double; 450€–1,300€ suite and junior suites; 2,000€–3,000€ Royal and Presidential suites. Métro: George V. **Amenities:** Bar, business center, concierge, dry cleaning, private parking (23€), restaurant, room service, free Wi-Fi.

Moderate

Hôtel Alison ★★   While the lobby decor at this comfortable, family-run hotel hasn't changed since at least 1982 (think Almodóvar movies), it's impeccably clean and shiny, as are the relatively spacious rooms. However you feel about beige walls and chocolate carpets, you should be pleased with the generally high level of comfort here, and the location is excellent: around the corner from the Madeleine and a short stroll to the Champs Elysées and the Place de la Concorde.

21 rue de Surène, 8th arrond. ☎ **01-42-65-54-00.** www.hotel-alison.com. 34 units. 129€–185€ double; 185€–205€ triple; 230€ family suite. Métro: Madeleine or Concorde. **Amenities:** Bar, free Wi-Fi.

Inexpensive

New Orient Hôtel ★★★   This lovely hotel, which offers comfortable rooms with high ceilings, 19th-century moldings, and antique headboards and armoires, may not be on top of the Champs Elysées, but it's not far, and it is close to stately Parc Monceau and a quick trot to the Saint Lazare train station. The friendly owners, inveterate flea market browsers, have refinished and restored the antique furniture themselves. Rooms (many of which have small balconies) are in tip-top shape, and bathrooms sparkle. Though there's an elevator, you'll have to negotiate stairs to get to it.

16 rue de Constantinople, 8th arrond. ☎ **01-45-22-21-64.** www.hotelneworient.com. 30 units. 130€–180€ double, 168€–205€ family room for 4. Métro: Villiers, Europe, or St-Lazare. **Amenities:** Computer in lobby, free Wi-Fi.

OPÉRA & GRANDS BOULEVARDS (2ND & 9TH ARRONDISSEMENTS)

This area offers a lovely mix of hip bars and restaurants and old-time Paris, with museums for a dose of culture. What the area lacks in big monuments, it makes up for with lower room rates and a more neighborhood-y feel.

Moderate

Hôtel Arvor Saint Georges ★★   Located in the charming "New Athens" neighborhood, where 19th-century Romantics like George Sand and Frédéric Chopin lived and worked, these spiffy lodgings offer an arty yet relaxed atmosphere, where fresh white walls show off modern photography and Daniel Buren graphics. Rooms are a little small, but simple and chic, with white walls, a splash of color, and a distinctive table or armchair. The airy lobby, with large windows and bookshelves is an invitation to kick back and read or sip a cup of tea. A tasty breakfast is served here or outside in the flower-filled patio. The friendly staff will give you a map of their favorite nearby restaurants; you can also check out the hotel's blog, which offers lots of tips (mostly in French) from real, live Parisians (www.jadooore.com).

8 rue Laferrière, 9th arrond. ☎ **01-48-78-60-92.** www.hotelarvor.com. 30 units. 139€–220€ double; 207€–280€ suite. Métro: St-Georges. **Amenities:** Bar, free Wi-Fi.

Inexpensive

Hôtel Chopin ★   Nestled at the back of the delightful Passage Jouffroy, this budget hotel has remarkably quiet rooms considering its location in the middle of the rush and bustle of the Grands Boulevards. The staircase is a little creaky (you have to climb a flight to get to the elevator), and the decor is nothing to write home about, but the rooms are clean and colorful and the bathrooms are spotless. Rooms on the upper floors get more light; many have nice views of Parisian rooftops.

10 bd. Montmartre or 46 passage Jouffroy, 9th arrond. ✆ **01-47-70-58-10.** www.hotel-chopin. com. 36 units. 102€–123€ double; 145€ triple. Métro: Grands Boulevards or Richelieu-Drouot. **Amenities:** Free Wi-Fi.

Hôtel Vivienne ★★★ Right around the corner from Passage des Panoramas, this family-run hotel offers comfortable, renovated, spotless lodgings at terrific prices. About half the hotel is decorated in a classic, if old-fashioned style; other rooms have been given a modern makeover. A few rooms have balconies with space for a small table; some have connecting doors, and there are some large suites that are great for families. If you don't mind sharing a toilet, there are several doubles that go for 88€. The location may not be exactly central, but it's a short walk to the Métro and a 10-minute stroll to the Palais Royal. If you are a light sleeper, ask for a room facing the courtyard as the street can be a little noisy.

40 rue Vivienne, 2nd arrond. ✆ **01-42-33-13-26.** www.hotel-vivienne.com. 44 units. 101€–160€ double; 196€ suite for 2–3. Métro: Grands Boulevards or Richelieu–Drouot. **Amenities:** Free Wi-Fi.

MONTMARTRE (18TH ARRONDISSEMENT)

Once you leave behind the tourist hordes that invade the Sacré-Coeur and Place du Tertre, you'll find a neighborhood of lovely little lanes and small houses, harkening back to the days when Picasso and the boys were at the Bateau Lavoir. Unfortunately, the pickings are slim if you want to actually sleep here. Another consideration: Although Montmartre is charming, it's on the northern edge of the city, so you'll need to budget extra time to get back down the hill to the center of town.

Moderate

Le Relais Montmartre ★★ These comfortable lodgings include small but impeccable rooms decked out in light, warm colors and a classic decor. Nothing particularly hip or stylish here, just quality accommodations in tasteful floral prints, plus reliable service. The one decorative quirk: exposed beams on the ceilings in shades of lavender and blue. The hotel is located on a peaceful little side street, right around the corner from a delicious stretch of food shops on Rue Lepic. There are connecting rooms for families and a lovely little patio for breakfasting in good weather.

6 rue Constance, 18th arrond. ✆ **01-70-64-25-25.** www.hotel-relais-montmartre.com. 26 units. 176€–259€ double; 218€–289€ triple. Métro: Blanche. **Amenities:** Concierge service, laundry service, iPad for guests, free Wi-Fi.

Inexpensive

Ermitage Sacré-Coeur ★★★ Built in 1890 by a rich gentleman for his mistress, this beautifully preserved townhouse has been lovingly converted into an intimate hotel. It may not offer room service (although a complimentary breakfast is served in your room) or much by way of amenities, but the ambience is unique. Tucked behind the Sacré-Coeur, this small mansion still feels like a private home. In fact, it virtually is: The Canipel family has run these unconventional lodgings for more than 40 years. Each of the five rooms is decorated in period prints and draperies, with beautiful antique bedsteads and armoires. The hotel has no elevator. The Canipels also rent nearby studios and apartments that sleep one to four.

24 rue Lamarck, 18th arrond. ✆ **01-42-64-79-22.** www.ermitagesacrecoeur.fr. 5 units. 115€–120€ double; 150€ triple; 170€ quad. Rates include breakfast. No credit cards. Métro: Lamarck-Caulaincourt. Parking 20€. **Amenities:** Free Wi-Fi.

RÉPUBLIQUE, BASTILLE & EASTERN PARIS (11TH & 12TH ARRONDISSEMENTS)

Encompassing the recently overhauled place de la République, as well as the historic place de la Bastille, this area is a good choice for both budget travelers and creatures of the night—it includes the bars and clubs of the Oberkampf and Charonne neighborhoods, and is close to the Marais.

Inexpensive

Cosmos Hotel ★★   Just around the corner from the animated Oberkampf neighborhood, this budget option is one of the best deals in town. The modern rooms are generally spotless; aside from a few nicks on the walls, everything from the bed linens to the floor covering looks spanking new. And such a deal: only 68€ to 75€ for a double. Furthermore, the staff is friendly and helpful. The only downside: Weekend nights can be noisy as people spill out of the busy bars and cafes nearby.

35 rue Jean-Pierre Timbaud, 11th arrond. www.cosmos-hotel-paris.com. ✆ **01-43-57-25-88.** 36 units. 68€–75€ double; 85€ triple; 94€ quad. Métro: Parmentier. **Amenities:** Free Wi-Fi.

Hôtel Résidence Alhambra ★   Recently reopened after a complete overhaul, this budget classic now sports a lobby in chic shades of gray and lots of polished concrete. Rooms are polished as well, with splashes of bright color. Tucked in the crook of this L-shaped hotel is a large, leafy garden with tables for alfresco breakfasts. You can even bring your own eats and picnic here after 10am. Eight of the guest rooms on the bottom floor open directly onto a balcony over the garden; about half of the others face onto it. Requests for garden views are taken, but there's no guarantee you'll get it.

13 rue de Malte, 11th arrond. ✆ **01-47-00-35-52.** www.hotelalhambra.fr. 53 units. 124€–200€ double; 169€–249€ triple; 209€–299€ quad; 209€–259€ family suite. Métro: Oberkampf. **Amenities:** Computer and printer in lobby, free Wi-Fi.

BELLEVILLE, CANAL ST-MARTIN & LA VILLETTE (10TH, 19TH & 20TH ARRONDISSEMENTS)

When historic arty neighborhoods like Saint-Germain and Montmartre became too expensive for up-and-coming artists, many immigrated to these more proletarian neighborhoods, giving the area a funky, bohemian feel. Even though it's gentrifying, Belleville is still known for artists' studios, while dozens of hip cafes and restaurants have popped up along the Canal St-Martin and the Bassin de la Villette. The young and adventurous will appreciate this part of town, but others may find it too much of a commute to the city center.

Moderate

Le Citizen ★★   Maybe it's the smiling young staff in jeans, or the ecological ethos, but there's something alternative in the air at this adorable boutique hotel on the Canal St-Martin. While the rooms are on the small side, they are light and airy, with lots of blonde wood and clean lines; all look out on the tree-lined canal. When you check in, you'll be handed an iPad loaded with information and apps on Paris. Minibar and a delicious buffet breakfast are included in your room rate.

96 quai de Jemmapes, 10th arrond. ✆ **01-83-62-55-50.** www.lecitizenhotel.com. 12 units. 189€–269€ double; 299€–329€ suite; 480€ apartment. Rates include breakfast. Métro: Jacques Bonsergent. **Amenities:** Minibar (free), iPad, room service, free Wi-Fi.

The Left Bank
LATIN QUARTER (5TH & 13TH ARRONDISSEMENTS)

Central and reasonably priced, the Latin Quarter is a long-time favorite for travelers in search of affordable accommodations. As a consequence, a few corners of this famously academic neighborhood are overrun with tourists and trinket shops. The streets immediately surrounding the place St-Michel (especially around rue de la Huchette) are where you'll find the worst tourist traps, both hotel and restaurant-wise; better prices and quality are to be had in the quieter and more authentic areas around the universities, a little farther from Notre-Dame but still within easy walking distance.

Expensive

Hôtel Design De La Sorbonne ★★   In the thick of the student quarter facing La Sorbonne, this cozy boutique hotel combines comfort with an unusual, but classy decor. Period furniture is covered in lively green, blue, and dark brown stripes; colorful wall fabrics put a modern spin on Victorian patterns, and excerpts from French literary classics are woven into the carpets. Each room has a desk with an iMac for guest's use. As pretty as they are, the rooms are small, and some have bathrooms that are downright tiny. If you need space, opt for a deluxe with a bathtub or the large room on the top floor with a view of the Sorbonne and the Pantheon.

6 rue Victor Cousin, 5th arrond. ✆ **01-43-54-58-08.** www.hotelsorbonne.com. 38 units. 130€–370€ double; 200€–400€ top floor double. Métro: Cluny–La Sorbonne. RER: Luxembourg. **Amenities:** Free Wi-Fi.

Hotel Seven ★★★   Weird and wonderful, this luxury concept hotel seems made for lovers in search of a night to remember. Mirrors and transparent showers abound here, as do huge beds, theatrical lighting and large sofas. Rooms are romantically space-age, with mobiles, pinpoint lights and in-room transparent double showers, while the suites go all out: "Sublime" is all white with a round double bed under a feathery ceiling; "The Black Diamond" features a faux crocodile headboard and a black bathtub studded with Swarovski synthetic diamonds. Most have "levitation" beds, which are suspended horizontally from the wall, as well as Nespresso machines, iPod docks, and fluffy bathrobes. The hotel is a bit out of the way, at the southern end of the Latin Quarter.

20 rue Berthollet, 5th arrond. ✆ **01-43-31-47-52.** www.sevenhotelparis.com. 35 units. 217€–397€ double; 477€–877€ suite. Métro: Les Gobelins. **Amenities:** Bar, concierge, laptop loans, massages by appointment, room service, wine cellar, free Wi-Fi.

Moderate

Hôtel des Jardins du Luxembourg ★★   Just around the corner from its glorious namesake, this is an excellent hideaway for a romantic honeymoon or cozy retreat. The building's claim to fame is that Sigmund Freud stayed here on his first visit to Paris; perhaps this has something to do with the 1930s and 1940s touches to the decor. The Art Deco ambience of the lobby and lounge invites deep reflection or at least a nice rest in one of the plush armchairs; for full relaxation, indulge in a visit to the sauna. While the standard rooms are quite pretty, with curly wrought-iron headboards and puffy comforters, the superior rooms, which cost only 10€ more, have nicer views, small balconies, snazzy bathrooms, and designer-fabric-covered walls.

5 impasse Royer-Collard, 5th arrond. ✆ **01-40-46-08-88.** www.les-jardins-du-luxembourg.com. 26 units. 110€–205€ double. Métro: Cluny–La Sorbonne. RER: Luxembourg. **Amenities:** Bar, free Wi-Fi.

Hôtel Saint-Jacques ★★ The spacious rooms in this delightful hotel retain lots of architectural details from its Belle Epoque past. Most of the ceilings are adorned with masses of curlicues, and some have restored 18th-century murals to gaze at while you laze in bed. Modern reproductions of famous French paintings hang on the walls; Second Empire–themed murals decorate the lobby and breakfast room. The romantic decor has a light, feminine feel, all shades of light blue, cream, and gray—considerably more inviting than when the hotel served as a set for the Audrey Hepburn/Cary Grant classic "Charade." Service is especially friendly here.

35 rue des Ecoles, 5th arrond. ✆ **01-44-07-45-45.** www.paris-hotel-stjacques.com. 26 units. 137€–326€ double; 217€–312€ triple. Métro: Maubert-Mutualité. RER: St-Michel–Notre-Dame. **Amenities:** Babysitting, bar, concierge, laundry service, loaner computer, free Wi-Fi.

Inexpensive

Hôtel des Grandes Ecoles ★★★ Tucked into a private garden on the slope of the Montagne St-Genviève, this hotel makes you feel as if you have just walked out of Paris and into the countryside. A path leads to a flower-bedecked interior courtyard, where birds chirp in the trees; the reception area adjoins an inviting breakfast room. The spotless rooms are filled with country-style furniture; crocheted bedspreads and framed etchings of flowers complete the look. The calm is such that the hotel has nixed TVs. What's more, this unique ambience comes at a reasonable price. Families will appreciate the six large suites that can sleep four.

75 rue de Cardinal-Lemoine, 5th arrond. ✆ **01-43-26-79-23.** www.hotel-grandes-ecoles.com. 51 units. 130€–160€ double; 180€ family room. Parking 30€. Métro: Cardinal Lemoine or Place Monge. **Amenities:** Free Wi-Fi.

ST-GERMAIN-DES-PRÉS & LUXEMBOURG (6TH ARRONDISSEMENT)

Sleek boutiques and restaurants abound in this legendary neighborhood; historic cafes and monuments lend plenty of atmosphere. Unlike some other Parisian neighborhoods, this one is lively even late at night; it is also centrally located and within walking distance of many top sights.

Expensive

Relais St-Germain ★★★ Fashioned from three adjoining 17th-century townhouses, this intimate hotel mixes old-world charm and jazzy modernity. Rooms are spacious, and even the smallest are equipped with a comfortable sitting area. The decor blends period furniture with modern prints, like the Louis XV armchair covered in zigzagged leather, or the 18th-century painting hung on a wall of mirrors. The effect is both stylish and deeply comforting. There are some extra stairs between floors, so if you have mobility issues, be sure to make that clear when you reserve. Guests have priority at the hotel restaurant, **Le Comptoir** (p. 82), where you might otherwise have a 6-month wait for a reservation. Book your room at least a month in advance.

9 carrefour de l'Odéon, 6th arrond. ✆ **01-44-27-07-97.** www.hotelrsg.com. 22 units. 285€–370€ double; 395€–440€ suite. Rates include breakfast if you reserve on the hotel's website. Métro: Odéon. **Amenities:** Restaurant, free Wi-Fi.

Inexpensive

Hotel Mayet ★★ The lobby of this young-at-heart hotel sports two murals, one by American graffiti artist JohnOne and the other by his French counterpart André. Rooms are snug but colorful, with white walls and touches of bright orange. The hotel has a lighthearted North African theme, with paintings of camels in the desert and vintage photos of beautiful Moroccan movie stars. This family-run enterprise also has an apartment for rent next door that sleeps four with a kitchen and washer-dryer.

3 rue Mayet, 6th arrond. ✆ **01-47-83-21-35.** www.mayet.com. 23 units. 102€–200€ double; 157€–240€ triple. Métro: Duroc. **Amenities:** Bar, free Wi-Fi.

EIFFEL TOWER & NEARBY (7TH ARRONDISSEMENT)

For some reason, many visitors to Paris clamor for hotels that are right near the Eiffel Tower, perhaps under the mistaken impression that this is a central location. It isn't. Still, there's no denying that this extremely posh area is beautiful, and there is something magical about wandering out of your hotel in the morning and seeing the Eiffel Tower looming in the background.

Expensive

Hôtel Signature St-Germain-des-Près ★★★   After undergoing a complete overhaul, the erstwhile Hôtel Lindberg has been reborn as a delightful boutique hotel. Run by the friendly Prigent family (who also run the Hôtel Londres Eiffel, see below), the new décor boasts interiors that are both stylish and welcoming. Bright colors on the walls blend harmoniously with subdued bedsteads and linens; mid-century reproduction furniture and faux antique phones take the edge off sleek modern lines. The "Prestige" rooms cost more, but are especially roomy (30 sq. meters/323 sq. feet). In addition to particularly attentive service, this hotel is also blessed with an excellent location for shopping addicts: it's just down the street from Bon Marché.

5 rue Chomel, 7th arrond. ✆ **01-45-48-35-53.** 26 units. 220€–350€ double; 380€ triple; 2-room connecting family suite 500€. Métro: Sèvres-Bablylone or St-Sulpice. **Amenities:** Concierge service, free Wi-Fi.

Moderate

Hôtel Eber Mars ★★   When you walk in the door, chances are you will be greeted by none other than Monsieur Eber himself, who has spent the last 10 years lovingly renovating his hotel. The 1930s-era decor is low-key and very Parisian. Walls in the spacious rooms are papered in period patterns in neutral colors, and lit by authentic Art Deco fixtures found at antiques fairs. Old-fashioned radiators have been scraped and lacquered; prints dating from the Universal Exposition of 1889 (which unveiled the Eiffel Tower) are hung on the walls. Rooms in this hotel are unusually large for Paris; the triples and connecting suites are ideal for families.

117 av. de la Bourdonnais, 7th arrond. ✆ **01-47-05-42-30.** www.hotelebermars.com. 25 units. 120€–280€ double; 200€–300€ triple. Métro: Ecole Militaire. **Amenities:** Bar, free Wi-Fi.

Hôtel Londres Eiffel ★★   From the moment you enter, you feel like you are in a private home. In fact, you may very well be welcomed by Samba, the lovely golden retriever, before you meet the Prigents, the hospitable owners. Polished wood banisters lead up spiral staircases to narrow hallways and cozy rooms decorated with a personal touch. Walls are covered with fabrics printed with tasteful 19th-century kitsch motifs, furniture is 1940s style, and the comfort level is terrific. A few rooms have views of the Eiffel Tower. It books up early. Connecting rooms are available for families.

1 rue Augereau, 7th arrond. ✆ **01-45-51-63-02.** 30 units. 160€–275€ double; 330€ triple. Métro: Ecole Militaire. **Amenities:** Free Wi-Fi.

Hôtel Muget ★★   Comfort is key at this personable hotel, where the conscientious staff has considered the smallest details of your stay. The lovely rooms are fitted with faux-antique furniture, big wood headboards hand-painted with a lily-of-the-valley (*muguet*) motif, and pretty new bathrooms with old-fashioned wooden washstands and mirror frames. Rooms are relatively large for Paris, and the triples are downright spacious. Five doubles have a great view of the Eiffel Tower, three others of Les Invalides; needless to say these book up months in advance. The others, which are equally comfy and less expensive, look out on either the quiet street or the airy courtyard.

11 rue Chevert 7th arrond. ✆ **01-47-05-05-93.** www.hotelmuguet.com. 43 units. 165€–280€ double; 250€–350€ triple. Métro: Varenne or La Tour Maubourg. **Amenities:** Computer and printer in lobby, free Wi-Fi.

Inexpensive
Hôtel du Champ de Mars ★★   An adorable and affordable little inn right around the corner from the food shops of rue Cler—what more could you ask for? Owners Françoise and Stéphane Gourdal offer all of their comfortable doubles at one great price: 130€. The impeccably maintained rooms are decorated with the kind of care people generally reserve for their own homes: thick cotton bedspreads, framed etchings, and warm colors. The friendly staff includes a delightful cocker spaniel named Cannelle.

7 rue du Champ de Mars, 7th arrond. ✆ **01-45-51-52-30.** www.hotelduchampdemars.com. 25 units. 130€ double. Métro: Ecole Militaire. **Amenities:** Laptop loan for guests, free Wi-Fi.

MONTPARNASSE & NEARBY (14TH & 15TH ARRONDISSEMENTS)

Montparnasse is more centrally located than it might seem—it's right on the border of St-Germain and close to the Luxembourg gardens. Also, the train station is a major transit hub for a bundle of Métro lines and bus routes. Though the utterly unaesthetic Tour Montparnasse now casts a shadow over this ancient artists' haunt (Henry Miller, Man Ray, Chagall, Picasso . . .), the little streets in the surrounding area are still full of personality.

Moderate
L'Apostrophe ★   Honoring the area's literary history (nearby writers' haunts include La Coupole and the Closerie des Lilas), this "poem hotel" is dedicated to the beauty and mystery of writing. The decor is a little off the wall, but very tastefully so, starting with an impressive silhouette of a tree on the hotel's facade. Rooms are themed: "Caligraphy" has Chinese characters set on royal blue walls; "Musique" features stenciled sheet music and instruments. Larger rooms include a Jacuzzi bathtub right in the room.

3 rue de Chevreuse, 6th arrond. ✆ **01-56-54-31-31.** www.apostrophe-hotel.com. 16 units. 169€–310€ standard double; 220€–353€ double with a Jacuzzi. Métro: Vavin. **Amenities:** Bar, free Wi-Fi.

Inexpensive
Hôtel des Bains ★★★   With cute, comfortable rooms and excellent rates, this friendly hotel is one of the best deals on the Left Bank, especially for families. It offers several good-sized, two-room suites for up to four people. Doubles are amply sized as well, with high ceilings; the largest ones face the pretty courtyard. The decor is simple but nicely accessorized with objects and artwork from the nearby Sunday art market. The elevator stops at a landing between floors, which have a few stairs.

33 rue Delambre, 14th arrond. ✆ **01-43-20-85-27.** www.hotel-des-bains-montparnasse.com. 42 units. 102.50€ double; 135€–170€ suites for 2–4 people. Métro: Vavin, Edgar Quinet, or Montparnasse. **Amenities:** Free Wi-Fi.

Alternative Accommodations

Hotels are all very well and good, but for some, nothing beats staying in a private home or apartment, particularly if you are a family on a budget. Fortunately, there are several Parisian options for travelers with an independent streak, including short-term rentals, bed-and-breakfasts, and "aparthotels," that is, short-term apartments with some hotel services.

SHORT-TERM RENTALS

There are dozens of agencies proffering hundreds of apartments smack in the center of the City of Light. Though the rates for two people are sometimes (but not always) significantly less than what you'd pay at a hotel, the advantages are many, not the least of which is the fact that you can cook some of your meals at home and save yourself a ton of time and money. Other benefits are privacy, independence, and a chance to see what it's like to live like a Parisian, even if it's just for a week.

If you are more than two, and especially if you are traveling *en famille,* the benefits can be huge. Family suites and/or adjoining rooms are rare in Parisian hotels, and you will almost always end up paying for two doubles—that is, somewhere around 250€ to 450€ per night—whereas you could rent a one-bedroom apartment with a foldout couch and/or extra bed in the living room for around 1,000€ to 1,400€ per week, a substantial savings.

In most cases, you will deal with the agency (not the owners), and the minimum stay is 4 days to 1 week. There are hundreds of agencies on the Internet, but here are a few well-established ones:

- **Parisian Home** (✆ **01-45-08-03-37;** www.parisianhome.com)
- **France Lodge** (✆ **01-56-33-85-85;** www.francelodge.fr)
- **Appartement de Ville** (✆ **01-42-45-09-08;** www.appartementdeville.com)
- **Paris Attitude** (✆ **01-42-96-31-46;** www.parisattitude.com)
- **Paris Appartements Services** (✆ **01-40-28-01-28;** www.paris-appartements-services.com)

Another less conventional agency option is the wildly popular **Airbnb** (www.airbnb.com), a vast network of accommodations offered directly by local owners. Its Paris page has hundreds of offers for rooms (shared or private) and entire apartments.

BED & BREAKFASTS

Though bed-and-breakfasts *(chambres d'hôtes)* are extremely common in the French countryside, in the big city, where privacy and anonymity are treasured, the idea of strangers living in one's home generally fills Parisians with horror. This is a city where despite the high rents, roommates are virtually unheard-of.

A terrific way to find a quality B&B is to visit the city's official B&B website: **Hôtes Qualité Paris** (www.hotesqualiteparis.fr). A partnership with Paris's most well-established and trusted B&B agencies, the site offers a wide range of rooms for about 50€ to 140€ per person per night, based on double occupancy. A couple of other recommended agencies are:

PARIS | Where to Stay

4

- **Alcôve & Agapes** (📞 01-44-85-06-05; www.bed-and-breakfast-in-paris. com)
- **Good Morning Paris** (📞 01-47-07-28-29; www.goodmorningparis.fr)

APARTHOTELS

Mostly designed for business travelers, these utilitarian lodgings are a cross between a hotel and an apartment. Short on charm, *aparthotels* are decidedly practical, as each unit comes with a kitchenette as well as hotel services such as fresh towels, dry cleaning, and a reception desk. Rates are generally higher than short-term rentals, but you do have the comfort of knowing you are dealing with a large company (if that makes you comfortable), with standardized apartments, organized websites, and customer service.

The best-known *aparthotel* company is **Citadines** (📞 01-41-05-79-05; www.citadines.com), which offers clean, comfortable units in excellent locations around the city. The cheapest rentals are the studios with pull-out beds, which range from 110€ to 320€ a night depending on the season and location.

WHERE TO EAT

Everywhere you look in Paris, someone is doing their best to ruin your waistline. *Boulangeries* (bakeries) with buttery croissants and decadent pastries lurk on every street corner; open-air markets tempt the senses; and restaurants with intriguing menus sprout up on every block.

Fortunately, you don't have to have a king-size budget to dine like royalty. Sure, there are those world-famous, multistarred restaurants that everyone has heard about. But recently, a whole new crop of "neo-bistros" has emerged, offering high-quality eats for a fraction of what you would pay in a gourmet palace. One outgrowth of this movement is the obsession with "noble" ingredients—high-quality, regional products, often from a small-scale farm or artisan, often organic, and always in keeping with the oldest and best traditions.

Note: Restaurants tend to be small in Paris, and when it comes to reservations, size matters. To be sure to get a table, reserve ahead for most of the restaurants listed below under the "Expensive" or "Moderate" categories.

Useful Websites for Foodies

- **Paris by Mouth** (www.parisbymouth. com) provides insider information (in English) on dining in the capital.

- **The Fork** (www.thefork.com) allows you to reserve restaurants online for free (according to area and type of food), and supplies a list of restaurant promotions—sometimes up to 50 percent off (check restrictions before you book).

- **Le Fooding** (www.lefooding.com) has a terrific list of Parisian restaurants as well as food-oriented events and news. The site is in French, but has some English translations.

- **David Lebovitz** (www.davidlebovitz. com) is a pastry chef and cookbook author who has a rocking website that discusses everything from restaurants and recipes to shopping and travel tips. A personal favorite.

The Right Bank
LOUVRE & ILE DE LA CITÉ (1ST ARRONDISSEMENT)

Dining near the Louvre can be an expensive and frustrating affair; it's rife with overpriced, mediocre tourist restaurants boasting menus in at least five languages. If you poke around some of the smaller streets however, you'll discover plenty of little restaurants where you can eat well and affordably. That said, if you are ready to spend, gourmet opportunities abound.

Expensive

Le Grand Véfour ★★★ CLASSIC FRENCH   Channel centuries of history at this illustrious restaurant, where Napoléon, Danton, Hugo, Colette, and Cocteau all once dined. Thanks to Guy Martin, chef and owner for the past decade, the food is as memorable as the magnificently preserved 18th-century salon: Signature dishes like Prince Rainier III pigeon and truffled oxtail parmentier share the menu with new creations with contemporary flavors like sumac and star anise. The desserts are incredible, especially the *palet* (a thick biscuit) with milk chocolate and hazelnuts, served with caramel and sea-salt ice cream. Reserve at least 2 weeks in advance, and note that the lunch fixed-price menu is a third of the price of the fixed-price dinner.

17 rue de Beaujolais, 1st arrond. ✆ **01-42-96-56-27.** www.grand-vefour.com. Main courses 88€–108€; fixed-price lunch 98€, fixed-price dinner 298€. Mon–Fri 12:30–1:45pm and 8–9:45pm. Closed Aug. Métro: Louvre–Palais-Royal or Pyramides.

Spring ★★★ MODERN FRENCH   One of the city's most talked-about restaurants has a chef who is—gasp—American! Try not to think about that and just enjoy the amazing dishes that come out of the kitchen. Chef Daniel Rose, native of Chicago, pays utmost respect to all things French while adding a dash of Yankee daring to his superb creations. The menu changes all the time, but it might start with quail eggs with lemony eggplant caviar, followed by filet of sole with mussels, smoked ham, and green tomatoes. It's a four-course fixed-price menu only, which doesn't seem to be a problem for diners, who fight for a seat here. The buzz is so strong and the capacity so small (40 diners max) that you should reserve around 3 months in advance.

6 rue Bailleul, 1st arrond. ✆ **01-45-96-05-72.** www.springparis.fr. Fixed-price dinner 84€. Tues–Sat 6:30–10:30pm. Closed 2nd week in Aug. Métro: Louvre-Rivoli.

Moderate

Le Fumoir ★★ MODERN FRENCH   With its high ceilings, subdued lighting, and large windows, this understatedly hip spot is a good place to regroup. During the day (except at lunch), dawdling is encouraged: magazines and newspapers are available, and there's a small lending library/book exchange in the back room. At night, well-dressed 30-somethings crowd around the magnificent wood bar—which once stood in a Philadelphia speakeasy—as they wait for their table. Like the surroundings, the seasonal menu has an international flair: offerings might include pork sautéed with kimchi or raviolis with Corsican *broccio* cheese and wild garlic pesto. On Sundays, there's a 26€ brunch complete with pancakes and eggs Benedict.

6 rue de l'Amiral Coligny, 1st arrond. ✆ **01-42-92-00-24.** www.lefumoir.com. Main courses 15€–26€; fixed-price menu lunch 23€–26€, fixed-price menu dinner 34€–38€. Daily 11am–2am, lunch served noon–3pm, dinner 7–11pm. Métro: Louvre-Rivoli.

It's 3pm. All of the restaurants are closed and you are dreaming of something light and healthy to eat. Fear not: Look for one of the following healthy gourmet chains that are multiplying around offices and shopping areas. Locations are listed on the restaurants' websites.

Cojean (21 locations; www.cojean.fr): A creation of an ex-McDonald's executive with an almost religious fervor for fresh, healthy food, these airy, modern boutiques serve innovative salads, as well as quiches, sandwiches, and fresh-squeezed juices. Many veggie options. Open until 4 or 5pm in most locations.

Exki (9 locations; www.exki.com): This Belgian chain (pronounced

"ex-KEY," like the French word for "exquisite") offers a terrific array of tasty, healthy sandwiches, soups, and desserts (vegetarian choices, too), until 9 or 10pm. It uses lots of organic, free-trade, seasonal ingredients and has a low ecological footprint.

Boco (3 locations; www.boco.fr): Organic takeout from Michelin-starred chefs for under 15€? Be still, my beating heart. Hot food, cold food, light meals, and desserts are served daily from 11am until 8 or 10pm (St-Lazare location closed weekends, Opèra location closed Sunday). Main dishes run 7€ to 10€, and, gasp, a fixed menu (changes daily) three-course meal costs 15€.

Pinxo ★★ MODERN FRENCH/TAPAS   Sample renowned chef Alain Dutournier's exquisite cooking in a relaxed atmosphere at this modern tapas restaurant, where food is made to be shared. Everyone grazes on small plates with magnificent mouthfuls (each dish is priced per person on the menu) such as lobster ravioli with artichoke emulsion; nuggets of lamb with *cépes* (wild mushrooms); or organic marinated salmon with herring and fennel. The best way to wash it all down is with a glass of wine (of course)—choose from 120 bottles, many of which are available by the glass.

9 rue d'Alger, 1st arrond. ☏ **01-40-20-72-00.** www.alaindutournier.com. Portions per person 6€–9€; meal per person 35€–40€. Mon–Fri 12:15–2:15pm and 7–10:30pm, Sat 7–10:30pm. Closed Aug. Métro: Tuileries.

Inexpensive

Aki ★ JAPANESE   Of the dozens of Japanese restaurants on rue Ste-Anne, this one, which specializes in *okonomiyaki*, stands out. This delicious dish is a sort of grilled omelet topped with meat or seafood and a yummy sauce. Watch the cooks create yours on a griddle in the open kitchen. It also serves udon and soba noodles. Arrive early or be prepared to wait in line.

11bis rue Sainte Anne, 1st arrond. ☏ **01-42-97-54-27.** Main courses 11€–15€. Mon–Sat 11am–10:45pm. Métro: Pyramides.

OPÉRA & GRANDS BOULEVARDS (2ND & 9TH ARRONDISSEMENTS)

Buzzing with cafes and theaters back in the 19th century, the long-overlooked Grand Boulevards have come back to life, especially near the Opéra and the hip part of the 9th arrondissement that borders Montmartre. Less trendy, but also less expensive, the little streets around the Bourse (the French stock exchange) have a wide range of restaurant options, especially at lunchtime.

Expensive

Casa Olympe ★★ MEDITERRANEAN/MODERN FRENCH Olympe Versini earned a Michelin star in her 20s and has been writing cookbooks and dazzling discerning palates ever since. One of the pioneers of "nouvelle cuisine" in the 1970s, she has since moved on to warmer climes, as reflected in the menu. There is a distinctly Mediterranean flair to dishes like marinated sardines, sweetbreads with Pantelleria capers, and roast shoulder of lamb with thyme. Finish off with whipped lemon sherbet with Prosecco.

48 rue St-Georges, 9th arrond. ✆ **01-42-85-26-01.** www.casaolympe.com. Main courses 20€–29€; fixed-price menu lunch 26€, fixed-price menu dinner 39€. Mon–Wed noon–2pm and 7:30–10:30pm; Thurs–Fri noon–2pm and 7:30–11pm. Closed 3 weeks in Aug. Métro: St-Georges.

Saturne ★★★ MODERN FRENCH There are not very many glass-roofed restaurants in Paris, and even fewer with a kitchen like this one. The chef's Scandinavian roots are evident in the décor, with its sleek blonde wood and white walls. But it's what's on the plate that makes it so hard to get a table here: exquisite combinations of flavors and textures, described on the menu as a list of ingredients. Resembling works of contemporary art, dishes might combine gnocchi, chestnuts, and truffles, or guinea hen with purple artichokes and spring garlic, and could be followed with a concoction of carrots, citrus, and olives. At lunch you can choose from a menu of three or six dishes; at dinner, it's one fixed-price six-course menu for one and all.

17 rue Notre-Dame-des-Victoires, 2nd arrond. ✆ **01-42-60-31-90.** www.saturne-paris.fr. Fixed-price lunch 40€–65€; fixed-price dinner 65€. Mon–Fri noon–2pm and 8–10:30pm. Closed first 3 weeks of Aug. Métro: Bourse.

Moderate

Chez Grenouille ★ TRADITIONAL FRENCH Chef Alexis Blanchard has won prizes for his pâtés and *boudins* (blood sausage), so you'll find all manner of charcuterie on the menu here, plus updated classics such as suckling pig with foie gras, duck parmentier, sweetbreads, oxtail, and pigs' feet, plus a fish dish or two for lighter eaters. The cooking may not be "heart smart," but it is delicious. Finish with a boozy baba au rhum.

52 rue Blanche, 9th arrond. ✆ **01-42-81-34-07.** www.restaurant-chezgrenouille-paris.com. Main courses 25€–36€; fixed-price lunch 23€; fixed-price dinner 35€. Mon–Fri noon–2:30pm and 7–11pm; Sat 7–11pm Métro: Trinité.

Le Pantruche ★★ TRADITIONAL FRENCH/BISTRO The name is old-fashioned slang for Paris, but this little bistro has a decidedly modern feel to it. Another case of a runaway chef from Michelin-starred restaurants, Le Pantruche offers deliciously updated bistro fare like braised sweetbreads with carrots in a licorice glaze, or suckling pig with pears, celery root, and chestnuts. It's hard to resist dessert when chocolate ganache or Grand Marnier soufflé are on the menu. Definitely reserve ahead, as the fixed-price menus are a terrific value and the tiny dining room fills quickly.

3 rue Victor Massé, 9th arrond. ✆ **01-48-78-55-60.** www.lepantruche.com. Lunch main courses 14€–25€; dinner main courses 21€–25€, fixed-price dinner 35€; fixed-price lunch 19€. Mon–Fri 12:30–2:30pm and 7:30–9:30pm. Closed first 3 weeks of Aug. Métro: Pigalle.

Inexpensive

Chartier ★★ TRADITIONAL FRENCH With a dining room that can seat over 300, this gargantuan establishment is one of the last of the *bouillons*, or workers' restaurants, found all over Paris back in the 19th century. The idea was to offer good food at modest prices, a concept that still speaks to working Parisians some 100 years later, if the line out the door is any indication. You come here for the experience more than for the food, which is tasty but certainly won't win any Michelin stars. The menu covers a wide variety of traditional dishes like roast free-range chicken with fries, or rump steak with pepper sauce. Service is fast and furious, but it's all part of the atmosphere, which is something that belongs to another time and place. It takes no reservations, so be prepared to wait.

7 rue du Faubourg Montmartre, 9th arrond. ℂ **01-47-70-86-29.** www.restaurant-chartier.com. Main courses 9€–13€. Daily 11:30am–10pm. Métro: Grands-Boulevards.

LE MARAIS (3RD & 4TH ARRONDISSEMENTS)

You should have no trouble finding good things to eat in the Marais. Between its working-class roots and its more recent makeover, it offers a wide range of choices, from humble falafel joints to trendy brasseries.

Expensive

Benoit ★★ TRADITIONAL FRENCH   This historic bistro had already hosted a century's worth of Parisian notables when Alain Ducasse took the helm in 2005. The dining room is still lined with mirrors, zinc, and tiles, while the classic menu has been given an extra dash of pizzazz. Dishes like escargots in garlic butter and brill braised with Jura wine share the stage with roasted milk-fed lamb from the Pyrenées and sautéed scallops *grenobloise*. The sommelier will help you navigate the huge wine list.

20 rue St-Martin, 4th arrond. ℂ **01-42-72-25-76.** www.benoit-paris.com. Main courses 26€–49€; fixed-price lunch 38€. Daily noon–2pm and 7:30–10pm. Closed first 3 weeks of Aug. Métro: Hôtel-de-Ville.

La Brasserie de l'Isle Saint-Louis ★ TRADITIONAL BRASSERIE   Owned by the same family for three generations, this lovely, old-fashioned brasserie serves healthy portions of classic Alsatian dishes, like choucroute garni—a small mountain of sauerkraut topped with slices of ham, sausage, and other smoked meats—in a relaxed atmosphere. Or try other classic brasserie fare like a tender entrecote (rib steak) or a breaded fillet of haddock. The decor is rustic without being kitsch. Despite the location, many of the diners are regulars. Eating's not a requirement; if you want, you can just enjoy a Mutzig (Alsatian beer) on the terrace and soak up a splendid view of the buttresses of Notre-Dame. Service is "nonstop."

55 quai de Bourbon, 4th arrond. ℂ **01-43-54-02-59.** www.labrasserie-isl.fr. Main courses 19€–32€. Thurs–Tues noon–11pm. Closed in Aug. Métro: Pont Marie.

Moderate

Café des Musées ★★ TRADITIONAL FRENCH/BISTRO   Weary culture vultures who've tried to do both the Picasso Museum and the Musée Carnavalet on the same day will appreciate this bustling corner cafe with its appealing sidewalk tables. This is not just any old corner cafe, mind you, but one where the inventive chef works wonders with bistro classics like steak frites and *andouillette* (tripe sausage) as well as lighter fare like fresh vegetable casserole with basil oil, or shrimp with Thai curry. The lunch fixed-price menu is a particularly good value.

49 rue de Turenne, 3rd arrond. ℂ **01-42-72-96-17.** Main courses 12€–21€; fixed-price lunch 17€; fixed-price dinner 27€. Daily noon–3pm and 7–11pm. Closed mid-Aug to early Sept. Métro: St. Paul or Chemin Vert.

Inexpensive

Breizh Café ★★ CREPERIE   After heading to Japan, where he found both a wife and professional success, Chef Bertrand Larcher started opening hugely popular creperies, first in Tokyo and then back in the home country. His Paris version is a warm and modern space that offers friendly service and great food. Start with oysters or head straight for a savory buckwheat *galette,* crisp and nutty and filled with high-quality organic ingredients, such as farm fresh eggs, Bordier butter, and seasonal produce. Try an artisanal cider, and save room for a sweet crepe, drizzled with chocolate or salted butter caramel. It gets very crowded here, so reserve ahead.

109 rue Vieille du Temple, 3rd arrond. ✆ **01-42-72-13-77.** www.breizhcafe.com. Main courses 8€–14€. Wed–Sat 11:30am–11pm; Sun 11:30am–10pm. Closed last 3 weeks in Aug. Métro: Filles du Calvaire.

L'As du Fallafel ★ FALAFEL/ISRAELI   This Marais institution offers, without a doubt, the best falafel in Paris. True, falafel joints are scarce in this city, but that doesn't take away from the excellence of these overstuffed beauties, brimming with cucumbers, pickled turnips, shredded cabbage, tahini, fried eggplant, and those crispy balls of fried chickpeas and spices. Wash it down with an Israeli beer. Service is fast and furious, but basically friendly—be prepared to deal with hordes of tourists and locals at lunch. Closed Friday afternoon and all day Saturday.

34 rue des Rosiers, 4th arrond. ✆ **01-48-87-63-60.** Main courses 8€–20€. Sun–Thurs 11am–midnight; Fri 11am–3pm. Métro: St. Paul.

Le Felteu ★★ TRADITIONAL BISTRO   It's easy to walk right by this unassuming restaurant, where locals crowd in to the clean but worn dining room for copious portions of excellent food. You'll usually find either Brigitte or her husband, Jerry, the longtime owners, behind the bar chatting with the regulars. Meanwhile, the kitchen is sending out grilled lamb, blood sausage (*boudin*) and sautéed apples, or other delicious bistro fare. Each dish comes with the vegetable du jour and/or a hearty portion of potato gratin.

15 rue Pequay, 4rd arrond. ✆ **01-42-72-14-51.** Main courses 15€–22€. No credit cards. Mon–Fri 12:30–2:15pm and 8–10:30pm; Sat 8–10:30pm. Métro: Rambuteau or Hôtel de Ville.

CHAMPS-ELYSÉES, TROCADÉRO & WESTERN PARIS (8TH, 16TH & 17TH ARRONDISSEMENTS)

Mobbed with tourists, oozing with opulence, the Champs-Elysées is a difficult place to find a good meal, unless you are willing to spend a lot of money. Mediocre chain restaurants abound on the grand avenue itself, and kebob joints mingle with frighteningly expensive gourmet palaces on the surrounding side streets.

Expensive

Caïus ★★ MODERN FRENCH   While the chef at this elegant dining room is a fan of spices and herbs from faraway lands, Jean-Marc Notelet's subtle cuisine also makes use of top-quality French ingredients, like mussels from Brittany, veal from Corrèze, and free-range pork raised on apples and acorns. Menu musthaves include cod with lemongrass and combava, grilled duck with sumac, and beef confit with tonka beans and niora. Be sure to reserve: Tables fill quickly with a devoted local clientele.

6 rue d'Armaillé, 17th arrond. ✆ **01-42-27-19-20.** www.caius-restaurant.fr. Main courses 20€–25€; fixed-price dinner 42€. Mon–Fri noon–2pm and 7:30–10:30pm. Closed 3 weeks in Aug. and last week in Dec. Métro: Argentine.

Lasserre ★★★ GOURMET FRENCH André Malraux, Salvador Dali, Audrey Hepburn, Marlene Dietrich—the list of celebrities who have dined at this legendary restaurant is understandably long. What famous person wouldn't want to eat in this superb dining room, where the ceiling opens when the weather is willing? A silk-draped, arch-windowed affair, the room glistens with fine porcelain, silver knickknacks, and crystal candelabras. The young chefs have recently brought new life to the classic menu, adding their own subtle creations, such as sea bass with vegetables in chardonnay, or roasted lamb confit with artichokes and apples. Reserve at least 2 weeks ahead. Dinner jackets required for men.

17 av. Franklin D. Roosevelt, 8th arrond. ✆ **01-43-59-02-13.** www.restaurant-lasserre.com. Main courses 85€–120€; fixed-price lunch 90€ and 120€; fixed-price dinner 220€. Thurs–Fri noon–2pm; Tues–Sat 7–10pm. Closed mid-July through Aug. Métro: Franklin Roosevelt.

Moderate
Publicis Drugstore Brasserie ★★ MODERN BRASSERIE You won't find toothpaste at this "drugstore," whose name comes from a former 1950s incarnation that consisted of a warren of shops, restaurants, and services "à l'americaine." This ultra-modern, oh-so-chic complex has replaced the funky original, but kept the multi-use concept in tact with shops, restaurants, and a cinema. The Brasserie is the most accessible eating option—a light-filled expanse with an incredible view of the Champs and the Arc de Triomphe. The food is high-end casual, featuring gourmet hamburgers, grilled fish, steak tartare, and fillet of sole delivered by a young and beautiful wait staff. Meals are served nonstop until 2am, a good bet for a late-night meal after sampling nearby nightlife. There's a terrific buffet brunch on Sundays.

133 av. des Champs Elysées, 8th arrond. ✆ **01-44-43-77-64.** www.publicisdrugstore.com. Main courses 19€–39€; fixed-price lunch 20€–25€; Sunday brunch 36€. Mon–Fri 8am–2am. Sat–Sun 10am–2am. Métro: Charles de Gaulle–Etoile.

Inexpensive
Boulangerie Joséphine ★ BAKERY/SANDWICHES/FRENCH This terrific bakery near the Arc de Triomphe has a nice outdoor terrace and a pretty upstairs dining room that fills quickly with local office workers and businesspeople. You can buy sandwiches and salads (and desserts, of course) to go, or sit down and sample one of the excellent daily specials, like stuffed vegetables, roast chicken, or osso bucco. Also open for breakfast from 8am.

69 av. Marceau, 8th arrond. ✆ **01-47-20-49-62.** www.josephine boulangerie.com. Main courses 5€–15€. Mon–Fri 8am–8pm. Métro: Charles de Gaulle–Etoile.

MONTMARTRE (18TH ARRONDISSEMENT)
When you get away from the tourist traps of Place du Tertre, you start to understand why this neighborhood is a favorite with the artsy-hipster set. And where there's art, you are bound to find an artist in the kitchen.

Moderate
Chéri Bibi ★ TRADITIONAL FRENCH Sitting pretty on the eastern side of the Sacré-Coeur, Chéri Bibi has become the unofficial canteen for the young and artsy Montmartre crowd. The affordable fixed-price two- or three-course menu features classic French fare with modern touches, like a tender flank steak with homemade chutney or beef stew with coriander. The decor is understated hip, with flea-market chairs and exposed stone walls. The crowd gathered around the restaurant's zinc bar sipping wine sometimes spills out onto the sidewalk on a warm night. Open only in the evenings.

15 rue André del Sarte, 18th arrond. ☏ **01-42-54-88-96.** Fixed-price dinner 26€–29€. Mon–Sat 8–11pm (until 2am for the bar). Métro: Barbes-Rochechouart or Château Rouge.

Nansouty ★★ MODERN FRENCH   Just north of the Butte de Montmartre, this popular wine bar will appeal to both gourmets and wine enthusiasts. Choose from more than 100 bottles on the massive blackboard, and supplement with top-quality nibbles. Can't make up your mind? Just ask the wait staff, who are wise in the ways of Bacchus. Success has been such that Nansouty is now open at both lunch and dinner, offering affordable fixed-price menus and seasonal specialties.

35 rue Ramey, 18th arrond. ☏ **01-42-52-58-87.** Main courses 18€; fixed-price lunch 17€; fixed-price dinner 30€. Tues–Fri noon–2:30pm and 8–11pm; Sat and Mon 8–11pm. Métro: Lamarck-Caulincourt or Château Rouge.

RÉPUBLIQUE, BASTILLE & EASTERN PARIS (11TH & 12TH ARRONDISSEMENTS)

Home to a mix of working-class families, hipsters, and *bobos* (bourgeois bohemians), the area between République and Nation is diverse, young, and fun. This might be why there are so many good restaurants around here. It's also a good neighborhood for discovering the flavors of Africa in restaurants featuring dishes from France's former colonies.

Expensive

La Gazzetta ★★ MODERN FRENCH   Just down the street from the bustling outdoor food market at Aligre, this beautiful, old-fashioned-looking bistro is helmed by a chef whose cooking is anything but traditional. How about spelt risotto with nettles, or mackerel with burnt spring onions—topped off with goat-cheese ice cream with roasted apricots for dessert? It may sound strange, but it tastes fantastic. Fans of experimental cooking can savor the 7-course tasting menu for 65€; at lunch a fixed-price menu offers 3 tiny appetizers and a main dish for 19€, an excellent price for this level of quality.

29 rue de Cotte, 12th arrond. tel] **01-43-47-47-05.** www.lagazzetta.fr. Fixed-price dinner 39€–65€; fixed-price lunch 19€. Tues–Sat noon–3pm and 7:30–10:30pm. Closed in Aug. Métro: Ledru-Rollin.

Moderate

Astier ★★ TRADITIONAL FRENCH/BISTRO   This beautiful old restaurant has kept its polished wood and checked tablecloths, as well as its classic menu. Wild boar terrine, rabbit in mustard sauce, rib steak with anchovy toasts, pike *quenelles* (a sort of elegant dumpling) and *tarte tatin* (apple tart) are menu regulars, plus the legendary cheese tray. It's a postcard version of a Paris bistro, minus the surly waiters. The fixed-price menu is your best bet, as the main courses can get pricey on their own.

44 rue Jean-Pierre Timbaud, 11th arrond. ☏ **01-43-57-16-35.** www.restaurant-astier.com. Main courses 22€–26€; fixed-price dinner 35€–45€; fixed-price lunch 25€–39€. Daily 12:15–2:15pm and 7–10:30pm. In July–Aug, closed Sat and Mon lunch, and all day Sun. Métro: Parmentier or Oberkampf.

Le Bistrot Paul Bert ★★ BISTRO/TRADITIONAL FRENCH   Ask any local food writer to name his or her favorite classic bistro, and there's a good chance you'll be directed here. The chalkboard menu changes with the seasons, but you can usually count on one of the city's best steak frites (here crowned with a glistening morsel of marrow), followed by a generous slice of *tarte tatin* (apple tart) served with thick crème fraîche. The decor is a jumble of wooden tables, cracked tile floors, flea-market finds, and polished zinc bar—exactly how you imagine a neighborhood bistro should be.

18 rue Paul Bert, 11th arrond. ✆ **01-43-72-24-01.** Main courses 27€; fixed-price lunch 19€ and 38€; fixed-price dinner 38€. Tues–Sat noon–2pm and 7:30–11pm. Closed in Aug. Métro: Faidherbe-Chaligny.

Mansouria ★★ MOROCCAN   Generally accepted as the queen of Moroccan cooking (she's published half a dozen cookbooks), Fatéma Hal rules suprême in the kitchen of this elegant restaurant. Naturally, it offers a wide variety of delicious couscous dishes, garnished with fragrant broths and grilled meats, but the real treat here are the *tagines,* or stews, like the one with chicken and walnut-stuffed figs, or another with lamb, eggplant, and preserved lemons. One dish, La Mourouzia, is prepared from a 12th-century recipe featuring lamb seared in real *ras al hanout*—an intense mixture of 27 spices—and stewed in honey, raisins, and almonds.

11 rue Faidherbe, 11th arrond. ✆ **01-43-71-00-16.** www.mansouria.fr. Main courses 18€–26€; fixed-price dinner 28€–36€. Mon 7:30–10:30pm; Tues–Sat noon–2pm and 7:30–11pm. Métro: Faidherbe-Chaligny.

Inexpensive
L'Ebauchoir ★ MEDITERRANEAN   Located in an unlikely corner of the 12th arrondissement, this neighborhood hangout offers a great selection of bistro cooking at reasonable prices. High ceilings, sunny yellow walls, and wooden fixtures create a friendly atmosphere for Mediterranean-inspired dishes like roast lamb with sweet garlic, polenta, and olives, or grilled bonito with a peach and preserved lemon salad. Vegetarian options include eggplant and feta with olives and fresh capers. Serving one of the few reasonable three-course lunches (15€), this place is jammed at noontime, so try to reserve.

43 rue des Citeaux, 12th arrond. ✆ **01-43-42-49-31.** www.lebauchoir.com. Main course dinner 19€–24€; fixed price lunch 13€–27€. Mon 8–11pm, Tues–Fri noon–2:30pm and 8–11pm, Fri–Sat noon–2:30pm and 7:30–11pm. Closed 1 week mid-Aug. Métro: Faidherbe Chaligny or Reuilly Diderot.

Waly Fay ★★ SENEGALESE   Take a gastronomic voyage to West Africa at this popular restaurant that has introduced umpteen Parisians to delicious Senegalese cuisine. A former French colony, Senegal has absorbed culinary influences from France, as well as its northern neighbors in the Magreb. Cool music and candlelight set the scene for some of the best poulet yassa (chicken marinated in lime and onions) in Paris; there also several versions of n'dolé, spinach-like leaves cooked with peanut sauce and mixed with shrimp, or fish, or meat. Less adventurous eaters might like the marinated brochettes, which are grilled over a wood fire. Fill out the meal with a side order of fried plantains or *atéké* (manioc). There's also a terrific selection of rums here, for cocktail hour.

6 rue Godefroy Cavalgnac, 11th arrond. ✆ **01-40-24-17-79.** www.walyfay.com. Main courses 13€–28€. Daily 7pm–midnight.

BELLEVILLE, CANAL ST-MARTIN & LA VILLETTE (10TH, 19TH & 20TH ARRONDISSEMENTS)
One of the last strongholds of Paris's bohemian set, here you can find both gourmet bistros and funky cheap eats, as well as a good number of wine bars that serve both nibbles and the fruit of the vine.

Moderate

Chez Michel ★★ BRETON/SEAFOOD Prices have barely budged in a decade at this popular restaurant, where chef Thierry Breton improvises on recipes from back home (Brittany), including lots of seafood dishes, like cotriade, a Breton fish stew, or fresh crab salad. A massive oven has been installed in the dining room itself, cooking up slow-cooked specialties like braised lamb. For dessert, try the copious rice pudding or the awe-inspiring Paris-Brest (a choux pastry filled with praline cream).

10 rue de Belzunce, 10th arrond. ✆ **01-44-53-06-20.** www.restaurant-chez-michel.com. Fixed-price lunch 29€; fixed-price dinner 35€. Tues–Fri noon–2pm and Mon–Fri 7pm–midnight. Closed Aug. Métro: Gare du Nord.

Rosa Bonheur ★ TAPAS This unconventional space is named after an unconventional 19th-century painter/sculptress. It's a restaurant and tapas bar, but it's also a sort of off-the-wall community center, hosting various expositions and events—it even has its own chorus and soccer team. Located in an old *buvette* (refreshment pavilion) inside the Parc des Buttes Chaumont, dating from the Universal Exposition of 1900, the restaurant boasts a sprawling terrace and one of the best panoramic views in town. A huge crowd gathers to drink and nibble tapas outside or sample dishes from the creative menu. An indoor play area and kids' menu make this a good family option.

2 allée de la Cascade, 19th arrond. ✆ **01-42-00-00-45.** www.rosabonheur.fr. Tapas 6€–9€; main courses 16€–22€. Thurs–Sun noon–midnight. Closed first 2 weeks in Jan. Métro: Botzaris.

Le Verre Volé ★ WINE BAR/MODERN FRENCH The sun is shining, the leafy trees are posing prettily along the Canal St-Martin, and you are walking over one of the Japanese-eque bridges that curve over the water. All that's missing is a table and a glass of wine. Luckily, this wine bar/restaurant is on hand to delight you with its vast selection. You could share a plate of sliced smoked meats and sausage, the usual accompaniment to a glass of red, or explore the menu, which might include a slice of milk-fed veal or mullet ceviche. Then select a bottle of wine from the shelves that line the walls, and enjoy it (for a nominal corkage fee) in this informal, if crowded, setting.

67 rue de Lancry, 10th arrond. ✆ **01-48-03-17-34.** www.leverrevole.fr. Main courses 15€–23€. Daily 12:30–2pm and 7:30–10:30pm. Métro: Jacques Bonsergent.

Inexpensive

Bob's Juice Bar ★ VEGETARIAN Hip Parisians are tripping all over themselves to try "smoossies" (that is, smoothies) these days, and some of the best can be found at this terrific vegetarian restaurant, which has muffins, bagels, soups, and other delicious goodies. The brainchild of Marc Grossman (alias "Bob"), an erstwhile New Yorker, this may not be the most authentically French experience, but it certainly is a tasty one. Sit down or take out here, or try the larger **Bob's Kitchen** in the Marais (74 rue des Gravilliers), which is open on weekends.

15 rue Lucien Sampaix, 10th arrond. ✆ **09-50-06-36-18.** Smoothies 4€–5€; main courses 5€–8€. Mon–Fri 7:30am–3pm. Métro: Jacques Bonsergent.

The Left Bank

LATIN QUARTER (5TH & 13TH ARRONDISSEMENTS)

Steer clear of the unbearably touristy area around rue de la Huchette and the often mediocre restaurants on rue Moufftard. Venture farther afield, where innovative restaurateurs have been cultivating a knowledgeable clientele of professors, professionals, and savvy tourists like yourself.

Expensive

Itinéraires ★★ FRENCH FUSION   After earning acclaim at 24 years old with his tiny tapas bistro in the 11th arrondissement, gifted chef Sylvain Sendra has opened this elegant enterprise devoted to finding the meeting point between French and more far-flung cuisines. The seasonal menu features lots of organic ingredients and might include a lamb confit with sweet spices and cauliflower couscous or poached cod in sage broth with mushrooms and aioli. Finish your meal with a Vahlrona chocolate soufflé tart with coffee ice cream.

5 rue de Pontoise, 5th arrond. ✆ **01-46-33-60-11.** www.restaurant-itineraires.com. Main dishes 27€–35€; fixed-price lunch 32€ and 38€; fixed-price dinner 55€—85€. Tues–Fri noon–2pm and 7–10:30pm, Sat 7–10:30pm. Closed Aug. Métro: Maubert-Mutualité.

La Tour d'Argent ★★ CLASSIC FRENCH   Sure, you come here for the pressed duck (the signature dish—each duck has been numbered since 1890), but the real reason to come to the "Silver Tower" is to sample its history, its view, and its incredible service. Five or six different waiters will visit your table at one time or another, accomplishing various tasks (opening wine bottles, pulling out your chair, and even leading you to the bathroom) with utmost professionalism and not a hint of snobbery. They then discreetly disappear into the rich décor as you gaze through the huge windows that give you a first-class view of Notre-Dame's flying buttresses. By the time you've finished your meal (which still merits its one Michelin star), you feel like a pasha. The fixed-price lunch is a good way to enjoy this singular experience without ruining your budget. Be sure to reserve at least a week in advance; jackets required for men at dinner.

15–17 quai de la Tournelle, 5th arrond. ✆ **01-43-54-23-31.** www.latourdargent.com. Main courses 70€–140€; fixed-price dinner 180€–200€; fixed-price lunch 80€. Tues–Sat noon–1pm; Tues–Sat 7–9pm. Closed in Aug. Métro: St-Michel or Maubert-Mutualité.

Moderate

Dans les Landes ★★ SOUTHWESTERN FRENCH/TAPAS   Chef Julien Duboué takes inspiration from his homeland and neighboring Basque country to create luscious tapas to be enjoyed with (many) glasses of great regional wines. Fried chipirions (small squid), polenta with smoked duck breast, Basque-style mussels—the list is long and tempting. It's packed at night, so get there early or reserve a table.

119 bis rue Monge, 5th arrond. ✆ **01-45-87-06-00.** Tapas 7€–23€. Daily noon–11pm. Closed last week of Dec, first week of Jan and 3 weeks in Aug. Métro: Censier-Daubenton.

Le Pré Verre ★★ MODERN FRENCH/ASIAN FUSION   This crowded and convivial gourmet wine bar offers dishes that are a scrumptious blend of traditional French and exotic ingredients—not particularly flashy or trendy or even spicy, just deliciously unexpected. One of the signature dishes is a meltingly tender *cochon de lait* (milk-fed pork) served with a smooth cinnamon-infused sauce and a delectably crunchy mass that turns out to be cabbage. The weekday lunch menu is a particularly great deal: You get an appetizer, a main dish, a glass of wine, and coffee for 15€.

8 rue Thenard, 5th arrond. ✆ **01-43-54-59-47.** www.lepreverre.com. Main courses 20€; fixed-price lunch 15€ and 32€; fixed-price dinner 32€. Tues–Sat noon–2pm and 7:30–10:30pm. Closed last week of Dec. Métro: Maubert-Mutualité or Cluny–La Sorbonne.

Inexpensive

Foyer Vietnam ★★ VIETNAMESE   This humble restaurant is usually crammed with students, professors, and working stiffs who come for the generous portions of Vietnamese classics. The Foyer is also a nonprofit dedicated to all things Vietnam, so you can enjoy art and seminars after you slurp your steaming bowl of *pho* (meat broth with vermicelli and vegetables) or *bò bún* (8€), a heap of rice vermicelli with sliced beef and a delicious tangy sauce. Finish with a Vietnamese *cà phê*, a drip coffee—the beans are roasted with butter and rum, giving it an exquisite flavor.

80 rue Monge, 5th arrond. ✆ **01-45-35-32-54.** www.foyer-vietnam.org. Main courses 7€–10€; fixed-price lunch 11€. No credit cards. Mon–Sat noon–2pm and 7–10pm. Closed Aug. Métro: Place Monge.

ST-GERMAIN-DES-PRÉS (6TH ARRONDISSEMENT)

Saint Germain is a mix of expensive eateries that only the lucky few can afford and stalwart holdouts from the days when poverty-stricken intellectuals and artists frequented the Café de Flore. Though the Marché St-Germain has been transformed into a type of mall, the restaurants hugging its perimeter offer a wide range of possibilities.

Expensive

Le Comptoir du Relais ★★★ TRADITIONAL FRENCH/BISTRO   The brainchild of super-chef Yves de Camdeborde, this small and scrumptious bistro is still bringing in the crowds almost a decade after it opened. During the day, it serves relatively traditional fare, say, a slice of lamb with thyme sauce or maybe the *panier de cochonaille,* a basket of the Camdeborde family's own brand of smoked meats. On weeknights, it's a temple to haute cuisine, with a five-course tasting menu. You'll need to reserve several weeks in advance for this meal, which changes every night and is nonnegotiable—the chef decides what you are going to eat. There are no reservations at lunch or on the weekends, when the bistro menu is served from noon to 11pm, so arrive early or be prepared to wait.

9 carrefour de l'Odeon, 6th arrond. ✆ **01-44-27-07-50.** www.hotel-paris-relais-saint-germain. com. Main courses weekends and weekdays 15€–29€; fixed-price dinner weeknights 60€. Daily noon–11pm. Métro: Odéon.

Le Relais Louis XIII ★★★ CLASSIC FRENCH   This acclaimed restaurant pays homage to traditional French cuisine at its most illustrious. No tonka beans or reduced licorice sauce here—Chef Manuel Martinez trains his formidable skills on classic sauces and time-honored dishes like sea-bass quenelles and roast duck, though he's not opposed to topping off the meal with a little lemon-basil sherbet. Signature dishes include lobster and foie gras ravioli, or braised sweetbreads with wild mushrooms. The atmospheric dining room, crisscrossed with exposed beams and ancient stonework, makes you wonder if the Three Musketeers might tumble through the doorway bearing your millefeuille with bourbon vanilla cream.

8 rue des Grands-Augustins, 6th arrond. ✆ **01-43-26-75-96.** www.relaislouis13.fr. Main courses 58€–59€; fixed-price lunch 55€; fixed-price dinner 85€–135€. Tues–Sat noon–2:30pm, 7:30–10:30pm. Closed Aug. Métro: Odéon or St-Michel.

Moderate

Mangetout ★★★ MODERN FRENCH   This affordable taste treat comes courtesy of Michelin-starred chef Alain Dutournier, the force behind Pinxo (see p. 73). For a relative pittance, you can get a delicious two- or three-course set meal that might start with a golden broth decked with fresh shrimp and vegetables, continue with a surprisingly light blanquette de veau (veal stew), and finish up with a tourtière, a flakey apple tart that is usually found in the French southwest, Dutournier's home sweet home. The quality of the ingredients and the cooking is superb and the price is right. As the dining room is tiny, dinner reservations are essential.

82 rue Mazarine, 6th arrond. ✆ **01-43-54-02-11.** www.alaindutournier.com/wp/mangetout. Main courses 17€–24€; fixed-price lunch 20€–25€; fixed price dinner 23€. Tues–Sat noon–2pm and 7–10:30pm. Closed in Aug. Métro: Mabillon or Odéon.

Le P'tit Fernand ★★ TRADITIONAL FRENCH/BISTRO   This tiny slice of a restaurant packs a flavorful punch. Red-checked tablecloths provide a homey background for excellent bistro dishes like thick steak with a confit of shallots and creamy mashed potatoes, or duck magret (breast) served with morello-cherry sauce. You could start with a nice light beet and rhubarb gazpacho or go nuts and order the homemade terrine of foie gras. Whatever it is, it will be executed with loving care and quality ingredients, which is why this restaurant has a devoted clientele.

7 rue Lobineau, 6th arrond. ✆ **01-40-46-06-88.** Main courses 18€–26€. Daily noon–2pm and 7–11:30pm. Métro: Mabillon.

Inexpensive
Restaurant Polidor ★ TRADITIONAL FRENCH/BISTRO   An unofficial historic monument, Polidor is not so much a restaurant as a snapshot of a bygone era. The decor has not changed substantially for at least 100 years, when Verlaine and Rimbaud, the bad boys of poetry, would come here for a cheap meal. In the 1950s, it was dubbed "the College of Pataphysics" by a rowdy group of young upstarts that included Max Ernst, Boris Vian, and Eugene Ionesco; André Gide and Ernest Hemingway were reputed regulars. The menu features hefty bistro standbys like boeuf bourguignon and *blanquette de veau* (veal stew), but you'll also find lighter fare like salmon with basil or chicken breast with morel sauce. These days, the artsy set has moved elsewhere; you'll probably be sharing the long wooden tables with other tourists, along with a dose of locals. Though the food is not particularly memorable, the ambience is unique.

41 rue Monsieur-le-Prince, 6th arrond. ✆ **01-43-26-95-34.** www.polidor.com. Main courses 11€–20€; fixed-price menu 22€–35€. No credit cards. Daily noon–2:30pm; Mon–Sat 7pm–12:30am; Sun 7–11pm. Métro: Odéon.

EIFFEL TOWER & NEARBY (7TH ARRONDISSEMENT)
Crowded with ministries and important people, this neighborhood is so grand, you half expect to hear trumpets blowing each time you turn a corner. Though it's a rather staid neighborhood, a few streets are fairly lively, namely rue Cler, a pretty market street, and rue St-Dominique, home to some of the best restaurants on this side of the Seine.

Expensive
L'Arpège ★★★ MODERN FRENCH   This is probably the only Michelin-three-star restaurant where vegetables are the stars. You can still find meat on the menu, but it takes a back seat to carrots, turnips, sweet peas, or whatever other lovely plant life is in season. The pristine produce comes from Chef Alain Passard's farm and is often picked the same day it's served. The menu comes in two sections: the "grand crus" of the vegetable garden, and the "memory" dishes: milk-fed lamb from the Aveyron with wild celery, or fresh fish from Brittany with

lovage and sweet peas. Don't miss the *tarte aux pommes bouquet de roses* (tart composed of apple ribbons rolled into tiny rosettes). Reservations are required at least 2 weeks in advance.

84 rue de Varenne, 7th arrond. ☎ **01-47-05-09-06.** www.alain-passard.com. Main courses 110€–225€; fixed-price lunch 140€, fixed-price tasting menu (lunch and dinner) 420€. Mon–Fri noon–2pm and 7–10:30pm. Métro: Varenne.

Restaurant Auguste ★★ MODERN FRENCH/SEAFOOD   It's not every famous chef that can call himself "Mr. Goodfish." Gael Orieux's love of the sea and everything in it has led him to become spokesperson for an association dedicated to protecting the oceans. That means what you eat is not only delicious, but also sustainable. Let's hope he makes an impact on his clientele, many of whom are politicians from the nearby Assemblée Nationale. Your dish will look like artwork, whether it's red mullet with sweet and sour cherries, turnips in coconut sauce and wild elderberries, or turbot with tomatoes, peppers, and quail eggs. Meat eaters may appreciate the veal with juniper berries served with sweet peas and rhubarb.

54 rue de Bourgogne, 7th arrond. ☎ **01-45-51-61-09.** www.restaurantauguste.fr. Main courses 36€–55€; fixed-price lunch 37€, fixed-price dinner 88€. Mon–Fri noon–2:30pm and 7–10:30pm. Closed 3 weeks in Aug. Métro: Varenne.

Moderate

Le Casse Noix ★★ TRADITIONAL FRENCH/BISTRO   The result of yet another great chef realizing his bistro dreams, this relaxed restaurant offers high-caliber food in a casual, affordable setting. The decor is nostalgic and the traditional French cooking is sincere and generous, featuring dishes like roast pork shoulder Ibaïona with olive puree, or a classic *petit salé* (lentils with smoky ham). About a 10-minute walk from the Eiffel Tower, this is a good bet for those looking for a bit of authenticity in an otherwise very touristy neighborhood. At dinnertime, the fixed-price menu is *obligatoire,* so no à la carte ordering. Lunch is more flexible.

56 rue de la Fédération, 15th arrond. ☎ **01-45-66-09-01.** www.le-cassenoix.fr. Main courses at lunch 19€–23€; fixed-price lunch 21€ and 26€, fixed-price dinner 33€. Mon–Fri noon–2:30pm and 7–10:30pm. Closed Aug and between Christmas and New Year. Métro: Dupleix.

La Fontaine de Mars ★★ BISTRO/SOUTHWESTERN FRENCH   Red and white checks are everywhere at this old-school bistro: on the tablecloths, the wicker chairs, and even the curtains. A venerable institution since it first opened in 1908, its low-key classy décor and traditional menu attracted the attention of President Obama, who made a surprise visit here with his wife Michele in 2009. The kitchen turns out reliable and succulent southwestern dishes like cassoulet, foie gras, and duck breast with black cherry sauce. Starters include *escargots* (snails) and *oeufs au Madiran* (eggs baked with red wine and bacon), and the dessert list is full of classics such as île flottante, crème brûlée, and dark chocolate mousse.

129 rue St-Dominique, 7th arrond. ☎ **01-47-05-46-44.** www.fontainedemars.com. Main courses 17€–49€. Daily noon–3pm and 7:30–11pm. Métro: Ecole Militaire.

Inexpensive

Café Constant ★★ TRADITIONAL FRENCH/BISTRO   Of the three Christian Constant restaurants on this street, this one is the most relaxed; you may find the master himself at the bar smoking a cigar here during his off-hours. The menu features modern versions of French comfort food like tangy poached cod with aioli, melt-in-your-mouth beef *daube* (stew) with carrots, or steak with shallots and creamy potato puree. The weekday lunch *formule* is a two-course meal (chef's choice) for 16€, a terrific deal for this level of quality. If you are hankering for a meal off-hours, between 3pm and 5pm you can select a dish from a more limited menu. No reservations.

139 rue Saint-Dominique, 7th arrond. ✆ **01-47-53-73-34.** www.maisonconstant.com. Main courses 16€–26€; fixed-price lunch 16€–23€. Daily noon–5pm and 7–11pm. Métro: Ecole Militaire.

Le Petit Cler ★ TRADITIONAL FRENCH/BISTRO   A mini-version of La Fontaine de Mars (see above), this cute little cafe tumbles out on to the rue Cler pedestrian market street and serves food of the same high quality as its upscale big sister, but simpler, and at a lower price. While you won't find as many red and white checks, you will find classic cafe fare (steaks with sautéed potatoes, omelets, and tartines—open-faced grilled sandwiches) as well as a daily special, which might be roast chicken (Sunday) or fresh fish (Friday, natch). You can also get a good continental breakfast here.

29 rue Cler, 7th arrond. ✆ **01-45-50-17-50.** www.fontainedemars.com. Main courses 11€–15€. Daily 8am–11pm. Closed 2 weeks in Aug. Métro: Ecole Militaire

MONTPARNASSE & NEARBY (14TH & 15TH ARRONDISSEMENTS)

The famous cafes where struggling writers and artists like Picasso, Hemingway, and Chagall once hung out are now much too expensive for most ordinary mortals, so having a drink is probably the best way to enjoy them. But there are plenty of other good options, from Breton creperies near the train station to a bundle of new gourmet bistros farther south.

Expensive

Cobéa ★★ MODERN FRENCH   Chef Philippe Bélissent invents concoctions that are as delicate and refined as the dining room in this pretty little house: Perfectly cooked veal with fava beans and polenta; freshly caught John Dory; or pigeon with artichokes and olives might show up on the mix-and-match menu. The concept at dinner is as follows: There is one menu, from which you decide whether you'd like to try four (75€), six (95€), or eight (115€) courses. Service is impeccable.

11 rue Raymond Losserand, 14th arrond. ✆ **01-43-20-21-39.** www.cobea.fr. Fixed-price lunch 49€–65€, fixed-price dinner 75€–115€. Tues–Sat 12:15–1:15pm, 7:15–9:15pm. Closed Aug. Métro: Gaïté or Pernety.

Moderate

La Régalade ★★ TRADITIONAL FRENCH/BISTRO   With its cracked tile floors, polished wood, and burgundy banquettes, chef Bruno Doucet's neo-bistro is an homage to the good things in life, like foie gras in asparagus bouillon or marinated sea scallops with basil and Parmesan. Main dishes are variations on French comfort food, such as a succulent pork breast with sweet peas, or lively innovations like a creamy squid risotto with sauteed prawns. Dessert could be a stinky Reblochon cheese, a molten Guanaja chocolate cake, or the house specialty, rice pudding. Reserve a week in advance.

14 av. Jean-Moulin, 14th arrond. ℭ **01-45-45-68-58.** Fixed-price menu 37€. Tues–Fri noon–2:30pm, Mon–Fri 7–11:30pm. Closed first 2 weeks of Aug. Métro: Alésia.

CAFÉ SOCIETY: PARIS'S top cafes

Cafe life is an integral part of the Parisian scene, and it simply won't do to visit the capital without joining in. Here are a few ideas for your own personal cafe tour.
Tip: Coffee or other drinks at the bar often cost half of what they do at a table.

Café de Flore ★   Every great French intellectual and artist seems to have had their moment here: Apollinaire, André Breton, Picasso, Giacometti, and of course, Simone de Beauvoir and Jean-Paul Sartre, who virtually lived here during World War II. The atmosphere today is less thoughtful and more showbiz, but it's still worth an overpriced cup of coffee just to come in and soak it up.

172 bd. St-Germain, 6th arrond. ℭ **01-45-48-55-26.** www.cafedeflore.fr. Daily 7am–2am. Métro: St-Germain-des-Prés.

Café de la Mairie ★   What could be nicer than sitting outdoors at a sidewalk cafe on the place St-Sulpice? Indoors, it's a 1970s archetype: Formica bar, boxy chairs, and an odd assortment of pensioners, fashion victims, students, and would-be novelists.

8 place St-Sulpice, 6th arrond. ℭ **01-43-26-67-82.** Mon–Fri 7am–2am, Sat 8am–2am, Sun 9am–2am. Métro: Mabillon or St-Sulpice.

Le Bistrot du Peintre ★   Artists, hipsters, and other fauna from the bustling rue de Charonne area flock to this popular spot, which sports an authentic Art Nouveau interior with the original peeling paint.

116 av. Ledru-Rollin, 11th arrond. ℭ **01-47-00-34-39.** www.bistrotdupeintre.com. Daily 7am–2am. Métro: Ledru-Rollin.

Les Deux Magots ★   The literary pedigree here is impressive: Poets Verlaine and Rimbaud camped out here, as did André Gide and Albert Camus. Sartre and de Beauvoir moved in postwar and stayed for decades. The outdoor terrace is pleasant early in the morning before the crowds awake.

6 place St-Germain-des-Prés, 6th arrond. ℭ **01-45-48-55-25.** www.lesdeuxmagots.fr. Daily 7:30am–1am. Métro: St-Germain-des-Prés.

Le Nemours ★   Cuddled up in a corner next to the Comedie Française, this beautiful cafe has a great terrace stretching out onto the Place Colette. The ideal spot for taking a load off after a day at the nearby Louvre.

2 place Colette, ℭ **01-42-61-34-14.** Mon–Fri 7am–midnight, Sat 8am–midnight, Sun 9am–8:30pm. Métro: Palais Royal–Musée du Louvre.

Inexpensive

Crêperie Josselin ★★ CREPERIE   This is one of the best of the dozens of crêperies concentrated near the Montparnasse train station. The cooks working the griddle know exactly how to achieve the lacy, golden edges of a perfect galette, and they are not shy with the butter. Josselin's specialty is the "couple," a double crepe that uses two of these lacy confections in one dish. It's delicious but filling; if you are not starving ask the waiter to make it a "simple." Tradition demands that this meal be accompanied by a bowl of hard cider (low alcohol content; for adults only). The easy prices, continuous service, and wide range of flavor combinations make this a great option for children as well. Closed on Monday, but you can wander down to No. 59, Le Petit Josselin, its sister restaurant (closed Sun).

67 rue du Montparnasse, 14th arrond. (?) **01-43-20-93-50.** Main courses 7€–11€; fixed-price menu 11€. No credit cards. Tues–Fri 11:30am–3pm and 6–11pm, Sat–Sun noon–11pm. Métro: Montparnasse-Bienvenüe.

EXPLORING PARIS

With more than 130 world-class museums to visit, scores of attractions to discover, extraordinary architecture to gape at, and wonderful neighborhoods to wander, Paris is an endless series of delights. Fortunately, you can have a terrific time in Paris even if you don't see everything. In fact, some of your best moments may be simply roaming around the city without a plan. Lolling on a park bench, dreaming over a drink at a sidewalk cafe, or noodling around an unknown neighborhood can be the stuff of some of your best travel memories.

The following pages highlight the best that Paris has to offer, from iconic sights known the world over to quirky museums and hidden gardens, from medieval castles to galleries celebrating the most challenging contemporary art.

One of Notre-Dame's famous gargoyles looks out on the roofs of Paris.

The Right Bank

LOUVRE & ILE DE LA CITÉ (1ST ARRONDISSEMENT)

This is where it all started. Back in the city's misty and uncertain beginnings, the Parisii tribe set up camp on the right bank of the Seine and started hunting on the **Ile de la Cité.** Many centuries later, the **Louvre** popped up, first as a fortress and now one of the world's mightiest museums. The city's epicenter packs in a high density of must-see monuments and museums, but don't miss the opportunity for aimless strolling, in the magnificent **Tuileries Gardens,** say, or over the **Pont Neuf.** *Note:* For simplicity's sake, the entire Ile de la Cité has been included in this section, though technically half of it lies in the 4th arrondissement.

Cathédrale de Notre-Dame ★★★ CATHEDRAL   This remarkably harmonious ensemble of carved portals, huge towers, and flying buttresses has survived close to a millennium's worth of French history and served as a setting for some of the country's most solemn moments. Napoléon crowned himself Emperor here, Napoléon III was married here, and the funerals of some of France's greatest generals (Foch, Joffre, Leclerc) were held here. In August 1944, the liberation of Paris from the Nazis was commemorated in the cathedral, as was the death of General de Gaulle in 1970.

Construction on the cathedral began in 1163 and lasted more than 200 years. The building was relatively untouched up until the end of the 17th century, when monarchs started meddling with its windows and architecture. By the time the Revolutionaries decided to convert it into a "Temple of Reason," the cathedral was already in sorry condition—and the pillaging that ensued didn't help. The interior was ravaged, statues were smashed, and the cathedral became a shadow of its former glorious self.

We can thank the famous "Hunchback" himself for saving Notre-Dame. Victor Hugo's novel "The Hunchback of Notre Dame" drew attention to the state of disrepair, and other artists and writers began to call for the restoration of the edifice. In 1844 Louis-Phillipe hired Jean-Baptiste Lassus and Viollet-le-Duc to restore the cathedral, which they finished in 1864.

Begin your visit at **Point Zéro,** just in front of the building on the parvis (the esplanade). This is the official center of Paris and the point from which all distances relative to other French cities are calculated. Before you are three enormous **carved portals** depicting (from left to right) the Coronation of the Virgin, the Last Judgment, and scenes from the lives of the Virgin and St. Anne. Above is the **Gallery of the Kings of Judah and Israel**—thought to be portraits of the kings of France, the original statues were chopped out of the facade during the Revolution; some of the heads were eventually found in the 1970s and now are in the Musée National du Moyen Age/Thermes de Cluny.

Cathédrale de Notre-Dame

Views from the Two Towers

The lines are long and the climb is longer, but the view from the **rooftop balcony** at the base of the cathedral's towers is possibly the most Parisian of all views. After trudging up some 255 steps (in a narrow winding staircase—not for small children or anyone with mobility concerns) you'll be rewarded with a panorama that not only encompasses the Ile de la Cité, the Eiffel Tower, and Sacré-Coeur, but is also framed by a collection of photogenic **gargoyles.** One of the most famous is the **Stryga,** a horned and winged beasty holding his head in his hands, pensively sticking his tongue out at the city below. Another 147 steps up a narrow stairway lead to the summit of the **south tower,** from which you get an endless view of Paris. Come in the morning before the crowds get thick, and avoid weekends (www.monuments-nationaux.fr; ✆ **01-53-40-60-80;** 9€ adults, 6€ under 26, free under 18; Apr–June and Sept 10am–6pm; July–Aug Mon–Fri 10am–6pm, Sat–Sun 10am–11pm; Oct–Mar 10am–5:30pm).

Upon entering the cathedral, you'll be immediately struck by two things: the throngs of tourists clogging the aisles, and, when you look up, the heavenly dimensions of the pillars holding up the ceiling. Soaring upward, these delicate archways give the impression that the entire edifice is about to take off into the sky. Up there in the upper atmosphere are three remarkable stained-glass **rose windows.** The north window retains almost all of its 13th-century stained glass; the other two have been heavily restored. An impressive **treasury** is filled with relics of various saints including the elaborate cases for the **Crown of Thorns,** brought back from Constantinople by Saint Louis in the 13th century. The crown itself is not on display; however, it can be viewed, along with a nail and some pieces of the Holy Cross, on the first Friday of

Soaring pillars and stained glass, Notre-Dame

the month (3pm), every Friday during Lent (3pm) and Good Friday (10am–5pm). For a detailed look at the cathedral, take advantage of the **free guided tours in English** (Wed–Thurs 2pm, Sat 2:30pm) or rent an **audioguide** for 5€.

When you leave, be sure to take a stroll around the outside of the cathedral to admire the other portals and the famous flying buttresses.

Place du Parvis Notre-Dame, 4th arrond. www.notredamedeparis.fr. ✆ **01-53-10-07-02.** Admission free to cathedral. Treasury 4€ adults, 2€ students and seniors, 1€ ages 6–12, free children 5 and younger. Cathedral Mon–Fri 8am–6:45pm; Sat–Sun 8am–7:15pm. Treasury Mon–Fri 9:30am–6pm; Sat 9:30am–6:30pm; Sun 1:30–6:30pm. Métro: Cité or St-Michel. RER: St-Michel.

The Conciergerie illuminated at night

Conciergerie ★ HISTORIC SITE   A dark relic of the Revolution, this famous prison commemorates the Reign of Terror, when murderous infighting between the various revolutionary factions engendered panic and paranoia that led to tens of thousands of people being arrested and executed. Many of the Revolution's most pivotal characters spent their final days here before making their way to the guillotine, including Marie Antoinette.

Though it's been a prison since the 15th century, the building itself is actually what remains of a 14th-century royal palace built by Philippe le Bel. The enormous **Salle des Gens d'Arms**, with its 8.4m-high (28-ft.) vaulted ceiling, is an impressive reminder of the building's palatial past. As for the prison, though the cells have been outfitted with displays and re-creations of daily life (including wax figures), it's a little difficult to imagine what it was like in the bad old days. However, the **Cours des Femmes** (the women's courtyard) virtually hasn't changed since the days when female prisoners did their washing in the fountain. In a curious attempt to spice up its offerings, the site has recently been hosting contemporary art exhibits.

2 bd. du Palais, 1st arrond. ☎ **01-53-40-60-80.** www.monuments-nationaux.fr. Admission 9€ adults, 6€ ages 18–25, free for 17 and younger. Daily 9:30–6pm. Métro: Cité, Châtelet, or St-Michel. RER: St-Michel.

A statue grouping in Jardin des Tuileries Garden

Jardin des Tuileries ★★★ GARDENS   This exquisite park spreads from the Louvre to the place de la Concorde. What you see today is based on the design by 17th-century master landscape artist André Le Nôtre—the man behind the gardens of Versailles. Le Nôtre's elegant geometry of flowerbeds, parterres, and groves of trees made the Tuileries Gardens the ultimate stroll for the era's well-to-do Parisians. It continues to delight both tourists and locals in the 21st century.

During World War II, furious fighting went on here, and many statues were damaged. Little by little in the postwar years, the garden put itself back together. Seventeenth- and eighteenth-century representations of various gods and goddesses were repaired, and the city added new works by modern masters such as Alberto Giocometti, Jean Dubuffet, and Henry Moore. Rodin's "The Kiss" and "Eve" are here, as well as a series of 18 of Maillol's curvaceous women, peeking out of the green **labyrinth** of hedges in the Carousel Gardens near the museum.

Pulling up a metal chair and sunning yourself on the edge of the large **fountain** in the center of the gardens (the **Grande Carrée**) is a delightful respite for tired tourists after a day in the Louvre; tots will enjoy playing with one of the wooden **toy sailboats** that you can rent from a stand (2.50€/half-hour).

Near place de la Concorde, 1st arrond. ☎ **01-40-20-90-43.** Free admission. Daily Apr–May 7am–9pm; June–Aug 7am–11pm; Sept 7am–9pm; Oct–Mar 7:30am–7:30pm. Métro: Tuileries or Concorde.

Musée des Arts Décoratifs ★★ MUSEUM   Possessing some 150,000 items in its rich collection, this fascinating museum offers a glimpse of history through the prism of decorative objects, with a spectrum that ranges from medieval traveling trunks to Philippe Starck stools. The collection is organized in more or less chronological order, so on your journey you will pass by paintings from the First Italian Renaissance, through a room filled with exquisite 15th-century intarsia ("paintings" made out of intricately inlaid wood), before gaping at huge, intricately carved 17th-century German armoires.

The collection weakens after 1930; it's hard to tell if this is due to a lack of imagination on the part of the museum or on the part of 20th-century designers. The chronological sequence can be hard to follow; note that the visit starts on the third floor. There are two other museums in the building (which is actually one of the extremities of the Louvre): the **Musée de la Publicité,** which takes on the history of advertising, and the **Musée de la Mode et du Textile,** which hosts exhibits on the many facets of clothing, including the works of famous couture houses like Jean-Paul Gaultier and Dior (both have the same hours as the main museum and are included in the ticket price to Arts Décoratifs).

Palais du Louvre, 107 rue de Rivoli, 1st arrond. ☎ **01-44-55-57-50.** www.lesartsdecoratifs.fr. Admission 9.50€ adults, 8€ ages 18–25, free children 17 and younger. Tues–Sun 11am–6pm. Métro: Louvre–Palais-Royal or Tuileries.

Musée du Louvre ★★★ MUSEUM   The best way to thoroughly visit the Louvre would be to move in for a month. Not only is it one of the largest museums in the world, with more than 35,000 works of art displayed over 60,000 sq. m (645,835 sq. ft.), but it's packed with enough masterpieces to make the Mona Lisa weep. Rembrandt, Reubens, Botticelli, Ingres, and Michelangelo are all represented here; subjects range from the grandiose (Antoine-Jean Gros's gigantic "Napoleon Bonaparte Visiting the Plague-Stricken in Jaffa") to the petite (Vermeer's tiny, exquisite "Lacemaker"). You can gape at a diamond the size of a golf ball in the royal treasury, or marvel over exquisite bronze figurines in the vast Egyptian section.

Today, the building is divided into three wings, Sully, Denon, and Richelieu, each one with its own clearly marked entrance, found under I.M. Pei's glass pyramid. Get your hands on a museum map (there's an excellent interactive map on the museum's website), choose your personal "must-sees," and plan ahead.

The Louvre at dusk, with I.M. Pei's famous pyramids

There's no way to see it all, but mercifully, the museum is well organized and has been very reasonably arranged into color-coded sections. If you're really in a rush or you just want to get an overall sense of the place, you can take the introductory guided tour in English (1½ hr.; 11:15am, 2pm; Wed–Sun except the first Sunday of the month; 12€).

The museum's three biggest stars are all located in the Denon wing. La Joconde, otherwise known as the **"Mona Lisa,"** now has an entire wall to herself, making it easier to contemplate her enigmatic smile. Another inscrutable female in this wing is the **"Venus de Milo,"** who was found on a Greek island in 1820. The **"Winged Victory of Samothrace,"** another magnificent Greek sculpture, stands at the top of a majestic flight of stairs, her powerful body pushing forward as if about to take flight. This headless deity originally overlooked the Sanctuary of the Great Gods on the island of Samothrace. At press time, the "Winged Victory" was undergoing a cleaning and was scheduled to be back on view in summer 2014.

Because a complete listing of the Louvre's highlights would fill a book, below is a decidedly biased selection of my favorite areas:

13TH- TO 18TH-CENTURY ITALIAN PAINTING A few standouts in the immense Italian collection include the delicate fresco by Botticelli called "Venus and the Three Graces Presenting Gifts to a Young Woman," Veronese's enormous "Wedding Feast at Cana," and of course, the "Mona Lisa." The Divine Miss M is in a room packed with wonders, including several Titians and Tintorettos. Once you've digested this rich meal, stroll down the endless Grande Galerie, past more da Vincis ("Saint John the Baptist," "The Virgin of the Rock"), as well as works by Raphael, Caravaggio, and Gentileschi.

GREEK & ROMAN SCULPTURE While the "Venus de Milo" and the "Winged Victory of Samothrace" are not to be missed, the Salle des Caryatides (the room itself is a work of art) boasts marble masterworks like "Artemis" hunting with her stag and the troubling "Sleeping Hermaphrodite," an alluring female figure from behind—and something entirely different from the front.

THE GALERIE D'APOLLON The gold-encrusted room is an excellent example of the excesses of 17th-century French royalty. Commissioned by Louis XIV, aka "The Sun King," every inch of this gallery is covered with gilt stucco sculptures and flamboyant murals invoking the journey of the Roman sun god Apollo (ceiling paintings are by Charles Le Brun). The main draw here is the collection of crown jewels. Among necklaces bedecked with quarter-sized sapphires and tiaras dripping with diamonds and rubies is the jewel-studded crown of Louis XV and the pearl-and-diamond diadem of Empress Eugenie.

THE EGYPTIANS   This is the largest collection outside of Cairo, thanks in large part to Jean-François Champollion, the 19th-century French scientist and scholar who first decoded Egyptian hieroglyphs. Sculptures, figurines, papyrus documents, steles, musical instruments, and of course, mummies, fill numerous rooms in the Sully Wing, including the colossal statue of Ramses II and the strangely moving Seated Scribe. He gazes intently out of intricately crafted inlaid eyes: A combination of copper, magnesite, and polished rock crystal create a startlingly lifelike stare.

LARGE-FORMAT FRENCH PAINTINGS   Enormous floor-to-ceiling (and these are high ceilings!) paintings of monumental moments in history cover the walls in

Greek and Roman sculpture galleries, Louvre

these three rooms. The "Coronation of Napoléon" by Jacques-Louis David depicts the newly minted Emperor crowning Josephine, while the disconcerted pope and a host of notables look on. Farther on are several tumultuous canvases by Eugène Delacroix, including "Liberty Guiding the People," which might just be the ultimate expression of French patriotism.

Note: When visiting the museum, **watch your wallets and purses**— there has been an unfortunate increase in pickpockets; organized groups even use children to prey on unsuspecting art lovers.

quai du Louvre, 1st arrond. Main entrance in the glass pyramid, cour Napoléon. © **01-40-20-50-50.** www.louvre.fr. Admission 12€ adults, children 17 and younger free. Sat–Mon and Thurs 9am–6pm; Wed and Fri 9am–9:30pm. Métro: Palais-Royal–Musée du Louvre.

Musée de l'Orangerie ★★ MUSEUM   Since 1927, this former royal greenhouse has been the home of Monet's "Nymphéas," or **water lilies,** which he conceived as a "haven of peaceful meditation." Two large oval rooms are dedicated to these masterpieces, in which Monet tried to replicate the feeling and atmosphere of his garden at Giverny. He worked on these enormous canvases for 12 years, with the idea of creating an environment that would soothe the "overworked nerves" of modern men and women.

The other highlight here is the Guillaume collection, an impressive assortment of late-19th- and early-20th-century paintings. The first light-filled gallery displays works by Renoir and Cezanne. The rest of the collection includes slightly sinister landscapes by Rousseau, enigmatic portraits by Modigliani, distorted figures by Soutine, as well as some kinder, gentler Picassos ("Les Adolescents" bathed in pink and rust tones).

Jardin des Tuileries, 1st arrond. © **01-44-77-80-07.** www.musee-orangerie.fr. Admission 10€ adults, 7.50€ ages 18–25, free children 17 and younger. Wed–Mon 9am–6pm. Métro: Concorde.

Palais Royal ★★ HISTORIC SITE/GARDEN   The gardens and long arcades of the Palais Royal are not only a delight to stroll through, they were also witness to one of the most important moments in French history. Built by Cardinal Richelieu, the lavish palace eventually came into the hands of a certain Duke Louis Philippe d'Orleans at the end of the 18th century. An inveterate spendthrift, the young lord soon found himself up to his ears in debt. To earn enough money to pay off his creditors, he came up with the shockingly modern idea of opening the palace gardens to development, building apartments on the grounds. The bottom floor of the galleries, which make up three sides of the enclosure you see today, were let out as shops, cafes, and boutiques. Gambling houses and bordellos sprang up between the shops and cafes, and the gardens became the central meeting place for revolutionaries. Things came to a head on July 12, 1789, when Camille Desmoulins stood up on a table in front of the Café de Foy and called the people to arms—2 days later, the mob would storm the Bastille, igniting the French Revolution. In more recent times, the palace was taken over by various government ministries, and the apartments were rented to artists and writers, including Colette and Jean Cocteau.

Today the shops in the arcades are very subdued, and very expensive— mostly antique toy and stamp dealers, a smattering of high-end designer clothes, and a couple of pricey restaurants, including the legendary Grand Véfour (p. 72). The *cour d'honneur* on the south end is filled with black-and-white-striped columns by Daniel Buren; though most Parisians have now gotten used to this unusual installation, when it was unveiled in 1987 it caused almost as much of a stir as Camille Desmoulins did on that fateful day.

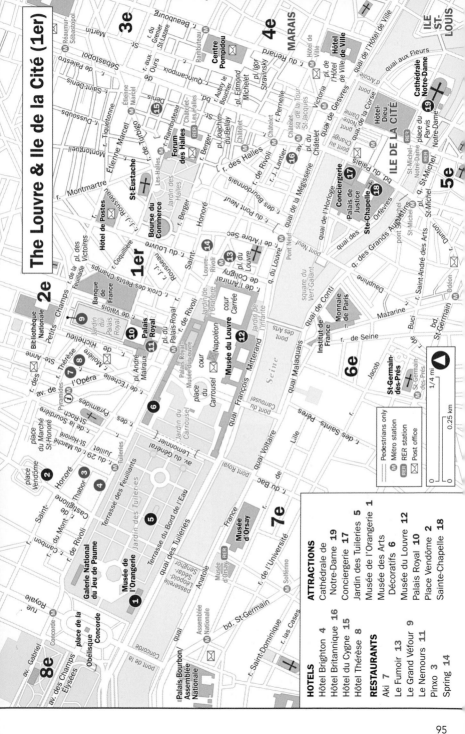

The Louvre & Ile de la Cité (1er)

2e
3e
4e MARAIS
ILE ST. LOUIS
1er
8e
7e
6e
5e
ILE DE LA CITÉ

Centre Pompidou
Cathédrale Notre-Dame **19**
Hôtel de Ville
Hôtel-Dieu
Conciergerie **17**
Palais de Justice
Ste-Chapelle **18**
Palais Royal **11**
Musée du Louvre **12**
Musée de l'Orangerie **1**
Galerie National du Jeu de Paume
place Vendôme **2**
Obélisque
place de la Concorde
Palais Bourbon/ Assemblée Nationale
Musée d'Orsay
Bibliothèque Nationale
Banque de France
Bourse du Commerce
St-Eustache
Forum des Halles
Hôtel de Postes
St-Roch
Institut de France
Monnaie de Paris

Pedestrians only
M Métro station
RER RER station
✉ Post office

0 0.25 km
0 1/4 mi

Place Vendôme ★★ SQUARE   In 1686, Louis XIV decided the time had come to design a magnificent square, at the center of which would stand a statue of His Royal Highness. Though the statue is long gone, this is still one of the classiest squares in the city. The work of Jules Hardouin-Mansart, this über-elegant octagonal ensemble of 17th-century buildings today is the home of the original Ritz Hôtel, as well as the world's most glitzy jewelry makers. When Napoléon took over, he erected a huge Roman-style column honoring his glorious army (yes, once again), this time documenting its victory at Austerlitz. A long spiral of bas-reliefs recounting the campaign of 1805 march up the Colonne de la Grande Armée, which is crowned by a statue of the Emperor himself.

Enter by rue de Castiglione, 1st arrond. Métro: Tuileries or Concorde.

Sainte-Chapelle ★★★ CHURCH   A wall of color greets visitors who enter this magnificent chapel. Stained-glass windows make up a large part of the upper level of the church, giving worshippers the impression of standing inside a jewel-encrusted crystal goblet. What isn't glass is elaborately carved and painted in gold leaf and rich colors: vaulting arches, delicate window casings, and an almost Oriental wainscoting of arches and medallions. The 15 windows recount the story of the Bible, from Genesis to the Apocalypse, as well as the story of St-Louis, who was responsible for the chapel's construction. During the Crusades, Louis IX (who was later canonized) brought home some of the holiest relics in Christendom from Constantinople: the crown of thorns and a piece of the Holy Cross. Such a treasure required an appropriately splendid chapel in the royal palace, and thus the chapel was built (the relics are now in the treasury of Notre-Dame). The record is not clear, but the architect may have been the illustrious Pierre de Montreuil, who worked on the cathedrals of St-Dennis and

Sainte-Chapelle

4

Exploring Paris

PARIS

Notre-Dame. What is sure is that the mysterious architect was brilliant: He managed to support the structure with arches and buttresses in such a way that the walls of the upper chapel are almost entirely glass.

The **lower chapel,** which was meant for the servants, has a low, vaulted ceiling painted in blue and red and gold and covered with fleur-de-lys motifs. Up a small staircase is the **upper chapel,** clearly meant for the royals. This masterpiece suffered both fire and floods in the 17th century and was pillaged by zealous Revolutionaries in the 18th. By the mid–19th century, the chapel was being used to store archives—2m (6½ ft.) of the bottom of each window was removed to install shelves. Fortunately, renewed interest in medieval art eventually led to a conscientious restoration by a team that was advised by master restorer Viollet-le-Duc. The quality of the work on the windows is such that it is almost impossible to detect the difference between the original and the reconstructed stained glass (which makes up about one-third of what you see).

Palais de Justice, 4 bd. du Palais, 1st arrond. © **01-53-40-60-80.** www.monuments-nationaux.fr 8.50€ adults, 5.50€ ages 18–25, free 17 and younger. Mar–Oct daily 9:30am–6pm; Nov–Feb daily 9am–5pm. Métro: Cité, St-Michel, or Châtelet–Les Halles. RER: St-Michel.

LE MARAIS (3RD & 4TH ARRONDISSEMENTS)

Home to royalty and aristocracy between the 14th and 17th centuries, the Marais still boasts remarkable architecture, some of it dating back to the Middle Ages. One of the few neighborhoods that was not knocked down during Baron Haussmann's urban overhaul, Marais has narrow streets still lined with magnificent *hôtels particuliers* (that is, mansions) as well as humbler homes from centuries past. The **Pompidou Center** is probably the biggest and most well-known attraction, but the Marais also harbors a wealth of terrific smaller museums, as well as the delightful **Place des Vosges.** The remnants of the city's **historic Jewish quarter** are found on rue des Rosiers, which has been invaded by chic clothing shops in recent years. These days, the real Jewish neighborhood is in the 19th arrondissement.

Centre Pompidou ★★ MUSEUM   The bizarre architecture of this building provokes such strong emotions, it's easy to forget that there is something inside. It was designed in 1971 by Italo-British architects Renzo Piano and Richard Rogers, whose concept was to put the support structure on the outside of the building, thereby liberating space on the inside for a museum and cultural center. The result was a gridlike exoskeleton with a tubular escalator inching up one side and huge multicolored pipes and shafts covering the other. To some, it's a milestone in contemporary architecture; to others, it's simply a horror. Either way, it's one of the most visited structures in France. For the Pompidou is much more than an art museum. Its some 100,000 sq. m (1,076,390 sq. ft.) of floor space includes a vast **reference library,** a **cinema archive,** bookshops, and a **music institute,** as well as a performance hall, a **children's gallery,** and areas for educational activities. The actual museum, the **Musée National d'Art Moderne,** is on the fourth and fifth floors.

Because the museum collection is in constant rotation, it's impossible to say what you're likely to see on your visit, but the emphasis is generally on works from the second half of the 20th century, with a good dose of surrealism, Dada, and other modern movements from the first half. It includes relatively tame abstracts by **Picasso** and **Kandinsky** to **Andy Warhol'**s multiheaded portrait of Elizabeth Taylor to a felt-wrapped piano by **Joseph Beuys.** Just outside of the front of the center is the **Atelier Brancusi,** where the sculptor's workshop has been reconstituted in its entirety.

Centre Pompidou

Take note of the monumental sculpture/mobile by Alexander Calder on the vast esplanade that slopes down towards the building, and don't miss the delightful **Stravinsky Fountain** around the side; kids are mesmerized by its colorful mobile sculptures by Niki de Saint Phalle and Jean Tinguely.

Place Georges-Pompidou, 4th arrond. ✆ **01-44-78-12-33.** www.centrepompidou.fr. Admission 11€–13€ adults, 9€–10€ students, free children 17 and younger; admission varies depending on exhibits. Wed–Mon 11am–10pm. Métro: Rambuteau, Hôtel de Ville, or Châtelet–Les Halles.

Gaîté Lyrique ★ CULTURAL CENTER   One of the newer additions to the city's cultural scene, this gallery space/concert hall/educational center is devoted to exploring mixed-media and digital art forms. Set in a abandoned 19th-century theatre (hence the name), the building has been transformed to host rotating exhibits that range from music and multimedia performances to design, fashion, and architecture to new media—there's even an interactive room dedicated to video games.

3 bis rue Papin, 3rd arrond. ✆ **01-53-01-52-00.** www.gaite-lyrique.net. Tues–Sat 2–8pm, Sun noon–6pm. Opening hours and admission prices may vary according to the exhibitions and events. Métro: Réaumur Sébastopol.

Hôtel de Ville ★ HISTORIC SITE   No, it's not a hotel. This enormous Neo-Renaissance wedding cake is Paris's city hall, and you can't go inside. But even if you can't get in to see the sumptuous halls and chandeliers, you will be able to feast on the lavish exterior, which includes 136 statues representing historic VIPs of Parisian history. Since the 14th century, this spot has been an administrative seat for the municipality; the building you see before you dates from 1873, but it is a copy of an earlier Renaissance version that stood in its place up until 1870, when it was burned down during the Paris Commune. The vast square in front of the building, which used to be called the place du Grève, was used for municipal festivals and executions, and it was also the stage for several important

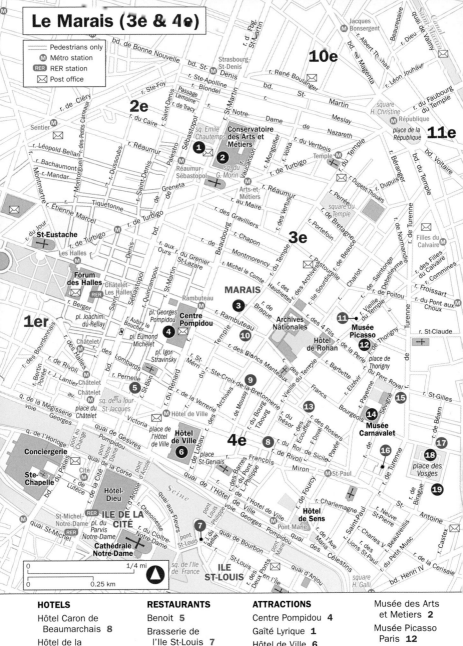

Le Marais (3e & 4e)

Pedestrians only
Ⓜ Métro station
RER RER station
✉ Post office

HOTELS

Hôtel Caron de
Beaumarchais **8**
Hôtel de la
Bretonnerie **9**
Hôtel Jeanne d'Arc
le Marais **16**
Pavillon de la Reine **17**

RESTAURANTS

Benoit **5**
Brasserie de
l'Ile St-Louis **7**
Breizh Café **11**
Café des Musées **15**
L'As du Fallafel **13**
Le Felteu **10**

ATTRACTIONS

Centre Pompidou **4**
Gaîté Lyrique **1**
Hôtel de Ville **6**
Maison de Victor Hugo **19**
Musée Carnavalet **14**
Musée de l'Art et
Histoire du Judaïsme **3**

Musée des Arts
et Metiers **2**
Musée Picasso
Paris **12**
Place des
Vosges **18**

The Pont Neuf

Since it's recently had a makeover, it does indeed look brand-spanking *neuf* (new), even though it is, in fact, the oldest bridge in Paris. The bridge was an instant hit when it was inaugurated by Henri IV in 1607: Ample sidewalks, and the fact that it was the first bridge sans houses, made it a delight for pedestrians. It still is, especially if you ignore the cars and just take in the lovely views.

The Pont Neuf

moments in the city's history, particularly during the Revolution: Louis XVI was forced to kiss the new French flag here, and Robespierre was shot in the jaw and arrested here during an attempted coup. Today the square is host to more peaceful activities: There's usually a merry-go-round or two to captivate the little ones, and in winter an **ice-skating rink** is set up.

29 rue de Rivoli, 4th arrond. © **01-42-76-43-43.** www.paris.fr. Free admission. Métro: Hôtel-de-Ville.

Maison de Victor Hugo ★ MUSEUM   The life of Victor Hugo was as turbulent as some of his novels. Regularly visited by both tragedy and triumph, the author of "The Hunchback of Notre Dame" lived in several apartments in Paris, including this one on the second floor of a corner house on the sumptuous place des Vosges. From 1832 to 1848, he lived here with his wife and four children. When Napoleon III seized power in 1851, this passionate advocate of free speech declared the new king a traitor of France. Fearing for his life, Hugo left the country and lived in exile until 1870 when he triumphantly returned and was elected to the senate. By the time he died in 1885 he was a national hero; his funeral cortege through the streets of Paris is the stuff of legend, and his body was one of the first to be buried in the Panthéon. The museum's collection charts this dramatic existence through the author's drawings, manuscripts, notes, furniture, and personal objects, which are displayed in rooms that recreate the ambiance of the original lodgings.

6 place des Vosges, 4th arrond. © **01-42-72-10-16.** www.musee-hugo.paris.fr. Free admission to the permanent collections. Tues–Sun 10am–6pm. Métro: St-Paul, Bastille, or Chemin-Vert.

Musée d'Art et Histoire du Judaïsme ★★ MUSEUM   Housed in the magnificent Hôtel de Saint Aignan, this museum chronicles the art and history of the Jewish people in France and in Europe. It features a superb collection of objects of both artistic and cultural significance (a splendid Italian Renaissance torah ark, a German gold-and-silver Hanukkah menorah, a 17th-century Dutch illustrated torah scroll, documents from the Dreyfus trial), which is interspersed with texts, drawings, and photos telling the story of the Jews and explaining the basics of both Ashkenazi and Sephardic traditions. The final rooms include a collection of works by Jewish artists, including Modigliani, Soutine, Lipchitz, and Chagall. In recent years, this museum has hosted some terrific temporary exhibits on offbeat subjects like the (Jewish) origins of Superman, Radical Jewish Culture, and the Walter Benjamin archives. Be prepared for airportlike security at the entrance.

71 rue du Temple, 3rd arrond. © **01-53-01-86-53.** www.mahj.org. Admission 8€ adults, 6€ ages 18–25, free 17 and younger. Mon–Fri 11am–6pm; Sun 10am–6pm. Métro: Rambuteau or Hôtel de Ville.

Musée des Arts et Métiers ★ MUSEUM   Here's a museum for the techies in your crowd. With a collection that runs from astrolabes to supercomputers, this place is a goldmine for geeks of all shapes and sizes. The goodies are organized into seven categories: scientific instruments, materials, construction, communication, energy, mechanics, and transportation. Learn how the metric system was born, what the first waterwheels looked like, and how the machine age got up to speed. See cyclotrons, gasometers, and microscopes. Probably the most famous item on display is Foucault's original pendulum, which still gracefully demonstrates the rotation of the Earth, just like it does in Umberto Eco's eponymous novel. The museum is housed in the ancient abbey of St-Martin-des-Champs.

60 rue Réaumur, 3rd arrond. © **01-53-01-82-00.** www.arts-et-metiers.net. Admission 6.50€ adults, 4.50€ students, free ages 17 and under. Tues–Wed and Fri–Sun 10am–6pm, Thurs 10am–9:30pm. Métro: Arts et Métiers.

Musée Carnavalet ★★ MUSEUM   Starting with a prehistoric canoe from 4600 b.c. and continuing into the 20th century, the history of Paris is recounted at this fascinating museum, through items as diverse as Gallo-Roman figurines, Napoléon's toiletry kit, and an 18th-century portrait of Benjamin Franklin when he was the U.S. ambassador to France.

The museum is housed in two magnificent 17th-century mansions. Little of the original interior decoration remains in either building, but this is made up for by the importation of entire rooms, including wall paneling and furniture, from various private mansions of different epochs. Highlights include the Louis XV–style **Salon des Philosophes,** with its beautiful *boiseries* (carved wood paneling) and historical objects like the inkwell of Jean-Jacques Rousseau; and the 18th-century **Café Militaire,** a room from an officer's cafe with gilded and sculpted wood paneling representing military motifs.

The section on the French Revolution includes several fascinating mementos, such as the keys to the Bastille prison and a copy of the "Declaration of the Rights of Man" that once hung behind the president of the Convention. Particularly moving are the personal objects of the royal family from their last days in prison—a lock of Marie Antoinette's hair, Louis XVI's razor and water glass, the

Paris Is No Longer Picasso-less

As this book was going to press, the **Musée Picasso Paris** (5 rue de Thorigny, www.museepicassoparis.fr, ℂ **01-42-71-25-21**) was about to reopen after several years worth of renovations. Ten additional exposition rooms will be added to house the works of the prolific painter, some 5,000 of which are in the collection. As the museum is being mysterious about when exactly it will open or what the opening hours and ticket prices will be, it's best to check the website before you to visit.

young Dauphin's writing exercises—reminders that these iconic figures were in fact made of flesh and blood.

23 rue de Sévigné, 3rd arrond. ℂ **01-44-59-58-58.** www.carnavalet.paris.fr. Free admission for permanent collection. Tues–Sun 10am–6pm. Métro: St-Paul or Chemin Vert.

Place des Vosges ★★★ PLAZA   Possibly the prettiest square in the city, this beautiful spot combines elegance, greenery, and quiet. Nowhere in Paris will you find such a unity of Renaissance-style architecture; the entire square is bordered by 17th-century brick townhouses, each conforming to rules set down by Henri IV himself, under which runs arched arcades. The square's history dates back to a mishap in 1559, when the site was occupied by a royal palace. During a tournament, feisty King Henri II decided to fight Montgomery, the captain of his guard. A badly aimed lance resulted in Henri's untimely death; his wife, Catherine de Medicis, was so distraught she had the palace demolished. His descendant, Henri IV, took advantage of the free space to construct a royal square. Over the centuries, a number of celebrities lived in the 36 houses, including Mme de Sévigny and Victor Hugo. Today the homes are for the rich, as are the chic boutiques under the arcades, but the lawns, trees, fountains, and playground are for everyone.

4th arrond. Métro: St-Paul.

OPÉRA & GRANDS BOULEVARDS (2ND & 9TH ARRONDISSEMENTS)

The grandiose **Opéra Garnier** reigns over this bustling neighborhood, which teems with office workers, tourists, and shoppers scuttling in and around the Grands Magasins (the big department stores) on Boulevard Haussmann. Which may account for why there are perhaps more opportunities for outstanding retail experiences here than for cultural ones.

Opéra Garnier ★★ OPERA HOUSE   Flamboyant, extravagant, and baroque, this opulent opera house is a splendid example of Second Empire architectural excess. Corinthian columns, loggias, busts, and friezes cover the **facade** of the building, which is topped by a gold dome. The interior of the building is no less dramatic. The vast **lobby,** built in a spectrum of different-colored marble, holds a spectacular double staircase that sweeps up to the different levels of the auditorium, as well as an array of glamorous antechambers, galleries, and ballrooms that make you wonder how the opera scenery could possibly compete. Mosaics, mirrors, gilt, and marble line these grand spaces, whose painted ceilings dance with fauns, gods, and nymphs. The main event, of course, is the **auditorium,** which might seem a bit small, considering the size of the building. In

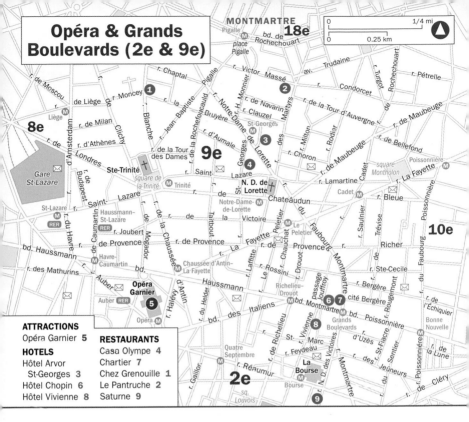

ATTRACTIONS

Opéra Garnier 5

HOTELS

Hôtel Arvor
St-Georges 3
Hôtel Chopin 6
Hôtel Vivienne 8

RESTAURANTS

Casa Olympe 4
Chartier 7
Chez Grenouille 1
Le Pantruche 2
Saturne 9

fact, it holds not even 2,000 seats. The beautiful **ceiling** was painted with color-ful images from various operas and ballets by Marc Chagall in 1964.

All of this (with the exception of the Chagall ceiling) sprang from the mind of a young, unknown architect named Charles Garnier, who won a competition launched by Napoléon III. Though the first stone was laid in 1862, work was held up by war, civil unrest, and a change in regime; the Palais Garnier was not inaugurated until 1875. Some contemporary critics found it a bit much (one called it "an overloaded sideboard"), but today it is generally acknowledged as a masterpiece of the architecture of the epoch.

And what about that phantom? Gaston Leroux's 1911 novel, "The Phantom of the Opera," clearly was inspired by the building's **underground lake,** which was constructed to help stabilize the building.

You can visit the building on your own, but you might want to take advantage of the **guided visits in English** (14€ adults, 12.50€ children under 10; Sept–June Wed, Sat–Sun 11:30am and 2:30pm; July–Aug daily 11:30am and 2:30pm). Either way, your visit will be limited to the lobby, the surrounding foyers, the museum, and if there's not a rehearsal in progress, the auditorium—sorry, you won't get to see the lake. Or simply **buy tickets to a show;** consult the Opéra website to see what's on at the Palais Garnier.

Corner of rue Scribe and rue Auber, 9th arrond. ✆ **08-92-89-90-90** (.34€ per min). www.opera-deparis.fr. Admission 10€ adults, 6€ students and ages 10–25, free children under 10. Oct to mid-July daily 10am–4:30pm, mid-July to Sept 10am–5:30pm. Métro: Opéra.

ABOVE: **Interior, Opéra Garnier;**
RIGHT: **Champs-Elysées at night, leading to Arc de Triomphe**

CHAMPS-ELYSÉES, TROCADÉRO & WESTERN PARIS (8TH, 16TH & 17TH ARRONDISSEMENTS)

Decidedly posh, this is one of the wealthiest parts of the city in both per-capita earnings and cultural institutions. While the **Champs-Elysées** is more glitz than glory, the surrounding neighborhoods offer high-end shops and restaurants as well as some terrific museums and concert halls. This is also where you will find grandiose architectural gestures, like the **Arc de Triomphe** and the **Place de la Concorde,** which book-end the Champs, and the **Grand Palais** and **Petit Palais,** leftovers from the legendary 1900 Universal Exposition.

Arc de Triomphe ★★★ MONUMENT   If there is one monument that symbolizes "La Gloire," or the glory of France, it is this giant triumphal arch. Crowning the Champs-Elysées, this mighty archway both celebrates the military victories of the French army and memorializes the sacrifices of its soldiers. Over time, it has become an icon of the Republic and a setting for some if its most emotional moments: the laying in state of the coffin of Victor Hugo in 1885, the burial in 1921 of the ashes of an unknown soldier who fought in World War I, and General de Gaulle's pregnant pause under the arch before striding down the Champs-Elysées to the cheering crowds after the Liberation in 1944.

   It took a certain amount of chutzpah to come up with the idea to build such a shrine, and sure enough, it was Napoléon who instigated it. In 1806, still glowing after his stunning victory at Austerlitz, the Emperor decided to erect a monument

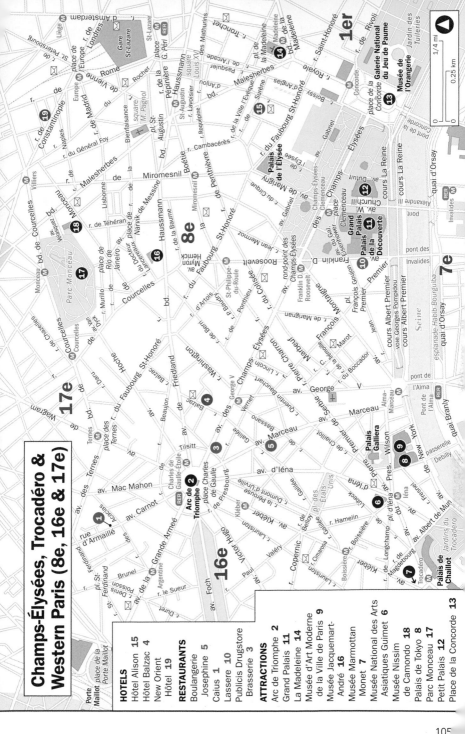

Champs-Élysées, Trocadéro & Western Paris (8e, 16e & 17e)

HOTELS
Hôtel Alison **15**
Hôtel Balzac **4**
New Orient
Hôtel **19**

RESTAURANTS
Boulangerie
Josephine **5**
Caius **1**
Lassere **10**
Publicis Drugstore
Brasserie **3**

ATTRACTIONS
Arc de Triomphe **2**
Grand Palais **11**
La Madeleine **14**
Musée d'Art Moderne
de la Ville de Paris **9**
Musée Jacquemart-
André **16**
Musée Marmottan
Monet **7**
Musée National des Arts
Asiatiques Guimet **6**
Musée Nissim
de Camondo **18**
Palais de Tokyo **8**
Parc Monceau **17**
Petit Palais **12**
Place de la Concorde **13**

LEFT: **Arc de Triomphe**; ABOVE: **Grande Arche de la Défense**

to the Imperial Army along the lines of a Roman triumphal arch. Unfortunately, the Empire came to an end before the arch was finished, and construction dragged on until 1836 when it was completed by Louis-Philippe.

The arch is covered with bas-reliefs and sculptures, the most famous of which is the enormous "Depart of the Volunteers" of 1792, better known as the Marseillaise, by François Rude. Just above is one of the many smaller panels detailing Napoleonic battles—in this case, Aboukir—wherein the Emperor trods victoriously over the Ottomans. At the base of the arch is the Tomb of the Unknown Soldier, over which a flame is relit every evening. The inscription reads ici repose un soldat français mort pour la patrie, 1914–1918 ("Here lies a French soldier who died for his country").

Don't try crossing the vast traffic circle to get to the arch; take the underpass near the Métro entrances. The panorama from the rooftop terrace is quite impressive; you will see the 12 boulevards that radiate from the star-shaped intersection (hence the moniker "Etoile"), most of which are named after Napoleonic battles. Out front is the long sweep of the Champs-Elysées, ending at place de la Concorde, behind which lurks the pyramid of the Louvre. In the other direction you will get a good gander at the modern Grande Arche de la Défense, a huge, hollow cubelike building that could fit Notre-Dame under its arch.

Place Charles de Gaulle–Etoile, 8th arrond. (C) **01-55-37-73-77.** www.monum.fr. Admission 9.50€ adults, 6€ ages 18–24, free 17 and under. Apr–Sept daily 10am–11pm; Oct–Mar daily 10am–10:30pm. Métro: Charles-de-Gaulle–Etoile.

Grand Palais ★★ HISTORIC SITE/MUSEUM   Built for the 1900 Universal Exhibition, this giant exhibition hall spans a total area of 72,000 sq. m (775,000 sq. ft.), with the biggest glass roof in Europe—an elegant lighting solution, since the building was constructed prior to electricity. After years of renovations, the Grand Palais is now as gorgeous as it was when it opened, and today it hosts a changing array of sporting and cultural events under the vast "Grand Nef" (or nave), as well as blockbuster temporary art exhibits (Edward Hopper, Chagall, Impressionists, and others). These tend to be mob scenes, so it pays to buy tickets in advance to big shows. The entrance to the big exhibits is usually at the side entrance, 3 ave. du Général Eisenhower.

Place Clemenceau, 8th arrond. ✆ 01-44-13 17,17, www.grandpalais.fr. Opening hours and admission prices vary according to the exhibitions and events. Métro: Champs-Elysées–Clémenceau.

La Madeleine ★ CHURCH   As you peer up the rue Royale from the place de la Concorde, you'll see something that very closely resembles a Roman temple. Whe the first stone was laid in 1763, it was destined to be a church with a neoclassical facade. But then the architect died, and then the Revolution broke out, and construction ground to a halt. No one knew what to do with the site until Napoléon finally strode onto the scene and declared that it would become the Temple de La Gloire, to honor the glorious victories of his army. He wanted something "solid" because he was sure that the monument would last "thousands of years." Unfortunately for him, military defeats and mounting debt would again delay construction until Napoléon decided that maybe it wouldn't be such a bad idea to make it a church after all—that way Rome would foot the bill. Once Napoléon was out of the picture for good, inertia sunk in again. It wasn't until 1842, under the Restoration, that La Madeleine was finally consecrated.

The inside of the church is pretty dark, due to a lack of windows, but there are some interesting works of art here, if you can make them out in the gloom. On the left as you enter is François Rude's "Baptism of Christ"; farther on is James Pradier's sculpture "La Marriage de la Vierge."

Place de la Madeleine, 8th arrond. ✆ **01-44-51-69-00.** www.eglise-lamadeleine.com. Free admission. Daily 9:30am–7pm. Métro: Madeleine.

Musée d'Art Moderne de la Ville de Paris ★ MUSEUM   Housed in a wing of the massive Palais de Tokyo, this municipal modern-art museum covers ground similar to that of the Pompidou Center but on a smaller scale. Though several big names are represented (Picasso, Rouault, and Picaba, to name a few), in general these are not their best-known works; highlights include a room dedicated to surrealism (the personal collection of André Breton) and a series of paintings by Delaunay and Léger. The contemporary section, from 1960 on, covers seriously abstract movements like Fluxus and Figuration. In recent years, the collection has acquired several new works from the 1980s on, but for the most recent cutting-edge ideas, you are probably better off at the Palais de Tokyo museum (see below) in the wing next door.

11 av. du Président-Wilson, 16th arrond ✆ **01-53-67-40-00.** www.mam.paris.fr. Free admission to permanent collections. Tues–Sun 10am–6pm. Métro: Iéna or Alma-Marceau.

Musée Jacquemart-André ★★★ MUSEUM   The love-child of a couple of passionate art collectors, this terrific museum takes the form of a 19th-century mansion filled with fine art and decorative objects. Not only is the collection superb, but it is also of a blissfully reasonable size—you can see a wide range of beautiful things here without wearing yourself to a frazzle.

Nélie Jacquemart and Edouard André devoted their lives to filling this splendid dwelling with primarily 18th-century French art and furniture. The paintings of Fragonard, Boucher, and Chardin are in evidence, as is an impressive assortment of Louis XV– and Louis XVI–era decorative objects. There are many superb portraits, including "Comte Français de Nantes" by David. The couple also amassed a number of 17th-century Dutch paintings, including a jaunty "Portrait of a Man" by Frans Hals, and Rembrandt's evocative "Pilgrims at Emmaus."

The peripatetic couple, who traveled frequently in search of new items for their collection, also took an interest in Renaissance Italian art; though at the time considered "primitive" by most art fans, that didn't stop them from snapping up Quattrocento masterpieces like Botticelli's "Virgin and Child." The Italian collection (on the second floor) is the most awe-inspiring part of the museum; not only are there works by masters like Bellini, Uccello, and Mantegna, they are presented in an intimate space with excellent lighting. You feel like you are walking into a jewel box. Enjoy a light lunch or tea in the lovely dining room.

158 bd. Haussmann, 8th arrond. ✆ **01-45-62-11-59.** www.musee-jacquemart-andre.com. Admission 11€ adults, 9.50€ students and children 7–17, free children 6 and younger. Daily 10am–6pm. Métro: Miromesnil or St-Philippe-du-Roule.

Musée Marmottan Monet ★★ MUSEUM

Boasting the world's largest collection of Monets, this museum offers an in-depth look at this prolific genius and some of his talented contemporaries. Among the dozens of Monet canvases is the one that provided the name of an entire artistic movement. Pressed to give a name to this misty play of light on the water for the catalog for an 1874 exposition that included Cézanne, Pissarro, Renoir, and Degas, Monet apparently said, "put 'impression.'" The painting, "Impression, Sunrise," certainly made one, as did the show—thereafter the group was referred to as the Impressionists. Monet never stopped being fascinated with the interaction of light and water, be it in a relatively traditional portrait of his wife and daughter against the stormy sea in "On the Beach at Trouville," or in an almost abstract blend of blues and grays in "Charing Cross Bridge." Monet often painted the same subject at different times of the day, as in his famous series on the Cathedral of Rouen, one of which is here: "Effect of the Sun at the End of the Day." Fans of the artist's endless water lily series will not be disappointed; the collection includes dozens of paintings of his beloved garden in Giverny.

Paintings by Renoir, Sisley, Degas, Gauguin and other contemporaries can be seen in the light-filled rooms on the upper floor, as are works by one of the only female members of the group, Berthe Morisot, who gets an entire room devoted to her intimate portraits and interiors.

2 rue Louis-Boilly, 16th arrond. ✆ **01-44-96-50-33.** www.marmottan.com. Admission 10€ adults, 5€ ages 8–24, free children 7 and younger. Tues–Wed and Fri–Sun 10am–6pm; Thurs 10am–8pm. Métro: La Muette. RER: Bouilainvilliers.

Musée National des Arts Asiatiques Guimet ★★ MUSEUM

Founded in 1889 by collector and industrialist Emile Guimet, today this vast collection of Asian art is one of the largest and most complete in Europe. Here you'll find room after room of exquisite works from Afghanistan, India, Tibet, Nepal, China, Vietnam, Korea, Japan, and other Asian nations. You could spend an entire day here, or you could pick and choose regions of interest (displays are arranged geographically); the free audioguide is a good bet for finding standouts and providing cultural context. Highlights include a Tibetan bronze sculpture ("Hevajra and Nairâtmya") of a multiheaded god embracing a ferocious goddess with 8 faces and 16 arms; a blissfully serene stone figure of a 12th-century Cambodian king ("Jayavarman VII") and superb Chinese scroll paintings, including a magnificent 17th-century view of the Jingting mountains in autumn. A few minutes' walk from the museum is the Panthéon Bouddhique (19 av. d'Iéna; ✆ 01-40-73-88-00; free admission; Wed–Mon 10am–5:30pm), an old mansion where Guimet's collection of Buddhist art from Japan is displayed.

6 place d'Iéna, 16th arrond. ✆ **01-56-52-53-00.** www.guimet.fr. Admission to permanent collection 7.50€ adults, 5.50€ ages 18–25, free for ages 17 and younger. Wed–Mon 10am–6pm. Métro: Iéna.

Musée Nissim de Camondo ★★ MUSEUM

In 1914 Count Moïse de Camondo built a mansion in the style of the Petit Trianon at Versailles and furnished it with rare examples of 18th-century furniture, paintings, and art objects. After the count's death in 1935, the house and everything in it was left to the state as a museum. This little-visited museum is a delight—the count's will stipulated that the house be left exactly "as is" when it was transformed into a museum, as a result you can wander through salons filled with gilded mirrors, inlaid tables, and Beauvais tapestries; a fully equipped kitchen; and a gigantic tiled bathroom—all in the same configuration as when Camondo and his family lived there. A special room displays the Buffon service, a remarkable set of Sèvres china decorated with a myriad of bird species, reproductions of drawings by the renowned naturalist, the Count of Buffon. Be sure to pick up a free English audioguide.

63 rue de Monceau, 8th arrond. ✆ **01-53-89-06-40.** www.lesartsdecoratifs.fr. Admission 7.50€ adults, 5.50€ ages 18–25, free for children 17 and younger. Wed–Sun 10am–5:30pm. Métro: Villiers.

Palais de Tokyo ★★ MUSEUM/PERFORMANCE SPACE   If you're traveling with cranky teenagers who've had enough of La Vieille France, or if you're also sick of endless rendezvous with history, this is the place to come for a blast of contemporary madness. This vast art space not only offers a rotating bundle of expositions, events, and other happenings, but it's also one of the only museums in Paris that stays open until midnight. While some might quibble over whether or not the works on display are really art, there's no denying that this place is a lot more fun than its stodgy neighbor across the terrace (see above). There's no permanent collection, just continuous temporary exhibits, installations, and events, which include live performances and film screenings. The center is now one of the largest sites devoted to contemporary creativity in Europe. In warm weather, you can eat on the splendid terrace or repair to its arty-cool restaurant, **Tokyo Eat.**

13 av. du Président-Wilson, 16th arrond. ✆ **01-81-97-35-88.** www.palaisdetokyo.com. Admission 10€ adults, 8€ ages 18–25, free for ages 17 and younger. Wed–Mon noon–midnight. Métro: Iéna.

Parc Monceau ★★ PARK/GARDENS   Marcel Proust used to laze under the trees in this beautiful park, and who could blame him? The lush lawns and leafy trees of this verdant haven would brighten the spirits of even the most melancholy writer. Located in a posh residential neighborhood and ringed by stately mansions, this small park, commissioned by the duke of Chartres in 1769, is filled with *folies,* faux romantic ruins, temples, and antiquities inspired by exotic faraway places. Don't be surprised to stumble upon a minaret, a windmill, or a mini-Egyptian pyramid here. The most famous *folie* is the **Naumachie,** a large oval pond surrounded in part by Corinthian columns. You'll find a sizeable **playground** in the southwest corner, as well as a **merry-go-round** near the north entrance.

35 bd. de Courcelles, 8th arrond. Free admission. 8am–sundown. Métro: Monceau or Villiers.

Petit Palais ★★ MUSEUM   The collection may not be exhaustive, and you may not see any world-famous works, but you will enjoy a wonderful mix of periods and artists at this small-ish municipal fine arts museum, whose chronology stretches from the ancient Greeks to World War I. The paintings of masters like Monet, Ingres, and Rubens are displayed here, as well as the Art Nouveau dining room of Hector Guimard, and the exquisite multilayered glass vases of Emile Gallé. Those interested in earlier works will find Greek vases, Italian Renaissance majolica, and a small collection of 16th-century astrolabes and gold-and-crystal traveling clocks. Intricately carved ivory panels and delicately sculpted wood sculptures stand out in the small Medieval section, and a series of rooms dedicated to 17th-century Dutch painters like Steen and Van Ostade is considered one of the best collections of its kind in France (after the Louvre). Refresh yourself after your visit at the cafe in the gorgeous inner courtyard.

Avenue Winston Churchill, 8th arrond. ✆ **01-53-43-40-00.** www.petitpalais.paris.fr. Free admission to permanent collection. Tues–Sun 10am–6pm. Métro: Champs-Elysées Clémenceau.

Place de la Concorde ★★★ PLAZA   Like an exclamation point at the end of the Champs-Elysées, the place de la Concorde is a magnificent arrangement of fountains and statues, with a 3,000-year-old Egyptian obelisk (a gift to France from Egypt in 1829) at its center. Looking at it today, it is hard to believe that this magnificent square was once bathed in blood, but during the Revolution, it was a grisly stage for public executions. King Louis XVI and his wife, Marie-Antoinette, both bowed down to the guillotine here, as did many prominent figures of the Revolution, including Danton, Camille Desmoulins, and Robespierre. Once the monarchy was back in place, the plaza hosted less lethal public events like festivals and trade expositions.

In 1835 the *place* was given its current look: Two immense fountains, copies of those in St. Peter's Square in Rome, play on either side of the obelisk; 18 sumptuous columns decorated with shells, mermaids, and sea creatures each hold two lamps; and eight statues representing the country's largest cities survey the scene from the edges of the action. On the west side are the famous **Marly Horses,** actually copies of the originals, which were suffering from erosion and have since been restored and housed in the Louvre. On the north side of the square are two palatial buildings that date from the 18th century: On the east side is the **Hôtel de la Marine,** and on the west side is the **Hôtel Crillon,** where in 1778, a treaty was signed by Louis XVI and Benjamin Franklin, wherein France officially recognized the United States as an independent country and became its ally.

Note: Cars tend to hurtle around the obelisk like racers in the Grand Prix; if you feel compelled to cross to the obelisk and you value your life, find the stoplight and cross there.

8th arrond. Métro: Concorde.

MONTMARTRE (18TH ARRONDISSEMENT)

Few places in this city fill you with the urge to belt out sappy show tunes like the *butte* (hill) of Montmartre. Admiring the view from the esplanade in front of the oddly Byzantine **Basilique du Sacré-Coeur,** you'll feel as if you've finally arrived in Paris, and that you now understand what all the fuss is about. Ignore the tour buses and crowds mobbing the church and the hideously touristy **place du Tertre** behind you and wander off into the warren of streets towards the **place des Abbesses** or up **rue Lepic,** where you'll eventually stumble across the **Moulin de la Galette** and **Moulin du Radet,** the two surviving windmills (there were once 30 on this hill).

Basilique du Sacré-Coeur ★★ CHURCH   Poised at the apex of the hill like a *grande dame* in crinolines, this odd-looking 19th-century basilica has become one of the city's most famous landmarks. After France's defeat in the Franco-Prussian War, prominent Catholics vowed to build a church consecrated to the Sacred Heart of Christ as a way of making up for whatever sins the French may have committed that had made God so angry at them. Since 1885, prayers for humanity have been continually chanted here (the church is a pilgrimage site, so dress and behave accordingly). Inspired by the Byzantine churches of Turkey

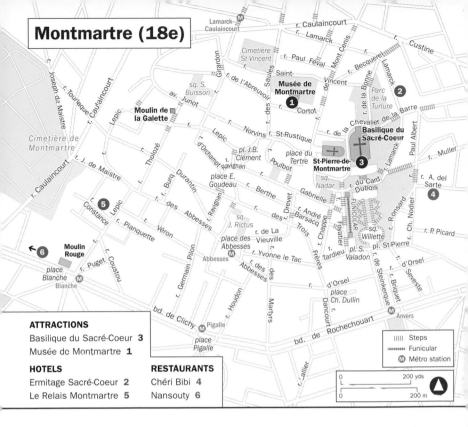

Montmartre (18e)

ATTRACTIONS
Basilique du Sacré-Coeur **3**
Musée de Montmartre **1**

HOTELS
Ermitage Sacré-Coeur **2**
Le Relais Montmartre **5**

RESTAURANTS
Chéri Bibi **4**
Nansouty **6**

|||| Steps
××××××× Funicular
Ⓜ Métro station

0   200 yds
0   200 m

and Italy, this multidomed confection was begun in 1875 and completed in 1914, though it wasn't consecrated until 1919 because of World War I. The white stone was chosen for its self-cleaning capabilities: When it rains, it secretes a chalky substance that acts as a fresh coat of paint. Most visitors climb the 237 stairs to the **dome,** where the splendid city views extend over 48km (30 miles).

35 rue Chevalier de la Barre, 18th arrond. ✆ **01-53-41-89-00.** www.sacre-coeur-montmartre.com. Free admission to basilica; joint ticket to dome and crypt 8€ adults, 5€ ages 4–16, free under 4. Basilica daily 6am–10:30pm; dome and crypt daily 8:30am–8pm May–Sept, 9am–5pm Oct–Apr. Métro: Abbesses; take elevator to surface and follow signs to funicular.

Sacré-Coeur at sunrise

Musée de Montmartre ★★ MUSEUM   The main reason to visit this small museum is to get an inkling of what Montmartre really was like back in the days when Picasso, Toulouse-Lautrec, Van Gogh, and so on were painting and cavorting up here on the *Butte*. While there are few examples of the artists' works here, there are plenty of photos, posters, and even films documenting the neighborhood's famous history, from the days when its importance was mainly religious, to the gory days of the Paris Commune, and finally to the artistic boom in the 19th and 20th centuries. Next to an original poster of Jane Avril by Toulouse-Lautrec, for example, you'll see a photo of the real Jane Avril, as well as other Montmartre cabaret legends like Aristide Bruant and La Goulue. The 17th century house that shelters the museum was at various times the studio and home of Auguste Renoir, Raoul Dufy, Susan Valadon, and Maurice Utrillo. Surrounded by gardens and greenery it offers a lovely view of the last scrap of the Montmartre vineyard.

12 rue Cortot, 18th arrond. ✆ **01-49-25-89-37.** www.museedemontmartre.fr. Admission 9€ adults, 7€ ages 18–25, 5€ ages 10–17, free under 10. Daily 10am–6pm. Métro: Lamarck-Caulaincourt.

RÉPUBLIQUE, BASTILLE & EASTERN PARIS (11TH & 12TH ARRONDISSEMENTS)

While you can't really point to any major tourist attractions in this area, this is a nice part of town for aimless wandering, especially if you are a) in search of youth-oriented nightlife, b) in search of youth-oriented clothing shops, or c) a history buff. The French Revolution was brewed in the workshops of the **Faubourg St-Antoine** and ignited at the **place de la Bastille.**

Place de la Bastille ★   The most notable thing about this giant plaza is the building that's no longer here: the Bastille prison. Now an enormous traffic circle where cars careen around at warp speed, this was once the site of an ancient stone fortress that became a symbol for all that was wrong with the French monarchy. Over the centuries, kings and queens condemned rebellious citizens to stay inside these cold walls, sometimes with good reason, other times on a mere

THE REBIRTH OF THE PARIS ZOO

After 10 years of purgatory and 2 years of reconstruction, the **Parc Zoologique de Paris** finally reopened in April 2014, to the delight of children and parents of both tourists and locals. Little remains of the old-fashioned zoo that once was. Today an ecologically-correct animal reserve invites visitors to five regions of the world, from the plains of Sudan to Europe, via Guyana, Patagonia, and Madagascar. Going for quality instead of quantity, the new zoo concentrates on certain areas of the world, with the goal of educating and inspiring visitors so that they will take home the desire to protect and nurture the natural world. Over a thousand different animals can be seen in replications of natural habitats: lemurs and lions, giraffes and jaguars, tortoises and tarantulas—as well as less famous but equally threatened species like tapirs, manatees, and the bright red tomato frog.

(Parc de Vincennes, 12th arrond. ✆ **01-44-75-20-10.** www.parczoologiquedeparis.fr. 22€ adults, 16.50€ students 12–25, 14€ children 3–11, free ages 2 and under. Mid-Oct to mid-Mar daily 10am–5pm, mid-Mar to mid-Oct Mon–Fri 10am–6pm, Sat–Sun and school holidays 9:30am–7:30pm).

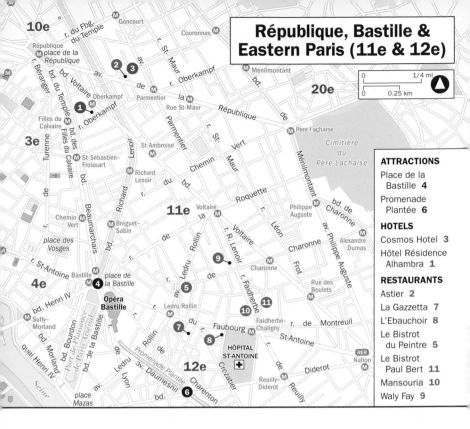

10e

r. du Fbg. du Temple

Goncourt

Couronnes

République
place de la
République

Béranger

bd. Voltaire

av.

Oberkampf

r. St-Maur

de

Ménilmontant

20e

0   1/4 mi

0   0.25 km

r. Oberkampf

Parmentier

la

r. Oberkampf

Rue St-Maur

République

de

Filles du
Calvaire

r. Oberkampf

Parmentier

3e

Turenne

bd. du Temple

bd. des Filles du Calvaire

St-Ambroise

Père-Lachaise

Cimitière
du
Père-Lachaise

St-Sébastien-
Froissart

Richard
Lenoir

Vert

r. St.

Maur

Ménilmontant

Chemin

Beaumarchais

Chemin
Vert

Richard
Lenoir

du

bd.

11e

Voltaire
la

Roquette

Philippe
Auguste

bd. de
Charonne

av. Philippe Auguste

Bréguet-
Sabin

de

av. Ledru Rollin

r. R. Lenoir

Voltaire

Léon

Charonne

Alexandre
Dumas

place des
Vosges

r. St-Antoine

Bastille

place de
la Bastille

r.

de

r. Faidherbe

Charonne

Frot

Rue des
Boulets

4e

bd. Henri IV

Opéra
Bastille

Ledru Rollin

r.

de

Faidherbe-
Chaligny

r. de   Montreuil

Sully-
Morland

quai Henri IV

bd. Bourdon

Port de Plaisance de Paris Arsenal

r. de la Bastille

du

Rollin

Faubourg

St-Antoine

RER
Nation

r. Morland

de

de

HÔPITAL
ST-ANTOINE

de

Diderot

Seine

Ledru

av. Daumesnil

Promenade Plantée

12e

Reuilly-
Diderot

de

Reuilly

place
Mazas

av. Lyon

bd.

Charenton

Crozatier

ATTRACTIONS

Place de la
  Bastille **4**
Promenade
  Plantée **6**

HOTELS

Cosmos Hotel **3**
Hôtel Résidence
  Alhambra **1**

RESTAURANTS

Astier **2**
La Gazzetta **7**
L'Ebauchoir **8**
Le Bistrot
  du Peintre **5**
Le Bistrot
  Paul Bert **11**
Mansouria **10**
Waly Fay **9**

whim. By the time the Revolution started to boil, though, the prison was barely in use; when the angry mobs stormed its walls on July 14, 1789, there were only seven prisoners to set free. Still, the destruction of the Bastille came to be seen as the ultimate revolutionary moment; July 14 is still celebrated as the birth of the Republic. Surprisingly, the giant bronze column in the center honors the victims of a different revolution, that of 1830.

12th arrond. Métro: Bastille.

La Promenade Plantée ★★ WALKING TRAIL Transformed from an unused train viaduct, this beautiful aerial garden walkway runs from the place de la Bastille to the Bois de Vincennes. The 4.5km (2.8-mile) pedestrian path runs along flower gardens, tree bowers, rose trellises, and fountains and takes you over the 12th arrondissement, past the Gare de Lyon, and through the Reuilly Gardens. At ground level along Ave. Daumesnil, the brick archways now shelter the **Viaduct des Arts,** a series of galleries and workshops that show off the work of highly skilled artisans.

Enter by the staircase on Avenue Daumesnil just past the Opéra Bastille, 12th arrond.

BELLEVILLE, CANAL ST-MARTIN & LA VILLETTE (10TH, 19TH & 20TH ARRONDISSEMENTS)

One of the most picturesque attractions in this area is the **Canal St-Martin** itself, which crosses a formerly working-class neighborhood that is now peopled by an arty mix of regular folk and *bobos* (bourgeois bohemians). The Belleville neighborhood is home to one of the city's bustling **Chinatowns,** as well as many artists' studios.

Cimetière du Père-Lachaise ★★★ CEMETERY   It's hard to believe that a cemetery could be a top tourist attraction, but this is no ordinary cemetery. This hillside resting place is wonderfully green and romantic, with huge leafy trees and narrow paths winding around the graves, which include just about every French literary or artistic giant you can imagine, plus several international stars. Proust, Moliére, La Fontaine, Colette, Delacroix, Seurat, Modigliani, Bizet, Rossini are all here, as well as Sarah Bernhardt, Isadora Duncan, Simone Signoret, and Yves Montand (buried side-by-side, of course), not to mention Oscar Wilde, whose huge stone monument is usually covered with lipstick kisses. Even the Lizard King, Jim Morrison, is here. Though the grave itself is unexceptional, the tomb of the '60s rock star is possibly the most visited in the cemetery. In 1971, battling drug, alcohol, and legal problems, the singer/musician came to Paris; 4 months later, he was found dead in a Parisian bathtub, at age 27.

A map is essential. You can find one at the newsstand across from the main entrance, on the website, or at the visitor's booth.

16 rue de Repos, 20th arrond. www.pere-lachaise.com. No telephone number. Admission free. Mon–Fri 8am–6pm; Sat–Sun 8:30am–6pm (closes at 5pm Nov to early Mar). Métro: Père-Lachaise or Philippe Auguste.

Cité des Sciences et de l'Industrie ★★ MUSEUM   This gigantic science-and-industry museum began life as an immense slaughterhouse. During construction in the 1960s, it was touted as the most modern of its kind. It turned out to be the center of a corruption scandal and was quickly abandoned when the city's abattoirs were transferred elsewhere. After years of head-scratching, the building was finally turned into this terrific museum, which includes a planetarium, a 3-D

Père-Lachaise Cemetery

movie theater, and a multimedia library, not to mention a real live submarine. The heart of the museum is Explora, two huge floors of interactive exhibits and displays, as well as excellent temporary exhibits. On the ground floor, parents will be delighted to find the Cité des Enfants (separate admission: 9€ adults, 6€ under 25 for a 1½-hr. session; see website for hours; reservations essential, particularly during French school vacations), which has separate programs for 2- to 7-year-olds and 7- to 12-year-olds. Kids get to explore their own sensations and the world around them in a series of hands-on activities and displays. If all this isn't enough, outside you can clamber into the Argonaut (3€), a real submarine that was one of the stars of the French navy in the 1950s, or dip inside the gigantic metal sphere, called the Geode (adults 12€, under 25 9€), an IMAX-type movie theater showing large screen films.

Parc de La Villette, 30 av. Corentine-Cariou, 19th arrond. ✆ **01-40-05-70-00.** www.cite-sciences.fr. Varied ticket packages 12€–19.50€ adults, 6€–15€ under 25, free ages 2 and under. Tues–Sat 10am–6pm; Sun 10am–7pm. Métro: Porte de La Villette.

Parc des Buttes Chaumont ★
PARK   Up until 1860, this area was home to a deep limestone quarry, but thanks to Napoléon III, the gaping hole was turned into an unusual park, full of hills and dales, rocky bluffs, and cliffs. It took 3 years to make this romantic garden; more than a thousand workers and a hundred horses dug, heaped, and blasted through the walls of the quarry to create green lawns, a cool grotto, cascades, streams, and even a small lake. By the opening of the 1867 World's

Belleville, Canal St-Martin & La Villette (10e, 19e & 20e)

ATTRACTIONS
Cimetière du
   Père-Lachaise 8
Cité des Sciences
   et de l'Industrie 1
Parc des Buttes
   Chaumont 3

HOTELS
Le Citizen 5

RESTAURANTS
Bob's Juice Bar 7
Chez Michel 2
La Verre Volé 6
Rosa Bonheur 4

Fair, the garden was ready for visitors. The surrounding area was, and still is, working-class; the Emperor built it to give this industrious neighborhood a green haven and a bit of fresh air. There are **pony rides** for the kids on weekends and Wednesdays, plus a **puppet theater,** a **carousel,** and **two playgrounds.**

Rue Botzaris, 19th arrond. Open 7am–11pm May 1–Sept 30; 7am–8pm Oct 1–Apr 30. Métro: Botzaris or Buttes Chaumont.

The Left Bank

LATIN QUARTER (5TH & 13TH ARRONDISSEMENTS)

What's so Latin about this quarter? Well, for several hundred years, the students that flocked here spoke Latin in their classes at the **Sorbonne** (founded in the 13th c.) and other nearby schools. The students still flock and the Sorbonne is still in business, and though classes are now taught in French, the name stuck. Intellectual pursuits aside, this youth-filled neighborhood is a lively one, packed with cinemas and cafes. History is readily visible here, dating back to the Roman occupation: The **rue St-Jacques** and **boulevard Saint-Michel** mark the former Roman cardo, and you can explore the remains of the **Roman baths** at the **Cluny Museum.**

Institut du Monde Arabe ★★ MUSEUM   In an age when Arab culture is all over the headlines, this is a good place to come to find out what the phrase actually means. The building, designed by architect Jean Nouvel in 1987, is worth the price of admission,. The south façade, which has a metallic latticework echoing traditional Arab designs, includes 30,000 light-sensitive diaphragms that regulate the penetration of light by opening and closing according to how bright it is outside. After a major overhaul, this museum, which used to be devoted solely to Islamic art, has now expanded its mission to include the many facets of the Arab world, specifically the 22 countries that helped create this institution in 1987. The collection includes beautiful examples of traditional calligraphy, miniatures, ceramics, woodwork, and carpets, as well as scientific objects, textiles, and illuminated manuscripts.

1 rue des Fossés St-Bernard, 5th arrond. ✆ **01-40-51-38-38.** www.imarabe.org. Admission to permanent collections 8€, 4€ under 26. Tues–Thurs 10am–6pm, Fri 10am–9:30pm, Sat–Sun 10am–7pm. Métro: Jussieu, Cardinal Lemoine, Sully-Morland.

Jardin des Plantes ★★ GARDENS   This delightful botanical garden, tucked between the Muséum National d'Histoire Naturelle (see below) and the Seine, is one of my favorite picnic spots. Created in 1626 as a medicinal plant garden for King Louis XIII, in the 18th century it became an internationally famed scientific institution thanks to naturalist, mathematician, and biologist Georges-Louis Leclerc, Count of Buffon, with the help of fellow-naturalist Louis-Jean-Marie Daubenton. Today the museums are still part academic institutions, but you certainly don't need to be a student to appreciate the lush grounds.

The garden also harbors a small, but well-kept zoo, the **Ménagerie du Jardin des Plants** (✆ **01-40-79-56-01;** 11€ adults, 9€ students 18–26 and children 4–16, free under 4; daily 9am–6pm). Created in 1794, this is the oldest zoo in the world. Because of its size, the zoo showcases mostly smaller species, in particular birds and reptiles, but it also has a healthy selection of mammals, including rare species like red pandas, Przewalski horses, and even Florida pumas.

rue Geoffroy-St-Hilaire, 5th arrond. ✆ **01-40-79-56-01.** www.jardindesplantes.net. Free admission to gardens. 8am–dusk. Métro: Gare d'Austerlitz.

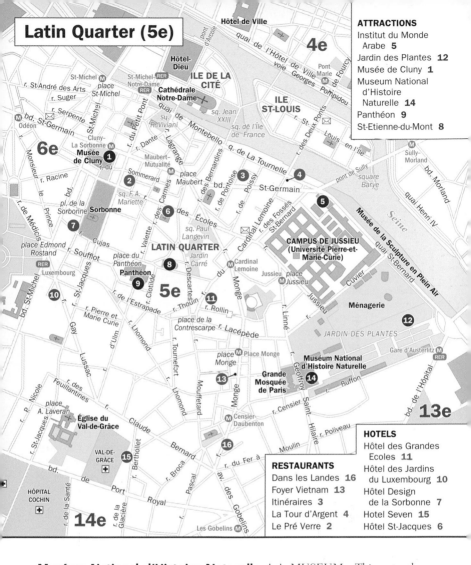

Latin Quarter (5e)

Hôtel de Ville

pont d'Arcole

quai de l'Hôtel de Ville

voie Georges Pompidou

4e

Pont Marie

r. de Fourcy

St-Michel Ⓜ

place St-Michel

St-Michel-RER
Notre-Dame RER

Hôtel-
Dieu

ILE DE LA
CITÉ

r. St-André des Arts

r. Suger

Cathédrale
Notre-Dame

ILE
ST-LOUIS

r. Serpente

quai du Petit Pont

sq. Jean XXIII

sq. de l'Île
de France

r. St-Louis

Odéon

bd. St-Germain

r. de la Bûcherie

sq. R. Viviani

quai de Montebello

pont de la Tournelle

r. des Deux Ponts

Louis-en-l'île

6e

Cluny-
La Sorbonne Ⓜ

Musée
de Cluny ❶

r. Dante

r. Lagrange

q. de La Tournelle

Sully-
Morland

Monsieur le Prince

r. Racine

bd. St-Michel

Maubert-
Mutualité

place
Maubert

bd. de Pontoise

r. de Poissy

St-Germain

pont de Sully

square Barye

bd. Morland

r. Sommerard

❷

r. des Bernardins

❸

❹

quai Henri IV

bd. St-Germain

sq. F. A. Mariette

r. des Carmes

r. de Pontoise

r. des Fossés St-Bernard

❺

Seine

r. de Médicis

pl. de la Sorbonne **Sorbonne**

des Écoles

r. Valette

Cardinal Lemoine

Musée de la Sculpture en Plein Air

❼

r. Cujas

sq. Paul Langevin

LATIN QUARTER

Jardin Carré

Cardinal Lemoine

CAMPUS DE JUSSIEU
(Université Pierre-et-
Marie-Curie)

quai St-Bernard

place Edmond Rostand

RER
Luxembourg

r. Soufflot

place du Panthéon

Panthéon ❾

❽

r. Descartes

du

r. Monge

Jussieu Ⓜ

place
Jussieu

Cuvier

bd. St-Michel

r. St-Jacques

5e

r. Clotilde

r. de l'Estrapade

❿

r. Pierre et
Marie Curie

r. Lhomond

⓫

r. Thouin

r. Rollin

r. Linné

r. Jussieu

Ménagerie

Gay

Lussac

r. d'Ulm

place de la
Contrescarpe

r. Lacépède

⓬

JARDIN DES PLANTES

Gare d'Austerlitz RER

r. des Feuillantines

r. P. Nicole

place
A. Laveran

r. St-Jacques

**Église du
Val-de-Grâce**

Claude

Bernard

r. Tournefort

Mouffetard

place
Monge

⓭

Ⓜ Place Monge

**Grande
Mosquée
de Paris**

r. Geoffroy Saint-Hilaire

r. Buffon

**Muséum National
d'Histoire Naturelle**

⓮

13e

bd. de l'Hôpital

VAL-DE-
GRÂCE

⓯

bd. de Port

Royal

Ⓜ Censier-
Daubenton

r. Censier

r. Poliveau

r. de la Glacière

HÔPITAL
COCHIN

14e

r. Broca

Pascal

r. du Fer à

av. des Gobelins

r. Fer à Moulin

⓰

Les Gobelins Ⓜ

Muséum National d'Histoire Naturelle ★★ MUSEUM   This natural-history museum was established in 1793 under the supervision of two celebrated naturalists, the Count of Buffon and Louis Jean-Marie Daubenton. This temple to the natural sciences contains a series of separate museums, each with a different specialty. The biggest draw is no doubt the **Grande Galerie de l'Evolution,** where a sort of Noah's ark of animals snakes its way around a huge hall filled with displays that trace the evolution of life and man's relationship to nature. Another interesting hall, the **Galerie de Minérologie et de Geologies,** includes a room full of giant crystals. For dinosaurs, saber-toothed tigers, ancient humans, and thousands of fossilized skeletons, repair to the **Galeries de Paléontologie et d'Anatomie Comparée.** A new **Galerie des Enfants** has hands-on interactive displays for the little tykes.

36 rue Geoffrey, 5th arrond. ℂ **01-40-79-54-79.** www.mnhn.fr. Admission to each gallerie 5€–9€ adults; 4€–7€ students, seniors 60 and older, and children 4–13. Wed–Mon 10am–6pm. Métro: Jussieu or Gare d'Austerlitz.

Musée National du Moyen Age/Thermes de Cluny (Musée de Cluny) ★★ MUSEUM   Ancient Roman baths and a 15th-century mansion set the stage for a terrific collection of Medieval art and objects at this museum. Built somewhere between the 1st and 3rd centuries, the baths (visible from bd. St-Michel) are some of the best existing examples of Gallo-Roman architecture. They are attached to what was once the palatial home of a 15th-century abbot, whose last owner, a certain Alexandre du Sommerard, amassed a vast array of Medieval masterworks. When he died in 1842, his home was turned into a museum and his collection put on display. Sculptures, textiles, furniture, and ceramics are shown, as well as gold, ivory, and enamel work. There are several magnificent tapestries, but the biggest draw is the late-15th-century **"Lady and the Unicorn"** series, one of only two sets of complete unicorn tapestries in the world (the other is in New York City).

Among the many sculptures displayed are the famous severed heads from the facade of Notre-Dame. Knocked off their bodies during the furor of the Revolution, 21 of the heads of the Kings of Judah were found by chance in 1977 during repair work in the basement of a bank. Other treasures include Flemish retables, Visigoth crowns, bejeweled chalices, wood carvings, stained-glass windows, and beautiful objects from daily life, like hair combs and game boards.

6 place Paul Painlevé, 5th arrond. ℂ **01-53-73-78-00.** www.musee-moyenage.fr. Admission 8€ adults, 6€ ages 18–26, free 17 and under. Wed–Mon 9:15am–5:45pm. Métro/RER: Cluny–La Sorbonne or St-Michel.

Panthéon ★ MAUSOLEUM   High atop the "montagne" (actually a medium-sized hill) of St-Geneviève, the dome of the Panthéon is one of the city's most visible landmarks. This erstwhile royal church has been transformed into a sort of national mausoleum—the final resting place of luminaries such as Voltaire, Rousseau, Hugo, and Zola. Initially dedicated to St-Geneviève, the church was commissioned by a grateful Louis XV, who attributed his recovery from a serious illness to the saint. The work of architect Jacques-Germain Soufflot, who took his inspiration from the Pantheon in Rome, the original must have been magnificent. However, during the Revolution, its sacred mission was diverted towards a new god—the Nation—and it was converted into a memorial and burial ground for Great Men of the Republic. This meant taking down the bells, walling up most of the windows, doing away with religious statuary, and replacing it with works promoting patriotic virtues. The desired effect was achieved—the enormous empty space, lined with huge paintings of great moments in French history, resembles a cavernous tomb. Though the building is of architectural interest, unless you're a fan of one of the men (or women) who are buried under the building (a staircase leads down to the actual crypt), it's probably best admired from the outside.

Place du Panthéon, 5th arrond. ℂ **01-44-32-18-00.** www.monuments-nationaux.fr. Admission 8.50€ adults, 5.50€ ages 18–25, free children 17 and younger. Apr–Sept daily 10am–6:30pm; Oct–Mar daily 10am–6pm. Métro: Cardinal Lemoine. RER: Luxembourg.

St-Etienne-du-Mont ★★ CHURCH   One of the city's prettiest churches, this ecclesiastical gem is a joyous mix of late Gothic and Renaissance styles. The 17th-century facade combines Gothic tradition with a dash of classical Rome; inside, the 16th-century chancel sports a magnificent **rood screen** (an intricately carved partition separating the nave from the chancel) with decorations inspired by the Italian Renaissance. Book-ended by twin spiraling marble staircases, this rood screen is the only one left in the city. A pilgrimage site, this church was once part of an abbey dedicated to St-Genviève (the city's patron saint), and stones from her original sarcophagus lie in an ornate shrine here. That's about all that is left of her—the saint's bones were burned during the Revolution and their ashes thrown in the Seine. The remains of two other great minds, Racine and Pascal, are buried here.

1 place St-Geneviève, 5th arrond. ℰ **01-43-54-11-79.** www.saintetiennedumont.fr. Free admission. Tues–Sat 8:45am–7:45pm, Sat–Sun 8:45am–noon and 2–7:45pm. Métro: Cardinal Lemoine or Luxembourg.

ST-GERMAIN-DES-PRÉS & LUXEMBOURG (6TH ARRONDISSEMENT)

In the 20th century, the St-Germain-des-Prés neighborhood became associated with writers like Jean-Paul Sartre, Simone de Beauvoir, Albert Camus, and the rest of the intellectual bohemian crowd that gathered at **Café de Flore** or **Les Deux Magots** (p. 86). But back in the 6th century, a mighty abbey founded here ruled over a big chunk of the Left Bank for 1,000 years. The French Revolution put a stop to that, and most of the original buildings were pulled down. Remains of both epochs can still be found in this now-tony neighborhood, notably at the 10th-century church **St-Germain-des-Prés** and the surviving bookstores and publishing houses that surround it.

Jardin du Luxembourg ★★★ GARDENS   Rolling out like an exotic Oriental carpet before the Italianate Palais du Luxembourg, this vast expanse of fountains, flowers, lush lawns, and shaded glens is the perfect setting for a leisurely stroll, a relaxed picnic, or a serious make-out session, depending on who you're with. At the center of everything is a fountain with a huge basin, where kids can sail toy wooden sailboats (2.50€ for a half-hour) and adults can sun themselves in the green metal chairs at the pond's edge. Sculptures abound: At

Fontaine de Observatoire, Luxembourg Gardens

Attention Bored Kids & Tired Parents

Frazzled parents take note: There are lots of activities in the Jardin de Luxembourg for kids who need to blow off steam. First off, there is the extra-large **playground** (1.20€ adults, 2.50€ under 12) filled with all kinds of things to climb on and play in. Then there are the wonderful wooden **sailboats** (2.50€ per half-hour) to float in the main fountain, as well as an ancient **carousel** (1.50€, next to the playground). At the **marionette theater** (4.70€ each for parents and children; Wed, Sat, Sun, and school vacation days; shows usually start after 3pm, Sat–Sun additional shows at 11am), you can see Guignol himself (the French version of Punch) in a variety of puppet shows.

every turn there is a god, goddess, artist, or monarch peering down at you from their pedestal. The most splendid waterworks is probably the Medici Fountain (reached via the entrance at place Paul Claudel behind the Odéon), draped with lithe Roman gods and topped with the Medici coat of arms, in honor of the palace's first resident, Marie de Medicis.

In 1621, the Italian-born French queen, homesick for the Pitti Palace of her youth, bought up the grounds and existing buildings and had a Pitti-inspired palace built for herself as well as a smaller version of the sumptuous gardens. During the Revolution, it was turned into a prison. American writer Thomas Paine was incarcerated there in 1793 after he fell out of favor with Robespierre; he narrowly escaped execution. On the plus side, the Revolutionaries increased the size of the garden and made it a public institution. Visitors can visit a horticulture school where pear trees have been trained into formal, geometric shapes, as well as beehives (yes, beehives) that are maintained by a local apiculture association.
Entry at Place Edmond Rostand, place André Honnorat, rue Guynemer, or rue de Vaugirard, 6th arrond. www.senat.fr/visite/jardin. 8am–dusk. Métro: Odéon. RER: Luxembourg.

Musée Zadkine ★★ MUSEUM   You could easily miss the alleyway that leads to this tiny museum in the small but luminous house where Ossip Zadkine lived and worked from 1928 to his death in 1967. A contemporary and neighbor of artists such as Brancusi, Lipchitz, Modigliani, and Picasso, this Russian-born sculptor is closely associated with the Cubist movement; his sober, elegant, "primitive" sculptures combine abstract geometry with deep humanity. Be sure to visit the artist's workshop, tucked behind the tranquil garden. *Note:* Due to the museum's small size, during temporary exhibits you'll have to pay to enter the permanent collection (which is usually free).
100 bis rue d'Assas, 6th arrond. ✆ **01-55-42-77-20.** www.zadkine.paris.fr. Free admission to permanent collections; temporary exhibits: 7€ adults, 5€ over 60, 3.50€ ages 14–26, free 13 and under. Tues–Sun 10am–6pm. Métro: Notre-Dame des Champs or Vavin.

St-Germain-des-Prés ★★ CHURCH   The origins of this church stretch back over a millennium. First established by King Childebert in 543, who constructed a basilica and monastery on the site, it was built, destroyed, and rebuilt several times over the centuries. Nothing remains of the original buildings, but the bell tower dates from the 10th century and is one of the oldest in France. The church and its abbey became a major center of learning and power during the Middle Ages, remaining a force to be reckoned with up until the French Revolution, when all hell broke loose: The abbey was destroyed, the famous library

St-Germain-des-Prés, Luxembourg & Montparnasse (6e & 14e)

1er

ILE DE LA CITÉ

ATTRACTIONS
Jardin du Luxembourg **20**
Les Catacombes **6**
Musée Zadkine **8**
St-Germain-des-Prés **11**
St-Sulpice **18**

6e

5e

15e

14e

HOTELS
Hôtel des Bains **3**
Hôtel Mayet **1**
L'Apostrophe **7**
Relais St-Germain **15**

RESTAURANTS
Café de Flore **9**
Café de la Mairie **16**
Cobéa **4**
Crêperie Josselin **2**
La Régalade **5**
Le Comptoir du Relais **14**
Le P'tit Fernand **17**
Le Relais Louis XIII **13**
Les Deux Magots **10**
Mangetout **12**
Restaurant Polidor **19**

burned, and the church vandalized. Restored in the 19th century, the buildings have regained some of their former glory, though the complex is a fraction of its original size.

Much of the interior is painted in a range of greens, and golds—one of the few Parisian churches to retain a sense of its original decor. The paint, however, is in a sorry state; the interior is scheduled to be restored during 2015. The heart of King Jean Casimir of Poland is buried here, as are the ashes of the body of René Descartes (his skull is in the collections of the Musée de l'Homme). On the left as you exit you can peek inside the **chapel of St-Symphorien,** where during the Revolution over 100 clergymen were imprisoned before being executed on the square in front of the church. The chapel was restored in the 1970s and decorated by contemporary artist Pierre Buraglio in 1992.

3 place St-Germain-des-Prés, 6th arrond. © **01-55-42-81-10.** www.eglise-sgp.org. Free admission. Mon–Sat 8am–7:45pm; Sun 9am–8pm. Métro: St-Germain-des-Prés.

St-Sulpice ★★ CHURCH   After years of renovations, the scaffoldings have finally come off the majestic facade of this enormous edifice. Construction started in the 17th century over the remains of a medieval church; it took over a hundred years to build, and one of the towers was never finished. Inside, the cavernous interior seems to command you to be silent; several important works of art are tucked into the chapels that line the church. The most famous of them are **three masterpieces by Eugène Delacroix,** "Jacob Wrestling with the Angel," "Heliodorus Driven from the Temple," and "St-Michael Vanquishing the Devil" (on the right just after you enter the church). Jean-Baptiste Pigalle's statue of the "Virgin and Child" lights up the Chapelle de la Vierge at the farthest most point from the entrance. A bronze line runs north–south along the floor; this is part of a **gnomon,** an astronomical device set up in the 17th century to calculate the position of the sun in the sky. A small hole in one of the stained glass windows creates a spot of light on the floor; every day at noon it hits the line in a different spot, climbing to the top of an obelisk and lighting a gold disk at winter equinox.

Place St-Sulpice, 6th arrond. © **01-42-34-59-98.** Free admission. Daily 7:30am–7:30pm. Métro: St-Sulpice.

EIFFEL TOWER & LES INVALIDES (7TH ARRONDISSEMENT)

The Iron Lady towers above this stately neighborhood, where the very buildings seem to insist that you stand up straight and pay attention. Stuffed with embassies and ministries, you'll see lots of elegant black cars with smoked glass cruising the streets, as well as many a tourist eyeing the **Eiffel Tower** or the golden dome of **Les Invalides,** and scurrying in and out of some of the city's best museums, like the **Musée du Quai Branly, Musée d'Orsay,** and **Musée Rodin.**

Eiffel Tower ★★★ MONUMENT   In his wildest dreams, Gustave Eiffel probably never imagined that the tower he built for the 1889 World's Fair would become the ultimate symbol of Paris and, for many, of France. Originally slated for demolition after its first 20 years, the Eiffel Tower has survived more than a century and is one of the most visited sites in the nation. No less than 50 engineers and designers worked on the plans, which resulted in a remarkably solid structure that despite its height (324m/1,063 ft., including the antenna) does not sway in the wind.

Eiffel Tower & Les Invalides (7e & 15e)

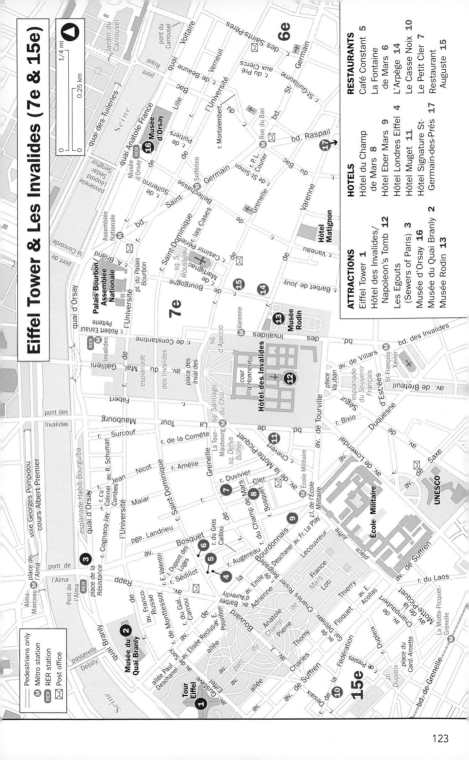

RESTAURANTS
Café Constant **5**
La Fontaine
de Mars **6**
L'Arpège **14**
Le Casse Noix **10**
Le Petit Cler **7**
Restaurant
Auguste **15**

HOTELS
Hôtel du Champ
de Mars **3**
Hôtel Eber Mars **9**
Hôtel Londres Eiffel **4**
Hôtel Muget **11**
Hôtel Signature St-
Germain-des-Prés **17**

ATTRACTIONS
Eiffel Tower **1**
Hôtel des Invalides/
Napoleon's Tomb **12**
Les Egouts
(Sewers of Paris) **3**
Musée d'Orsay **16**
Musée du Quai Branly **2**
Musée Rodin **13**

But while the engineers rejoiced, others howled. When the project for the tower was announced, a group of artists and writers, including Guy de Maupassant and Alexandre Dumas, published a manifesto that referred to it as an "odious column of bolted metal." Others were less diplomatic: Novelist Joris-Karl Huysmans called it a "hole-riddled suppository." Despite the objections, the tower was built—over 18,000 pieces of iron, held together with some 2.5 million rivets. In this low-tech era, building techniques involved a lot of elbow grease: The foundations, for example, were dug entirely by shovel, and the debris was hauled away in horse-drawn carts. Construction dragged on for 2 years, but finally, on March 31, 1889, Gustave Eiffel proudly led a group of dignitaries up the 1,710 steps to the top, where he unfurled the French flag for the inauguration.

Eiffel Tower

Over 100 years later, the tower has become such an integral piece of the Parisian landscape that it's impossible to think of the city without it. Over time, even the artists came around—the tower's silhouette can be found in the paintings of Seurat, Bonnard, Duffy, Chagall, and especially those of Robert Delaunay, who devoted an entire series of canvases to the subject. It has also inspired a whole range of stunts, from Pierre Labric riding a bicycle down the stairs from the first level in 1923 to Philippe Petit walking a 700m-long (2,296-ft.) tightrope from the Palais de Chaillot to the tower during the centennial celebration in 1989. Eiffel performed his own "stunts" towards the end of his career, using the tower as a laboratory for scientific experiments. By convincing the authorities of the tower's usefulness in studying meteorology, aerodynamics, and other subjects, Eiffel saved it from being torn down.

The most dramatic view of the tower itself is from the wide esplanade at the Palais de Chaillot (Métro: Trocadéro) across the Seine. From there it's a short walk down through the gardens and across the Pont d'Iena to the base of the tower. The first floor has been closed for the last two years for major renovations. By autumn 2014, visitors should be able to enjoy chic new pavilions and displays, and part of the floor will be glassed over—so you can virtually walk on air. Personally, I think the view from the second level is the best; you're far enough up to see

A Workout & a Bargain at the Eiffel Tower

No need to go to the gym after marching up the 704 steps that lead you to the second floor of the Eiffel Tower. Not only will you burn calories, but you'll save money: At 5€ adults, 4€ ages 12 to 24, and 3€ ages 4 to 11, this is the least expensive way to visit. Extra perks include an up-close view of the amazing metal structure and avoiding long lines for the elevator.

the entire city, yet close enough to clearly pick out the various monuments. But if you are aching to get to the top an airplanelike view awaits. The third level is, mercifully, enclosed, but thrill-seekers can climb up a few more stairs to the outside balcony (entirely protected by a grill).

Champ de Mars, 7th arrond. ✆ **01-44-11-23-23.** www.tour-eiffel.fr. Lift to 2nd floor 9€ adults, 7.50€ ages 12–24, 4.50€ ages 4–11; lift to 2nd and 3rd floors 15€ adults, 13.50€ ages 12–24, 10.50€ ages 4–11; stairs to 2nd floor 5€ adults, 4€ ages 12–24, 3€ ages 4–11. Free admission for children 3 and under. Mid-June to Aug daily 9am–midnight, Sept to mid-June daily 9.30am–11pm; Sept to mid-June stairs open only to 6pm. Métro: Trocadéro or Bir Hakeim. RER: Champ de Mars–Tour Eiffel.

Hôtel des Invalides/Napoléon's Tomb ★★ MUSEUM   This grandiose complex houses a military museum, church, tomb, hospital, and military ministries, among other things. Commissioned by Louis XIV, who was determined to create a home for soldiers wounded in the line of duty, it was built on what was then the outskirts of the city. The first war veterans arrived in 1674—between 4,000 and 5,000 soldiers would eventually move in, creating a mini-city with its own governor. An on-site hospital was constructed for the severely wounded, which is still in service today.

As you cross the main gate, you'll find yourself in a huge courtyard, the *cour d'honneur,* once the site of military parades. The surrounding buildings house military administration offices and the recently renovated **Musée de l'Armée,** one of the world's largest military museums, with a vast collection of objects testifying to man's capacity for self-destruction. The most impressive section is **Arms and Armor,** a panoply of 13th- to 17th-century weaponry. Viking swords, Burgundian battle axes, 14th-century blunderbusses, Balkan *khandjars,* Browning machine guns, engraved Renaissance serpentines, musketoons, grenadiers—if it can kill, it's enshrined here. There is also a huge wing covering the exploits of everyone from **Louis XIV** to **Napoléon III,** another on the two **World Wars,** and a shrine to **Charles de Gaulle.** Also onsite is the **Musée des Plans et Reliefs,** a somewhat dusty collection of scale models of fortresses and battlefields.

The **Eglise du Dôme** is split in two, the front half being the light-filled "Soldier's Church," decorated with magnificent chandeliers and a collection of flags of defeated enemies. On the other side of the glass partition the **Tomb of Napoléon** lies under one of the most splendid domes in France. Designed by Hardouin-Mansart, it took over 2 decades to build. The interior soars 107m (351 ft.) up to a skylight, which illuminates a brilliantly colored cupola. Ethereal light filters down to an opening where you can look down on the huge porphyry sarcophagus, which holds the emperor's remains, encased in five successive coffins (one tin, one mahogany, two lead, and one ebony). Surrounding the sarcophagus are the tombs of two of Napoléon's brothers, his son, and several French military heroes. Don't blame the over-the-top setting on Napoléon; the decision to transfer his remains to Paris was made in 1840, almost 20 years after his death. Tens of thousands crowded the streets to pay their respects as the coffin was carried under the Arc de Triomphe and down the Champs-Elysées to Les Invalides, where it waited another 20 years until the tomb was finished.

Place des Invalides, 7th arrond. ✆ **01-44-42-37-72.** www.invalides.org. Admission to all the museums, the church, and Napoléon's Tomb: 9.50€ adults, free 17 and younger. Apr–Oct 10am–6pm, Nov–Mar 10am–5pm. Métro: Latour-Maubourg, Varenne, or Invalides. RER: Invalides.

Musée d'Orsay ★★★ MUSEUM   What better setting for a world-class museum of 19th-century art than a beautiful example of Belle Epoque architecture? In 1986, the magnificent Gare d'Orsay train station, built to coincide with

Musée d'Orsay

the 1900 World's Fair, was brilliantly transformed into an exposition space. The huge, airy central hall lets in lots of natural light, which is artfully combined with artificial lighting to illuminate a collection of treasures.

The collection spans the years 1848 to 1914, a period that saw the birth of many artistic movements, but today it is best known for the emergence of Impressionism. All the superstars of the epoch are here, including Monet, Manet, Degas, and Renoir, not to mention Cézanne, and Van Gogh.

The top floor is now the home of the most famous Impressionist paintings, like Edouard Manet's masterpiece, "Le Déjeuner sur l'Herbe." Though Manet's composition of bathers and friends picnicking on the grass draws freely from those of Italian Renaissance masters, the painting shocked its 19th-century audience, which was horrified to see a naked lady lunching with two fully clothed men. Manet got into trouble again with his magnificent "Olympia," a seductive odalisque stretched out on a divan. There was nothing new about the subject; viewers were rattled by the unapologetic look in her eye—this is not an idealized nude, but a real woman, and a tough cookie to boot.

The middle level is devoted to the post-Impressionists, with works by artists like Gauguin, Seurat, Rousseau, and Van Gogh, like the latter's "Church at Auvers-sur-Oise," an ominous version of the church in a small town north of Paris where he moved after spending time in an asylum in Provence. This was 1 of some 70 paintings he produced in the 2 months leading up to his suicide.

1 rue de la Légion d'Honneur, 7th arrond. ☎ **01-40-49-48-14.** www.musee-orsay.fr. Admission 11€ adults, 8.50€ ages 18–25, free ages 17 and younger. Tues–Wed and Fri–Sun 9:30am–6pm; Thurs 9:30am–9:45pm. Métro: Solférino. RER: Musée d'Orsay.

Musée du quai Branly ★★★ MUSEUM   It's just a few blocks from the Eiffel Tower, but this museum's wildly contemporary design has forever changed the architectural landscape of this rigidly elegant neighborhood. Its enormous central structure floats on a series of pillars, under which lies a lush garden, separated from the noisy boulevard out front by a huge glass wall. However you feel about the outside, you cannot help but be impressed by the inside: The vast space is filled with exquisite examples of the traditional arts of Africa, the Pacific Islands, Asia, and the Americas. Designed by veteran museum-maker Jean Nouvel, this intriguing space makes an ideal showcase for a category of artwork that too often has been relegated to the sidelines of the museum world.

This magnificent collection is displayed in a way that invites you to admire the skill and artistry that went into the creation of these diverse objects. Delicately carved headrests from Papua New Guinea in the form of birds and crocodiles and intricately painted masks from Indonesia vie for your attention. Look at and listen to giant wooden flutes from Papua New Guinea, displayed with an on-going recording. A selection of "magic stones" from the island nation of Vanuatu includes smooth abstract busts reminiscent of Brancusi sculptures. A fascinating collection of Australian aboriginal paintings segues into the Asian art section, and the journey continues into Africa, starting with embroidered silks from Morocco and heading south through magnificent geometric marriage cloths from Mali and wooden masks from the Ivory Coast. The Americas collection includes rare Nazca pottery and Inca textiles, as well as an intriguing assortment of North American works, like Haitian voodoo objects and Sioux beaded tunics.

37 quai Branly and 206 and 218 rue de Université, 7th arrond. ℰ **01-56-61-70-00.** www.quaibranly.fr. Admission to permanent exhibitions 9€ adults, free children 17 and younger. Tues–Wed and Sun 11am–7pm; Thurs–Sat 11am–9pm. Métro: Alma-Marceau. RER: Pont d'Alma.

Musée Rodin ★★★ MUSEUM There aren't many museums that can draw thousands of visitors who never even go inside. But the grounds of this splendid place are so lovely that many are willing to pay 2€ just to stroll around. Behind the Hôtel Biron, the mansion that houses the museum, is a formal garden with benches, fountains, and even a little cafe. Of course, it would be foolish *not* to go inside and drink in the some of the 6,600 sculptures in this excellent collection (don't worry, not all are on display), but it would be equally silly not to take the

Gardens at the Musée Rodin

time to admire the large bronzes in the garden, which include some of Rodin's most famous works. Take, for example, "The Thinker." Erected in front of the Panthéon in 1906 during a political crisis, Rodin's first public sculpture soon became a Socialist symbol and was quickly transferred here by the authorities, under the pretense that it blocked pedestrian traffic. Other important outdoor sculptures include the "Burghers of Calais," "Balzac," and the "Gates of Hell," a monumental composition that the sculptor worked on throughout his career.

Indoors, marble compositions prevail, although there are also works in terra-cotta, plaster, and bronze, as well as sketches and paintings on display. The most famous of the marble works is "The Kiss," which was originally meant to appear in the "Gates of Hell." In time, Rodin decided that the lovers were too happy for this grim composition, and he explored it as an independent work. As usual with Rodin's works, the critics were shocked by the couple's overt sensuality, but not as shocked as they were by the large, impressionistic rendition of "Balzac," exhibited at the same salon, which critic Georges Rodenbach described as "less a statue than a strange monolith, a thousand-year-old menhir." The museum holds hundreds of works, many of them legendary, so don't be surprised if after a while your vision starts to blur. That'll be your cue to head outside and enjoy the garden. **Note:** Don't be surprised if parts of the building are closed for renovation during your visit. The most famous pieces should still be on display, and the statues in the garden will all be present and accounted for.

79 rue de Varenne, 7th arrond. ☏ **01-44-18-61-10.** www.musee-rodin.fr. Admission 9€ adults, 7€ ages 18–25, free children 17 and younger. Tues and Thurs–Sun 10am–5:30pm, Wed 10am–8:30pm. Métro: Varenne or St-Francois-Xavier.

MONTPARNASSE (14TH & 15TH ARRONDISSEMENTS)

Even though it had its heart ripped out in the 1970s when the original 19th-century train station was torn down and the ugly Tour Montparnasse was erected, this neighborhood still retains a redolent whiff of its artistic past. Back in the day, artists like Picasso, Modigliani, and Man Ray hung out in cafes like **Le Dôme, La Coupole, La Rotonde,** and **Le Sélect,** as did a "Lost Generation" of English-speaking writers like Hemingway, Fitzgerald, Faulkner, and Joyce. Today the famous cafes are mostly filled with tourists, but you can still find quiet corners. Amazingly, **La Ruche,** the legendary artists' studio from the Golden Years, is still standing (www.la-ruche.fr).

Les Catacombes ★ CEMETERY/HISTORIC SITE   Definitely not for the faint of heart, the city's catacombs are filled with the remains of millions of ex-Parisians, whose bones line the narrow passages of this mazelike series of tunnels. In the 18th century, the Cimetière des Innocents, a centuries-old, overpacked cemetery near Les Halles, had become so foul and disease-ridden that it was finally declared a health hazard and closed. The bones of its occupants were transferred to this former quarry, which were later joined by those of other similarly pestilential Parisian cemeteries.

In 1814, the quarry stopped accepting new lodgers. Rather than leaving just a hodgepodge of random bones, they organized them in neat stacks and geometric designs, punctuating the 2km (1¼ miles) with sculptures and pithy sayings carved into the rock. The one at the entrance sets the tone: stop—here is the empire of death. The visit will be fascinating for some, terrifying for others; definitely not a good idea for claustrophobics or small children. You'll want to wear comfortable shoes and bring a sweater of some sort, as it's cool down here (around 57°F/14°C).

Les Catacombes

1 avenue du Colonel Henri Rol-Tanguy, 14th arrond. ☎ **01-43-22-47-63.** www.catacombes. paris.fr. Admission 8€ adults, 6€ seniors, 4€ ages 14–26, free for children 13 and younger. Tues–Sun 10am–5pm (last entry at 4pm). Métro: Denfert-Rochereau.

SHOPPING IN PARIS

Like us, most Parisians can't actually afford to buy the French luxury brands so revered around the world—and yet they manage to look terrifically put together. What's their secret? Read on as I attempt to shed some light on this puzzling mystery; the shops and services listed below will give you a good point of departure for your Parisian shopping adventure.

Business Hours

In general, shops are open from 9 or 10am to 7pm; many are closed on Monday, and most are closed on Sunday. Unfortunately, that means that the stores are jam-packed on Saturday, so don't say I didn't warn you.

Some smaller, family-run operations sometimes still close between noon and 2pm for lunch, but most stores stay open all day. Many larger stores and most department stores stay open late (that is, until 9pm) 1 night a week (called a *nocturne*). For food and toiletry emergencies, tiny minimarkets (called *alimentations*) stay open late into the night 7 days a week. ***Note:*** Many shops close down for 2 or 3 weeks in July or August, when the vacation exodus empties out major portions of the city.

Great Shopping Areas
STREETS FOR BARGAIN HUNTING

You can find clothes and knickknacks at significantly reduced prices at discount shops, which tend to conglomerate on certain streets. **Rue d'Alésia** (14th arrond., Métro: Alésia) is lined with outlet stores *(déstock)* selling discounted wares, including designer labels like Sonia Rykiel; and **Rue St-Placide** (6th arrond., Métro: Sèvres-Babylone) has both outlet stores and discount shops like Mouton à Cinq Pattes (p. 133).

MIDRANGE SHOPPING HUBS

Several areas have high concentrations of chain and midrange stores where you can get a lot of shopping done in a small area. They are: **Rue de Rennes** (6th arrond.; especially near the Tour Montparnasse); **Les Halles** (1st arrond.; the Forum des Halles underground mall is still open during the reconstruction of Les Halles above; don't ignore the many nearby shops above); **Rue de Rivoli** (1st arrond., btw. rue du Pont Neuf and Hôtel de Ville); and **Grands Magasins** (9th arrond.)—be sure look in the little streets that weave around the Printemps and Galeries Lafayette department stores (see below).

CHIC BOUTIQUE-ING

Paris has an endless number of darling boutiques, ranging from funky to fantastic. A few of the best streets for boutique shopping or simply *lèche-vitrine* (window shopping) are: **Rue des Abbesses** (18th arrond.; Métro: Abbesses), for affordable chic and the shops of hip, young startup designers; **Rue de Charonne** (11th arrond.; Métro: Bastille), a youth-oriented street that has recently taken a turn upscale with a dose of tony boutiques; **Rue des Francs Bourgeois** (4th arrond.; Métro: St-Paul), for a cornucopia of fashionable/cool/hip stores, most of which are open on Sunday; and **Rue Etienne Marcel** (2nd arrond.; Métro: Etienne Marcel), next to the hip Montorgueil pedestrian zone, with stylish boutiques galore.

THE SKY'S THE LIMIT

If you don't look at price tags and are always searching for the ultimate everything, Paris does not disappoint. For centuries, Paris has been the capital of luxury goods, many of them for sale on **Avenue Montaigne** (8th arrond.; Métro: Franklin D. Roosevelt), with breathtakingly expensive designer flagships like Dior and Chanel; the **Place Vendôme** (1st arrond.; Métro: Concorde or Tuileries), with eye-popping jewelry shops (Cartier, Boucheron, and so on); and **Rue du Faubourg St-Honoré** (8th arrond.; Métro: St-Philippe du Roule), where deeply elegant boutiques are filled with choice morsels of designer goods.

Markets: Food & Flea

Marchés (open-air or covered markets) are small universes unto themselves where nothing substantial has really changed for centuries. These markets are great local spots to hunt for fresh food or browse flea-market finds.

FOOD MARKETS

Paris's food markets are noisy, bustling, joyous places where you can buy fresh, honest food. Following is a short list of food *marchés*; you can find more on the municipal website (www.paris.fr; click on the little green basket labeled "Marchés" in the upper righthand corner). ***Note:*** Unless you see evidence to the contrary, don't pick up your own fruits and vegetables with your hands. Wait until the vendor serves you.

MARCHÉ D'ALIGRE ★★★ (also called Marché Beauveau, place d'Aligre, 12th arrond.; outdoor market Tues–Sun 9am–1pm, covered market Tues–Sat 9am–1pm and 4–7:30pm, Sun 9am–1:30pm; Métro: Ledru Rollin or Gare de Lyon):

One of the city's largest markets, this sprawling affair invades a whole neighborhood, with both outdoor stalls and a covered market.

MARCHÉ BATIGNOLLES ★★ (bd. Batignolles, btw. rue de Rome and Place Clichy, 17th arrond.; Sat 9am–3pm; Métro: Rome): A terrific, all-organic Saturday market with fresh regional produce and close proximity to pretty sidewalk cafes for an after-marché coffee.

MARCHÉ RASPAIL ★★ (bd. Raspail, btw. rue de Cherche-Midi and rue de Rennes, 6th arrond.; Tues and Fri 7am–2:30pm; organic Sun 9am–3pm; Métro: Rennes): Stretching several blocks down the center divider of a wide avenue, this outdoor market makes a delicious gourmet stroll.

FLEA MARKETS

MARCHÉ AUX PUCES DE PARIS ST-OUEN–CLIGNANCOURT ★ (Porte de Clignancourt, 18th arrond.; www.marcheauxpuces-saintouen.com; Sat 9am–6pm, Sun 10am–6pm, Mon 11am–5pm; Métro: Porte de Clignancourt): At the northern edge of the city, this claims to be the world's largest antiques market. It was once a bargain-hunter's dream, but prices now often rival those of antiques dealers. Hard-core browsers will get a kick out of wandering the serpentine alleyways of this Parisian medina. *Note:* Beware of pickpockets.

MARCHÉ AUX PUCES DE LA PORTE DE VANVES ★★ (Av. Georges-Lafenestre, 14th arrond.; www.pucesdevanves.typepad.com; Sat and Sun 7am–2pm; Métro: Porte de Vanves): This weekend event sprawls along two streets and is the best flea market in Paris—dealers swear by it. Look for old linens, vintage Hermès scarves, toys, ephemera, costume jewelry, perfume bottles, and bad art. Get there early—the best stuff goes fast.

Shopping A to Z
ANTIQUES & COLLECTIBLES

L'Objet qui Parle ★★ This delightful and quirky shop sells a jumble of vintage finds, including framed butterflies, teapots, furniture, chandeliers, crockery, hunting trophies, religious paraphernalia, and old lace. Great for souvenir shopping. 86 rue des Martyrs, 18th arrond. ☏ **06-09-67-05-30.** Métro: Abbesses.

Village St-Paul ★★ When you pass through an archway on rue St-Paul, you come upon a lovely villagelike enclosure, the remnant of a centuries-old hamlet that was swallowed up by the city. Today, it's a village of antiques dealers and design shops, selling everything from old bistro chairs and vintage lingerie to Brazilian eco-furniture and Iranian kilim rugs. www.levillagesaintpaul.com. No phone. Métro: St-Paul.

BEAUTY & PERFUME

The Different Company ★★ This independent perfume house makes its own unique fragrances with mostly natural materials. Signature scents include Osmanthus, Sel de Vétiver, and Rose Poivrée, but let your nose lead the way when you visit the store. 10 rue Ferdinand Duval, 4th arrond. ☏ **01-42-78-19-34.** www.thedifferentcompany.com. Métro: St-Paul.

Editions de Parfums Fréderic Malle ★★ This chic temple to the nose offers a superb range of original fragrances. Sample M. Malle's wares in special "smelling columns," round, phone-booth-like tubes where you can experience aromas like Noir Epice and Lipstick Rose. There are two other stores at 140 avenue Victor Hugo in the 16th arrondissement, and 21 rue du Mont Thabor in the 1st. 37 rue de Grenelle, 7th arrond. ✆ **01-42-22-76-40.** www.fredericmalle.com. Métro: Rue du Bac.

Make Up Forever ★ This French cosmetics company, which trains professional makeup artists, also runs this boutique where you can buy products and get a **makeup lesson** (25 min. for 25€, 60 min. for 60€; call to reserve). A second location is at 5 rue de la Boétie in the 8th arrondissement. 5 rue des Francs Bourgeois, 4th arrond. ✆ **01-42-71-23-19.** www.makeupforever.fr. Métro: St-Paul.

BOOKS

Galignani ★★ This old-fashioned shop has thrived since 1810. Owned by the literary Gagliani family, whose ancestor used one of the first printing presses back in 1520, the store is filled with a terrific range of both French and English books, with a special emphasis on French classics, modern fiction, sociology, and fine arts. 224 rue de Rivoli, 1st arrond. ✆ **01-42-60-76-07.** www.galignani.com. Métro: Tuileries.

San Francisco Book Company ★★ Since new books in English can be very expensive in Paris, there's a steady traffic in used ones in the expatriate community, with a couple of bookstores devoted to the task. This centrally located shop has a good stock of both hardback classics and paperback airplane reading, as well as rare and out-of-print editions. 17 rue Monsieur Le Prince, 6th arrond. ✆ **01-43-29-15-70.** www.sanfranciscobooksparis.com. Métro: Odéon.

Shakespeare & Company ★★★ This venerable shrine is a must on any Parisian literary tour. Run by George Whitman for some 60 years before he passed away in 2011 at 98, today it is helmed by his daughter, Sylvia, who was named for Sylvia Beach (who founded the original bookshop in 1919). Many a legendary writer has stopped in over the decades for tea; many an aspiring author has camped out in one of the back rooms (Whitman liked to think of this store as a "writer's sanctuary"). Today, Whitman's presence is still felt at this historic bookshop, which sells used and new books. Check the website for ongoing readings and other events. 37 rue de la Bûcherie, 5th arrond. ✆ **01-43-25-40-93.** www.shakespeareandcompany.com. Métro/RER: St-Michel–Notre-Dame.

CLOTHING & ACCESSORIES

Antoine & Lili ★★ Hot pink is the signature color at this wacky store, where the gaily painted walls are hung with oodles of colorful objects from around the world. The women's clothes are innovative and fresh yet wearable, and come in a range of bright colors. It has five other branches in town; check the website for addresses. 95 quai de Valmy, 10th arrond. ✆ **01-40-37-41-55.** www.antoineetlili.com. Métro: Jacques-Bonsergent.

Sale Mania

Despite recent changes to the laws that restricted sales to certain times of the year, stores still follow the traditional sale (*soldes*) seasons. Two times a year, around the second week in January and the second week in July (specific dates are plastered all over the city), retailers go hog-wild and slash prices; the rest of the year sale prices don't dip down much below 30 percent. When opening day finally arrives, chaos ensues. There are good deals to be had, but try to avoid the first days of havoc and especially the weekends.

Des Filles à la Vanille ★   Marrying "parfum et couture," this store smells as good as it looks. It has a great selection of big, fuzzy, funky sweaters, unusual long slit skirts, and gauzy dresses, as well as its own line of perfumes, including a vanilla-scented number, *bien sûr*. Another branch is at 150 bd. St-Germain in the 6th. 56 rue St-Antoine, 4th arrond.; ✆ **01-48-87-90-02.** www.desfillesalavanille.com. Métro: St-Paul.

French Trotters ★   Airy and spacious, this Marais emporium is the flagship store for this temple of urban chic. While the original store (which is still open, 30 rue de Charonne, 11th arrond.) featured both hot local French labels and the store's own brand of relaxed *branchitude* (hipness), this one sells all that plus housewares, books, and stationary. Terrific styles for both men and women. 128 rue Vieille du Temple, 3rd arrond. ✆ **01-44-61-00-14.** www.frenchtrotters.fr. Métro: Saint Sébastien–Froissart or Files du Calvaire.

Children
Lilli Bulle ★★   If you are looking for something a little different and original, this is a good place to start. These cool and colorful clothes will make your kids look like they live in this fun and funky neighborhood. 3 rue de la Forge Royale, 11th arrond. ✆ **01-43-73-71-63.** www.lillibulle.com. Métro: Faidherbe-Chaligny.

Marie Puce ★★   A little softer and gentler than Lilli, Marie offers easy elegance for tots who need to dress up (at least a little) but can't stand frills. Most of the clothing here is 100 percent Made in France. 60 rue du Cherche Midi, 6th arrond. ✆ **01-45-48-30-09.** www.mariepuce.com. Métro: Sèvres-Babylone or St-Placide.

Discount
Mouton à Cinq Pattes ★   Sift through the packed racks of designer markdowns and you just might find Moschino slacks or a Gaultier dress at a fabulous price. If you do, grab it fast—it might not be there tomorrow. The store at No. 8 is women's apparel only; No. 18 serves both sexes, and a third store at 138 bd. St-Germain is just for men. 8 and 18 rue St-Placide, 6th arrond. ✆ **01-45-48-86-26.** www.moutonacinqpattesparis.com. Métro: Sèvres-Babylone.

Lingerie
Orcanta ★   This chain has a great selection of name brands (such as Lise Charmel, Chantal Thomas, and Huit) and usually at least a rack or two of discounted items. More locations on the website. 60 rue St-Placide, 6th arrond. ✆ **01-45-44-94-44.** www.orcanta.fr. Métro: St-Placide.

Tab Lingerie ★★   Deep discounts on major brands (Léjaby, Simone Pérèle) can be found at this cramped treasure trove, which tempts passersby with a rack stuffed with lacy things at 30 to 70 percent off. The store entrance is at the end of the narrow corridor. 52 rue de la Chausée d'Antin. ✆ **01-48-74-41-11.** Métro: Chausée d'Antin–Lafayette.

CONCEPT STORES
Over the last few years, these hard-to-categorize stores with eclectic collections have popped up in several parts of the city. These are good places to hunt for that atypical gift you've been seeking.

Bü ★   A cross between Colette (see below), Ikea, and an upscale hardware store, this new and enigmatically named store (it's French, not Scandinavian) has reasonably priced housewares, stationary, leather handbags, luggage, and toys, as well as regional edibles. 45 rue Jussieu, 5th arrond. ✆ **01-40-56-33-22.** www.bu-store.com. Métro: Jussieu or Cardinal-Lemoine.

Colette ★★ What can you say about a store that sells both Hermès scarves and knitted hot dogs? This shopping phenom offers both high style and high concept—basically, if it's utterly cool and happening, they sell it. Karl Lagerfeld jeans, heart-shaped sunglasses, psychedelic nail polish, designer toilet brushes, and so forth. 213 rue St-Honoré, 1st arrond. ✆ **01-55-35-33-90.** www.colette.fr. Métro: Tuileries.

DEPARTMENT STORES

Le Bon Marché ★★★ Founded in the mid-1800s, this was one of the world's first department stores. Despite its name (*bon marché* means affordable), this is the most expensive of Paris' *grand magasins*. It is also the most stylish, with beautiful displays and fabulous clothes of every imaginable designer label, both upscale and midrange. Right next door is its humongous designer supermarket, **La Grande Epicerie** (see "Specialty Groceries," below). 24 rue de Sèvres, 7th arrond. ✆ **01-44-39-80-00.** www.lebonmarche.com. Métro: Sèvres–Babylone.

Galeries Lafayette ★★ The biggest of the *grand magasins* (department stores) sports an over-the-top Art Nouveau dome under which oodles of fashionable goodies are displayed for style-conscious shoppers. A bit less expensive than its more glamorous rival next door (see Printemps, below), it's also so huge that you can usually find just what you are looking for. It has everything from luxury labels to kids' stuff, not to mention books, stationary, wine, and a gourmet shop. 40 bd. Haussmann, 9th arrond. ✆ **01-42-82-34-56.** www.galerieslafayette.com. Métro: Chausée d'Antin–Lafayette.

Galeries Lafayette

Printemps ★★ The glistening domes of this 19th-century building bring to mind a grand hotel on the French Riviera. High fashion gets priority here; four of the seven floors of women's wear are devoted to designer labels. If you can't handle the crowds inside, you can always enjoy the famed *vitrines*, or **window displays,** outside. Better yet, ride to the top of Printemps Beauté/Maison and enjoy the splendid **panoramic view;** it even has a cafe at the top where you can lunch. 64 bd. Haussmann, 9th arrond. ✆ **01-42-82-50-00.** www.printemps.com. Métro: Havre-Caumartin or St-Lazare.

FOOD & DRINK

Chocolate
Michel Chaudun ★★★ If you are looking for a chocolate cellphone, look no further. Or how about chocolate pliers or ping-pong paddles? Known for his sculpting skills, Chaudun is also renowned for the exquisite taste of his

masterworks. Be sure to try the pavés—melt-in-your-mouth little squares of chocolate ganache made to resemble cobblestones. 149 rue de l'Université, 7th arrond. ✆ **01-47-53-74-40.** Métro: Invalides.

Patrick Roger ★★ This cutting-edge chocolate boutique could easily be mistaken for a jewelry shop. Here you can sample chocolates with names like "Insolence" (almond and chestnut) and "Zanzibar" (thyme and lemon), as well as candied fruits, nougat, and other delicacies. Five other stores in the city. 108 bd. St-Germain, 6th arrond. ✆ **01-43-29-38-42.** www.patrickroger.com. Métro: Odéon.

Specialty Groceries

Fauchon ★ Some (like me) find it overhyped and overpriced; others think it's heaven on Earth. Founded in 1886, this tea-room-cum-luxury-food-emporium has been wowing the crowds for over a century, and the crowds are certainly still coming. In 2004, the establishment received a shocking pink makeover and expanded exponentially—now you can find Fauchon from Hamburg to Ho Chi Min City. 26 and 30 place de la Madeleine, 8th arrond. ✆ **01-70-39-38-00.** www.fauchon. com. Métro: Madeleine.

La Grande Epicerie Paris ★★ This humongous gourmet grocery mecca, an outgrowth of Le Bon Marché department store (see above) stocks every imaginable gourmet substance you could possibly imagine, and many that you couldn't. Sculpted sugar cubes, designer mineral waters, truffled basalmic vinegar, pink salt from the Himalayas—need I go on? It also has an excellent (if expensive) takeout department for picnic items. 38 rue de Sèvres, 7th arrond, ✆ **01-44-39-81-00.** www.lagrandeepicerie.fr. Métro: Sèvres-Babylone.

Wines

Before you start planning to stock your wine cellar back home, consider this sad truth: Most non–EU countries won't let you bring back much more than a bottle or two. Your best bet is to drink up while you're here.

Les Domaines Qui Montent ★ This association of some 150 wine producers offers a vast selection of wines that come from small, independent vineyards where the emphasis is on quality and *terroir*, not quantity. An on-site wine bar also serves meals. There is a second location at 136 bd. Voltaire in the 11th arrondissement and a third on the corner of rue Ballu and rue Vintimille in the 9th. 22 rue Cardinet, 17th arrond. ✆ **01-42-27-63-96.** www.lesdomainesquimontent.com. Métro: Courcelles or Wagram.

Legrand Filles et Fils ★★ More than just a wine store, this is a place where you can learn everything there is to know about the sacred grape. 1 rue de la Banque, 2nd arrond. ✆ **01-42-60-07-12.** www.caves-legrand.com. Métro: Bourse.

JEWELRY

Bijoux Blues ★★ Hand-crafted, unique jewelry at reasonable prices made in an atelier in the Marais—who could ask for more? Designs are fun and funky, yet elegant. Pieces can be custom-designed. 30 rue St-Paul, 4th arrond. ✆ **01-48-04-00-64.** www.bijouxblues.com. Métro: St-Paul.

White Bird ★ If you are looking for a unique engagement ring or present for your sweetheart, this is a good bet. It has a terrific selection of jewelry made by talented, independent craftspeople/designers. 38 rue du Mont Thabor, 1st arrond. ✆ **01-58-62-25-86.** www.whitebirdjewellery.com. Métro: Concorde.

STATIONERY

L'Art du Papier ★★   This delightful stationery store has a fabulous selection of colored papers and envelopes, as well as ink-stamps, sealing wax, and the essentials for hobbies like calligraphy and "le scrapbooking." It has three other locations: 16 rue Daunou in the 2nd arrondissement, 197 bd. Voltaire in the 11th, and 17 ave. de Villiers in the 17th. 48 rue Vavin, 6th arrond.; ℂ **01-43-26-10-12.** www.art-du-papier.fr; Métro: Vavin.

ENTERTAINMENT & NIGHTLIFE

Paris blooms at night; its magnificent monuments and buildings become even more beautiful when they're cloaked in their evening illuminations. The already glowing Eiffel Tower bursts out in twinkling lights for the first 10 minutes of every hour. While simply walking around town can be an excellent night out, the city is also a treasure trove of rich evening offerings: bars and clubs from chic to shaggy, sublime theater and dance performances, top-class orchestras, and scores of cinemas and art-film houses.

With few exceptions, the city's major concert halls and theaters are in action between September and June, taking off during the summer months during the annual vacation exodus. On the upside, summer is the time for several wonderful music festivals, including the **Festival Chopin** and **Jazz à La Villette** (p. 137), many of which take place in Paris's lovely parks and gardens.

GETTING TICKETS   You can get tickets in person at **Fnac,** the giant bookstore/ music chain that has one of the most comprehensive box offices in the city (follow the signs to the "Billeterie"). You can also **order your tickets online in English** at www.fnactickets.com or by phone at ℂ **08-92-68-36-22** (.34€ per min.). **Ticketnet.fr** offers a similar service where you can buy tickets either online (www.ticketnet.fr) or by phone (ℂ **08-92-39-01-00;** .34€ per min.).

Ile de la Citte with Notre Dame at night

For up-to-the-minute dates and schedules for what's happening in music, theater, dance, and film, pick up the **weekly listing magazines "Pariscope"** or **"l'Officiel des Spectacles"** (both .50€) the Parisian bibles for weekly events. Both come out on Wednesdays and are available at any newsstand. Online,

Télérama's website has good listings (www.telerama.fr; click on "sortir") as does **Evene** (www.evene.fr). For reviews, try the **"Paris Voice"** (www.parisvoice.com) an English-language online magazine that regularly reviews shows around town.

Discount hunters can stand in line at one of the city's three **half-price ticket booths,** all run by **Le Kiosque Théâtre** (www.kiosquetheatre.com; Tues–Sat 12:30–8pm, Sun 12:30–4pm). There's one in front of the Montparnasse train station; a second is on the west side of the Madeleine; and a third in the center of Place des Ternes (17th arrond.). Half-price tickets for same-day performances go on sale here at 12:30pm. You can also find plenty of ticket discounts online at **BilletRéduc** (www.billetreduc.com, in French).

Theater

Paris has hundreds of theaters, many of which have nightly offerings. Although most of it is in French, you can find a few English-language shows (see "Belly Laughs in English," below). Of course, avant-garde shows combining dance, theater, and images really need no translation.

Comédie-Française ★★   Established by Louis XVI in 1680, this legendary theater is the temple of classic French theater (Corneille, Racine, Molière), though in recent decades the troupe has branched out into more modern territory. In addition to the gorgeous just-restored main theater **(Salle Richelieu),** the company presents its offerings in its two other theaters: the medium-size **Théâtre du Vieux Colombier** (21 rue du Vieux Colombier, 6th arrond.; ✆ **01-44-39-87-00;** Métro: St-Sulpice or Sèvres–Babylone) and the smaller **Studio-Théâtre** (Galerie du Carrousel du Louvre, under the Pyramid, 99 rue de Rivoli, 1st arrond.; ✆ **01-44-58-98-58;** Métro: Palais Royal–Musée du Louvre). Place Colette, 1st arrond. ✆ **08-25-10-16-80** (.15€ per min). www.comedie-francaise.fr. Métro: Palais-Royal–Musée du Louvre.

Théâtre National de Chaillot ★★   Dance and theater are on equal footing at this beautiful Art Deco theater in the Palais de Chaillot, where contemporary choreographers and theater directors share a jam-packed program. There is a lot of blurring of lines here between the two disciplines; dance programs often include video and text, and theater productions often incorporate the abstract. 1 place du Trocadéro, 16th arrond; ✆ **01-53-65-30-00;** www.theatre-chaillot.fr. Métro: Trocadéro

Opera, Dance & Classical Concerts

Cité de la Musique ★★   This modern complex offers a wide range of music options, from classical to contemporary to jazz. Young musicians and rising stars are highlighted; small orchestras and chamber musicians also show up on the program. The Jazz à La Villette festival in August/September is not to be missed.

Ticket prices are very democratic, running from 15€ to around 45€. 221 av. Jean-Jaurès, 19th arrond. ✆ **01-44-84-44-84.** www.cite-musique.fr. Métro: Porte de Pantin.

Opéra de Paris ★★★ This mighty operation includes both the **Palais Garnier** (place de l'Opéra, 9th arrond.; see p. 103), an attraction in itself, and the **Opéra Bastille** (2 place de la Bastille, 12th arrond.) a slate-colored behemoth that has loomed over the place de la Bastille since 1989. The company has since split its energies between the two venues. In theory, more operas are performed at the Bastille, which has more space and top-notch acoustics, and the Garnier, home of the **Ballet de l'Opéra de Paris,** focuses more on dance, but the reality is you can see either at both. ✆ **08-92-89-90-90** (.34€ per minute); from outside of France: ✆ **(0)1-71-25-24-23.** www.operadeparis.fr.

Salle Pleyel ★★★ The Paris equivalent of Carnegie Hall, this mythic concert hall has hosted stars from Otto Klemperer to Louis Armstrong. The **Orchestre de Paris** makes its home here, and the **Radio France Philharmonic** also makes numerous appearances. Jazz and highbrow also pop up on the agenda. 252 rue du Faubourg-St-Honoré, 8th arrond. ✆ **01-42-56-13-13.** www.sallepleyel.fr. Métro: Ternes or Charle de Gaulle–Etoile.

Cabaret

Some visitors feel they simply haven't had the true Paris experience without seeing a show at the Moulin Rouge or the Lido, even though there is nothing particularly Parisian, or even French, about them these days. Today's audiences are more likely to arrive in tour buses than touring cars, and the shows are more Vegas than Paris. What you will see here is a lot of scenic razzmatazz and many sublime female bodies, mostly *torse nue* (topless).

The Crazy Horse ★ This temple to "The Art of the Nude" presents an erotic dance show with artistic aspirations. Be advised that unlike the other shows, this one is known for what the girls *aren't* wearing. The performers, who slither, swagger, and lip-synch with panache, have names like Zula Zazou and Nooka Karamel. Note that while it has no dining on site, it has dinner-show packages with nearby restaurants. 12 av. George V, 8th arrond. ✆ **01-47-23-32-32.** www.lecrazyhorse paris.com. 65€ show only with seats at the bar; 105€ show only seated; from 125€ show and champagne; show plus dinner packages 184€–215€. Métro: George V or Alma Marceau.

Moulin Rouge ★ When it opened in 1889, the Moulin Rouge was the talk of the town, and its huge dance floor, multiple mirrors, and floral garden inspired painters like Toulouse-Lautrec. Times have changed—today's Moulin Rouge relies heavily on lip-synching and pre-recorded music, backed up by dozens of befeathered Doriss Girls, long-legged ladies who prance about the stage. Be prepared for lots of glitz and not much else. 82 bd. Clichy, place Blanche, 18th arrond. ✆ **01-53-09-82-82.** www.moulinrouge.fr. 99€ show alone; 109€ show with half-bottle of champagne; 180€–210€ show with dinner. Métro: Blanche.

The Moulin Rouge

Jazz Clubs

Paris has been a fan of jazz from its beginnings, and many legendary performers like Sidney Bechet and Kenny Clark made the city their home. Still a haven for jazz musicians and fans of all stripes, Paris offers dozens of places to duck in and listen to a good set or two. Here are a few of the best:

Caveau des Oubliettes ★   There are not too many jazz clubs in the world where you can both listen to music and admire an authentic, French Revolution–era guillotine. Located in the Latin Quarter, just across the river from Notre-Dame, this underground nightspot was once a medieval prison. Today patrons laugh, drink, talk, and flirt in the narrow passageways and listen to jazz in the lounge. 52 rue Galande, 5th arrond. ✆ **01-46-34-23-09.** www.caveaudesoubliettes.fr. Free cover, 1 drink min. (from 5.50€). Métro: St-Michel.

New Morning ★★★   If you are looking for big names and hot acts, look no further. This place has incredible lineups, including jazz giants, pop legends, and international superstars, as well as top-grade local talent. This relatively large club (the room holds 300) fills up quickly, and no wonder: This truly is one of the best jazz venues in town, and the top ticket price is only around 30€. 7 rue des Petites-Ecuries, 10th arrond. ✆ **01-45-23-51-41.** www.newmorning.com. Cover 18€–28€. Métro: Château-d'Eau.

Le Sunset/Le Sunside ★★   One of several famous jazz clubs on the rue des Lombards (and it's a short street!), this one has a split personality. Le Sunset Jazz, is dedicated to electric jazz and international music, whereas le Sunside is devoted to acoustic jazz for the most part. Some of the hottest names in French jazz appear here regularly (Jacky Terrasson, Didier Lockwood) along with a new crop of international stars. 60 rue des Lombards, 1st arrond. ✆ **01-40-26-46-60.** www.sunset-sunside.com. Tickets 15€–30€. Métro: Châtelet.

The Bar Scene

Paris may not be the 24-hour party city some other international capitals claim to be, but it has plenty of places to sip, flirt, and be merry. In general, bars stay open until around 2am.

Andy Wahloo ★★ A play on the name of the famous pop artist, this is a tiny temple to 1970s North African culture and kitsch. Sip your drink beneath a silk-screened Moroccan coffee ad and listen to some of the best Algerian raï around. 69 rue des Gravilliers, 3rd arrond. ℭ **01-42-71-20-38.** www.andywahloo-bar.com. Métro: Arts et Métiers.

Le Bar du Plaza Athénée ★★ Knock yourself out and order a shockingly expensive drink at this classy, historic joint, which simply drips with glamour and fabulousness. The bar itself literally glows (it's lit from inside), fashioning an even more luminous aura around the sleek patrons. Hotel Plaza-Athénée, 25 av. Montaigne, 8th arrond. ℭ **01-53-67-66-65.** www.plaza-athenee-paris.fr. Métro: Alma-Marceau.

Experimental Cocktail Club ★ If you're looking for a sophisticated spot to spot stars, you've come to the right place. Known, not surprisingly, for its gourmet cocktails, this cosmopolitan lounge has the feel of a retro speakeasy. 37 rue St-Sauveur, 2nd arrond. ℭ **01-45-08-88-09.** www.experimentalcocktailclub.com. Métro: Sentier.

WINE BARS

Le Baron Rouge ★ This neighborhood institution spills out onto a corner that it shares with the sprawling Marché d'Aligre, a giant outdoor and covered market. It only has a few tables, but most people stand at the counter or outside, glass in hand, especially during market hours. It's a little rough-and-tumble getting your drink order in at the bar. 1 rue Théophile Roussel, 12th arrond. ℭ **01-43-43-14-32.** Métro: Ledru-Rollin.

Les Caves Populaires ★★ This is a neighborhood wine bar (yes, they have those in Paris), where locals come to shoot the breeze. The waiters are friendly, the decor low-key, and the wine and cheese-and-sausage platters cheap. 22 rue des Dames, 17th arrond. ℭ **01-53-04-08-32.** Métro: Place de Clichy.

The Club Scene

If you want to go out to a *boîte de nuit* (nightclub), you'll have plenty to choose from in Paris. Keep in mind that the French love their fashion, so dressing to impress is obligatory—sneakers will rarely get you past the line outside. Most clubs don't really get going until at least 11pm, if not later.

NIGHTCLUBS

Batofar ★★ For more than 15 years, this bright red boat has been the site of music and dancing and general good times. Docked on the quai François Mauriac, this multifunctional floating venue includes a dance club, a bar, a restaurant, and a terrace for cocktail hour and low-key soirees. On good nights, hundreds of gyrating dancers move in rhythm to house, garage, techno, and live jazz music. Facing 11 quai François Mauriac, 13th arrond. ℭ **01-53-60-17-00.** www.batofar.org. Métro: Quai de la Gare.

Nouveau Casino ★★ This former movie theater is now a giant dance club with live music, a huge bar that vaguely resembles an iceberg, hanging chandeliers, and a terrific program that includes all sorts of avant-garde dance music and bands with names like Flatbush Zombies and Moon Safari Club. 109 rue Oberkampf, 9th arrond. ℭ **01-43-57-57-40.** www.nouveaucasino.net. Métro: St-Maur, Parmentier, or Ménilmontant.

GAY & LESBIAN BARS & CLUBS

Paris has a vibrant gay nightlife scene, primarily centered around the **Marais.** Pick up one of the magazines devoted to the subject—like **"Qweek"** (www. qweek.fr)—for free in gay bars and bookstores. Also look for **"Têtu"** magazine at newsstands—it has special nightlife sections.

Le 3w Kafe ★   The most popular lesbian bar in the Marais, this is a good place to come to find company. Downstairs, a DJ spins on weekends, when there's dancing. Men can only enter the premises if accompanied by a woman. 8 rue des Ecouffes, 4th arrond. ✆ **01-48-87-39-26.** Métro: St. Paul.

Le Cox ★   You'll know it when you get here; it's where the crowd is spilling out onto the sidewalk. This place still gets big crowds, even though it's been here for years; people come for the bar as well as the great DJs. The clientele is a pleasant mix, everything from hunky American tourists to sexy Parisians. 15 rue des Archives, 4th arrond. ✆ **01-42-72-08-00.** www.cox.fr. Métro: Hôtel de Ville.

Open Café ★   More relaxed and more diverse than neighboring Le Cox, this cafe-bar has a busy sidewalk terrace that's usually full both day and night. Everyone from humble tourists to sharp-looking businessmen to TV stars hang out here. 17 rue des Archives, 4th arrond. ✆ **01-42-72-26-18.** www.opencafe.fr. Métro: Hôtel-de-Ville.

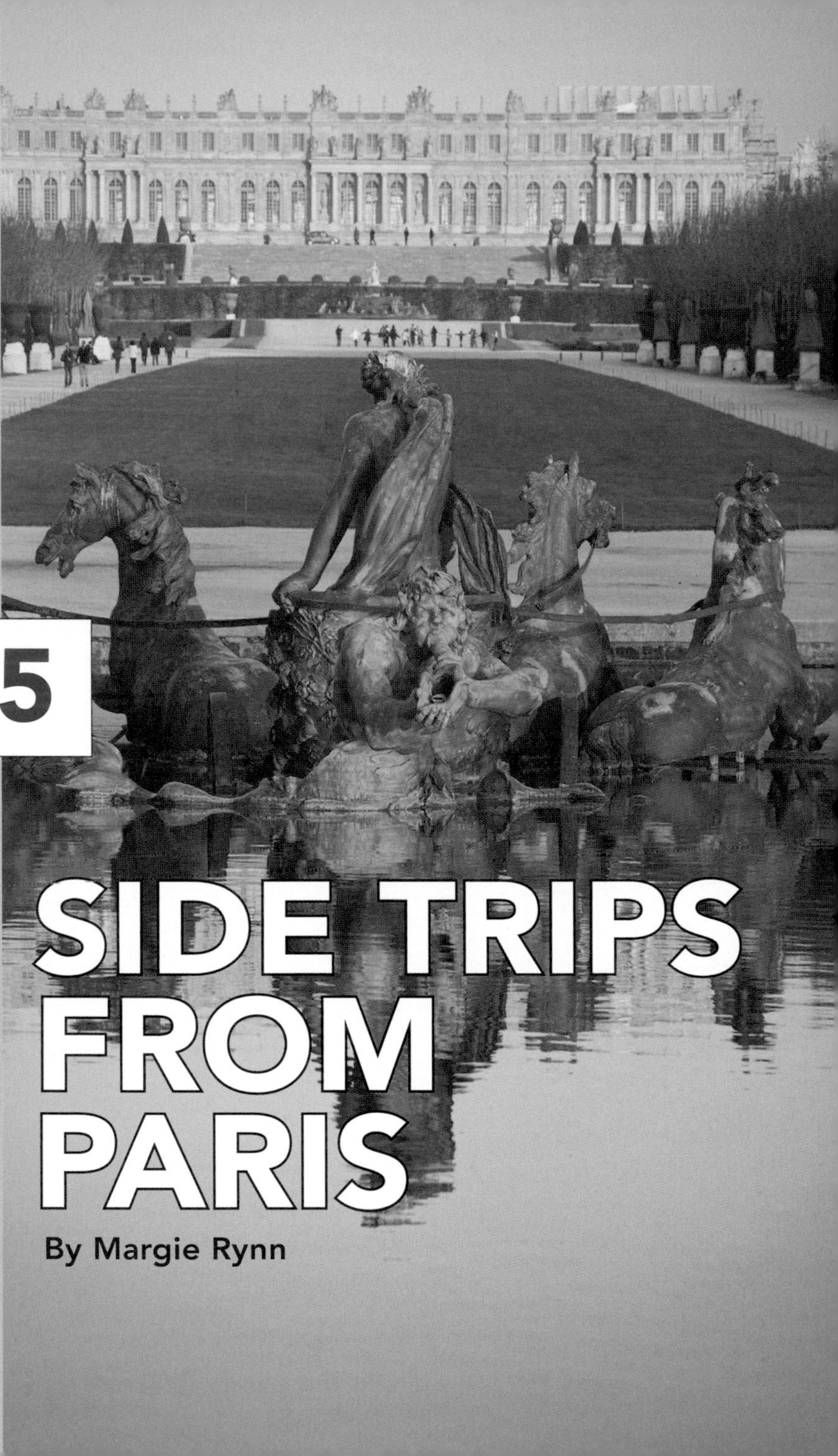

5

SIDE TRIPS FROM PARIS

By Margie Rynn

Whether you are escaping Paris for the day or embarking on an adventure to another part of France, there are plenty of wonderful destinations just an hour from the capital. Royal castles like **Versailles** and **Fontainebleau,** Monet's famous garden at **Giverny,** the stained glass windows of the cathedral of **Chartres,** and even **Disneyland** are all within the borders of the Ile-de-France, which is not an island but a region encompassing Paris and its outer environs. Just outside its borders but still within reach is the cathedral and champagne of **Reims.**

Your main problem will be deciding where to go. If you've never been there, your first choice should probably be the château and gardens of **Versailles.** They're close by, easily accessible by train, and truly not to be missed. **Chartres** would be my second choice, for its breathtaking Gothic cathedral, winding streets, and half-timbered houses. After that, it's a toss-up. If castles are your game, **Fontainebleau** and **Vaux-le-Vicomte** should be high on your list. Fans of Claude Monet will love exploring the gardens at **Giverny,** and families with kids in tow will appreciate **Disneyland Paris.** To get a taste of another French city (and try some champagne), **Reims** is a good choice.

VERSAILLES ★★★

21km (13 miles) SW of Paris; 71km (44 miles) NE of Chartres

The grandeur of the Château of Versailles is hard to imagine until you are standing in front of it. Immediately, you start to get an idea of the power (and ego) of the man who was behind it, King Louis XIV. One of the largest castles in Europe, it is also forever associated with another, less fortunate king, Louis XVI and his wife Queen Marie Antoinette, who were both forced to flee when the French Revolution arrived at their sumptuous doorstep. The palace's extraordinary gardens, designed by the legendary landscape architect André Le Nôtre, are almost worth the visit on their own.

Don't feel you have to see everything—for many, a visit to the palace is enough culture, and a nice relaxing stroll/picnic/nap in the park is a great way to finish off the day. If you can't handle crowds but you still want to get a taste of life during the Ancien Régime, you could just visit Marie Antoinette's Estate—you'll miss the palace, but you'll get to revel in a beautiful garden and see the pretty Trianons, hamlet, and other small buildings.

Essentials

ARRIVING   Take the **RER C** (www.transilien.fr; 30 min. from the Champs de Mars station) to **Versailles Rive Gauche–Château de Versailles.** Make sure the final destination for your train is Versailles Rive Gauche and *not* Versailles Chantier, which will leave you on the other end of town, a long walk from the

Château. Even worse, the Versailles Chantier trains actually run in the opposite direction, touring all around Paris before arriving at Versailles, which will add an hour or so to your journey. Assuming you've taken the right train, it's about a 5-minute walk from the train station to the château. For a little more (4.20€ adults), you can also take the **SNCF** Transilien suburban train (www.transilien. fr; 45 min.) from the Gare St-Lazare station to **Versailles-Rive Droite,** and then walk about 10 minutes to the Château (around 45 min. total).

Unless you have a **Paris Visite** or other pass that includes zones 1–4, you will need to buy a special ticket (one-way fare 3.45€ adults; 1.70€ children 4–10; free under 4); a regular Métro ticket will not suffice. Another option is to buy a 1-day **Mobilis** pass for zones 1–4 (11.20€), which gives you unlimited travel in those zones for the day. You can buy a ticket from any Métro or RER station; the fare includes a free transfer to the Métro.

TICKETS   If you are made of tough stuff and want to see everything, you can buy the all-inclusive **Château Passeport,** which grants you access to the main château, the gardens, the Trianon Palaces, and the Marie Antoinette Estate (Nov–Mar 18€ adults; free 17 and under; Apr–Oct including *Les Grandes Eaux Musicales* 25€ adults; free 17 and under). If you are merely human, you can buy a **ticket to just the Palace** (15€ adults; free 17 and under) or **just the Trianons and Marie Antoinette's Estate** (10€). A **Paris Museum Pass** will get you into everything except *Les Grandes Eaux Musicales* (Apr–Oct), so you'll have to buy a separate ticket to get into the gardens (9€).

VISITOR INFORMATION   **Château de Versailles,** ✆ 01-30-83-78-00, www. chateauversailles.fr. **Versailles Tourist Office,** 2 bis av. de Paris, ✆ 01-39-24-88-88, www.versailles-tourisme.com.

EVENING SHOWS   From mid-June to mid-September, there are spectacular **fountain night shows** (24€ adults; 20€ 6–17 years old) where you stroll around the gardens and enjoy illuminated fountains, music, and fireworks.

DAYTIME SHOWS   From April to October on weekends and Tuesdays, fountains play to Baroque music throughout the gardens closest to the castle, otherwise known as *Les Grandes Eaux Musicales* (depending on your ticket, this could be included, otherwise 9€; 7€ ages 6–17). If your ticket does not offer you entrance to this part of the gardens, the rest of the park is accessible from side entrances and is free of charge.

TICKETS   Purchase tickets to the shows at the château, online at www.chateau-versailles-spectacles.fr, or from any Fnac store (✆ 08-92-68-36-22, .34€ per min; www.fnacspectacles.com).

Where to Eat & Stay

Nuance ★ MODERN FRENCH   A cozy dining room, a modern menu, and reasonable prices are enough to keep locals crowding into this gourmet eatery, which is about a 10-minute walk from the Château of Versailles. Roast pork with honey and rosemary, sautéed scallops in a Thai bouillon, or a simple chicken brochette with curry sauce might be on the menu, depending on the season and your appetite.

10 bd. du Roi. ✆ **01-39-49-58-35.** www.restaurant-nuance.com. Main courses 13.90€–22.20€. Tues–Fri noon–1:30pm and 7:30–9:30pm, Sat 7:30–9:30pm.

Trianon Palace ★★★   Versailles is close enough to Paris that you don't need to spend the night, but if you are celebrating something special, this is one of the poshest hotels in the Ile de France. Elegant gardens and grounds, an indoor

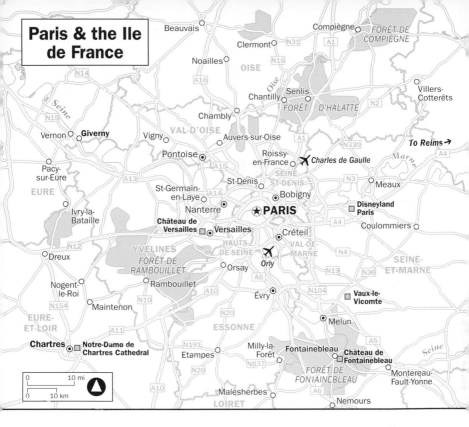

heated pool, 19th-century frills, luxurious rooms, and a two-star Michelin restaurant with a famous Scottish chef, **Gordon Ramsey au Trianon** (fixed-price menus at dinner start at 147€). A more low-key dining option is La Veranda, and if you need total relaxation, there's a Guerlain spa.

1 bd. de la Reine. **℃ 01-30-84-50-00.** www.trianonpalace.com. 199 units. 230€–600€ doubles, 350€–810€ junior suites, 1,000€–4,000€ suites. Parking 20€. **Amenities:** Bar, concierge, indoor pool, restaurants, spa, Wi-Fi (25€ per day).

The Château of Versailles

Back in the 17th century, after having been badly burned by a nasty uprising called Le Fronde, Louis XIV decided to move his court from Paris to Versailles, a safe distance from the intrigues of the capital. He also decided to have the court move in with him, where he could keep a close eye on them and nip any new plots or conspiracies in the bud. This required a new abode that was not only big enough to house his court (anywhere from 3,000 to 10,000 people would be palace guests on any given day), but also one that would be grand enough to let the world know who was in charge.

There was already a château on the site when Louis came to town; his father, Louis XIII, had built a small castle, "a hunting lodge," there in 1623. Louis, aka the "Sun King," brought in architects, artists, and gardeners to enlarge the castle and give it a new look. In 1668, architect Louis Le Vau, began work on the enormous "envelope," which literally wrapped the old castle in a second building.

Château of Versailles

Meanwhile, legendary garden designer André Le Notre was carving out formal gardens and a huge park out of what had been marshy countryside. Thousands of trees were planted, and harmonious geometric designs were achieved with flower beds, hedges, canals, and pebbled pathways dotted with sculptures and fountains.

Construction involved as many as 36,000 workers and ground on for years; in 1682 the King and his court moved in, but work went on right through the rest of his reign and into that of Louis XV. Louis XVI and his wife, Marie Antoinette, made few changes, but history made a gigantic one for them: On October 6, 1789, an angry mob of Parisians marched on the palace and the royal couple was forced to return to Paris. Versailles would never again be a royal residence.

The palace was ransacked during the Revolution, and in the years after it fell far from its original state of grace. Napoleon and Louis XVIII did what they could to bring the sleeping giant back to life, but by the early 1800s, during the reign of Louis-Philippe, the castle was slated for demolition. Fortunately for us, this forward-thinking king decided to invest his own money to save Versailles for future generations, and in 1837 the vast structure was made into a national museum. Little by little, precious furniture and art objects were retrieved or re-created; paintings, wall decorations, and ceilings were restored. Not surprisingly, restoration is ongoing, so be prepared for the unexpected when you arrive. Even if a few areas are closed, the place is so huge that should you feel so inclined, you can still tour yourself into a 17th-century stupor.

Touring the Palace

The "envelope," or the newer part of the building, includes a series of rooms called the **Grand Apartments,** used primarily for ceremonial events (a daily occurrence), the **Queen's Apartments,** and the **Galerie des Glaces.** These, along with the **King's Apartments,** and the **Chapel,** are the must-sees of the palace. If you have time and fortitude, you can take a **guided visit** to the royal

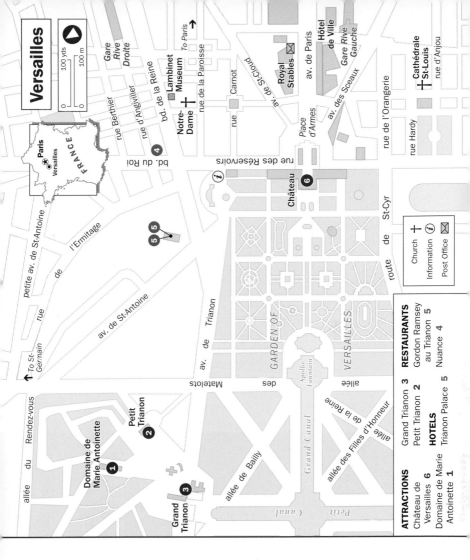

family's private apartments (16€, some in English, check website for schedule) to see a more intimate look at castle life.

Each room in the **Grand Apartments ★★★** is dedicated to a different planet, and each has a fabulous painting on the ceiling depicting the god or goddess associated with said heavenly sphere. The first and probably the most staggering paintings are in the **Salon d'Hercule ★★**: an enormous canvas by Paolo Veronese, *Christ at Supper with Simon,* and a splendid, divinity-bedecked ceiling portraying Hercules being welcomed by the gods of Olympus by Antoine Lemoyne. The **Salon d'Apollon ★**, not surprisingly, was the throne room, where the Sun King would receive ambassadors and other heads of state.

The ornate **Salon de Guerre ★** and **Salon de Paix ★** bookend the most famous room in the place, the recently restored **Galerie des Glaces (the Hall** of Mirrors) ★★★. Louis XIV commanded his painter-in-chief, Charles Le Brun, to paint the 12m-high (40-ft.) ceiling of this 73m-long (240-ft.) gallery with representations of his accomplishments. This masterwork is illuminated by light from the 17 windows that overlook the garden, which are matched on the opposite wall by 17 mirrored panels. This splendid setting was the scene of a historic event in a more recent century: In 1919, World War I officially ended when the Treaty of Versailles was signed here.

The **Queen's Apartments** ★★ include a gorgeous bedroom with silk hangings printed with lilacs and peacock feathers, which looks exactly as it did in 1789, when the Queen, Marie Antoinette, was forced to flee revolutionary mobs through a secret door (barely visible in the wall near her bed). The **King's Apartments** ★★★ are even more splendiferous, though in a very different style: Here the ceilings have been left blank white, which brings out the elaborate white and gold decoration on the walls. The **King's bedroom** ★★★, hung from top to bottom with gold brocade, is fitted with a banister that separated the King from the 100 or so people who would watch him wake up in the morning.

You should also make sure to see the **Chapel** ★★★, a masterpiece of light and harmony by Jules Hardouin Mansart, where the kings attended mass. This lofty space (the ceiling is over 25m/82 ft. high) reflects both Gothic and Baroque styles, combining a vaulted roof, stained glass, and gargoyles with columns and balustrades typical of the early 18th century.

Touring the Domaine de Marie Antoinette

Northwest of the fountain lies the **Domaine de Marie Antoinette** ★★★ (if you don't have a Château passport or museum pass you'll pay a separate ticket to get in). It was here that the young queen sought refuge from the strict protocol and infighting at the castle. Her husband gave her the **Petit Trianon** ★★, a small manor that Louis XV used for his trysts, which she transformed into a

The Hall of Mirrors, Versailles

stylish haven. She created an entire world around it, including a splendid **English garden ★**, several lovely pavilions, a jewel-like **theater ★★**, and even a small **hamlet ★** with a working farm and a dairy, where she and her friends would play cards and gossip, or just stroll in the "country." Although the **Grand Trianon ★** is not really linked to the story of Marie Antoinette, it is worth a brief visit. Built by Louis XIV as a retreat for himself and his family, this small marble palace consists of two large wings connected by an open columned terrace from which there is a delightful **view ★** of the gardens. The furniture and decor dates from the Napoleonic era.

Touring the Gardens & Park

The entire 800-hectare (2,000-acre) park is laid out according to a precise, symmetrical plan. From the terrace behind the castle, there is an astounding **view ★★★** that runs past two parterres, down a central lawn (the Tapis Vert), down the **Grand Canal ★★** and seemingly on into infinity. Le Nôtre's masterpiece is the ultimate example of French-style gardens; geometric, logical, and in perfect harmony—a reflection of the divine order of the cosmos. A solar theme is reflected in the statues and fountains along the main axis of the perspective; the most magnificent of these is the **Apollo Fountain ★★★** where the sun god emerges from the waves at dawn on his chariot. On the sides of the main axis, near the castle, are a set of six groves, or **bosquets ★**, leafy

One of many fountains in the gardens at Versailles

mini-gardens hidden by walls of shrubbery; some were used as small outdoor ballrooms for festivities, others for intimate rendezvous out of reach of the prying eyes of the court. Today, you can **picnic, bike ride** (bikes can be rented next to the restaurant), or even **row a boat** on a sunny day.

Place d'Armes. ✆ **01-30-83-78-00.** www.chateauversailles.fr. Palace 15€ adults, free for 18 and under. Marie Antoinette's Estate 10€ adults, everything free for children 17 and younger. Palace Apr–Oct Tues–Sun 9am–6:30pm; Nov–Mar Tues–Sun 9am–5:30pm. Marie Antoinette's Estate Apr—Oct Tues–Sun noon–6:30pm; Nov–Mar Tues–Sun noon–5:30. Garden and park: Apr–Oct 8am–8:30pm; Nov–Mar 8am–6pm.

CHARTRES ★★★

88km (58 miles) SW of Paris; 76km (47 miles) NW of Orléans

You'll see it long before you see the actual town: the spire of the cathedral of Chartres rising above a sea of wheat fields. About an hour from Paris, you can easily visit this stunning church and its inspiring stain-glassed windows and still have enough time to wander through the narrow streets of the old town.

Essentials

ARRIVING   Direct **trains** leave from Paris' Gare Montparnasse and take about an hour (15.60€ one-way). For information visit www.voyages-sncf.com or call ✆ **36-35.** If **driving** from Paris take A10/A11 southwest and follow signs to Le Mans and Chartres. (The Chartres exit is marked.)

VISITOR INFORMATION   The **Office de Tourisme** in the Maison du Saumon, 8 rue de la Poissonerie (✆ **02-37-18-26-26;** www.chartres-tourisme.com).

Where to Stay & Eat

Le Grand Monarque ★★   Located in the town center, this grand old hotel has been in the same family for decades and is a Chartres institution. The comfortably chic rooms have a classic French appeal; many open up onto an Italian-style patio. The hotel is famed for its gourmet restaurant, **Le Georges,** a Michelin-starred affair that draws food lovers from far and wide (fixed-price menus start at 51€). The menu highlights local products like rabbit stuffed with foie gras, or farther flung steamed sea bass with truffles.

22 place des Epars, Chartres. ✆ **02-37-18-15-15.** www.bw-grand-monarque.com. 55 units. 99€–206€ double; 200€–265€ suite. Parking 8€. **Amenities:** 2 restaurants, babysitting, bar, laundry service, room service, spa, free Wi-Fi.

Exploring the Cathedral

With its carved portals and three-tiered flying buttresses, this cathedral would be a stunning sight even without its legendary **stained-glass windows**—though the world would be a drearier place. For these ancient glass panels are truly glorious: a kaleidoscope of colors so deep, so rich, and so bright, it's hard to believe they are some 700 years old. Meant as teaching devices more than artwork, the windows functioned as a sort of enormous cartoon, telling the story of Christ through pictures to a mostly illiterate populace. From its beginnings, pilgrims came from far and near to see a piece of cloth that believers say was worn by the Virgin Mary during Christ's birth. The **relic** is still here, but these days it's primarily a different sort of pilgrim that is drawn to Chartres: Over 1.5 million tourists come here every year.

A Romanesque church stood on this spot until 1194, when a fire burnt it virtually to the ground. All that remained were the towers, the Royal Portal, and a few remnants of stained glass. The locals were so horrified that they sprung to action; in a matter of only 3 decades a new cathedral was erected, which accounts for its remarkably unified Gothic architecture. This was one of the first churches to use buttresses as a building support, allowing the architect (whose name has

Stained glass rose window at Chartres Cathedral

Tours, Guided & Otherwise

For over 3 decades, Malcolm Miller has been studying the cathedral and giving terrific **guided tours in English.** The 75-minute tour usually begins at noon and sometimes also at 2:45pm Monday through Saturday (10€ adults; 5€ students). No need to reserve; a sign inside at the entrance to the gift shop indicates that day's tour schedule. You can also rent an audioguide (in English) for 6.20€.

been lost) to build its walls at twice the height of the standard Romanesque cathedrals and make space for its famous windows. The new cathedral was dedicated in 1260 and has miraculously survived the centuries with relatively little damage. The French Revolution somehow spared the cathedral. During World War I and World War II, the precious windows were carefully dismounted piece by piece and stored in a safe place in the countryside.

The cathedral's **facade ★★** is a remarkable assemblage of religious art and architecture. The tower to your right (the **Old Tower,** or South Tower) is topped by its original sober Romanesque spire; that on your left (**New Tower,** or North Tower) was blessed with an elaborate Gothic spire in the early 1500s, when the original burned down. Below is the **Royal Portal ★★★**, a masterpiece of Romanesque art. Swarming with kings, queens, prophets, and priests, this sculpted entryway tells the story of the life of Christ. You can **climb to the top of the New Tower** to take in the **view ★**; just remember to wear rubber-soled shoes, as the 300 steps are a little slippery after all these centuries.

As you enter the cathedral, the dimness is pierced by the radiant colors of the **stained-glass windows ★★★**. Three windows on the west side of the building, as well as the beautiful rose window to the south called **Notre Dame de la Belle Verière ★** date from the earlier 12th-century structure; the rest, with the exception of a few modern panels, are of 13th-century origins. The scenes depicted in glass, read from bottom to top, recount stories from the Bible as well as the lives of the saints. You will soon find yourself wondering how medieval artists, with low-tech materials, managed to create such vivid colors. The blues, in particular, seem to be divinely inspired. In fact, scientists have pierced at least part of the mystery: The blue was made with sodium and silica compounds that made the color stand up to the centuries better than other colors.

Another marvel is the **chancel enclosure ★★★**, which separates the chancel (the area behind the altar) from the ambulatory (the walkway that runs around the outer chapels). Started in 1514 by Jehan de Beauce, this intricately sculpted wall depicts dozens of saints in a recounting of the lives of the Virgin and Christ. Back in the ambulatory is the Chapel of the Martyrs, where the cathedral's cherished **relic** resides: a piece of cloth that the Virgin Mary apparently wore at the birth of Christ, which was a gift of Charles the Bald in 876.

Chartres also harbors a rare **labyrinth ★**, which is traced on the floor of the cathedral near the nave. A large circle, divided into four parts, is entirely filled by a winding path that leads to the center. *Note:* The cathedral asks that visitors not talk or wander around during mass, which is generally held in the late morning and early evening. You are welcome to sit in on services, of course.

16 Cloître Notre-Dame. ✆ **02-37-21-22-07.** www.cathedrale-chartres.monuments-nationaux.fr. General admission to the cathedral is free, admission to the towers 7.50€ adults, 4.50€ adults 18–25, free for children 17 and under. Cathedral open daily 8:30am–7:30pm.

Exploring the Old Town

Give yourself a little time to explore the medieval cobbled streets of the **Vieux Quartier (Old Town)** ★. There are several gabled houses in the narrow lanes near the cathedral, including the colorful facades of **rue Chantault,** one of which is 8 centuries old. Seek out rue du Bourg, where you'll find the famous **Salmon House** (which houses the tourist office) and some lovely sculptures (including a certain fish). In the lower town, you can stroll along the picturesque **Eure River** with its stone bridges and ancient wash-houses. If you go on a Saturday or Wednesday morning there is a covered farmers market in **place Billard** (until 1pm), the perfect place to grab some supplies for a lunch in the park behind the cathedral or along the river.

Musée des Beaux-Arts de Chartres ★   Housed in an impressive former Episcopal palace, this museum of fine arts boasts a collection covering the 16th to 20th centuries, including the work of masters such as Zurbarán, Watteau, and Soutine.

29 Cloître Notre-Dame. ✆ **02-37-90-45-80.** May–Oct Wed and Sat 10am–noon and 2–6pm, Sun 2–6pm; the rest of the year, until 5pm. Admission 3.40€ adults, 1.70€ students, free 17 and under.

FONTAINEBLEAU ★★★

60km (37 miles) S of Paris, 74km (46 miles) NE of Orléans

Napoleon called it "the house of the centuries; the true home of kings," and he had a point: Fontainebleau was a royal residence for more than 700 years. Elegant and dignified, this grand château carries the architectural imprint of many a monarch, in particular, Francis I, Henri IV, and Napoleon I. Surrounded by a dense forest and verdant countryside, a trip out here is a relaxing green interlude to your Parisian trip.

Essentials

ARRIVING   **Trains** to Fontainebleau leave from the Gare de Lyon (schedules at www.transilien.fr). The 40-minute trip costs 8.75€ for adults and 4.35€ for ages 4–10 one-way. From the Fontainebleau–Avon train station take the local bus (line 1) direction Lilas, to the Château; the fare is 1.90€ one-way. Buses are timed to arrive with the train from Paris. If you're **driving** from Paris, take the A6 south, exit Fontainebleau.

VISITOR INFORMATION   The **Office de Tourisme** is at 4 rue Royale, Fontainebleau (✆ **01-60-74-99-99;** www.fontainebleau-tourisme.com), opposite the main entrance to the château.

Where to Stay

Hôtel Aigle-Noir ★★   This 18th-century mansion, once the home of Cardinal de Retz, is just down the street from the château. You'll pass through mighty gates and a grand courtyard before you enter the hotel, which is one of Fontainebleau's most elegant. Rooms are decked out with antiques and reproductions, walls are covered with period prints, and the staff will make you feel that you are one of the Cardinal's close friends. A Napoléon III-style bar completes the picture.

27 place Napoleon–Bonaparte. ✆ **01-60-74-60-00.** www.hotelaiglenoir.com. 53 units. 115€– 320€ double; 240€–480€ suite. Parking 12€. **Amenities:** Bar, concierge, laundry service, room service, free Wi-Fi.

Where to Eat

Auberge de la Croix d'Augas ★ SAVOYARD   This country inn is located
2.5km (1½ miles) from the château in the forest of Fontainebleau. The decor and
the menu resemble that of an Alpine chalet; Savoyard specialties like fondue,
raclette, and tartiflette figure prominently here. Don't worry, if you aren't up for
these cheese, potato, and ham-laden dishes there are also pasta, fish, and steak
choices. The rustic setting has lots of wood beams and a lovely terrace for outdoor dining in good weather.

Exit Fontainebleau on bd. de Maréchal Foch (rte. D606) to rte. D116, about 1km (½ mile) into the
forest. © **01-64-23-49-25.** www.restaurant-fontainebleau.fr. Main courses 9.90€–20.60€; fixed-
price menu lunch 14.90€, fixed-price menu dinner 20.80€. Daily noon–2pm and 7:15–10pm.

L'Axel ★★★ MODERN FRENCH   If, after a few hours experiencing life in
a castle you feel like treating yourself to a royal meal, this is the place to find one.
Widely hailed as a rising culinary star, chef Kunihisa Goto creates exciting French
dishes with a dash of Japanese *je ne sais quoi*, like Wagyu steak with sweet potatoes and onions, or sea bass and oysters with crispy soybeans and truffles. Reservations are a must.

43 rue de France. © **01-64-22-01-57.** www.laxel-restaurant.com. Main courses 39€–50€; fixed-
price lunch 33€; fixed-price dinner 52€–90€. Apr–Oct Thurs–Sun 12:15–2pm and 7:30–9:30pm,
Mon and Wed 7:30–9:30pm. Nov–Mar Thurs–Sun 12:15–2pm and 7:30–9:30pm, Wed
7:30–9:30pm.

Exploring Fontainebleau

Though kings were already living here by the 12th century, it was during the
Renaissance that Fontainebleau really took on its regal allure. In 1528, inveterate
castle-builder King François I decided to completely rebuild Fontainebleau and
make it into a palace that would rival the marvels of Rome. He tore down most
of the medieval castle, and hired an army of architects and artisans to construct
a new one. He also imported a passel of Italian painters, including Il Rosso and
Primaticcio, whose style of painting, featuring frescoes in bright colors with sen-
suous (often nude) figures in mythological landscapes, became known as the
School of Fontainebleau.

After François' death, work continued, but it wasn't until Henri IV arrived
on the scene in the 17th century that there were more major transformations.
Henri added several wings and a courtyard (the **Cour des Offices**), and invited
a new clutch of artists, who established a second School of Fontainebleau. This
time, the artists were of French and Flemish origins (Ambrose Dubois, Martin
Fréminet, and others), and used oil paint and canvas instead of frescos. Louis
XIV, preferring Versailles, didn't bother much with Fontainebleau, but both Louis
XV and Louis XVI left their mark. Napoleon also made a lasting imprint on the
castle's interior. Fontainebleau made an imprint on the Emperor as well: On April
20, 1814, he abdicated here, before being sent off to exile on the island of Elba.

Touring the Château

Most of what you'll want to see (and what I describe below) is in the **Grands
Appartements.** The **Petits Appartements,** a series of rooms that were Napoleon's private residence, requires an additional ticket.

Your first stop will be the **Cour du Cheval Blanc** ★★ at the entrance to
the palace. It was in this grand square, which is surrounded by wings of the castle

on three sides, that Napoleon said adieu to his faithful imperial guards. "Continue to serve France," he pleaded. "Her welfare was my only concern." The sumptuous **horseshoe staircase ★★** was contributed by Henri II. On the left, as you enter, is the **Chapelle de la Trinité ★**. When he was 7, Louis XIII climbed up the scaffolding to watch Martin Fréminet, his art instructor, paint the glorious ceiling. Linking the chapel with the royal apartments is the **Gallery of François I ★★★**, a stunning example of Renaissance art, whose walls are covered with exceptional frescos, moldings, and boiseries (carved woodwork). Throughout the gallery (and elsewhere in the castle) you will see the salamander, François' official symbol.

The other major must-see is the **Salle de Bal ★★★**. This 30m (98-ft.) long ballroom is a feast of light and color; the frescos by Primaticcio and Nicolo dell'Abate have been completely restored, and their rich hues radiate like they were painted yesterday. The monumental fireplace at the far end was designed by 16th-century architect Philibert Delorme.

The **Royal Apartments ★★** were decorated and redecorated by successive monarchs. Louis XIII was born in the **Salon Louis XIII ★**, a fact that is symbolized in the ceiling mural showing Love riding a dolphin. Though several different queens slept in the **Chambre de l'Impératrice ★★**, its current setup reflects the epoch of Empress Josephine (Napoleon's first wife). The sumptuous bed, crowned in gilded walnut and covered in embroidered silk, was made for Marie Antoinette in 1787. The queen would never see it; the Revolution exploded before she could arrange a royal visit to the château. Napoleon transformed the Kings' bedroom into the **Salle du Trône ★**, or Throne Room. It's easy to imagine the emperor receiving his subjects up there in blue velvet, bookended by two huge Napoleonic standards.

The life of the emperor is celebrated at the **Musée Napoléon Ier ★**, located in the Louis XV wing, displaying historic memorabilia and artwork relating to his reign, like the tent he slept in during military campaigns, and a remarkable mechanical desk. With an additional ticket, you can visit the **Petits Appartements,** which date from Louis XV, but were redecorated in Empire style for Napoleon and his Empress (first Josephine, then Marie-Louise).

Touring the Gardens

The formal gardens must have been beautiful when André Le Nôtre put his hand to them in the 17th century, but today, though well-kept, they look a little arid. More lush is the **Garden of Diane ★**, a quiet spot of green on the north side of the castle created during the time of François I, which centers around a statue of the goddess surrounded by four dogs. The **English Garden ★**, complete with an artificial stream and lush groves of tall trees, was added by Napoleon. The vast

---

Hiking Along Trails Left by French Kings

The Forest of Fontainebleau is riddled with *sentiers* (hiking trails) made by French kings and their entourages who went hunting in the forest. A *Guide des Sentiers* is available at the tourist information center (see above, you can also download trail maps from their website).

Bike paths also cut through the forest. You can rent bikes at **A La Petite Reine,** 14 rue de la Paroisse, a few blocks from the château (© **01-60-74-57-57;** www. alapetitereine.com; 8€ per hour, 15€ for a full day.)

Carp Pond ★, which extends directly from the south side of the **Cour de la Fontaine,** has a small island with a pavilion where an afternoon snack would be served to royal residents. Surrounding the gardens and its park is the enormous **Fontainebleau Forest ★★**, which, if you have the time, is definitely worth the visit (see box, below).

Place du Général-de-Gaulle. ℂ **01-60-71-50-70.** www.musee-chateau-fontainebleau.fr. *Grands appartements* 11€ adults, 9€ students 18–25; ticket to *petits appartements* 6.50€ adults, 5€ students 18–25; all admissions free 17 and under. Apr–Sept Wed–Mon 9:30am–6pm; Oct–Mar Wed–Mon 9:30am–5pm.

VAUX-LE-VICOMTE ★★★

47km (29 miles) SE of Paris; 24km (15 miles) NE of Fontainebleau

This jewel of a castle comes with a story that reads like a Hollywood screenplay. Nicolas Fouquet, the château's original owner, was a brilliant finance minister and lover of arts and leisure. In the early 1700s he was the toast of Paris. His circle included France's top artists and intellectuals, drawn to his gorgeous home in the country. Unfortunately, Fouquet underestimated the jealousy of his superiors, in particular the young king, Louis XIV.

Things came to a head one fateful night in the summer of 1661. As Voltaire put it, "On August 17, at 6 in the evening, Nicolas Fouquet was the King of France; at two in the morning, he was nobody." Oblivious to the fact that the king was already fed up with his penchant for stealing the spotlight, Fouquet organized a stupendous party in his honor. He pulled out all the stops: There was a sumptuous meal, a play written and performed by Molière, and a fireworks display—no one had seen anything like it. Three weeks later, Fouquet was arrested on trumped-up charges of embezzlement. The king seized the castle, confiscated its contents, and hired its artists and architects to work on Versailles. Though writers

Château de Vaux-le-Vicomte

like Madame de Sévigné and La Fontaine pleaded with the king on Fouquet's behalf, the once untouchable financial minister spent the rest of his life in prison.

Essentials

ARRIVING   Though it's close to Paris, Vaux-le-Vicomte is hard to reach by mass transit. By **car,** take the A4 east to the N104 south to Vert Saint-Denis, then the D82 east to Vaux-le-Vicomte. There are **trains** from Gare de Lyon to Melun (30 min; 8.10€ adults, 4.05€ children 4–10), but then you'll need to take a taxi from the station 6.5km (4 miles) to Vaux-le-Vicomte (18€–20€ each way). On weekends and holidays between April and October, there is a shuttle bus ("Chateaubus") from the Melun train station (7€ per person round trip, free under 12). From April to October there are also **day tour packages** including transport from the center of Paris and château tickets (www.pariscityvision.com; from 61€ per person).

VISITOR INFORMATION   The nearest **tourist office** is in Melun, at 18 rue Paul Doumer (www.ville-melun.fr; ✆ **01-64-52-64-52**).

Where to Eat & Stay

Château de Courtry ★   Unless you want to sleep in uninspiring Melun, your best overnight bet is to find a bed-and-breakfast, like this lovely little château. While the inside might not be quite as impressive as its noble exterior, the three guest rooms are quite comfortable, and your hosts also offer various meal possibilities, from brunch to gourmet picnics to candlelight dinner (17€–39€).

12 rue du Château, Sivry-Courtry, 6km (3.7 mi) from the château on the D215 and the D126. ✆ **01-60-69-36-01** or 06-62-79-78-20. www.chateaudecourtry.com. 3 units. 90€ doubles, 93€–96€ family room for up to 5 people. Rates include breakfast. **Amenities:** Meals for guests, free Wi-Fi (on ground floor only).

Touring the Château

Though his reaction was extreme, Louis XIV's jealousy is not too hard to understand when you are standing in front of Vaux-le-Vicomte; the edifice is the epitome of 17th-century elegance. The castle was eventually released to Fouquet's widow, and has remained in private hands ever since. The ancestors of the current owners, Jean-Charles and Alexandre de Vogüé, bought the palace in 1875, when they started a much-needed restoration program to restore Vaux to its original splendor. The château is now entirely restored and filled with splendid tapestries, carpets, and art objects.

One of its most impressive rooms was actually never finished: the oval **Grand Salon ★★**, which Fouquet never got a chance to paint or furnish. Here, you actually don't miss all the decorative trimmings; the bare white pilasters and detailed carvings have a classical beauty that stands on its own. For something more ornate, there is the **King's bedroom ★★**; this lavish ensemble of chandeliers, brocade, and painted ceiling (by Le Brun) was a model for the King's Apartments in Versailles. The **Salon des Muses ★** also gets a fabulous ceiling by Le Brun, as well as several fine tapestries covering its walls. To help imagine what Fouquet's dinner parties were like, take a stroll through the elaborately decorated **Salle à Manger ★** (dining room), where a table is set with stacks of rare fruits and gold candlesticks, and a sideboard displays a set of extraordinary majolica. You can see life on the other side of the banquet table downstairs in the **kitchen,** with its more humble servants' dining area.

The **gardens ★★★** are almost as spectacular as the château. The carefully calculated geometry of the flowerbeds and alleyways makes this a study in harmony, even if you couldn't call them exactly natural. Nature is lurking close by, however—the entire ensemble is surrounded by seemingly endless forest. Just behind the castle are two enormous beds of boxwood trimmed into elaborate designs; Le Nôtre took his inspiration from the patterns in Turkish carpets. The far end of the gardens is crossed by a large **canal.** There you will also find a series of grottos, each sheltering a statue of a different river god. Finally, from the last basin, turn around and take in the lovely **view ★** of the gardens with the château rising in the background.

77950 Maincy. ✆ **01-64-14-41-90.** www.vaux-le-vicomte.com. Admission 16.50€ adults, 13.50€ students, seniors and children 6–16, free for children 5 and under. Mar to mid-Nov 10am–6pm. Closed mid-Nov to Feb, except for certain days during the Christmas holidays.

GIVERNY ★★

74km (46 miles) NW of Paris

In 1883, Claude Monet and his family moved to a tiny town north of Paris, where they rented a house that came with almost 1 hectare (2½ acres) of land. He didn't know it then, but he would spend the rest of his life there, painting scenes from the fabulous garden that he would create out of the grassy slope behind his house. Today, the **Fondation Claude Monet à Giverny** is open to the public, and for a small fee, you too can wander in and out of the brilliant flower beds, lush bowers, and shady arbors that inspired this impressionist master.

Essentials

ARRIVING **Trains** (SNCF, for schedules visit www.voyages-sncf.com) leave every hour or two from the Gare St-Lazare train station to Vernon, the closest stop to Giverny, which is about 7km (4.5 miles) away. The trip takes around 45 minutes and costs 14.30€ one-way. From Vernon you can either take a shuttle bus (8€ round-trip) or rent a bike at the station (L'Arrivé de Giverny, ✆ **02-32-21-16-01;** 14€ for the day) and pedal there on the marked bike path.

If you're **driving,** take the Autoroute A14 to the A13 toward Rouen. Take exit 14 for Vernon/Bonnières and cross the Seine on to Bennecourt. From here, a direct road with signs leads to Giverny.

VISITOR INFORMATION The **Office de Tourisme des Portes de l'Eure** is right next to the Fondation Monet, at 80 rue Claude Monet (✆ **02-32-51-39-60;** www.cape-tourisme.fr).

Where to Eat & Stay

Le Jardin des Plumes ★★   Top chef and local boy Eric Guerin recently turned this Anglo-Norman mansion into a chic yet comfy hotel and restaurant, offering colorful and fresh accommodations and excellent cuisine to Monet fans (and others). Half of the eight guest rooms are in the main house, the others are in a modern annex; some look out on a lovely garden. The restaurant shares the garden view; the exquisite fixed-price menus start at 29€ at lunch and 39€ at dinner.

1 rue de Milieu, a short walk from the gardens. ✆ **02-32-54-26-35.** www.lejardindesplumes.fr. 8 units. 160€–200€ doubles, 250€–290€ suites. Nov–Mar closed Mon–Tues; closed all Jan. **Amenities:** Restaurant, free Wi-Fi.

Exploring Giverny

When you enter this green haven, you'll quickly realize that Monet wasn't just a brilliant painter; he was also a gifted gardener. By the end of his life, the garden was just as much a work of art as the paintings, or perhaps they *were* the paintings. If you have already visited the Orangerie in Paris, and seen his magical Nympheas, or water lilies, spread across huge canvases in two oval-shaped rooms, in a way, you have already visited this garden; they were painted here, with the aim of faithfully recreating the feeling you would have if you were looking at the same flowers at Giverny.

There are actually two gardens here: The first and closest to the house is the **Clos Normand ★★**, a French-style garden that is resolutely orderly and geometric, despite the riot of colors. Gladioli, larkspur, phlox, daisies, and asters clamor for your attention; irises and oriental poppies brighten the western lawn. Monet painted here, but his famous water lily series was born in the **Water Garden ★★★**. Monet bought this piece of property in 1893 with the intention of building a garden that resembled those in the Japanese prints he collected; the ornate **Japanese**

Monet's garden and pond at Giverny

bridge ★ figures prominently in several of his canvases. Today the garden looks much as it did when Monet was immortalizing it. Willows weep quietly into the ponds, heather, ferns, azaleas, and rhododendrons carpet the banks. This garden was a sanctuary for the painter, who came here to contemplate and explore one of his favorite subjects: the complex interplay of water and light.

At **Monet's house** ★ you can see the artist's living spaces as well as his **Japanese print collection.** Unfortunately, none of his paintings are on display.

Be advised that it will be virtually impossible to experience the gardens as Monet did—more or less alone. This is an extremely popular outing for both individuals and tour groups, so your best bet is to come on a slow day like Monday or Wednesday, and/or to arrive after 3pm, when the groups have left.

84 rue Claude-Monet. ✆ **02-32-51-28-21.** www.fondation-monet.com. Admission 9.50€ adults, 5€ students, free for children 6 and under. Apr–Oct daily 9:30am–6pm. Closed Nov–Mar.

REIMS ★★

143km (89 miles) E of Paris; 29km (18 miles) N of Epernay

Blessed with a gorgeous cathedral, site of royal coronations for a thousand years, Reims (pronounced "rahns") is the largest city in the region and the unofficial capital of that deliciously fizzy nectar known as champagne. While it was almost obliterated by bombing during World War I, parts of the historic center have survived, including the above-mentioned cathedral, which has been beautifully restored. If it is not as quaint as other French cities, it is a lively and interesting place to visit, with a large pedestrian-only shopping district and plenty of historic monuments.

The main draw here though, aside from the cathedral, is bubbly. Some of the most famous names in champagne are found here, including Pommery, Mumms, and Ruinart; all offer tours and tastings. Reims makes a good base for exploring the Champagne region, and is just a short hop from the vineyards of Epernay.

Essentials

ARRIVING   High-speed, direct **TGV trains** leave for Reims from Paris's Gare de l'Est several times per day (trip time: 45–50 min.; 34€–59€ one-way). There are 8 to 10 direct trains per day from Strasbourg into the Champagne Ardennes TGV station 8km (5 miles) outside of town, with connections to the center (trip time: approximately 2 hr.; 55€–75€ one-way). For information, visit www.voyages-sncf. com or call ✆ **36-58.** If you are **driving** from Paris, take the A4 east.

The **Tourist Office** is next to the cathedral, 2 rue Guillaume de Machault (📞 **03-26-77-45-00;** www.reims-tourisme.com).

Where to Eat & Stay

Best Western Hôtel de la Paix ★★
Sleek rooms with contemporary furniture draw tourists to this moderately priced hotel located just a few minutes walk from the cathedral. If that's not enough to convince you, maybe the lovely indoor pool and fitness center will. The hotel's restaurant, Café de la Paix, specializes in well-executed seafood dishes, but there's a good range of traditional brasserie fare (meat) on the menu as well (fixed-price dinner menus start at 19€).

9 rue Buirette, Reims. 📞 **03-26-40-04-08.** www.hotel-lapaix.fr. 165 units. 125€–230€ double; 350€–400€ suite. Parking 14€. **Amenities:** Bar, exercise room, indoor pool, room service, restaurant, sauna, free Wi-Fi.

Les Crayères ★★★
This palatial neoclassic château is one of the region's most wanted accommodations, and it's not hard to understand why. Located in a 7-hectare (17-acre) park, the château fulfills all of your country manor fantasies, with a lush, classically French décor, rich fabrics, ornate paneling and opulent details. The guest rooms range from the relatively small and sedate "Baronne" category, to the splendid "Imperatrice" suite the size of a small apartment. The restaurant, **Le Parc,** is equally exquisite, complete with two Michelin stars and a heavenly menu (fixed-price dinner menus 120€–210€). Less heady fare is on offer at the **Le Jardin,** a more casual option (fixed-price menus 31€–47€).

64 bd. Henri-Vasnier, Reims. 📞 **03-26-24-90-00.** www.lescrayeres.com. 20 units. 370€–735€. Closed last week in Dec and first 2 weeks of Jan. **Amenities:** 2 restaurants, bar, babysitting, concierge service, laundry service, room service, tennis court, free Wi-Fi.

Where to Eat

Le Millénaire ★★★ MODERN FRENCH
This is yet another gourmet institution in a city that doesn't lack for good food. You'll be served in a streamlined modern room with lofty ceilings and an amazing menu: lobster roasted with wild mushrooms, sweetbreads with truffles—this is the place to *se faire un petit plaisir*, that is, spoil yourself. Desserts are just as delicious—the problem is saving room for them.

4-6 rue Bertin. 📞 **02-26-08-26-62.** www.lemillenaire.com. Main courses 38€–59€; fixed-price menus 35€–94€. Mon–Fri noon–2pm and Mon–Sat 7–10pm.

Le Jamin ★ FRENCH
Classic, unpretentious dishes are given a dash of modern flair at this popular restaurant, where the chef is wont to come out and chat with the customers at the end of the meal service. The menu might include a sautéed cod in champagne, or steak with a light mustard sauce. Finish off with a slice of local Brie de Meaux.

18 bd. Jamin. 📞 **03-26-07-37-30.** www.lejamin.com. Main courses 15.50€–24€; fixed-price menus 23.50€–36€. Tues–Sun noon–2:30pm, Tues–Sat 7:30–9:30pm.

Exploring the City

Cathédrale Notre-Dame de Reims ★★★ CATHEDRAL
This mighty cathedral has survived the centuries (it was damaged but left standing when the city was bombed to smithereens in World War I) and today draws tourists (and the faithful) from far and wide who come to admire its magnificent Gothic

Reims

To Laon

r. du Mont d'Arène
r. de St-Brice
bd. L. Roederer
Gare de Reims
bd. du Gén. Leclerc
pl. Drouet d'Erlon
r. Chátivesle
r. Burette
r. de Talleyrand
r. de l'Etape
Condorcet
r. de Thillos
Vesle

To Epernay

Centre des Congrès

ERLON

HINCMAR

To Soissons

chaussée Bocquaine

To Paris

autoroute de l'Est

bd. P. Doumer

r. Clovis

rue du Jard

rue des

rue de Venise

rue Capucins

des Moulins

rue F. Roosevelt
rue de Laon

Porte Mars

rue

bd. Foch

bd. Joffre

rue Thiers

cours J.-B. Langlet

pl. du Forum

place Royale

r. Carnot

r. du Trésor

Notre-Dame de Reims

Palais du Tau

rue Chanzy

r. Libergier

rue

Cimetière du Nord

r. du Champs de Mars

r. J.-J. Rousseau

place A. Briand

rue Cérès

rue Voltaire

bd. de la Paix

rue de l'Université

r. Lt. Herduin

r. du Gerbert

LA BARBÂTRE

rue Gambetta

rue Barbâtre

Ancien Collège des Jésuites

r. du Ruisselet

r. du Grand Cerf

FLECHAMBAULT

bd. Docteur Henrot

Veste

r. Simon

Basilique St-Rémi

place des Droits-de-l'Homme

bd. Lundy
rue Andrieux

r. C. Lenoir

bd. Jamin

To Rethel

Jean

Jaurès

av.

de Cernay

rue

rue G. Laurent

St-Marceaux

bd. de la Paix

bd.

r. de Sillery

LES COUTURES

r. Ponsardin

r. du

bd. Pasteur

r. de

bd. Victor Hugo

r. des Salines

pl. St Nicaise

bd. Henry

bd. Diancourt

bd. Vasnier

bd. Pommery

place du Général Gourand

av. du Gén. Giraud

To Verdun

FRANCE
Paris ★ Reims

0   1/4 mi
0   0.25 km

ATTRACTIONS
Cathédral Notre-Dame de Reims **7**
Mumm **2**
Musée de la Reddition **1**
Musée des Beaux Arts **6**
Palais du Tau **8**
Pommery **10**
Taittinger **9**

HOTELS
Best Western Hôtel de la Paix **4**
Les Crayères **11**

RESTAURANTS
Le Jamin **3**
Le Millénaire **5**

Information (i)
Post Office ✉

A4

architecture and elaborate statuary, not to mention some stunning stained glass windows. The official setting for royal coronations for a thousand years, perhaps its most dramatic moment was the one engineered by Joan of Arc. Instructed by voices, the teenage shepherdess made it her mission to get Charles VII back on the throne, and to get the English out of France. Though she accomplished the first here at Reims in 1429, she was unfortunately burned at the stake before she could complete the second.

Back in the 5th century, France's first king, Clovis I, was baptized in a small church on this site, giving the site a royal reputation that would follow it through the centuries. The current cathedral dates from the 13th century, and harbors 2,303 statues carved into its facades and decorating its interior. Its western and northern facades are graced with elaborate portals carved with hundreds of saints and angels. Inside, the narrow nave reaches 38 meters (125 ft.) giving the impression that the soaring arches reach all the way to heaven. Some of the original stained glass survived the war (including the rose window on the western facade); in 1974, Marc Chagall created the three stained glass windows in the axial chapel.

Place du Cardinal Luçon. **© 03-26-47-55-34.** www.cathedrale-reims.com Free admission. Daily 7:30am–7:30pm.

Cathédrale Notre-Dame de Reims

Musée des Beaux-Arts ★

MUSEUM   This fine arts museum has a remarkable collection that stretches from the 15th to 20th centuries. In fact, the collection has grown too big for the current building and in 2018, the museum will be moving to a spiffy new one designed by British architect David Chipperfield. In the meantime, many of the older works are being restored and prepped for the move, so the collection focuses on modern movements like fauvism, cubism, and surrealism, as well as contemporary works.

8 rue Chanzy. **© 03-26-35-36-00.** www.reims.fr. Admission 4€ adults, free for students and children 16 and under. Wed–Mon 10am–noon and 2–6pm.

Musée de la Reddition ★ HISTORIC SITE/MUSEUM

This humble site, a former technical school, was the setting for one of the 20th century's turning points: the surrender of the Germans to the Allies, which ended World War II. General Eisenhower himself was on hand on the fateful day, May 7, 1945, and the room hasn't changed since the papers were signed: battle maps line the walls and the wood table and chairs, complete with ashtrays, are as they were. The exhibit includes military uniforms, historic objects, and a short film in French, German, and English.

12 rue Franklin Roosevelt. **© 03-26-47-84-19.** www.reims.fr. Admission 4€ adults, 3€ ages 18–25 and over 65, free for students and children under 18. Wed–Mon 10am–noon and 2–6pm.

Palais de Tau ★ MUSEUM

On the southern side of the cathedral lies the former Archbishop's Palace, which now houses a museum dedicated to the royal coronations that took place next door. The collection includes items from the cathedral's treasury, including Saint Rémi's 12th-century coronation chalice and the Sainte-Ampoule, a holy flask that held the oil used to anoint new kings. Learn about the coronation rituals in displays in the vast banquet room, the Salle de Tau.

2 Place du Cardinal Luçon. **© 03-26-47-81-79.** http://palais-tau.monuments-nationaux.fr. Admission 7.50€ adults, free for children under 18. May–Aug Tues–Sun 9:30am–6:30pm; Sept–Apr Tues–Sun 9:30am–12:30pm and 2–5:30pm.

Exploring the Champagne Cellars ★★

Underneath Reims is a vast network of tunnels left over from centuries of chalk extraction. The former quarries turned out to be the perfect spot to store champagne, and today there are some 200km (124 miles) of champagne cellars lying 20 to 40 meters (65 to 131 feet) under the city, holding millions of bottles of bubbly in various stages of fermentation. Most of the top champagne *maisons* offer daily tours of their operations; many insist you reserve in advance. Below are three of the most popular; for a complete listing of available tours in both **Reims** and **Epernay** (a half-hour drive south on the D951), visit the official site of the **Union des Maisons de Champagne** (www.maisons-champagne.com).

Mumm ★ WINERY   One of the most venerable names in champagne, the Mumm family started this enterprise in 1827. The 1-hour visit includes a descent into the tunnels and a tour of the museum, accompanied by an introduction to champagne basics and a glass of Cordon Rouge.

34 rue du Champ-de-Mars. ✆ **03-26-49-59-70.** www.mumm.com. Reservations required. Tours (in English) 10€–20€ adults, 5€ ages 11–18, free for children 10 and under. Mar–Oct daily 9am–6pm; Nov–Feb Sat–Sun 9am–noon and 2–6pm.

Pommery ★ WINERY   Be ready to descend a grand 116-step stairway into the effervescent world of the Pommery cellars. There are a variety of visits on offer here, starting with a 30-minute visit and a glass of Pommery Brut (13€ adults) to a 1-hour "Prestige" tour with a glass of Cuvée Louise (31€ adults). Other tours combine champagne with contemporary art—another passion of the Pommery enterprise.

5 Place du Général-Gouraud. ✆ **03-26-61-62-56.** www.pommery.com. Reservations required. Admission 13€–31€ adults, 7€–9€ children 10–18, free for children 9 and under. Daily 10am–6pm.

Taittinger ★ WINERY   Taittinger is a *grande marque* of French champagne, one of the few still controlled by members of the family that founded it in 1932. The cellars were dug as chalk mines during the Gallo-Roman era and contain vestiges of a long-gone abbey. Tours last about an hour and include everything from how a corking machine works to the art of sediment removal.

TINY bubbles

The difference between champagne and other wines is a second, in-the-bottle fermentation. Once the wine has completed its first fermentation in tanks, it is blended, bottled, sugar and yeast are added, and the bottles sealed with metal caps. Placed horizontally, the bottles are then inverted and turned at regular intervals, allowing the yeast to settle in the neck. This process (called *remuage*, or "riddling") is mostly done by machines now, but some houses still employ *remueurs*, professionals who can hand-turn up to 40,000 bottles per day. Next, the bottles are dipped neck-first into a freezing agent to create an easily removed plug containing the sediment (*dégorgement*). Finally, they are topped up with a mixture of wine and sugar syrup (the *dosage*), the classic corks are inserted, and the finished product goes to the caves, where it ages anywhere from 2–10 years.

9 place St-Nicaise. ☎ **03-26-85-45-35.** www.taittinger.com. Admission 12€ adults, free for children 11 and under. Mid-Mar to mid-Apr Mon–Sat 9:30am–1pm and 1:45pm–5:30pm; mid-Apr to mid-Nov daily 9:30am–5:30pm; mid-Nov to mid-Mar Mon–Fri 9:30am–1pm and 1:45pm–5:30pm.

DISNEYLAND PARIS ★

41km (25 miles) E of Paris

It might not be particularly French, but there's no denying that this is a fun place to visit—especially if you're traveling with kids. Once there, even curmudgeons like myself cannot resist getting swept up by the fun rides and the good cheer. There are two parks here, **Disneyland Paris** and **Disney Studios;** depending on your stamina, you can do them both in a day.

Essentials

ARRIVING   You could arrive by **TGV** (the French railway's high-speed train), but a less spectacular and less complicated option is to simply climb on the **RER A** (www.transilien.fr; 40 min.; 7.50€ adults, 3.75€ ages 4–10 one-way) and take it all the way to its terminus at Marne-la-Vallée–Chessy (just make sure that this is the terminus—the RER A has multiple destinations). When you get out, you'll be about a 5-minute walk from the entrance. By **car,** head east on the A4 and take the Parcs Disney exit.

VISITOR INFORMATION   **Disneyland Paris Guest Relations Office,** located in City Hall on Main Street, U.S.A. (☎ **08-25-30-05-00,** .15€ per min; www. disneylandparis.com). For general tourist information for the region, visit the **Espace de Tourisme,** between the train station and Disney Village (☎ **01-60-43-33-33;** www.tourisme77.fr).

ADMISSION   Admission varies depending on the season. In peak season, a 1-day park ticket (for either the main park or Walt Disney Studios) costs 64€ for adults, 58€ for children 3 to 11, and is free for children 2 and under; a 2-day park-hopper ticket is 139€ for adults, 126€ for kids; and a 3-day park-hopper ticket is 169€ for adults, 156€ for kids. There are oodles of special offers throughout the year, some that include transportation to and from Paris; check the website for details.

HOURS   Hours vary throughout the year, but often they are 10am to 7pm with later closings in the summer months. Check the website for exact hours.

Where to Stay

You can easily make Disney a day trip from Paris—the transportation links are excellent—or you can spend a night . . . or two. Most overnight guests take a package that includes park entry, breakfast, and a couple of nights in a hotel. The per-night hotel prices listed below can range wildly, depending on the package you book, the number of days you stay, the time of year, and so on. Your best bet is to study the website or call the reservations service shared by the resort's seven theme hotels. If you'd like to reserve by phone, call ☎ **407/W-DISNEY** [934-7639] in North America, or ☎ **08-25-30-02-22,** (.15€ min.) in France. Otherwise, you can always reserve online at www.disneylandparis.com.

VERY EXPENSIVE

Disneyland Hotel ★★   Looking like a cartoon version of a Victorian resort, this giant pink pagoda is Disney's most luxurious hotel. Rooms are spacious and comfortable (at these prices they better be); many overlook Sleeping Beauty's

Castle and Big Thunder Mountain. Some less desirable units open onto a parking lot, so specify when you reserve. There are extras galore here, including an indoor pool, multiple restaurants, and a spa.

Disneyland Paris, Marne-la-Vallée. ℘ **01-60-45-65-89.** www.disneylandparis.com. 495 units. 579€–1,172€ double; from 1,260€ suite. **Amenities:** 2 restaurants, babysitting, bar, cafe, health club w/indoor pool, room service, sauna, spa, free Wi-Fi.

EXPENSIVE

Newport Bay Club ★★   This gargantuan hotel on the edge of Lake Disney strives to resemble a New England harbor-front inn (ca. 1900). The yacht club atmosphere carries over to the nautically decorated blue and cream rooms, arranged in various shapes and sizes. As this book went to press, about half of the rooms were being given a nautically themed make-over, but don't worry, that leaves another 500 at your disposal.

Disneyland Paris, Marne-la-Vallée. ℘ **01-60-45-55-00.** www.disneylandparis.com. 1,093 units. 255€–468€ double; from 320€ suite. **Amenities:** 2 restaurants, bar, health club, indoor and outdoor pools, room service, sauna, Wi-Fi (15€ per day).

MODERATE

Hotel Cheyenne/Hotel Santa Fe ★   These two Old West–style lodgings stand side by side, vaguely resembling a movie set. The Cheyenne is a collection of western-looking two-story buildings along Desperado Street; the desert-themed Santa Fe is a clutch of 42 adobe-style pueblos. Kids will enjoy sleeping in a hotel that looks like a park attraction; parents will appreciate the indoor/outdoor playgrounds and kid-friendly atmosphere.

Disneyland Paris, Marne-la-Vallée. ℘ **01-60-45-63-12** (Cheyenne) or **01-60-45-79-22** (Santa Fe). www.disneylandparis.com. 2,000 units. 140€–410€ double. **Amenities:** Bar, restaurant, free Wi-Fi (in common areas only).

Where to Eat

You won't starve at Disneyland Paris, which offers some 70 restaurants and snack bars. You can live on burgers and fries, or try one of the following upscale restaurants. One way or another, the bill will probably be higher than you bargained for. For all restaurant **reservations,** call ℘ **01-60-30-40-50.**

California Grill ★ CALIFORNIAN/FRENCH   For a meal with class, this is Disney's gourmet restaurant, tucked into the swank Disneyland Hotel. While it may not rival the gourmet palaces back in Paris, the menu features well-executed French classics, as well as a few "Californian" dishes like gourmet burgers and grilled vegetable platters. This is a quiet, mostly adult venue (though they do have nice children's menus); the restaurant is open only for dinner. You'll need to make reservations here.

In the Disneyland Hotel. ℘ **01-60-45-65-76.** Fixed-price menu 85€–120€; children's menu 29.50€. Daily 6:30pm–10:30pm.

Inventions ★ INTERNATIONAL   This may be the only restaurant in Europe where Disney characters go table-hopping. This is not *grande cuisine*, but the quality is much better than your average buffet, with dishes such as chilled asparagus, Italian prosciutto, or even escargot and bouillabaisse, plus lots of kid-friendly dishes from spaghetti to Buzz Lightyear éclairs.

In the Disneyland Hotel. ℘ **01-60-45-65-76.** Buffet 54.50€ adults, 29.50€ children 7–11, 22€ children 3–6. Daily 12:30–3pm and 6–10:30pm.

Exploring Disney

In the U.S., there are Disneyland and Disney World; in France, you could call it Disney Universe. There are two parks in this giant resort, the classic Disneyland, complete with the Matterhorn and Space Mountain, and Disney Studios, where you can try your hand at cinematography or delve into the world of cartoons. But the parks are just the beginning of your excellent adventure in Marne-la-Vallée: There are also seven hotels, a golf course, tennis courts, and an ice skating rink, not to mention Disney Village, with its boutiques, restaurants, discotheque, cinema, and IMAX theater. For the purposes of this guide, we'll just stick with parks. In general, Disneyland is a better choice for the under-7 crowd; though even the little ones will still get a kick out of the cartoon attractions at Disney Studios.

Disneyland Park

Isn't it comforting that some things never change? Here you are in France, and yet there is Frontierland, Adventureland, and Fantasyland, just the way you remember them back home. Okay, not exactly. For one thing, everyone's speaking French. And Japanese. And Bulgarian, Hindi, and Farsi. The success of this resort is its international appeal. When you enter the park, you'll step right into **Main Street USA,** that utopian rendition of early-20th-century America, complete with horse and buggies and barbershop quartets. Here you'll find the **information center** as well as a train, which leaves from Main Street Station. The train, which does a circuit around the park, will whisk you off to **Frontierland,** where you'll find a paddle-wheel steamboat, a petting zoo, and the Lucky Nugget saloon, among other things. Next, you'll chug through **Adventureland,** with old favorites like the Swiss Family Robinson treehouse and the Pirates of the Caribbean, as well as newer attractions like Aladdin's Oriental Palace. Onward towards **Fantasyland** with Sleeping Beauty's Castle (Le Château de Belle au Bois Dormant), whizzing teacups, flying Dumbos, and "It's a Small World." Last stop is **Discoveryland,** home of Space Mountain and the submarine Nautilus, as well as "Buzz Lightyear's Laser Blast." There are parades virtually every afternoon on Main Street, and a spectacular light and fountain show, Disney Dreams, around closing time.

Disney Studios

Though the primary draw here, of course, is Disneyland Park, Disney Studios makes an interesting alternative for older kids who have already done Disney and are up for something different. The main entrance to the studios, called the **Front Lot,** consists of Disney Studio 1, an elaborate sound stage complete with film props, shops, and restaurants. You then move inside the park, where there are film-oriented attractions like **Disney Animation Studios,** where you can learn how cartoons are made, and the **Back Lot,** with its special effects and stunt shows.

Naturally, there are fun rides here, too, like the **Tower of Terror** (based on the *Twilight Zone* TV show), **Crush's Coaster** and the **Rock 'n' Rollercoaster** (featuring Aerosmith tunes). Smaller visitors will appreciate **Toy Story Playland,** where they can speed around on the **RC Racer** or soar through the skies on the **Toy Soldiers Parachute Drop.**

THE LOIRE VALLEY

By Lily Heise

J ust 2 hours south of Paris, the Loire Valley enchants visitors with a stunning landscape of castles and vineyards straight out of a fairy tale. King François I and his Renaissance court left a spectacular cultural legacy, earning the entire valley a place on the World Heritage Site list. History buffs can trace Joan of Arc from Orléans to Chinon; romantics fall in love with the story-book châteaux of Chenonceau, Azay-le-Rideau, and Ussé; garden lovers revel in the verdant paradise of Chaumont and Villandry; gastronomes tantalize their palates at Michelin-starred restaurants and rustic *auberges;* and outdoor adventurers can see it all by bike.

As its name would imply, the region's rolling hills and forests hug the winding Loire River, encompassing 800 sq. km (308 sq. miles) of land south of Ile-de-France, from the city of Orléans and extending west to Nantes on the Atlantic coast. Most visitors use Tours or Orléans as their starting point; however, the towns of Blois, Amboise, or Saumur make excellent bases for exploring the region.

Most visitors to the Loire arrive via Paris; there are about six direct trains daily from the TGV station at Charles de Gaulle airport to the Tours TGV station Saint-Pierre (1 hr., 40 min; 39€–70€ one-way). At least one high-speed train (TGV) an hour runs to both Orléans and Tours, convenient starting points for anyone not renting a car directly in Paris.

The Loire Valley has **two regional tourist offices** that can help you plan your stay in advance: **Comité Régional de Tourisme Val de Loire,** 37 av. de Paris, Orléans 45000 (www.visaloire.com; ✆ **02-38-79-95-28**), and **SEM Régionale des Pays de la Loire,** 1 place de la Galarne, BP 80221, Nantes 44202 Cedex 2 (www.westernloire.com; ✆ **02-40-48-24-20**). Local tourist offices are listed throughout the chapter.

ORLÉANS ★

119km (74 miles) SW of Paris; 72km (45 miles) SE of Chartres

Ever since **Joan of Arc** relieved the besieged city from the Burgundians and the English in 1429, the city has honored the "Maid of Orléans." This deliverance is

Sleep Like a King (or Queen)

As one of the most visited regions of France, it's not surprising to find a great variety of accommodation options. Sleep like a king or queen in one of the Loire's many châteaux hotels, from the medieval **Hostellerie Gargantua** (p. 202) to the opulence of the **Château d'Artigny** (p. 191) or the **Château de Marçay** (p. 201). The valley is dotted with thousands of unique *gîtes* (**B&Bs**) including medieval towers, houseboats, and even troglodyte caves. For details and reservations, go to http://en.gites-de-france. com.

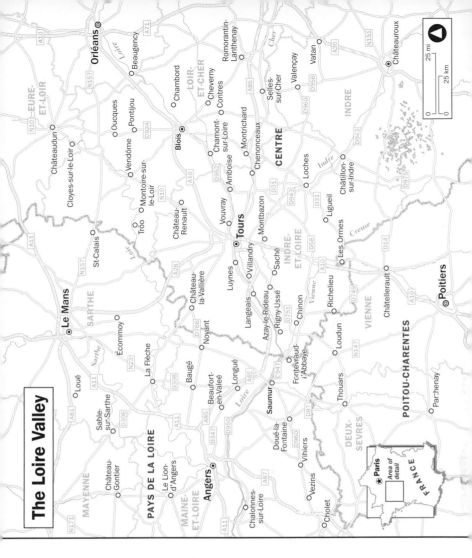

The Loire Valley

celebrated every year on May 8, the anniversary of her victory. But even if you aren't in town for the celebration, it's impossible to overlook the city's affection for the warrior; her name adorns everything from streets and cafes to chocolates and candies. Though it suffered damage in World War II, the city's downtown still remains quaint, though it has gradually been losing its regional prominence to the more prosperous Tours.

Essentials

ARRIVING   About two **trains** per hour arrive from Paris's Gare d'Austerlitz (1 hr., 10 min.; 20€–25€ one-way); there are also a dozen connections from Tours (50–70 min.). The one-way fare from Tours to Orléans is about 20€. Orléans lies on the road between Paris and Tours. If you're **driving** from Paris, take A10 south; from Tours, take A10 north.

VISITOR INFORMATION   The **Office de Tourisme** is at 2 place de L'Etape (www.tourisme-orleans.com; ☎ **02-38-24-05-05**).

Getting Around

ON FOOT   Orléans's city center is small and many streets are pedestrianized. For short stays, it's easiest to explore the town on foot.

BY BICYCLE   Orléans has a Paris style bike-sharing scheme, **Vélo'+** (www.aggloveloplus.fr). There are 350 bikes available at 33 stations around the city. You can register online (where you can also download a map of the city's bike stations) or directly at one of 8 bike stands where credit cards are accepted; fees are 1€ per day.

BY CAR   All the sites in the city can be explored on foot. Underground parking is well sign-posted; there are convenient lots beside the Hotel de Ville, the Cathedral, and near the river at Place du Châtelet.

BY TAXI   **Taxis Orléans** (www.taxis-orleans.fr; ☎ **02-38-53-11-11**) can be found throughout the city. They can be ordered or there are ranks in front of the train station and at the corner of rue Royal and place du Martroi.

BIKING YOUR WAY through THE LOIRE

Trains serve some towns, but the best way to see this relatively flat region is by car or bike. Ten years and several million euros later, the vast program called **La Loire à Vélo** ("The Loire on a Bike"; www.cycling-loire.com) has completed the 800km-long (496-mile) **Loire à Vélo trail,** so you can now safely pedal from Sancerre to the sea on a dedicated bike path past châteaux, villages, and natural areas or easily bike from one château to another. The path was designed for low-key cycling and is linked to cycling-friendly hotels and bike-rental outfits along the way (look for the accueil vélo signs). More paths are added every year, and the trail will hook up to an even more massive project called **EuroVelo 6,** a cycling path that leads all the way to the Black Sea.

La Loire à Vélo has partnered with various tourist offices and travel agencies to offer a range of bike-trip packages that include hotel, meals, bike rental, and baggage transport (very important if you don't want to haul extra weight). For more information, visit **www.cycling-loire.com,** or one of the two regional tourist offices (listed above). The website also has detailed information on dozens of bike-rental outfits along the route, as well as brochures and links to guidebooks on various sections of the path.

One of the better-known outfitters is **Detours de Loire,** 35, rue Charles Gille, Tours (www.locationdevelos.com; ☎ **02-47-61-22-23**), which has three other shops in Blois, Saumur, and

Nantes, as well as 20 or so associated outlets up and down the Loire à Vélo circuit. This means that you can pick up your bike in one town and leave it in any partner outlet along the way without backtracking. If you are arriving in the Loire Valley by train, the four main shops are all located close to the town station. Prices for all-purpose bikes run from 15€ to 22€ per day, with discounts for multi-day rentals. A 300€ deposit (usually a credit card imprint) is required. Detours de Loire can also organize hotel-bike packages, deliver your bike to your hotel, and store your bags while you are pedaling. **Note:** Most outlets are open only from April to October.

Orléans

Gare
d'Orléans

↑To Chartres & Paris
Bus Station

To Sens
& Gien
→

←To Blois
& Tours

ATTRACTIONS
Cathédrale Ste-Croix **6**
Eglise St-Aignan **7**
Hôtel Groslot **4**
Musée des Beaux-Arts **5**

HOTELS
Best Western
Hôtel d'Arc **1**
Hôtel de l'Abeille **2**

RESTAURANTS
Chez Jules **8**
La Vieille Auberge **3**

Church +
Information (i)
Post Office ✉

BY PUBLIC TRANSPORT Orléans has both buses and trams that snake through the city run by the **TAO** (www.reseau-tao.fr; ✆ **08-00-01-20-00**). Trams will serve your visit best; line A reaches the train station and line B goes by the cathedral. Tickets (1.50€) can be purchased from automatic kiosks at the Tram station, or for the bus (1.60€) directly from the driver.

[FastFACTS] ORLÉANS

ATMs/Banks   The city center has plenty of banks, especially around shopping hub Place du Châtelet.

Doctors & Hospitals   **Centre Hospitalier Régionale d'Orléans,** 1 rue Porte Madeleine (www.chu-orleans.fr; ✆ 02-33-51-44-44).

Internet Access   **Mondial Phone,** 84 rue des Carmes (✆ 02-38-72-17-52), has computers with Internet and international phone call services.

Mail & Postage   **La Poste,** 19 rue Royale (✆ 36-31).

Pharmacies   **Pharmacie du Châtelet,** 38 Place du Châtelet (✆ 02-38-53-34-50).

Where to Stay

Best Western Hôtel d'Arc ★ Located minutes from the station and close to the city center, this hotel is a good option for a quick and convenient stopover in town. Built in the 1920s, the four-story building has an elegant Art Deco facade. The friendly staff makes you feel you're at a family run establishment and not a chain hotel. The bedrooms have classic appeal and many have been recently updated, including one very modern deluxe room. Try to book rooms ending in 2, which are slightly larger, and if possible, interior rooms instead of ones on the somewhat noisy front rue de la République.

37 ter rue de la République, Orléans 45000. ✆ **02-38-53-10-94.** www.hoteldarc.fr. 35 units. 143€–230€ double. Parking 11€. **Amenities:** Room service; free Wi-Fi.

Hôtel de l'Abeille ★★ If you're taking some time to get to know Orléans before embarking on château country this is the city's most charming hotel. Stepping into the foyer, you will be instantly transported back to the 19th century. In fact, the hotel dates from 1903 and has been run for four generations by the same family. The cozy Belle Epoque feel flows into the guest rooms, each decorated with vintage prints and antiques. Throughout the building are ornamental nods to both Napoleon, whose symbol was the bee and the namesake of the hotel, and Joan of Arc, the liberator of Orléans. Take a late afternoon break or morning coffee on its peaceful rooftop terrace.

64 rue Alsace-Lorraine. ✆ **02-38-53-54-87.** www.hoteldelabeille.com. 27 units. 98€–135€ double; 140€–195€ family suite. Parking 10€. **Amenities:** Bar; room service; free Wi-Fi.

Where to Eat

Chez Jules ★★ TRADITIONAL FRENCH Yvan and Isabelle Cardinaux take the idea of "chez" to a whole new level with the warm welcome and delectable dishes at one of the best restaurants in town. Service and quality prevail; don't expect fine crystal and a maitre d'. The extremely reasonable menu features seasonal refined dishes such as roebuck with pumpkin mousse topped with chorizo shavings and half-roasted pigeon with ginger. To finish we loved the Roquefort cheese *tartine* with pear sorbet drizzled in pear liqueur and the poached Clementine draped in chocolate sauces and served with vanilla ice cream. Reservations almost always a must.

136 rue de Borgogne. ✆ **02-38-54-30-80.** Main courses 16€–22€; fixed-price lunch 19€, dinner 22€–33€. Tues–Sat noon–2pm and 7–9:30pm. Closed 2–3 weeks in July.

La Vieille Auberge ★ MODERN FRENCH Take a trip to the French countryside in the heart of the city at this charming restaurant housed in a 17th-century building. Dine inside in a stylish room or, on sunny days, enjoy your creative creations in a lovely garden. The menu changes with the season to take advantage of the freshest available ingredients and may start with foie gras with candied figs, before moving on to glazed confit de canard with sweet potatoes sprinkled with apple chips or their famous Rossini beef filet.

2 rue du Faubourg St-Vincent. ✆ **02-38-53-55-81.** www.lavieilleauberge45.com. Main courses 24€–30€; fixed-price lunch 25€, dinner 35€–49€. Mon–Thurs noon–2pm and 7–9:30pm; Fri–Sat noon–2pm and 7–10pm; Sun noon–2pm.

Exploring the Town

Orléans, pop. 116,000, is the chief town of Loiret, on the Loire, and beneficiary of many associations with the French aristocracy. It gave its name to the dukes and duchesses of Orléans. Wander the narrow lanes of the city center to get the feel for what the city might have been like during Joan of Arc's time. Note the equestrian statue of Jeanne d'Arc on place du Martroi. From the square, you can walk past the elegant arched galleries on rue Royal (rebuilt in 18th-c. style) across pont George-V (erected in 1760). A simple cross marks the site of the Fort des Tourelles, which Joan of Arc and her men captured.

Cathédrale Ste-Croix ★ CATHE-DRAL   Begun in 1287 after a Romanesque church here collapsed from old age, the cathedral was burned by the Huguenots in 1568. Henri IV laid the first stone of the present building in 1601; work continued until 1829. The cathedral boasts a 17th-century organ and woodwork from the early 18th century in its chancel, the masterpiece of Jules Hardouin-Mansart and other artists associated with Louis XIV.

Place Ste-Croix. ✆ **02-38-77-87-50.** Free admission. May–Sept daily 9:15am–6pm; Oct–Apr daily 9:15am–noon and 2–6pm.

Street in Orléans

Eglise St-Aignan ★ CHURCH   One of the most frequently altered churches in the Loire Valley, St-Aignan was consecrated in 1509 in the form you see today. It possesses one of France's earliest vaulted hall crypts, complete with polychromed capitals. Scholars of pre-Romanesque art are interested in its rare 10th- and 11th-century aesthetics. Above ground, the church's Renaissance-era choir and transept remain, but the Protestants burned the nave during the Wars of Religion. In a wood-carved shrine are the remains of the church's patron saint.

Place St-Aignan. No phone. Crypt can be visited only on a guided tour; sign up at the tourist office.

Hôtel Groslot ★ HISTORIC HOME   This brick Renaissance mansion was begun in 1550 and embellished in the 19th century. François II (the first husband of Mary, Queen of Scots) lived here during the fall of 1560 and died on December 5. It was here that his brother and successor Charles IX met his lovely Marie Touchet. Between the Revolution and the mid-1970s, it functioned as the town hall. Marriage ceremonies, performed by the town's magistrates, are still held here. The statue of Joan of Arc praying was the work of Louis-Philippe's daughter, Princesse Marie d'Orléans. In the garden, you can see the remains of the 15th-century Chapelle St-Jacques.

Place de l'Etape (northwest of the cathedral). ✆ **02-38-79-22-30.** Free admission. July–Sept Mon–Fri and Sun 9am–6pm, Sat 5–8pm; Oct–June Mon–Fri and Sun 10am–noon and 2–6pm, Sat 5pm–7pm (occasionally closed Sat for weddings).

Musée des Beaux-Arts ★★ MUSEUM   The best art museum in the region, the fairly large collection is made up of mostly French, but also Italian,

Dutch, and Flemish works from the 15th to 20th centuries. It includes some impressive treasures by Tintoretto, Boucher, Van Dyke, and Vélasquez as well as a variety of portraits, including one of Mme. de Pompadour by Drouais. The museum also holds one of the countries best collections of pastels with works by Quentin de la Tour and Chardin.

Place Saint-Croix. ✆ **02-38-79-21-55.** www.coeur-de-france.com/orleans-beauxarts.html. Admission 4€ adults, 2€ students, free for children 18 and under and for all visitors on Sun. Tues–Sun 10am–6pm.

BEAUGENCY

150km (93 miles) SW of Paris; 85km (53 miles) NE of Tours

On the right bank of the Loire, the charming town of Beaugency boasts many medieval sites including a long 12th-century bridge with 23 arches, said to have been built by the Devil himself.

Essentials

ARRIVING If you're **driving** from Blois to Beaugency, take N152 northeast. About 20 **trains** per day run between Beaugency and either Blois or Orléans; each trip takes about 20 minutes, and the one-way fare is 6.20€. For railway information, visit www.voyages-sncf.com or dial ✆ **36-35.** From Orléans, about 4 to 8 **buses** a day go to Beaugency. For bus schedules and information, visit www.ulys-loiret.com.

Where to Eat & Stay Nearby

For lunch in the center of Beaugency, the **Relais du Château** (8 rue du Pont; ✆ **02-38-44-55-10**), at the foot of the castle, serves up satisfying traditional dishes and lunch menus from 16€.

La Tonnellerie ★★ Situated a short drive south of Beaugency, this 19th-century manor house makes for the perfect restful stay in the immediate area. This isn't one of the regions grand château-hotels; nevertheless, rooms are comfortable and tastefully appointed with reproduction antiques and period prints. Your experience is complete lounging in the luxuriant garden with a period book by Balzac or Flaubert. The restaurant serves regional classics (main courses from 20€) and is open to nonguests, though reservations are required.

12 rue des Eaux-Bleues, Tavers, Beaugency 45190. ✆ **02-38-44-68-15.** www.tonelri.com. 20 units. 108€–180€ double; 180€–199€ suite; family rooms available. Closed Dec 15–Jan 31. Take A10, exit at Beaugency, and then take N152 to Beaugency/Tavers. **Amenities:** Restaurant, bar, bike rental, outdoor pool, free Wi-Fi.

Princess de la Loire Youth Hostel ★ The best bargain for bikers on a budget, this youth hostel near Beaugency offers the most reasonable accommodation in the whole of the Loire. Clean and bright, the hostel has dormitories with four to six beds, a common kitchen, and laundry facilities. Share your Loire touring routes with other travelers at the sociable barbecue and picnic areas. Bike rentals are available directly from the hostel or in town at the Détours shop near the train station.

152 rue de Châteaudun (2km from Beaugency on the D925). ✆ **02-38-44-61-31.** www.hihostels. com. 116 beds. 16€ shared dormitory. Closed mid-Nov to mid-March. **Amenities:** Bike rental, laundry room, shared kitchen, free Wi-Fi.

Exploring the Town

A major medieval event took place here: the 1152 annulment of the marriage of Eleanor of Aquitaine and her cousin, Louis VII. She then married Henry II of England, bringing southwestern France as her dowry, an act that set off the Hundred Years' War. This remarkable woman was the mother of Richard the Lion-Hearted. (The film "The Lion in Winter" dramatizes these events.)

The 15th-century **Château Dunois** is currently closed for renovations and may not reopen again until 2015 or beyond, so you'll have to see it from its exterior. The château is brooding and impressive, its historical links stretching back to almost-mystical medieval antecedents. The current castle was built by Jean d'Orléans, who fought alongside Joan of Arc in the siege of Orléans, on the foundations of an earlier 10th-century fortress that belonged to the lords of Beaugency, whose feudal power extended throughout the region. Astride the street (la rue du Pont) that leads to one of the château's secondary entrances, the **Voûte St-Georges (St. George's Vault)** is an arched gateway from the earlier château.

More medieval moodiness is on hand at **La Tour César,** a 36m-tall (118-ft.) castle keep that is all that remains of an 11th-century citadel. It's a fine example of Romanesque military architecture, but the interior is in ruins.

Eglise Notre-Dame, place Saint-Fermin, a 12th-century abbey, was rebuilt after it was burned during the Wars of Religion (1562–98). You can still see traces of its original Romanesque architecture in the chancel and transept. Nearby, the 16th-century **Tour St-Fermin,** a bell tower with a panoramic view of the valley, is famous for bells that ring out a traditional tune three times a day.

The 10th-century **Eglise St-Etienne,** place du Martroi, is one of the oldest churches in France. Now deconsecrated, it is owned by the municipality and is open only for temporary exhibitions of painting and sculpture.

BLOIS

180km (112 miles) SW of Paris; 60km (37 miles) NE of Tours

The star attraction in this town of 52,000 is unquestionably the **Château de Blois,** but if time remains after a château visit, you may want to wander around the quaint historic core to get a feel for a real Loire Valley town.

Essentials

ARRIVING A dozen or so **trains** run from Paris's Gare de Austerlitz every day (1 hr., 45 min.; 28€ one-way), and several others depart from the Gare Montparnasse, which involves a change in Tours (around 1 hr., 50 min.; 33€–70€). From Tours, trains run almost every hour (trip time: 40 min.), at a cost of 11€ one-way. For information and schedules, visit www.voyages-sncf.com or dial ✆ **36-35.** From June

Château de Blois

to September, you can take a **bus** (www.tlcinfo.net; ☏ **02-54-58-55-44**) from the Blois train station to tour châteaux in the area, including Chambord, Chaumont, Chenonceau, and Amboise. If you're **driving** from Tours, take RN152 east to Blois, which runs along the Loire; if you want to get there fast, take the A10 autoroute. If you'd like to explore the area by **bike,** check out **Traineurs de Loire,** 1 rue Chemonton (www.traineursdeloire.com; ☏ **02-54-79-36-71**). Rentals start at 6€ per hour, 13€ per day, open April to October.

VISITOR INFORMATION   The **Office de Tourisme** is at 23 place du Château (www.bloispaysdechambord.com; ☏ **02-54-90-41-41**).

Where to Eat & Stay

Côté Loire–Auberge Ligérienne ★   Even though its decor is akin to a seaside resort, you won't feel lost at sea staying at this quaint hotel on the banks of the Loire. Only a 5-minute walk from the château, it's a great option for travelers touring the region without a car. There is plenty of character at this B&B-like inn, from the vintage maritime posters, pillows with sailboat motifs, and ancient building features from the 12th, 15th, and 16th centuries. Most rooms are rather large for the size of the establishment, though beware of the narrow staircase. A tiny restaurant on the ground floor is open to outside guests, with one of the owners doing double duty as chef. His love of the region shines in such culinary creations as savory blancmange with goat cheese and tomatoes confit or local Sandre fish with butter sauce.

2 place de la Grève. ☏ **02-54-78-07-86.** www.coteloire.com. 8 units. 59€–95€ double. Restaurant fixed-price menu 30€, main course 18€. Open Tues–Sat. Closed Jan to mid-Feb. **Amenities:** Restaurant, bar, free Wi-Fi.

Le Médicis ★★ TRADITIONAL FRENCH   It's worth the short 1km (½ mile) trip from the center of town to dine at this Michelin-starred restaurant and inn. It will be hard to choose from original dishes like lobster in puff pastry with Thai-style shrimp spring rolls, pigeon suprême with gnocchi of green peas and beans, or veal sweetbreads with spinach ravioli. Even more difficult will be selecting an accompanying bottle from an extensive wine list of over 300 labels. The inn also rents 10 elegant rooms; double rates are 79€ to 150€.

2 allée François 1er. ☏ **02-54-43-94-04.** www.le-medicis.com. Reservations required. Main courses 20€–30€; fixed-price menu 34€–51€. Daily noon–1:15pm and 7–9pm. Closed Jan 3–31, and Sun night and Mon Nov–Mar. Bus: 2.

L'Orangerie du Château ★★★ TOURAINE   The king's blessing has been bestowed on this wonderful restaurant located in a former outbuilding of the castle, the perfect majestic lunch spot after a morning inside the château. The classic dining room is also bustling with local fans of chef Jean-Marc Molveaux.

He passionately prepares scallop and vegetable tortellini, frogs' legs with watercress gnocchi and veal sweetbreads served with parsnip mousseline. There's even a special children's menu for *petits gourmands*. Your regal feast is made complete in summer when you can dine on the outdoor terrace facing the castle.

1 av. Jean-Laigret. ✆ **02-54-78-05-36.** www.orangerie-du-château-fr. Main courses 25€–40€; fixed-price menu 38€–83€; children's menu 15€. Tues–Sat noon–1:30pm and 7:15–9:15pm. Closed mid-Feb to mid-Mar.

Exploring the Town & the Château

Blois is a piece of living history, with cobblestone streets and restored white houses with slate roofs and redbrick chimneys. Some of its "streets" are mere alleyways originally laid out in the Middle Ages or lanes linked by a series of stairs. If you have time for **shopping,** head for the area around **rue St-Martin** and **rue du Commerce** for high-end items such as clothing, perfume, shoes, and jewelry. On Saturday, a daylong **food market** is on place Louis XII and place de la République, lining several blocks in the center of town at the foot of the château.

Château de Blois ★★★ CASTLE   On the misty morning of December 23, 1588, Henri I, the duc de Guise, had just left a warm bed of one of Catherine de Médicis' ladies-in-waiting. His archrival, King Henri III, had summoned him, but when the duke arrived, only the king's minions were about. The guards approached with daggers. Wounded, the duke made for the door, where more guards awaited him. Staggering, he fell to the floor in a pool of his own blood. Only then did Henri III emerge from behind the curtains. "Mon Dieu," he reputedly exclaimed, "he's taller dead than alive!" The body couldn't be shown: The duke was too popular. Quartered, it was burned in a fireplace.

The murder of the duc de Guise is only one of the events associated with the Château de Blois, begun in the 13th century by the comte de Blois. Blois reached the apex of its power in 1515, when François I moved to the château. For that reason, Blois is often called the "Versailles of the Renaissance," the second capital of France, and the "City of Kings." But Blois soon became a palace of exile. Louis XIII banished his mother, Marie de Médicis, to the château, but she escaped by sliding into the moat down a mound of dirt left by the builders.

If you stand in the courtyard, you'll find that the château is like an illustrated storybook of French architecture. The Hall of the Estates-General is a beautiful 13th-century work; Louis XII built the Charles d'Orléans gallery and the Louis XII wing from 1498 to 1501. Mansart constructed the Gaston d'Orléans wing between 1635 and 1637. Most remarkable is the François I wing, a French Renaissance masterpiece containing a spiral staircase with ornamented balustrades and the king's symbol, the salamander.

41000 Blois. ✆ **02-54-90-33-33.** www.chateaudeblois.fr. Admission 9.80€ adults, 7.50€ students, 5€ children 6–17, free for children 5 and under. Additional fees for light shows and special events. July–Aug daily 9am–7pm; Apr–June and Sept daily 9am–6:30pm; Oct daily 9am–6pm; Nov–Mar daily 9am–12:30pm and 1:30–5:30pm.

CHAMBORD ★★★

91km (118 miles) SW of Paris; 18km (11 miles) E of Blois

The Château de Chambord, the grandest of the region's castles, is the culmination of François I's two biggest obsessions: hunting and architecture. It's a must for any Loire castle itinerary.

Essentials

ARRIVING   It's best to **drive** to Chambord. Take D951 northeast from Blois to Saint Dyé, turning on to the rural road to Chambord. You can also rent a **bicycle** in Blois and ride the 18km (11 miles) to Chambord, or take a **tour** to Chambord from Blois in summer. From May to September, **Transports du Loir et Cher** (www.tlcinfo.net; ✆ **02-54-58-55-44**) operates bus service to Chambord.

Exploring the Château

The Château de Chambord ★★★ CASTLE   Built as a hunting lodge, this colossal edifice is a masterpiece of architectural derring-do. Some say Leonardo da Vinci had something to do with it, and when you climb the amazing double spiral staircase, that's not too hard to believe. The staircase is superimposed upon itself so that one person may descend and a second ascend without ever meeting. While da Vinci died a few months before construction started in 1519, what emerged after 20 years was the pinnacle of the French Renaissance and the largest château in the Loire Valley. The castle's proportions are of exquisite geometric harmony, and its fantastic arrangement of turrets and chimneys makes it one of France's most recognizable châteaux.

Construction continued for decades; François I actually stayed at the château for only a few weeks during hunting season, though he ensured Chambord would forever carry his legacy by imprinting his "F" emblem and symbol, the Salamander, wherever he could. After he died, his successors, none too sure what to do with the vast, unfurnished, and unfinished castle, basically abandoned it. Finally, Louis XIII gave it to his brother, who saved it from ruin; Louis XIV stayed there on several occasions and saw to restorations, but not a single monarch ever really moved in. The state acquired Chambord in 1932, and restoration work has been ongoing ever since.

Château de Chambord at sunset

Interior, Château de Chambord

Four monumental towers dominate Chambord's facade. The three-story keep has a spectacular terrace from which the ladies of the court watched the return of their men from the hunt. Many of the vast rooms are empty, though several have been filled with an impressive collection of period furniture and objects, giving an idea of what the castle looked like when parts of it were occupied. The château lies in a park of more than 5,260 hectares (12,992 acres), featuring miles of hiking trails and bike paths, as well as picnic tables and bird-watching posts.

📞 **02-54-50-40-00.** www.chambord.org. Admission 11€ adults, free 17 and under accompanied by an adult. Open daily April to Sept 9am–6pm, and Oct–Mar 9am–5pm.

CHEVERNY ★

192km (119 miles) SW of Paris; 19km (12 miles) SE of Blois

Unlike most of the Loire castles, Cheverny is the residence of the original owner's descendants, offering a rare glimpse into the normally very private life of French aristocrats.

Essentials

ARRIVING   Cheverny is 19km (12 miles) south of Blois, along D765. It's best reached by **car** or on a **bus tour** (Apr–Aug only) from Blois with **TLC Transports du Loir et Cher** (www.tlcinfo.net; 📞 **02-54-58-55-44**). Bus no. 4 leaves from the railway station at Blois once or twice per day; see the TLC website for the schedule. You can also take a **taxi** (📞 **02-54-78-07-65**) from the railway station at Blois.

Where to Eat & Stay

The **Orangerie** on the castle grounds is also a nice option for a quick bite, serving a variety of snacks, lunch, and teatime fare.

St-Hubert ★ TRADITIONAL FRENCH   If you can't get invited to lunch by the château owners, your appetite can be pleasantly satisfied at this nearby excellent-value inn. It offers fixed-price menus of regional specialties such as Muscadet-infused rabbit terrine with pear compote; local free-range Touraine Géline chicken with pommes darphin (thick potato pancake), topped with a tomato caviar; and for "dessert" Ste. Maure goat cheese or Sologne strawberry melba. While it's a far cry from the luxurious bedrooms of the castle, the St-Hubert offers economic **lodging** with 20 conservatively decorated rooms for 50€ to 65€ for a double.

122 rte. Nationale. ✆ **02-54-79-96-60.** www.hotel-sthubert.com. Main courses 18€–22€; fixed-price menu 19€–29€; children's menu 12€. Daily noon–2pm and 7–9pm. Closed Sun night off-season.

Exploring the Château

Château de Cheverny ★ CASTLE
The family of the vicomte de Sigalas can trace its lineage from Henri Hurault, the son of the chancellor of Henri III and Henri IV, who built the château in 1634. Designed in classic Louis XIII style, it is resolutely symmetrical. Its elegant lines and sumptuous furnishings provoked the Grande Mademoiselle, otherwise known as the Duchess of Montpensier, to proclaim it an "enchanted castle."

You, too, will be impressed by the antique furnishings, tapestries, and objets d'art. A 17th-century French artist, Jean Mosnier, decorated the fireplace with motifs from the legend of Adonis. The Guards' Room contains a collection of medieval armor; also on display is a Gobelin tapestry depicting the abduction of Helen of Troy. In the king's bedchamber, another Gobelin traces the trials of Ulysses. Most impressive is the stone stairway of carved fruit and flowers. To complete the regal experience, your arrival or departure from the château might be heralded by red-coated trumpeters accompanied by an enthusiastic pack of hunting hounds.

✆ **02-54-79-96-29.** www.chateau-cheverny.fr. Admission 9.50€ adults, 6.50€ students under 25 and children 7–18, and free children 6 and under (additional fee for exhibits), boat and golf cart rentals also available. Daily Nov–Mar 9:45am–5pm; April–June and Sept 9:15am–6:15pm; July–Aug 9:15am–6:45pm; and Oct 9:45am–5:30pm.

VALENÇAY ★★

233km (144 miles) SW of Paris; 56km (35 miles) S of Blois

One of the Loire's most handsome Renaissance châteaux, Valençay combines the wonders of châteaux-hopping and family fun, and even has a special museum for car lovers.

Essentials

ARRIVING   If you're **driving** from Tours, take A85 east, turning south on D956 (exit 13 to Selles-sur-Cher) to Valençay. From Blois, follow D956 south.

Exploring the Château & Park

Château de Valençay ★★ CASTLE
Talleyrand acquired it in 1803 on the orders of Napoleon, who wanted his minister of foreign affairs to receive dignitaries in style. The d'Estampes family built Valençay in 1520. The dungeon and

Château de Valençay

west tower are of this period, as is the main body of the building, but other wings were added in the 17th and 18th centuries. The effect is grandiose, all domes and turrets. The apartments are sumptuously furnished, mostly in the Empire style, but with Louis XV and Louis XVI trappings as well. A star-footed table in the main drawing room is said to have been the one on which the final agreement of the Congress of Vienna was signed in June 1815 (Talleyrand represented France).

After your visit to the château, take a walk through the garden and deer park. There are plenty of activities here for kids, including a giant labyrinth, a miniature farm, a playground, a golf cart circuit through the forest, and, in high season, historic reenactments (at 3pm, 4pm, and 5pm). A few nights each summer the château and its grounds return to the Renaissance, decked out with thousands of candles, costumed performers, and musical entertainment (see website for details).

Classic car enthusiasts' motors can get revved up at the **Musée de l'Automobile de Valençay,** situated 200m (656 ft.) from the château. The exhibit shows the evolution of the automobile with over 60 antique vehicles, including a rare tandem style pulley-operated Bédélia (ca. 1914).

2 rue de Blois. ✆ **02-54-00-10-66.** www.château-valencay.fr. The Automobile Museum is located at 12 av. de la Résistance (✆ **02-54-00-07-74;** www.musee-auto-valencay.fr). Admission for castle, automobile museum, and park 12€ adults, 8.50€ students, 3€ children 4–6, and free ages 5 and under. Open daily mid-March to April 10:30am–6pm; May 10am–6pm; June 9:30am–6:30pm; July–Aug 9:30am–7pm; Sept 10am–6pm; Oct–Nov 9 10:30am–5:30pm.

Kitchen in Château de Valençay

AMBOISE ★★

219km (136 miles) SW of Paris; 35km (22 miles) E of Tours

Amboise is on the banks of the Loire in the center of vineyards known as Touraine-Amboise. The good news: This is a real Renaissance town. The bad news: Because it is so beautiful, tour buses overrun it, especially in summer. Other than the myriad of notable royal residences, the town has also played host to Leonardo da Vinci, who spent his last years here, and more recently, royal rocker Mick Jagger, lord of a nearby château.

Essentials

ARRIVING About a dozen **trains** per day leave from both Tours and Blois. The trip from Tours takes 20 minutes and costs 5.60€ one-way; from Blois, it takes 20 minutes and costs 7€ one-way. Several conventional trains a day leave from Paris's Gare d'Austerlitz (trip time: about 2 hr., 15 min.), and several TGVs depart from the Gare Montparnasse, with a change to a regular train at St-Pierre-des-Corps, next to Tours (trip time: 1 hr., 30 min.). Fares from Paris to Amboise start at 26€. For information, visit www.voyages-sncf.com or call ✆ **36-35.**

If you prefer to travel by bus, **Fil Vert Buses** (www.tourainefilvert.com), which operates out of Gare Routière in Tours, just across from the railway station, runs about six to eight **buses** every day between Tours and Amboise. The one-way trip takes about 45 minutes and costs 2.20€.

If you're **driving** from Tours, take the D751, following signs to Amboise.

VISITOR INFORMATION   The **Office de Tourisme** is on quai du Général-de-Gaulle (www.amboise-valdeloire.com; ✆ **02-47-57-09-28**).

Where to Eat & Stay

Chez Hippeau Brasserie de l'Hotel de Ville ★ FRENCH   If you need a quick lunch in the town's historic core, this bustling Paris-style brasserie is a good option, particularly in pleasing hungry little bellies. And the city ambience is what you'll get with busy waiters and packed tables, yet the wide menu and the speed will refuel you for the rest of your day of touring. On the menu are the usual suspects of standard *steak-frites*, grilled salmon with vegetables and *canard confit* with honey and rosemary—as well as a range of lighter salads, *croque-monsieurs*, and omelets.

1 and 3 rue François 1er. ✆ **02-47-57-26-30.** Main courses 8€–20€; fixed-price menu 11.50€– 23€; children's menu 7.90€. Daily 11am-11pm.

Le Choiseul ★★★ Composed of three mansions dating from the 15th through 18th centuries and nestled on the banks of the Loire River, Le Choiseul is the best hotel in Amboise and serves its best cuisine. Its rooms are opulent with traditional charm and all the modern comforts of a luxury hotel. Be sure to explore the grounds, where an outdoor pool is surrounded by Italian sculptures; ask the staff about visiting the impressive "Greniers de César" troglodyte caves nearby. New chef Mickaël Renard has brought his creativity and savoir-faire to its recently reinvented restaurant **Le 36** (open to nonguests). His refined menu of beautifully presented dishes might include sea elms with Jerusalem artichoke mousse and truffle juice or filet of duckling, with nougat, tender turnips, with orange sweet-and-sour sauce. Lunch ranges from 29€ to 36€, with dinner going for 50€ to 85€.

36 quai Charles-Guinot. ✆ **02-47-30-45-45.** www.le-choiseul.com and www.le36-amboise.fr (restaurant). 32 units. 200€–325€ double; 385€ suite. **Amenities:** Restaurant, bar, bicycles, outdoor pool, room service, free Wi-Fi.

Le Fleuray ★★ The welcome couldn't be warmer at this lovely ivy-covered manor house run by a family of English expatriates, a short drive from Amboise. With their cross-cultural approach, the Newingtons turned a rundown farmhouse into the perfect mélange of Anglo-Saxon comfort and French sophistication. This attention to detail is evident from the intimate foyer to the spacious guest rooms; several of which have private terraces. With peaceful surroundings

The Loire at sunset from a bridge in Amboise

and plenty to do on the extensive grounds, this is an excellent base for château touring and some family fun. The hotel also has an excellent restaurant serving food infused with regional and international flavors. Items on the fixed-price menus (29€–39€) might include guinea fowl stuffed with chestnuts drizzled in maple syrup, tandoori-style monkfish medallions with sweet potato and ginger purée, or wild mushroom risotto topped with baby glazed onions and mature parmesan shavings.

Route D74, near Amboise. ✆ **02-47-56-09-25.** www.lefleurayhotel.com. 23 units. 88€–148€ double. Free parking. From Amboise, take the D952 on the north side of the river, following signs to Blois; 12km (7½ miles) from Amboise, turn onto D74, in the direction of Cangey. **Amenities:** Restaurant, bar, free bikes, golf course, Jacuzzi, massage, outdoor pool, room service, tennis court, free Wi-Fi.

Le Manoir Les Minimes ★★   In the shadow of the looming castle is this welcoming and reasonably priced hotel, set in a magical restored 18th-century mansion. Built on the foundations of an ancient convent, the hotel is made up of the main building, draped in wisteria, and a small annexed cottage, centered by a tranquil garden. Once inside, you feel like you've entered a fine aristocratic home, with tasteful furnishings and decorations chosen with a careful eye to detail. The most charming rooms are in the main building, especially those in the attic with their beautiful exposed beams (though tall guests might have trouble with the slanted ceilings). The rooms in the annex aren't as quaint, but are more spacious. Many second- and third-floor rooms open to views of the Loire or the château. Some rooms only have a bathtub (with a shower head), which may not appeal to all guests.

34 quai Charles Guinot. ✆ **02-47-30-40-40.** www.manoirlesminimes.com. 15 units. 139€–225€ double; 305€–530€ suite. **Amenities:** Parking; free Wi-Fi.

Exploring the Town

Château d'Amboise ★★ CASTLE   On a rocky spur above the town, this medieval château was rebuilt in 1492 by Charles VIII, the first in France to reflect the Italian Renaissance.

Visitors enter on a ramp that opens onto a panoramic terrace fronting the river. At one time, buildings surrounded this terrace, and fêtes took place in the enclosed courtyard. The castle fell into decline during the Revolution, and today only about a quarter of the once-sprawling edifice remains. You first come to the Flamboyant Gothic **Chapelle de St-Hubert,** distinguished by its lacelike tracery, which holds the **tomb of Leonardo da Vinci,** who died in Amboise. Tapestries cover the walls of what's left of the château's grandly furnished rooms, which include **Logis du Roi (King's Apartment).** The vast **Salle du Conseil,** bookended by a Gothic and a Renaissance fireplace, was once the venue of the lavish fêtes. Exit via the **Tour des Minimes** (also known as the Tour des Cavaliers), noteworthy for a ramp up which horsemen could ride. The other notable tower is the Heurtault, which is broader than the Minimes, with thicker walls.

✆ **02-47-57-00-98.** www.chateau-amboise.com Admission 10.70€ adults, 9.20€ students, 7.20€ ages 7–14, free children 6 and under. Open daily Jan 9am–12:30pm and 2–4:45pm; Feb 9am–12:30pm and 1:30–5pm; Mar 9am–5:30pm; Apr–June 9am–6:30pm; July–Aug 9am–7pm; Sept–Oct 9am–6pm; Nov 2–15 9am–5:30pm; Nov 16–Dec 31 9am–12:30pm and 2–4:45pm.

Château du Clos-Lucé ★ HISTORIC HOME/MUSEUM   Within 3km (1¾ miles) of the base of Amboise's château, this brick-and-stone building was constructed in the 1470s. Bought by Charles VII in 1490, it became the summer residence of the royals and also served as a retreat for Anne de Bretagne, who, according to legend, spent a lot of time praying and meditating. Later, François I installed "the great master in all forms of art and science," Leonardo himself. Da Vinci lived here for 3 years, until his death in 1519. Today the site functions as a small museum, where you can step back into the life and imagination of da Vinci. The manor contains furniture from his era; examples of his sketches; models for his flying machines, bridges, and cannon; temporary exhibits; and an annual Renaissance musical festival late September (a nod to da Vinci's musical talents).

2 rue de Clos-Lucé. ✆ **02-47-57-00-73.** www.vinci-closluce.com. Mar–Nov 15 admission 14€ adults, 10€ students, 9€ children 6–18, 36€ family ticket (2 adults, 2 children), free children 5 and under. Open daily Jan 10am–6pm; Feb–June 9am–7pm; July–Aug 9am–8pm; Sept–Oct 9am–7pm; Nov–Dec 9am–6pm.

CHENONCEAUX ★★★

224km (139 miles) SW of Paris; 26km (16 miles) E of Tours

Chenonceau is one of the most remarkable castles in France. Its impressive setting, spanning a whole river, along with an intriguing history and renowned residents, make it many visitors' favorite château in the whole country. (*Note:* The village, whose year-round population is less than 300, is spelled with a final *x*, but the château isn't.)

Essentials

ARRIVING   About a dozen daily **trains** run from Tours to Chenonceaux (trip time: 30 min.), costing 6.80€ one-way. The train deposits you at the base of the château; from there, it's an easy walk. For information, visit www.voyages-sncf. com or call ✆ **36-35.** If you're **driving,** from the center of Tours follow the signs to the D40 east, which will take you to the signposted turnoff for Chenonceaux.

Where to Eat & Stay

From March to November a gourmet lunch can be enjoyed at the **Orangerie** of the château; there is also a tea salon, a snack bar, and picnic areas on the grounds.

Auberge du Bon-Laboureur ★★   This inn, within walking distance of the château, is your best bet in town for a comfortable night's sleep and exceptional Loire Valley cuisine. A former coach house opened in 1786, the hotel authentically evokes the era with its tiled, turreted tower, ivy-covered walls and antique furniture. Spread across various buildings, guest rooms are generally spacious and some have fireplaces or open out onto the garden with private terraces. Dine like a *reine* at its Michelin-starred restaurant; its seasonal menu uses produce direct from the hotel's garden and may include green pea and langoustine *millefeuille*, with beetroot puree or shoulder of veal with its sweetbreads. The excellent value menu at lunch is 30€; dinner menus run from 51€ to 85€ and a vegetarian menu is also available.

6 rue du Dr. Bretonneau, Chenonceaux 37150. ✆ **02-47-23-90-02.** www.bonlaboureur.com. 25 units. 129€–185€ double; 210€–310€ suite. Closed mid-Nov to mid-Dec and Jan 7–Feb 14. **Amenities:** Restaurant, bar, outdoor pool, room service, free Wi-Fi.

Au Gâteau Breton ★ TRADITIONAL FRENCH   A brief jaunt from the château, this restaurant is ideal for a casual lunch or tea. This pretty 18th-century inn was formerly a grocery store run by natives of neighboring Brittany. The shady terrace offers ample outdoor dining or cozy up over their hardier dishes in the rustic interior. Worthwhile dishes include homey favorites like local andouillette sausage, coq au vin, and their specialty poulet Tourangelle (sautéed chicken with mushroom and cream sauce).

16 rue du Dr. Bretonneau. ☏ **02-47-23-90-14.** Main courses 15€–20€; fixed-price menus 17.50€–28.50€. Apr–Sept daily noon–2:30pm, 7–10pm; Nov–Mar daily noon–2:30pm.

Exploring the Château, Museum & Gardens

Château de Chenonceau ★★★ CASTLE   A Renaissance masterpiece, the château is best known for the dames de Chenonceau, who once occupied it. Built first for Katherine Briçonnet, the château was bought in 1547 by Henri II for his mistress, Diane de Poitiers. For a time, this remarkable woman was virtually queen of France, infuriating Henri's dour wife, Catherine de Médicis. Diane's critics accused her of using magic to preserve her celebrated beauty and keep Henri's attentions from waning. Apparently, Henri's love for Diane continued unabated, and she was in her 60s when he died in a jousting tournament in 1559.

When Henri died, Catherine became regent (her eldest son was still a child), and one of the first things she did was force Diane to return the jewelry Henri had given her and abandon her beloved home. Catherine then added her own touches, building a two-story gallery across the bridge—obviously inspired by her native Florence. The gallery, which was used for her opulent fêtes, doubled as a military hospital in World War I. It also played a crucial role in World War II, serving as the demarcation line between Nazi-occupied France and the "free" zone.

Gobelin tapestries, including one depicting a woman pouring water over the back of an angry dragon, and several important paintings by Poussin, Rubens, and Tintoretto adorn the château's walls. The chapel contains a marble Virgin and Child by Murillo, as well as portraits of Catherine de Médicis in black and white. There's even a portrait of the stern Catherine in the former bedroom of her rival, Diane de Poitiers. In François I's Renaissance bedchamber, the most interesting portrait is that of Diane as the huntress Diana.

Château de Chenonceau

The women of Chenonceau are the subject of the **Musée de Cire (Wax Museum),** located in a Renaissance-era annex a few steps from the château.

The château boasts vast grounds that include a maze, a vegetable garden, and a beautiful *jardin à la française,* open on summer evenings for an illuminated "night walk" accompanied by Italian classical music (weekends in June; nightly July–Aug 9:30pm–11:30pm).

✆ **02-47-23-90-07.** www.chenonceau.com. Admission 12.50€ adults and 9.50€ students and children 7–17; combination ticket château and wax museum 14€ adults, 12€ children 7–17; free 6 and under; admission for evening garden light show 5€ adults, free children under 7. Open daily 9am–8pm July–Aug; 9am–7pm last 2 weeks of March; 9am–7:30pm June and Sept; 9am–6pm Oct; 9am–5pm rest of the year.

CHAUMONT-SUR-LOIRE ★★

200km (124 miles) SW of Paris; 40km (25 miles) E of Tours

The connections of this lesser-visited castle to Diane de Poitiers make it an excellent château to pair with a visit to the Château de Chenonceau. It is also a wonderful stop for garden enthusiasts.

Essentials

ARRIVING   Several **trains** a day travel to Chaumont from Blois (trip time: 10–15 min.) and Tours (about 40 min.). The one-way fare is 3.60€ from Blois, 8.60€ from Tours. The railway station serving Chaumont is in Onzain, a nice 2.4km (1½-mile) walk north of the château. For train schedules and ticketing information, visit www.voyages-sncf.com or call ✆ **36-35.**

Where to Eat & Stay

From April to October, the château grounds are home to four places you can dine or obtain snacks, the best being the **Grand Velum** restaurant with refined dishes mainly using local or organic ingredients.

Le Domaine des Hauts de Loire ★★   A 3km (1¾ miles) drive from the Château de Chaumont, this is one of the finest château-hotels on the eastern Loire circuit. Perched on the north side of the Loire, this estate house was built by the owner of a Paris-based newspaper in 1840. He referred to it as his "hunting lodge," much in the lines of Louis XIII and his grand Versailles. Rooms are decorated in Louis Philippe or Empire style, each with its own individual touches such as vintage tiles or rustic wooden beams. Most are quite large; though those in the half-timbered annex that was originally the stables are less coveted. The large park is perfect for a sunset stroll.

Its Michelin-two-starred restaurant is definitely a highlight. The creative menu may offer red mullet with grilled artichokes and smoked marrow or the decadent wild boar with truffle cream and quince purée. Main courses range from 52€ to 69€, with fixed-price menus ranging from 49€ to 99€.

Rte. d'Herbault. ✆ **02-54-20-72-57.** www.domainehautsloire.com. 36 units. 190€–315€ double; 350€–690€ suite. Closed Dec–Feb. **Amenities:** Restaurant, bar, outdoor pool, room service, Wi-Fi (10€/hour).

Exploring the Château & Garden

Château de Chaumont ★★ CASTLE   On the morning when Diane de Poitiers first crossed the drawbridge, the Château de Chaumont looked grim.

Henri II, her lover, had recently died. The king had given her Chenonceau, but his angry widow, Catherine de Médicis, forced her to trade her favorite château for Chaumont, a comparatively virtual dungeon for Diane, with its medieval battlements, pepper-pot turrets and perch high above the Loire.

The château belonged to the Amboise family for 5 centuries. In 1465, when one of them, a certain Pierre, rebelled against the rule of Louis XI, the king had the castle burned to the ground as a punishment. Pierre and his descendants rebuilt for the next few decades. The castle's architecture spans the period between the Middle Ages and the Renaissance, and the vast rooms still evoke the 16th and 17th centuries. In the bedroom occupied by Catherine de Médicis, you can see a portrait of the Italian-born queen. The superstitious Catherine housed her astrologer, Cosimo Ruggieri, in one of the tower rooms (a portrait of him remains). He reportedly foretold the disasters awaiting her sons.

The château passed through the hands of various owners and was eventually acquired and restored by the eccentric Marie Say and Amédée de Broglie in the late 18th century, who also added elaborate stables, a farm, and gardens. Since 1992, the latter has hosted the **International Garden Festival,** a world-renowned gathering of cutting-edge landscape designers that lasts from mid-April to mid-October and is open to the public. Each year, a dozen different gardens are created, using thousands of different plants and innovative garden designs. Since 2008, the château has also been a site for contemporary art and photography exhibits; check the website for this year's program.

© **02-54-51-26-26.** www.domaine-chaumont.fr. Admission is 10.50€ adults, 6.50€ children 12–18, 4€ children 6–11, and free ages 5 and under. Full pass including the festival 16€ adults, 11€ children 12–18, 5:50€ children 6–11, and free 5 and under. Open daily Nov–Mar 10am–5pm; April–June 10am–6:30pm; July–Aug 10am–7pm; Sept 10am–6:30pm; and Oct 10am–6pm.

TOURS ★

232km (144 miles) SW of Paris; 113km (70 miles) SW of Orléans

Though it doesn't have a major château, Tours (pop. 137,000), at the junction of the Loire and Cher rivers, is known for its food and wine. Many of its buildings were bombed in World War II, and 20th-century apartment towers have taken the place of castles. But the downtown core is quite charming, and because Tours is at the doorstep of some of the most magnificent châteaux in France, it makes a good base from which to explore.

Essentials

ARRIVING As many as 14 high-speed TGV **trains** per day depart from Paris's Gare Montparnasse and arrive at St-Pierre des Corps station, 6km (3¾ miles) east of the center of Tours, in an hour. Free *navettes*, or shuttle buses, await your arrival to take you to the center of town (the Tours Centre train station). A limited number of conventional trains also depart from Gare d'Austerlitz and arrive in the center of Tours, but these take twice as long (about 2¼ hrs.). One-way fares range from 22€ to 65€. For information, visit www.voyages-sncf.com or call © **36-35.** If you're **driving,** take highway A10 to Tours.

VISITOR INFORMATION The **Office de Tourisme** is at 78–82 rue Bernard-Palissy (www.ligeris.com; © **02-47-70-37-37**).

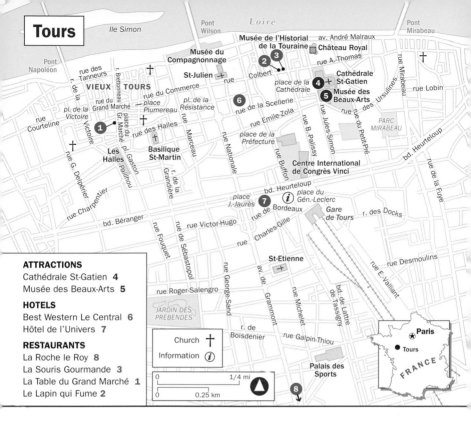

ATTRACTIONS
Cathédrale St-Gatien **4**
Musée des Beaux-Arts **5**

HOTELS
Best Western Le Central **6**
Hôtel de l'Univers **7**

RESTAURANTS
La Roche le Roy **8**
La Souris Gourmande **3**
La Table du Grand Marché **1**
Le Lapin qui Fume **2**

Getting Around

ON FOOT   Besides the TGV train station which is in the suburb of St-Pierre des Corps, most other sites of interest in Tours are accessible on foot.

BY BICYCLE   There are safe and extensive bike paths in Tours. You can rent a bike at **Detours de Loire,** 35 rue Charles Gilles (www.locationdevelos.com; ✆ 02-47-61-22-23), at a cost of 15€ per day. A deposit is required.

BY CAR   If you have a car for exploring the Loire, you can find a number of underground parking garages downtown. There is a convenient one at the Tours Centre train station and another at rue Nationale and rue de la Préfecture. You can rent a car at **Avis** (www.avis.fr; ✆ 02-47-20-53-27), located in the Tours Centre station, or **Europcar,** at the St-Pierre des Corps station (www.europcar.fr; ✆ 02-47-63-28-67).

BY TAXI   The most extensive taxi network is **Taxis Tours** (www.taxis-tours.fr; ✆ 02-47-20-30-40). Their hotline has some English-speaking operators or you can usually find one in front of the train.

BY PUBLIC TRANSPORT   Tours has both buses and one brand new tram line, a network called **Le Fil Bleu,** 9 rue Michelet (www.filbleu.fr; ✆ 02-47-66-70-70). Tickets (2€) can be purchased from automatic kiosks at a Tram station, from bus drivers or from their office.

[FastFACTS] TOURS

ATMs/Banks   The city center has plenty of banks, especially around Place Gaston Paillhou or along rue Nationale.

Doctors & Hospitals   **Centre Hospitalier Régionale de Tours,** 2 Bd Tonnellé (www.chu-tours.fr; ✆ 02-47-47-47-47).

Internet Access   **Top Communication,** 129 rue Colbert (✆ 02-47-60-98-10).

Mail & Postage   **La Poste,** 17 rue Nationale (✆ 36-31).

Pharmacies   **Pharmacie du Centre,** 28 rue des Halles (✆ 02-47-05-65-20).

Where to Stay

Most visitors use Tours as a starting point for their Loire exploration. Staying in a small town or the countryside is ideal for discovering the region; see the suggestions throughout the chapter.

Best Western Le Central ★   If you're spending more time touring the sites of Tours or taking in an evening in town, this central hotel is a good headquarters. Despite being walking distance from the station and the cathedral, the surrounding greenery gives it an almost country feel. Parts of the building face a leafy garden, reducing street traffic noise, though it makes the hotel a little tricky to find. Many of its rooms have been recently refurbished and decor remains classic and conservative, though a big plus are their size, generous for French standards.

21 rue Berthelot, Tours 37000. ✆ **800/528-1234** in the U.S. and Canada, or 02-47-05-46-44. www.bestwesterncentralhoteltours.com. 37 units. 104€–160€ double; 200€–260€ suite. Parking 10€. **Amenities:** Bar, babysitting, room service, free Wi-Fi.

Hôtel de l'Univers ★★   This grand old 19th-century hotel has recently undergone a much-needed facelift, returning its former grandeur as top hotel in town. Its star-studded line of guests has included Rockefeller, Churchill, and Hemingway. Its midsize rooms are decorated in a conservative contemporary style in beiges and creams accented with splashes of vibrant color. The bathrooms have also been renewed with shower/tubs, some with Jacuzzi functions. Its restaurant serves a good quality and value menu at 28€ if you don't adventure out into the city. On weekdays, the hotel is popular with business travelers; thus on most weekends it offers greatly reduced rates.

5 bd. Heurteloup, Tours 37000. ✆ **02-47-05-37-12.** www.oceaniahotels.com. 85 units. 200€–245€ double; 210€–300€ suite. Parking 15€. **Amenities:** Restaurant, bar, room service, free Wi-Fi.

Where to Eat

Restaurants in Tours can be pricey, but you can keep costs low by dining at **La Souris Gourmande,** 100 rue Colbert (http://lasourisgourmande.com; ✆ **02-47-47-04-80**), where the chef is respected for the diversity of his cheese selection. You may be asked to join a communal table. Main courses cost 13€ to 15€. At the raffish but cheerful bistro **Le Lapin qui Fume,** 90 rue Colbert (www.aulapinquifume.fr; ✆ **02-47-66-95-49**), a fixed-price menu costs 10€ to 15€ at lunch and 15€ to 26€ at dinner and features standard bistro fare and, as the name suggests, rabbit.

La Roche le Roy ★★ MODERN FRENCH   Serious gastronomes need not tour the Tours dining scene; head straight to this tasty and tasteful restaurant. Alain Couturier's culinary finesse is accentuated by the picturesque setting of this charming 18th-century manor south of the center. Couturier's repertoire includes lobster tails with vanilla bourbon, Brittany "pearl" oysters baked in cheese and champagne, and his masterpiece of "Apicius" suprême of Racan pigeon. For dessert, try the warm orange soufflé flavored with Grand Marnier.

55 rte. St-Avertin. ✆ **02-47-27-22-00.** www.rocheleroy.com. Main courses 25€–38€, lunch menu 35€, dinner menu 58€–72€. Tues–Sat noon–1:30pm and 7:30–9:30pm. Closed 2 weeks in Feb and 3 weeks in Aug. From the center of town, take av. Grammont south (follow signs to St-Avertin–Vierzon).

La Table du Grand Marché ★ MODERN FRENCH   This little gem in the heart of Tours is an excellent value, creative bistro. The booths of its simple yet appealing dining room are packed with locals who come back time and time again for its refined seasonal menu. Chef Flavien Lelong gathers inspiration from near and far with such dishes as the local Touraine "burger" of *rillons* and *rillettes* (potted meats) topped with Saint Maure cheese and prune coulis, ray fish wings with black rice and grapefruit butter, or the gamey parmentier of hare and skewer of doe with blueberry sauce.

25 rue du Grand Marché. ✆ **02-47-64-10-62.** www.la-table-du-grand-marche.com. Main courses 18€–26€; fixed-price menu lunch 18€, dinner 31€–35€. Tues 7–10pm; Wed–Sat 12:30–2pm and 7–10pm; Sun 12:30–2pm.

Where to Eat & Stay Near Tours

Château d'Artigny ★★★   If you want to have the utmost castle experience, this is the glitziest château-hotel in the valley. Nestled in a forest 1.5km (1 mile) west of the hamlet of Montbazon and 15km (9¼ miles) south of Tours, the château is newer than it looks, built in 1912 for the perfume and cosmetics king François Coty, who spared no cost for this perfect architectural beauty. Much of this character remains today, with fine antiques, Louis XV–style chairs, and various bronze and marble statuary. Only 31 units are in the main building; the others are in four annexes: a former chapel, gatehouse, mill, and staff dormitory. Each have their own charm, yet might not be what you're expecting so be careful when booking. Complete your château experience at the Artigny's regal restaurant **L'Origan** (lunch menu from 29€, dinner from 55€).

Rte. des Monts (D17). ✆ **02-47-34-30-30.** www.artigny.com. 65 units. 150€–430€ double; 440€–550€ junior suite. From Tours, take N10 south for 11km (6¾ miles) to Montbazon, and then take D17 1.5km (1 mile) southeast. **Amenities:** Restaurant, bar, babysitting, exercise room, outdoor pool, room service, sauna, spa, 2 tennis courts, free Wi-Fi (in some).

Château de Beaulieu ★★   With a lack of special hotels inside Tours, it's well worth driving out to this lovely and reasonably priced 18th-century manor. Situated only 5km (3 miles) south of the city, the refined estate sits on a 3-hectare park. The grounds include fountains and a manicured French garden. A gracious double-curving stairway takes you to the welcoming reception hall. Guest rooms have elegant wooden furniture, fireplaces, and refitted bathrooms. The nine best rooms are in the main château; the other ten are in the nearby turn-of-the-20th-century pavilion. Before heading out on your castle touring, relax in the steam room or get a massage in the new Magnolia spa. The restaurant is appreciated around the area for its inventive cuisine and extensive wine list (lunch menu 29€, dinner menu 45€–75€).

67 rue de Beaulieu, Joué-les-Tours 37300. ✆ **02-47-53-20-26.** www.chateaudebeaulieu37.com. 19 units. 97€–197€ double. From Tours, take av. de Grammont south, and turn right on bd. Winston Churchill and then left on av. de Pont Cher and right on rue de Beaulieu. **Amenities:** Restaurant, bar, bike rental, spa, free Wi-Fi.

Exploring the City

Pilgrims en route to Santiago de Compostela in northwest Spain once stopped here to pay homage at the tomb of St-Martin, the "Apostle of Gaul" and bishop of Tours in the 4th century. One of the most significant conflicts in European history, the 732 Battle of Tours checked the Arab advance into Gaul. In the 15th century, French kings set up shop here and Tours became the capital of France, a position it held for more than 100 years.

Most Loire Valley towns are rather sleepy, but Tours is where the action is, where streets and cafes bustle with a large student population. The heart of town is **place Jean-Jaurès.** The principal street is **rue Nationale,** running north to the Loire River. Head west along rue du Commerce and rue du Grand-Marché to Vieux Tours/Vieille Ville (old town). If you turn left on rue du Commerce toward the old town center, you can explore the streets and courtyards for regional specialties, books, toys, and crafts. A hotbed for antiques is east of rue Nationale (toward the cathedral), along **rue de la Scellerie.** Up rue Nationale toward the river are more shops and upscale boutiques and a small mall with chain stores.

Place Plumereau (often shortened to "place Plume"), a square of medieval buildings, houses a concentration of restaurants and bars. In the warmer months, the square explodes with tables that fill with people who like to people-watch (and be watched themselves). This is a good place to start if you're going out in the evening; otherwise, venture to the trendy bars on **rue Colbert,** which lies in the heart of Tours, midway between the place Plumereau and the cathedral. Allow a morning, afternoon, or evening to see Tours.

Cathédrale St-Gatien ★ CATHEDRAL   This cathedral honors a 3rd-century evangelist and has a Flamboyant Gothic facade flanked by towers with bases from the 12th century. The lanterns date from the Renaissance. The choir is from the 13th century, with new additions built in each century through the 16th. Sheltered inside is the handsome 16th-century tomb of Charles VIII and Anne

Place Plumereau, Tours

Château-Hopping Made Easy

If you aren't renting a car, several tour companies in Tours arrange full- and half-day visits to nearby castles, and three of them offer minibus tours that leave daily from the tourist office. **Acco-Dispo** (www.accodispo-tours.com; ✆ **06-82-00-64-51**), **Saint-Eloi Excursions** (http://saint-eloiexcursions.com; ✆ **06-70-82-78-75**), and **Quart de Tours** (www.quart detours.com; ✆ **06-30-65-52-01**) all offer minibus tours that depart around 9am;

you can reserve on the tourist office web-site (www.visaloire.com) or directly on the company websites. Costs range from 20€ to 55€ per person. The price usually does not include meals or admission to the châteaux, but participation in the tour qualifies you for reduced group rates. Keep in mind that less is sometimes more when it comes to castle viewing; after two or three, you may not be able to remember which was which.

de Bretagne's two children. Some of the glorious stained-glass windows are from the 13th century.

5 place de la Cathédrale. ✆ **02-47-70-21-00.** Free admission. Daily 9am–7pm.

Musée des Beaux-Arts ★ ART MUSEUM   For an art fix in Tours, stop by this provincial museum, worth visiting just to see the lovely rooms and gardens of the former Archbishop's palace, with parts dating to the 12th century. Hanging on the walls are works by Rubens, Delacroix, Rembrandt, and Boucher; the sculpture collection spans Roman busts to moody Rodin.

18 place François Sicard. ✆ **02-47-05-68-73.** www.mba tours.fr. Admission 5€ adults, 2.50€ seniors and students, free for children 12 and under. Wed–Mon 9am–12:45pm and 2–6pm. Bus: 3.

Tours Nightlife

Long a student town, Tours has a lively young population. Much of the evening action centers around Place Plumereau **and rue Colbert.** The twenty-something crowd gets early evening drinks at **Le Baron,** 11 rue des Ofèvres (✆ **02-47-20-13-97**). You can then sip the city's most inventive cocktails in the cool lounge vibe of **Mango,** 28 rue du Grand Marché (www.facebook.com/mangobartours).

In summer, many locals camp out at **La Guinguette,** a vast open-air "bar" by the Pont Wilson along the Loire River, much in the spirit of Paris Plages. The daytime activities extend nightly with concerts, dancing, food, drink, and games. It's open mid-May to mid-September and only cash is accepted.

If you have the urge for more dancing, the hottest place in town is **L'Excalibur,** 35 rue Briçonnet (✆ **02-47-64-76-78**), with an electro beat and video system. A clientele of all ages, many from the surrounding countryside, heads to **Le Pyms,** 170 av. de Grammont (www.lepyms.com; ✆ **02-47-66-22-22**), where there are two spaces, one playing '80s nostalgia and the other contemporary electro.

VILLANDRY ★★★

253km (157 miles) SW of Paris; 32km (20 miles) NE of Chinon; 18km (11 miles) W of Tours; 8km (5 miles) E of Azay-le-Rideau

The Renaissance Château de Villandry should be at the top of the list for any garden lover. Its 16th-century-style *jardins* are celebrated throughout Touraine and amaze visitors from around the world with their beauty and faithful historic preservation.

Essentials

ARRIVING Three daily **buses** operate from Tours from July to October only; the trip takes about 30 minutes and costs 2.20€. For bus information, visit www.tourainefilvert.com or call ✆ **02-47-05-30-49.** Villandry has no train service. The nearest connection from Tours is in Savonnières; the trip takes around 15 minutes and costs 3.90€ one-way. For information, visit www.voyages-sncf.com or call ✆ **36-35.** From Savonnières, you can walk along the Loire for 4km (2½ miles) to reach Villandry, rent a **bike** at the station, or take a **taxi.** You can also **drive,** following D7 from Tours.

Where to Eat & Stay

Le Cheval Rouge ★ MODERN FRENCH   Next to the château, this is a surprising country restaurant serving up sophisticated versions of French classics. The bright dining room is welcoming or there is a large enclosed terrace with individual tables shaded with umbrellas. The chef carefully prepares fois gras profiteroles with fig jam, bass poached in sparkling Vouvray wine, and rump steak with goat cheese sauce. On a hot day, finish off with the frozen soufflé with Cointreau. The inn also rents 41 recently renovated rooms, decorated with modern appeal and furnishings. A double is 69€; the hotel also has several family rooms renting for 78€ to 99€.

9 rue Principale. ✆ **02-47-50-02-07.** www.lecheval-rouge.com. Main courses 15€–18€; fixed-price menu 20€–36€. Daily noon–2:30pm and 7–9pm.

Exploring the Gardens & Château

Château de Villandry ★★★ CASTLE/GARDENS   Every square meter of the gardens is like a geometric mosaic. Designed on a trio of superimposed cloisters with a water garden on the highest level, the gardens were restored by the Spanish doctor and scientist Joachim Carvallo, great-grandfather of the present owner. The grounds contain 17km (11 miles) of boxwood sculpture, which the

Château de Villandry

gardeners cut to style in only 2 weeks each September. The borders symbolize the faces of love: tender, tragic (represented by daggers), and crazy (with a labyrinth that doesn't go anywhere). The arbors, citrus hedges, and walks keep 6 men busy full-time. The vegetable garden is being reverted to all-organic.

A feudal castle once stood at Villandry. In 1536, Jean le Breton, François I's finance minister and former ambassador to Italy, acquired the property and built the present château with influences of the Italian Renaissance. The buildings form a U and are surrounded by a moat. Near the gardens is a terrace from which you can see the small village and its 12th-century church. A tearoom on-site, **La Doulce Terrasse** (☎ 02-47-50-02-10; closed mid-Nov to mid-Feb), serves regional cuisine, including vegetables from the garden, fresh-baked bread, and homemade ice cream. For a more gourmet meal, try **Le Cheval Rouge** (see above).

☎ 02-47-50-02-09. www.chateauvillandry.com. Admission to gardens and château 9.50€ adults, 5.50€ children 8–18, free for children 7 and under; entrance to gardens only 6.50€ adults, 4€ children 8–18. Gardens open daily 9am–5 or 7:30pm, depending on the hour of sunset; château open daily 9am–4:30 or 6:30pm, depending on a complicated seasonal schedule.

LANGEAIS ★

259km (161 miles) SW of Paris; 26km (16 miles) W of Tours

Dominating the town on a steep slope, this medieval fortress is one of the few châteaux actually on the Loire. Crossing over its drawbridge and through its massive towers takes you back 500 years to the start of the golden age of the Loire.

Essentials

ARRIVING   Several **trains** per day stop here en route from Tours or Saumur. The one-way fare from Saumur is 8.10€; the one-way fare from Tours 5.60€. Transit time from both cities is around 20 minutes. For schedules and information, visit www.voyages-sncf.com or call ☎ 36-35. If you're **driving** from Tours, take D952 southwest to Langeais.

Exploring the Château

Château de Langeais ★★ CASTLE   On December 6, 1491, 15-year-old Anne de Bretagne was wed to Charles VIII at Langeais, permanently attaching Brittany to France. The original castle was built in the 10th century when Fulk III (972–1040), Count of Anjou, sometimes called the "Black Falcon," seized Langeais from the Count of Blois. He erected the first keep, the ruins of which can still be seen. The present structure was built in 1465 in the late medieval style. The interior is well preserved and furnished, thanks to Jacques Siegfried, who not only restored it over 20 years, but also bequeathed it to the Institut de France in 1904.

The rooms recreate the ambience of a regal residence of the late Middle Ages, rich with ornamental fireplaces and tapestries. A remarkable 15th-century millefleurs tapestry decorates the Chambre de la Dame, and seven superb tapestries known as the "Valiant Knights" cover the walls of the Salle des Preux.

The Banquet Hall features a mantelpiece carved to resemble a fortress, complete with crenellated towers. The Wedding Hall includes a re-creation of the marriage of Anne de Bretagne and Charles VIII with lavishly costumed wax figures. In the Luini Room is a large 1522 fresco by that artist, removed from a chapel on Lake Maggiore, Italy. It depicts Saint Francis of Assisi and Saint Elizabeth of Hungary with Mary and Joseph. Kids can learn medieval castle construction with interactive displays, or have some fun exploring the tree house and the two playgrounds.

☎ **02-47-96-72-60.** www.chateau-de-langeais.com. Admission 9€ adults, 7.50€ students and ages 18–25, 5€ children 10–17, free for 9 and under. Open daily Apr–June and Sept to mid-Nov 9:30am–6:30pm; mid-Nov to Jan 10am–5pm; Feb–Mar 9:30am–5:30pm; July–Aug 9am–7pm.

AZAY-LE-RIDEAU ★★

261km (162 miles) SW of Paris; 21km (13 miles) SW of Tours

With its idyllic location and fairy-tale turrets, the Renaissance Château d'Azay-le-Rideau was deemed by neighboring writer Honoré de Balzac to be "a facetted diamond set in the Indre."

Essentials

ARRIVING To reach Azay-le-Rideau, take the **train** from Tours or Chinon. From either starting point, the trip time is about 30 minutes; the one-way fare is 5.10€ from Chinon, 5.80€ from Tours. For the same fare, the SNCF railway also operates a bus between Tours and Azay; the trip takes 50 minutes. For schedules and information, visit www.voyages-sncf.com or call ☎ **36-35.** If you're **driving** from Tours, take D751 southwest to Azay-le-Rideau.

Where to Eat

L'Aigle d'Or ★★ TRADITIONAL FRENCH   In this practically one-horse town this isn't merely a watering hole. The tiny town of Azay holds one of the area's best value gastronomic gems. It might not look very special from the outside, which helps keep away the masses; however, the dining room's toasty fireplace and rustic wooden beams reveal its true character. For decades now chef Jean Luc Fèvre has been wowing guests with his signature filet of beef Chinon and his seasonal creations such as crab parmentier with shrimp cream, sandre fish stew with local Azay wine, or chocolate baba with Cointreau and orange salad. Treat yourself to the wine-pairing menu, a steal at only 72€ and featuring wines produced in the vicinity of the château.

10 av. Adélaïde-Riché. ☎ **02-47-45-24-58.** www.laigle-dor.fr. Main courses 16€–25€; fixed-price menus lunch 21€–23€, dinner 30€–58€. Mon–Tues and Thurs–Sat noon–1:30pm and 7:30–9pm, Sun noon–1:30pm. Closed Jan to mid-Feb.

Exploring the Château

Château d'Azay-le-Rideau ★★ CASTLE   Its machicolated towers and blue-slate roof pierced with dormers give it a medieval air; however, its defensive-fortress-like appearance is all for show. The château was actually commissioned in the early 1500s for Gilles Berthelot, François I's finance minister, and his wife, Philippa, who supervised its construction. They didn't have long to enjoy their elegant creation: In 1527, Berthelot was accused of misappropriation of funds and forced to flee, and the château reverted to the king. He didn't live here, but granted it to Antoine Raffin, one of his high-ranking soldiers. It became the property of the state in 1905.

Before you enter, circle the château and note the perfect proportions of this crowning achievement of the Renaissance in the Touraine. Check out its most fancifully ornate feature, the bay enclosing a grand stairway with a straight flight of steps. From the second-floor Royal Chamber, look out at the gardens. This lavish bedroom housed Louis XIII when he came through in 1619. The private apartments are lined with rich tapestries dating from the 16th and 17th centuries and feature examples of rare period furniture. Azay hosts a sound-and-light show most nights in July and August (details below).

C **02-47-45-42-04.** www.azay-le-rideau. monuments-nationaux.fr/. Admission 8.50€ adults, 5.50€ youth 18–25, free 17 and under. Open daily July–Aug 9:30am–7pm; April–June and Sept 9:30am–6pm; Oct–Mar 10am–12:30pm and 2–5:30pm. Admission to the evening sound-and-light show 9€ adults, 4€ children 5–12, free 4 and under; show is nightly mid-July to late Aug 8:30pm–midnight.

Château d'Azay-le-Rideau in autumn

LOCHES ★★

258km (160 miles) SW of Paris; 40km (25 miles) SE of Tours

Forever linked to legendary beauty Agnès Sorel, Loches is an exquisite medieval village, situated on the banks of the Indre River.

Essentials

ARRIVING   Six to ten **buses** run daily from Tours, run by the SNCF railway; the 50–70 minute trip costs 9.40€ one-way. For schedules, visit www.voyages-sncf. com or call *C* **02-47-05-30-49.** If you're **driving** from Tours, take N143 southeast to Loches.

VISITOR INFORMATION   The **Office de Tourisme** is near the bus station on place de la Marne (www.loches-tourainecotesud.com; *C* **02-47-91-82-82**).

Where to Eat & Stay

Hotel de France ★   Located in the medieval center of Loches, this charming hotel was a postal relay station until the mid–19th century. In 1932, three floors were added, converting it into an inn. Though the rooms have been upgraded and redecorated, the place keeps its classic provincial charm. The quietest rooms overlook the courtyard; however, the front rooms might be preferred for their balconies. This atmosphere is carried over into the excellent quality and value of the restaurant; guests and day-trippers can dine in the graceful dining room or in the peaceful paradise of the verdant courtyard (menus 18€–24€).

6 rue Picois, Loches 37600. *C* **02-47-59-00-32.** http://h.france.loches.free.fr. 17 units. 64€–95€ double. Parking 5€. Closed Jan 5 to early Feb and mid-Nov to mid-Dec. **Amenities:** Restaurant, bar, room service, free WiFi.

Where to Eat

Galerie B ★   For a creative meal in this traditional town, Galerie B is the place to go. Located in a former art gallery, it has retained an artsy ambiance with contemporary furniture and local artwork adorning the walls, though hints of history are apparent with the ceiling beams. This old-meets-new is also reflected in Chef David Béguin's traditional-with-a-contemporary-edge cuisine. The beautifully presented dishes may include salmon steak with squid ink, spaghetti drizzled with combava sauce, or saddle of rabbit stuffed with apples, chanterelle mushrooms and nuts. They also do take out, a rarity in France. This can make for quite the gourmet picnic near the château.

26–28 Grande rue, Loches 37600. ✆ **02-36-05-45-32.** www.restaurant-lagalerieb.fr. Main courses 15€–29€; fixed-price menus 16€ weekday lunch and 30€ gourmet lunch or dinner. May–Sep Tues evening to Sun noon, Oct–Apr Wed noon–Sun noon. Closed 2 weeks mid-Feb.

Exploring the Town

Sitting high on a bluff overlooking the valley, the château and its satellite buildings form a complex called the **Cité Royale ★**. The House of Anjou, from which the Plantagenets descended, owned the castle from 886 to 1205. Its royal legacy continued with its occupation by the kings of France from the mid-13th century, until Charles IX became king in 1560.

Château de Loches ★★, 5 place Charles-VII (www.chateau-loches.fr; ✆ **02-47-59-01-32**), one of the region's best examples of medieval architecture, is remembered for the *belle des belles* (beauty of beauties) Agnès Sorel, who lived there in the 15th century. Maid of honor to Isabelle de Lorraine, Charles VII became so enamored by Agnès that he gifted his new mistress the château. She bore the king three daughters and wielded great influence over him until her mysterious death. She was immortalized on canvas posthumously by Fouquet as a nearly topless Virgin Mary–with a disgruntled Charles VII looking on. (The original is in Antwerp; the château has a copy.) The château also contains the oratory of Anne de Bretagne, decorated with ermine tails. One of its outstanding treasures is a triptych of *The Passion* (1485) from the Fouquet school.

The massive 36 meter-high (118 feet) keep, or *donjon,* of the comtes d'Anjou was built in the 11th century and turned into a prison by Louis XI. The Round Tower contains rooms used for torture; a favorite method involved suspending the victim in an iron cage. In the 15th century, the duke of Milan, Ludovico Sforza, was imprisoned in the Martelet and painted frescoes on the walls to pass the time; he died here in 1508.

You can visit the château, the keep, and medieval garden without a guide daily. It's open April to September from 9am to 7pm, and October to March 9:30am to 5pm; in August a medieval festival is usually held at the castle.

Tickets to the château and the dungeon cost 8.50€ for adults, 6.50€ for students and children 7-18. Children 6 and under enter free.

The tomb of Agnès Sorel rests nearby at the Romanesque **Collégiale St-Ours (Collegiate Church of St-Ours),** 1 rue Thomas-Pactius (✆ 02-47-59-02-36), which was erected in the 11th and 12th centuries. Sculpted figures of saints and animals decorate the portal. Stone pyramids *(dubes)* surmount the nave; the carving on the west door is exceptional. The church is open daily from 9am to 7pm, except during mass; admission is free.

Finally, you may want to walk the ramparts and enjoy the view of the town, including a 15th-century gate and Renaissance inns.

SAUMUR

299km (185 miles) SW of Paris; 53km (33 miles) SE of Angers

Saumur lies in a region of vineyards, where the Loire separates to encircle an island. It makes one of the best bases for exploring the western Loire Valley. A small but thriving town, it doesn't entirely live off its past: Saumur produces some 100,000 tons per year of the mushrooms the French adore. Balzac left us this advice: "Taste a mushroom and delight in the essential strangeness of the place." The cool tunnels for the *champignons* also provide the ideal resting place for the region's celebrated sparkling wines. Enjoy both of these local favorites at a neighborhood cafe.

Essentials

ARRIVING **Trains** run frequently between Tours Centre and Saumur. Some 20 trains per day arrive from Tours (trip time: 30–40 min.); the one-way fare is 12€. From the station, take bus A into town. For schedules and information, visit www.voyages-sncf.com or call ✆ **36-35.** If you're **driving** from Tours, follow D952 or the A85 autoroute southwest to Saumur.

VISITOR INFORMATION The **Office de Tourisme** is on place de la Bilange (www.ot-saumur.fr; ✆ **02-41-40-20-60**).

Where to Stay

Hôtel St-Pierre ★ Sophisticated Saumur style shines through at this reasonably priced hotel. In the shadows of the Eglise St-Pierre, this 500-year-old building has been brought up to 21st-century standards with creative care to every last detail. Guest rooms have been uniquely decorated with artistic touches and many showcase their architectural aspects such as stone fireplaces or thick wooden beams; the prestige rooms are the best and well worth the splurge. The

---

Going Underground

As you drive along the Loire, something other than castles may catch your eye along the riverbanks. The region of Anjou holds the largest concentration of troglodyte caves in all of France. The beige limestone of the area was put to good use building the many châteaux, and the empty caverns from the excavated stone were not left abandoned.

Not surprisingly, the caves were first used to store bottles of the region's bubbly wine; more recently, however, many have been converted into homes, art galleries, and even restaurants. For a true troglodyte experience, stop in at the bustling and mainly underground artist town of **Turquant,** 10 km (6 miles) east of Saumur (www.turquant.fr).

Rock-carved troglodytes near Saumur

small French town ambience is completed by listening to the tolling church bells while relaxing in the garden terrace.

Rue Haute-Saint-Pierre. ☎ **02-41-50-33-00.** www.saintpierresaumur.com. 14 units. 110€–240€ double, one suite 250€. **Amenities:** Free parking, babysitting, room service, free Wi-Fi.

Where to Eat

If you're just breezing through town or looking for a casual bite, try **Les Tontons** (www.bistrotlestontons-saumur.blogspot.fr; ☎ **02-41-59-59-40**), a welcoming English-friendly bistro with great-value daily lunch specials and a fabulous local wine list. If you're visiting the equestrian center, you can rub shoulders with the riders at nearby **Le Carrousel** (www.le-resto-du-carrousel.com; ☎ **02-41-51-00-40**), showcasing regional cuisine for 13€ for lunch and from 20.50€ at dinner.

Le Gambetta ★★ MODERN FRENCH   For cuisine as chic as the city of Saumur, book a table at this avant garde address. The contemporary decor matches the inventive menu of Michelin-starred chef Mickael Pihours. He takes French cuisine far afield with wild turbot smoked with Oolong tea accompanied by parsnip soup, venison with truffle oil with porcini and bacon lasagna, and adventurous desserts such as pumpkin topped with Valrhona grand cru chocolate and caramel.

12 rue Gambetta. ☎ **02-41-67-66-66.** www.restaurantlegambetta.com. Main courses 20€–30€; lunch menu 25€, dinner menu 31€–97€. Tues and Thurs–Sun noon–2pm; Tues and Thurs–Sat 7–9pm. Closed 2 weeks in Jan, 3 weeks in Aug.

Exploring the Area

Of all the Loire cities, Saumur remains the most bourgeois; perhaps that's why Balzac used it for his classic characterization of a smug little town in "Eugénie Grandet." Saumur is also famous as the birthplace of the *couturière* Coco Chanel.

The men of Saumur are among the best equestrians in the world. Founded in 1768, the city's riding school, **Cadre Noir de Saumur ★**, avenue de l'Ecole Nationale d'Equitation (www.cadrenoir.fr; ☎ **02-41-53-50-50**), is one of the grandest in Europe, rivaling Vienna's, enough so to be deemed a UNESCO World Heritage Site in 2011. The stables house some 350 horses. Mid-February to October, 1-hour tours (8€ adults, 6€ children) run from 9:30 to 11am and 2pm to 4pm from Monday afternoon to Saturday afternoon. Tours depart about every 20 minutes. Some 48km (30 miles) of specialty tracks wind around the town—to see a rider carry out a curvet is a thrill. The performances peak during the **Carrousel de Saumur ★★** on the third weekend in July.

After lengthy restoration work, the **Château de Saumur** (www.chateau-saumur.com; ☎ **02-41-83-31-31**) has reopened to the public. The 12th-century château was the royal residence of Philippe II in the early 13th century and hasn't changed much since being immortalized in the September scene of the famous illuminated manuscript "Les Très Riches Heures" in 1410. The interior of the castle has displays recounting the history of the château as well as examples of tapestries, porcelain, furniture, and other decorative arts. An evening equestrian-and-light show is held in July and August in front of the château (Thurs–Sat; admission 18€ adults, 14€ children). Admission to the château museum from June to September is 9€ adults, 5€ children 7–16, free under 7; spring and autumn 5€ adults, 3€ children (open daily Apr to mid-June and mid-Sept to Oct 10am–1pm and 2–5:30pm; mid-June to mid-Sept 10am–6:30pm; closed Nov–Apr).

The area surrounding the town has become famous for its delicate sparkling wines. In the center of Saumur, you can wander the many aisles of **La Maison du Vin,** 7 quai Carnot (www.vinsvaldeloire.fr; ✆ **02-41-38-45-83**), and choose from a large stock direct from the surrounding vineyards.

An alternative is to travel east of Saumur to the village of **St-Hilaire,** where you'll find a host of vineyards. One of the better ones is **Veuve Amiot,** 21 rue Jean-Ackerman (www.veuveamiot.fr; ✆ **02-41-83-14-14**), where you can tour the wine cellars, taste different vintages, and buy bottles right in the showroom (open daily except Sundays in January and February).

Mushroom enthusiasts can learn about the cultivation of the local fungi first-hand at the **Musée du Champignon** (www.musee-du-champignon.com; ✆ **02-41-50-31-55**). Don't miss the annual mushroom festival in October. Admission to the museum is 8.20€ adults, 6€ children under 18 (open daily Feb to mid-Nov 10am–6pm and until 7pm Apr–Sept).

CHINON ★★

283km (175 miles) SW of Paris; 48km (30 miles) SW of Tours; 31km (19 miles) SW of Langeais

In the film "Joan of Arc," Ingrid Bergman identified the dauphin as he tried to conceal himself among his courtiers. This took place in real life at the Château de Chinon, one of the oldest fortress-châteaux in France. Charles VII centered his government at Chinon from 1429 to 1450. In 1429, with the English besieging Orléans, the Maid of Orléans prevailed upon the dauphin to give her an army. The rest is history. The seat of French power stayed at Chinon until the end of the Hundred Years' War.

Essentials

ARRIVING The SNCF runs about seven **trains** and four **buses** every day to Chinon from Tours (trip time: 45 min. by train; 1 hr., 15 min. by bus); the one-way fare is 9.70€. For schedules and information, visit www.voyages-sncf.com or call ✆ **36-35.** Both buses and trains arrive at the train station, which lies at the edge of the very small town. If you're **driving** from Tours, take D751 southwest through Azay-le-Rideau to Chinon.

VISITOR INFORMATION The **Office de Tourisme** is at place Hofheim (www.chinon-valdeloire.com; ✆ **02-47-93-17-85**).

Where to Eat & Stay

Château de Marçay ★★★ Fairytale dreams come true without breaking the bank at this unique château-hotel. The reverie begins as you drive onto the grounds of this imposing medieval fortress surrounded by vineyards. The 21st century has made it to the interior with all the modern comforts. Guest rooms feature vintage floral prints and most rooms have massive exposed beams to augment the castle charm; the less-expensive rooms are located in the Pavillon des Vignes annex. The restaurant is one of the best in the region, where you can dine on regional seasonal specialties accompanied by the château's own wine (fixed-price menus at lunch 30€–35€ and dinner 48€–85€). Try your hand at creating the same dishes during one of the chef's cooking classes (70€ per person).

Marçay. ✆ **02-47-93-03-47.** www.chateaudemarcay.com. 30 units. 110€–225€ double; 280€–310€ suite. Closed mid-Jan to mid-Mar. Take D116 for 7km (4¼ miles) southwest of Chinon. **Amenities:** Restaurant, bar, outdoor pool, room service, tennis court, free Wi-Fi.

Hostellerie Gargantua ★   This is the one of the most original economic hotels in all of the Loire. Located in the heart of town at the foot of the Château de Chinon, the castle-like 15th-century building used to be a courthouse where the father of writer François Rabelais (see "Musée Rabelais–La Devinière," below) worked as a lawyer. A highlight is its early Renaissance spiral staircase. The hotel has its quirks, but these are overruled by the large high-ceilinged guest rooms; most have canopy beds and some have stone fireplaces and/or views of the castle. Dine in its medieval hall, where you can sample some tasty local freshwater sandre prepared with Chinon wine, or duckling with dried pears and smoked lard.

73 rue Haute St. Maurice. ✆ **02-47-93-04-71.** www.hotel-gargantua.com. 7 units. 59€–89€ double. Closed Dec. **Amenities:** Restaurant, bar, free Wi-Fi. Parking from Apr–Nov 6€.

Where to Eat

Les Années 30 ★ FRENCH   Tucked away on the oldest street in Chinon is the town's most cutting-edge cuisine. Set in an appealing 16th-century building the interior is decorated with paintings and photos from the 1930s, hence the restaurant's name. Its excellent-value menu could include such dishes as rabbit terrine with grapefruit mousse and ginger sorbet, or duck with cherry reduction and poached pear. The raspberry millefeuille with thyme ice cream is the perfect way to end a summertime lunch on the vine-draped terrace.

78 Rue Haute St Maurice. ✆ **02-47-93-37-18.** www.lesannees30.com. Reservations recommended. Main courses 16€–28€; fixed-price lunch menu during the week 18€, dinner menu 26€–43€. Thurs–Mon 12:15–2pm; Tues 7:30–10pm in Jul–Aug. Closed June 14–Jul 1 and Nov 20–Dec 6.

Exploring the Town & the Château

On the banks of the Vienne, the winding streets of Chinon are lined with many medieval turreted houses, built in the heyday of the court. The most typical street is **rue Voltaire,** lined with 15th- and 16th-century townhouses. At no. 44, Richard the Lion-Hearted died on April 6, 1199, from a wound suffered during the siege of Chalus in Limousin. The Grand Carroi, in the heart of Chinon, was the crossroads of the Middle Ages. For the best view, drive across the river and turn right onto quai Danton. From this vantage point, you'll be able to see the castle in relation to the town and the river.

Chinon is known for its delightful red wines. After you visit the attractions, stop for a glass on one of Chinon's terraced cafes or visit a few local vineyards.

Château de Chinon ★★ CASTLE   The château, which was more or less in ruins, has undergone a massive excavation and restoration that started in 2003 and so far has resulted in beautifully restored ramparts, castle keep, and royal apartments, which now look more or less as they did in the good old days. After being roofless for 200 years, the apartments sport pitched and gabled slate roofs and wood floors, and the keep is once again fortified. The restoration, while not exact (due to the state of the original building), gives the overall impression of what the castle looked like around the time of Joan of Arc's visit. The buildings are separated by a series of moats, adding to its medieval look. A new building has been constructed on the foundations of the Fort of St-George, which serves as an entrance hall and museum, featuring new archeological finds discovered during the restoration, as well as objects and interactive displays that recount the story of Joan of Arc, Charles VII, and the history of the castle.

Btw. rue St-Maurice and av. Francois Mitterrand. ✆ **02-47-93-13-45.** www.forteressechinon.fr. Admission 8.50€ adults, 6.50€ students, free for children 12 and under. Open daily May–Aug 9:30am–7pm; Mar, Apr and Sept 9am–6pm; Oct–Feb 9:30am–5pm.

Chinon is famous for its wines, which crop up on prestigious lists around the world. Supermarkets and wine shops throughout the region sell them; families that have been in the business longer than anyone can remember maintain the two most interesting stores. At **Caves Plouzeau,** 94 rue Haute-St-Maurice (www.plouzeau.com; ✆ **02-47-93-32-11**), the 12th-century cellars were dug to provide building blocks for the foundations of the château. The present management dates from 1929; bottles of red or white wine cost from 6€ to 12€. You're welcome to climb down to the cellars (open for visits and wine sales Apr–Sept Tues–Sat 11am–1pm and 3–7pm and Oct–Mar Thurs–Sat 2–6pm).

The cellars at **Couly-Dutheil,** 12 rue Diderot (www.coulydutheil-chinon.com; ✆ **02-47-97-20-20**), are suitably medieval; many were carved from rock. This company produces largely Chinon wines (mostly reds); the popularity of its Bourgueil and St-Nicolas de Bourgueil has grown in North America in recent years. Tours of the caves and a *dégustation des vins* (wine tasting) require an advance call and cost 4€ to 6€ per person. Tours held year-round 8am–noon and 1:45–5:45pm.

Musée Rabelais–La Devinière ★ MUSEUM   The most famous son of Chinon, François Rabelais, the earthy humanist Renaissance writer, lived in town on rue de la Lamproie. (There's a plaque marking the spot where his father practiced law and maintained a home and office.) The museum in his honor, just outside the hamlet of Scuilly 5.5km (3½ miles) west of Chinon, was an isolated cottage at the time of his birth. Spending the early years of his life here profoundly affected the writer, and the area served as inspiration for parts of his most famous work, "Gargantua." Exhibits are spread out on the three floors of the main building, in the dovecote and the wine cellars, each area dedicated to an aspect of Rabelais, his times, and his role in Chinon. It is still an active vineyard, producing 4,000 bottles of excellent wine that would do the writer proud.

La Devinière, just outside of Seuilly off the N751. ✆ **02-47-95-91-18.** www.monuments-touraine. fr. Admission 5€ adults, 4€ students, free for children 11 and under. Open daily Apr–June 10am–12:30pm and 2–6pm; July–Aug 10am–7pm; Sept 10am–12:30pm and 2–6pm; Oct–Mar Wed–Mon 10am–12:30pm and 2–5pm. From Chinon, follow the road signs pointing to Saumur and the D117.

USSÉ ★

295km (183 miles) SW of Paris; 14km (8¾ miles) NE of Chinon

The Château d'Ussé is truly a fairy-tale castle. At the edge of the dark forest of Chinon in Rigny-Ussé, it was the inspiration for Perrault's legend of "The Sleeping Beauty" ("La Belle au Bois Dormant").

Essentials

ARRIVING   The château is best visited by car or on an organized bus tour from Tours. If you're driving from Tours or Villandry, follow D7 to Ussé.

Exploring the Château

Château d'Ussé ★ CASTLE   Conceived as a fortress in 1424, this complex of steeples, turrets, towers, and dormers was erected at the dawn of the

Château d'Ussé

Renaissance on a hill overlooking the Indre River. The terraces, laden with orange and lemon trees, were laid out by the royal gardener Le Nôtre. When the need for a fortified château passed, the north wing was demolished to open up a greater view. The château was later owned by the duc de Duras and then by Mme. de la Rochejacquelin; its present owner, the marquis de Blacas, has opened many rooms to the public, most recently the private dining room and the dungeon. The visit begins in the Renaissance chapel, with its sculptured portal and handsome stalls. You then proceed to the royal apartments, furnished with tapestries and antiques. One gallery displays an extensive collection of swords and rifles. A spiral stairway leads to a tower with a panoramic view of the river and a waxwork Sleeping Beauty waiting for her prince to come.

✆ **02-47-95-54-05.** www.chateaudusse.fr. Admission 14€ adults, 4€ students and children 8–16, free 7 and under. Open daily mid-Feb to March 10am–6pm; April–Aug 10am–7pm; and Sept–Nov 10am–6pm; closed the rest of the year.

FONTEVRAUD-L'ABBAYE ★★

304km (188 miles) SW of Paris; 16km (10 miles) SE of Saumur

The Plantagenet dynasty is buried in the Abbaye Royale de Fontevraud. The kings, whose male line ended in 1485, were also the comtes d'Anjou, and they wanted to be buried in their native soil. This regal patronage led to the building of one of Europe's largest medieval monastery complexes.

Essentials

ARRIVING   If you're **driving,** take D147 about 4km (2½ miles) from the village of Montsoreau. In season, you can take a **bus** (Line 1) from Saumur; schedules vary according to school holidays—visit the bus company's website, www.agglo bus.fr, to download the schedule or call ✆ **02-41-51-11-87.** The one-way fare for the 30-minute trip is 1.50€.

Where to Eat

La Licorne ★ MODERN FRENCH   Luckily the frugal monks' lifestyle of the Fontevraud Abbey isn't replicated at this nearby popular dining spot. Located on a walkway between the abbey and the parish church, this 18th-century bourgeois home exudes the grace of the *ancien régime*. However, the service isn't quite as regal and can be somewhat slow. So sit back and relax in its walled garden; the excellent-value menu is certainly worth the wait. It includes refined dishes such as filet of local Féra freshly caught from lake Léman; royal Maine d'Anjou pigeon topped with Chinon truffles; scampi ravioli with wild morel mushroom sauce; and such delectable desserts as local Alienor pastries.

Allée Ste-Catherine. ✆ **02-41-51-72-49.** www.restaurant-gastronomique-licorne.fr. Main courses 15€–30€; fixed-price menu 29€–65€. Nov–Apr Tues–Sun noon–2pm; Tues and Thurs–Sat 7–9pm; May–Oct daily noon–2pm and 7–9pm. Closed 2 last weeks of Dec.

Exploring the Abbey

Fontevraud-l'Abbaye ★★ ABBEY In this 12th-century Romanesque church—with four Byzantine domes—lie the remains of two English kings and princes, including Henry II of England, the first Plantagenet king, and his wife, Eleanor of Aquitaine, the most famous woman of the Middle Ages. Her crusading son, Richard the Lion-Hearted, is also entombed here. The Plantagenet line ended with the death of Richard III at the 1485 Battle of Bosworth. The tombs fared badly during the Revolution, when mobs desecrated the sarcophagi and scattered their contents on the floor.

More intriguing than the tombs is the octagonal **Tour d'Evraud,** the last remaining Romanesque kitchen in France. Dating from the 12th century, it contains five of its original eight *apsides* (half-rounded indentations originally conceived as chapels), each crowned with a conically roofed turret. A pyramid tops the conglomeration, capped by an open-air lantern tower pierced with lancets. Robert d'Arbrissel, who spent much of his life as a recluse, founded the abbey in 1101. Aristocratic ladies occupied one part; many, including discarded mistresses of kings, had been banished from court. The four youngest daughters of Louis XV were educated here. Since 1975, the abbey has also functioned as a cultural center, offering expositions, concerts, and seminars.

✆ **02-41-51-73-52.** www.abbaye-fontevraud.com. Admission 9.50€ adults, 7€ students, free 8 and under. Open daily April–June and Sept–Oct 9:30am-6pm; daily July–Aug 9:30am–7pm; daily Nov–Dec 10am–5:30pm; and Feb–Mar Tues–Sun 10am–5:30pm; closed Jan.

ANGERS ★★

288km (179 miles) SW of Paris; 89km (55 miles) E of Nantes

Once the capital of Anjou, Angers straddles the Maine River at the western end of the Loire Valley. Though it suffered extensive damage in World War II, it has been restored, blending provincial charm with a hint of sophistication. The bustling regional center is often used as a base for exploring the châteaux to the west. Young people, including some 30,000 college students, keep this vital city of 155,700 jumping until late at night.

Essentials

ARRIVING High-speed **trains** make the 1½-hour trip every hour from Paris's Gare Montparnasse; the cost is 28€ to 61€ one-way. From Tours, about 10 trains per day make the 1-hour trip; a one-way ticket is 17€. The Angers train station is a convenient walk from the château. For schedules and information, visit www.voyages-sncf.com or call ✆ **36-35.** From Saumur, there are direct **bus** connections (1½ hrs.); visit www.angoubus.fr or call ✆ **08-20-16-00-49** (.12€ per minute) for schedules. If you're **driving** from Tours, take the A85 autoroute west and exit at Angers Centre.

VISITOR INFORMATION   The **Office de Tourisme,** 7 place Kennedy (www. angers-tourisme.com; ℭ **02-41-23-50-00**), is opposite the entrance to the château.

Where to Eat & Stay

La Salamandre ★★ CLASSIC FRENCH   Located in the Best Western Hotel d'Anjou, this elegant restaurant celebrates the king who put the Loire Valley on the map: François I. His symbol, the salamander, appears cleverly throughout the decor. Enjoy royal service and regal ambiance with its large wooden fireplace, and stately furniture and wallpaper. Its menus could feature traditional pot aux feu soup à l'ancienne, or the more adventurous zucchini flower soufflé with lobster mousse, or you can't go wrong with the divine Anjou pigeon with truffles.

Built in 1846, the hotel continues on with the same royal themes. It rents 55 comfortable, spacious rooms that are slightly dated, though not as far back as the building itself (from 115€–185€).

In the Hotel d'Anjou, 1 bd. du Maréchal Foch. ℭ **02-41-88-99-55.** www.restaurant-lasalamandre.fr. **For the hotel:** ℭ **02-41-21-12-11;** www.hoteldanjou.fr. Main courses 21€–38€; fixed-price menu lunch 24€, dinner 29€–69€. Open daily noon–2pm and Mon–Sat 7:30–9:30pm.

L'Hôtel de France ★   Situated right across from the railway station, this comfortable 19th-century hotel is the best place to overnight in Angers. It has been in the careful hands of the Bouyer family since 1893. The spacious rooms are decorated in mainly cream and beige tones with smart classic furnishings. It is a common stopover for business travelers and room rates go up 15€ to 25€ per night during trade shows.

8 place de la Gare, Angers 49100. ℭ **02-41-88-49-42.** www.hoteldefrance-angers.com. 55 units. 127€–147€ double; 183€ suite. Parking 7€. **Amenities:** Restaurant, bar, room service, free Wi-Fi.

Provence Caffè ★ PROVENÇAL   If you've had your fill of Loire specialties, come here for the flavors of Provence. From the outside, it doesn't look like much, but that helps keep it a good local secret. Decor is modern and simple; the best tables are by the windows with the wonderful view of the main town square. Chef François Derouet has a fondness for fish, serving up red mullet salad with pistou, sea bream with ratatouille tart and Niçois crumble with goat cheese. To cleanse your palate, order a *Versinthe*, the lesser-known Provençal cousin to absinthe.

9 place du Ralliement. ℭ **02-41-87-44-15.** www.provence-caffe.com. Main courses 16€; fixed-price menu 19€–34€. Tues–Sat noon–2pm and 7–10pm.

Exploring the Town

If you have time for shopping, wander to the pedestrian zone in the center of town. Its boutiques and small shops sell everything from clothes and shoes to jewelry and books. To satisfy your sweet-tooth stop in at **Benoit,** 2 rue Lices (www.chocolats-benoit.com; ℭ **02-41-88-94-52**). The best chocolate shop in Angers was passed from father to daughter and Anne-Francoise's new recipes have garnered her enough awards and renown to open boutiques in Paris and Lille.

Oenophiles will not be disappointed with the selection at the **Maison du Vin de l'Anjou,** 5 bis place Kennedy (www.vinsdeloire.fr; ℭ **02-41-88-81-13**), where you can learn about the area's vineyards and buy a bottle or two for gifts or a picnic.

Cathédrale St-Maurice ★★ CATHEDRAL   The cathedral dates mostly from the 12th and 13th centuries; the main tower is from the 16th century. The

statues on the portal represent everybody from the Queen of Sheba to David at the harp. The tympanum depicts Christ Enthroned. The stained-glass windows from the 12th through the 16th centuries have made the cathedral famous. The oldest one illustrates the martyrdom of St. Vincent; the most unusual is of St. Christopher with the head of a dog. The 12th-century nave, a landmark in cathedral architecture, is a work of harmonious beauty. If you're interested in a guided tour, call the church's presbytery at the number below. Tours are conducted erratically, often by an associate of the church, and usually with much charm and humor. The tours are available in French, English (offered July–Aug), and Italian.

Cathédrale St-Maurice, Angers

Place Freppel. ✆ **02-41-87-58-45.** Free admission; donations appreciated. Daily 9am–7pm.

Château d'Angers ★★★ CASTLE   The château, dating from the 9th century, was the home of the comtes d'Anjou. The notorious Black Falcon lived here, and in time, the Plantagenets took up residence. From 1230 to 1238, the outer walls and 17 enormous towers were built, creating a fortress. King René favored the château, and during his reign, a brilliant court life flourished until he was forced to surrender to Louis XI. Louis XIV turned the château into a prison. In World War II, the Nazis used it as a munitions depot, and the Allies bombed it in 1944.

Visit the castle to see the **Apocalypse Tapestries ★★★**. They weren't always so highly regarded—they once served as a canopy to protect orange trees and were also used to cover the damaged walls of a church. Woven in Paris by Nicolas Bataille from cartoons by Jean de Bruges around 1375 for Louis I of Anjou, they were purchased for a nominal sum in the 19th century. The series of 77 sections, illustrating the Book of St. John, stretches 100m (328 ft.).

In 2009, the roof of the Logis Royal burned in an electrical fire and the château suffered damage (fortunately, the tapestries are housed in a separate

---

A Toast with the Home-Brew—Cointreau

Another libation unique to Angers is Cointreau. Two confectioner brothers set out to create a drink of "crystal-clear purity." The result was Cointreau, a twice-distilled alcohol from the peels of two types of oranges, bitter and sweet. The factory has turned out the drink since 1849. Cointreau flavors such drinks as the cosmopolitan and the sidecar. Recent marketing campaigns, including one featuring seductress Dita Von Teese, have helped modernize the brand and today some 13 million bottles of Cointreau are consumed annually.

La Carée Cointreau, 2 bd. des Bretonnières (www.cointreau.fr; ✆ **02-41-31-50-50**), is in the suburb of St-Barthèlemy, a 10-minute drive east of the town center. If you call ahead to reserve, you can take a 1½-hour guided tour of the distillery and then visit the showroom, where you can sample and stock up on the fruity liqueur. Hours are variable; tours run on Saturdays only from October to April, and Tuesday through Saturday the rest of the year (10€ adults, 3.80€ children 12–17, free 11 and under).

LOIRE FOR kids

The Loire is a wonderful family holiday destination, and the highlights, of course, are the castles (**Valençay, Langeais,** and **Loches** being the best to include for children). But the two most frequently visited attractions for families are located at the same address: the **Aquarium du Val de Loire** and the **Parc des Mini-Châteaux** (www.decouvrez-levaldeloire.com; ✆ 02-47-23-44-44), 9.5km (6 miles) west of Amboise, near the village of Lussault-sur-Loire.

The **Parc des Mini-Châteaux** holds replicas of France's most famous castles, built at 1/30 the size of the originals. Chambord, for example, is less than 3.5m (11 ft.) tall. It's all very patriotic—a sort of learning game that teaches French schoolchildren the glories of their *patrimoine* (heritage) and collects some of the most celebrated architecture in Europe. Admission is 14€ adults, 10.50€ students and children 4–14, and free children 3 and under; for a full day of fun get a discounted joint ticket with the Aquarium 22€ and 15€ (daily early Apr–May 10:30am–7pm; June–Aug 10am–7pm/8pm; Sept–Nov 14 10:30am–6pm; closed mid-Nov to early Apr). The **aquarium** is home to some 10,000 freshwater and saltwater fish. Admission is 14€ adults, 10.50€ children 4–14 (daily Jan–Mar and Sept–Dec 10:30am–6pm; Apr–May 10:30am–7pm; June to late July 10am–7pm; and late July to mid-Aug 10am–8pm; closed 2 weeks in Nov and Jan).

There are also plenty of activities for outdoor adventures in the area. Take a break from navigating the castles of the Loire by paddling it. **The Canoe Company** (www.canoe-company.fr; ✆ 06-37-01-89-92) rents canoes on both the Loire River at Rochecorbon and on the Cher at the foot of the Château de Chenonceau (open daily, starting at 14 € per person for 2 hours).

building and were untouched), however, the Logis, which includes the royal apartments, has undergone careful renovations and is now reopened to the public. A full visit should also include the ramparts, windmill tower, and 15th-century chapel. Once you've paid the entrance fee, you can take an hour-long guided tour focusing on the architecture and history of the château, or a tour devoted to the Apocalypse Tapestries. Both are available only in French; a self-guided tour with audio guide is available in English.

2 promenade du Bout-du-Monde. ✆ **02-41-86-48-77.** www.angers.monuments-nationaux.fr. Admission 8.50€ adults, 5.50€ seniors and students 18–25, free children 17 and under and on 1st Sun/month. Sept–Apr daily 10am–5:30pm; May–Aug daily 9:30am–6:30pm.

Musée Jean Lurçat ★★ MUSEUM There are actually four museums in town, but the most interesting is in the Ancien Hôpital St-Jean. A hospital established in 1174, visitors now come for its famous tapestry, *Le Chant du Monde (The Song of the World),* created by Jean Lurçat between 1957 and 1966. This monumental work of 10 panels is a symphony of the artist's interpretation of the destiny of the world, from awe-inspiring space travel to the horrible apocalypses of war. Save time to visit the 17th-century dispensary, equipped with shelves of earthenware jars and trivets. Don't miss the Romanesque cloister with its secret garden on your way out.

4 bd. Arago. ✆ **02-41-24-18-45.** www.musees.angers.fr. Admission 4€ adults, 3€ students, free for 25 and under. June–Sept daily 10am–6:30pm; Oct–May Tues–Sun 10am–noon and 2–6pm.

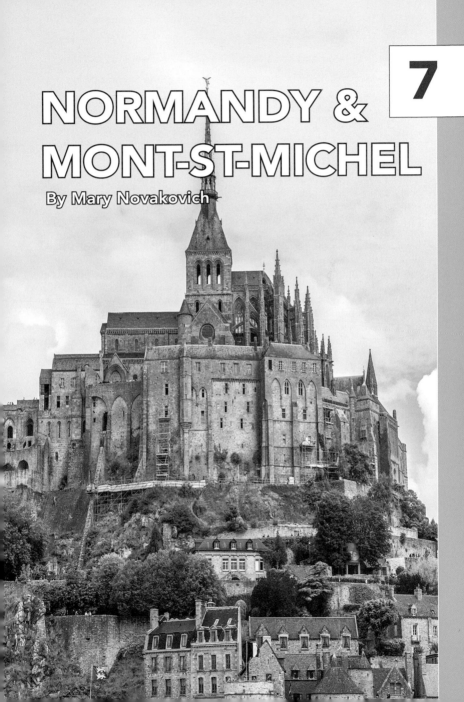

NORMANDY & MONT-ST-MICHEL

By Mary Novakovich

There's a gentleness in Normandy's rich rolling landscape that gives little clue to the region's long and turbulent history. Look a little closer, however, and you see haunting reminders of some of the Second World War's most dramatic and decisive battles. The Allied landings on Normandy's beaches in June 1944 changed the course of the Second World War. Although the embarkation beaches teem with visitors in the summer, they remain living memorials to bravery, determination, and ingenuity.

But these sights don't exclusively define the region. Fashionable Deauville and its family-friendly neighbor Trouville have been drawing sun-seekers since the 19th century. As the age of the railway expanded during the Victorian era, so too did genteel seaside resorts that dot this stretch of France's northern coast.

Bayeux attracts lovers of history and art, many to see the extraordinary tapestry that recounts another battle that altered the course of history: the Norman Conquest. Honfleur is a place of arty pilgrimage, and Rouen's history and bustling restaurant scene attract foodies hungry for culture. At the western border is Mont-St-Michel, which has stood guard for a millennium. A new pedestrian walkway will link the coastline with this castle in the sand for the first time.

Head inland to savor the cream of Normandy produce: namely the pungent cheeses from Camembert, Pont l'Evêque and Livarot. Instead of the vineyards that characterize the South of France, Normandy has apple orchards that produce the region's renowned cider and Calvados brandy.

ROUEN ★★

135km (84 miles) NW of Paris; 89km (55 miles) E of Le Havre

Normandy's capital buzzes from dawn 'til dusk, thanks to its busy port and lively university. Its agreeable atmosphere invites leisurely strolls along medieval lanes, where some of Normandy's most delicious produce sits temptingly in shop windows. Former celebrated residents of Rouen include writer Gustave Flaubert (who grew up along the city's enchanting cobbled streets), Claude Monet (who endlessly painted Rouen's Cathédrale de Notre-Dame), and Joan of Arc, who met her tragic end in the place du Vieux Marché, the Old Marketplace, in 1431.

Rouen suffered greatly during World War II when half of it was destroyed, mostly by Allied bombers. During the reconstruction of the old quarters, some of the almost-forgotten crafts of the Middle Ages were revived. Today its metropolitan area is home to half a million people, with about 100,000 clustered in the large center.

Essentials

ARRIVING   From Paris's Gare St-Lazare, **trains** leave for Rouen about once an hour (trip time: 1½ hr.). The one-way fare is 23€, but you can get deals online for as little as 10€. For rail information and schedules, visit www.voyages-sncf.com

PREVIOUS PAGE: **Mont-St-Michel**

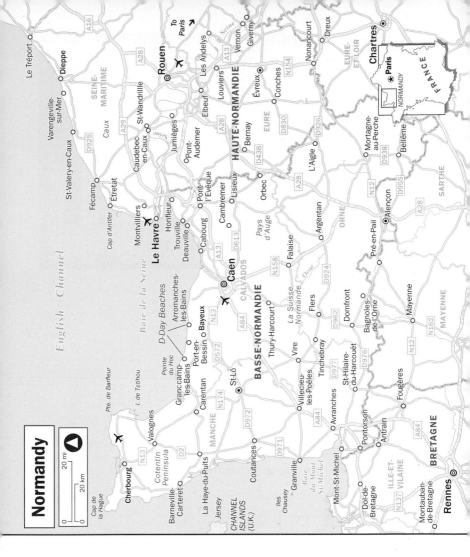

or call ✆ **36-35**. To **drive** from Paris, take A13 northwest to Rouen (trip time: 1½ hr.).

VISITOR INFORMATION   The **Office de Tourisme** is at 25 place de la Cathédrale (www.rouentourisme.com; ✆ **02-32-08-32-40**).

CITY LAYOUT   As in Paris, the Seine splits Rouen into a **Rive Gauche** (Left Bank) and **Rive Droite** (Right Bank). The old city is on the Rive Droite.

Getting Around

ON FOOT   Rouen's old town is compact and best navigated on foot, as many of its medieval streets are pedestrianized. The Tourist Office offers free maps marked with two easy-to-follow walking tours around the city.

Half-timbered houses in Rouen

BY BICYCLE Like many French cities, Rouen has its own bike-sharing scheme, **Cy'clic** (http://cyclic.rouen.fr). You can register online or directly at one of Rouen's 21 bike stands; fees range from 1€ for 1 day to 5€ for a week.

BY CAR **Rouen Park** (www.rouenpark.com) details the city's five central public parking lots, with information on exact location, number of parking places, and hourly prices.

BY TAXI **Les Taxi Blancs** (📞 02-35-61-20-50).

BY PUBLIC TRANSPORT Rouen's **Métro** (www.crea-astuce.fr) has one line running north-south through the city, underground on Rive Droite and at street level on Rive Gauche. The most central stations in Rive Droite are Théâtre des Arts, Palais de Justice, and the train station, Gare-Rue Verte. Tickets cost 1.50€ and are on sale at automatic kiosks at each station.

[FastFACTS] ROUEN

ATMs/Banks Dozens of banks are all around the city center, with six along rue Jeanne d'Arc.

Business Hours As in most of France, shops are closed from about noon until at least 2pm, or even 3 or 4pm. They might open briefly on Sunday mornings, and most will be closed for a day early in the week, usually a Monday or a Tuesday.

Doctors & Hospitals **Centre Hospitalier Universitaire de Rouen** (www.chu-rouen. fr; 📞 **02-32-88-89-90**).

Emergencies The Tourist Office lists a full range of emergency contacts—from a poison center to an emergency cardiology unit—on its website (www.rouentourisme.com). Click on "General Information," then "Emergency Numbers."

Mail & Postage **La Poste,** 112 rue Jeanne d'Arc (📞 **36-31**).

Pharmacies **Grande Pharmacie du Centre,** 29 place Cathédrale (📞 **02-35-71-33-17**).

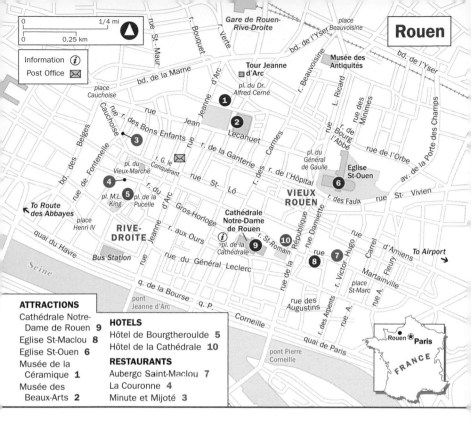

ATTRACTIONS
Cathédrale Notre-
  Dame de Rouen 9
Eglise St-Maclou 8
Eglise St-Ouen 6
Musée de la
  Céramique 1
Musée des
  Beaux-Arts 2

HOTELS
Hôtel de Bourgtheroulde 5
Hôtel de la Cathédrale 10

RESTAURANTS
Auberge Saint-Maclou 7
La Couronne 4
Minute et Mijoté 3

Where to Stay

Hotel de Bourgtheroulde ★★   Just steps from place du Vieux-Marché and rue de l'Horologe is Rouen's only five-star hotel and prettiest hideaway. When you step into the ornate 16th-century courtyard, the last thing you expect to see when you enter this historic mansion is a screamingly chic and modern galleried restaurant and bar, where locals meet for an after-work drink. Each elegant room is a one-off—some contemporary, others more classic—with interesting features such as exposed stone walls and beams, wood paneling, and bathrooms tiled in chunky, earthy mosaics. At the **Spa du Drap d'Or,** a steam bath, sauna, and Normandy's largest indoor pool await after a day of sightseeing.

15 place de la Pucelle. ✆ **02-35-14-50-50.** www.hotelsparouen.com. 78 units. 260€–320€ double; 450€–550€ suite. Parking 18€. **Amenities:** 2 bars; indoor swimming pool; 2 restaurants; spa; free Wi-Fi.

Hôtel de la Cathédrale ★   This incredibly charming hotel is one of Rouen's most appealing affordable options. The location—just off a pedestrian street midway between the cathedral and the Eglise St-Maclou—is unbeatable. Guestrooms are simple, but each has its own character, with quirky wallpaper, plump leather armchairs, or wooden beamed ceilings. In summertime, a buffet breakfast is served in the cobble-covered courtyard.

12 rue St-Romain. ✆ **02-35-71-57-95.** www.hotel-de-la-cathedrale.fr. 26 units. 90€–120€ double; 140€ triple; 160€ quadruple. Public parking 11€ nearby. **Amenities:** Breakfast room; free Wi-Fi.

Where to Eat

Don't be surprised to find plenty of fresh, succulent seafood in France's fourth largest port. Rouen lives up to its status as Normandy's capital in offering a superb selection of restaurants serving fantastic Norman cuisine. Restaurants are dotted all around the city, with many found in the antiques quarter near Eglise St-Maclou and, inevitably, in the old market square. Key local ingredients include fresh fish, rich cream, butter, and apples, which are on tantalizing display in the **daily market,** place du Vieux Marché (Tues–Sun 6:30am–1:30pm). A much larger **food market** is in the place St-Marc east of the cathedral (Tues, Fri, Sat 6am–6pm, Sun 6am–1:30pm).

Auberge Saint Maclou ★ TRADITIONAL FRENCH   In a picturesque half-timbered building on the edge of Rouen's antiques district, this lively neighborhood restaurant adds a Norman touch to French classics. Try the duck breast in a rich cider sauce, or a delicately roasted plaice served with shrimp bisque. On summer evenings, sidewalk tables spill out into the shadow of Eglise St-Maclou.

222 rue Martainville. ✆ **02-35-71-06-67.** Main courses 16.40€–26.20€. Tues–Fri noon–2pm and 7–10pm, Sat 7–10pm, Sun noon–2pm.

La Couronne ★★★ NORMAN   It's so easy to feel utterly cocooned in the cozy half-timbered interior of France's oldest *auberge*, which has been feeding travelers since 1345. Photos of the great and the good cover the entrance and the upper floor, and a few have left their mark on the menu, too. One is Julia Child, whose first-ever French lunch menu in 1948—oysters and *sole meunière*—you can have for 65€. Another menu replicates some of the dishes enjoyed by the Impressionists (35€), including pigs' cheeks that have been braised seemingly forever and are, frankly, sublime.

31 place du Vieux Marché. ✆ **02-35-71-40-90.** www.lacouronne.com.fr. Main courses 25€–48€; fixed-price lunch menu 25€–75€; fixed-price dinner menu 35€–75€. Daily noon–2:30pm and 7–10:30pm.

Minute et Mijoté ★★ FRENCH   You won't be able to take your eyes off the wonderfully retro decor of this tiny bistro near the Vieux Marché. Practically every collector's item from the 1950s and 60s is crammed into this adorably kitsch and very friendly space. Start with a creamy foie gras flan in cider sauce, or grilled gambas served with chorizo risotto. And the house specialty, slow-cooked lamb shoulder wrapped in savoy cabbage, just melts in the mouth.

58 rue de Fontenelle. ✆ **02-32-08-40-00.** www.gill.fr. Main courses 21€; fixed-price menu 26€–31€. Tues–Sat noon–2pm and 7:45–10pm.

Exploring Rouen

The city's main sights—and the old town— are on the Right Bank of the Seine. Visitors usually make a beeline for **place du Vieux Marché**. Their first impression is often one of bafflement when they see the giant modernist Church of Ste-Jeanne in the place where Joan of Arc was executed for heresy on May 30, 1431. Surrounded by medieval half-timbered restaurants and shops, the church's 1970s architecture comes as a bit of a shock. But it somehow works, with its enormous stained-glass windows and a swirling roof that nudges the neighboring market stalls. A simple sign in the church's garden marks the spot where France's greatest heroine was burnt at the stake. This square was also the former home of Rouen's Joan of Arc Museum, which closed in 2012. A new Joan of Arc Visitors' Center is currently under construction and is expected to open in 2015.

The pedestrianized "Street of the Great Clock"—**rue du Gros Horloge**—runs between Rouen's cathedral and place du Vieux Marché and is one of the hubs of the city. It's named for an ornate gilt Renaissance clock mounted on an arch over the street and is connected to a bell tower; this had been the clock's home until it was lowered in 1529 so that the Rouennais could get a closer look at it. You can climb the bell tower, stopping at the exhibition rooms along the way to learn about the structure's history and watch the bells in action. At the top are lovely views of the old town and cathedral. Open Tuesday to Sunday 10am to 1pm and 2 to 7pm from April to October, and from 2 to 6pm November to March. Admission 6€ for adults and 3€ for under 18, including audio guide.

Cathédrale Notre-Dame de Rouen ★★★ CATHEDRAL

Monet immortalized Rouen's cathedral in more than 30 paintings. Consecrated in 1063, the cathedral, a symphony of lacy stonework, was reconstructed after suffering damage in World War II. Two towers distinguish it: **Tour de Beurre** was financed by the faithful who were willing to pay for the privilege of eating butter during Lent. Containing a carillon of 56 bells, the 1877 **Tour Lanterne** rises to almost 150m (492 ft.), making its spire the tallest in France.

Inside, the cathedral's choir is a masterpiece, with 14 soaring pillars. Particularly interesting is the **Chapelle de la Vierge,** adorned with Renaissance tombs of the cardinals of Amboise. Also entombed here is the heart of Richard the Lion-Hearted. Along the south-facing side of the cathedral is an entrancing collection of statues of saints that had previously adorned the exterior.

Behind the cathedral is the **Palais de l'Archevêché (Archbishop's Palace).** The broken arches and rosette windows witnessed the trial of Joan of Arc in 1431, and her rehabilitation was proclaimed here in 1456.

For a bird's-eye view over the cathedral and square, visit **Le Balcon** (admission 2€; accessed via the Tourist Office), a top-floor viewing platform that tells the story of the cathedral. Worth a look are the photographs of the damage inflicted on this great structure during World War II.

Cathédrale Notre-Dame de Rouen

Interior, Cathédrale Notre-Dame de Rouen

Place de la Cathédrale. ✆ **02-35-71-51-23.** www.cathedrale-rouen.net. Free admission. Apr–Oct Mon 2–7pm, Tues–Sat 9am–7pm; Nov–Mar Mon 2–6pm, Tues–Sat 9am–noon and 2–6pm; Sun and holidays year round 8am–6pm. Closed during Mass and some holidays.

Eglise St-Maclou ★★ CHURCH   St-Maclou was built in the Flamboyant Gothic style with a step-gabled porch and cloisters. It's known for the 16th-century panels on its doors; look out for the Portail des Fontaines on the left. The church was built in 1200, rebuilt in 1432, and consecrated in 1521. Its lantern tower is from the 19th century, and its exterior was completely renovated in 2013.

Well worth a peek is the nearby **Aître Saint-Maclou,** 184 rue Martainville (✆ **02-76-08-81-13**). Half-timbered buildings, decorated with creepy skull motifs, mark the site of a cemetery dedicated to victims of the 1348 Great Plague. It now houses the regional Ecole des Beaux-Arts. From April to October it's open daily 9am to 7pm; from November to March it's open Saturday and Sunday 9am to 6pm, plus during French school holidays. Admission is free.

3 place Barthélémy. ✆ **02-35-08-69-00.** Free admission. Apr–Oct Sat–Sun 10am–noon and 2–6pm; Nov–Mar Sat–Sun 10am–noon and 2–5:30pm.

Musée de la Céramique ★ MUSEUM   Rouen has been an important center for ceramics and pottery production since the 16th century. This small museum highlights local treasures, from reddish-hued 17th- and 18th-century Rouen *faïence* (opaquely glazed earthenware) to two new rooms dedicated to 19th- and 20th-century Sèvres porcelain.

1 rue Faucon. ✆ **02-35-07-31-74.** www.rouen-musees.com. Admission 3€ adults, 2€ students, free for children 17 and under. Wed–Mon 2–6pm.

Musée des Beaux-Arts ★★ MUSEUM   More than 8,000 artworks ranging from medieval primitives to contemporary paintings are housed in this imposing 19th-century edifice. You'll find paintings by Ingres (such as his "La Belle Zélie") and a salon devoted to Géricault, including his portrait of Delacroix. Other works are by Veronese, Velázquez, Caravaggio, Rubens, Poussin, Fragonard, and Corot, and by Impressionists such as Renoir, Sisley, and Monet, including several of the latter's paintings of the Rouen cathedral.

Esplanade Marcel Duchamp. ✆ **02-35-71-28-40.** www.rouen-musees.com. Admission 5€ adults, 3€ students, free for children 17 and under. Wed–Mon 10am–6pm.

Shopping

Rouen was once one of France's major producers of the fine decorative ceramic ware known as ***faïence de Rouen.*** For contemporary faïence, your best bet is **Faïencerie Augy,** 26 rue St-Romain (✆ **02-35-88-77-47**). Rouen is also an antiques capital, with dozens of vendors in the Old Town. The best hunting ground is along **rue Damiette,** and **rue St-Romain.** A **flea market** joins the food stalls in place St-Marc on Fridays and Saturdays. Other antiques shops worth visiting are **Michel Bertran,** 108 rue Molière (✆ **02-35-98-24-06**), with a good selection of 18th- and 19th-century paintings, especially by School of Rouen Impressionists; and **Etienne Bertran,** 110 rue Molière (✆ **02-35-70-79-96**), with its collection of antique books.

Chocolate lovers are spoiled for choice, with delectable treats at **Le Cacaotier,** 5 rue Guillaume le Conquérant (www.lecacaotier.com; ✆ **02-35-62-71-06**) and **Auzou,** 163 rue du Gros Horloge (www.auzou-chocolat.fr; ✆ **02-35-70-59-31**).

On Normandy's Cider & Calvados route

Normandy might not have the vineyards of other parts of France, but it does have endless apple orchards that produce the acclaimed Calvados brandy, refreshing alcoholic cider, and *pommeau*, a mixture of Calvados and apple juice. In the lush rolling hills of the Pays d'Auge east of Caen, producers open their half-timbered farms (mostly by appointment) to thirsty tourists eager to try the different varieties of apple nectar. Some of the region's most delightful villages lie on this 40km (25-mile) Route du Cidre (www.larouteducidre.fr), notably Cambremer and Beuvron-en-Auge, the latter being one of the designated Most Beautiful Villages of France (www.beuvron cambremer.com).

Nightlife

Opéra de Rouen, 7 rue du Docteur Rambert (www.operaderouen.fr; ✆ 02-35-98-74-78), schedules year-round ballet, opera, and classical music. A variety of concerts takes place at **Abbatiale Saint-Ouen,** place du Général-de-Gaulle. And at the former hangar **Le 106,** quai Jean de Béthancourt (www.le106.com; ✆ 02-32-10-88-60), there's a jam-packed lineup of French and international pop and rock shows. Check the Tourist Office's website for the latest events.

Le Vicomté, rue de la Vicomté (✆ 02-35-71-24-11), attracts everyone from the after-work crowd to clubbers, with five levels devoted to fun and food. There's a club with live bands and DJs, classy fireside cocktail bar, restaurant, patio, and even a billiard room.

HONFLEUR ★★

201km (125 miles) NW of Paris; 63km (39 miles) NE of Caen

This exquisite fishing port dating from the 11th century has been the focus of artists for hundreds of years—native son Eugène Boudin, Gustave Courbet and Claude Monet, to name but three. Stroll the Vieux Bassin (old harbor) and you can still see art students with their sketchbooks trying to capture the enchanting light that dances off the white boats and glistening water. Impossibly tall 18th-century townhouses tower over the harbor, where cafes and restaurants crowd around the pleasure boats.

It's busy and, yes, full of tourists from all over the world. But it's such a beguiling place that it's worth putting up with the throngs. Time your visit so that you have lunch a bit early, about noon. Then you'll have the streets to yourself while everyone else is still eating.

The approach from the east is along the impressive Pont de Normandie bridge that spans the Seine River from Le Havre. And the Côte de Grace—the start of the alluring Côte Fleurie—meanders westwards from here, passing half-timbered Norman homes and ancient chapels en route to Trouville.

Essentials

ARRIVING   There's no direct **train** service into Honfleur. From Paris, take one of the half-dozen or so daily trains from Gare St-Lazare to Trouville-Deauville (from 25€ one-way). There are cheaper fares if booked in advance online. From there, **Bus Verts du Calvados** (www.busverts.fr; ✆ 08-10-21-42-14) no. 20 makes the 25-minute ride to Honfleur; the one-way fare is 2.40€. From Rouen,

Sailboats in Honfleur harbor

take the train to Le Havre (15€ one-way; journey time around an hour) and transfer to bus no. 50 (4.65€ one-way), for the 30-minute ride to Honfleur. Several buses (no. 20) run daily between Caen and Honfleur (trip time: 2 hr.); the one-way fare is 8.20€.

To **drive** from Paris (trip time: 2–2½ hr.; 20.80€ in tolls), take A13 west, then the A29 north in the direction of Le Havre. From Pont l'Evêque or other points southwest, D579 leads to Honfleur's major boulevard, rue de la République.

VISITOR INFORMATION The **Office de Tourisme** is on quai Lepaulmier (www.ot-honfleur.fr; ✆ **02-31-89-23-30**).

[FastFACTS] HONFLEUR

ATMs/Banks Half a dozen banks are along rue de la Foulerie, place Pierre Berthelot and rue des Longettes.

Mail & Postage **La Poste,** 7 cours Albert Manuel (✆ **36-31**).

Pharmacies **Pharmacie du Dauphin,** 5 rue Dauphin (✆ **02-31-89-10-80**).

Where to Stay

Absinthe Hôtel ★★ You can't fault the Absinthe Hotel's location right by the quayside and down an atmospheric street of 16th-century houses. Most of the rooms are in what used to be a church presbytery, with more in an annex with views of the port. The decor is a handsome blend of the traditional and the contemporary. Each room has its own whirlpool bath; one suite features a private sauna. The elegant **Absinthe Restaurant,** on the ground floor, peeks out over the town's port.

1 rue de la Ville. ✆ **02-31-89-23-23.** www.absinthe.fr. 11 units. 130€–210€ double; 255€–265€ suite. Parking 13€. **Amenities:** Restaurant; free Wi-Fi.

La Maison de Lucie ★★   Walk less than 10 minutes from the busy port and step into a tranquil world in this 18th-century townhouse. The incredible warmth comes not only from the roaring fire in the reception room but also from the friendly owners. Pleasingly old-fashioned rooms (but with modern fittings) cluster around the internal courtyard, some of which open directly onto this pretty little flower-filled space. There's also a separate pavilion that houses one of the hotel's attractive suites, complete with fireplace. Nip downstairs into the vaulted cellar of the main house for a relaxing session in the Jacuzzi.

44 rue des Capucins. ✆ **02-31-14-40-40.** www.lamaisondelucie.com. 12 units. 170€–200€ double; 250€–330€ suite. Parking 15€. **Amenities:** Spa 40€; free Wi-Fi.

Les Maisons de Léa Hotel & Spa ★★★   In the bustle of the central place Sainte-Catherine is this ivy-covered collection of 16th-century buildings that make up one of the region's most appealing hotels. The themes vary in this converted salt warehouse and adjoining houses, from Maison Romance—all pale florals and agreeably overstuffed armchairs—to the nautical tones of the Maison Capitaine. Afternoon tea in the cozy library is tough to resist. Its intimate **Restaurant de Léa**, with deep red walls and a roaring fire, comes up with some beautiful creations. Try the chestnut soup topped with whipped foie gras, or succulent cod on a bed of mushroom risotto. Menus from 28€ to 56€.

Place Sainte-Catherine, Honfleur 14600. ✆ **02-31-14-49-49.** www.lesmaisonsdelea.com. 30 units. 160€–205€ double; 260€–305€ suite. **Amenities:** Restaurant; bar; spa; free Wi-Fi.

Where to Eat

There are numerous mediocre restaurants in Honfleur, especially along the Vieux Bassin. Too many cater to large groups on day trips, knowing that these patrons are unlikely to come back. If you're happy with a bowl of so-so mussels, then by all means take in the lively atmosphere of the harborside restaurants. If you want better quality food, then check out the back streets.

Le Bistro des Artistes ★★ NORMAN   The back of this friendly restaurant overlooks the harbor, so book ahead if you want one of the two tables with waterside views. Chef and owner Anne Marie Carneiro changes her menu regularly but will usually include such regional classics as veal chops *à la normande,* monkfish in cider, skate in mustard sauce, or *teurgoule,* a rich Norman rice pudding. Anne Marie dishes out the food herself, so don't be too impatient if the service is a little slow. She also runs an adorable bed-and-breakfast, **Logis St-Léonard**, on the south side of town. There are only two rooms (125€ and 155€), but there is also a two-bedroom house to rent for 750€ for weekends or 1,500€ for a week.

30, place Pierre-Berthelot. ✆ **02-31-89-95-90.** www.logis-saint-leonard.com. Main courses 15€–27€. July–Sept Thurs–Tues noon–2:30pm and 7–10pm, Wed 7–10pm; Oct–June Fri–Tues noon–2:30pm and 7–10pm.

Le Hamelin ★ NORMAN   This bustling bistro across the square from SaQuaNa offers seafood of better quality and value than you're likely to find in the Vieux Bassin just around the corner. Giant bowls of mussels, delectable shellfish platters, and poached skate with capers keep fish fans happy while carnivores can feast on slow-cooked lamb and rosemary or veal tenderloin Vallée d'Auge style with apples and a deliciously rich sauce of butter, cream, and Calvados.

16 place Hamelin. ✆ **02-31-89-16-85.** www.restaurantlehamelin.com. Main courses 7.90€–48€. Fixed-price menu 18€–46€. Daily noon–3pm and 7–10pm.

Restaurant SaQuaNa ★★★ CONTEMPORARY FRENCH   In case you were wondering about the strange name, it's a mash-up of "Saveurs, qualité, nature." Given a different spelling, it becomes "sakana", which is Japanese for fish. That pretty much sums up Chef Alexandre Bourdas's philosophy; he trained in Japan, and has taken an Asian minimalist approach in everything from the food to the decor. In this Zen atmosphere, the food is exquisite and reaches taste buds you didn't know you had. There are only two menus—one five courses, the other nine—both of which change all the time and feature plenty of fish. It could include sea bream with cabbage leaves, salmon and saffron, or foie gras and lentils. Sounds deceptively simple, but you'll soon see why the restaurant has two Michelin stars.

22 place Hamelin. ✆ **02-31-89-40-80.** www.alexandre-bourdas.com. Fixed-price menu 75€– 115€. Thurs–Sun 12:30–2:30pm and 7:30–9:30pm.

Exploring Honfleur

Begin your tour of Honfleur by picking up a map from the Tourist Office. Each one is printed with three handy walking routes, all detailing points of interest around town. Stroll along the scenic quays, past the fishing boats and narrow, slate-roofed houses that line the **Vieux Bassin**. On the north side of the harbor, the former governor's house, the imposing **Lieutenance,** dates from the 16th century. Nearby is France's largest wooden church, **Eglise Ste-Catherine,** place Ste-Catherine (✆ **02-31-89-11-83**), which was built by 15th-century shipbuilders. The church is open July and August daily from 8am to 8pm, September through June daily 8:30am to noon and 2 to 6pm.

See the village from a different perspective on one of the regular **boat trips** (www.promenade-en-bateau-honfleur.fr; 45–90 min.; 6€–9.50€) that depart from jetties east of the Vieux Bassin. The 45-minute ride on *La Calypso* explores the harbors that make up the port of Honfleur, while the 90-minute journey on *La Jolie France* takes you out into the Seine estuary.

Les Maisons Satie ★★ MUSEUM   Erik Satie—composer, painter, friend to the Surrealists and Dadaists—was born in this house in 1866, and it's fitting that the museum paying homage to him is just as wonderfully eccentric as the man himself. The giant pear sculpture you see at the beginning sets the stage for some seriously wacky exhibits, enhanced by a suitably strange audio guide. It might not be to everyone's taste, and it's useful if you know even a little about his background. *Tip:* Be prepared to apply a little pedal power for one of the exhibits.

67 bd. Charles V. ✆ **02-31-89-11-11.** www.musees-honfleur.fr. Admission 6€ adults, 4.50€ ages 10–17, free children 9 and under. May–Sept Wed–Mon 10am–7pm; Oct–Dec and Feb 16–Apr Wed–Mon 11am–6pm. Closed Jan–Feb 15.

Musée Eugène Boudin ★★ MUSEUM   Located in the former chapel of an Augustinian convent, this museum vividly evokes the reasons why so many painters were drawn to Honfleur over the centuries. The pastels and paintings of Honfleur's native son, Eugène Boudin, form part of a fine collection of artworks including Impressionist paintings by Dubourg, Monet, Courbet, and Dufy. Additional displays include local photographs (snapped between 1880–1920), Norman tourism posters, and antiques.

Rue de l'Homme de Bois. ✆ **02-31-89-54-00.** www.musees-honfleur.fr. Admission 5.50€ adults, 2.50€ students and children 10 and over. Mar 15–June Wed–Mon 10am–noon and 2–6pm; July– Sept Wed–Mon 10am–noon and 2–6:30pm; Oct–Dec and Feb 16–Mar 14 Mon and Wed–Fri 2:30–5:30pm, Sat–Sun 10am–noon and 2:30–5:30pm. Closed Jan–Feb 15.

Monet's Garden at Giverny

Claude Monet spent the last 43 years of his life in creative contentment in his house and sprawling gardens in the Normandy village of Giverny, 75km (47 miles) northwest of Paris. It's just as enchanting as when he lived there with his wife and eight children surrounded by colorful gardens and ponds decked with the water lilies and green Japanese bridge seen in so many of his paintings. The house and gardens are open daily from April 1–November 1, 9:30am–6pm; admission 9€ adults, students 5€, children under 7 free. If travelling from Paris, take the train from St-Lazare to Vernon, and catch the shuttle to Giverny. Trains cost from 14.30€ each way; the shuttle costs 8€ round-trip. www.fondation-monet. com. See chapter 5, "Side Trips from Paris," for more on a visit to Giverny.

NaturoSpace ★★ MUSEUM   Discovering France's largest tropical butterfly house in Honfleur is an unexpected delight. Thousands of colorful specimens—more than 50 species from South America, Asia, Africa, and Oceania—flutter through a greenhouse-like labyrinth of exotic foliage, from orchids and birds of paradise to palms. Visit in the morning to watch chrysalises crack open and brand-new butterflies make their first flight.

Bd. Charles V. ✆ **02-31-81-77-00.** www.naturospace.com. Admission 8.50€ adults, 6.60€ students and children 3 to 13, family package 33€. Apr–June and Sept daily 9:30am–1pm and 2–6:30pm, July–Aug daily 9:30am–6:30pm; Oct–Nov and Feb–Mar 9:30am–1pm and 2–5:30pm. Closed Dec and Jan.

DEAUVILLE ★★★

206km (128 miles) NW of Paris; 47km (29 miles) NE of Caen

Deauville has been associated with the rich and famous since the Duc de Morny, Napoleon III's half-brother, founded it as an upscale resort in 1859. In 1913, it entered sartorial history when Coco Chanel launched her career here, opening a boutique selling tiny hats that challenged the fashion of huge-brimmed hats loaded with flowers and fruit. Chanel cultivated a tradition of elegance that dominates Deauville. It's classy, restrained, and understated—precisely the qualities that have been attracting well-heeled Parisians in overwhelming numbers since the early 20th century. They're the ones who unselfconsciously call Deauville the 21st arrondissement of Paris.

Colored parasols on the beach at Deauville

Essentials

ARRIVING   There are five to nine daily **rail** connections from Paris's Gare St-Lazare (trip time: 2 hr., but 3hr. if changing trains in Lisieux); prices start at 15€ one-way. The rail depot lies midway between Trouville and Deauville, within walking distance of both resorts. **Bus Verts du Calvados**(www.busverts.fr;✆08-10-21-42-14) serves the Normandy coast from Caen to Le Havre. To drive from Paris (trip time: 2½ hr.), take A13 west to Pont L'Evêque, and then follow D677 north to Deauville.

VISITOR INFORMATION   The **Office de Tourisme** is at 112 rue Victor Hugo (www.deauville.org; ✆ **02-31-14-40-00**).

SPECIAL EVENTS   For 10 days in late August/early September, the **Deauville American Film Festival** (www.festival-deauville.com; ✆ **02-31-14-40-00**) honors movies made in the United States. Actors, producers, directors, and writers, from Brad Pitt to Steven Spielberg, flock here and briefly eclipse the high rollers at the casinos and the polo crowd. Unlike many film festivals, Deauville is open to the general public.

[Fast FACTS] DEAUVILLE

ATMs/Banks   A half-dozen banks cluster on and around rue Eugène-Colas.

Internet Access   Various bars and cafes offer free Wi-Fi, including **Le Morny's Café,** 6 place Morny (✆ **02-31-87-32-06**), as well as the Office de Tourisme.

Mail & Postage   **La Poste,** 20 rue Robert Fossorier (✆ **36-31**).

Pharmacies   **Pharmacie de Garde,** 8 rue Désiré Le Hoc (✆ **02-31-14-61-70**).

Where to Stay

L'Augeval ★   Two Norman-style villas make up this immensely charming three-star hotel just west of the Hippodrome de Deauville–La Touques. It's less than a 10-minute walk from the center, yet it seems a world away in its calm and friendly atmosphere. Rooms in the Trait de l'Union villa are generally more spacious, and those rooms that aren't tucked in under the mansard roof have a balcony or terrace. (One even has an adorable little loggia.) On still evenings you can hear the gentle whinnying of the horses in nearby stables. All have elegant French furnishings, with sumptuous brocades and comfy chairs, and some of the bathtubs have whirlpool jets. Flowers fill the surrounding gardens, which are enhanced by a small but heated swimming pool.

15 av. Hocquart-de-Turtot. ✆ **02-31-81-13-18.** www.augeval.com. 42 units. 74€–248€ double; 206€–345€ suite. Parking 8€. **Amenities:** Bar; babysitting; billiards and darts room; exercise room; outdoor pool; room service; sauna and steam room 26€ for 30 min.; free Wi-Fi.

Les Manoirs de Tourgéville ★★★   An inspired base for families touring the Normandy coast, Les Manoirs, a 6km (4 miles) hop from Deauville, is an ultra-friendly grand hotel built around an ancient Norman mansion. Borrow one of the hotel's free bikes for a slow ride past the deer and rabbits living in the 7 hectares (17 acres) of tranquil grounds. Light and airy guestrooms in the mansion combine period features with fine linens and furnishings. Suites in the newer building are ultra-modern and can interlink to accommodate large families.

Chemin de l'Orgueil, Tourgéville. ✆ **02-31-14-48-68.** www.lesmanoirstourgeville.com. 57 units. 160€–320€ double; 270€–590€ suite. **Amenities:** 2 restaurants; bar; bikes; cinema; health club; parking; indoor pool; room service; sauna; free Wi-Fi.

Royal Barrière ★★★   No single hotel epitomizes the epic grandeur of Deauville like the Royal Barrière. Push through its gilded revolving doors to find photo portraits of a thousand famous former guests: Sean Connery, Harrison Ford, Barack Obama, among them. Guest rooms and suites are a palatial medley of crushed red velvet, plush carpet, and cool marble. Guests enjoy complimentary access to the Royal's beach club and Olympic-size pool or a golf lesson at the prestigious Golf Barrière Club. Non-guests may sit at Deauville's top table by dining at **Restaurant l'Etrier** (fixed-price menus 67€–115€). This temple of seafood gastronomy is overseen by chef Eric Provost, a one-time understudy of Alain Ducasse and Joël Robuchon.

Boulevard Cornuché. ✆ **02-31-98-66-22.** www.lucienbarriere.com. 252 units. 222€–800€ double; 830€–2,300€ suite. Parking 15€. Closed Jan–Feb. **Amenities:** Restaurant; children's dining room; bar; babysitting; exercise room; heated outdoor pool; room service; steam room; 2 tennis courts; Wi-Fi (10€/day).

Where to Eat

As expected, Deauville has its share of fine-dining restaurants, and simply those that are touristy and overpriced, particularly along rue Eugène Colas. You also pay a premium to sit at one of the restaurants along the beachfront promenade Les Planches, but sea views don't come cheap.

La Cantine de Deauville ★ FRENCH   You won't leave hungry from this lively brasserie with an airy, modern ambience. It's the place to come for hearty plates of beef, notably huge steaks (suitably called "Gargantua") and steak tartare prepared at the table. If you want something a bit lighter, try the herb-crusted grilled sea bass or salmon saltimbocca with goat's cheese. The two-course lunchtime menu at 15.90€ is a particularly good value. La Cantine is certainly a breath of fresh air among the more touristy restaurants along Eugène Colas.

90 rue Eugène Colas. ✆ **02-31-87-47-47.** www.lacantinedeauville.fr. Main courses 17€–29€. Open daily 9am–11pm.

Le Ciro's Barrière ★★★ FRENCH/SEAFOOD   From its excellent vantage point on Les Planches, you get some of Deauville's best people-watching to go with some top-class seafood. It may be pricey, but Norman chef Jérôme Taquet's superb cuisine is worth it. For a luxurious appetizer, try grilled langoustines with foie gras and chestnuts. If you want a seafood blowout, go for the *plateau de fruits de mer royal* (79€), a tower of local lobster, Isigny oysters, and super-fresh shellfish.

Planches de Deauville, boulevard de la Mer. ✆ **02-31-14-31-31.** www.lucienbarriere.com. Main courses 33€–52€. Thurs–Mon noon–2:30pm and 7:30–10pm. Open daily July–Aug. Closed 2 weeks in Jan.

Il Parasole ★ ITALIAN   This reliable, jolly, and good-value pizzeria proves that you don't have to spend a fortune in Deauville to have an enjoyable meal. Pizzas have perfectly thin crusts and are generous in size, as are the classic pasta dishes such as seafood spaghetti and risotto with gambas. It gets busy, especially on the outside terrace, so you might want to book a table a few hours ahead. There's another branch just over the Touques River in neighboring Trouville.

6 rue Hoche. ✆ **02-31-88-64-64.** www.ilparasole.com. Main courses 8.90€–23.90€. Daily noon–3pm and 7–midnight. Open non-stop in July and Aug.

Exploring Deauville

Some of the architecture looks as if it had stepped out of a gothic fairy tale. The style is ostensibly Norman—lots of half-timbered buildings mostly in suitably muted shades. But then you see turrets sprouting here and there, with gables and balconies wedged into every nook and cranny. It's as if a French version of the Addams Family had a hand in designing some of these glorious confections. The overall effect is delightful, enhanced by the profusion of flowers in the public spaces. With its golf courses, casinos, deluxe hotels, La Touques and Clairefontaine racetracks, regattas, yacht harbor, polo grounds, and tennis courts, Deauville hums with upper-class patronage. Soak up the exclusive vibe with an afternoon spent people-watching, particularly along boutique-lined **rue Eugène-Colas, place Morny** (named for the resort's founder), and **place du Casino.**

Outdoor Activities

BEACHES   Deauville's boardwalk, **Les Planches,** is an impossibly pretty promenade running parallel to the town's 2km (1-mile) beach, **Plage de Deauville.** Beaux Arts and half-timbered Norman-inspired buildings line its edges. Deauville's distinctively primary-colored parasols dot the sands—even out of season. Visitors parade along the boardwalk past private bathing cabins, each one's entrance stenciled with the names of Hollywood film stars who have attended the Deauville American Film Festival. It's hard not to smile at some of the misspellings.

Access to every beach in Normandy is free, although beach clubs cover some stretches of sand. You can rent a beach umbrella for 10€ a day and a sun-lounger for 5€. Rent two sun-loungers and an umbrella for 18€. A bathing cabin costs from 10€–20€ a day. Parking costs from 2€ per hour in the public lots beside the sea.

The **Piscine Municipale,** boulevard de la Mer (© 02-31-14-02-17), is a large indoor seawater pool. Depending on the season, bathers pay 4€ to 5€ per person. Swimming caps are compulsory and, as in every municipal swimming pool in France, men have to wear Speedo-style trunks. No baggy shorts allowed.

HORSE RACES/POLO   You can watch horses—either racing or competing at polo—most days from late June to early September. The venues are the **Hippodrome de Deauville-La Touques,** 45 av. Hocquart de Turtot (www.france-galop.com; © 02-31-14-20-00), in the heart of town near the Mairie de Deauville (town hall); and the **Hippodrome de Deauville Clairefontaine,** route de Clairefontaine (www.hippodrome-deauville-clairefontaine.com; © 02-31-14-69-00), within the city limits, 2km (1 mile) west of the center. Tickets normally cost 3€ for adults, free for those under 18.

Shopping

Luxury boutiques such as Hermès, Ralph Lauren, and Louis Vuitton cluster around the **place du Casino**. If you're looking for more inclusive and slightly more affordable shops, including a lovely Norman-style Printemps department store, take a stroll along **rue Eugène-Colas** and **place Morny.**

To see Norman produce in all its glory, head for the **Marché Publique** (open-air market) in place du Marché beside place Morny. In July and August, it's open daily 8am to 1pm. The rest of the year, market days are Tuesday, Friday, and Saturday, as well as Sunday from March to June and September through October. In addition to fruits, vegetables, poultry, cider, wine, and cheese, you'll find cookware, porcelain tableware, and cutlery.

Nightlife

The **Casino de Deauville,** rue Edmond Blanc (www.lucienbarriere.com; © 02-31-14-31-14), has been one of France's foremost casinos since it opened in 1912. Over the years, the original Belle Epoque has expanded to include a theater,

Le Brummel nightclub, three restaurants, two bars, and a huge collection of slot machines (*machines à sous*). The casino distinguishes areas for slot machines from more formal zones containing such games as roulette, baccarat, blackjack, and poker. The slots are open daily 10am to 2am (to 3am Fri and 4am Sat) and have no dress code. The areas containing *les jeux de table* (table games) are open Monday to Thursday 4pm to 2am (to 3am Fri and 4am Sat) and Sunday 2:30pm to 2am. Entrance is free, and you must present a passport or ID to gain admission.

Clubbers head for **Le Chic,** 14 rue Désiré-le-Hoc (www.lechicdeauville.fr; ✆ 02-31-88-30-91), a favorite with French actors and off-duty jockeys. Polo players frequent the perennially popular **Brok Café,** 14 av. du Général-de-Gaulle (✆ 02-31-81-30-81)—if you're keen to join them, make sure you hit this Cuban-style venue before midnight.

Les Planches, Domain du Bois Lauret, Blonville (www.lesplanches.com; ✆ 02-31-87-58-09), 4km (3 miles) from Deauville, attracts gilded young Parisians with its world-class DJs, large dance floor, and even a swimming pool next to the indoor/outdoor bar. It's open from 11pm until dawn every Saturday night except in January and February, and daily in July and August.

TROUVILLE ★★★

206km (128 miles) NW of Paris; 47km (29 miles) NE of Caen

Hugging the eastern bank of the Touques River is Deauville's less fashionable—but no less fascinating—neighbor Trouville. Deauville might have the chic boutiques, but Trouville has the soul of a working fishing port. Cross the Touques at the Pont des Belges and you immediately see the change in atmosphere. The large fish market, Marché aux Poissons, is a hive of activity and teems with small cafes selling the freshest seafood. More restaurants line the quayside, which becomes even livelier every Wednesday and Sunday when the open-air food market sets up its stalls.

Essentials

ARRIVING   There are **rail** connections from Gare St-Lazare in Paris to Trouville (see the "Deauville" section, earlier in this chapter). **Bus Verts du Calvados** (www.busverts.fr) links Trouville, Deauville, and the surrounding region with the rest of Normandy. For bus information, call the **Gare Routière** (✆ 08-10-21-42-14).

VISITOR INFORMATION   The **Office de Tourisme** is at 32 bd. Fernand-Moureaux (www.trouvillesurmer.org; ✆ 02-31-14-60-70).

Exploring Trouville

The bustle of Trouville's quayside carries on into the narrow alleyways that wind behind the port. It's a pleasure to get lost here among the many restaurants and little shops that somehow squeeze into the haphazard collection of lanes. Eventually you'll come to the grand Victorian villas along **Les Planches**, the first seaside boardwalk on the Normandy coast, which dates back to 1867. In those days, artists and writers including Gustave Flaubert, Marguerite Duras, Claude Monet, and Eugène Boudin flocked to Trouville's beach, **Plage de Trouville,** captivated by the light and fresh air. Nowadays it's a firm favorite with families, with a giant children's play area, donkey rides, tennis courts, and the **Piscine de Trouville** (✆ 02-31-14-48-10), an indoor freshwater pool that gets very crowded in summer. Depending on the season, bathers pay 6€ to 7€ per person.

Hours are July to August daily 9:30am to 7:30pm, June and September daily 10am to 7pm, and October to May daily 10:30am to 7pm.

If you want to cross over to Deauville, you can take the little foot ferry that trundles back and forth at high tide (daily May–Sept; weekends and holidays only Oct–Apr; 1.20€) or the pedestrian walkway (same charge). Or just walk south to the permanent bridge, the Pont des Belges, which spans the Touques. On the Trouville quayside, you can rent bikes of all shapes and sizes by the hour at **Les Trouvilllaises** (www.lestrouvillaises.fr; ✆ **02-31-98-54-11**; open from Mar 15–Oct 30).

[Fast FACTS] TROUVILLE

ATMs/Banks   Banks are along bd. Fernand Moureaux, rue Victor Hugo and Place Foch.

Internet Access   Various bars and cafes along the quayside offer free Wi-Fi. Don't hesitate to ask for the access code.

Mail & Postage   **La Poste,** rue Amiral de Maigret (✆ **36-31**).

Pharmacies   **Pharmacie Centrale du Port,** 138 bd. Fernand Moureaux (✆ **02-31-88-10-59**).

Where to Stay

Best Western Hostellerie du Vallon ★   Trouville's best hotel is tucked away on a quiet street up from the busy port area. Behind its traditional Norman exterior—with lots of half-timbering draped in flowers—are attractively and comfortably furnished bedrooms with private balconies. Its indoor pool makes this warm four-star a good year-round option, but be aware of the high prices charged by the bar—when it's open, that is. Golfers get a 15 percent discount at the Golf de Deauville St-Gatien course.

12 rue Sylvestre Lasserre. ✆ **02-31-98-35-00.** www.hostellerie-du-vallon.com. 62 units. 135€–210€ double. Free parking. **Amenities:** Bar; billiard room; exercise room; Jacuzzi; indoor pool; sauna; steam room; free Wi-Fi.

Hotel Flaubert ★   You can't get any closer to the beach than at the Flaubert. This 1930s Norman-style three-star is right on Les Planches. This is old-school seaside charm, with decent-sized rooms traditionally furnished, and many with balconies. It's worth paying the extra money to get a view of the sea, but be aware that it might get a bit noisy in high season. If you're a light sleeper, you might prefer a street-facing room.

Rue Gustave Flaubert. ✆ **02-31-88-37-23.** www.flaubert.fr. 31 units. 100€–165€ double; 150€–260€ suite. Closed mid-Nov to mid-Feb. **Amenities:** Bar; free Wi-Fi.

Where to Eat

Trouville's 60-odd restaurants are well served by the constant supply of seafood that comes into the port. It doesn't have the fine-dining scene of Deauville—nor, for the most part, its high prices. That doesn't mean it's particularly cheap, but you can find a delicious lunch in one of the many quayside bistros and cafes. A visit to the Marché aux Poissons is a must: browse its stalls and take your pick of whatever seafood is on offer—from oysters and tiny shrimps to whelks and scallops. Then get the stallholder to cook it for you. Grab a glass of chilled muscadet and perch on one of the high tables surrounding the market. One of the best stalls is **Poissonnerie Pillet-Saiter** (www.poissonnerie-pilletsaiter.fr; ✆ 02-31-88-02-10).

La Petite Auberge ★ NORMAN   The earth meets the sea in this cozy, Norman bistro tucked away in a narrow lane not far from the beach. Prices match the level of cooking, with filets of red mullet simmered in a rich broth, or a turbot with a delicate sauce of cider and cream. Meat lovers can opt for roast duckling, wood pigeon, or just a perfectly cooked filet steak. It's a tiny place with 30 seats at most, so reservations are vital in season.

7 rue Carnot. ✆ **02-31-88-11-07.** www.lapetiteaubergesurmer.fr. Main courses 29€–34€; fixed-price menu 38€–55€. Thurs–Mon noon–2:30pm and 7:15–9:30pm. Closed Jan 15–30 and Jun 15–30.

Les Mouettes ★ SEAFOOD/NORMAN   What used to be a classic fishermen's hangout continues to serve good-quality seafood and meat dishes in convivial surroundings near the port. If you want something different, try the *grand aïoli*—steamed cod, mussels, and vegetables served with luscious garlicky mayonnaise—or the *choucroute de poissons*, haddock, cod, and mussels on a bed of sauerkraut—a taste of Alsace on the Normandy coast.

11 rue des Bains. ✆ **02-31-98-06-97.** www.le-central-trouville.com. Main courses 8.90€–18.80€; fixed-price menu 13.90€–29.50€. Open daily 9am–11pm.

Trouville Nightlife

Trouville's casino, **Casino Barrière de Trouville,** place du Maréchal-Foch (www.lucienbarriere.com; ✆ 02-31-87-75-00), is smaller and less stuffy than Deauville's, with more of a New Orleans–style environment in its Louisiane Café bar. Entrance to the slot machines is free. Entrance to the more formal area—with roulette, blackjack, and craps—costs 14€ per person. You must present a passport or ID card to gain admission, and be age 18 or over. The formal area is open Sunday through Thursday 9pm to 2am, Friday 9pm to 3am, and Saturday 9pm to 4am. The casino's nightclub, Embellie, is open Saturdays from 10am to 5am. Entrance is free, with drinks starting at 12€. There is no formal dress code as such, but you should dress smartly.

CAEN ★

238km (148 miles) NW of Paris; 119km (74 miles) SE of Cherbourg

Situated on the banks of the Orne, the port of Caen suffered great damage in the 1944 invasion of Normandy. Mercifully, though, the twin abbeys founded by William the Conqueror and his wife, Mathilda, were spared. Today much of Caen is both cosmopolitan and commercial, with a vibrant, welcoming vibe. The capital of Lower Normandy, it's home to a student population of 30,000 and several great museums, and serves as a convenient base for exploring the surrounding coast.

Essentials

ARRIVING   From Paris's Gare St-Lazare, between 12 and 15 **trains** a day arrive in Caen (trip time: 2–2½ hr.). The fare is 26.80€ one-way. One-way fares from Rouen (trip time: 1 hr., 45 min.) start at 26€. To **drive** from Paris, travel west along A13 to Caen (drive time: 2½–3 hr.).

VISITOR INFORMATION   The **Office de Tourisme** is on place St-Pierre in the 16th-century Hôtel d'Escoville (www.caen-tourisme.fr; ✆ 02-31-27-14-14).

CITY LAYOUT   Downtown Caen stretches from Abbaye aux Dames in the east to Abbaye aux Hommes in the west. The pedestrianized rue St-Pierre bisects the town's main shopping district. The train station is southeast of the city center. The towering ramparts of the hilltop Château de Caen make an ideal spot to get your bearings.

Getting Around

ON FOOT   Caen's city center is small and much of it is pedestrianized. For short stays, it's easiest to explore the town on foot.

BY BICYCLE   Caen has its own bike-sharing scheme, **V'eol** (www.veol.caen.fr). You can register online (where you can also download a handy map of the city's bike paths) or directly at one of Caen's 40 bike stands; fees start at 1€ for the first 30 minutes.

BY CAR   It's best to park your wheels and explore the city center on foot. The Tourist Office website offers a downloadable map (under "Transport"), clearly marked with the town's major parking lots. Among others, there is one behind the train station and three just south of the Château and one underground in front of the Château.

BY TAXI   **Taxis Abbeilles,** 54 place de la Gare (www.taxis-abbeilles-caen.com; ✆ 02-31-52-17-89).

BY PUBLIC TRANSPORT   The **Twisto bus and tram network** (www.twisto.fr; ✆ 02-31-15-55-55) crisscrosses the city. Most useful for visitors is the tram: The two north-south lines (A and B) overlap through the city center, passing all of Caen's major monuments en route. Tickets (1.35€) can be purchased from automatic kiosks at each station.

[Fast FACTS] CAEN

ATMs/Banks   The city center has plenty of banks, including five on rue Jean Eudes.

Doctors & Hospitals   **Centre Hospitalier Universitaire de Caen,** av. de la Côte de Nacre (www.chu-caen.fr; ✆ 02-31-06-31-06).

Internet Access   Various bars and cafes along the quayside offer free Wi-Fi. Don't hesitate to ask for the access code.

Mail & Postage   **La Poste,** 2 rue Georges Lebret (✆ 36-31).

Pharmacies   **Pharmacie du Château,** 27 av. Libération (✆ 02-31-93-64-78).

Where to Stay

Best Western Hotel le Dauphin ★   Three separate buildings—one built on the site of a 15th-century priory—make up this friendly and rather quirky hotel. The location is wonderfully central, just steps away from the Château and the pedestrianized streets of restaurants and shops. The rooms can be a bit compact but they're full of charm, some with exposed brickwork and cute little alcoves. Ask for a room in the tower, which will give you lovely views of the Château.

29 rue Gémare. ✆ 02-31-86-22-26. www.le-dauphin-normandie.com. 37 units. 100€–190€ double. Parking free but limited. **Amenities:** Restaurant; bar; room service; spa; free Wi-Fi.

A Proustian Remembrance of "Balbec"

If you read Marcel Proust's *Remembrance of Things Past*, you'll discover that the resort of "Balbec" was really Cabourg, 24km (15 miles) northeast of Caen. Guests can check into the **Grand Hôtel,** Les Jardins du Casino, promenade Marcel Proust, 14390 Cabourg (www.mgallery.com; ✆ **02-31-91-01-79**, doubles from 160€ to 455€), a holdover from the opulent days when it was first built in 1855. What used to be Marcel Proust's favorite room has been restored from a description in his novel. Film buffs will also recognize the Grand Hotel's dining room from the 2011 French hit comedy-drama *The Untouchables*, with its majestic floor-length windows overlooking the sea.

The town of Cabourg (www.cabourg.net) is just as charming, its Victorian streets fanning out from the grand circle where the hotel stands. Beneath the hotel is the indoor municipal swimming pool, where locals flock when it's too cold to take to the huge stretch of sands in front of Promenade Marcel Proust. Every June, the beach becomes the setting for the Romantic Film Festival, when a giant screen shows dozens of romance-themed films over five days. The large covered market is worth a visit, too, on Wednesdays, Fridays, and weekends (daily in July and August), when farmers bring their fresh Normandy produce.

Le Clos St-Martin ★★ Sylvie and Jean Noël run this intimate, four-room *chambres d'hôtes,* or bed-and-breakfast. The three antique-splashed suites (one of which can be booked as a family room) and one double are set over three floors of a rambling 16th-century mansion, just a short stroll from the Abbaye aux Hommes. Breakfast is superb, and often includes Sylvie's baked treats, such as *teurgoule,* Norman rice pudding.

18bis place Saint Martin. ✆ **02-31-50-08-71.** www.leclosaintmartin.com. 4 units. 108€ double; 118€–160€ suite, including breakfast. Public parking nearby. **Amenities:** Free Wi-Fi.

Where to Eat

A large student population helps make Caen's dining scene one of the most dynamic in Normandy. Sidewalk cafes and restaurants line rue du Vaugueux and the surrounding neighborhood, east of the Château.

A Contre Sens ★★ FRENCH/NORMAN Anthony Caillot's Michelin-starred restaurant has been steadily building up a buzz in Caen since it opened in 2009. And no wonder: This highly inventive chef has put the fun back into dining. You could play it safe and go à la carte, but it's much more rewarding to put yourself in Caillot's hands for the "surprise" menu of five or seven courses (three at lunch). The menu changes constantly, and Caillot relies heavily on seasonal market produce. But his little Asian touches such as kimchi with foie gras are inspired. The restaurant is tiny, so reservations must be made at least several weeks ahead.

8 rue des Croisiers. ✆ **02-31-97-44-48.** www.acontresenscaen.fr. Main courses 27€–32€; fixed-price lunch 25€–52€; fixed-price dinner 52€–62€. Wed–Sat noon–2pm; Tues–Sat 7:30–9:15pm.

Le Bouchon du Vaugueux ★★ FRENCH Everything comes together perfectly in this lively yet intimate little bistro: warm and friendly ambience, excellent service and, above all, beautifully prepared and unfussy regional dishes. The seasonal menu changes but could include slow-cooked duck legs with pureed parsnips, beef braised in cider, and of course, a selection of superb Normandy cheeses. There aren't many tables, so it's best to book ahead.

12 rue Graindorge. ✆ **02-31-44-26-26.** www.bouchonduvaugueux.com. Fixed-price lunch 16€–24€; fixed-price dinner 21€–33€. Tues–Sat noon–2pm, Tues–Thurs 7–10pm, Fri–Sat 7–10:30pm. Closed 2 weeks Sept.

Exploring Caen

A fun way to visit Caen's major sites, including both Abbayes and the Château, is to follow the self-guided **William the Conqueror Circuit.** Maps can be picked up at the Tourist Office, from which the walking tour departs.

Abbaye aux Dames ★ RELIGIOUS SITE   William the Conqueror's wife Mathilda founded this abbey around 1060, which embraces Eglise de la Trinité and its Romanesque towers. Its spires were destroyed in the Hundred Years' War. The 12th-century choir houses the tomb of Queen Mathilda.

Place Reine Mathilde. ✆ **02-31-06-98-45.** Free admission. Daily 2–5:30pm. Free guided 1-hr. tour of choir, transept, and crypt (in French) daily 2:30 and 4pm.

Abbaye aux Hommes ★★ RELIGIOUS SITE   Founded by William the Conqueror in 1066 to ensure a papal pardon for marrying his distant cousin Mathilda, this abbey is next to the Eglise St-Etienne. During the Allied invasion, residents of Caen fled to St-Etienne for protection. Twin Romanesque towers 84m (276 ft.) tall dominate the church. A marble slab inside the high altar marks the site of William's tomb. The hand-carved wooden doors and an elaborate wrought-iron staircase are exceptional.

Esplanade Jean-Marie Louvel. ✆ **02-31-30-42-81.** 4.50€ adults, 3.50€ students, free for children 17 and under. Obligatory tours (50–90 min.; in English and/or French) July–Aug daily 9:30am, 10:15am, 11am, 2:30pm, 3:15pm, 4pm and 5:15pm; Feb–June and Sept–Nov daily 9:30am, 11am, 2:30pm and 4pm; Jan and Dec Mon–Fri 9:30am, 11am, 2:30pm and 4pm, Sat–Sun no tours but cloisters open Mon–Sat 9am–1pm and 2–6:30pm, Sun 2–6:30pm.

Le Château de Caen ★★ CASTLE   This castle complex was built on the ruins of a fortress erected by William the Conqueror in 1060. As soon as the weather warms up, much of the population picnics in the surrounding grounds. Climb to the top of the extensive ramparts for sublime views over Caen. Within the medieval compound are two museums, as well contemporary sculptures. The **Musée de Normandie** (www.musee-de-normandie.caen.fr; ✆ **02-31-30-47-60**) displays local archaeological finds, along with a collection of regional sculpture, paintings, and ceramics. Admission is 3.10€, and it's open daily 9:30am to 6pm (closed Tues Nov–May). Also within the walls is the **Musée des Beaux-Arts** (www.mba.caen.fr; ✆ **02-31-30-47-70**), a collection of Old Masters including Veronese, Tintoretto, and Rubens. Admission is free excluding temporary shows, which cost 3.10€ to 9€. It's open Wednesday through Monday 9:30am to 6pm.

Esplanade de la Paix, rue de Geôle, av. de la Libération. www.chateau.caen.fr.

Le Mémorial de Caen (Caen Memorial) ★★★ MONUMENT/MEMORIAL   This is not a museum to be rushed through, as it explores history from 1918 to the present day in engrossing and thought-provoking exhibits. It puts the 20th century in context by starting with the end of the First World War, leading to the horrors of the Second World War and beyond to the Cold War and the Berlin Wall. Civilian stories are told in heartbreaking detail, along with tales of courage and ingenuity of Allied soldiers. Not surprisingly, there is a large exhibition dedicated to the D-Day landings, as well as the reopening of the head-quarters used by German General Richter during the war. The museum's cafe is reasonably priced and a good spot to relax in between exhibitions.

Esplanade Général Eisenhower. ✆ **02-31-06-06-44.** www.memorial-caen.fr. Admission Apr–Sept 19€ adults, 17€ students and children 10–18; Oct–Mar 19€ adults, 16€ students and children 10–18; free to World War II veterans, those with war disabilities, war widows, and children 9 and under. Feb 15–Nov 11 daily 9am–7pm; Nov 12–Dec 31 and Jan 28–Feb 14 Tues–Sun 9:30am–6pm. Closed Jan.

Shopping

Caen has some excellent boutique-lined shopping streets, including **boulevard du Maréchal-Leclerc, rue St-Pierre,** and **rue de Strasbourg. Antiques** hunters should check out the shops along **rue Ecuyère.** The **market** at place Courtonne on Sunday morning sells secondhand goods.

For foodie souvenirs, **Chocolaterie Charlotte Corday**, 114 rue St-Jean (✆ **02-31-86-33-25**), has an irresistible collection of chocolate and other sweet goodies. Find regional items at **Le Comptoir Normand,** 7 rue de Geôle (✆ **02-31-86-34-13**), including Calvados, charcuterie products, and Caen-style tripe.

Nightlife

Take a walk down rue de Bras, rue St-Pierre, and rue Vaugueux to size up the action. Young hipsters go to **Le Chic,** rue des Prairies St-Gilles (✆ **02-31-94-48-72**), where dance music begins around 11:30pm and carries on until 6am. For offbeat international gigs, head to **Le Cargö,** 9 cours Caffarelli, Port de Caen (www.lecargo.fr; ✆ **02-31-86-79-31**).

BAYEUX ★★

267km (166 miles) NW of Paris; 25km (16 miles) NW of Caen

Bayeux's alluring medieval heart was spared bombardment in 1944, and was the first town to be liberated—the day after D-Day, in fact. Its half-timbered houses, stone mansions, cobblestoned streets, and ancient watermills have remained more or less intact, making this immensely pleasant town a joy to explore. It does get busy in the summer—with the double whammy of the nearby D-Day beaches and the extraordinary historical document that is the Bayeux Tapestry—but it retains its agreeable Norman atmosphere and the sense that it exists beyond the tourist crowds.

Bayeux

Essentials

ARRIVING Nine **trains** depart daily from Paris's Gare St-Lazare. The 2½-hour trip to Bayeux costs from 25.50€. Most journeys require a change in Caen. Travel time between Caen and Bayeux is about 15–20 minutes and costs 6.60€. To **drive** to Bayeux from Paris (trip time: 3 hr.), take A13 to Caen and E46 west to Bayeux.

VISITOR INFORMATION The **Office de Tourisme** is at Pont St-Jean (www. bessin-normandie.com; ✆ **02-31-51-28-28**).

SPECIAL EVENTS   The town goes wild on the first weekend in July during **Fêtes Médiévales** (www.fetesmedievales.bayeux.fr; ✆ **02-31-92-03-30**); the streets fill with market stalls, medieval dress, and themed treats during 2 days of medieval revelry. In mid-June, Bayeux is the finishing point for the annual **Tour de Normandie** (www.tourdenormandie.com; ✆ **06-28-33-00-75**), a classic car race that winds through the Normandy countryside in elegant style.

[Fast FACTS] BAYEUX

ATMs/Banks   There are banks throughout town, particularly along rue Saint-Malo.

Internet Access   **Médiathèque Municipale,** Centre Guillaume Le Conquérant, rue aux Coqs (✆ **02-31-51-20-20**), has Internet access and Wi-Fi.

Mail & Postage   **La Poste** rue Larcher (✆ **36-31**).

Pharmacies   **Pharmacie St Martin,** 20 rue St Martin (✆ **02-31-92-00-22**).

Where to Stay

Hôtel d'Argouges ★★   The subtle stone archway with the dark green door is not always easy to spot within the bustle of Rue St-Patrice, with its shops and Bayeux's Saturday food market. But inside find an enchanting 18th-century mansion that has been turned into a friendly and comfortable three-star hotel. Some of the rooms can be on the small side, but the handsome antique-style furnishings and modern bathrooms make up for it. So does the beautiful tree-shaded garden, where breakfast is served on warm days.

21 rue St-Patrice. ✆ **02-31-92-88-86.** www.hotel-dargouges.com. 28 units. 70€–188€ double; 165€–340€ suite. Free parking. **Amenities:** Breakfast room; free Wi-Fi.

Hôtel Tardif ★★   Set within an 18th-century *hôtel particulier*, or private home, this luxurious guesthouse is just steps from Bayeux's town center. Within the elegant foyer, a suspended wooden staircase sweeps up to first-floor rooms, each one decked out in period furnishings and overlooking either the *cour d'honneur* courtyard or botanical gardens.

16 rue Nesmond or 57 rue Larcher. ✆ **02-31-92-67-72.** www.chateauhotelbayeux.com. 6 units. 65€–195€ double; 180€–270€ suite. Free parking. **Amenities:** Lounge-library; free Wi-Fi.

Villa Lara ★★★   In a dreamy spot by the watermills of the Aure River is what is probably the best hotel in Bayeux. Four-star Villa Lara has been open only since 2012, but it has already built up a dedicated following. Its spacious rooms—some with balconies and views of Bayeux's cathedral—have sumptuous French furnishings of velvet and brocade, complemented by modern marble bathrooms. Its contemporary exterior is subtle and classy enough not to stand out like a sore thumb among its medieval neighbors. You'll find it hard to tear yourself away from the cozy lounge with its library and fireplace, but when you do, you'll find a welcoming staff eager to organize tours to the D-Day beaches and daily trips to Mont-St-Michel.

6 place de Québec. ✆ **02-31-92-00-55.** www.hotel-villalara.com. 28 units. 180€–340€ double; 290€–510€ suite. Free parking. **Amenities:** Breakfast room; gym; free Wi-Fi. Closed Dec–Feb.

Where to Eat

Bayeux has plenty of informal cafes offering quick snacks for visitors touring the D-Day beaches or just popping in to visit the tapestry. There are, however, a couple of special places worth checking out.

Le P'tit Resto ★ NORMAN   Tucked just behind the town's cathedral, this small restaurant stands out among Bayeux's more tourist-targeted eateries. Chef Yannick Yon's cuisine puts a creative spin on traditional Norman dishes. Think beef tartare with wasabi and roasted sesame seeds, or coconut-crusted cod and honey-caramelized leeks. It seats just 20 diners, plus 8 more on a small terrace, so reservations are highly recommended.

2 rue du Bienvenu. ✆ **02-31-51-85-40.** www.restaurantbayeux.com. Main courses 17€; fixed-price menus 19€–33€. Mon 7–9pm, Tue–Sat noon–2pm and 7–9pm.

Le Volet qui Penche ★★ NORMAN   Pierre-Henri Lemessier's wine shop doubles as a wine bar and bistro with only one three-course menu. It's a picky eater's nightmare, and a delight for everyone else who enjoys beautifully cooked regional cuisine matched with expertly chosen wines in a warm, convivial atmosphere. The menu depends on what Pierre-Henri has picked up at the market, and could include a starter of goat's cheese salad followed by flash-fried calf's liver. Pierre-Henri certainly knows his wines and will suggest the perfect match for your tastes—and budget.

3 impasse de l'Islet. ✆ **02-31-21-98-54.** www.levoletquipenche.com. Fixed-price menus 9.50€–16€. May–Dec Tues–Fri 9am–8:30pm, Mon and Sat 5–8:30pm; Mar–Apr Tues–Fri 9am–8:30pm, Sat 5–8:30pm; and Jan–Feb Tues–Fri 7am–7pm. Closed Feb 17–Mar 3, Mar 24–31, and Oct 27–Nov 11.

Exploring Bayeux

This compact town is best explored on foot. At its heart in rue du Général de Dais is **Cathédrale Notre-Dame de Bayeux,** a Norman medieval structure consecrated in 1077 in the presence of William the Conqueror. It's open daily 9am to 5pm mid-Nov to Feb; 9am to 6pm Mar to Jun; and 9am to 7pm July to mid-Nov. Entrance is free.

Musée d'Art et d'Histoire Baron Gérard (MAHB) ★ MUSEUM   This bright and airy museum, which opened in 2013, is set within the town's ancient bishop's palace, much of it constructed during the Middle Ages. Exhibitions range from local archaeological finds to regional lacework and delicate porcelain, as well as more than 600 regional artworks created between the 15th and 20th centuries.

37 rue du Bienvenu. ✆ **02-31-92-14-21.** Admission 7€ adults, 4€ students and children, free for children 9 and under. May–Sept daily 9:30am–12:30pm and 2–6:30pm; Oct–Apr daily 10am–12:30pm and 2–6pm. Closed Jan–Feb 15.

Musée de la Tapisserie de Bayeux ★★★ MUSEUM   This, arguably the most famous tapestry in the world, is actually an elaborate embroidery on linen, measuring 69m (226 ft.) long and 50cm (20 in.) wide. It depicts 58 scenes in 8 colors and was likely created in Kent between 1066 and 1077.

Housed in a 270-degree glass case that sweeps along a low-lit tunnel-like room, this masterpiece tells the story of the conquest of England by William the Conqueror. Make certain you use the free and informative audio guide: it really brings the story to life. And don't ignore the detail in the motifs at the top and bottom of the cloth: some of them will surprise you.

Detail of the Bayeux Tapestry

In 2013, the museum inaugurated a new area dedicated to the creation of the Bayeux Tapestry, and which also vividly evokes life in the Middle Ages. Displays include maps, scale models, and a film about the Battle of Hastings.

Centre Guillaume le Conquérant, 13 bis rue de Nesmond. ℂ **02-31-51-25-50.** www.bayeux museum.com. Admission 9€ adults, 4€ students, free for children 9 and under. Mar 15–Nov 15 daily 9am–6:30pm (May–Aug until 7pm); Nov 16–Mar 14 daily 9:30am–12:30pm and 2–6pm. Closed 3 weeks in Jan.

Musée Memorial de la Bataille de Normandie ★ MUSEUM   On June 7, 1944, Bayeux was the first strategic town to be liberated during the Battle of Normandy (June 6–Aug 29, 1944). Here, in a low-slung bunker-like building are window displays of military history, details of the beach landings, and examples of the tanks and weapons used to win the battle. A 25-minute film showcases news clips from the period. Across from the museum, the **Commonwealth Cemetery** contains 4,144 graves of British soldiers who were killed during the Battle of Normandy.

Bd. Fabian Ware. ℂ **02-31-51-46-90.** www.bayeuxmuseum.com. Admission 6€ adults, 4€ students and children, free for children 9 and under. May–Sept daily 9:30am–6:30pm; Oct–Apr daily 10am–12:30pm and 2–6pm. Closed Jan–Feb 15.

THE D-DAY BEACHES ★★

Arromanches-les-Bains: 272km (169 miles) NW of Paris, 11km (6¾ miles) NW of Bayeux; Grandcamp-Maisy (near Omaha Beach): 299km (185 miles) NW of Paris, 56km (35 miles) NW of Caen

A visit to the beaches, where the greatest invasion force of all time landed, is a must for anyone visiting Normandy's north coast. The 70th anniversary of the invasion in 2014 was the occasion for new museums, exhibitions, and events to mark this momentous event in modern history.

It was a rainy week in early June 1944 when the greatest armada ever was assembled along the southern coast of England. A full moon and cooperative tides were needed for the cross-Channel invasion. Britain's top meteorologist for the USAAF and RAF—Sir James Stagg—forecast a small window in the inclement weather. Over in France, Normandy's German occupiers lacked such a detailed weather forecast, so many Nazi officers drifted home for the weekend in the belief that no landing could take place soon.

Supreme Allied Commander Dwight D. Eisenhower believed Stagg's reports—and knew that further delays would hinder his element of surprise. With the British invasion commander, Field Marshal Montgomery, at his side, Eisenhower made the ultimate call.

At 9:15pm on June 5, the BBC announced to Normandy's French Resistance that the invasion was imminent by way of coded messages. The underground movement started dynamiting the region's railways to hinder German troop movement.

Before midnight, Allied planes began bombing the Norman coast. By 1:30am on June 6 ("the Longest Day", and what the French call *Jour-J*), members of the 101st Airborne were parachuting to the ground on German-occupied French soil. At 6:30am, the Americans began landing on the beaches, code-named Utah and Omaha. An hour later, British and Canadian forces made beachheads at Juno, Gold, and Sword, swelling the number of Allied troops in Normandy to a massive 135,000. That evening a joint beachhead had been formed and yet more troops, tanks, trucks, and other *matériel* poured into Normandy. The push to Paris—and Berlin—had begun.

Essentials

ARRIVING A **car** is practically essential to explore the D-Day Beaches at leisure. Each monument, museum, and beach has plenty of parking, too.

Bus Verts (www.busverts.fr; ✆ 08-10-21-42-14) runs buses from Bayeux to Arromanches (no. 75) and from Bayeux to Omaha Beach and the American Cemetery (no. 70) every few hours for 2.40€ per trip.

Several group tours also cover the D-Day Beaches. From Bayeux, **Normandy Tours,** Hotel de la Gare (www.normandy-landing-tours.com; ✆ 02-31-92-10-70), runs a 4-hour tour (in English) to Arromanches, Omaha Beach, the

The beach at Arromanches, with the remains of Mulberry Harbour in the distance

American Military Cemetery, and Pointe du Hoc for 62€ adults and 55€ students and seniors from April to October. From Caen, the **Caen Memorial Museum,** Esplanade Général Eisenhower (www.memorial-caen.fr; ✆ **02-31-06-06-45**), conducts full-day (115€) tours along the same route from April to December, including lunch and access to Caen's museum. A half-day trip costs 64€ or 81€, depending on time of departure.

VISITOR INFORMATION The **Office de Tourisme,** 4 rue Maréchal-Joffre, Arromanches-les-Bains (www.ot-arromanches.fr; ✆ **02-31-22-36-45**), is open year-round except in January.

Reliving the Longest Day

Few places in the world have a more concentrated—or more moving—selection of sights than Normandy's D-Day Beaches. More than 30 memorials, cemeteries, and museums, which range from coastal batteries to museums dedicated to underwater military finds, are spread out along this 50km (31-mile) stretch of coast. The most spellbinding site for all nationalities is the **Normandy American Visitor Center ★★★,** behind Omaha beach at Colleville-sur-Mer (www.abmc.gov; ✆ **02-31-51-62-00**). The graves of 10,000 Allies who liberated mainland France lie within 70 hectares (173 acres) of manicured grounds above the cliffs. The visitor center retells the dramatic story of the American landings—and those of British, Canadian, Polish, Free French, and other allies—on the morning of June 6, 1944. Most dramatic are the personal tales, often told via video and interactive displays. Make certain you leave enough time for a good look at the exhibitions; they really are captivating. Admission is free. The cemetery is open daily 9am to 6pm from April 14 to Sept 15, and until 5pm the rest of the year. Visitors may also wander down to Omaha Beach itself and explore the bunkers and memorials. At 4:30pm, you can watch the Lowering of the Colors, where the American flag is lowered in a poignant ritual.

Normandy American Visitor Center and Cemetery, Omaha Beach

The **Overlord Museum,** Colleville-sur-Mer (www.overlordmuseum.com; ✆ 02-31-22-00-55), opened in summer 2013, half a mile uphill from the Normandy American Visitor Center. More than 10,000 pieces of *matériel* and 35 military vehicles are showcased in D-Day dioramas around a great hall. Admission is 6.90€ adults and 4.90€ students and children; free for children under 10. Open daily 10am to 5pm Feb, Nov, Dec; 10am to 6pm Mar to May and Oct; 9:30am to 7pm June to Aug; and 9:30am to 6pm Sept; closed Jan.

Farther west along the coast, you'll see the jagged lime cliffs of the **Pointe du Hoc.** A cross honors a group of American Rangers who scaled the cliffs using hooks to get at the gun emplacements. The pockmarked landscape has a lunar look, with giant craters showing where the bombs fell. Farther along the Cotentin Peninsula is **Utah Beach,** where the 4th U.S. Infantry Division landed at 6:30am. A U.S. monument commemorates their heroism.

Eastward along the coast in the British invasion sector is the seaside resort of **Arromanches-les-Bains.** A deep-water port was deemed essential to Allied success, so in June 1944, two mammoth prefabricated ports known as Mulberry Harbours were towed across the Channel. The one that landed in Arromanches was nicknamed Port Winston. "Victory could not have been achieved without it," Eisenhower later said. Indeed, in 10 months this "temporary" artificial harbor delivered 2.5 million men and countless vehicles into northern France. The wreckage is still visible just off the beach. Arromanches's **Plage Musée du Débarquement,** place du 6-Juin (www.musee-arromanches.fr; ✆ 02-31-22-34-31), illuminates the scale of the D-Day landings through maps, models, a cinema, photos, and a diorama of the landing beaches. Admission is 7.50€ adults and 5.50€ students and children. May to September, hours are daily 9am to 7pm (Oct–Apr daily 10am–12:30pm and 1:30–5pm; closed Jan).

Eastward again through the British and Canadian invasion sectors is **Musée Gold Beach ★★,** 2 place Amiral Byrd, Ver-sur-Mer (www.goldbeachmusee.fr; ✆ 02-31-22-58-58). The museum focuses on the heroism of Britain's RAF and Royal Navy and the meticulous Allied coordination that went into the D-Day landings. Admission is 4.50€ adults and 2.50€ students and children. From April to October, hours are daily 10:30am to 5:30pm (closed Tues Apr–June and Sept–Oct); open November to March only by appointment.

Just eastward along the coast in Courseulles-sur-Mer is the **Centre Juno Beach ★★,** voie des Français Libres (www.junobeach.org; ✆ 02-31-37-32-17). This gem of a museum details Canada's entire war effort, with particular focus on the Battle of the Atlantic and the march through Germany. Outside the museum is a stark memorial to the Canadian dead of D-Day, their names inscribed simply on blue towers. Walk towards the beach and pause in front of the sculpture with the words to Paul Verlaine's poem "Chanson d'Automne": this was the code the BBC used to alert the French Resistance on June 5. Admission is 7€ adults and 5.50€ students and children, with reduced rates for visits only to the park or temporary exhibits. From April to September, hours are daily 9:30am to 7pm (Mar, Oct 10am–6pm; Feb, Nov–Dec 10am–5pm; closed Jan).

Where to Eat & Stay near the D-Day Beaches

Ferme de la Rançonnière ★   This manor house dating from the 13th to the 15th centuries is now a snug, immensely charming country hotel only a few miles south of the coast near Asnelles. Exposed stone, beamed ceilings, half-timbered walls, rich fabrics, communal rooms with giant fireplaces—all add up to a romantic, relaxing hideaway. The restaurant's menu is as sumptuous as the interior, with rich pickings including roast venison and grilled halibut on fixed-price menus at 30.80€ and 42.80€. The restaurant is open to the public, and guests have the option of half board.

Route de Creully, 14480 Crépon. ✆ **02-31-22-21-73.** www.ranconniere.fr. 35 units. 70€–170€ double; 180€–265€ suite. Free parking. **Amenities:** Restaurant; bar; breakfast room; free Wi-Fi.

Hôtel de la Marine ★   History buffs will be pleased to know that this three-star hotel directly faces Gold Beach, where the British landed on D-Day. The bedrooms are furnished quite simply and could stand a bit of updating, but the sea views make up for the rustic look. The restaurant is open daily noon to 2pm and 7 to 9:30pm, and serves fixed-price hearty French meals from 24.50€ to 42€ each.

1 quai du Canada, Arromanches-les-Bains 14117. ✆ **02-31-22-34-19.** www.hotel-de-la-marine.fr. 33 units. 61€–110€ double; 144€–235€ apartments. Free parking. **Amenities:** Restaurant; bar; free Wi-Fi.

La Marée ★ NORMAN   Set beside the port, this small, nautically decorated restaurant serves mostly fish, and only fish caught in the English Channel or within a reasonable distance out in the Atlantic. Meat-eaters aren't ignored, however, with dishes such as duck breast with garlicky mashed potatoes. On warm days, tables spill out towards the water's edge.

5 quai Henri Chéron, 14450 Grandcamp Maisy. ✆ **02-31-21-41-00.** www.restolamaree.com. Fixed-price menus 16€–27€. Daily 12:30–2:30pm and 7–9:30pm. Closed Jan 1–Feb 7.

Mercure Omaha Beach ★   This modern spa and golf hotel is a comfortable and convenient base for touring the beaches, and golfers have knockout views of the Normandy coast on the hotel's course. As a bonus, the pretty village of Port-en-Bessin is only a 15-minute walk away. Contemporary rooms veer on the business-like, but they're spacious and many have balconies. The hotel's **restaurant** has an impressive selection of seafood (from 8.90€) as well as meat and fish dishes including luscious steak tartare (15.90€) and grilled sea bass (18.90€).

Chemin du Colombier, 14520 Port-en-Bessin. ✆ **02-31-22-44-44.** www.hotel-omaha-beach.com. 74 units. 120€–210€ double; 190€–220€ suite. Free parking. **Amenities:** Restaurant; bar; breakfast room; gym; pool; spa; free Wi-Fi.

MONT-ST-MICHEL ★★★

324km (201 miles) W of Paris; 129km (80 miles) SW of Caen; 48km (30 miles) E of St-Malo

A UNESCO World Heritage Site, Mont-St-Michel is one of the most alluring spots on France's northern coast. The fortified island seems to float on a shifting bed of sand and sea. Once a bastion marking the border between Normandy and Brittany, then a place of monastic retreat, this Disney-like castle now attracts 3 million visitors every year. In high summer it's exceptionally busy, but enthralling nevertheless.

Essentials

ARRIVING   The most efficient way to reach Mont-St-Michel is to **drive.** From Caen, follow A84 southwest towards Avranches, eventually taking the D43 and following signs to its end at Mont-St-Michel. Total driving time from Paris is about 3½ hours.

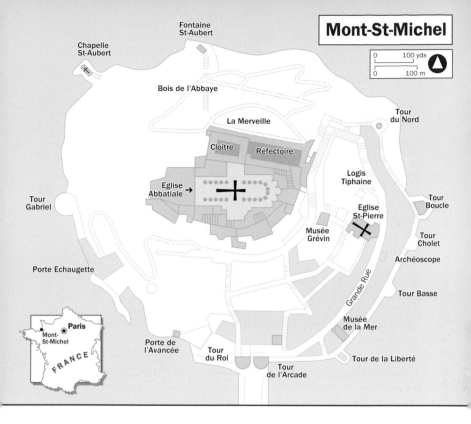

There are no direct **trains** between Paris and Mont-St-Michel. One option is to take a local TER train from Paris's Gare St-Lazare to Caen (www.voyages-sncf.com; ✆ **36-35**), then another local TER train to Pontorson, where a 3€ shuttle bus ferries passengers directly to the new visitor center. Another is to take a TGV (fast train) from Paris to Rennes in Brittany, from where a coach takes you to Mont-St-Michel for 12.70€ each way.

VISITOR INFORMATION The **Tourist Information Center** is Lieu-dit le Bas Pays, 50170 Beauvoir (www.bienvenueaumontsaintmichel.com; ✆ **02-14-13-20-15**).

Where to Eat & Stay

If you plan to stay overnight on the island, be prepared to pay a premium. It is, however, an unforgettable experience, as you can explore the island in the evening in peace after the crowds have left. But **travel light:** the hotels are a long, mostly uphill walk from where the shuttle bus drops you off, and the cobblestoned streets don't make it easy to transport your luggage. And don't expect to have a late supper; most restaurants close soon after the day-trippers leave, apart from hotel restaurants. But there are advantages to staying overnight—particularly in the summer, when evening concerts are staged in the abbey and sound-and-light shows illuminate the island.

Mont-St-Michel

Auberge Saint-Pierre ★ The sheer charm of this 15th-century half-timbered inn makes up for the small size of the rooms. But they are cozy and comfortable, with half-timbered walls and exposed beams. Some of the rooms are in the Chapeau Blanc Logis, a secluded former fisherman's cottage a few minutes' (uphill) walk from the hotel. Ask for a room with a view of the bay, especially if you're staying in the Logis, which has small terraces with gorgeous views. The restaurant is just as charming, with set menus from 20€ to 65€, which include *agneau du pré salé*, local lamb raised on salt marshes, and the especially fluffy Mont-St-Michel omelet.

Grande Rue. ✆ **02-33-60-14-03.** www.auberge-saint-pierre.fr. 23 units. 217€–247€ double; 264€–299€ suites. **Amenities:** Restaurant; bar; free Wi-Fi.

Crêperie La Sirène ★ NORMAN This bustling, cheerful crêperie makes an appealing stop for lunch of the savory buckwheat crepes known as galettes, stuffed with gooey cheese and ham. Then follow with a sweet crepe for dessert, all washed down with Normandy cider.

Grande Rue. ✆ **02-33-60-08-60.** Main courses 3.50€–10€. Daily 9am–10:30pm; closed Jan.

Exploring Mont-St-Michel

France's biggest tourist attraction outside of Paris has been undergoing major changes over the past few years. Before 2012, the causeway linking the island with the mainland was rammed with parked cars, and the bay was in danger of silting up. To restore Mont-St-Michel to its island status, the authorities have built a **new approach** and banished cars to a parking lot by a new visitor center. Free shuttle buses take visitors to the island 2.5km (1½ miles) away. Parking costs 12€ for 24 hours, but is free if you stay less than 30 minutes.

Otherwise it's a 50-minute hike to the island across the shifting sands. Those with their own bike can pedal over. A ride across in a horse-drawn carriage costs 5€ per person. An additional **Office de Tourisme** is on the island itself, to the left of the gates (www.ot-montsaintmichel.com;℡02-33-60-14-30). Both tourist centers are open daily year-round.

Once you reach the island, you'll have a steep climb up Grande Rue, lined with 15th- and 16th-century houses and souvenir shops, to reach its famous **abbey** (www.mont-saint-michel.monuments-nationaux.fr; ℡02-33-89-80-00). Ramparts encircle the church and a three-tiered ensemble of 13th-century buildings called **La Merveille** (The Wonder) that rise up to the abbey's pointed spire. This terraced complex is one of Europe's most important Gothic monuments. On the

The Grande Rue, Mont-St-Michel

second terrace of La Merveille is one of Mont-St-Michel's largest and most beautiful spaces, a 13th-century hall known as the **Salle des Chevaliers.** Crowning the mount's summit is the spellbinding **Eglise Abbatiale** church.

The abbey is open daily May to August 9am to 7pm, and September to April 9:30am to 6pm. Entrance includes an English-language group tour when available, but you can also explore on your own. Admission is 9€ adults, 5.50€ students and ages 18 to 25, and free for children 17 and under.

Most visitors are content to wander around the medieval ramparts. Those seeking a little more sightseeing may head to the **Musée de la Mer,** Grande Rue (℡ 02-33-89-02-02), which showcases marine crafts throughout history and the ecology of the local tidal flats. Another museum worth visiting is the **Logis Tiphaine,** Grande Rue (℡ 02-33-89-02-02), a 15th-century home originally under the control of the Duguesclin family. Both museums are open daily from 9:30am to 5pm, and cost 9€ for adults, free for children 18 and under. You can buy a pass for 18€ that covers the cost of four museums.

For a different perspective of Mont-St-Michel, join one of the guided walks from the mainland to the island, tracing the original pilgrim route. **Chemins de la Baie** (℡ 02-33-89-80-88; www.cheminsdelabaie.com) takes groups on various barefoot walks across the sands. Ones that come with a commentary in English cost 10.30€ and last 3½ hours.

BRITTANY

By Lily Heise

8

"L ittle Britain," as it was called by the 4th- and 5th-century Celts who came to settle this northwestern peninsula, always seems apart from the rest of France. While this was once politically true (the region resisted conquer and incorporation into Charlemagne's Frankish empire, remaining an independent duchy until 1532), even today's Bretons hold fast to their traditions, and their independent spirit is undeniable. The original Breton language, with its roots in Welsh and Cornish, though once suppressed, has experienced a revival. The *Gwenn-ha-du*—the black-and-white Breton flag—still flies proudly in every town. This unique cultural identity, along with its wild coast, succulent seafood, rustic hamlets, and medieval fortresses make it one of the most authentic areas of France.

Brittany is home to some of the nicest towns in the country. You can't help but be charmed strolling the streets of the former fortress town of St-Malo or medieval Dinan. Quimper is the bastion of Breton culture and Nantes is becoming a cool outpost for Parisians.

The region is a perfect destination for nature or beach lovers with its promontories, coves, and traffic-free islands dotting the rocky coastline, some 1,207km (748 miles) long. There's the posh resort of Dinard for more glamorous sunbathers.

The British, just a channel-hop away, think of Brittany as a resort region. But the French typically go south to chase their sun. Therefore, you'll never run into huge tourist masses, yet popular beaches can get crowded in summer.

If you're coming from Mont-St-Michel, use St-Malo, Dinan, or Dinard as a base to explore northern Brittany. Visitors from the eastern Loire Valley can reach the coastline of southern Brittany in under 3 hours.

ST-MALO ★★★

414km (257 miles) W of Paris; 69km (43 miles) N of Rennes; 13km (8 miles) E of Dinard

Despite past lives as a fortress and the site of a monastery, St-Malo is best known for the *corsaires* who used it as a base during the 17th and 18th centuries. During wartime, a decree from the French king sanctioned the seafaring mercenaries to intercept British ships and requisition their cargo. During peacetime, they acted as intrepid merchant marines, returning from Asia and the Americas with gold, coffee, and spices. Indeed, the sea is in the hearts of all *Malouins*, as natives of St-Malo are called—especially during the city's famous transatlantic sailing race, the *Route du Rhum*, which is held every 4 years and finishes in Guadeloupe.

Walking the ramparts and cobblestone streets, it's hard to imagine that 80 percent of St-Malo was destroyed in World War II. What you see today is thanks to a meticulous, decades-long restoration.

PREVIOUS PAGE: **Ramparts at St-Malo**

St-Malo encompasses the communities of St. Servan and Paramé, but most tourists head for the walled city, or *Intra-muros*. In summer, the Grande Plage du Sillon towards Paramé is dotted with sun-seekers; year-round it's sought after for its deluxe seawater spa. St. Servan's marina is adjacent to a large terminal where ferries depart for and arrive from the Channel Islands and England.

Essentials

ARRIVING   From Paris's Gare Montparnasse, about 14 TGV **trains** per day make the journey; a one-way ticket ranges from 43€ to 76€. Three of these trains are nonstop, making the journey in 2¾ hours; transferring at Rennes takes 4 hours. For information, visit www.voyages-sncf.com or call ✆ **36-35**. If you're **driving** from Paris, take A13 west to Caen and continue southwest along N175 to the town of Miniac Morvan. From there, travel north on N137 directly to St-Malo. Driving time is 4 hours from Paris.

VISITOR INFORMATION   The **Office de Tourisme** is on esplanade St-Vincent (www.saint-malo-tourisme.com; ✆ **08-25-13-52-00**).

SPECIAL EVENTS   The **Festival de la Musique Sacrée,** from mid-July to mid-August, stages evening concerts twice a week in the cathedral. The famous transatlantic yacht race the **Route du Rhum** (www.routedurhum.com) departs from St-Malo every 4 years in November (the next isn't until 2018).

Getting Around

ON FOOT   With its layout and tiny one-way streets, its best to tour the city on foot.

BY BICYCLE   Many of the city's streets have bike lanes. You can rent bikes in St-Malo, Dinard, and Dinan and even have them delivered to your hotel from **Vélo Emeraulde** (www.velo-corsaire.fr; ✆ **06-58-02-24-61**). Rentals are 12€ daily for adults and 8€ for children (weekend/week-long rates available).

BY CAR   There are several parking lots along Quai Saint-Vincent, but they fill up quickly in summer months. You can rent a car at the TGV train station from **Europcar** (www.europcar.fr; ✆ **02-99-56-75-17**) or **Avis** (www.avis.fr; ✆ **02-99-40-18-54**).

BY TAXI   There are usually taxis in front of the station or call **Saint Malo Taxi** (www.taxi-st-malo.com; ✆ **02-23-18-18-18**).

BY PUBLIC TRANSPORT   The local bus service does not go into the old city but you can get a bus (line C1 or C2) from the station to the city walls; **the network is run by KSMA** (www.ksma.fr; ✆ **02-99-40-19-22**). Buy your one-way tickets (1.25€) directly from the bus driver.

[Fast FACTS] ST-MALO

ATMs/Banks   There are several ATMs around the cathedral or along rue Broussais.

Doctors & Hospitals   **Centre Hopitalier de Saint Malo,** 1 rue de la Marne (www.ch-stmalo.fr; ✆ **02-99-21-21-21**).

Internet Access   **Cyber Café Le Memphis,** in the Hotel aux Voyageurs, 2 bd des Talards (✆ **02-99-56-30-35**).

Mail & Postage   **La Poste,** 6 Place du Prieuré (✆ **36-31**).

Pharmacies   **Pharmacie des Cotes d'Emeraude,** 3 rue Broussais (✆ **02-99-40-85-54**).

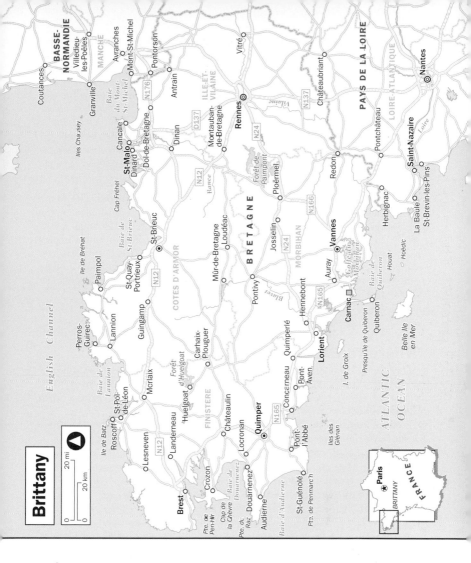

Where to Stay

While some hotels inside the city walls are up to snuff, others are a bit run down. An alternative is to stay along the Plage du Sillon and walk the 10 minutes into the historic center.

Hotel Alba ★   Facing the shimmering sea, this is the perfect beach-based hotel in St-Malo. You almost have the impression of staying on a boat, due to its proximity to the water; the smallish rooms gain in size thanks to their expansive views. Each is tastefully decorated in earthy tones, with modern, comfortable furnishings. The best rooms feature balconies and there are also several family rooms. If you're not strolling on the beach at sunset, enjoy a drink on its terrace or its scenic bar.

17 rue des Dunes, St-Malo 35400. ☎ **02-99-40-37-18.** www.hotelalba.com. 22 units. 99€–171€ double; 200€ family room. Free parking. **Amenities:** Bar; room service; free Wi-Fi.

Hôtel France et Chateaubriand ★★   To experience the 19th-century hey-day of the Emerald coast, there's no better place than at the birthplace of one of its heroes: writer Chateaubriand. Located inside the walls of old St-Malo, upon stepping into the flowering courtyard it's like you've entered the Romantic era. Common areas still have this bygone feeling; however, guestrooms are being brought into the 21st century, the best and most modern rooms being the *chambres supérieures*. Request a room with views of the ramparts or the sea. Sip cool cocktails in the chic bar or dine in the regal restaurant with gold-trimmed Corinthian columns.

12 pl. Chateaubriand, St-Malo 35412. ✆ **02-99-56-66-52.** www.hotel-fr-chateaubriand.com. 80 units. 106€–205€ double. Parking 15€. **Amenities:** Restaurant; cafe; bar; babysitting; room service; free Wi-Fi.

Quic en Grogne ★   Ideally positioned on a quiet street close to shops and the beach, this is the perfect budget hotel *intra-muros*. The hotel finished a lengthy renovation in early 2014, giving it a fresh, contemporary feel. The small guest-rooms have a subtle nautical theme while staying clear of kitsch. All bathrooms have been refitted; the more expensive ones have bathtubs. The best rooms look over a flowery courtyard. Breakfast is served in a glass-covered sunroom, and its convenient private parking allows guests to avoid the hassle of parking outside the ramparts.

8, rue d'Estrées, Saint-Malo 35400. ✆ **02-99-20-22-20.** www.quic-en-groigne.com. 15 units. 85€–112€ double. Parking 13€. Closed end of Dec–Jan. **Amenities:** Free Wi-Fi.

Where to Eat

Quench your summer thirst with the best ice cream in St-Malo at **Sanchez**, 9 rue Vieille Boucherie (www.sanchez-artisan-glacier.fr; ✆ **02-99-56-67-17**). With over 120 flavors, it'll be hard to choose, but we love their signature flavor "Le péché Malouin."

For a formal meal, **Hôtel France et Chateaubriand** (see above) has one of the finest dining rooms in town.

La Brasserie du Sillon ★ SEAFOOD/FRENCH   Outside the city walls you'll find St-Malo's most innovative restaurant. Set in a lovely stone building facing the Sillon beach, the interior is refined and the best tables overlook the sea. Dishes are beautifully presented, though on the pricey side *à la carte*, savings can be made with their great value fixed-priced menus. Savor specialties such as fisherman's *choucroute,* scallops in butter sauce or filet mignon of pork with chestnuts, or you might be easily tempted by 13 different *plateaux de fruit de mer*, overflowing with freshly caught shrimp, periwinkle, crab and lobster.

3 Chaussée du Sillon. ✆ **02-99-56-10-74.** www.brasseriedusillon.com. Main courses 17€–35€; fixed-price menus 22€–35€. Daily noon–2pm; Sun–Thurs 7–10pm; Fri–Sat 7–10:30pm.

Le Chalut ★★ SEAFOOD/FRENCH   French for "fish-net," here's where you'll find the freshest catches in town. The kitschy nautical decor keeps this 1-Michelin-starred pearl well hidden. Some of Chef Jean-Philippe Foucat's creations include red mullet filets with marinated capers and artichokes drizzled with orange oil, John Dory with asparagus and fresh coriander, scallops with ginger and celery mousse or turbot with regional white Paimpol beans and lobster cream. Save a little room for the Chivas whiskey soufflé with citrus and passion fruit caramel. Reservations required.

8 rue de la Corne-de-Cerf. ✆ **02-99-56-71-58.** Main courses 19€–29€; fixed-price menu lunch 23€, dinner 28€–58€. Wed–Sun noon–1:30pm and 7–9:30pm.

Exploring the City

The 15th-century **Porte St-Vincent**, with a Belle Epoque carrousel just in front of it, is the main entrance to St-Malo *Intra-muros*. Walk to your right past the restaurant terraces on place Chateaubriand—a portal leads to steps up to the **ramparts ★★★**. Built and rebuilt over several centuries, some parts of these walls date from the 14th century. Weather cooperating, they're an ideal place to start a walking tour and take in sweeping views of the English Channel and the **Fort National** (see below).

About halfway round, you'll see an islet called the **Ile du Grand-Bé ★★**; during low tide you can walk to it and visit French Romantic novelist **Chateaubriand's tomb.** His last wish was to be buried here, where he'd "hear only the sounds of the wind and the ocean." Also within sight is the **Piscine de Bon-Secours,** a 1930s outdoor swimming pool whose three walls catch receding seawater. On warm days you'll see brave divers leaping from its cement platform.

If it's too windy, get off the ramparts by descending the ramp that joins rue de la Crosse. Turn left onto rue de la Pie Qui Boit and follow it until you reach rue Broussais. Alternatively, continue along the ramparts (where the view just keeps getting better) until you reach the **Porte de Dinan.** The street below it, rue de Dinan, becomes rue Broussais. Both routes lead to **place de Pilori** back in the center. Head back toward the Porte St-Vincent for the greatest concentration of shopping and dining options.

Cathédrale St-Vincent ★★★ CATHEDRAL   Transformation of a monastic church into this cathedral began in 1146. Over the centuries, various architects added Romanesque, Gothic, and Neoclassical elements—only to have the steeple knocked off and the transept destroyed during fierce fighting in 1944. It took nearly 30 years to restore the structure and its magnificent stained glass. A floor mosaic commemorates the 1535 blessing of St-Malo native Jacques Cartier before he set off to discover Canada. Cartier's tomb is here, along with that of René Duguay-Trouin, a legendary privateer so successful he was made a commander in the French navy.

12 rue St-Benoît. ✆ **02-99-40-82-31.** Free admission.

Fort National ★ HISTORIC SITE   Designed by famed military architect Sébastien de Vauban, construction of this fortress began in 1689. You can access it by walking 300m (984 ft.) over sand at low tide (heed the tidal information, or you may find yourself wading back). Thirty-five-minute guided tours take you into the dungeon and explain the fort's history; it's equally rewarding to wander on your own and enjoy the views of the bay.

Grande Plage de Sillon. ✆ **06-72-46-66-26.** www.fortnational.com. Tours: 5€ adults, 3€ ages 6–16, free children 5 and under. Open Jun–Sept. Hours, which depend on the tide, vary. Call in advance or look to the fort itself (when the French flag is flying, it's open to visitors).

Musée d'Histoire de St-Malo ★★ MUSEUM   This museum is perfect for understanding the history and commercial importance of St-Malo. The buildings themselves, the keep and gatehouse of the Château de St-Malo, add to the experience. Exhibits use artifacts, ship models, and imagery to tell the stories of the city's most famous citizens—Chateaubriand, Jacques Cartier, and the privateers Duguay-Trouin and Surcouf. A section is reserved for photos of the extensive damage the city incurred during World War II.

Porte St-Vincent. ✆ **02-99-40-71-57.** Admission: 6€ adults, 3€ ages 8–18, free for children 7 and under. Apr–Oct daily 10am–12:30pm and 2–6pm; Nov–Mar Tues–Sun 10am–noon and 2–6pm.

Beaches

Along the coast, stretches of sand intersperse with rugged outcroppings that suggest fortresses protect Brittany from Atlantic storms. Both the **Grande Plage du Sillon** and the **Plage de Bon Secours,** west of the city walls, are very popular. Situated between the two, the **Plage de l'Eventail** is small and especially rocky.

Shopping

If you're in St-Malo on Tuesday or Friday between 8am and 1pm and want to experience a great Breton market, head for the **Halle au Blé,** in the heart of the old city. You can't miss the bustle and the hawking of seafood, fresh produce, local dairy products, and baked goods.

Check out **Marin-Marine,** 5 Grand Rue (✆ 02-99-40-90-32), for men's and women's fashions including mariner's shirts and Breton wool sweaters. **Gauthier Marines,** 2 rue Porcon de la Barbinais (www.gauthiermarines.com; ✆ 02-99-40-91-81), is a walk-in treasure chest of model ships, wooden sculpture, and marine-themed gift items.

Brittany's most revered chef and modern-day spice hunter, Olivier **Roellinger,** has an eponymous shop at 12 rue Saint-Vincent (www.epices-roellinger. com; ✆ 06-18-80-44-10). His beautifully presented blends, made from spices found all over the world, are worth collecting. And just try leaving **Maison Larnicol,** 6 rue St Saint-Vincent (www.chocolaterielarnicol.fr; ✆ 02-99-40-57-62), empty handed. It specializes in Breton sweets including baked goods, chocolates, and a variety of flavored caramels.

St-Malo Nightlife

For an evening of gambling, head to **Le Casino Barrière,** 2 chaussée du Sillon (✆ 02-99-40-64-00). You can also order dinner, sometimes accompanied by live music. A passport must be presented.

For dancing, consider **L'Escalier,** La Buzardière (www.escalier.fr; ✆ 02-99-81-65-56), open Thursday to Saturday midnight to 7am. The cover

Fort National, St-Malo

LUNCH ON THE half-shell

If you're driving east from St-Malo to Mont-St-Michel, consider a stop in **Cancale** ★★★—a harbor town famous for its oysters since the 17th century, when Louis XIV had them delivered regularly to Versailles.

Head to the northernmost end of the Port de la Houle, just beyond the jetty, where you'll see a handful of blue and white covered stalls selling shellfish out of crates. Come armed with a baguette and half-bottle of muscadet (easily found on the port's main street) and order a dozen oysters to go. The sellers will shuck them immediately and hand them to you on a plastic plate. Find a spot on a bench or the rocks, slurp down your mollusks and toss the shells onto the sun-bleached pile below.

For a second course, pop in to the **Crêperie du port,** 1, place du Calvaire, 7 quai Thomas (© **02-99-89-60-66**) for inventive buckwheat *galettes* and dessert crepes.

Oysters at Cancale

doesn't exceed 14€. You'll need wheels, as the club is in the countryside 5km (3 miles) east of town. It does have a free shuttle, however; for information and reservations call **06-85-31-27-64. Le 109,** 3 rue des Cordiers (www.le-109. com; © **02-99-56-81-09**), is a futuristic bar and dance club in a 300-plus-year-old vaulted cellar. It isn't as fashionable as L'Escalier, but is accessible without a car. It's open Tuesday to Sunday 8pm to 3am; the price of your first drink (10€–12€) is considered the cover charge.

Popular pubs include **L'Aviso,** 12 rue du Point du Jour (© **02-99-40-99-08**), offering 300 types of beer and Breton beer on tap, and **Pub Saint Patrick,** 24 rue Sainte-Barbe (© **02-99-56-66-90**), serving 50 different Irish whiskeys, along with Breton beer. Concerts are regularly scheduled at the latter.

DINARD ★★

417km (259 miles) W of Paris; 23km (14 miles) N of Dinan

Dinard (not to be confused with its inland neighbor, Dinan) sits on a rocky promontory at the top of the Rance River, opposite St-Malo. Once a small fishing community, by the late 19th century it was a favorite of the European jet set, thanks largely to wealthy British families who built grand Victorian villas along the coast.

Though its golden age has tarnished somewhat, Dinard is still one of France's best-loved resorts. It's also a destination for cinephiles, who flock to film festival here every October.

Essentials

ARRIVING If you're **driving,** take D186 west from St-Malo to Dinard. SNCF **trains** go only as far as St-Malo; from there, take bus no. 16A, which departs from the St-Malo rail station daily for the 30-minute ride to Dinard. The one-way fare is 2.30€. **Buses** arrive from many towns and cities in Brittany, including Rennes. Schedule and fare information is available via **Illenoo** (www.illenoo-services.fr; ✆ **08-25-13-81-30**). Between April and October, **Compagnie Corsaire,** Gare Maritime de la Bourse, St-Malo (www.compagniecorsaire.com; ✆ **02-23-18-15-15**), operates ferryboats from St-Malo to Dinard. The trip takes 10 minutes and costs 4.90€ one-way. A **taxi** to Dinard from St-Malo is another option; it costs 25€ during the day, with a 50 percent surcharge after 7pm and on Sundays and holidays. For information, call ✆ **06-84-92-55-73.**

VISITOR INFORMATION The **Office de Tourisme** is at 2 bd. Féart (www.ot-dinard.com; ✆ **02-99-46-94-12**).

[FastFACTS] DINARD

ATMs/Banks Easy-access ATMs are on avenue Edouard VII and Place Rochaid.

Doctors & Hospitals Centre Hopital Arthur Gardiner, 1 rue Henri Dunant (http://centre-hospitalier.ehpadhospiconseil.fr; ✆ **02-99-16-88-88**).

Internet Access Hotel Beaurivage has computers with internet available for non-guests, 2 Place du Général de Gaulle (✆ **02-99-46-14-34**).

Mail & Postage La Poste, 8 Place Rochaid (✆ **36-31**).

Pharmacies Pharmacie Centrale Franca, 15 bd Féart (✆ **02-99-46-22-68**).

Where to Stay

Didier Méril (see "Where to Eat," below) also rents rooms.

Grand Hôtel Barrière de Dinard ★★ The glory of the Victorian era lives on at one of the Emerald coast's grandest hotels. Part of the Lucien Barrière luxury chain, this 1858 hotel epitomizes Second Empire style. A short walk from downtown, the majestic two-winged building overlooks the Vicomté bay. Luxury knows no bounds, from the spacious foyer to the deluxe pool and spa. Guestrooms have modern elegance, the balconies being a major plus. However, the perfect sea-views are best admired from the four balconies of the new 70m² executive suite. In the evening you can savor succulent seafood in the regal restaurant or a cocktail in the swanky bar.

46 av. George V, Dinard 35801. ✆ **02-99-88-26-26.** www.lucienbarriere.com. 90 units. 171€–454€ double; 1,050€–1,700€ suite. Closed mid-Nov to early April. **Amenities:** Restaurant; bar; babysitting; kids' club; fitness center; indoor pool; room service; rooms for those w/limited mobility, sauna; spa; tennis; free bicycle rental; free Wi-Fi.

Hôtel Printania ★ The keys to Breton hospitality are handed to you at this quaint hotel. Considered by its family-run management as a *musée-hôtel*, you will definitely feel at home here if you're looking for a warm, cultural experience right down to the staff dressed in folkloric costumes. The decor seems frozen from when the hotel was opened in 1920 with solid wooden furniture, traditional floral wallpaper, and grandmother-style nautical antiques and artwork. Your room might even feature *lits clos*—Breton-style beds akin to ships' bunks. Don't worry, there are also modern flat-screen TVs and wireless Internet. It's only 5 minutes from the beach, which you can appreciate from the glassed-in terraces or great restaurant that, not surprisingly, serves up tasty local classics.

5 av. George-V, Dinard 35801. © **02-99-46-13-07.** www.printaniahotel.com. 56 units. 90€–167€ double; 238€–314€ suite. Closed mid-Nov to mid-Mar. **Amenities:** 3 restaurants; bar; free Wi-Fi.

Where to Eat

The **Grand Hôtel Barrière de Dinard** (see above) offers fine dining.

Didier Méril ★★ FRENCH/BRETON   The best meal in Dinard comes with the best views. Located right on the Bay of Prieuré, this historic stone building has been refurbished with designer furniture. This new-meets-old is carried over on Chef Didier Méril's refined menu with such dishes as cod with Avruga caviar and champagne butter and minced beef with foie gras cream and roasted duck drizzled with salty caramel. The wine list is equally impressive, with over 450 labels. If those aren't enough, the view of the bay from its summer terrace will certainly leave you awe-struck.

Above the restaurant are six stylish bedrooms for rent, some with sea views; rates range from 85€ to 160€.

1 place du Gen. de Gaulle. © **02-99-46-95-74.** www.restaurant-didier-meril.com. Main courses 20€–75€; fixed-price menu 31€–80€. Daily noon–2pm and 7–9:30pm.

La Passerelle du Clair de Lune ★ SEAFOOD   As its name indicates, this restaurant is located at one end of the Promenade du Claire de Lune, a perfect spot to enjoy the views of the sea and its excellent catches. The menu is a steal granted its location. The exotic hints in its decor are also sprinkled in the foie gras with kumquat chutney, Brittany lobster grilled with cocoa beans, or the steamed sea bass with smoked carrots and ginger sauce. On a hot summer night, finish off with the pineapple carpaccio with saffron cream.

3 avenue George-V. © **02-99-16-96-37.** www.la-passerelle-restaurant.com. Main courses 20€–60€; fixed-price menu 25€–35€. Daily noon–2:30pm and 7–9:30pm.

Enjoying the Resort

Most visitors come to Dinard for the beach. It's a 10-minute walk from the town's historic core to the Pointe du Moulinet and encircles most of the old town with its haunting 19th-century villas and encompasses views as far away as St-Malo.

BEACHES & SWIMMING   Dinard's main beach is the **Plage de l'Ecluse** (La Grande Plage), the strip of sand between the peninsulas that defines the edges of the old town. Favored by families and vacationers, it's crowded on hot days. Smaller and more isolated is the **Plage de St-Enogat** (you pass through the village of St-Enogat on the 20-min. hike east from Dinard). The **Plage du Prieuré,** a 10-minute walk from the center, has a few trees that shade the sand. Because there's such a difference between high and low tides, the municipality has built swimming pool–style basins along the Plage de L'Ecluse and the Plage du Prieuré to catch the seawater.

The **Piscine Olympique,** boulevard du Président-Wilson, next to the casino (© **02-99-46-22-77**), is a covered, heated seawater pool open year-round. Entrance is 4.80€ for adults, 3.80€ for ages 5 to 17, and free for children 4 and under. From July to mid-September, it's open Monday to Friday 10am to 12:30pm and 3 to 7:30pm, weekends 10am to 12:30pm and 3 to 6:30pm. Hours vary the rest of the year according to the needs of school groups and swim teams (inquire at the tourist office).

SHOPPING   For shops and boutiques, concentrate on rue du Maréchal-Leclerc, rue Levavasseur, and boulevard Féart. In the 15th-century house containing **Galerie d'Art du Prince Noir,** 70 av. George-V (© **02-99-46-29-99**), you'll find paintings and sculptures by some of the most talented artists in France. The gallery is closed from October to April. Another worthwhile destination is **L'Ancien Temple,** 29 rue Jacques-Cartier (© **02-99-46-82-88**), in a former Protestant church. The high-ceilinged showrooms feature upscale porcelain, stoneware, kitchen utensils, gift items, and fresh flowers.

Dinard Nightlife

Like many French beach resorts, Dinard has a casino. **Le Casino Barrière,** 4 bd. Du Président-Wilson (www.lucienbarriere.com; © **02-99-16-30-30**) is liveliest from Easter to late October with games including roulette, blackjack, and slot machines and two bars and a restaurant in-house. Hours are Sunday through Thursday from 11am to 2am, Friday and Saturday from 11am to 3am. Admission is free. An alternative is **La Suite,** 2 rue la Ville Biais, off of route du Barrage (www.lasuitedinard.fr; © **02-99-46-46-46**), a nightclub and dance club on the outskirts with a loyal following thanks to a good wine selection and amiable ambience. It's open Thursdays through Saturdays, with varying cover charges and free shuttle-bus service to Dinard and St-Malo. According to its club rules, "Homosexuality is not a problem—but homophobia is."

In the evenings from June to September, tourists stroll the **Promenade du Clair de Lune** to admire specially illuminated buildings and gardens and hear all kinds of music performed outside.

DINAN ★★★

396km (246 miles) W of Paris; 52km (32 miles) NW of Rennes

Once a fortified stronghold of the Dukes of Brittany, Dinan is one of the prettiest and best-preserved towns in the region. It's noted for its *maisons à piliers,* medieval half-timbered houses built on stilts over the sidewalks. For centuries the town has served as a hub of cultural and commercial activity, from the original merchants and traders to today's artists and craftspeople. There's tourist bustle on a busy day, but it's hard not to be moved by a walk atop the ramparts or a visit to the basilica.

Essentials

ARRIVING   Dinan has an SNCF **train** station, but service is infrequent. The trip from Rennes, with one stop, takes about 1 hour and costs 15.30€. From St-Malo it takes about as long and costs 10€. Most rail passengers just transfer to one of the **buses** that line up in front of the train stations. The trip time is almost the same, but tickets are 2€. For information on bus schedules visit www.tibus.fr or call © **08-10-22-22-22.** If you're **driving** from Dinard, take highway D166 south to Dinan.

VISITOR INFORMATION   The **Office de Tourisme** is at 9 rue du Château (www.dinan-tourisme.com; © **02-96-87-69-76**).

SPECIAL EVENTS   One of the biggest medieval festivals in the world, the **Fêtes des Remparts** is held the third weekend of July in even-numbered years. Mingle amongst the knights and maidens and enjoy authentic street entertainment, food, and crafts. Take in an archery competition or even a jousting match.

Medieval houses in Dinan

[FastFACTS] DINAN

ATMs/Banks   Several ATMs are located in Place Duclos or on rue Thiers.

Doctors & Hospitals   **Centre Hopitalier Dinan/St Brieuc,** avenue Saint-Jean de Dieu (www.chdinanstbrieuc.fsjd.fr; ✆ **02-96-87-18-00**).

Internet Access   The stylish **Le Patio** bar and restaurant has Wi-Fi, 9 Place du Champ Clos (✆ **02-96-39-84-87**).

Mail & Postage   **La Poste,** 7 Place Duclos (✆ **36-31**).

Pharmacies   **Pharmacie Centrale Gildas Morvan,** 8 Place Duclos (✆ **02-96-39-07-10**).

Where to Stay

Hôtel Arvor ★★   The entrance to this former 14th-century Jacobin convent ushers you into the most romantic hotel in town. The building was first refurbished in the 18th century in a Renaissance style, and thankfully, again in 2011 bringing it up to 21st-century standards. Guestrooms carry on in an amorous ambiance with colorful drapery, plush armchairs and even some heart-shaped throw pillows. The rooms are rather spacious, in contrast to the small, though well-equipped bathrooms. Families will be able to spread out in their spacious duplex suite that sleeps six.

5 rue Pavie, Dinan 22100. ✆ **02-96-39-21-22.** www.hotelarvordinan.com. 22 units. 82€–125€ double. Parking 6€. Closed Jan. **Amenities:** Free Wi-Fi.

Hôtel d'Avaugour ★★   Set in a stone house just inside the ramparts, this is a perfect and comfortable base for exploring Dinan. The entire hotel is tastefully decorated in a contemporary style and the ground floor has recently been renovated, the additional windows now shedding delicate daylight onto readers in the comfortable lounge. The guestrooms have simple yet plush furnishings with hints of Brittany in the decor. The verdant window views either showcase the surrounding historic buildings or the large and lovely backyard garden, where you can take tea in the afternoon.

1 place du Champs, Dinan 22100. © **02-96-39-07-49.** www.avaugourhotel.com. 24 units. 125€–
260€ double; 230€–350€ suite. Closed Nov–Mar 1. **Amenities:** Free Wi-Fi.

Where to Eat

For a less formal meal there are lighter eateries on rue de la Poissonnerie. Stop in
at busy **Creperie Ahna,** no. 7 (© **02-96-39-09-13**), which has been run by the
same family for four generations.

L'Auberge du Pélican ★ FRENCH/BRETON   Locavores reign supreme at
this *auberge.* They know exactly where their fresh fish is caught and they even
make their own bread. The modern look does not take away from their traditional
philosophies perfectly carried out in their sea "choucroute" with fresh fish filets
in *beurre blanc* sauce, *confit de canard* and from October to March, a special tasting menu of fresh scallops caught right in the bay.

3 rue Haute Voie. © **02-96-39-47-05.** Main courses 14€–28€; fixed-price menus 21€–60€. July–
Aug daily noon–2pm and 7–10pm (except Mon noon); Sept–June Tues– Sat noon–2pm and
7–10pm and Sun noon–2pm. Closed Jan.

Exploring the Town

Dinan's ramparts, which include 14 watchtowers and four gates, extend for
almost 3.5km (2 miles) around the town. The tourist office can provide you with
a printed walking guide.

An authentic and appealing street is the sloping rue du Jerzual, flanked with
15th-century dwellings and shops with craftspeople selling their wares. In the
middle is the **Porte du Jerzual,** a 13th- and 14th-century gate—you can still see
traces of its drawbridge in the stone. In the direction of the river the street
becomes **rue du Petit-Fort** and leads to the town's small port and its Gothic
style bridge.

Basilique St-Sauveur ★★ CHURCH   Built between the 12th and 16th
centuries, this church has Romanesque, Gothic, Baroque, and Classical elements. A monument holds the heart of Bertrand du Guesclin, the beloved Breton
knight who defended Dinard during the Hundred Years' War. Just behind the
basilica, the terraced **Jardin Anglais (English Garden)** provides a panoramic
view of the Rance Valley and direct access to the ramparts.

place St-Sauveur. © **02-96-39-06-67.** Free admission.

Château Musée de Dinan ★ MUSEUM   Three medieval structures
reunited in the 16th century form this fascinating municipal museum. The dungeon of this colossal 14th-century fortress was a residence for the Duke of Brittany before being converted into a jail. It contains displays on Dinan's history
dating back to prehistory, and the chapel contains holy artifacts, furniture, and
silver. The visit is worthwhile merely to see the castle interior.

rue du Château. (© **02-96-39-45-20.** Admission: 4.60€ adults, 1.90€ ages 12–18, free for
children 11 and under. June–Sept daily 10am–6:30pm, Oct–May daily 1:30–5:30pm. Closed Jan.

Tour de l'Horloge ★ HISTORIC SITE   This structure boasts a clock made
in 1498 and a bell donated by Anne de Bretagne in 1507. After 158 steps you'll
be rewarded with a view of Dinan from the 23m (75-ft.) belfry—one of only two
intact belfries in all of Brittany. Its main bell is named after Anne—three smaller
ones are engraved with the names Jacqueline, Françoise, and Noguette.

rue de l'Horloge (© **02-96-87-58-72.** Admission: 4€ adults, 3€ ages 13–18, free for children 12
and under. Apr–May 2–6pm; June–Sept 10am–6:30pm.

AN idyll ON AN ILE

The **Ile de Bréhat** is home to some 350 hearty folk who live most of the year in isolation—until the summer crowds arrive. The tiny island (actually two islands, Ile Nord and Ile Sud, linked by a bridge, Le Pont Vauban) is in the Gulf of St-Malo, north of Paimpol. A visit to Bréhat is an adventure, even to the French. The only settlement on the islands is Le Bourg, in the south. The only bona fide beach is a strip of sand at Guerzido.

Walking is the primary activity, and it's possible to stroll the footpaths around the island in a day. Cars, other than police and fire vehicles, aren't allowed. Tractor-driven carts carry visitors on an 8km (5-mile) circuit of Bréhat's two islands, charging 9€ for the 45-minute jaunt (it's 4€ for children 4–11, free for 3 and under). A number of places rent bikes, but they aren't necessary. The rich flora here astonishes many visitors, who arrive expecting a wind-swept island only to discover a more Mediterranean clime. Flowers abound in summer, though both the gardens and houses appear tiny because of the scarcity of land. At the highest point, Chapelle St-Michel, you'll be rewarded with a panoramic view.

The **tourist office,** place du Bourg, Le Bourg (www.brehat-infos.fr; ✆ **02-96-20-83-16**), is open Monday to Saturday mid-June to mid-September.

To reach Paimpol, **drive** west on D768 from Dinard to Lamballe, then take E50 west to Plérin and D786 north to Paimpol. To reach the island, take D789 4km (2½ miles) north of Paimpol, where the peninsula ends at the Pointe de l'Arcouest. From Paimpol, 6 to 10 **Tibus** (www.tibus.fr; ✆ **08-10-22-22-22**) buses make the 10-minute run to the point for a one-way fare of 2€. Then catch one of the **ferries** operated by **Les Vedettes de Bréhat** (www.vedettesdebrehat.com; ✆ **02-96-55-79-50**). Ferries depart about every 30 minutes in summer, around 7 times per day in the off-season; the round-trip costs 9.50€ for adults, 8€ for ages 4 to 11, and is free for children 3 and under. Visitors in April, May, June, and September will find the island much less crowded than in July and August. Cars are not allowed on the ferry.

QUIMPER ★★

570km (353 miles) W of Paris; 205km (127 miles) NW of Rennes

Quimper, the town that pottery built, is the historic capital of Brittany's most traditional region, La Cornouaille. It takes its name from the Breton word *kemper*, the meeting of two rivers—in this case the Odet and the Steir. There's no better place to get a feel for southern Breton culture, whether during its annual festival or just trolling the *vieux centre* for Quimperware, the hand-painted *faience* that's symbolized Brittany for centuries. Modern-day Quimper is somewhat bourgeois, home to some 67,000 *Quimperois* who walk narrow streets spared from World War II damage.

Essentials

ARRIVING   Speedy **TGV trains** take only 4½ hours from the Montparnasse station in Paris. The one-way fare is around 67€. For information, visit www.voyages-sncf.com or call ✆ **36-35.** If you're **driving,** the best route is from

Rennes: Take E50/N12 west to just outside the town of Montauban, continue west along N164 to Châteaulin, and head south along N165 to Quimper.

VISITOR INFORMATION   The **Office de Tourisme** is on place de la Résistance (www.quimper-tourisme.com; ✆ **02-98-53-04-05**).

SPECIAL EVENTS   For 6 days around the third week of every July, the **Festival de Cornouaille** celebrates Breton culture. The festivities include parades in traditional costume and Celtic and Breton concerts throughout the city. For information, contact the tourist office.

[Fast FACTS] QUIMPER

ATMs/Banks   Several ATMs can be found on rue du Parc and rue René Madec.

Doctors & Hospitals   **Centre Hopitalier de Cornouaille,** avenue Yves Thépot (www.ch-cournouaille.fr; ✆ **02-98-52-60-60**).

Internet Access   **C.com C@fé**, 9 Quai du Port au Vin (✆ **02-98-95-81-62**).

Mail & Postage   **La Poste**, 37 bd Amiral de Kerguélen (✆ **36-31**).

Pharmacies   **Pharmacie de la Cathédrale,** 24 Place Saint-Corentin (✆ **02-98-95-00-20**).

Where to Stay

Hôtel Kregenn ★   For a solid sleep in the center, this is your best option. Located on a quiet street a block from the river, this hotel is an excellent value for the money. Though a Best Western, the hotel is still family-run, with an exceptionally friendly staff. Guestrooms are relatively spacious and have a simple yet stylish decor. The interior garden-terrace is the place to retire for a relaxing break. A coffee or glass of wine can be had at the bar; however, breakfast, for 13€, is the only meal served.

11–15 rue des Réquaires, Quimper 29000. ✆ **02-98-95-08-70.** www.hotel-kregenn.fr. 32 units. 109€–180€ double, 185€–220€ suite. Parking 7€. Pets 15€. **Amenities:** Bar; limited room service; free Wi-Fi.

Where to Eat

For a drink or meal at any time of the day, sit down at the stylish **Brasserie de l'Epée,** 14 rue du Parc (www.quimper-lepee.com; ✆ **02-98-95-28-97**). The oldest "brasserie" in Brittany, it dates back to 1830 and serves elegant bistro fare, and, of course, copious seafood options.

Ambroisie ★ BRETON/FRENCH   Breton cuisine at its best is prepared in this popular establishment in the heart of Brittany's cultural capital. For more than 25 years, Gilbert Guyon has honed his culinary arts, earning himself the only Michelin star in Quimper. His focus is in the kitchen; however, the dining room hasn't been neglected and has nice contemporary furniture and large paintings inspired by English painter Francis Bacon. Guyon's menu features modern takes on regional traditions such as his signature buckwheat galette with prawns. You might also like cocotte of duck cooked in cider or mussels with Breton artichokes. Pursue this local theme for dessert with an excellent selection of cheese straight from the farm or homemade fromage blanc sorbet.

49 rue Elie Fréron. ✆ **02-98-95-00-02.** www.ambroisie-quimper.com. Fixed-price menu 41€–70€; children's menu 15€. Tues–Sun noon–1:30pm; Tues–Sat 7:30–9:15pm.

Where to Stay Nearby

Manoir du Stang ★★   Hidden away in the Fouesnant Forest is one of Brittany's loveliest manor-hotels. Only 13km (8 miles) from Quimper, this refined 16th-century estate has changed hands only once in its 400-year history. The imposing stone walls and impeccably maintained grounds are proof of this test of time. The 10 hectares (25 acres) of natural woodland are perfect for idyll strolls, and golfers delight in teeing off at the neighboring 18-hole course. The lounge is cozy with a toasty fireplace and is furnished with antiques and patterned armchairs. Guestroom decor is a little old fashioned, but this adds to its homey Breton feel. There's no restaurant, but breakfast can be brought to your bed.

La Forêt-Fouesnant 29940. ✆ **02-98-56-96-38.** www.manoirdustang.com. 22 units. 116€–146€ double. Free parking. Closed end-Sept to late April. Drive 1.5km (1 mile) north of the village center and follow signs from N783; access is by private road. **Amenities:** Bar; free Wi-Fi.

Exploring the Town

In some quarters, Quimper maintains its old-world atmosphere, with narrow medieval streets and footbridges spanning the rivers.

Cathédrale St-Corentin ★★ CATHEDRAL   Characterized by two towers that climb 75m (246 ft.), this cathedral was built between the 13th and 15th centuries. The twin steeples were added in the 19th. Inside, note the 15th-century stained glass—windows on the north side were funded by religious donors, those on the south by secular ones.

pl St-Corentin. ✆ **02-98-95-06-19.** Free admission. Sept–Jun daily 9:45am–noon and 1:30–6:30pm; July–Aug daily 9:45am–6:30pm, except during Sun morning services.

Musée des Beaux-Arts ★★ MUSEUM   This museum is a nice cultural surprise along the mostly outdoorsy Brittany coast. First opened in 1872, it underwent renovations and extension work in the early 1990s. The collection features some impressive names including Rubens, Boucher, Fragonard, and

A sunny day in Quimper

Corot, in addition to a strong collection of the Pont-Aven school (Gaugin, Sérusier, Bernard, Lacombe, Maufra, Denis). A special tribute is also paid to Quimper native Mac Jacob, a Surrealist poet and painter.

40 pl St-Corentin. ✆ **02-98-95-45-20.** www.mbaq.fr. Admission 5€ adults, 3€ ages 12–26, free for 11 and under. July–Aug daily from 10am–7pm; Apr–Jun and Sept–Oct Wed–Mon 9:30am–noon and 2–6pm; and Nov–Mar Wed–Mon 9am–noon and 1:30–5pm, Sun 2–5pm.

Musée Departemental Breton ★★★ MUSEUM Located in the medieval Palais des Eveques de Cornouaille (Palace of the Bishops of Cornwall), next to the cathedral, this is a highlight of any visit to Quimper. Renovations over the last decade have revamped its displays of the archaeological and decorative history of the region. It is one of the best ways to learn about the customs and traditions of Brittany, illustrated in items of stained glass, sculpture, furniture, painting, and *faience* (see below), in addition to four rooms showcasing everyday and ceremonial Breton costumes.

1–3 rue Roi Gradlon. ✆ **02-98-95-21-60.** www.museedepartementalbreton.fr. Admission: 4€ adults, 2.50€ ages 18–25, free for children 17 and under. Free on weekends from Jan–May and Oct–Dec. Tues–Sat 9am–noon and 2–5pm.

Shopping

Quimper's proximity to the rivers gave it plenty of access to clay; it's been known as a pottery town since the late 1600s. *Faience,* the French term for glazed earthenware (as opposed to porcelain, manufactured to be more delicate) is your go-to souvenir here. Quimperware is recognized for its bright, hand-painted motifs, often Breton figures, fruits, and flowers. One of the most popular designs is a male *Breton* or female *Bretonne,* both in profile and in traditional costume. Today this 19th-century motif is copyrighted and fiercely protected.

The best shopping streets are **rue Kéréon** and **rue du Parc,** where you'll find Breton products including pottery, dolls and puppets, clothing made from regional cloth and wool, jewelry, lace, and beautiful Breton costumes.

One site that produces stoneware is open for tours. From April to September, Monday to Friday 10am to 12:45pm and 1:45 to 4:30pm, five to seven tours per day depart from the visitor information center of **HB-Henriot Faïenceries de Quimper,** rue Haute, Quartier Locmaria (www.hb-henriot.com; ✆ **02-98-90-09-36**). Tours in English, French, or both last 40 to 45 minutes and cost 5€ for adults, 2.50€ for children 8 to 14, and are free for children 7 and under. On site, a store sells the most complete inventory of Quimper porcelain in the world. You can invest in first-run (nearly perfect) pieces or slightly discounted "seconds," with almost imperceptible flaws. Everything can be shipped.

For more Breton pottery, as well as fine tablecloths, linens, and other household items, visit **François le Villec,** 4 rue Roi-Gradlon (www.levillec.com; ✆ **02-98-95-31-54**).

CONCARNEAU ★★

539km (334 miles) W of Paris; 93km (58 miles) SE of Brest

This port is a favorite of painters, who never tire of capturing the subtleties of the fishing fleet. It's also unique among the larger coastal communities because fishing, not tourism, is its main industry (Concarneau's canneries produce most of the tuna in France). Walk along the quays, especially in the evening, and watch the Breton fishers unload their catch; later, join them for a pint of cider in the taverns.

Essentials

ARRIVING   There's no rail service to Concarneau. If you're driving, the town is 21km (13 miles) southeast of Quimper along D783. A bus runs from Quimper to Concarneau (trip time: 30 min.); the one-way fare is 2€. The bus from Rosporden, site of another SNCF railway station, runs about eight times per day (trip time: 20 min.) for a fare of 2€. For information call (© 08-10-81-00-29).

VISITOR INFORMATION   The **Office de Tourisme** is on quai d'Aiguillon (www.tourismeconcarneau.fr; © 02-98-97-01-44).

Where to Stay

Les Sables Blancs ★★   Overlooking Concarneau's loveliest beach, you can't have a better seaside stay than at this boutique hotel. Recent renovations made to this 1960s building transformed it into a glass paradise. Every room has expansive windows facing the sea in addition to small private terraces. Most rooms are vastly white with only small hints of color in pillows or artwork; the never-ending sea is decoration enough. For some sophisticated surf and turf grab a table on the terrace or in the stylish dining room of the hotel's restaurant, Le Nautile.

Plage des Sables Blancs, Concarneau 29900. © **02-98-50-10-12.** www.hotel-les-sables-blancs.com. 16 units. 125€–260€ double; 270€–410€ suite. Always open. **Amenities:** Free Wi-Fi.

Where to Eat

La Coquille ★ SEAFOOD/TRADITIONAL FRENCH   Located right on the port, you can practically see your dinner being reeled in at the freshest venue in town. While it might not look sophisticated from the outside, the dining room features stone walls, ceiling beams, century-old oil paintings from the School of Pont-Aven, and a spectacular view of the harbor. Not surprisingly, you'll find a lot of seafood on menu at La Coquille (the shell). The menu varies according to the latest catches. It could include scallops with algae butter, grilled lobster with Kari Gosse sauce or, to please the carnivores, filet of beef with red wine reduction sauce. The friendly staff will make you want to stay for dessert; try the "palette" of sorbets, inspired by the colorful local paintings on the walls. Reservations a must in season.

1 quai du Moros, at Nouveau Port. © **02-98-97-08-52.** www.lacoquille-concarneau.com. Main courses 9.80€–43€; fixed-price menu 30€–46€. Tues–Sun noon–1:30pm; Tues–Sat 7:30–9:30pm.

Exploring the Area

The town is built on three sides of a natural harbor whose innermost, sheltered section is the **Nouveau Port.** In the center of this is the heavily fortified **Ville Close ★★**, an ancient hamlet surrounded by ramparts, some from the 14th century. From the quay, cross the bridge and descend into the town. Souvenir shops have taken over, but don't let that spoil it. You can spend an hour wandering the alleys, gazing up at the towers, peering at the stone houses, and stopping in secluded squares.

For a splendid view of the port, walk the **ramparts ★**. They're open to pedestrians daily 10am to 7:30pm, with seasonal variations.

Also in the old town is a fishing museum, **Musée de la Pêche ★**, 3 rue Vauban (www.musee-peche.fr; © 02-98-97-10-20). The 17th-century building displays ship models and exhibits chronicling the development of the fishing industry; you can also view the ship *Hemerica,* which has recently undergone extensive restorations. Admission is 4.50€ for adults and free for 18 and under.

It's open daily February, March, and October from 10am to 12:30pm and 2 to 6pm, from April to June and September 10am to 6pm, and July to August 9:30am to 7pm. Closed January to mid-February.

BEACHES Concarneau's largest, most beautiful beach, popular with families, is the **Plage des Sables Blancs,** near the historic core. Within a 10-minute walk are the **Plage de Cornouaille** and two small beaches, the **Plage des Dames** and **Plage de Rodel,** where you'll find fewer families with children. The wide-open **Plage du Cabellou,** 5km (3 miles) west of town, is less crowded than the others.

SEA EXCURSIONS Boat rides are usually fine between June and September but can be treacherous the rest of the year. The dazzling Glenans archipelago, 10 miles off the coast, is a must if you have the time and sea legs. For excursions, contact Vedettes Glenn (www.vedettes-glenn.fr; ✆ **02-98-97-10-31**) or Vedettes de l'Odet (www.vedettes-odet.com; ✆ **02-98-57-00-58**). In midsummer, you can arrange deep-sea fishing with the captain of the Santa Maria (www.santamariapeche.com; ✆ **06-62-88-00-87**).

PONT-AVEN ★★

522km (324 miles) W of Paris; 32km (20 miles) SE of Quimper; 16km (10 miles) S of Concarneau

Paul Gauguin loved this inland village, with its white houses flanking the River Aven on its gentle course to the Atlantic. It's also known for 15 *moulins,* or water mills, that once operated along the waterways. Only one of them is still functional, but the rest have been restored for historical and aesthetic purposes. With such picturesque surroundings, one might suspect Pont-Aven of being a tourist trap, but its modest, pleasant atmosphere endures.

Essentials

ARRIVING If you're **driving** from Quimper, go southeast on N165 and follow signs into Pont-Aven. From Quimperlé, head west along D783 until N165 and follow signs. SNCF **trains** stop at Quimper, where you can transfer to between four and six daily **buses** to Pont Aven (trip time: 30 min.; one-way fare 2€). For bus information, call the Pont-Aven tourist office (see below). For train information visit www.voyages-sncf.com or ✆ **36-35.**

VISITOR INFORMATION The **Office de Tourisme** is at 5 place de l'Hôtel-de-Ville (www.pontaven.com; ✆ **02-98-06-04-70**).

Where to Eat & Stay

Le Moulin de Rosmadec ★★★
TRADITIONAL FRENCH You will be impressed by more than just the Impressionists of Pont-Aven if you dine

Picturesque Pont-Aven

at this picturesque 15th-century stone mill, easily southern Brittany's best restaurant. The dining room is classy and contemporary, but it's the shady terrace that is highly coveted. Chef Frédéric Sébilleau has earned his Michelin star with his famous grilled lobster with two butter sauces, freshly caught abalone from Glénan with coco de Paimpol beans and algae, and rack of lamb with polenta fries and eggplant caviar. On Thursdays when the Moulin is closed, stop in at Sébillau's brother's less-formal restaurant, **Sur Le Pont,** 11 Place Paul Gauguin, (www.surlepont-pontaven.fr; ✆ 02-98-60-16-16).

The Moulin also rents four pleasant double rooms for 98€ to 105€. Not as fancy as the food, they are modern and comfortable, plus as the mill is at the end of a cul-de-sac, it's quiet and calm.

Pont-Aven 29123. ✆ **02-98-06-00-22.** www.moulinderosmadec.com. Main courses 30€–50€; fixed-price menu 43€–79€. Tues–Sun 12:30–2pm and Tues–Sat 7:30–9pm. Closed Jan and Feb.

Exploring the Area

In the village there are themed walking tours possible, such as the artists' trail or the *promenade des moulins*—the tourist office can provide maps. You can also visit one of the shops that produce the famous *galette de Pont-Aven*, a round, butter-rich cookie that Bretons like to dunk in their coffee. **Traou Mad,** rue du Port (✆ 02-98-06-18-18), has a second shop on the bridge. **Délices de Pont-Aven,** 1, quai Théodore Botrel (✆ 02-98-06-02-75), offers tours of their nearby production facilities in July and August (Tues and Thurs at 10am; admission 2€ and free 18 and under).

The 16th-century **Chapelle de Trémalo,** lieu-dit Trémalo (✆ 02-98-06-01-68), is 1.2km (¾ mile) north of the town center. Here is the wooden crucifix that inspired two of Gauguin's best-known paintings, *The Yellow Christ* (displayed today in a museum in Buffalo, New York) and his *Self-Portrait with the Yellow Christ* (displayed at the Musée d'Orsay in Paris). On private lands which still belong to descendants of the family who originally built and consecrated it in 1532, the chapel is unlocked every morning at 10am and closed at 5pm (6pm July–Aug). It's still a place of worship, so masses are conducted from time to time. Plunk a coin or two into a machine to briefly illuminate the interior—otherwise, midday sunlight from the windows is sufficient.

In the Footsteps of Gauguin

In the summer of 1886, Paul Gauguin arrived in the Breton village of Pont-Aven. Lesser-known artists, including Maurice Denis, Paul Sérusier, and Emile Bernard, soon followed. Breaking from mainstream Impressionism, the Pont Aven School—as the style of Gauguin and his 20 or so followers came to be known—emphasized pure colors, shunned perspective and shadowing, and simplified human figures. Both *The Yellow Christ* and *The Green Christ*, two of Gauguin's most memorable works, exemplify this method, also known as Synthetism.

The **Musée des Beaux-Arts de Pont-Aven,** place de l'Hôtel de Ville (www.museepontaven.fr; ✆ 02-98-06-14-43), provides a comprehensive exhibit of these 19th-century painters. Expect muted greens and blues and lots of Breton patriotism as interpreted through the most famous artistic movement to emerge from Brittany. At time of print, the museum was closed for renovation until at least spring 2015. Upon reopening, check website for updated hours and admission fees.

CARNAC ★★

486km (301 miles) W of Paris; 37km (23 miles) SE of Lorient; 100km (62 miles) SE of Quimper

Aside from being a popular beach resort, Carnac is home to the largest mega-lithic site in the world. Spread out over 4km (2½ miles), **Les Alignements,** as three fields of huge, upright stones are known, date back more than 6,000 years to Neolithic times. Scholars have debated their purpose for centuries, though most suggest they had astronomical or religious significance. One theory is that the stones marked burial sites. Another legend claims they are Roman soldiers turned to stone by the wizard Merlin. In all, the town contains 2,732 *menhirs,* some rising to heights of 20m (66 ft.).

Carnac's five beaches stretch over nearly 3km (1¾ miles). Protected by the Quiberon Peninsula, they back up onto sand dunes and shady forests. **Carnac-Plage** is a family resort and camping hotspot beside the ocean and along the waterfront boulevard de la Plage. The area is packed in July and August.

Essentials

ARRIVING **Driving** is the most convenient way to get to Carnac. From Pont-Aven, travel southeast along N165, passing through Hennebont. At the intersection with D768, continue south along the signposted road to Carnac. From Nantes, take N165 northwest to Auray and then D768.

Links to Carnac by public transport are inconvenient, as there's no railway station. **Train** travelers leave the SNCF network at either Quiberon or Auray and take a bus into town. An additional option, available between June and August only, is to get off the train at Plouharnel-Carnac station, 3km (1¾ miles) from Carnac. For more information about bus transit from any of these hamlets, call ✆ **08-10-10-10-56.**

VISITOR INFORMATION The **Office de Tourisme** is at 74 av. des Druides (www.ot-carnac.fr; ✆ **02-97-52-13-52**).

Where to Eat & Stay

Auberge le Ratelier ★★ BRETON A true taste of Brittany is savored at this converted farmhouse, situated a short stroll from the center of Carnac. The stone building is draped in vines and the interior is equally charming with rustic decor, a fireplace, and wooden beams. Due to its seaside location the menu showcases local seafood, particularly celebrated in its "trip around lobster" set menu. You can also enjoy non-fish dishes like smoked duck with Breton artichokes and Camembert toasts, or the saddle of rabbit stuffed with foie gras.

Upstairs, the inn has eight small, slightly old-fashioned but comfortable guest rooms with showers. They are a steal at 55€ to 70€.

4 chemin du Douët. ✆ **02-97-52-05-04.** www.le-ratelier.com. Main courses 19€–34€; fixed-price menu 23€–48€. Sept–June Thurs–Mon noon–2:30pm and 7:30–9:30pm; July–Aug daily (same hours). Closed mid-Nov to mid-Dec and Jan.

Camping La Grande Métairie ★ A 5-minute drive from the center of Car-nac is this family fun paradise. The large complex next to the Megaliths is sur-rounded by trees and is a short drive to the beach. There is plenty to do onsite with a large pool complex, water slides, a tree adventure park, mini-golf, tennis and more. They even have a little farm and a circus school. You can either pitch your own tent or rent a variety of equipped mobile homes or for something differ-ent, opt for one of their tree-houses perched safely in the branches.

The Wild, Wild Coast

Follow the D768 south from Carnac over the isthmus connecting the mainland to **Quiberon,** with its crescent of white sand. You'll probably see weathered Breton fishers hauling in their sardine catch.

The entire **Côte Sauvage,** or Wild Coast, is rugged and dramatic, with waves breaking ferociously against the reefs. Winds, especially in winter, lash the dunes, shaving the short pines that grow here. On the landward side, the beach is calm and relatively protected.

A 45-minute ferry ride from Quiberon is **Belle-Ile-en-Mer,** an 83 sq. km (32 sq. miles) outpost of sand, rock, and vegetation. It feels blissfully isolated, despite a scattering of hotels and seasonal restaurants. Depending on the season, 5 to 15 **ferries** depart daily from Port Maria in Quiberon (✆ **08-20-05-61-56**). A round-trip ticket costs 33.65€ for adults, 21.90€ for ages 4 to 17, and free for children 3 and under. In summer, you must reserve space for your car, as well as for passengers. The ferry docks at **Le Palais,** a fortified 16th-century port that is the island's window to mainland France. The Office de Tourisme is here, on Quai Bonnelle Le Palais (✆ **02-97-31-81-93**).

Excellent accommodation and dining can be found in **Port de Goulphar,** an inlet on the southern shore framed by cliffs. The standout is the 63-unit Relais & Châteaux property **Castel Clara,** (www.castel-clara.com; ✆ **02-97-31-84-21**) with restful rooms, two heated swimming pools (one seawater), and extensive spa services. Ideal service and first-class cuisine add to the sense of peace. Depending on the season, and on the view from the room (sea or garden), rates range from 120€ to 385€ in a double, 335€ to 515€ in a suite. The hotel is closed from mid-November to mid-December.

A fitting souvenir are sardines from **La Belle-Iloise boutique** on the Place de la République (www.labelleiloise.fr; ✆ **02-97-31-29-14**). Even if you don't like sardines, the attractive tins make unusual *objets*. The last cannery in Belle-Ile-en-Mer closed in 1975, but production continues in Quiberon, and Belle-Iloise boutiques can be found in most Breton towns.

BELOW: **Beach at Quiberon**

Route des Alignements de Kermario–Kerlescan 56342 Carnac. ✆ **02-97-52-24-01.** www.lagrandemetairie.com. From 14€ tent lots, 96€–295€ mobile homes, discounts on weekly rates. Closed mid-Sep to Apr. **Amenities:** Restaurant; babysitting; bar; disco; grocery; Jacuzzi; pool; Wi-Fi in central bar.

Château de Locguénolé ★★★ Crowning a small bay enveloped by a 120-hectare (297-acre) forest, this is the most graceful hotel in southern Brittany.

Located near the town of **Hennebont,** 29km (18 miles) northwest of Carnac, the château has been in the same family for over 2 centuries, enough time to perfect this excellent combination of French elegance and maritime personality. While strolling the beautifully maintained gardens you can watch sailboats idly cruise by. The stately main building is filled with tasteful antiques, tapestries, and paintings. Guestrooms are very spacious; though the decor is a touch dated, this also adds to its charm. Rooms in the renovated 1720 Breton cottage annex are well appointed, but lack the sea view. The elegant drawing room now serves as the hotel's Michelin-starred restaurant, the best place to enjoy local seafood and shellfish.

Rte. De Port-Louis en Kervignac, Hennebont 56700. ✆ **02-97-76-76-76.** www.chateau-de-locguenole.com. 22 units. 159€–240€ double; 258€–422€ suite. Closed Jan 21 to mid-Feb. From Hennebont, follow hotel signs, 4km (2½ miles) south. **Amenities:** Restaurant; babysitting; outdoor pool; room service; 2 saunas; free Wi-Fi.

Exploring the Area

Out of fear of vandalism, the local tourist authorities have fenced in the mega-liths and now allow visitors to wander freely among the *menhirs* only between October and March, when the park is open daily from 10am to 5pm, and when entrance is free. From April to September, the park can be visited only as part of a rigidly controlled 1-hour guided tour, priced at 6€ per person (5€ for students or anyone between 18 and 24; under 18 are free). Tours are usually in French but, depending on the perceived need, may include some additional commentary in English. The only way to be sure is to call the **visitor center, La Maison des Mégalithes,** at ✆ **02-97-52-29 81,** for a rundown on the tours arranged for the day of your intended visit. For more information, visit www.carnac.monuments-nationaux.fr.

At Carnac Ville, **Musée de Préhistoire,** 10 place de la Chapelle (www.museedecarnac.com; ✆**02-97-52-22-04**), displays collections from 450,000 BC to the 8th century. Admission is 6€ for adults, 2.50€ for ages 6 to 18, and free for children 5 and under. Hours are as follows: July and August daily 10am to 6pm; October to March Wednesday to Monday 10am to 12:30pm and 2 to 5:30pm; April to June and September Wednesday to Monday 10am to 12:30pm and 2 to 6pm.

NANTES ★★★

385km (239 miles) W of Paris; 325km (202 miles) N of Bordeaux

Technically, Nantes (pop. 288,000) is outside of Brittany. In 1941, the Vichy Government transferred it from the region into a newly-created one, the Pays de la Loire. This administrative action did nothing to change Nantes' deeply Breton soul, however, and no guide to Brittany would be complete without its inclusion.

The capital of Brittany is Rennes (pop. 208,000), but when comparing the two cities, many agree that Nantes is more vibrant. It's best known for its busy port, which suffered great damage in World War II, and for the 1598 Edict of Nantes, which guaranteed religious freedom to Protestants (this was later revoked). During the Middle Ages, Nantes expanded from an island in the Loire to the northern edge of the river, where its center lies today. Many famous people, from Molière to Stendhal, have lived here.

Despite a lackluster reputation, Nantes is becoming a kind of Atlantic Coast Parisian annex for young *bobos* and families tired of the capital's rat race.

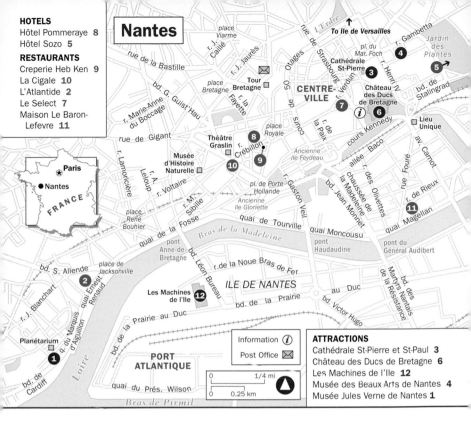

Impressive revitalization is changing the city, as once-dreary industrial suburbs are being transformed into places you'd actually like to visit.

Essentials

ARRIVING The **TGV train** from Paris's Gare Montparnasse takes about 2 to 2½ hours to get to Nantes and costs range from 48€ to 65€. For information, visit www.voyages-sncf.com or call ✆ **36-35.** Nantes's **Gare SNCF,** 27 bd. de Stalingrad, is a 5-minute walk from the town center. If you're **driving,** take A11 for 385km (239 miles) west of Paris. The trip takes about 4 hours. **Aéroport Nantes-Atlantique** (✆ **02-40-84-80-00**) is 12km (7½ miles) southeast of town. **Air France** (www.airfrance.fr; ✆ **36-54** within France only) offers daily flights from Paris. A shuttle bus between the airport and the Nantes train station takes 25 minutes and costs 7.50€. A taxi from the airport costs 30€ to 35€ and takes about 20 minutes.

VISITOR INFORMATION The **Office de Tourisme** is at 9 rue des Etats (www.nantes-tourisme.com; ✆ **08-92-46-40-44**).

PASS NANTES Available at the airport, tourist office, and certain hotels, the pass allows you to enter museums and ride any of the city's public conveyances, including buses, trams, and some of the boats that cruise through town along Erdre River. The pass costs 17€ for 1 day, 24€ for 2 days, and 40.50€ for 3 days; passes for families of 4 are a good value.

Getting Around

ON FOOT The downtown, cathedral, castle, and the island are accessible on foot and the central train station helps for visitors without wheels.

BY BICYCLE Nantes has a Paris-style bike-sharing program called **Bicloo** (www.bicloo.nantesmetropole.fr; ✆ **09-69-39-36-67**). With over 103 stations it's a great way to get around. You can register online at machines at most stations or at the tourist office. Fees are 1€ for a day pass or 5€ for a weekly pass.

BY CAR As the downtown core is highly pedestrianized, it's best to park your car; around the station there are ideal official lots. Otherwise, there is another at the cathedral. You can rent a car near the train station through **Europcar,** 325 rue Marcel Paul (www.europcar-atlantique.fr; ✆ **02-40-47-19-38**) or **Hertz,** rue Cornulier (www.hertz.fr; ✆ **02-40-35-78-00**).

BY TAXI For an English-speaking service call **Taxis Nantes** (www.taxisnantes.fr; ✆ **06-88-28-16-29**).

BY PUBLIC TRANSPORT Nantes has an extensive transit system of trams, buses, and ferries run by the **TAN** (www.tan.fr; ✆ **02-40-44-44-44**). A one-way ticket costs 1.50€ and can be purchased from a machine at tram stations or 2€ from the bus driver or an unlimited day pass is 4.60€.

[Fast FACTS] NANTES

ATMs/Banks   There are easy-access ATMs in front of the cathedral or around Place Royale.

Doctors & Hospitals   **Centre Hopitalier Universitaire de Nantes,** 85 rue Saint-Jacques (www.chu-nantes.fr; ✆ **02-40-08-33-33**).

Internet Access   **KpointCom,** 15 allée Dugay Trouin at Place du Commerce (✆ **02-51-82-27-71**) or free Wi-Fi available at the tourist office.

Mail & Postage   **La Poste,** 2 Place de Bretagne (✆ **36-31**).

Pharmacies   **Grand Pharmacie de Paris,** 17 rue Orléans (✆ **02-40-48-64-48**).

Where to Stay

Hôtel Pommeraye ★ Situated in the heart of town, this is a convenient option for a reasonably priced overnight in Nantes. It's surrounded by a multitude of shops, restaurants, and the historic Passage Pommeraye. The compact rooms are decorated with contemporary furnishings and creative touches. The organic and low-carbon-footprint breakfast is delicious and you can ask for a tray to be delivered to your room for free. Rooms on the street side can be noisy, so for a peaceful sleep request a room facing the courtyard.

2 rue Boileau, Nantes 44000. ✆ **02-40-48-78-79.** www.hotel-pommeraye.com. 74 units. 69€–169€ double; 118€–268€ suite. Small pets 5€. **Amenities:** Restaurant; bar; free packing nearby; room service; free Wi-Fi.

Hôtel Sozo ★★★ Located in a renovated 19th-century chapel across from the Jardin des Plants, this exceptional boutique hotel is more than just a place to lay your head, it's a philosophy. Sozo means creation and imagination in Japanese; the driving force behind the hotel's inception and its ongoing spirit. Guestrooms are small though extremely well appointed; each one features characteristics of the chapel from stained glass to pillars and arches. The room size matters less since the monumental foyer is the place to be. Enjoy a cocktail on its designer furniture or take your turn at the grand piano, that is, unless it's already occupied by a famous musician—the hotel is a favorite for visiting artists and performers.

16 Rue Frédéric Cailliaud, Nantes 44000. ✆ **02-51-82-40-00.** http://sozohotel.fr. 28 units. 197€– 347€ double. Parking 10€. **Amenities:** Room service; free Wi-Fi.

Where to Eat

You can't beat a traditional Breton crepe to satisfy hunger and the best in town are flipped at **Creperie Heb Ken,** 5 rue de Guérande (www.heb-ken.fr; ✆ 02-40-48-79-03). Adventurous eaters should try the scallops with saffron sauce. Or for brunch, a light lunch, or afternoon tea surrounded by crystal chandeliers and stuffed animal heads with sunglasses, pop into the hip **Le Select**, 14 rue du Château (www.leselect.fr; ✆ 02-40-89-04-49).

For a fancier *chocolat chaud* or *confit de canard* settle in at the glitzy Belle Epoque brasserie **La Cigale**, 4 place Gralin (www.lacigale.com; ✆ **02-51-84-94-94**).

L'Atlantide ★★★ MODERN FRENCH   The panoramic view rivals the amazing culinary creativity at the best restaurant in Nantes. Situated on the fourth floor of the city's chamber of commerce building, the Jean-Pierre Wilmotte designed dining room has a wall of windows looking out onto the city and Loire River. Chef Jean-Yves Guého took his knives around the world before returning to his native Brittany. His travels have influenced his innovative menu, which may include ravioli of merlan and Thai basil served in a seafood and lemongrass broth, sea bass with truffles and Jerusalem artichoke purée, or ginger-glazed veal sweetbreads with braised Brussels sprouts. These are best enjoyed with some muscadet or anjou from the excellent cellar stocked mostly with Loire Valley wines.

Centre des Salorges, 16 quai Ernest Renaud. ✆ **02-40-73-23-23.** www.restaurant-atlantide.net. Main courses 27€–70€; fixed-price lunch 38€, dinner 48€–118€. Mon–Fri noon–2pm; Mon–Sat 8–9:45pm. Closed Aug and late-Dec to early Jan.

Maison Le Baron-Lefevre ★ TRADITIONAL FRENCH   Located in a former wholesale market building, excellent food traditions are carried on at this locavore restaurant—so local that all the vegetables come from their own garden. Chef Jean Charles Baron sticks to classic dishes in order to focus on the flavor of the products. His seasonal menu may feature creamy squash soup, sole meunière with *pot à feu* vegetables, or supreme of chicken with new potatoes. Service is very attentive, with personal touches like seasonal fruit or nuts with your coffee. They also sell a range of their preserves and products.

33 rue de Rieux. ✆ **02-40-89-20-20.** www.baron-lefevre.fr. Main courses 16€–33€; weekday lunch menu 18.50€, dinner 26€. Tue–Sat noon–2pm, 7–11pm.

Exploring the City

Cathédrale St-Pierre et St-Paul ★★ CATHEDRAL   Begun in 1434, this cathedral wasn't finished until the late 19th century. Still, it managed to remain architecturally harmonious—a rare feat. Two square towers dominate the facade; more impressive is the 100m-long (328-ft.) interior. Its *pièce de résistance* is the Renaissance tomb of François II, duc de Bretagne, and his second wife, Marguerite de Foix. The couple were the parents of Anne de Bretagne, who commissioned sculptor Michel Colombe to create their final resting place. White walls and pillars contrast with the rich colors of the stained-glass windows; helpful signs explain the significance of most objects.

Place St-Pierre. ✆ **02-40-47-84-64.** Free admission. Daily 8:30am–6:15pm. Crypt: Sat–Sun 3–6pm.

Château des Ducs de Bretagne ★★ CASTLE/MUSEUM This enormous complex, seat of the Dukes of Brittany, was constructed in the 9th or 10th century, enlarged in the 13th century, destroyed, then rebuilt into its present shape by François II in 1466. The Duchesse du Berry, royal courtesan, was imprisoned here, as was Gilles de Retz (aka "Bluebeard"), one of France's most notorious mass murderers. The castle's rich inventory has been presented as a museum since the 17th century. About 30 rooms are devoted to the history of the port, displaying evocative objects such as scale models of the city during different eras. The museum charges admission, but you can visit the courtyard and stroll along the ramparts for free.

4 place Marc-Elder. ✆ **08-11-46-46-44.** www.chateau-nantes.fr. Ramparts free daily 10am–7pm (July–Aug until 8pm, Sat until 11pm). Museum 5€ adults, 3€ students 25 and under, free for children 17 and under. Sept–June Tues–Sun 10am–6pm; July–Aug daily 10am–7pm. Closed public holidays.

Musée des Beaux-Arts de Nantes ★ MUSEUM Built mainly on the collection amassed in the late 18th century by the Cacault brothers, the museum features a fine array of paintings from the 12th to the late 19th centuries. There is a strong Italian representation (Perugino, Tintoretto, Gentileschi) due to François Cacault's travels as a diplomat. The municipality added to this foundation with purchases of 19th-century works by Delacroix, Rousseau, Renoir, and Gauguin, in addition to modern and contemporary artists. At print time the museum was closed for extensive renovations, reopening date planned for mid-2016. Until then, temporary exhibits are display in the chapel.

On the Rivers

Nantes might not be on the sea, but it's still highly connected to water with its two rivers: the Loire and the Erdre. You can hop on the Loire's **Navibus** public watertaxi and in 15 minutes you disembark at the charming former fishing village of **Trentemoult**. You wouldn't know you were in the Nantes suburbs while strolling its narrow lanes lined with colorful three-story houses, artist studios, and secret gardens. On your way back, grab a coffee at one of the cafes by the ferry dock. The small ferries depart regularly from the Nantes Gare Maritime on the Quai de la Fosse; the journey goes for a regular bus/tram ticket.

The Erdre River, deemed by King François I as "the most beautiful river of France," empties into the Loire, hidden underground through downtown, but it pops above not far from la Tour de Bretagne. A visit to its **Ile de Versailles** offers various pleasures, namely its tranquil Japanese garden. In summer, you can rent small boats from its tip. Or better yet, take a leisure cruise along the Erdre to admire its beautiful plush landscape and graceful castles; these are arranged by **Bateaux Nantais** (http://bateaux-nantais.fr; ✆ **02-40-14-51-14**) and depart just north of Ile de Versailles on the Quai de la Motte. The cruise lasts 1 hour, 45 minutes and costs 12.50€; they also run lunch and dinner options.

The Jules Verne Museum, Nantes

10 rue Georges Clemenceau. ✆ **02-51-17-45-00.** www.museedesbeauxarts.nantes.fr. Admission 2€ adults, 1€ students 19–26, free for children 18 and under. Wed–Mon 10am–6pm (Thurs until 8pm).

Musée Jules Verne de Nantes ★ MUSEUM   Nantes's most historic figure is certainly the novelist Jules Verne ("Journey to the Center of the Earth," "Around the World in Eighty Days"). Born in Nantes in 1828, he sat for hours on end, looking out his window at the busy port, imagining the exotic destinations the ships had traveled from. His adventures best come to life not at the museum, but at **Les Machines de L'Ile** (see "Brittany for Kids" box at the end of the chapter). However, fans of the author and young explorers will enjoy the museum's displays of memorabilia and artifacts inspired by his writings, from ink spots to a "magic" lantern with glass slides. Die-hard fans can seek out his former residence at 4 rue de Clisson in the Ile-Feydeau, though it is privately owned and not open to the public.

3 rue de l'Hermitage. ✆ **02-40-69-72-52.** Admission 3€ adults, 1.50€ students, free for ages 18 and under. Wed–Sat and Mon 10am–noon and 2–6pm; Sun 2–6pm.

Shopping

As the bustling regional capital, Nantes overflows with shops and boutiques. The principal shopping streets are rue du Calvaire, rue Crébillon, rue Boileau, rue d'Orléans, rue de la Marne, and rue de Verdun. Most of these encompass the shopping districts around place Graslin, place Royale, the château, and the cathedral. The Passage Pommeraye, a historic gallery that dates back to 1843, houses a small, upscale shopping center.

A handful of antiques shops can be perused on rue Jean Jaures such as **Ecritoire Antiquités Poidras,** at no. 12 (✆ **02-40-47-78-18**), offering 18th- and 19th-century furniture and decorative pieces such as historic mantels. Further historic knickknacks can be picked through every Saturday and Sunday morning at the flea market in **Place Viarme.**

BRITTANY FOR kids

St-Malo is a great destination for families. Not only is there the beach, but kids will also love exploring the ramparts, the château, and the fort (see p. 247). In summer, gigantic mazes are created in the cornfields south of the town, the biggest and easiest to get to is the **Labyrinthe du Corsaire** (www.labyrintheducorsaire. com; ✆ **02-99-81-17-23**), located 6km (3½ miles) from the center. There are also inflatable jumping castles and other games. Entrance is 8€ and it's open daily 10:30am-7pm July and August.

To cool down or burn some energy, head to the side-by-side **Cobac Parc & Aqua'Fun Park** (www.cobac-parc.com; ✆ **02-99-73-80-16**). A day's worth of fun is had zooming down its waterslides, swinging clubs at the mini-golf, and twirling around on its small amusement park rides. Cobac Parc is open daily 10:30am to 6:30pm in July and August and sporadic hours, usually including weekends, April to June and September (consult website calendar); Aqua'Fun is open the same days but from 1pm. A joint ticket

for both parks is 23€ for 12 and up and 19.50€ for children 11 and under.

One of the regional highlights for families is Nantes's **Les Machines de l'Ile,** 3 rue de l'Hermitage (www.lesmachines-nantes.fr; ✆ **02-40-69-72-52**), a fantastical workshop based on hometown writer Jules Verne's imagined creatures and the mechanical drawings of Leonardo da Vinci. A 12m (147-ft.) elephant, made from 45 tons of wood and steel, takes 50 passengers at a time for a stroll around the premises. Don't leave without a ride on the massive Carrousel des Mondes Marins (Marine Worlds Carousel) that takes 300 "voyagers" at a time on a trip through its three levels representing the ocean, seabed, and abyss. One ticket gives access to the rides, another admits you to the Galerie, where you can see future creations taking shape. Admission is 8€ adults, 5.50€ ages 18 and under. Because the site is a functioning workshop, its opening hours change weekly; check the English pages of their website for details.

For some local gastronomic specialties, start filling your basket at **La Fraiseraie**, 10 rue des Carmes (www.lafraiseraie.com; ✆ **02-40-20-47-23**) which sells a variety of jams, juices, and candies made from famous Pornic strawberries. More tasty treats can be picked up at **Gautier Debotte,** 9 rue de la Fosse (✆ **02-40-48-23-19**), a historic *chocolatier* established in 1823, and makers of "Le Muscadet Nantais"—a chocolate-covered white grape macerated in local muscadet wine. Other Debotte boutiques are at 2 rue des Hauts Pavé, 3 rue de Budapest and 15 rue Crébillon (the latter two have tea salons). Finish off your food shopping with some actual bottles of muscadet or other regional wines; a great selection is stocked at the **Maison des Vins de la Loire,** 15 Place du Commerce (www.vinsvaldeloire.fr; ✆ **02-40-89-75-98**).

Nantes Nightlife

When the sun goes down, the town turns into one big party. On **place du Bouffay, place du Pilori,** and the pedestrian streets in between, you'll find lots of cafes and pubs, many with live music and fun people. A younger crowd rules **rue Scribe.**

Live music fans can catch blues, jazz, or rock concerts at **L'Univers Café,** 16 rue Jean-Jacques-Rousseau (✆ **02-40-73-49-55**) while oenophiles won't be disappointed with the wine lists at the modern **Comédie des Vins**, 4 Rue Suffren (www.lacomediedesvins-nantes.com; ✆ **02-40-73-11-68**) or the rustic **Café de Provence,** 2, rue Vauban (www.baravinslaprovencenantes.com; ✆ **02-40-48-78-71**). On warm summer nights, amble along the **Ile de Nantes** to the **Le Hangar des Bananes** (www.hangarabananes.com). These former storage buildings for exotic fruit from the colonies have been converted into a line of bars and restaurants with large terraces.

The hippest location in Nantes, and the town's leading cultural center, is **Le Lieu Unique,** 2 rue de la Biscuiterie (✆ **02-51-82-15-00**). Converted from a 19th-century biscuit factory, the venue offers presentations ranging from plays (in French) to art exhibitions. Admission is free to the dimly lit, concrete-floored bar at ground level, which is frequented by students and artists who pack the dance floor. There is also a restaurant with the same vibe. The bar is open Monday 11am to 8pm, Tuesday and Wednesday 11am to 1am, Thursday 11am to 2am, Friday and Saturday 11am to 3am, and Sunday 3 to 8pm.

For dancing, the over-30 crowd heads to the vintage 1970s gay-friendly disco **L'Evasion,** 3 rue de l'Emery (✆ **02-40-47-99-84**). Other discos include **Le Royal Club Privé,** 7 rue des Salorges (www.leroyal.fr; ✆ **02-40-69-11-10**). Don't wear jeans to any of these places, and be prepared to pay 15€ to 20€.

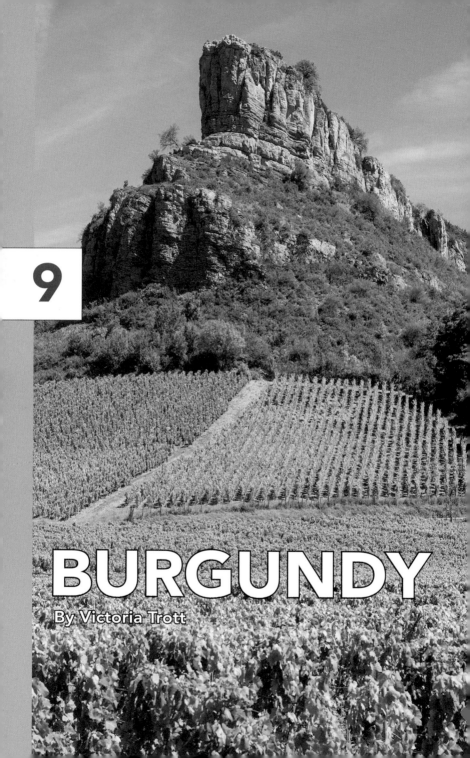

9

BURGUNDY

By Victoria Trott

Bordered by the River Saône to the east and the River Loire to the west, Burgundy is an agricultural region famed for its wines: The major growing areas are Chablis, Côte de Nuits, Côte de Beaune, Côte Chalonnaise, and Mâconnais. Needless to say, good food plays a large part, too. Cistercian monasteries and medieval churches mark the landscape, along with centuries-old honey-colored villages. Burgundy is crossed by several canals, making it a popular destination for water-based holidays, while walkers and cyclists can explore miles of towpaths and routes through the vines. From 1032 until 1477, when it was annexed by France, the Duchy of Burgundy was an independent province whose territory included Luxembourg, Belgium, and the Netherlands; its legacy is a rich cultural heritage.

The Côte d'Or evokes mythical Premier Cru appellations such as Richebourg and Vosne-Romanée, while the region's grassy agricultural plains are home to mouth-watering offerings such as Charolais beef, garlic-infused snails, and pungent Epoisses cheese. Sleepy historic towns and villages have been awoken by the appeal of Michelin-starred restaurants: L'Espérance in Vézelay, Le Relais Bernard Loiseau in Saulieu, and Maison Lameloise in Chagny. Today Burgundy offers many opportunities for wine tourism, from free tastings to private tours.

DIJON ★★★

312km (193 miles) SE of Paris; 320km (198 miles) NE of Lyon

Located in the north of the region, Dijon is the capital of Burgundy. Founded by the Romans, this city of 152,000 residents has undergone a 400 million-euro facelift since 2010, including a new tramway, an Olympic-size swimming pool, pedestrianized shopping streets, and restored landmark squares.

On the doorstep of the illustrious Côte d'Or wine region, Dijon combines world-class wines with good food, including four restaurants with Michelin stars. As well as being famed for its mustard, the city is also the home of *Kir* (a mix of white Aligoté wine and Crème de Cassis blackcurrant liqueur, named after former Dijon mayor Canon Félix Kir). After admiring the city's impressive Gothic churches and the sumptuous Palais des Ducs et des Etats de Bourgogne, make time to get lost in Dijon's medieval heart: Here you'll happen upon extravagant stone-facaded *hôtels particuliers* (private mansions), some of which have colorful roof tiles, a practice that dates back to the 14th century and is found throughout the region.

The city has some interesting events throughout the year; pick up an agenda from the tourist office. In May, vintage motorbike fans arrive for the **Coupes Moto Légende** to race their bikes around the Prenois race track. Every June, the **Estimate** comes to town: a nine-day festival of outdoor dance and music

A colorful town square in Dijon

concerts. In November, the city hosts one of France's largest food fairs, the **Foire internationale et gastronomique de Dijon.**

Essentials

ARRIVING   If you are **driving,** from Paris follow the A6 southeast to Pouilly-en-Auxois, and then go east along A38 and finally onto the D905 (around Plombières-lès-Dijon) into central Dijon. A dozen or so TGV **trains** arrive from Paris's Gare de Lyon each day (trip time: 1 hr., 35 min.); the standard one-way fare is 51€ to 71€. For information, visit www.voyages-sncf.com or call *℃* **36-35.**

VISITOR INFORMATION   The **Office de Tourisme** is at 11 rue des Forges (www.visitdijon.com; *℃* **08-92-70-05-58**).

Getting Around

BY TAXI   There is a taxi rank at the train station. To reserve in advance, contact **Taxis Dijon** (www.taxis-dijon.fr; *℃* **03-08-41-41-12**).

BY PUBLIC TRANSPORT   Dijon has a good network of **buses** and **trams,** although the city is easy to get around on foot. Tickets cost 1.20€ and you can buy them on the bus/tram or in the Divia office at 16 place Darcy.

BY BIKE   **Velodi** (www.velodi.net; *℃* **08-00-20-03-05**) offers self-service and drop-off points all around town including Forges-Notre Dame by the tourist office and place Ste-Bénigne.

[FastFACTS] DIJON

Hospital   **Hôpital Général,** 2 rue de l'Hôpital; *℃* **03-80-40-28-29.**

Pharmacy   Dijon's pharmacies take turns staying open after 11pm. Ask at the police station in place Suquet (*℃* **03-80-44-55-00**). **Pharmacie Barbier** at 28 rue Monge (*℃* **03-80-30-20-06**) is usually open until 11pm.

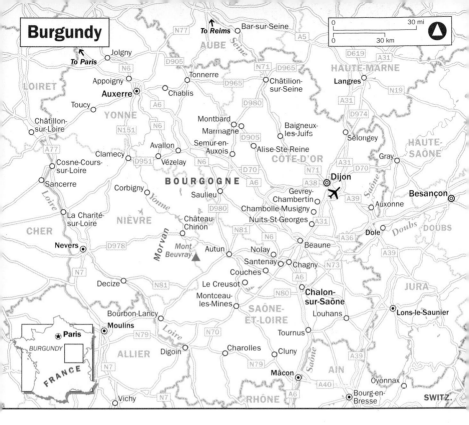

Where to Stay

Hostellerie du Chapeau Rouge ★★ Instantly recognizable by its pink facade and white shutters, the four-star "Hotel Red Hat" is our favorite luxury abode in Dijon for its style (we particularly like the top-floor Signature suites with Nespresso machines) and friendly staff. It's only a 10-minute walk from the train station, too. Some of the rooms have had a contemporary makeover; others, including the four-person family rooms and superior rooms, have a more traditional style. After a hard day's sightseeing, the sauna, hammam and hydromassage showers in the basement spa are a welcome sight, and a small range of spa treatments are on the menu. Talking of menus, the hotel restaurant, overseen by William Frachot, is the best in town with two Michelin stars.

5 rue Michelet, 21024 Dijon. ✆ **03-80-50-88-88.** www.chapeau-rouge.fr. 29 units. 110€–199€ double, 149€–189€ family rooms, 169€–239€ suites. Breakfast 17€. Valet parking 15€. Menus: fixed-price lunch 42€, fixed-price dinner 78€–150€. **Amenities:** Restaurant; bar; concierge; room service; spa; free Wi-Fi.

Hôtel Le Jacquemart ★★ If you're looking for budget accommodation in the center of Dijon then this is the place to come. Housed in an 18th-century building in the middle of the antiques district, two-star Le Jacquemart (named after the bell-clanging automaton on the top of the city's Eglise Notre Dame), has rooms with shared bathrooms to family rooms sleeping four. The decor is a little, er, 1970s, but that and the occasional original feature such as a marble fireplace add to its charm. There are even a couple of courtyard balconies for smokers.

32 rue Verrerie, 21000 Dijon. ✆ **03-80-60-09-60.** www.hotel-lejacquemart.fr. 33 units. 39€–85€. Breakfast 6.50€. Parking: 6€. **Amenities:** Bar; free Wi-Fi.

Hôtel Wilson ★   This three-star former coaching inn, dating back to the 17th century, is the ideal stop for drivers as it's on the southeast edge of town. Rooms have oodles of character with beams, creaky floors and dark-wood antique furniture, while the bathrooms have been redone in white contemporary style. Enjoy a good buffet breakfast by the impressive stone fireplace before embarking on the 15-minute walk into the town center. Later, try one of the regional aperitifs in the bar, then if you're feeling flush, head to the Michelin-starred restaurant of Stéphane Derbord next door (dinner menus from 53€).

1 rue de Longvic, 21000 Dijon. ✆ **03-80-66-82-50.** www.wilson-hotel.com. 27 units. 89€–142€ double, 137€–210€ family rooms. Breakfast 13.50€. Parking 10€. **Amenities:** Bar; beauty treatments; room service; free Wi-Fi.

In recent years a number of boutique-style self-catering apartments have sprung up in Dijon, including **Les Appartements à Part** (www.appartements-a-part. com; ✆ **06-81-00-50-77**) from 105€ per night and **Un Ours en Ville** (www. gite-ours.com; ✆ **03-80-35-46-77**) from 80€ per night. There is even a waterside **campsite** 20-minutes' walk from the town center (www.camping-du-lac-dijon.com; ✆ **03-80-30-54-01**), which is open from April to mid-October.

Where to Eat

Dijon has four restaurants with Michelin stars: **Loiseau des Ducs** (www.bernard-loiseau.com; ✆ **03-80-30-28-09**), where lunch menus start at 20€; **Stéphane Derbord** (www.restaurantstephanederbord.com; ✆ **03-80-67-74-64**) and **Le Pré aux Clercs** (www.jeanpierrebilloux.com; ✆ **03-80-38-05-05**), which all have one star; and **William Frachot at Hostellerie du Chapeau Rouge** (see "Where to Stay"), who has two. For a snack head to **rue de la Chouette** and the very quaint **Maison Millière** (www.maison-milliere.fr; ✆ **03-80-30-99-99**) at No. 10–14 or **La Rose de Vergy** (www.rosedevergy.com; ✆ **03-80-61-42-22**) at No.1.

DZ'Envies ★★   BURGUNDIAN/ JAPANESE/MOROCCAN   You won't find any beams or exposed stonework in this white-and-orange minimalist restaurant opposite Les Halles, but you will encounter plenty of local diners. Chef David Zuddas used to have a Michelin star at his previous establishment but decided to open a new "bistrogastro" in the city center to give himself more creative freedom. The lunch menu changes daily: expect the likes of eggs poached in shitake bouillon with smoked mackerel for starters, traditional beef cheeks in red Burgundy for a main, followed by pain d'épices panna cotta with pear marmalade. In the evening you can choose from three to five *envies* ("desires" aka dishes). A breath of fresh air.

Boeuf bourguignon, a Burgundy specialty

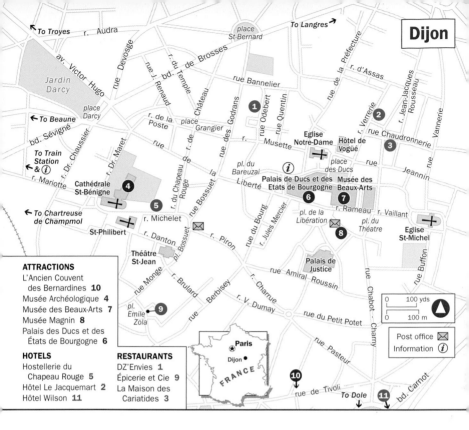

12 rue Odebert, 21000 Dijon. ℘ **03-80-50-09-26.** www.dzenvies.com. Main courses 16€–22€; fixed-price lunch 16€–19.90€, dinner 29€, 32€ or 36€. Mon–Sat noon–2pm and 7–10pm. Closed first 11 days in Jan.

Epicerie et Cie ★ BURGUNDIAN   The chaotic service can set our teeth on edge, but this little restaurant in one of Dijon's prettiest squares offers a unique experience. The moment you walk through the door you're transported back to 1950s France: Georges Brassens on the gramophone, retro advertising posters on the walls, mismatched wooden furniture. The menu focuses on the dishes that "grandma used to make": Burgundian specialty oeufs en meurette (poached eggs in red wine sauce), slow-cooked jarret de porc (pork knuckle) and Charolais steak tartare (raw minced beef). Be sure to save room for dessert—we like the pain d'épices or Marc de Bourgogne–flavor ice cream.

5 place Emil Zola. ℘ **03-80-30-70-69.** Main courses 15€–30€. Daily noon–2pm and 7–10pm (until 11pm Fri and Sat).

La Maison des Cariatides ★★★ BURGUNDIAN   Opened in 2011, this gourmet restaurant in one of Dijon's most striking *hôtels particuliers*, is named after the 12 male and female statues carved into the facade. Inside the 17th-century walls, originally built to house a successful wine merchant and his family, you'll find exposed stones and chic contemporary furniture. Thomas Collomb's cuisine includes such local specialties as jambon persillé (ham and parsley terrine) and tête de veau (calf's head); although, there is plenty to attract the less adventurous. The two-course lunch is a good value at 18€, while in the evening the 52€ tasting menu changes daily.

28 rue Chaudronnerie, 21000 Dijon. ✆ **03-80-45-59-25.** www.lamaisondescariatides.fr. Main courses 26€–45€; fixed-price lunch 18€–25€; fixed-price dinner 38€–52€. Tues–Sat noon–1:45pm; 7:30–9:30pm. Closed 2 weeks in Aug.

Exploring Dijon

One of the most historic buildings in this ancient province is the **Palais des Ducs et des Etats de Bourgogne,** which symbolizes the independent (or semi-independent, depending on the era) status of this fertile region. Capped with an elaborate tile roof, the complex is arranged around a trio of courtyards. The oldest section, only part of which you can visit, is the **Ancien Palais des Ducs de Bourgogne,** erected in the 14th and 15th centuries. The newer section is the **Palais des Etats de Bourgogne,** constructed in the 17th and 18th centuries for the Burgundian parliament; check out the **Chapelle des Elus** (free access via the tourist office), which dates from 1738 and was designed by Jacques Gabriel, the king's architect. Today the palace is *la mairie* (the town hall); all of its newer section and much of its older section are reserved for the municipal government and not open to the public. However, there are fabulous views from the top of **Tour Philippe le Bon** (316 steps; days and times vary; 2.50€ adults) and a fine museum, the **Musée des Beaux-Arts** (see below).

The **Musée Archéologique,** 5 rue du Docteur Maret (www.musees-bourgogne.org; ✆ 03-80-48-83-70), contains findings unearthed from Dijon's archaeological digs. Admission is free, and it's open Wednesday to Sunday 9am to 12:30pm and 1:30 to 6pm; from mid-May to September the museum is also open on Mondays.

A medieval nunnery, **L'Ancien Couvent des Bernardines,** 17 rue Ste-Anne (✆ 03-80-48-80-90), is home to two museums. The chapel holds the **Musée d'Arts Sacrés,** devoted to art from regional churches, and the cloister contains the **Musée de la Vie Bourguignonne,** which exhibits folkloric costumes, farm implements, and some 19th- and early-20th-century storefronts from Dijon's center. Admission is free to both museums (Oct–Apr Wed–Mon 9am–noon and 2–6pm, and May–Sept 9am–12:30pm and 1:30–6pm).

Chartreuse de Champmol ★ MONASTERY   Although the fancy tombs of the dukes of Burgundy are in what is now the Musée des Beaux-Arts, their bodies are actually buried in this charterhouse at the western edge of Dijon. Now a psychiatric hospital, it's still possible to visit: the main sights are the church portal and magnificent Well of Moses, which features six prophets from the Old Testament; both were the work of influential Dutch sculptor Claus Sluter. Guided tours are available via the tourist office.

1 bd Chanoine-Kir, 21000 Dijon. ✆ **08-92-70-05-58.** Admission 3.50€, free for children under 18. Daily 9:30am–12:30pm and 2–5pm (Apr–Oct until 5:30pm). Bus L3 direction Fontaine d'Ouche: stop at CHS La Chartreuse.

Musée des Beaux-Arts ★★★ MUSEUM   The area of the ducal palace housing France's fifth most important national art collection was partially renovated between 2008 and 2013, and further improvements are due to be made from 2015 to 2018 as part of a 60 million-euro scheme. Now 14 rooms display 500 restored European works dating from the 5th to 16th centuries while the rest of the building showcases (mainly) European art leading up to the present day. The highlight of the visit has to be the tombs of the dukes of Burgundy (who aren't actually buried here), complete with gilded angels at their heads and lions at their feet. One of the best additions is undoubtedly the multimedia tablets that place the works in context; there are also interactive activities for children. The new courtyard bar is perfect for a drink or a snack on fine days.

In the Palais des Ducs et des Etats de Bourgogne, cour de Bar. ✆ **03-80-74-52-09.** Free admission. May–Oct Wed–Mon 9:30am–6pm; Nov–Apr Wed–Mon 10am–5pm.

Musée Magnin ★★ MUSEUM Housed in a beautiful 17th-century *hôtel particulier,* this museum, which is one of France's national museums, boasts an impressive collection of around 2,000 artworks by mainly French, Italian, and Flemish artists from the 14th to the 19th centuries. They were bequeathed to the state in 1938 by Maurice and Jeanne Magnin and are displayed around the house like an amateur collector's "cabinet of curiosities" in accordance with the couple's wishes. The inner courtyard is particularly attractive.

4 rue des Bons-Enfants, 21000 Dijon. ✆ **03-80-67-11-10.** www.musee-magnin.fr. Admission 4.50€ adults, 2.50€ ages 13–25, free for age 12 and under. Tues–Sun 10am–noon and 2–6pm.

Shopping

Your shopping list may include regional wines, mustard, antiques, *pain d'épices* (spiced bread), and the blackcurrant liqueur, Crème de Cassis. The best shopping streets are rue de la Liberté, rue du Bourg, rue Bossuet, Place Grangier for designer shops and rue Verrerie for antiques. The market at **Les Halles,** rue Odebert, sells fruit, vegetables, and foodstuffs on Tuesday, Thursday, and Friday from 8am to noon, and Saturday from 8am to 5pm.

Dijon has several great *fromageries* (cheese shops) including **Le Chalet Comtois** (28 rue Musette; ✆ 03-80-30-48-61); look out for the regionally made semi-soft Cîteaux, made by monks in the abbey of the same name, and pungent, unctuous Epoisses. For bread, look no further than **Tartin'art** (8 rue Musette; ✆ 03-80-30-97-31), which also offers sandwiches, quiches, and salads. For wine, we like **Dr. Wine** (5 rue Musette; ✆ 03-80-53-35-16); they also have a good restaurant and do delicious platters of ham and cheese. You won't be able to pass **Carbillet** (58 rue des Forges; ✆ 03-80-30-38-82) without going in to buy some cakes or chocolates. At **La Boutique Maille,** 32 rue de la Liberté (✆ 03-80-30-41-02), you can purchase many varieties of the world-famous mustard while **Bourgogne Street** (61 rue de la Liberté; ✆ 03-80-30-07-10) is a one-stop-shop for regional produce. **Mulot et Petitjean** (their ornately paneled flagship store is at 13 place Bossuet; ✆ 03-80-30-07-10) is the place to go for homemade *pain d'épices.*

For antiques and interiors, head to the half-timbered streets around rue Verrerie: **Antiquaires Golmard,** 3 rue Auguste Comté (✆ 03-80-67-14-15), specializes in objects originating on private estates in the region. **Le Consortium,** 37 rue de Longvic (www.leconsortium.fr; ✆ 03-80-68-45-55), is Dijon's most interesting modern-art gallery.

For the last 30 years, **Le Baldaquin,** 13 rue Verrerie ✆ 03-80-30-59-69), has been a children's treasure trove of wooden toys and mobiles.

Nightlife

Bal'tazar, 20 avenue Garibaldi (www.bal-tazar.fr; ✆ 06-25-82-76-71) is a chic club where champagne is the tipple of choice and top-name DJs spin the decks; it's open Friday and Saturday from 11pm. Bordello chic reigns at another popular venue, **Le Cercle Jamaïque,** 14 place de la République (www.lecerclejamaique. com; ✆ 03-80-73-52-19); it's a bar and nightclub rolled into one, with jazz, rock, and Latin tunes until 4am. The barge **Péniche Cancale,** 14 avenue Jean Jaurès (© **03-80-43-15-72**), is open from Thursday to Sunday from 6pm to 2am and provides an intimate setting for music concerts.

Lined with classic paperbacks and original printing paraphernalia, **L'Edito,** 2 place Darcy (www.brasserie-ledito.fr; © **03-80-30-69-43**) is an atmospheric place for a beer or a cocktail while **Dr. Wine** (see "Shopping") has around 200 references on its wine menu.

The opera season (www.opera-dijon.fr; © **03-80-48-82-82**) in Dijon stretches from October to May. Operas, dance recitals, and concerts are held in two venues: **Grand Théâtre de Dijon,** place du Théâtre (where you can pop along anytime Tues–Sat from 11am–6pm to buy tickets) and **L'Auditorium,** place Jean Bouhey (that opens just 1 hr. before each performance). You can also pick up tickets at FNAC on rue du Bourg.

Several cinemas show films in their original version including **Eldorado,** 21 rue Alfred de Musset (© **03-80-66-51-89**), and **Devosge,** 6 rue Devosge (© **03-80-30-74-79**).

Where to Stay & Eat Nearby

La Gentilhommière ★★ BURGUNDIAN/FRENCH About 20-minutes' drive south of Dijon on the A31 is Nuits-St-Georges, world famous for its legendary wines such as Romanée-Conti. On the way into this sweet little town is The Gentleman's Residence, a three-star family-friendly hotel and gourmet restaurant, Le Chef Coq, in a former hunting lodge surrounded by fields and forest. On the menu you'll find the likes of quail pie with Madeira wine jelly and boeuf bourguignon; we particularly like the hot-and-cold blackberry gratin for dessert. There is an excellent wine list and they make a mean Kir, too, which is best sipped next to the fireplace in winter. The contemporary-design rooms are in two separate 1980s blocks.

13 vallée de la Serrée, 21700 Nuits-St-Georges. © **03-80-61-12-06.** www.lagentilhommiere.fr. 31 units. 115€–200€. Breakfast 15€. Free parking. Main courses 27€–31€; fixed-price lunch 23.50€; dinner 31€–59€. Daily noon–2pm and 7–9pm. Restaurant closed Tues eve and Sat lunch. Hotel closed mid-Dec to mid-Jan. **Amenities:** Restaurant; bar; children's playroom; parkland; pool; tennis court; free Wi-Fi.

AUXERRE ★★

154km (95 miles) SE of Paris; 148km (92 miles) NW of Dijon

On a hill overlooking the River Yonne, Auxerre (pronounced "*Ausserre*") was founded by the Gauls and enlarged by the Romans; at the bottom of rue des Pêcheurs you can see the remains of a Gallo-Roman tower underneath the medieval one. Joan of Arc spent several days in the town in 1429 and Napoleon Bonaparte stopped here on his return from Elba in 1815.

Although these days it's arguably best known for its soccer team, Auxerre's AOC wines produced on the surrounding hills are renowned, too: try Irancy and Chitry.

The city, which has around 40,000 inhabitants, is a pleasant place to spend a couple of days exploring the narrow, cobbled streets admiring the 700 or so beautifully preserved *colombage* (half-timbered) buildings. The most charming district is the Quartier St-Nicolas, the old fishermen's quarter. However, the main reason to visit is to see the rare crypt murals (see "Exploring Auxerre").

Restored half-timbered houses, Auxerre

Auxerre has a full events calendar. In June, the free three-night **Catalpa** world music festival includes the French "air guitar" championships. In July and August, the **"Garçon la note!"** festival presents free music concerts each evening in the city's bars and restaurants. A market takes place every Tuesday and Friday morning in place de l'Arquebuse.

Essentials

ARRIVING   Visitors often **drive** here because Auxerre is near A6/E15 (the Autoroute du Soleil) motorway from Paris. There are TER **trains** every hour from Paris (Gare de Bercy; trip time: 1hr., 45 min.), and the fare is 28.30€ one-way. For train information, visit www.voyages-sncf.com or call ✆ **36-35.**

VISITOR INFORMATION   The **Office de Tourisme** is at 1–2 quai de la République (www.ot-auxerre.fr; ✆ **03-86-52-06-19**).

Getting Around

BY TAXI   If you're arriving by train you might want to book a taxi. Contact **Taxis Auxerrois** on ✆ **03-86-46-78-78.**

BY BIKE   You can rent bikes from the tourist office. Prices range from 6€ for 2 hours to 83€ for 7 days.

Where to Stay

Hôtel Le Maxime ★★   This onetime salt storehouse on the banks of the River Yonne is our favorite hotel in town. The style is classical and elegant from the public areas to the rooms; book one at the front for a view of the water. There is a grand fireplace in the beamed lounge; however, for a drink in even more atmospheric surroundings, head downstairs into the vaulted cellar. There isn't a restaurant, but there is 24-hour room service and plenty of eating places nearby. Massage treatments are available on site.

2 quai de la Marine, 89000 Auxerre. ✆ **03-86-52-14-19.** www.lemaxime.com. 26 units. 96€–139€ double; 139€–157€ triple; 149€–247€ suite. Breakfast 12.50€. Parking 9€. **Amenities:** Bar; in-room massage; laundry service; room service, free Wi-Fi.

Le Seignelay ★   On the western edge of town, this two-star former coaching inn dating from the 18th century is a good budget option and it's got a well-regarded traditional restaurant, too. Rooms are basic but bright and cheerful and individually decorated; some overlook the garden, others the courtyard. We like the fact that the owners specialize in selling wines direct from producers in the north of Burgundy.

2 rue du Pont, 89000 Auxerre. ✆ **03-86-52-03-48.** www.leseignelay.com. 17 units. 53€–90€. Breakfast 7.50€. Parking 7.50€. Closed Feb. **Amenities:** Restaurant; free Wi-Fi.

Where to Eat

Le Saint-Pèlerin ★★ BURGUNDIAN   It's well worth making a pilgrimage to "The Holy Pilgrim" for good-quality, good-value Burgundian food. We adore the beef slow-cooked in Irancy red wine accompanied by one of the house potatoes (like creamy mash served in its skin). The cheese board is usually well stocked with regional names like Epoisses and all dishes are homemade, including the bread and ice cream. In summer there's an outside terrace and in winter the wood-fired oven in the rustic dining room keeps diners warm, as well as turns out some tasty grills year-round.

56 rue Saint-Pèlerin, 89000 Auxerre. ✆ **03-86-52-77-05.** Main courses 12€–25€; fixed-price menu 14.90€–35€. Tues–Sat noon–2pm and 7–10pm. Closed 1 week in May and 2 weeks at Christmas and New Year.

Exploring Auxerre

The railway station is at the eastern edge of town, about 1.5km (1 mile) from the historic center. Most of Auxerre is on the western bank of the Yonne. Its heart is between place du Maréchal-Leclerc (near the Hôtel de Ville [city hall]) and the Cathédrale St-Etienne. A little electric bus, *Voyager*, takes visitors on a 45-minute guided tour daily in July and August (Sat–Sun only Apr–June and Sept) from 10am–5:30pm for 5€; it's particularly useful for families with small children or those with reduced mobility, due to the hilly nature of some of the streets.

You could also while away quite a few hours "messing about on the river" from April to September, either in your own rented electric boat (ask at the tourist office), which is fun for families, or during a cruise aboard *L'Hirondelle II* (www.bateauxauxerrois.com; ✆ **06-30-37-66-17**); every Thursday in July and August there is a gourmet cruise showcasing regional food and wine (15€ adults, 8€ children 4–12).

Abbaye St-Germain ★★★ ABBEY   This Benedictine abbey was founded in the 5th century by St-Germain, a former bishop of Auxerre, after who it is named; he is buried here. Its school was once reputed throughout Christendom. The main reason to visit is to see the **crypt murals** depicting the stoning of St. Stephen, which date back to the 9th century and are the oldest in France. The lovely 17th-century cloister hosts art exhibitions and concerts in summer, including during the Catalpa festival. Also here is the town's archaeology museum, whose exhibits date from prehistoric times.

2 bis Place St-Germain à Auxerre, 89000 Auxerre. ✆ **03-86-18-02-90.** Admission to crypt 6€ adults, children under 16 go free as do students under 26; free entry to museum. **Abbey:** Wed–Mon May–Sept 9:45am–6:45pm (guided tours of crypt 10am, 11am, noon, 1:45pm, 2:45pm, 3:45pm, 4:45pm, 5:45pm); Oct–Apr 10am–noon and 2–5pm (guided tours of crypt 10am, 11am, 2pm, 3pm and 4pm). **Museum:** Wed–Sun May–Sept 10am–noon, 2–6.30pm (until 5pm Oct–Apr).

Cathédrale St-Etienne ★★ CATHEDRAL   Dominating the River Yonne, this Gothic cathedral, the city's most emblematic sight, is also one of its most interesting. The stained-glass windows, which date from the 13th to the 16th century are some of France's finest while the crypt protects a rare 11th-century **mural** of Christ on a horse.

Place St-Etienne, 89000 Auxerre. ✆ **03-86-51-29-20.** Admission to crypt 3€ adults, children under 12 free. Cathedral: mid-Mar–mid-Nov Mon–Sat 7.30am–7pm, Sun 8.30am–7pm, mid-Nov–mid-Mar Mon–Sat 7.30am–5.30pm, Sun 8.30am–5.30pm. Crypt open mid-Mar–Oct Mon–Sat 9am–6pm, Sun 2–6pm, Nov–mid-Mar Mon–Sat 10am–5pm.

Where to Stay & Eat Nearby

La Côte Saint Jacques ★★★ BURGUNDIAN   In 2009 the restaurant of this family-friendly luxury hotel was named the top hotel restaurant in Europe in the Prix Villégiature Awards, which recognize the finest establishments in Europe, Africa, and Asia. The accommodation is chic and contemporary, and the spa was voted the best in the Relais & Châteaux group in 2012. But the main reason to come here is for the Michelin-three-star cuisine of Jean-Michel Lorain. Each recipe is a work of art: Bresse chicken cooked by champagne steam and chocolate sphere with a tender passion fruit center are just two dishes that display Lorain's love of mixing flavors from around the world. You can even learn the chef's secrets during one of his off-season cookery classes.

14 Faubourg de Paris (N6), 89300 Joigny (30km/19 miles NW of Auxerre on the D606). ✆ **03-86-62-09-70.** www.cotesaintjacques.com. 32 units. 225€–640€. Breakfast 28€. Free parking. Fixed-price lunch (from Wed–Sat) 75€ and 89€; dinner 144€–255€. Restaurant open Tues 7:30–9:45pm, Wed–Sun 12:15–2pm and 7:30–9:45pm. Hotel and restaurant closed Mon and early to late Jan. **Amenities:** Restaurant; fitness room; indoor pool; kids' playroom; sauna; shop; spa; free Wi-Fi.

VÉZELAY ★★

217km (135 miles) SE of Paris; 52km (32 miles) S of Auxerre

Vézelay, a living museum of French antiquity, stands frozen in time. For many, the town is the high point of a trip through Burgundy. During the 12th century, it was one of the great pilgrimage sites of the Christian world as it contained the alleged tomb of St. Mary Magdalene, that "beloved and pardoned sinner."

Today the medieval charm of Vézelay is widely known throughout France, and visitors virtually overrun the town in summer. The hordes are especially thick on July 22, the official day of homage to La Madeleine.

Essentials

ARRIVING   If you're **driving** from Paris, take A6 south to Auxerre, then continue south along N6 to Givry and then D951 to Vézelay. Eight **trains** a day travel from Paris Gare de Bercy to Sermizelles, taking 2½ hours and costing 33€ one-way. For train information, visit www.voyages-sncf.com or call ✆ **36-35.** You'll need to take a taxi or the shuttle bus into town (details on tourist office website).

VISITOR INFORMATION The **Office de Tourisme** is at 12 rue St-Etienne (www.vezelaytourisme.com; ✆ **03-86-33-23-69**).

Where to Stay

Le Compostelle ★★   On the main square at the bottom of the hill, this two-star hotel in a renovated 19th-century house is our favorite in Vézelay. Rooms are bright and minimally furnished; 12 have views of the garden and surrounding lush countryside while 3 others overlook the town. As you'd suspect, given its name, the hotel is on the pilgrimage route to Santiago de Compostela and is a popular stopping-off point for pilgrims. The terrace is an attractive spot for breakfast in summer.

Place du Champ de Foire, 89450 Vézelay. ✆ **03-86-33-28-63.** www.lecompostellevezelay.com. 18 units. 55€–69€ double; 79€–89€ triple or quad. Breakfast 9.50€. Parking nearby. Closed Dec to mid-Feb. **Amenities:** Bar; free Wi-Fi.

Where to Eat

L'Espérance ★★★ MODERN FRENCH   If you are a foodie with cash to splash, this Michelin three-star restaurant and hotel is an unmissable experience. Self-trained chef Marc Meneau made his name by creating new versions of ancient recipes: oysters in seawater jelly, eggs Florentine, and strawberries Marie Antoinette are just a taste of what's on offer. He enjoys marrying flavors—beetroot with foie gras and scallops, for example—and says, "I want to find the primary taste of the product I'm cooking; if it's veal it must taste of veal." A successful *vigneron* with his own AOC wines, Meneau offers cooking classes for adults and children. Those on a budget will be pleased to know that the hotel's Bistro Gainsbourg, inspired by the late singer Serge, has a three-course menu for 39€.

Saint-Père-en-Vézelay, 89450 Vézelay. ✆ **03-86-33-39-10.** www.marc-meneau-esperance.com. Main courses 76€–122€; fixed-price lunch 60€–96€, dinner 135€–198€. Thurs–Sun noon–2pm; Wed–Mon 7:30–9:30pm. Closed mid-Jan to early Mar.

A La Fortune du Pot ★★ BURGUNDIAN   It might be called "Pot Luck" but you can be sure of good-value Burgundian cooking in this old village house at the bottom of the hill: like *boeuf bourguignon*, chicken Gaston Gérard (cooked in a mustard and white wine sauce) and andouillette (tripe sausage) with Epoisses cheese. We particularly like the crème brulée Grand Marnier dessert and the wine list specializes in wines from the area, including several chablis. The dining room is "smart-rustic" and there is an outside terrace for warm days.

6 place du Champ de Foire, 89450 Vézelay. ✆ **03-86-33-32-56.** www.fortuntedupot.com. Main courses 13.50€–15.50€; fixed-price menus 16€–24€. Daily noon–2pm and 7–9pm. Closed Mon eve, Tue, and mid-Nov to mid-Feb.

Exploring Vézelay

On a hill surrounded by countryside, Vézelay is one of France's most spiritual places as its basilica (see below) is said to house the remains of Mary Magdalene; both it and the hill are UNESCO World Heritage Sites. The town, which is known for its sculptured doorways, mullioned windows and corbelled staircases, began as an abbey founded in 858 by Girart de Roussillon, Comté de Bourgogne.

On March 31, 1146, St. Bernard preached the Second Crusade here; in 1190, the town was the rendezvous point for the Third Crusade, drawing such personages as Richard the Lion-hearted and King Philippe-Auguste of France. Later, St. Louis IX came here several times on pilgrimages.

Park outside the town hall and walk through the medieval streets lined with 15th-, 16th-, and 18th-century houses and flower-filled gardens. Download a free guided tour to your smartphone from www.guidigo.com to help you get around. **Musée Zervos** at 14 rue St-Etienne (www.musee-zervos. com; *©* **03-86-32-39-26;** July–Aug daily 10am–6pm, closed Tue rest of year and mid-Nov to mid-Mar), is worth a look for its fine collection of modern art, including works by Picasso.

If you're in the mood to shop, head for rue St-Etienne and rue St-Pierre; you'll find an assortment of stores selling religious books and statuary. For a bottle or two of Vézelay wine go to **Cave Henry de Vézelay,** 4 route de Nanchèvres, St-Père-sous-Vézelay (*©* **03-86-33-29-62**). There is also a brewery, **Brasserie de Vézelay**, on rue du Gravier (*©* **03-86-34-98-38**) about 2km (1.4 miles) east of the town, which makes organic beer.

Old house in Vézelay

Basilique Ste-Madeleine ★★★ CHURCH   Visible for miles around due to its hilltop location, the basilica was founded in the 9th century and then restored by architect Viollet-le-Duc in the 19th century, who famously also renovated Notre Dame de Paris. This Romanesque jewel is at its most atmospheric when the monks sing during the daily services (see website for details), and to get the most out of your visit it's advisable to go on a guided tour led by one of the brothers. In the crypt are the supposed remains of Mary Magdalene, which attract pilgrims from around the world; many are en route to Santiago de Compostela. The basilica's interior is the backdrop for the "Vézelay S'Enflamme" *son et lumière* at the start of August.

Place de la Basilique, 89450 Vézelay. *©* **03-86-33-39-50.** www.basiliquedevezelay.org. Free admission. Tours 3.60€. Daily 7am–8pm. Guided visits Tues–Sat 9–11am and 2:30–5pm; Sun 9–10:30am and 2:30–5pm.

AVALLON ★

214km (133 miles) SE of Paris; 52km (32 miles) SE of Auxerre; 96km (60 miles) NW of Dijon

This fortified town sits behind ancient ramparts, upon which you can stroll. A medieval atmosphere permeates Avallon, where you'll find many 15th- and 16th-century houses. At the town gate on Grande Rue Aristide-Briand is a 1460 clock tower. The Romanesque **Collégiale St-Lazare** dates from the 12th century and has fantastic doorways, an artfully lit interior, and impressive woodwork. The church, open daily from 8am to 7pm, is said to have received the head of St. Lazarus in 1000 ad, thus turning it into a pilgrimage site. A good day to visit is Saturday for the local produce market in place Général de Gaulle, which attracts foodies from miles around.

Essentials

ARRIVING If you're **driving,** travel south from Paris along A6 past Auxerre to Avallon. **Trains** arrive daily from Paris Gare de Bercy every 2 hours (trip time: almost 3 hr.; 34.70€ one-way). Bus service from Dijon takes 2 hours and costs 1.50€ one-way; purchase tickets on the bus. For train information, visit www. voyages-sncf.com or call ✆ **36-35.**

VISITOR INFORMATION The **Office de Tourisme** is at 6 rue Bocquillot (www. avallon-morvan.com; ✆ **03-86-34-14-19**).

Where to Stay

Château de Vault de Lugny ★★★ This fairytale château is the only five-star hotel in the Yonne department and is the place to stay if you want to feel like a king or queen for a few days. In fact, there is even a suite called "Le Roy" which was set aside for the kings of France, complete with monumental fireplace, four-poster bed, double bath tub, and Gothic chairs; the other rooms are a bit more sedate and are mainly decorated in *toile de Jouy.* You certainly won't get bored with 40 hectares (100 acres) of parkland to explore, including a river with fishing rights and a 400-year-old sycamore tree. The indoor pool is in an attractive stone cellar while the gourmet restaurant, which features seasonal food from its own garden, is housed in the 17th-century former kitchen. Unsurprisingly, Romanée-Conti, the world's most expensive wine, is one of the references on the wine list.

11 rue du Château, 89200 Vault-de-Lugny (6km/4 miles west of Avallon on the D606 then D128). ✆ **03-86-34-07-86.** www.lugny.fr. 15 units. 290€–465€; 495€–915€ suites. Breakfast 25€. Closed mid-Nov to Apr. Take D957 from Avallon, turn right in Pontaubert (after the church) and follow signs; Vault-de-Lugny is about 3km (1¾ miles) away. **Amenities:** Babysitting; bar; butler; indoor pool; mountain bikes; restaurant; room service; tennis court; valet parking; free Wi-Fi.

Moulin des Ruats ★ In a wooded valley at the gates of the Morvan Regional Natural Park, this 18th-century former flour mill is now a stylish three-star hotel. The rooms, some of which have balconies overlooking either the garden or the river, are individually decorated with designs ranging from Pop Art to Rococo; some have muted tones. The restaurant, where gourmet Burgundian cuisine is on the menu, has a waterside dining room and, pleasingly, all meals can be enjoyed outside in summer. Massage treatments are available.

23, rue des Isles Labaumes, 89200 Avallon (4km/3 miles west of Avallon on the D427). ✆ **03-86-34-97-00.** www.moulindesruats.com. 25 units. 88€–140€ double; 160€ suite. Breakfast 13.50€. Free parking. Closed mid-Nov to mid-Feb. Take D427 3km (1¾ miles) west outside town. **Amenities:** Restaurant; bar; lounge; free Wi-Fi.

Where to Eat

Le Vaudésir ★★ BURGUNDIAN Award-winning chef Cécile Riotte-Jeanne worked in several top restaurants, including Joël Robuchon in Monaco, before returning to her native Burgundy in 2012. In this 1930s-style restaurant, she uses the finest regional products to create excellent-value traditional favorites such as steak tartare and *oeufs en meurette* (poached eggs in red wine sauce). Eat in the garden on warm days or by the fire in the chic-traditional dining room in winter; we love the black-and-white diamond-pattern floor.

84 rue de Lyon, 89200 Avallon. ✆ **03-86-34-14-60.** www.levaudesir.com. Main courses 14€–19€; fixed-price menu 14€–20€. Noon–2pm and 7–9pm. Closed Sun eve, Tue eve, and Wed.

SAULIEU ★

250km (155 miles) SE of Paris; 76km (47 miles) NW of Beaune

Saulieu is interesting, but its food put it on the international map. The town (pop. 3,000) has enjoyed a reputation for cooking since the 17th century and is one of France's *Sites Remarquables du Goût* for its Fête du Charolais (festival of Charolais cows) in August; a food festival, Les Journées Gourmandes, also takes place here at the end of May. Both Mme. de Sévigné and Rabelais praised Saulieu's culinary attributes.

The main sight is the 12th-century **Basilique St-Andoche,** place Docteur Roclore, which has some interesting decorated capitals. Next door, in the **Musée**

Charolais cows

François-Pompon, (closed Mon pm and Tue; ✆ **03-80-64-19-51**), you can see works by François Pompon (d. 1933), the well-known sculptor of animals; his large statue of a bull stands on a plaza off N6 at the entrance to town. Also in the museum are archaeological remnants from the Gallo-Roman era, sacred medieval art, and a room dedicated to France's great chefs including Bernard Loiseau (see "Where to Stay & Eat"). Randomly, Europe's largest festival of Cajun music is held in Saulieu in July.

Essentials

ARRIVING If you're **driving,** head along A6 from Paris or Lyon. The **train** station is northeast of the town center. Passengers coming from Paris sometimes opt to take the TER from Paris Bercy, getting off in Montbard, 48km (30 miles) to the north. There are about six trains a day to Montbard and the journey takes over 2 hours and costs from 36.20€. From Montbard, a series of **buses** timed to the arrival of the trains carry passengers on to Saulieu for a one-way fare of 1.50€. For bus information, call **Transco** (www.mobigo-bourgogne.com; ✆ **03-80-63-33-59**); for rail information, visit www.voyages-sncf.com or call ✆ **36-35.**

VISITOR INFORMATION The **Office de Tourisme** is at 24 rue d'Argentine (www.saulieu.fr; ✆ **03-80-64-00-21**).

Where to Stay & Eat

La Borne Impériale ★ This two-star hotel in an attractive ochre-colored old village house is a good option for those who want to experience Saulieu's foodie delights without breaking the bank. The smart-rustic restaurant, whose walls are hung with works by contemporary local artists, specializes in traditional Burgundy cuisine (yes, there are snails on the menu) and grills (the steaks are naturally from the Charolais breed). Chef Jean trained under the legendary Roger Verger of the Moulin de Mougin on the Côte d'Azur and passes on his know-how to amateurs via private cooking lessons. For warmer days, there is a terrace that overlooks the pretty rose garden; as do the six rooms, which have all been renovated and decorated in contemporary style. Madame can be a little, how shall we say, "brusque"?

16 rue d'Argentine, 21210 Saulieu. ☏ **03-80-64-19-76.** www.borne-imperiale.com. 6 units. 62€–82€ double. Breakfast 10€. Free parking. Main courses 19€–32€. Menus 19€–48.50€. Closing times vary with the seasons. **Amenities:** Restaurant; free Wi-Fi.

Le Relais Bernard Loiseau ★★★   A few doors along from La Borne Impériale is one of France's great restaurants, named after the late chef who created it. The attached five-star hotel and empire, which includes satellite restaurants in Dijon, Beaune and Paris, is now run by Bernard's wife, Dominique, while the Michelin-three-star cuisine is overseen by Patrick Bertron, who has worked in the kitchen since 1982. As well as Patrick's own dishes, you'll also find Bernard's classics on the menu including frogs' legs with garlic purée and parsley jus, crispy-skin pike with shallot marmalade and red wine sauce, and "pure chocolate dessert rose with candied orange coulis. Wine connoisseurs can choose from 900 references. The decor throughout is "rustic luxury" with wooden beams and Burgundy-tile floors. In the rooms, plush fabrics cover the sofa and beds; the suite has its own fireplace and we love the wrought-iron staircase and balcony in the junior suite duplex. Children are very welcome: They have their own game room and gourmet menu and the dwarf geese are a popular distraction.

2 rue Argentine, 21210 Saulieu. ☏ **03-80-90-53-53.** www.bernard-loiseau.com. 23 units. 148€–375€ double; 420€–585€ suite. Breakfast 28€. Menus 70€–215€. Closed Tues and Wed (except on public holidays), Jan 21–Feb 27. **Amenities:** Restaurant; bar; exercise room; indoor and outdoor pools; kids' playroom; pétanque; room service; sauna; shop; spa; free Wi-Fi.

AUTUN ★★

293km (182 miles) SE of Paris; 85km (53 miles) SW of Dijon; 48km (30 miles) W of Beaune; 60km (37 miles) SE of Auxerre

Autun is one of the oldest towns in France. Founded by the Romans, it was called Augustodunum: "the other Rome." Some relics still stand, including a section of its ramparts, which date from 1 BC. Also here are the remains of the largest

Roman amphitheatre at Autun

theater in Gaul, the Théâtre Romain (free entry). It was nearly 150m (492 ft.) in diameter and could hold some 20,000 people. In July and August, it hosts a magnificent *son et lumière* with a 1000-strong cast recounting Julius Caesar's time in Burgundy.

Autun is a thriving provincial town of 14,000, but because it's off the beaten track, the hordes go elsewhere. Still, it has its historical associations—Napoleon Bonaparte studied here in 1779 at the military academy (today the Lycée Bonaparte). Don't miss the Passage Balthus, a 19th-century neo-Renaissance arcade with its original features.

Essentials

ARRIVING   If you're **driving,** take A6 south until reaching A38, then turn onto N81 towards Autun. Rail links to Autun are awkward. Six high-speed TGV **trains** a day from Paris's Gare de Lyon run to Le Creusot-Montceau, 40km (25 miles) south of Autun (59€–111€ one-way) taking under 1½ hours. From there, take a 30-minute bus connection to Autun. In Autun, **buses** arrive at a parking lot by the railway station on avenue de la République (1.50€ one-way). For bus information, visit www.buscephale.fr or call ✆ **03-80-11-29-29.** For railway information, visit www.voyages-sncf.com or call ✆ **36-35.**

VISITOR INFORMATION   The **Office de Tourisme** is at 13 rue Général Demetz (www.autun-tourisme.com; ✆ **03-85-86-80-38**).

Where to Stay & Eat

La Tête Noire ★   Decorated in the sunny colors of Provence, this three-star family-run hotel offers the best value stay in Autun. The focus of the menu, naturally, is the dishes and produce of Burgundy: we like the starter of apple salad with Bleu de Bresse cheese and ham from the Morvan Regional Natural Park, then the duck breast in reduced red wine sauce for main. From some bedrooms you can see the cathedral and from others the surrounding countryside; and breakfast is a wonderful spread of charcuterie, cheese, and artisanal jams.

3, rue de l'Arquebuse, 74100 Autun. ✆ **03-85-86-59-99.** www.hoteltetenoire.fr. 31 units. 84€ - 114€ double; 109€ family room. Breakfast 11.50€. Free parking nearby. Menus 19€–48€. **Amenities:** Restaurant; free Wi-Fi.

Exploring Autun

Autun was an important Roman link on the road from Lyon to Boulogne. A legacy of that period is the 17m (56-ft.) high **Porte d'Arroux,** once the city's northern gate, which has two archways now used for cars and smaller ones used for pedestrians. Also exceptional is the **Porte St-André (St. Andrew's Gate),** northwest of the Roman theater. Rising 20m (66 ft.), it has four doorways and is surmounted by a gallery of 10 arcades.

Cathédrale St-Lazare ★★   CATHEDRAL   Built in the 12th century to house the relics of Lazarus (who turned out to be the bishop of Aix and not the one that rose from the dead, as was originally believed), this cathedral is one of France's finest examples of Romanesque architecture and was inspired by the famous Cluny Abbey. The steeple, however, dates from the 1460s. Its main attractions are the carving of the Last Judgment on the west tympanum, and the capitals, whose carvings depict the three Magi, the flight to Egypt, and the suicide of Judas (amongst others). It is fortunate that they all survived as the canons here in the 18th century covered them with plaster, thinking them ugly. At the entrance to the sacristy is the "The Martyrdom of Saint Symphorian," by Dominique Ingres.

Place St-Louis, 74100 Autun. Free admission. Daily 8am–7pm.

Musée Rolin ★ MUSEUM   Housed in the 15th-century birthplace of Nicolas Rolin, founder of the Hospices de Beaune (see p. 293), this museum has a rich collection of artifacts from the Gallo-Roman era to the Middle Ages, as well as French and European paintings from the 17th to the 20th centuries. Highlights include mosaics from ancient Augustodunum; "The Temptation of Eve," originally the lintel of the cathedral's north door; and a 12-minute film, "Revelation: The Great Door of Autun," which explores the cathedral's "Last Judgment" tympanum in high-definition 3D.

3 rue des Bancs, 74100 Autun. ℂ **03-85-52-09-76.** Admission 5.20€ adults, 3.50€ students and children. June 21–Sept 21 daily 10am–1pm and 2–6pm; Apr–June 20 Wed–Mon 9:30am–noon and 1:30–6pm; Oct–Nov and Feb 22–Mar 31 Wed–Mon 10am–noon and 2–5pm (Sun pm only). Closed November 1 and 11, Dec–Feb 21.

BEAUNE ★★★

316km (196 miles) SE of Paris; 39km (24 miles) SW of Dijon

Beaune is the perfect base for exploring the **Côte d'Or** wine region that stretches to the North and South of the city. Burgundy's most influential wine merchants are all based here: Louis Jadot, Joseph Drouhin, and Bouchard Père et Fils, to name but a few. Beaune was a Gallic sanctuary, then a Roman town and some of its ramparts are still intact; you can even walk on them. Until the 14th century, Beaune was the residence of the ducs de Bourgogne. When the last duke, Charles the Bold, died in 1477, Louis XI annexed the town. The main sight is the **Hôtel-Dieu** (see "Exploring Beaune"), also known as the Hospices de Beaune. The Swiss-born Chevrolet brothers, who moved to the US and created one of the world's best-known car brands, were brought up here.

Hôtel-Dieu, Beaune

Essentials

ARRIVING If you're **driving,** note that Beaune is a few miles from the junction of three highways—A6, A31and A36. Beaune has good railway connections with Dijon, Lyon, and Paris. From Paris's Gare de Lyon, there are several TGV **trains** per day (trip time: just over 2 hr.; 56.60€–81€ one-way), with many more possibilities via a transfer in Dijon. For train information and schedules, visit www. voyages-sncf.com or call *℃* **36-35.**

VISITOR INFORMATION The **Office de Tourisme** is at 6 bd. Perpreuil (www. beaune-tourism.com; *℃* **03-80-26-21-30**).

Getting Around

BY TAXI The train station is a 15-minute walk from the town center so you might want to get a taxi to your accommodation. Try **Taxi Franon** *℃* **06-07-77-77-55.**

BY BIKE The best way to see this vine-planted land is by bike. Near Beaune train station, **Bourgogne Randonnées,** 7 av. du 8 septembre (www.bourgogne-randonnees.fr; *℃* **03-80-22-06-03**), rents bikes for 18€ per day.

Where to Stay

Le Grillon ★★ If you're coming by car and fancy getting away from it all but want to be within walking distance of town (20 min.), this is the place to stay. Three-star Le Grillon, a stylishly decorated, pink-washed 19th-century gentleman's residence named after the current owners, has a large garden and an outdoor pool around which you can relax on fine days. Rooms are painted in muted tones with contemporary fabrics and wallpaper providing splashes of color; most have the famous red Burgundy tiles. A new wing has four spacious suites with their own terraces. Rental bikes are available to explore the surrounding countryside.

21 route de Seurre, 21200 Beaune. *℃* **03-80-22-44-25.** www.hotel-grillon.fr. 20 units. 75€–87€ double; 110€–135€ suite. Breakfast 10€. Free parking. **Amenities:** Bar; laundry service; lounge; free Wi-Fi.

Hôtel Le Cep ★★★ This four-star hotel, which takes its name from the roots of a vine, is our favorite in Beaune. Created from several adjoining *hôtels particuliers* dating from the 16th century (Louis XIV stayed in one), the atmosphere here is of old-fashioned luxury with first-class service to match. We particularly like sitting by the lounge fire in winter and the vaulted breakfast room; a small fitness center at the top of a tower in the courtyard offers great views over the town. The 27 suites, each individually designed in traditional French style and furnished with antiques, have Nespresso machines and a Night Cove, which helps guests to sleep and wake up naturally; a dish of fresh fruit is delivered daily. Loiseau des Vignes (see "Where to Eat, below") is the hotel restaurant.

27 rue Jean-Francois Maufoux, 21200 Beaune. *℃* **03-80-22-35-48.** www.hotel-cep-beaune. com. 61 units. 178€–238€ double; 328€ suite; 528€ apartment. Breakfast 20€. Parking 18€. **Amenities:** Restaurant; bar; exercise room; massage treatments; room service; free Wi-Fi.

Beaune also has some great B&Bs, from the luxury **La Terre d'Or** (www. laterredor.com; *℃* **03-80-25-90-90**), with five rooms ranging from 180€ to 250€ in a lovely location overlooking the town, to the charming **Les Planchottes,** (http://lesplanchottes.free.fr; *℃* **03-80-22-83-67**), an old winegrower's house which has two pretty rooms costing 100€. Accommodation under 70€ per night is hard to find in Beaune, but there is a municipal four-star campsite,

Les Cent Vignes (© 03-80-22-03-91), open from Easter to October, which has 116 pitches, hot showers, a tennis court, and a restaurant.

Where to Eat

21 Boulevard ★★ BURGUNDIAN/FRENCH   This chic restaurant housed in a 15th-century wine cellar is the place to go if you're looking to make a night of it, as they also have an attached club that is open until 2am. We like the chicken breast with Epoisses cheese and the French toast dessert made with Mulot et Petitjean's *pain d'épices*. The wine list has more than 600 references, including a couple of pages of champagnes.

21 boulevard St-Jacques, 21200 Beaune. © **03-80-21-00-21.** www.21boulevard.com. Main courses 18€–36€; fixed-price menus 28€–45€. Tues–Sat noon–2pm and 7–10pm.

Loiseau des Vignes ★★★ BURGUNDIAN   Part of Hôtel Le Cep (see "Where to Stay," above) and a satellite of the Relais Bernard Loiseau in Saulieu (see p. 288), this restaurant has one Michelin star and is our favorite in Beaune. Although the furniture is contemporary, the atmosphere is decidedly 16th century: think beams and stone walls. As well as the gourmet French-Burgundian food created by Mourad Haddouche, with lunch menus starting at 20€, the main attraction is the "wine library" which has around 70 wines, some of them rare, and many available by the glass (5€–45€). On warm days, meals are served in the listed courtyard.

31 rue Maufoux, 21200 Beaune. © **03-80-24-12-06.** www.bernard-loiseau.com. Main courses 24€–128€; fixed-price lunch menus 20€–28€; dinner menus 59€–95€. Tues–Sat noon–2pm and 7–10pm. Closed Feb.

Les Vins de Maurice ★ FRENCH   Primarily a shop selling wines from across France, Maurice also offers snacks such as platters of cheese and ham as well quiches and desserts created according to the mood of the chef: we like the caramel and chocolate biscuit cake. Service is fast and friendly, the decor is 1950s retro, and there's a little courtyard for warmer days. Only opened in 2012, it's the hippest place in town.

8 rue Fraisse, 21200 Beaune. © **09-80-39-85-87.** www.lesvinsdemaurice.com. Main courses 8€–25€; fixed-price menu from 15€. Tues–Sat 10am–10pm.

Exploring Beaune

Known as "the daughter of Cluny," the **Collégiale Notre-Dame,** place du Général Leclerc, is a Romanesque church dating from 1120. Some remarkable 15th-century tapestries illustrating scenes from the life of the Virgin Mary are on display in the sanctuary and you can view them from Easter to mid-November (days and times vary). Admission is 3€ for adults, 2€ for children 11 to 18, and free for children 10 years and under.

Opened in 2011, **Dalinéum,** at 26 place Monge (© **03-80-22-63-13;** daily 11am–7pm; 7€ adults, 5€ ages 12–18; free for under 12s), is a permanent private collection of works by Salvador Dalí.

The best **shopping** streets are rue de Lorraine, rue d'Alsace, rue Maufoux, and place de la Madeleine. For smaller boutiques, stroll down the pedestrian rue Carnot and rue Monge. You'll encounter plenty of designer labels, vintners, and antiques dealers.

Every Wednesday and Saturday morning, the streets around place de la Halle and place de Fleury are chock-a-block with Burgundy's liveliest market. The most serious meat and cheese producers have their stalls in Les Halles. Consider taking a tour with American expat chef Marjorie Taylor of **The Cook's**

Atelier (www.thecooksatelier.com; ✆ **06-84-83-16-18**), then making your own lunch under her supervision. And be sure to visit **Edmond Fallot** at 31 rue du Faubourg (www.fallot.com; ✆ **03-80-22-10-10**) on the southwestern outskirts of town to buy mustard and have a look around the factory.

Hôtel-Dieu des Hospices Civils de Beaune ★★★ Famous for its excellent wines, produced by vineyards bequeathed to it by grateful patients over the years, this hospital was founded in 1443 by Nicolas Rolin (see "Exploring Autun"), chancellor to the Duke of Burgundy, and his wife Guigone. The sick are now treated in a state-of-the-art building on the outskirts of town, built and maintained thanks to money earned from the hospital's annual wine auction, which takes place on the third weekend of November: the *Vente des Vins des Hospices de Beaune*. The interesting sights are many, including the colorful tiled roof, the vast "room of the poor," and "The Last Judgment" polyptych by Flemish artist Roger van der Weyden. An audioguide, included in the entrance fee, provides an entertaining and informative commentary by "Nicolas" and "Guigone."

Rue de l'Hôtel-Dieu, 21200 Beaune. ✆ **03-80-24-45-00.** www.hospices-de-beaune.com Admission 7€ adults, 3€ ages 10–18, free for children 9 and under. Mid-Mar to mid-Nov daily 9am–6:30pm; mid-Nov to mid-Mar daily 9–11:30am and 2–5:30pm.

Musée des Beaux-Arts ★ ART MUSEUM This museum is particularly rich in works by Flemish and Dutch artists from the 16th and 17th centuries. Also on display are paintings by Beaune-born Félix Ziem of the 19th century Barbizon School, lithographs by Picasso and Le Corbusier, and a 12th-century polychrome "Virgin with Child."

6 bd. Perpreuil (Porte Marie de Bourgogne), 21200 Beaune. ✆ **03-80-24-56-92.** Admission (includes Musée du Vin de Bourgogne) 5.70€ adults, 3.60€ students and children 11–18, free for children 10 and under. Daily 11am–1pm and 2–6pm (Dec–Mar closed Tues).

Musée du Vin de Bourgogne ★ MUSEUM Although the presentation is a bit old-fashioned for modern tastes, this museum housed in the former home of the Dukes of Burgundy, provides an overview of winemaking from antiquity to the 20th century. We love the collection of Aubusson tapestries, inspired by vineyard scenes.

Rue d'Enfer. ✆ **03-80-22-08-19.** Admission 5.70€ adults, 3.70€ students and children 11–18, free for children 10 and under. Apr–Nov 9:30am–6pm; Dec–Mar 9:30am–5pm (closed Tue Jan–March).

Where to Stay & Eat Nearby

Les Charmes ★ In the heart of the village of Meursault, this family-run three-star hotel in a shuttered 18th-century winegrower's house offers a stylish and relaxing stay. The five spacious "Grand Cru" rooms are in the main house and individually decorated in traditional style, while the seven "Villages" rooms in the renovated outbuildings overlooking the courtyard are more contemporary. In summer, guests can enjoy the large gardens and swimming pool. There isn't a restaurant but there are good eating places in the village and area, not to mention plenty of wineries for tastings. You might also like to visit the spa at nearby château-hotel **La Cueillette** (www.laceuillette.com; ✆ **03-80-20-62-80**).

10 place Murger, 21190 Meursault (9km/6 miles southwest of Beaune on the D973). ✆ **03-80-21-63-53.** www.hotelescharmes.com. 13 units. 85€–128€ double; 120€–143€ triple. Breakfast 12€. Free parking. **Amenities:** Bar; laundry; reading room; room service; pool; free Wi-Fi.

Maison Lameloise ★★★ BURGUNDIAN Not only does it have three Michelin stars, but this gourmet eating place, housed in a coaching inn dating from the 15th century, was voted the world's best restaurant in Trip Advisor's

A taste **OF THE CÔTE D'OR**

Beaune is the epicenter of Burgundian winemaking with many of the world's most coveted and expensive wine appellations within an hour's drive. To the north lies the **Côte de Nuits,** famed for its red Pinot Noir vineyards with mythical appellations such as **La Romanée** and **Richebourg.** To the south lies **Côte de Beaune,** home to the great names of white chardonnay wines such as **Meursault** and **Chassagne-Montra-chet.** At the time of writing, the area was waiting to hear if its unique land and climate had been granted UNESCO World Heritage status. You may want to start your wine tour in Beaune where many of Burgundy's *négociants* (wine merchants who process and bottle the produce of smaller winemakers and then sell under their own name) have their bases. As well as being able to simply turn up with no appointment, you'll often be able to taste a wider variety of appellations than at an individual vine-yard. **Patriarche Père et Fils** (www. patriarche.com; ✆ **03-80-24-53-78**) offers 1-hour visits to its fabulous 13th- to 14th-century vaulted tasting cellars

where millions of bottles are held along 5km (3 miles) of underground cellars; it's open daily from 9:30 to 11:30am and 2 to 5pm, and admission is 16€. **Bouchard Père et Fils,** 15 rue du Château, (www. bouchard-pereetfils.com; ✆ **03-80-24-80-45**) has cellars in the 15th-century Castle of Beaune, a former royal fortress. A guided tour in English and tasting of six wines takes place at 10am (and at 4pm Apr–Nov) from Monday to Saturday and costs 19€. Just opposite the cel-ebrated Hôtel-Dieu, the **Marché aux Vins** (www.marcheauxvins.com; ✆ **03-80-25-08-20**) is housed in a for-mer Cordeliers church. With over 100 hectares (247 acres) of vineyards, this wine *négociant* offers a wide range of appellations to taste. Tastings of 7 wines cost 11€ and 10 wines cost 15€. It's open daily Apr to Oct from 10am to 6:30pm; Nov to Mar from 10am to noon and 2 to 6pm. On the northern outskirts of town on the D18, American-owned **Maison Louis Jadot** (www.louisjadot.com; ✆ **03-80-26-31-98**), is open for free tastings Mon to Fri from 3 to 7pm and Saturday from 11am to 5:30pm. You can

Travelers' Choice Restaurant Awards in 2013. From 1921 to 2008, the kitchen was run by the Lamy family but now Eric Pras, their protégé, is in charge. Five dining rooms, each with its own ambiance (a mix of stones, beams, and contem-porary furnishings), provide the backdrop for the mouthwatering Burgundian-inspired culinary creations: frogs' legs with spinach perfumed with lemon and ginger, and milk-fed lamb with caramelized garlic and saffron to name but two. The 16 rooms are elegantly furnished in opulent traditional fabrics and furniture. 36 place d'Armes, 71150 Chagny (16km/10 miles southwest of Beaune on the D974). ✆ **03-85-87-65-65.** www.lameloise.fr. 16 units. 180€–350€. Breakfast 25€. Fixed-price lunch 78€; fixed-price dinner 130€–180€. Thurs–Mon noon–1:45pm and 7:30–9:30pm (open daily for lunch in summer). Closed mid-Dec to mid-Jan.

MÂCON

397km (247 miles) SE of Paris; 127km (79 miles) S of Dijon; 87km (54 miles) S of Beaune.

On the banks of the River Saône, in the south of Burgundy, Mâcon is a workaday town whose historic center is a pleasant place to spend a day just strolling around also pre-book a tasting and a visit to its modern cellars at 3pm Mon to Fri and 10am on Saturdays, which costs 20€.

If you fancy visiting vineyards outside Beaune, head south along D974 to Pommard. **Château de Pommard,** 15 rue Marey Monge (www.chateaudepommard.com; ✆ **03-80-22-12-59**). Built for Messire Vivant de Micault equerry and secretary of Louis XVI in 1726, this castle was bought in 2003 by Maurice Giraud. Visits to the cellars that hold 300,000 bottles, the castle museum with its collection of antique vintners' tools, the gardens, and the art gallery cost 21€. It's open daily from 9:30am to 6:30pm. Next, you can head farther along the D974 to the **Château de Meursault** (www.meursault.com; ✆ **03-80-26-22-75**). This domaine owns over 60 hectares (148 acres) of vineyards covering appellations including Aloxe Corton, Pommard, Puligny-Montrachet, and of course Meursault. You can turn up without prior reservation for a visit to the cellars of this fabulous 19th-century castle, followed by a tasting of five wines in the old castle kitchens for 18€. It is open daily 9:30am to noon and 2 to 6pm (no lunchtime closure May to September). You may like to stop for a wine-tasting lunch along the way at **La Table d'Olivier Leflaive** (www.Olivier-leflaive.com; ✆ **03-80-21-37-65**), 10 place du Monument in Puligny-Montrachet, which costs 25€ plus 25€–45€ for accompanying wine.

For those who'd like to visit independent, family winegrowers but don't know where to start, **Burgundy by Request** (www.burgundybyrequest.com; ✆ **06-85-65-83-83**), run by English expat Tracy Thurling, should be your first port of call. Cristina Otel of **Taste Burgundy Wine School** (www.tasteburgundywineschool.org; ✆ **06-68-84-24-28**), is a highly qualified winemaker whose courses and tours offer a more in-depth knowledge of the local AOCs. A good introduction to grape varieties is also offered by **Vin Sensation** at 1 rue d'Enfer in Beaune (www.sensation-vin.com; ✆ **03-80-22-17-57**) during their "Essential Burgundy" session that lasts 1½ hours and costs 35€.

the narrow streets and along the quayside. Founded by the Celts and developed by the Romans, Mâcon is famous for being the birthplace of Romantic poet and politician Alphonse de Lamartine (see "Exploring Mâcon"). A good time to visit is during the **Vin'Estival** wine festival at the end of April, which includes a competition to find France's best *grand vin*; the surrounding area is famous for its Mâconnais and Beaujolais wines. The town is particularly lively from mid-June until the end of August when the **Eté Frappé** festival takes place, featuring music concerts, open-air cinema, and children's entertainment.

Essentials

ARRIVING   If you're **driving,** take A6 south past Beaune and onto Mâcon. Six direct TGV **trains** a day from Paris's Gare de Lyon run to Mâcon Loche TGV station (7km/4 miles outside Mâcon and connected to the centre by shuttle bus from Monday to Saturday) taking 1½ hours with fares starting at 64€ one-way. For railway information, visit www.voyages-sncf.com or call ✆ **36-35.**

VISITOR INFORMATION   The **Office de Tourisme** is at 1 place Saint-Pierre (www.macon-tourism.com; ✆ **03-85-21-07-07**).

Where to Stay

Hôtel d'Europe et d'Angleterre ★★   Reopened in 2013 with new owners and a stylish new look, this three-star hotel is our favorite place to stay in town. Dating from 1800, anyone who is anyone has stayed here over the years from Winston Churchill to Catherine Deneuve; and even the first giraffe to set foot on European soil (Zarafa, in 1827). Rooms are decorated in neutral tones, with armchairs and lampshades providing splashes of color. Most rooms overlook the courtyard but we like the deluxe rooms, which have a river view (99€–130€). There's organic produce at breakfast including award-winning jams and the '50s-retro wine bar has a good selection of local wines.

92–109 quai Jean Jaurès, 71000 Mâcon. ✆ **03-85-38-27-94.** www.hotel-europeangleterre-macon. com. 31 units. 67€–154€ double. Breakfast 13.50€. Parking 10€. **Amenities:** Babysitting; bar; breakfast room; laundry; massage service; free Wi-Fi.

Where to Eat

The top restaurant in town is **Pierre** (www.restaurant-pierre.com; ✆ **03-85-38-14-23**) at 7 rue Dufour, which has one Michelin star and does a weekday lunch menu for 25€. **Le Saint-Laurent** (www.georgesblanc.com; ✆ **03-85-39-29-19**) on the other side of the river (cross via the 11th-century Saint Laurent bridge) at 1 quai Bouchacourt, has welcomed world leaders; lunch menus start at 20€.

Le Lamartine ★ BURGUNDIAN/FRENCH   This quayside brasserie named after Mâcon's most famous son has been serving good traditional food since 1804. House specialties include frogs' legs, tête de veau (veal's head) and boeuf bourguignon; there are also about a dozen salads from which to choose. Everything is homemade and we particularly like the crème brulée dessert. The decor is stylish, too, with brass-topped wooden banquettes, 1920s-style tables and chairs, and a black-and-white diamond-pattern floor. It's always buzzing with local voices.

259 quai Lamartine, 71000 Mâcon. ✆ **03-85-35-16-63.** www.lelamartine.com. Main courses 14€–44€; fixed-price menu 14€–25€. Daily 11am–11pm.

Exploring Mâcon

Mâcon has two churches worth a visit: the Neo-Roman Eglise Saint Pierre on place St-Pierre, the town's largest church, and 19th-century Cathédral Saint Vincent on Square de la Paix. There are two museums of note in town: the **Musée Lamartine** at 41 rue de Sigorgne (✆ **03-85-39-90-38;** Tues–Sun 10am–noon and 2–6pm; admission 2.50€ adults, free for children under 18), housed in an 18th-century *hôtel particulier,* is of interest to fans of the writer and politician who was born in Mâcon in 1790; and the **Musée des Ursulines** at 5 rue des Ursulines (same details as Musée Lamartine; a combined ticket for both museums can be bought for 3.40€), named after the 17th-century convent in which it is based, whose collections comprise archaeological finds from the area, a floor dedicated to local life in times past, and also French and Flemish landscape paintings dating from the 16th to 19th centuries. From May to September, you can take boat trips along the River Saône for an afternoon or a day (book at the tourist office). However, the most interesting sights are within a half-hour drive of the town.

Day Trips from Mâcon

A fun way to explore the vineyards is on foot or by bike, which can be hired from the old train station (now a tourist office; ✆ **03-85-21-07-14**) at Charnay-lès-Mâcon, a 10-minute drive from town on the D54. The former railway line is now a "green route." If driving, you might like to stop off at **Terres Secrètes** on che-min du Val de Grosne in Prissé (www.terres-secretes.com; ✆ **03-85-37-88-06**) to buy some wine and local produce.

Grand Site Solutré-Pouilly-Vergisson ★★★ NATURAL SITE   Domi-nating the Pouilly-Fuissé vineyards, the Rock of Solutré and its environs, includ-ing the Rock of Vergisson, have been inhabited by man for 57,000 years. In 2013, the area received the label "Grand Site de France." Visitors can find out more about the site's history in the **Musée Départemental de Préhistoire** (www.musee-prehistoire-idf.fr, at the base of the Rock of Solutré, before walking to the top for panoramic views (493m; takes about 30 min.). Be sure to arrive early for a car parking space in summer.

71960 Solutré-Pouilly (10km/6miles west of Mâcon on the D54). ✆ **03-85-35-85-24.** Daily Apr–Sept 10am–6pm; Oct–Mar 10am–noon and 2–5pm. Admission 3.50€ adults; free for under 18s.

Hameau Duboeuf ★★ THEME PARK   Deep in Beaujolais country, this "wine village" created by well-known wine merchant Georges Duboeuf, is an interesting day out for the family. Visitors can learn about the evolution of wine over 2,000 years via entertaining films and automated puppet shows; you can even "fly" over the surrounding countryside. In summer, stroll around the Beaujolais garden, ride on the mini train, and play a round of adventure golf. You could easily spend a day here and there is also a zoo nearby, **Touroparc** (www.touroparc.com; ✆ **03-85-35-51-53**).

796 route de la Gare, 71570 Romanèche-Thorins (17km/11 miles south of Mâcon on the D906). ✆ **03-85-35-22-22.** www.hameauduboeuf.com. Daily 10am–6pm. Admission 19€ adults, 1 child (ages 4–15) goes free with 1 paying adult.

Where to Stay & Eat Nearby

Four generations of Blanc chefs have dominated the restaurant scene around Mâcon. The original Mère Blanc's Bresse chicken in a cream sauce with basmati rice is so legendary that this free-range chicken has become a Blanc trademark. The Blanc restaurant empire now extends from Lyon to its postcard-perfect hub in the village of Vonnas (www.georgesblanc.com).

La Courtille de Solutré ★★   In an idyllic location in the middle of the Pouilly-Fuissé vineyards, beneath the Rock of Solutré, is this gourmet "restaurant with rooms." Contemporary and original features work well together in this old stone village house. On the menu you'll find snails with chorizo, and Charolais steak with bone marrow à la tapenade; look out for the AOC Mâconnais: a hard, mild goats' cheese. There are six stylish rooms, each individually decorated in white and muted tones; all but two have views over the vines.

71960 Solutré-Pouilly (10km/6 miles west of Mâcon on the D54). ✆ **03-85-35-80-73.** www.lacourtilledesolutre.fr. 6 units. 85€–110€ double. Breakfast 10€. Free parking. Lunch menus 23€–27€, dinner menus 38€–42€. Restaurant closed Sun eve–Tues (hotel open daily). **Amenities:** Bar; terrace; free Wi-Fi.

There are some gorgeous B&B accommodations in this area including **Domaine la Source des Fées** (www.lasourcedesfees.com; ✆ **03-85-35-67-02**) in Fuissé, where rooms start at 118€; and the magnificent **Château de Pierre-clos** (www.chateaudepierreclos.com; ✆ **03-85-35-73-73**), which has five rooms starting at 155€. The **Manoir des Grandes Vignes** (www.manoir-des-grandes-vignes.com; ✆ **03-85-37-84-99**) in Prissé provides gîte accommodation from 20€ per person per night. **Camping du Lac** (www.lac-cormoranche.com; ✆ **03-85-23-97-10**) is a four-star campsite next to a lake in Cormoranche-sur-Saône.

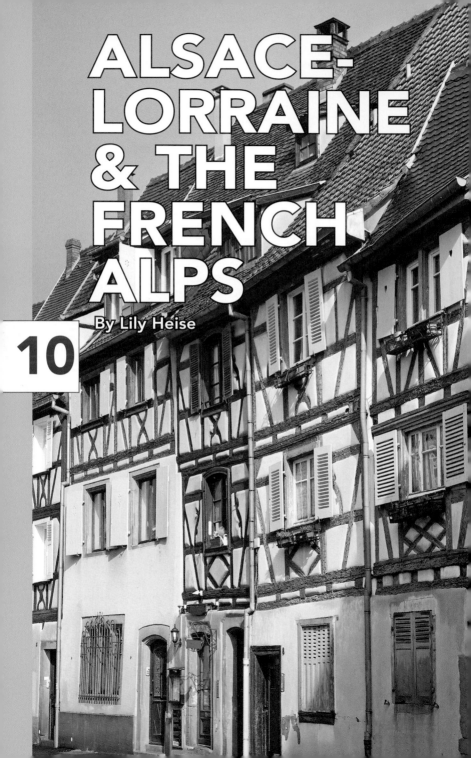

ALSACE-LORRAINE & THE FRENCH ALPS

By Lily Heise

10

The easternmost regions of France, Alsace and Lorraine, with ancient capitals at Strasbourg and Nancy, were the object of a centuries-old dispute between Germany and France. In fact, they were annexed by Germany between 1870 until after World War I and from 1940 to 1944. Though they've remained part of France since the end of World War II, Alsace especially is still reminiscent of the Black Forest, with its flower-laden half-timbered houses and traditional *winstub* taverns serving *choucroute* and sausage.

With this cultural mélange, it's not surprising Strasbourg became the base of the European parliament. Whereas Lorraine, with its rolling landscape and regal architecture, appears and feels more distinctly French in character and is even the homeland of one of the country's greatest heroines: Joan of Arc. Ponder these local traits while wandering through the quaint towns of the Alsatian Wine Road or through the natural splendor of the Vosges Mountains.

ALSACE-LORRAINE

Strasbourg ★★★

483km (300 miles) SE of Paris; 217km (135 miles) SW of Frankfurt

Situated about 483km (300 miles) southeast of Paris and tucked in the elbow of northwest France, Strasbourg ping-ponged between Germany and France for centuries. Today this capital of wine-growing Alsace blends Teutonic might with a cosmopolitan flair. With the majestic gothic Cathédrale Notre-Dame and its astronomical clock, the maze of cobbled streets, half-timbered houses and the poetic canals of La Petite France, this UNESCO World Heritage Site on the River Ill weaves fairy-tale charm with the European Parliament's political clout.

ESSENTIALS

ARRIVING The **Strasbourg-Entzheim Airport** (Aéroport International Strasbourg; www.strasbourg.aeroport.fr; ✆ **03-88-64-67-67**), 15km (9¼ miles) southwest of the city center, receives daily flights from many European cities, including Paris, London, Rome, Amsterdam, and Moscow. The **shuttle train** (look for the signs to pedestrian footbridge connecting the airport to the station platform) whisks you to Strasbourg main station in 9 minutes. The shuttles run every 15 minutes from 5am until 10pm Monday through Friday, twice an hour on Saturday between 6am and 9pm, and once to twice per hour on Sundays between 8am and 9pm. The one-way cost is 4€ and includes connection to the municipal tram system. For information, call ✆ **03-88-77-70-70**.

The superfast TGV **train** makes round-trips from Paris to Strasbourg, cutting travel time nearly in half to 2 hours, 20 minutes. At least 15 **trains** a day arrive from Paris's Gare de l'Est; the one-way fare is 47€ to 89€. For information and schedules, call ✆ **36-35**.

PREVIOUS PAGE: **Old houses in downtown Colmar, Alsace**

La Petite France, Strasbourg

By **car,** the giant A35 crosses the plain of Alsace, with occasional references to its original name, the N83. It links Strasbourg with Colmar and Mulhouse.

VISITOR INFORMATION   The **Office de Tourisme** is on 17 place de la Cathédrale (www.otstrasbourg.fr; ✆ **03-88-52-28-28**). There is a second branch inside the main train station (same telephone number as above).

STRASBOURG PASS   If you plan to do several tourist activities or museums, you can save with the Strasbourg Pass. Valid for 3 days, it grants free entrance to cathedral towers, clock, one museum, free boat cruise ticket, half-day free bike rental, 50 percent discount on second museum and other discounts; 14.90€ for adults and 7.45€ for children, available at the tourist office.

SPECIAL EVENTS   The Classical Music Festival runs for 2 weeks in June, and the Festival de Jazz runs in early July (both www.festival-strasbourg.com; ✆ **03-88-15-29-29**). They feature international artists and draw large crowds. Ticket prices range from 24€ to 75€ and go on sale in mid-April. Wolf Music, 24 rue de la Mésange (http://wolf-musique.musicunivers.com; ✆ **03-88-32-43-10**), arranges ticket sales for these festivals. The Association Musica (www.festival-musica.org; ✆ **03-88-23-46-46**) organizes the Festival International des Musiques d'Aujourd'hui. It takes place from the end of September to the first week of October and combines contemporary concerts with movies and modern opera performances. Tickets (8€–25€) go on sale at the end of June.

In late November and December, the place de Cathédrale erupts with the magical **Marché de Noël** (Christmas Market), where you can purchase handmade ornaments and gifts and warm up with hot *vin chaud* (mulled wine).

CITY LAYOUT   The center of Strasbourg is mainly located on **Grand Ile,** a large island hugged by two branches of the Ill River. **Petit France** is the area between these two branches; with its crooked streets and half-timbered houses, it's a major visitor destination.

GETTING AROUND

ON FOOT   Most of the main sites are accessible on foot and the city center is highly pedestrianized.

BY BICYCLE   Like a growing number of French cities, Strasbourg has a bike-sharing program called **Vélhop** (www.velhop.strasbourg.eu; ✆ 09-69-39-36-67). You can register in their boutiques at 3 rue d'Or or in the Strasbourg station; fees are 1€ per hour or 5€ per day. A deposit is required.

BY CAR   If you have a car for exploring Alsace, there are convenient under-ground parking lots in Place Gutenberg, Place Kléber, and near the train station. You can rent a car at **Avis** (www.avis.fr; ✆ 08-20-61-16-98), located at the train station or in the Kléber parking garage, or **Europcar,** at the station (www.europcar.fr; ✆ 08-25-85-74-79).

BY TAXI   To serve the many business travelers there are a good number of taxis circulating around the city. You can also order one from **Centre Alsace Taxis** (www.centre-alsace-taxis.fr; ✆ 03-88-85-15-15).

BY PUBLIC TRANSPORT   Strasbourg has an extensive transit network of trams and buses run by the **CTS** (www.cts-strasbourg.eu; ✆ 02-47-66-70-70). A one-way ticket costs 1.60€ or an unlimited day pass is 4.10€. Tickets can be pur-chased from automatic kiosks at a tram station or from a bus driver.

[FastFACTS] STRASBOURG

ATMs/Banks   The city center has plenty of banks; you'll definitely find one around Place Kléber.

Doctors & Hospitals   **Hopitaux Universitaires de Strasbourg,** 1 Place de l'Hopital (www.chru-strasbourg.fr; ✆ **03-88-11-67-68**).

Internet Access   **Linkys,** 22 rue des Frères (✆ **03-88-35-08-31**).

Mail & Postage   **La Poste,** 5 Place du Chateau (✆ **36-31**).

Pharmacies   **Pharmacie de l'Homme de Fer,** 2 Place de l'Homme de Fer (✆ **03-88-32-55-55**).

WHERE TO STAY

Cour du Corbeau ★★★ Originally opening in the 17th century, this is one of the oldest hotels in all of France and certainly the most enchanting one in Strasbourg. Though situated in the heart of the historic center, its traditional half-timbered architecture makes you feel like you're at a country inn. The interior has mostly been redone and features classy contemporary furnishings; however, some rooms have wooden beams and lovely old-fashioned windows that bring out its heritage. They have a number of deluxe rooms and almost 20 spacious suites. In the evening you can enjoy a cocktail at the swanky bar.

5 rue des Bouchers, Strasbourg 67000. ✆ **03-90-00-26-26**. www.mgallery.com search Strasbourg. 57 units. 305€–355€ double; 415€–485€ suite. **Amenities:** Babysitting; bar; fitness room; parking; free Wi-Fi.

Hôtel Gutenberg ★ This is a great-value, centrally located hotel with character. From the street, admire the former 18th-century mansion's elegant facade. Once inside, you've entered the 21st century. Guest rooms have been redone with Scandinavian design, a testament to Strasbourg's espousement of Europe. Other modern features include flatscreen TVs and refitted, yet small bathrooms.

31 rue des Serruriers, Strasbourg 67000. ✆ **03-88-32-17-15**. www.hotel-gutenberg.com. 42 units. 150€–195€ double. **Amenities:** Free Wi-Fi.

Romantik Hôtel Beaucour ★★ For a restful night's sleep in the boisterous city-center, book at this peaceful hotel. Hidden away on a private street a few blocks from the cathedral, it's hard to imagine that this charming 17th-century building with timbered ceilings used to be an umbrella factory. The welcome is as warm as the foyer's toasty fireplace. Alsatian hospitality and character are sprinkled throughout, so expect a small dose of gingham and hearts. Rooms are on the large size for European hotels and another plus is the presence of whirlpool tubs. The generous breakfast buffet will prep you for your next day of touring.

5 rue des Bouchers, Strasbourg 67000. ✆ **03-88-76-72-00**. www.hotel-beaucour.com. 49 units. 153€–186€ double; 214€–247€ suite. Parking 8.50€. **Amenities:** Babysitting, free Wi-Fi.

WHERE TO EAT

For a quick good-value meal, stop in at the **Brasserie de l'Ancienne Douane**, 6 rue de la Douane. (www.anciennedouane.fr; ✆ **03-88-15-78-78**), a large brasserie serving Alsatian specialties like "sauerkraut of the Customs officers" and foie gras of Strasbourg. Alternatively, try **Maison Kammerzell,** 16 place de

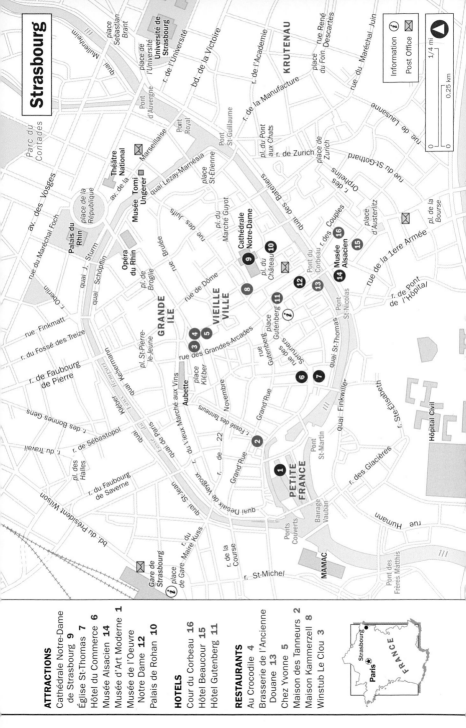

Strasbourg

la Cathédrale (www.maison-kammerzell.com; ✆ **03-88-32-42-14**). Conveniently located on the main square, this fairytale gingerbread-house is a marvel for young and older palates.

For a *choucroute*-free lunch, track down **VertuOse,** 19 rue d'Austerlitz (www.vertuose.eu; ✆ **03-88-23-63-32**); their daily specials, salads, and inventive "Schpeck'Nini" sandwiches please both carnivores and vegetarians.

Chez Yvonne ★★ FRENCH/ALSATIAN   Opened in 1873, this is one of the oldest and most charming *winstub* in town. Located near the cathedral, it is frequented by journalists and other political dignitaries. With its neat lines of tables and red-checked curtains, it's a mix of bourgeois home and sophisticated bistro. The menu features refined versions of some of the best regional cuisine such as *maennerstolz* (smoked beef and pork sausage), black pudding with apple compote, and the house specialty coq au Riesling with spaëtzle pasta.

10 rue du Sanglier. ✆ **03-88-32-84-15.** www.chez-yvonne.net. Main courses 13€–25€. Daily noon–2:15pm and 6pm–midnight.

Au Crocodile ★★★ ALSATIAN   No, exotic meats are not a specialty here as its name might suggest, notwithstanding, this is easily the most innovative restaurant in Strasbourg. Originally a 14th-century Benedictine monastery, it was converted into an *auberge* in 1801 by a captain of Napoleon's army on his return from the Egyptian campaign (he brought the infamous crocodile, now stuffed and on display, with him). Its brilliant chefs have earned three Michelin stars and have served major French celebrities and heads of state (notably Barack Obama). Current chef Philippe Bohrer's creations could include spider crab cannelloni with oyster juice and caviar from Aquitaine or roebuck with dates and wild mushrooms infused with licorice.

10 rue de l'Outre. ✆ **03-88-32-13-02.** www.au-crocodile.com. Main courses 45€–75€; fixed-price menu lunch 72€, dinner 96€–139€. Tues–Sat noon–1:30pm and 7:30–9:30pm. Closed last 3 weeks of July and Dec 24–29.

Maison des Tanneurs ★ ALSATIAN   Referred to by locals as "la Maison de la Choucroute," come here for the best sauerkraut-and-pork in town. Set in a former tannery dating from 1572, this antiques-filled restaurant was opened in 1949. It sits idyllically on the water, its terrace opening onto the canal. If you're not tempted by its signature dish, the chef also prepares veal kidneys with local white wine, the Belle Strabourgeoise foie gras or the stuffed guineafowl on a bed of choucroute. Save room for the Kougelhopf glazed with sweet Gewürztraminer liqueur or the Alsatian fruit tart.

42 rue du Bain-aux-Plantes. ✆ **03-88-32-79-70.** www.maison-des-tanneurs.com. Main courses 20€–25€; fixed-price lunch 24€–26€. Tues–Sat noon–1:45pm and 7–10pm (also Sun noon–2pm in Dec). Closed first 2 weeks in Jan.

Winstub Le Clou ★ ALSATIAN   Warmth and hearty Alsatian goodness exude from this great-value, authentic *winstub*. Wood-paneled walls, folkloric artwork, and communal tables add to its charm. They specialize in typical regional fare, like Alsatian snails, *bibeleskas* (thick cream sauce) with country-style potatoes, or a house favorite Pinot Noir–braised *wädele* (Alsatian sauerkraut with hearty knuckle of ham).

3 rue de Chaudron. ✆ **03-88-32-11-67.** www.le-clou.com. Main courses 13€–25€; fixed-price menu 17€–26€. Mon–Tues and Thurs–Sat 11:30am–2:15pm; Mon–Sat 5:30–midnight.

Place Kléber, Strasbourg

EXPLORING STRASBOURG

Despite World War I and World War II damage, much remains of Old Strasbourg, including covered bridges and towers from its former fortifications, plus
many 15th- and 17th-century dwellings with painted wooden fronts and carved
beams.

The city's traffic hub is **place Kléber** ★, dating from the 15th century. Sit
here with a tankard of Alsatian beer and get to know Strasbourg. The bronze
statue in the center is of J. B. Kléber, born in Strasbourg in 1753; he became one
of Napoleon's most noted generals and was buried under the monument. Apparently, his presence offended the Nazis, who removed the statue in 1940. This
Alsatian bronze was restored to its proper place in 1945.

From here, take rue des Grandes-Arcades southeast to **place Gutenberg,**
one of the city's oldest squares. The central statue (1840), by David d'Angers, is
of Gutenberg, who perfected his printing press in Strasbourg in the winter of
1436 and 1437. The former town hall, now the **Hôtel du Commerce,** was built
in 1582 and is one of the most significant Renaissance buildings in Alsace. The
neighborhoods within a few blocks of the city's **Notre Dame Cathedral** are
loaded with medieval references and historical charm.

La Petite France ★★ is the most interesting quarter of Strasbourg. A virtual island, it's surrounded by scenic canals on four sides, and its 16th-century
houses reflect in the waters of the Ill River. In "Little France," old roofs with gray
tiles have sheltered families for ages, and the cross-beamed facades with roughly
carved rafters are in typical Alsatian style. For a good view, walk along rue des
Moulins, branching off from rue du Bain-aux-Plantes.

Cathédrale Notre-Dame de Strasbourg ★★★ CATHEDRAL The
city's crowning glory is an outstanding example of Gothic architecture, representing a transition from the Romanesque. Construction began in 1176. The pyrami-
dal tower in rose-colored stone was completed in 1439; at 141m (462 ft.), it's the
tallest one from medieval times. This cathedral is still in use; religious ceremonies, particularly on feast days, meld perfectly with the architectural majesty.
Individual tourists can visit the tower only in the summer (you may have to wait

to climb it). The Office de Tourisme (see above) organizes tours for groups; call for the schedule.

Four large counterforts divide the **main facade ★★★** into three vertical parts and two horizontal galleries. Note the **rose window,** which looks like stone lace. The facade is rich in decoration: On the portal of the south transept, the *Coronation and Death of the Virgin* in one of the two tympanums is the finest such medieval work. In the north transept, see also the facade of the **Chapelle St-Laurence,** a stunning achievement of the late Gothic German style.

A Romanesque **crypt** lies under the chancel, which is covered with square stonework. The stained-glass window is the work of Max Ingrand. The **nave** is majestic, with windows depicting emperors and kings on the north Strasbourg aisle. Five chapels cluster around the transept, including one built in 1500 in the Flamboyant Gothic style. In the south transept stands the **Angel Pillar ★★,** illustrating the Last Judgment, with angels lowering their trumpets.

The **astronomical clock ★** was built between 1547 and 1574. It stopped during the Revolution, and from 1838 to 1842, the mechanism was replaced. Each day at 12:30pm, crowds gather to see its show of allegorical figures. On Sunday, Apollo drives his sun horses; on Thursday, you see Jupiter and his eagle. The body of the clock has a planetarium based on the theories of Copernicus. Close-up views of the clock are available Monday to Saturday from noon to 12:30pm; tickets (2€ adults, 1.50€ ages 5–18 and students) are on sale in the mornings at the post-card stand or from 11:45am at a kiosk in the south portal.

Place de la Cathédrale. ✆ **03-88-32-75-78** for times of services. www.cathedrale-strasbourg. fr. **Cathedral:** Daily 7am–7pm. Free admission to cathedral. **Tower:** ✆ **03-88-43-60-40.**

Stained-glass rose window, Cathédrale Notre-Dame de Strasbourg

Apr–Sept daily 9am–7:15pm (July until 9:45pm, early Aug until 8:45 and late Aug 7:45pm); Oct–Mar daily 10am–5:15pm. Tower admission 4.70€ adults, 2.30€ children 17 and under and students, free to all the 1st Sun of the month.

Eglise St-Thomas ★ CHURCH   Built between 1230 and 1330, this Romanesque church was one of the first converted to Protestantism when the movement arrived in Alsace in 1524. It contains the **mausoleum ★★** of Maréchal de Saxe, a masterpiece of French art by Pigalle (1777), and a magnificent 12th-century sarcophagus of Archbishop Aledoch.

Rue Martin-Luther (along rue St-Thomas, near pont St-Thomas). ✆ **03-88-32-14-46.** www.saint-thomas-strasbourg.fr. Free admission. Apr–Oct daily 10am–6pm; Nov–Dec & Mar daily 10am–5pm. Closed Jan to mid-Feb.

Musée Alsacien ★ MUSEUM   Housed in three mansions from the 16th and 17th centuries, this lovely museum takes visitors on a voyage through the ages of Alsatian history via its impressive collection of paintings, furniture, and other decorative arts.

23 quai St-Nicolas. ✆ **03-88-52-50-01.** www.musees.strasbourg.eu. Admission 6.50€ adults, 3.50€ students and seniors, free for children 17 and under. Wed–Mon 10am–6pm.

Musée of Modern and Contemporary Art (MAMC) ★ MUSEUM   In the heart of La Petite France, this is Strasbourg's showcase of modern European art from 1870 to the present. While it's not quite the level of the Orsay or Pompidou in Paris, it's worth a meander for true art lovers. The collection itself was started in 1919 and has grown thanks to donations from local arts patrons. The layout of the museum starts with a historical section tracing the emergence of modern art and going forward to the 21st century, including works by Rodin, Monet, Picasso, and Kandinsky. It also has an art library, a museum shop, and a cafe-restaurant on the terrace.

1 place Jean-Hans Arp. ✆ **03-88-23-31-31.** www.musees.strasbourg.eu. Admission 7€ adults, 3.50€ students 24 and under and seniors, free for children 17 and under. Tues–Sun 10am–6pm.

Musée de l'Oeuvre Notre-Dame ★★★ MUSEUM   This museum, located in excellently restored buildings from the era, illustrates the art of the Middle Ages through the Renaissance and the beginnings of the Reformation, making it a perfect stop for fans of ecclesiastic art and medieval history. The collection displays many pieces that were previously displayed in the cathedral (where copies have since been substituted). The most celebrated is a stained-glass head of Christ from about the 11th century. Other noteworthy works are the 13th-century sculpture hall with the wise and foolish virgins from 1280, the winding Renaissance staircase, and 16th- and 17th-century artifacts by Strasbourg goldsmiths.

3 place du Château. ✆ **03-88-52-50-00.** www.musees.strasbourg.eu. Admission 6.50€ adults, 3.50€ students 24 and under and seniors, free for children 17 and under, includes free audio-guide. Tues–Sun 10am–6pm.

Palais de Rohan ★★ PALACE   This palace south of the cathedral was built from 1732 to 1742 for the Prince-Bishop of Strasbourg, the illegitimate son of Louis XIV. Echoing Parisian Rococo style, it is noted for its facades and sumptuous interior, making it one of the crowning design achievements in eastern France. Impressive works by Rubens, Rembrandt, Van Dyck, Goya, and Renoir are displayed on the first floor fine-arts museum (Musée des Beaux-Arts). On the main floor is a decorative-arts museum featuring ceramics and the original machinery of the cathedral's first astronomical clock. There is also an

10

ALSACE-LORRAINE

Strasbourg

archaeological museum with precious artifacts excavated from nearby digs, focused on art and utilitarian objects from the Roman and early medieval eras.

2 place du Château. ✆ **03-88-52-50-00.** Admission 6.50€ adults, 3.50€ students, free for children 17 and under. Wed–Mon noon–6pm.

SHOPPING

Strasbourg overflows with antiques shops, artisans, craftspeople, and beer makers. Every well-accessorized home in Alsace owns some of the napkins, aprons, tablecloths, and tea and bath towels of the Beauvillé textile mills. **Nappes d'Alsace,** 6 rue Mercière, near the cathedral (www.antiquites-bastian.com; ✆ **03-88-22-69-29**), has one of the widest selections of textiles in town.

Bastian, 22–24 place de la Cathédrale (✆ **03-88-32-45-93**) has been a family affair since 1861. They specialize in 18th- and 19th-century ceramic tureens that Alsace produced in abundance. There's also a selection of Louis XV and Louis XVI furniture, crafted in the region during the 18th and 19th centuries following Parisian models from the same era.

One of the most appealing shops in Strasbourg is **Arts et Collections d'Alsace,** 4 place du Marché aux Poissons (www.arts-collections-alsace.com; ✆ **03-88-14-03-77**), which sells copies of art objects and utilitarian ware from museums and private collections through Alsace in addition to upscale gift items for the home and kitchen and fabric by the yard.

STRASBOURG NIGHTLIFE

A hub of outdoor entertainment is **place de la Cathédrale,** where you can find an assortment of performers and artists. Dancers perform spontaneously against the illumination of the cathedral. From mid-July to early August, folk dances take place in La Petite France on Monday night in place des Tripiers, Tuesday in place Benjamin Zix, and Wednesday in place du Marché aux Cochons de Lait. Performance dates vary; check with the Office de Tourisme (www.otstrasbourg.fr; ✆ **03-88-52-28-29**) for a schedule.

THE PERFORMING ARTS   For opera and ballet, seek out the **Opéra du Rhin,** 19 place Broglie (www.operanationaldurhin.fr; ✆ **03-88-75-48-23**); tickets cost 12€ to 80€. The **Orchestre Philharmonique de Strasbourg** performs at the Palais de la Musique et des Congrès, place de Bordeaux (www.philharmonique-strasbourg.com; ✆ **03-69-06-37-00**). Tickets cost 14.50€ to 63€. The **Théâtre National de Strasbourg** plays a busy schedule at 1 av. de la Marseillaise (www.tns.fr; ✆ **03-88-24-88-00**). Tickets cost 5.50€ to 27€.

BARS & CLUBS   The streets surrounding place de la Cathédrale, in particular rue des Frères, rue des Soeurs, and rue de la Croix, are bustling with cafes and bars. **Jeannette et les Cycleux,** 3 rue des Tonneliers (www.lenetdejeannette.com; ✆ **03-88-23-02-71**), is a quirky retro bar filled with trendy young locals sipping on wine or nibbling at their tasty "planchettes."

Despite being known for its white wines, Alsace is also the number one beer-producing region of France, not surprising due to its historical links and proximity to Germany. This tradition is being maintained at the artisan brewery **Au Brasseur,** 22 rue des Veaux (www.aubrasseur.fr; ✆ **03-88-36-12-13**); additionally, a wide variety of local and international pints can be sampled at **Les Freres Berthom,** 18 rue des Tonneliers (www.lesberthom.com; ✆ **03-88-32-81-18**).

For a late night with the stylish 20-35 strasbourgeois, go underground at **Le Seven,** 25 rue des Tonneliers (www.lesevenstrasbourg.com; ✆ **03-88-32-77-77**), and groove to the beats of contemporary dance and electro music.

La Route Du Vin (Wine Road) ★★★

The fastest route between Strasbourg and Colmar, 68km (42 miles) south, is N83. But if you have time, the famous Route du Vin, the oldest "wine road" in France established in 1950, makes a rewarding experience. It rolls through 60 charming villages and is flanked by the Vosges foothills, with medieval towers and feudal ruins evoking faded pageantry. The vine-covered slopes sometimes reach a height of 435m (1,427 ft.), and an estimated 20,000 hectares (49,400 acres) of vineyards line the road. Some 30,000 families earn their living tending the grapes.

Serious oenophiles will want to select specific vineyards to visit; however, the picturesque scenery and quaint towns are a highlight for any visitor to the region. The best villages are described below; charming Kaysersberg is a convenient place for lunch, while most overnights are done in the largest town, Colmar. The best time to go is for the harvest in September and October when there are festivals throughout the area (especially in Ribeauvillé). Useful additional information can be found at **www.alsace-wine-route.com.**

WHERE TO EAT & STAY ALONG LA ROUTE DU VIN

If you don't opt for one of the detailed entries below, a tasty pit stop can be made in Andlau at the unpretentious bistro **Au Boeuf Rouge,** 6 rue du Dr. Stoltz (✆ **03-88-08-96-26**), serving up hearty standard classics.

If you're visiting Ribeauvillé, you can satisfy hungry bellies of all ages at quaint **La Flammerie,** 9 Grand Rue (www.flammerie-ribeauville.com; **03-89-73-61-08**); as the name indicates, they have excellent flammekueche tarts, in addition to a wide range of traditional dishes and even some salads, a rarity in Alsace. Or for finer dining in the same town try **Le Clos St-Vincent,** Rte. de Bergheim (www.leclossaintvincent.com; ✆ **03-89-73-67-65**). At this lovely inn overlooking the vineyards, you might enjoy the Chapotin family's food so much that you'll want to stay the night in one of their balconied guestrooms.

The most authentic way to experience the Alsatian Wine Road is to actually sleep amongst the vines, something you can do at one of the area's many

Route du Vin, the oldest wine road in France

BIKING THE wine road

A lovely way to experience the Wine Road is to leisurely breeze through the vines and villages by bicycle. The Strasbourg tourist office provides maps showing bike routes that fan out from the city into the countryside, with emphasis on cycle lanes (*les pistes cyclables* in French) that prohibit cars. One of these is a 27km (17-mile) stretch that runs southwest from Strasbourg to the wine hamlet of Molsheim. It has a forest on one side, the banks of the Brûche River (a tributary of the Rhine) on the other, and little car traffic. You can rent bikes from **Esprit Cycles,** 18 rue Jacques Krutenau (www.espritcycles.com; ✆ **03-88-36-18-41**). Their rates are 18€ daily, 28€ for the weekend, and 80€ weekly. It's open Monday to Friday 8am to 12:30pm and 1:30 to 7pm, and Saturday 10am to 6pm.

charming **B&Bs.** You can peruse an extensive list and book directly on the regional tourism website, **www.alsace-wine-route.com.**

Le Chambard ★★★   The old-fashioned town of Kaysersberg hides one of the best restaurant-hotels along the Wine Road. Entering the town, you will be instantly charmed with its 18th-century main building, exuding quintessential Alsatian charm. However, the guestrooms are as cutting edge as the kitchen's cuisine. The large rooms have sleek furnishings often with a zebra pattern. The relaxing spa will prep you for more touring.

Their Winstub bistro on the ground floor is ideal for a casual meal, but it's their gastronomic restaurant that serves up the best food in town. Bestowed with the high honor of Meilleur Ouvrier de France, Chef Olivier Nasti applies his talent to such marvels as the "freshwater" platter of frog, pike, and crawfish in a Riesling cream or the locally caught hare *à la royale* with regional kasknopfle pasta and wild mushrooms. Main courses start at 32€, lunch menus are 40€ and dinner 91€–133€ (open Thurs–Sun noon–2pm and 7–9pm).

9–13 rue du Général-de-Gaulle, Kaysersberg 68240. ✆ **03-89-47-10-17.** www.lechambard.com. 32 units. 120€–292€ double, 320€–375€ suite. **Amenities:** Restaurant; pool; spa; free Wi-Fi.

Winstub Gilg ★   Located in the center of the scenic village of Mittelbergheim, this is one of the best bargains for a meal or overnight along the Wine Road. Started in 1614, the comfy inn features a two-story stone staircase, classified as a historic monument. Furnishings are simple and slightly dated, yet rooms are warmly decorated. Some have exposed beams and stone walls, and all have modern bathrooms with a tub/shower. Locals faithfully flock to its restaurant, where chef Vincent Reuschlé prepares regional specialties with creative flare such as the house specialty "wine-maker's" ham puff pastry, saddle of rabbit with mixed mushrooms and cocotte of veal sweetbreads with späetzle dumplings (menus 33€–68€, restaurant closed on Tues and Wed).

1 rte. du Vin, Mittelbergheim, Barr 67140. ✆ **03-88-08-91-37.** www.hotel-gilg.com. 15 units. 68€–98€ double. **Amenities:** Restaurant; free Wi-Fi. Hotel and restaurant closed Jan and from late June to early July.

MITTELBERGHEIM

The loveliness of Mittelbergheim, 43km (27 miles) from Strasbourg, has earned the town a place on the list of "most beautiful villages of France." Houses in the Renaissance style border its **place de l'Hôtel-de-Ville.** Around town are a number of medieval wells and ancient wine presses.

ANDLAU

This gardenlike resort, 42km (26 miles) from Strasbourg, was the site of an abbey founded in 887 by the disgraced wife of Emperor Charles the Fat. It has now faded into history, but a church remains that dates from the 12th century. In the tympanum are noteworthy Romanesque carvings. The **Office de Tourisme,** 5 rue du Général-de-Gaulle (www.pays-de-barr.com; *℡* **03-88-08-22-57**), is open Monday through Friday 9am to noon.

DAMBACH ★

One of the delights of the Wine Road, Dambach (48km/30 miles from Strasbourg) is the largest wine-producing village in Alsace, from where one of the finest Alsatian wines, the Grand Cru Frankstein, comes. The town, formally Dambach-la-Ville, has ramparts and three fortified gates and was once protected by the medieval Bernstein castle, today in ruins above the town. Its timbered houses are gabled with galleries, and many contain oriels. Wrought-iron signs still tell you if a place is a bakery or a butcher shop. A short drive from the town is the **Chapelle St-Sebastian,** with a 15th-century ossuary. The **Office de Tourisme** (www.dambach-la-ville.fr; *℡* **03-88-92-61-00**) is in La Mairie (town hall), place du Marché.

Between Dambach and Ribeauvillé is the region's most impressive castle: the **Château Haut Koenigsbourg ★★**. Clinging to the mountainside, it has a sprawling view of the whole valley. Presumed to date from the 12th century, it has typical medieval fortress features including thick defensive walls, turrets, and a tall keep. It was highly damaged and subsequently abandoned during the Thirty Years' War. It was eventually restored under German Emperor Wilhelm II in the early 20th century, although the accuracy of the restoration is somewhat dubious; nonetheless, it's a spectacular site. Entrance is 8€ adults, 6€ students, and free for children under 17. It's open daily November to February 9:30am to noon and 1 to 4:30pm; March to May, September and October 9:15am to 5pm and June to August until 6pm (www.haut-koenigsbourg.fr; *℡* **03-69-33-25-00**).

RIBEAUVILLÉ ★★

At the foot of vine-clad hills dotted with castle ruins, Ribeauvillé (87km/54 miles from Strasbourg) is picturesque, with old shop signs, pierced balconies, turrets, and flower-decorated houses. The town is noted for its Riesling and Gewürztraminer wines. See its Renaissance fountain and **Hôtel de Ville,** place de la Mairie, which has a collection of silver-gilt medieval and Renaissance tankards known as *hanaps.* For information, go to the tourist office at 1 Grand' Rue (www.ribeauville-riquewihr.com; *℡* **03-89-73-23-23**). Guided tours showcase the *hanaps,* the building's architecture, and the history of the town. The free 90-minute tours run from May to September, on Sunday and Tuesday through Friday at 10am, 11am, and 2pm. On tour days at 3pm, the same guide leads a 90-minute walking tour of the town. Tours are in French, German, or halting English.

Also of interest in Ribeauvillé is the **Tour des Bouchers** (Butcher's Tower), built in stages from the 13th to the 16th century.

Every year on the first Sunday in September, visitors fill the town for its **Pfifferdaj** or **Jour des Menetriers (Day of the Minstrels),** the oldest festival in Alsace dating back to the Middle Ages. Beginning at 3pm and lasting almost 2½ hours, it features a parade of flute players from Alsace, the rest of France, Switzerland, and Germany, and as many as 600 parade participants. You can stand anywhere to watch the spectacle, but seats on the medieval stone benches line each side of the parade route.

KAYSERSBERG ★★

Once a free city of the empire, Kaysersberg (93km/58 miles from Strasbourg) lies at the mouth of the Weiss Valley, between two vine-covered slopes; it's crowned by a castle ruined in the Thirty Years' War. From one of the many ornately carved bridges, you can see the city's medieval fortifications along the top of one of the nearby hills. Many of the houses are Gothic and Renaissance, and most have half-timbering, wrought-iron accents, leaded windows, and multiple designs carved into reddish sandstone.

In the cafes, you'll hear a combination of French and Alsatian. The age of the speaker usually determines the language—the older ones remain faithful to the dialect of their grandparents.

Dr. Albert Schweitzer, who received the 1952 Nobel Peace Prize for his philosophy of "Reverence for Life," was born here in 1875; his house is near the bridge over the Weiss. You can visit the **Musée du Albert Schweitzer,** 126 rue du Général de Gaulle (✆ **03-89-47-36-55**), from April to November daily from 9am to noon and 2 to 6pm. Admission is 2€ adults and 1€ for students and children 11 and under.

The **Office de Tourisme** is at 39 rue du Général-de-Gaulle (www.kaysersberg.com; ✆ **03-89-78-22-78**).

AMMERSCHWIHR

Ammerschwihr, 9km (5½ miles) north of Colmar (79km/49 miles from Strasbourg), is a good stop to cap off your Wine Road tour. Once a free city of the empire, the town was almost destroyed in 1944 and has been reconstructed in the traditional style. More and more travelers visit to sample the wine, especially Käferkopf. Check out the town's gate towers, 16th-century parish church, and remains of early fortifications.

ROUFFACH

Rouffach is south of Colmar. One of the highest of the Vosges Mountains, Grand-Ballon shelters the town from the winds that bring rain, which makes for a dry climate and a special grape. Make a beeline for the excellent vineyard **Clos St-Landelin** (www.mure.com; ✆ **03-89-78-58-00**), on the Route du Vin, at the intersection of RN83 and route de Soultzmatt. A clerical estate from the 6th century until the Revolution, it has been celebrated over the centuries for the quality of its wine. Clos St-Landelin covers 21 hectares (52 acres) at the southern end of the Vorbourg Grand Cru area. Its steep slopes call for terrace cultivation.

The soil that produces these wines is anything but fertile. Loaded with pebbles, sand, and limestone, the high-alkaline earth produces low-yield, scraggly vines whose fruit goes into superb Rieslings, Gewürztraminers, and pinot noirs. Members of the Muré family have owned these vineyards since 1648. In their cellar is a 13th-century wine press, the oldest in Alsace, and one of only three like it in France. (The other two are in Burgundy.) The family welcomes visitors who want to tour the cellars and ask about the wine, which is for sale. It's open Monday to Friday 8am to 6:30pm, and Saturday 10am to 1pm and 2 to 6pm.

Colmar ★★★

440km (273 miles) SE of Paris; 140km (87 miles) SE of Nancy; 71km (44 miles) SW of Strasbourg

One of the most attractive towns in Alsace, Colmar is a must for any visitors to the region. Colmar has been so well restored, you'd never guess it was hard hit in two world wars. You can't help but be charmed by its medieval and early Renaissance buildings, half-timbered structures, gables, and gracious loggias. Tiny gardens and washhouses surround many of the homes. Its old quarter looks more German than French, filled with streets of unexpected twists and turns. The third-largest town in Alsace, its geographic location makes it a natural gateway to the Rhine country, near the vine-covered slopes of the southern Vosges.

ESSENTIALS

ARRIVING If you're **driving,** take N83 from Strasbourg; trip time is 1 hour. Because of the narrow streets, we suggest that you park and walk. Leave the car in the Champ-de-Mars, or in the underground Place Rapp for a fee of around 1.50€ per hour, northeast of the railway station, and then walk a few blocks east to the old city; or park in the lot designated parking vieille ville, accessible from rue de l'Est at the edge of the Petite Venise neighborhood, and walk a few blocks southeast to reach

Balcony of Maison Pfister in Colmar

the old city. **Trains** link Colmar to Nancy, Strasbourg, and Mulhouse, as well as to Germany via Strasbourg, across the Rhine. Twenty to twenty-two trains per day arrive from Paris's Gare de l'Est (trip time: 4–6 hr.); the one-way fare is 47€ to 89€. For information, call ✆ **36-35,** or 08-92-35-35-35 from outside France.

VISITOR INFORMATION The **Office de Tourisme** is at 4 rue Unterlinden (www.ot-colmar.fr; ✆ **03-89-20-68-92**). For information on wines, vintages, and winery visits, contact the **CIVA** (Alsace Wine Committee), Maison du Vin d'Alsace, 12 av. de la Foire-aux-Vins (www.vinsalsace.com; ✆ **03-89-20-16-20**). It's usually open Monday to Friday 8:15am to noon and 2 to 5pm. Make arrangements far in advance.

SPECIAL EVENTS Alsatian **folk dances** on place de l'Ancienne-Douane begin around 8pm on Tuesday from mid-May to mid-September. If you want to listen to classical music, visit during the first 2 weeks in July for the **Festival International de Musique de Colmar** (www.festival-colmar.com; ✆ **03-89-20-68-97**), which schedules 24 concerts in venues around the city, such as churches and public monuments. Tickets for these cost 10€ to 15€. **Les Mardis de la Collégiale,** at place de la Cathédrale (✆ **06-71-06-50-18**), stages free concerts every Tuesday at 8:45pm from the end of July to mid-September. You can get complete information on any of the events in town at the Office de Tourisme.

[FastFACTS] COLMAR

ATMs/Banks You'll find ATMs in Place de la Cathédrale or at the intersection of rue Kléber, avenue de la République and rue Stanislas.

Doctors & Hospitals **Hopitaux Civils de Colmar,** 39 avenue de la Liberté (www.ch-colmar.fr; ✆ **03-89-12-40-00**).

Mail & Postage   **La Poste,** 34 avenue de la République (📞 **36-31**).

Pharmacies   **Pharmacie du Cigne,** 31 rue des Tetes (📞 **03-89-41-30-09**).

WHERE TO STAY

Rooms are also available in **La Maison des Têtes** (see "Where to Eat," below).

Le Colombier ★   New York meets Colmar at this revamped historic home. The facade, old beams, and spiral staircase are virtually all that's left of the 16th century, for the rooms have all been redone with sleek contemporary furnishings and art. They come in a variety of shapes due to the age of the building; ceilings are high, but often slanted. Modern comfort is accentuated with cushy beds covered in fine linens. Bathrooms are small and only have showers. Request a room with a view of the canals or the timbered courtyard.

7 rue Turenne, Colmar 68000. 📞 **03-89-23-96-00.** www.hotel-le-colombier.fr. 28 units. 94€–229€ double; 220€–264€ suite. Parking 10€. **Amenities:** Bar; room service; free Wi-Fi.

Hostellerie Le Maréchal ★★   Alsatian charm shines brightly at this hotel located in three 16th-century houses in the heart of la Petite Venice. Guestrooms are named after   different composers, to whom decorative nods are dotted throughout the hotel. Rooms are on the small side and are roughly divided between classical or modern style, some with canopy beds. Most bathrooms have been redone with contemporary fittings and tiles; the more expensive doubles and both suites have Jacuzzi tubs. The east annex is less desirable with a timbered, sloping ceiling and no Internet. It's worth reserving at its gastronomic restaurant where you can enjoy duck breast with caramelized potatoes and turnips beside the fireplace or in summer, fish cooked in Riesling samosas on its canal-side terrace.

4–6 place des Six-Montagnes-Noires, Colmar 68000. 📞 **03-89-41-60-32.** www.hotel-le-marechal.com. 30 units. 115€–225€ double; 275€ suite. Parking 15€. **Amenities:** Restaurant; room service; entirely smoke-free; free Wi-Fi.

WHERE TO EAT

La Maison des Têtes ★ TRADITIONAL FRENCH   The beauty of this historic building will capture your eye, and the chef's exceptional skills will quickly entice your palate at one of the top restaurant-hotels in town. Set in a unique, centrally located 17th-century house, lunch here after visiting the Unterlinden Museum or stop in for a romantic dinner. The refined dining room is surrounded by aged-wood beams and paneling and lit by lovely Art Nouveau lighting fixtures; period stained glass finishes the elegant look. Dishes include homemade goose foie gras with Riesling, sea bass with pike mousse and Champagne sauce, and fillet of lamb with eggplant caviar. Paired with Alsatian wines, it's sheer culinary perfection. There are also 21 classically furnished rooms with minibars, safes, air-conditioning, and TVs; suites have Jacuzzis. Rates are 145€ to 168€ for a double, 198€ to 270€ for a suite.

In the Hôtel des Têtes, 19 rue des Têtes, Colmar 68000. 📞 **03-89-24-43-43.** www.la-maison-des-tetes.com. Main courses 19€–33€; fixed-price menu lunch 25€, dinner 38€–66€. Wed–Sun noon–2pm; Tues–Sat 7–9:30pm. Closed Feb.

Winstub Le Cygne ★★★ ALSATIAN   Hidden from the tourist masses down an obscure side street, this is a best *winstub* in town. Savor authentic Alsatian specialties in the cozy wood-paneled dining room bustling with locals. You might need to bring your Alsatian dictionary to decipher the excellent value menu items such as fleischschnackas (regional pot-au-feu soup), jambonneau à l'ancienne (leg of pork), and lawerknaepfla (quenelle dumplings of various meats). For the less courageous, they prepare a variety of reliable and tasty flammekueche tarts. To complete your experience, order a portion of Muster or Roquefort cheese. The kitchen is open until midnight.

17 rue Edouard Richard, Colmar 68000. ✆ **03-89-23-76-26.** www.winstublecygne.fr. Main courses 12€–20€ Sun–Fri noon–2pm; Tues–Sat 7pm–midnight.

WHERE TO EAT & STAY NEARBY

Die-hard gourmets flock to **Illhaeusern** to dine at the Auberge de l'Ill, one of the greatest restaurants in all of France. It's situated on a well-signposted route 18km (11 miles) from Colmar, east of the N83 highway,

Auberge de l'Ill ★★★ MODERN FRENCH   Alsatian cuisine is not all choucroute and pork, especially not at the region's best restaurant. The Haeberlin family opened their first *auberge* over a hundred years ago, gradually building up their reputation to obtain a first Michelin star in 1952 and 15 years later, their third. With incredible finesse and foreign flares, Chef Marc Haeberlin transforms Alsatian traditions into *la grande cuisine*. His exquisite creations vary from sautéed bass and Beluga black lentil makis with lime emulsion to caramelized veal sweetbreads in a chestnut crust with malt, foie gras and leak ravioli, in addition to the local filet of roebuck with mango compote and bubespitzle (German-style "gnocchi"). Some dishes may require 24 hours' notice, so check when you make reservations.

To enjoy your meal without having the worry of driving back into town, stay at their **Hôtel des Berges.** It has 13 rustic but regal rooms overlooking the Ill River. The rates are 300€ to 350€ for a double, 400€ to 550€ for a suite, and 500€ for a decade-old cottage on the grounds.

Rue de Collonges, Illhaeusern 68970. ✆ **03-89-71-89-00.** www.auberge-de-l-ill.com. Main courses 42€–172€; fixed-price menu lunch 129€, dinner 174€. Wed–Sun noon–2pm and 7–9pm. Closed 1st week of Jan and mid-Feb to mid-Mar.

EXPLORING COLMAR

Colmar is rich with historic houses, many half-timbered and, in summer, accented with geranium-draped window boxes. One of the most beautiful is **Maison Pfister,** 11 rue des Marchands, at the corner of rue Mercière, a 1537 building with wooden balconies. On the ground floor is a wine boutique, **Vinium** (see "Wineries," below). If you take pont St-Pierre over the Lauch River, you'll have an excellent view of Old Colmar and can explore **Petite Venise,** which is filled with canals.

Eglise des Dominicains ★ CHURCH   This church contains one of Colmar's most famous treasures: Martin Schongauer's painting *Virgin of the Rosebush,* or *Vierge au buisson de rose* (1473), all gold, red, and white, with fluttering birds. Look for it in the choir. At print time, the church was temporarily housing the **Issenheim Altarpiece** (see **Unterlinden Museum,** below); it will return to the museum in spring 2015.

Place des Dominicains. ✆ **03-89-24-46-57.** Admission until spring 2015 included in Unterlinden Museum ticket 8€ adults, 5€ students under 30 and children 12–17, free for children 11 and under. Afterwards, admission may return to 1.50€ adults, 1€ students, .50€ ages 12–16, free for children 11 and under. Apr–Dec daily 10am–1pm and 3–6pm.

Eglise St-Martin ★★ CHURCH   In the heart of Old Colmar is this Gothic collegiate church, considered the most beautiful in town. Begun in 1235, it was built on the site of former Carolingian and Romanesque churches. Its 70m (230 ft.) steeple beacons visitors from afar, whereas its spacious interior features soaring pointed arches, delicate medieval statuary and a choir erected by William of Marburg in 1350.

Place de la Cathédrale. ✆ **03-89-41-27-20.** Free admission. Daily 8am–6:30pm (until 7pm May–Oct). Closed to casual visitors during Mass and Sun mornings.

Musée Bartholdi ★ MUSEUM   American history buffs and New Yorkers should stop here to pay homage to Frédéric-Auguste Bartholdi, sculptor of the Statue of Liberty. This museum is located in the house where he was born in 1834. The display focuses on his masterpieces, especially the Statue of Liberty, with scale models, plans and documents linked to its construction. A reconstruction of Bartholdi's Paris apartment, with furniture and memorabilia, gives insight into the artist's life and inspirations. Also of note are rooms dedicated to paintings of Egypt Bartholdi amassed during his travels in 1856 and another with a fine collection of Jewish art.

30 rue des Marchands. ✆ **03-89-41-90-60.** www.musee-bartholdi.com. Admission 5€ adults, 2.50€ students and children 12–18, free for children 11 and under. Wed–Mon 10am–noon and 2–6pm. Closed Jan–Feb, May 1, Nov 1, and Christmas.

Musée d'Unterlinden (Under the Linden Trees) ★★★ MUSEUM Housed in a former Dominican convent, Alsace's most visited museum is a highlight of any trip to Colmar. The seat of Medieval and Renaissance Rhenish mysticism, it was converted into a museum in 1653 and features a remarkable collection of ecclesiastic treasures, archaeology finds, modern paintings, and decorative arts.

The main highlight is the 1516 **Issenheim Altarpiece (Le Retable d'Issenheim) ★★★**, by Würzburg-born Matthias Grünewald, "the most furious of realists." A masterpiece of the German Renaissance, this dramatic altar screen vividly illustrates the Crucifixion and the Incarnation, framed by the Annunciation and the Resurrection. The carved altar screen portrays the Temptation of St. Anthony; the amazingly detailed work also contains birds, monsters, and other ghastly animals (housed until spring 2015 in the **Eglise des Dominicains,** see above). Other gems include an altarpiece (dating from 1470) of Jean d'Orlier by Martin Schongauer, an extensive collection of religious woodcarvings and stained glass from the 14th to the 18th centuries, Gallo-Roman artifacts, armory from the Romanesque to the Renaissance, and paintings by the likes of Picasso and Nicolas de Staël.

In 2007 the city commenced an ambitious project to double the exhibition space to show off its modern and contemporary art collection. The expansion includes the neighboring former municipal baths, an Art Nouveau building, and a new structure designed by Swiss architects Herzog and de Meuron, The grand opening of these new spaces is scheduled for fall 2014.

1 rue d'Unterlinden. ✆ **03-89-20-15-58.** www.musee-unterlinden.com. Admission 8€ adults, 5€ students under 30 and children 12–17, free for children 11 and under. May–Oct daily 9am–6pm; Nov–Apr Wed–Mon 9am–noon and 2–5pm. Closed national holidays.

SHOPPING

The best shopping can be achieved in the old town of Colmar, particularly rue de Clefs, Grand' Rue, rue des Têtes, and rue des Marchands.

ANTIQUES   Antiques abound in Colmar and shops that deserve particular attention include **Geismar Dany,** 32 rue des Marchands (✆ **03-89-23-30-41**), specializing in antique painted furniture, and **Antiquités Guy Caffard,** 56 rue des Marchands (www.caffard-antiquites.com; ✆ **03-89-41-31-78**), with its mishmash of furniture, postcards, books, toys, bibelots, and the like. Also worth noting are **Lire & Chiner,** 36 rue des Marchands (www.lire-et-chiner.fr; ✆ **03-89-24-16-78**), and **Antiquité Arcana,** 13 place l'Ancienne Douane (✆ **03-89-41-59-81**).

WINERIES   Colmar being at the heart of the wine-producing Rhine country, local wine is one of the best purchases you can make here. If you don't have time to visit the vineyards along the Wine Road, stop in **Vinium** in **la Maison Pfister,** 11 rue des Marchands (www.vinum.pro; ✆ **03-89-41-33-61**), owned by a major Alsace winegrower, **Muré,** proprietor of the vineyard Clos St-Landelin. A vast selection of wines and liqueurs from the region and the rest of France is stocked at the **Cave du Musée,** 11 rue Kléber (www.lacavedumusee.com; ✆ **03-89-23-85-29**).

You can drive to one of the most historic vineyards in Alsace-Lorraine. **Domaines Schlumberger** (www.domaines-schlumberger.com; ✆ **03-89-74-27-00**) lies 26km (16 miles) southwest of Colmar in Guebwiller. The cellars, established by the Schlumberger family in 1810, are an unusual combination of early-19th-century brickwork and modern stainless steel. These grapes become such famous wines as Rieslings, Gewürztraminers, muscats, sylvaners, and pinots (blanc, gris, and noir). Views of the vineyards and tasting rooms are available without an appointment, but group tours of the cellars are conducted only when a staff member is available, so call before you go. The vineyard is only open to tastings Monday to Thursday 8am to 6pm and to 5pm on Fridays. They are also closed 2 weeks in August and the end of December (varies each year—call for details).

La Route Des Cretes ★★

From Basel, Switzerland, to Mainz, Germany, a distance of some 242km (150 miles), the Vosges Mountains stretch along the west side of the Rhine Valley, bearing a similarity to the Black Forest of Germany. Many German and French families spend their summer vacation exploring the Vosges. Travelers with less time may want to settle for a quick look at the ancient mountains that once formed the boundary between France and Germany. They are filled with tall hardwood and fir trees, and a network of twisting roads with hairpin curves traverses them. The depths of the mountain forests are the closest France comes to wilderness.

EXPLORING THE AREA

You can explore the mountains by heading west from Strasbourg, but there's a more interesting route from Colmar. La Route des Crêtes (Crest Road) begins at **Col du Bonhomme,** west of Colmar. The French High Command created it during World War I to carry supplies over the mountains. From Col du Bonhomme, you can strike out on this magnificent road, once the object of bitter fighting but today a series of panoramic vistas, including one of the Black Forest.

By **Col de la Schlucht,** 62km (38 miles) west of Colmar, you'll have climbed 1,472m (4,828 ft.). Schlucht is a summer and winter resort and one of the most beautiful spots in the Vosges, with a panoramic view of the Valley of Münster and the slopes of Hohneck. As you skirt the edge of this glacier-carved valley, you'll be in the midst of a land of pine groves with a necklace of lakes. You may want to turn off the main road and go exploring in several directions; the scenery is that tempting. But if you're still on the Crest Road, you can circle **Hohneck,** one of the highest peaks, at 1,590m (5,215 ft.), dominating the Wildenstein Dam of the Bresse winter-sports station.

At **Markstein,** you'll come to another resort. From here, take N430 and then D10 to **Münster,** where the savory cheese is made. You'll go via the Petit-Ballon, a landscape of forest and mountain meadows with grazing cows. Finally, **Grand-Ballon,** at 1,400m (4,592 ft.), is the highest point you can reach by car in the Vosges. Get out of your car and go for a walk; if it's a clear day, you'll be able to see the Jura, with the French Alps beyond.

Nancy ★★★

370km (229 miles) E of Paris; 148km (92 miles) W of Strasbourg

Nancy, in France's northeast corner, was the capital of old Lorraine. The city was built around a fortified castle on a rock in the swampland near the Meurthe River. A canal a few blocks east of the historic center connects the Marne to the Rhine.

The city is serenely beautiful, with a history, cuisine, and architecture all its own. It once rivaled Paris as the center for the design and production of Art Nouveau. Nancy has three faces: the medieval alleys and towers around the old Palais Ducal where Charles II received Joan of Arc, the rococo golden gates and fountains, and colorful Art Nouveau architecture from the turn-of-the-20th-century heyday of the Ecole de Nancy.

With a population of more than 100,000, Nancy remains the hub of commerce and politics in Lorraine. Home to a large university, it's a center of mining, engineering, metallurgy, and finance. Its 30,000 students, who have a passion for *le cool jazz,* keep Nancy jumping at night.

ESSENTIALS

ARRIVING The fast **TGV train** from Paris's Gare de l'Est arrives in Nancy after just 90 minutes, making the city a virtual commute from Paris. Many Parisians now visit for *le weekend.* The one-way fare ranges between 48€ and 80€. Trains from Strasbourg arrive in Nancy every hour, a one-way fare costing 25€. For

Place Stanislas in historical center of Nancy, a UNESCO World Heritage Site

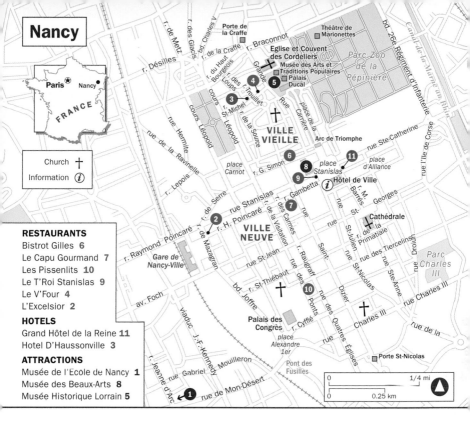

information and schedules, call ✆ **36-35,** or 08-92-35-35-35 from outside France. If you're **driving** to Nancy from Paris, follow N4 east (trip time: 4 hr.).

VISITOR INFORMATION   The **Office de Tourisme** is at place Stanislas (www. ot-nancy.fr; ✆ **03-83-35-22-41**).

PASSE-MUSÉE   This combination ticket gives access to six museums in town, all for a net price of 10€ per person (another 16€ also includes a 24-hour transit pass, an audioguide for the city, and other discounts). Included in the pass is access to the Musée de l'Ecole de Nancy, the Musée des Beaux-Arts, and the Musée Historique Lorraine (which is also known as the Musée des Arts et Traditions Populaires). Ask about the ticket at the tourist office or any participating museum.

SPECIAL EVENTS   Serious jazz lovers come to town for 2 weeks in October to attend **Jazz Pulsations** (www.nancyjazzpulsations.com; ✆ **03-83-35-40-86**). Some kind of performance takes place every night around sundown in a tent in the Parc de la Pépinière, a very short walk from the place Stanislas. Some performances are free, others charge varying rates from 10€ to 35€.

GETTING AROUND

ON FOOT   The train station is a 10-minute walk to the heart of the city and many main sites are within walking distance.

BY BICYCLE You can rent bikes from **VelOstan,** at the Nancy station in the Thiers entrance (www.grand-nancy.org/velostanboutic; ✆ **06-08-05-16-43**). Their reasonable rates are 2€ half-day and 3€ full day.

BY CAR You can park your car right at the station or south of Place Stanislas at the **Vinci Parking,** 6 rue Claude Charles. Car rentals can be found at the train station at **Avis** (www.avis.fr; ✆ **08-20-61-17-03**), or just outside the station at **Europcar,** (www.europcar.fr; ✆ **08-25-35-83-58**).

BY TAXI There are always taxis outside the train station and some circulating around. You can order one in advance from **Nancy Taxis** (www.taxis-nancy.com; ✆ **03-83-37-65-37**).

BY PUBLIC TRANSPORT Nancy has a well-serviced bus and tram system called the **Reseau Stan** (www.reseau-stan.com; ✆ **03-83-30-08-08**). A one-way ticket costs 1.50€ and can be purchased from automatic kiosks at a tram station or from a bus driver.

[Fast FACTS] NANCY

ATMs/Banks The city center has scores of ATMs, several are along rue Saint-Jean or Saint-Dizier.

Doctors & Hospitals **Hopital Central de Nancy,** 29 avenue du Maréchal de Lattre de Tassigny (www.chu-nancy.fr; ✆ **03-83-85-85-85**).

Mail & Postage **La Poste,** 10 rue Saint-Dizier (✆ **36-31**).

Pharmacies **Pharmacie du Point Central,** 35 rue Saint-Dizier (✆ **03-83-32-08-57**).

WHERE TO STAY

Grand Hôtel de la Reine ★★ Right on place Stanislas, a royal stay is assured at Nancy's grandest hotel. Constructed along with the harmonious square in the mid-18th century, it was formerly a splendid private mansion. While the rooms might be a little dated, they are regally appointed in Louis XV–style furniture and drapery with Venetian chandeliers and gilt-framed mirrors. All guestrooms have spacious bathrooms with tub/showers. Your noble experience is complete with a room facing the square; however, they come at a princely supplement. There is a comfortable bar with leather sofas, a lounge hung with portraits of local aristocrats, and an elegant restaurant serving classic and modern dishes.

2 place Stanislas, Nancy 54000. ✆ **800/777-4182** in the U.S. and Canada, or 03-83-35-03-01. www.hoteldelareine.com. 43 units. 107€–220€ double; 300€ suite. **Amenities:** Restaurant; bar; babysitting; room service; free Wi-Fi.

Hotel D'Haussonville ★★ Set in a 15th-century classified historic mansion, this is a special find in the elegant former capital of the Duchy of Lorraine. Close to the beautiful Eglise Saint Epvre, the townhouse has a unique gothic balcony and a Renaissance balustrade. The wings surround a quaint courtyard adorned with flowers and a fountain. Each of the seven suites has its own international theme. Most have high ceilings, luxurious bathrooms, and the best have views of the church.

9 rue Mgr. Trouillet, Nancy 54000. ✆ **03-83-35-85-84.** www.hotel-haussonville.fr. 7 units. 140€–230€ double. Closed most of Aug and first 2 weeks of Jan. **Amenities:** Breakfast room.

WHERE TO EAT

For a light lunch or snack near place Stanislas, stop in at **Le T'Roi Stanislas,** 3 rue Stanislas (☏ **03-83-28-07-70**). Open non-stop 10am to 8pm and until midnight in summers, it serves the local specialty quiche Lorraine (the egg, ham, and cheese tart), crepes, salads and a variety of beverages including their creative DIY "choco-cho" hot chocolates in 10 different flavors.

A range of restaurants line rue des Maréchaux, nicknamed Gourmet Street. The best for inventive cuisine is **Bistrot Gilles** at no. 31 (http://lebistrotdegilles.e-monsite.com; ☏ **03-83-35-43-73**). For great market-base cuisine try the tiny **Le V'Four,** 10 rue St-Michel (www.levfour.fr; ☏ **03-83-32-49-48**), where you can get a special fixed-price lunch for 1€ and dinner from 31€ to 67€.

You might end your day of sightseeing by calling at the century-old brasserie **L'Excelsior,** 50 rue Henri Poincare (www.brasserie-excelsior.com; ☏ **03-83-35-24-57**), which is an amazing period piece from 1911 with stained-glass windows and polished brass chandeliers. Just a block from the rail station, it serves Lorraine specialties with fresh oysters, a delight in season.

Le Capu Gourmand ★★ MODERN FRENCH   The perfect mix of Nancy's classicism and artistic pizzazz is found in dishes of this leading restaurant located a mere 5-minute walk from place Stanislas. The dining room has sophisticated furnishings with tones of gray. The menu adds rebellious twists to traditional dishes such as foie gras flavored with black chocolate, tartare of salmon with Gewurztraminer jelly, red mullet on a salad of Granny Smith apples, pistachios drizzled with balsamic vinaigrette or the roasted pineapple with acacia honey and lavender cream.

31 rue Gambetta. ☏ **03-83-35-26-98.** www.lecapu.com. Main courses 30€–40€; fixed-price menu weekday lunches 25€, dinner 34€–62€. Tues–Fri and Sun noon–2pm; Tues–Sat 7:30–10pm.

Les Pissenlits (The Dandelions) ★ TRADITIONAL FRENCH   This cozy little brasserie is a gem on Nancy's dining scene. The dining room is instantly welcoming with Nancy-made Art Nouveau antiques. Local traditions carry over onto Chef Jean-Luc Mengin's economical menu with such specialties as dandelion salad with fried bacon and creamy meurotte vinaigrette, veal kidneys following Grandma's recipe served with homemade späetzle noodles and matelote of freshwater zander with shallots cooked with local gris de Toule wine. Consult Danièle, the chef's wife, for your accompanying wine; she's one of the few accredited female wine stewards in France. They also run the wine bar and cellar next door, **Vins et Tartines** (www.vins-et-tartines.com).

27 bis rue des Ponts. ☏ **03-83-37-43-97.** www.les-pissenlits.com. Main courses 13€–20€; fixed-price menu 22€–40€. Tues–Sat 11:45am–2:30pm and 7:15–10:30pm.

EXPLORING NANCY

The most monumental square in eastern France, and the heart of Nancy, is **place Stanislas ★★★**, named for Stanislas Leszczynski, the last of the ducs de Lorraine, ex-king of Poland, and father-in-law of Louis XV. His 18th-century building programs transformed Nancy into one of Europe's most palatial cities. The square stands between Nancy's two most notable neighborhoods: the **Ville Vieille** (old town), in the medieval core, centered on the cathedral, Grande Rue, and the labyrinth of narrow meandering streets that funnel into it; and the **Ville Neuve,** in the southwest. Built in the 16th and 17th centuries, when streets were laid out in straight lines, Ville Neuve centers on rue St-Jean.

Place Stanislas was laid out from 1752 to 1760 according to the designs of Emmanuel Héré. Its ironwork gates are magnificent. The square is fabled for the brilliant and fanciful railings, the work of Jean Lamour. His gilded railings with flowery decorations and crests evoke Versailles. The entire plaza is an all-pedestrian zone.

The **Arc de Triomphe,** constructed by Stanislas from 1754 to 1756 to honor Louis XV, adjoins the place de la Carrière, a tree-lined promenade leading to the 1760 **Palais du Gouvernement.** This governmental palace adjoins the **Palais Ducal,** built in 1502 in the Gothic style with Flamboyant Gothic balconies.

Musée des Beaux-Arts ★★ MUSEUM   Housed in an 18th-century building on place Stanislas, this outstanding regional museum dates back to the Revolution, its collection built on local bequeaths such as Mme Henri Galilée's donation of 117 modern works from Bonnard to Modigliani. On display is a remarkable Manet portrait of the wife of Napoleon III's dentist. Other highlights are by Tintoretto, Caravaggio, Rubens, and Delacroix.

3 place Stanislas. ✆ **03-83-85-30-72.** http://mban.nancy.fr. Admission 6€ adults, 4€ students 12–25, free for children 11 and under and for all first Sun of the month. Wed–Mon 10am–6pm.

Musée de l'Ecole de Nancy ★★ MUSEUM   In a building from the époque is a fascinating museum on the city's famous Art Nouveau movement. It features glasswork, furniture, and ceramics from the school's leading artists. Highlights include Emile Gallé's "Dawn and Dusk" bed, and "Mushroom Lamp," Eugène Vallin's oak entrance door and dining room set. Afterwards, amble through the garden in search of the intriguing stained-glass "aquarium" pavilion.

36–38 rue Sergent-Blandan. ✆ **03-83-40-14-86.** www.ecole-de-nancy.com. Admission 6€ adults, 4€ students, free for children 17 and under. Free for students on Wed. Wed–Sun 10am–6pm.

Musée Historique Lorrain ★★★ MUSEUM   The art and history of the Lorraine region from ancient times is showcased in this museum set in the former Ducal Palace and the Cordeliers convent. The collection presents a chronological overview from Gallo-Roman artifacts to portraits of the regional aristocracy. The engravings of local artist Jacques Callot include a famous yet dark series on "the Miseries and Misfortunes of War" (a later inspiration for Goya). There are also works by his contemporaries Jacques Bellange, Georges de la Tour, and Claude Deruet.

The exhibit continues next door in the Flamboyant Gothic **Eglise des Cordeliers ★**, the burial site of the dukes of Lorraine. The most remarkable burial monuments are those of René II (1509; attributed to the sculptor Mansuy Gauvain) and a reclining statue of his second wife, Philippa of Gueldres, by Ligier Richier. The rest of the display tells the story of the daily life of the area's country folk with artwork, rooms from period homes, and farming equipment. The Ducal Palace section of the museum will be closed for renovation works from early 2015, but the Cordelier chapel and convent section will remain open.

In the Palais Ducal, 64 Grande-Rue. ✆ **03-83-32-18-74.** www1.nancy.fr. Admission 6€ adults, 4€ students and children 12–18, free for children 11 and under (combo ticket for Palais Ducal and Eglise des Cordeliers). Free for students first Sun of each month. Tues–Sun 10am–12:30pm and 2–6pm.

SHOPPING

The famous French *macaron* almond flour cookie is said to have been invented in Nancy by Benedictine nuns. Their original recipe is followed at **Maison des Soeurs Macarons,** 21 rue Gambetta (www.macaron-de-nancy.com; ✆ **03-83-32-24-25**). Another good place to acquire them in addition to another traditional

Nancy specialty, Bergamotte candies, is at the pretty shop **Lefèvre Lemoine,** 7 rue Henri Poincaré (☎ **03-83-30-13-83**).

Though larger and more expensive, Art Nouveau antiques also make excellent souvenirs of Nancy. Visit **Denis Rugat,** 13 rue Stanislas (☎ **03-83-35-20-79**), for the best pieces. It stocks Lalique crystal, brightly colored vases, and enameled boxes made with a technique known locally as *les émaux de Longwy,* plus an assortment of glass-shaded lamps.

You'll find more glass and crystal by **Daum,** at more reasonable prices than virtually anywhere else in France. The company's premier outlet is **Boutique Daum,** 14 place Stanislas (☎ **03-83-32-21-65**), where the most perfect specimens from the Daum factory are sold at prices that are usually about 30 percent less than what you'd pay in other glass galleries in France. Or for savings of 30 to 40 percent less than what's sold in the above-mentioned boutique, you can seek out Daum's factory outlet, **Magasin d'Usine Daum,** 17 rue Cristallerie (☎ **03-83-30-80-24**), a 5-minute walk from the place Stanislas, its pieces are slightly flawed.

NANCY NIGHTLIFE

As night approaches, most of the student population heads to the Old Town. Young *Nancéiens* start their night with a drink at **Le Pinnachio,** 9 Place Saint Epvre (☎ **03-83-35-55-95**); its terrace facing the Saint Epyre church is the best place to enjoy a pint or glass of chilled wine in summer.

Nancy's most popular dance club is **Les Caves du Roy,** 9 place Stanislas (☎ **03-83-35-24-14**), where a techno crowd flails around in a chrome-and-metallic space. It's open Tuesday to Thursday 11pm to 4am, Friday 11pm to 5am, and Saturday midnight to 6:15am.

The fashionable of Nancy dance the night away at the stylish **l'Etage discothèque** (www.letage-club.fr; ☎ **09-50-96-01-01**). Music varies per night with hip-hop, funk and Latino theme nights during the week, house and electro on weekends. There's usually no cover; its open Wednesday and Thursday 10pm to 4am and Friday and Saturday 10pm to 5am.

Domremy-La-Pucelle

443km (275 miles) SE of Paris; 10km (6¼ miles) NW of Neufchâteau

Most often visited on a day trip, Domrémy is a plain village that would have slumbered in obscurity, but for the fact that Joan of Arc was born here in 1412. Today it's a pilgrimage center attracting fans of the heroine from all over the world.

THE other CENTRE POMPIDOU

Since 2010 the vast collections of Paris's Centre Pompidou have been shared with its much-talked-about satellite in Metz, the capital city of Alsace's neighboring region, Lorraine. Located in a building more avant-garde than the art on the walls, you can peruse rotating masterpieces from the main museum's huge collection in addition to thematic temporary exhibits. Film screenings and guest lectures can extend your visit to a full day. Metz is a 30- to 35-minute train ride from Nancy; trains run every 20 minutes (11€ one-way). The **museum** is located at 1 parvis des Droits de l'Homme (www.centrepompidou-metz.fr; ☎ **03-87-15-39-39**; admission 7€–12€ adults (depending on the exhibit), free for seniors and children 26 and under). Open Mon and Wed to Fri 11am to 6pm, Sat 10am to 6pm, and Sun 10 to 6pm.

ESSENTIALS

ARRIVING   If you're **driving,** take N4 southeast of Paris to Toul, and then A31 south toward Neufchâteau/Charmes. Then take N74 southwest (signposted in the direction of Neufchâteau). At Neufchâteau, follow D164 northwest to Coussey. From there, take D53 into Domrémy.

There is no railway station in Domrémy—you must take one of four **trains** daily going to either Nancy or Toul, where you can make bus and rail connections to Neufchâteau, 9.5km (6 miles) away. You can also take a **taxi,** MBM Assistance 88 (*C* **03-29-06-12-13**), for about 100€ each way.

EXPLORING JOAN'S LEGACY

Her four-room family's house is known as **Maison Natale de Jeanne d'Arc,** 2 rue de la Basilique (*C* **03-29-06-95-86**). Here you can see the chamber where she was born. The **Centre Johannique,** a museum beside the house, illustrates the life and times of St. Joan. The house is open April to September Wednesday to Monday 10am to 6pm, and October to March Wednesday to Monday 10am to noon and 2 to 5pm. Admission is 3€ for adults, free for children 9 and under. The house is closed in January.

Adjacent to the museum, on rue Principale, is **Eglise St-Rémi;** repairs and partial reconstructions from the 19th century have masked its 12th-century origins. All that remains from the age of Joan of Arc are a baptismal font and some stonework. On a slope of the Bois-Chenu 1.5km (1 mile) uphill from the village is a monument steeped in French nationalism, the **Basilique du Bois-Chenu,** built on the spot Joan is said to have heard the voices. Made of local Vosges pink granite, and decorated with mosaic and monumental statues celebrating the saint, it was begun in 1881 and consecrated in 1926. To reach it, follow signs from the center and along rue de la Basilique.

Verdun ★★

261km (162 miles) E of Paris; 66km (41 miles) W of Metz

Built on both banks of the Meuse and intersected by a series of canals, Verdun has an old section, the Ville Haute, on the east bank, which includes the cathedral and Episcopal palace. Today stone houses on narrow cobblestone streets give Verdun a medieval appearance. However, most visitors come to see the famous World War I battlefields, 3km (1¾ miles) east of the town, off N3 toward Metz. With the centennial anniversary of the Great War from 2014–18, many special events and exhibits will be commemorating this at the various sites throughout the region.

Verdun Memorial Museum, built on the site of the 1916 battle

ESSENTIALS

ARRIVING   Two **trains** arrive daily from Paris's Gare de l'Est; you'll have to change at Châlons-en-Champagne. Several daily trains also arrive from Metz, after a change at Conflans. The one-way fare from Paris is 33€ to 40€; from Metz, it's 13€.

ALSACE-LORRAINE FOR kids

One of the best family sites in the region is the **Ecomuseum in Ungersheim** between Colmar and Mulhouse (www.ecomusee-alsace.fr; ✆ **03-89-62-43-00**). It's a reconstructed turn-of-the-20th-century Alsatian village of 73 buildings, including houses, farms and traditional artisanal workshops. Kids can watch a potter at work, learn about beekeeping, poke their head into a schoolroom or take a ride on a horse-drawn cart. Entrance is 14€ adults, 9.50€ children 4 to 14, free 3 and under. Open daily 10am to 6pm April, May, September and October; and daily 10am to 7pm June through August and December to early January.

The Vosges mountains have plenty of activities for outdoor adventurers, especially the **Parc Ballon** (mentioned above in "La Route des Cretes"). If hiking or biking is not for you, take a ride on the historic **Abreschviller train,** 2 Place Norbert Prévot, Abreschviller (train-abreschviller.fr; ✆ **03-87-03-71-45**). Started in 1884 for logging, today old-fashioned steam or diesel trains take visitors on a 6km (4-mile) circuit around the area. The round-trip journey takes 90 minutes. It runs in April and October on Wednesday, Sunday and holidays at 3pm, and more frequently May to September; check website for timetable. Tickets are 7€ adult one-way and 11€ round-trip, for children it's 5€ and 8.50€ respectively.

For a family break in Lorraine, stop in at the **Muséum-Aquarium de Nancy,** 34 rue Sainte-Catherine (www.museum aquariumdenancy.eu; ✆ **03-83-32-99-97**) with 57 aquariums and a display of 600 preserved animal and archaeological specimens. Open daily 10am to noon and 2 to 6pm. Admission is 4.20€ adults; 2.20€ seniors, students and children 12–17; free children 11 and under and all visitors the first Sunday of the month.

For train information and schedules, call ✆ **36-35** or 08-92-35-35-35. **Driving** is easy; Verdun is several miles north of the Paris-Strasbourg autoroute (A4).

VISITOR INFORMATION The **Office de Tourisme** is on place de la Nation (www.verdun-tourisme.com; ✆ **03-29-84-14-18**). It's closed on bank holidays.

TOURING THE BATTLEFIELDS

At this garrison town in eastern France, Marshal Pétain proclaimed, "They shall not pass!" And they didn't. Verdun is where the Allies held out against a massive assault by the German army in World War I. Near the end of the war, 600,000 to 800,000 French and German soldiers died battling over a few miles along the muddy Meuse between Paris and the Rhine. Two monuments commemorate these tragic events: Rodin's *Defense* and Boucher's *To Victory and the Dead.*

The local tourist office provides maps for two tours of the brutal and bloody battlefields that helped define World War I. The "Circuit Champs de Bataille Rive Droite" encompasses the better-known battlegrounds on the River Meuse's right bank. It's a 4-hour, 32km (20-mile) route, and takes in **Fort Vaux,** where Raynal staged a heroic defense after sending his last message by carrier pigeon.

After passing a **French cemetery** of 16,000 graves—an endless field of crosses—you arrive at the **Ossuaire de Douaumont** (www.verdun-douaumont. com, ✆ **03-29-84-54-81**), where the bones of those blown to bits were embedded. Nearby, at the **Fort de Douaumont,** the "hell of Verdun" was unleashed. From the roof, you can look out at a vast field of corroded tops of "pillboxes."

Then you proceed to the **Tranchée des Baïonettes (Trench of Bayonets).** Bayonets of French soldiers entombed by a shell seemingly burst forth from this unique memorial.

Within a few paces of the Tranchée des Baïonettes, you'll see the **Mémorial de Verdun** (built around 1967), Fleury Devant Douaumont (www.memorial-de-verdun.fr; ✆ **03-29-84-35-34**). The museum dis-

Douaumont Ossuary

plays weapons, uniforms, photographs, and geography of one of the bloodiest battles of World War I (currently closed for enlargement works, it will reopen in late 2015).

The second self-guided tour, known as **"Circuit Champs de Bataille Rive Gauche"** (or "Circuit de l'Argonne"), also requires about 4 hours, and during its 97km (60 miles), it focuses on mostly outdoor sites. It takes in the **Butte de Montfaucon,** a hill on which Americans erected a memorial tower, and the moving **Cimetière Américain at Romagne** (www.abmc.gov/cemeteries), the largest American cemetery in Europe with over 14,000 graves. Because public transportation is inadequate, only visitors with cars should attempt to make these circuits. The British Battlefield Tours Research Society offers group and private tours of the area (www.battlefieldtours.co.uk; ✆ **+44-1-21-430-5348**).

THE FRENCH ALPS

No part of France has more dramatic scenery than the Alps; the western ramparts of the mountains and their foothills are truly majestic. From the Mediterranean to the Rhine, they stretch along the southeastern flank of France. The skiing here is the best in Europe. From January to March, skiers flock to resorts like Courchevel, Megève, Val d'Isère, and **Chamonix–Mont Blanc,** the capital of Alpine skiing, with its 19km (12-mile) Vallée Blanche run. Mont Blanc, at 4,810m (15,777 ft.), is the highest mountain in Western Europe. From July to September, spa fans head to Evian-les-Bains, culture lovers to charming Annecy, and anyone will enjoy a boat cruise on the scenic Lake Léman (Lake Geneva).

Evian-les-Bains ★★★

576km (357 miles) SW of Paris; 42km (26 miles) NE of Geneva

On the château-dotted southern shore of Lac Léman, Evian-les-Bains is one of the leading spa resorts in France. Its lakeside promenade, lined with trees and lawns, has been fashionable since the 19th century. Evian's waters became famous in the 18th century, and the first spa buildings were built in 1839. In the days when Marcel Proust came to enjoy the Belle Epoque grandeur, Evian was the haunt of the very rich. Proust modeled his "Balbec baths" on Evian's. Today the spa, with its promenade and elegant casino, attracts a broader range of guests—it's not just for the rich anymore.

ESSENTIALS

ARRIVING   The best way to approach Evian-les-Bains by **train** from the French Alps is from the gateway city of Annecy. (Many trains from other parts of France and Switzerland require transfers to the railway junction of Bellegarde.) The one-way fare from Annecy is 17€. For train information and schedules, call ✆ **36-35** or 08-92-35-35-35.

The French Alps

Popular **ferries (CGN)** leave Geneva from quai du Mont-Blanc, at the foot of the rue des Alpes, or from Le Jardin Anglais. From May 28 to September 21, a first-class, one-way ticket costs 64€, a second-class ticket 46€. For ferry information and schedules, visit www.cgn.ch or call ✆ **+41 848/811-848** or 04-50-70-73-20.

VISITOR INFORMATION   The **Office de Tourisme** is on place d'Allinges (www.eviantourism.com; ✆ **04-50-75-04-26**).

WHERE TO EAT & STAY

Hôtel-Restaurant Le Bourgogne ★ TRADITIONAL FRENCH   Come here for a delicious meal without breaking the bank, plus the beautiful view is free. The restaurant's reliable menu may include homemade foie gras and mango ceviche, fillet of Fera straight from Leman Lake with emulsion of arugula, or filet of beef with cream of morel mushrooms. Your dinner will go down better with some regional wines such as Crépy and Rousette. The inn also offers 30 comfortable, simply decorated rooms with TVs for 87€ to 92€ double and has a Jacuzzi and spa.

73 rue Nationale, Evian-les-Bains 74500. ✆ **04-50-75-01-05.** www.hotel-le-bourgogne-evian-les-bains.com. Main courses 20€–25€; fixed-price menu 16.50€–45€. Tues–Sun noon–2pm; Tues–Sat 7–10pm. Closed Jan.

Hôtel de la Verniaz ★★★   The essence of Haute-Savoie exudes at this charming country house. Situated on a hillside with a view of woods, lake and mountains, the main building is covered in flowers. The individual chalets have their own gardens and more privacy, but come at a high cost. All guestrooms are refined, with classical furnishings and antiques; some have fireplaces. The restaurant's creative menu could include supreme of farm-raised chicken or filet of Simmental beef cooked in malt beer; main courses run from 28€ to 38€; fixed-price menus are 38€ to 85€.

Avenue D'Abondance, à Neuvecelle Eglise, Evian-les-Bains 74500. ✆ **800/735-2478** in the U.S. and Canada, or **04-50-75-04-90.** www.verniaz.com. 36 units. 125€–235€ double; 270€–460€ suite; 255€–505€ chalet. Closed mid-Nov to mid-Mar. **Amenities:** Restaurant; bar; babysitting; outdoor pool; room service; 2 tennis courts; free Wi-Fi.

TAKING THE WATERS AT EVIAN

The clear, cold waters at Evian, legendary for their health and beauty benefits, attract a clientele with both the time and the money to appreciate them. The most luxurious way to immerse yourself in the resort's hydro-rituals is to check into either of these hotels, both of which maintain private spa facilities open only to well-heeled guests: **Hôtel Royal,** boulevard de Royal, or **Hôtel Ermitage,** avenue du Léman (contact for both: www.royalparcevian.com or ✆ **04-50-26-85-00**). They offer expensive packages perfect for pampering patrons' bodies, souls, and egos.

More reasonably priced are the spa facilities at **Les Thermes Evian,** place de la Libération (www.lesthermesevian.com; ✆ **04-50-75-02-30**). This public spa is adjacent to Débarcadère (the dock), just uphill from the edge of the lake. The hotel spas are more likely to emphasize beauty regimens and stress therapies; the public facility offers a broader range of services, including tanning, massage, and skin and beauty care (but no facilities for overnight guests). Depending on the program you select, you will spend 20€ to 220€. The spa is open Monday to Saturday, usually from 9am to 8pm.

Annecy ★★★

538km (334 miles) SE of Paris; 56km (35 miles) SE of Geneva; 140km (87 miles) E of Lyon

Lac d'Annecy is the jewel of the Savoy Alps. The regional capital Annecy makes the best base for touring the Haute-Savoie. Once a Gallo-Roman town, the seat of the Comtes de Genève, Annecy opens onto one of the best views of lakes and mountains in the French Alps. Since the 1980s, Annecy has become a booming urban center that has managed to preserve its natural setting. In summer, its lakefront promenade is crowded and active.

A summer day on Annecy Lake

ESSENTIALS

ARRIVING   A car is useful but not essential in the Alps. Annecy has rail links with Paris and Lyon. Nine **trains** arrive daily from Lyon (trip time: 5 hr.), with a one-way fare from 25€ to 36€. About six trains daily arrive from Paris's Gare de Lyon (around 5 hr., transfer at Lyon or Bellegarde); the fare starts at 35€ to 96€ one-way. For information, call ✆ **36-35.**

VISITOR INFORMATION   The **Office de Tourisme** is at 1 rue Jean-Jaurès (www.lac-annecy.com; ✆ **04-50-45-00-33**).

WHERE TO EAT & STAY

Le Belvédère ★ FRENCH/SEAFOOD   You can't beat the amazing views and the excellent value gourmet cuisine at this cozy restaurant. On a belvedere lookout above Annecy, you will be enthralled by the spectacular views over mountains and lakes. Chef Vincent Lugrin has earned one Michelin star with his varied menu. Try his signature foie gras with a fig compote and vanilla-flavored bourbon sauce or tempt your palate with the truffle and potato millefeuille or freshly caught Lake Annecy Féra with carrots and lemon zest. You might want to finish with a selection of cheeses from the local Crèmerie du Lac or the irresistible extra dark Guayaquil chocolate lava cake.

They rent 10 recently revamped rooms, each with a contemporary look and fitted with designer furnishings. Rooms go for 135€ to 200€ double.

7 chemin du Belvédère, Annecy 7400. ✆ **04-50-45-04-90.** www.belvedere-annecy.com. Reservations recommended. Main courses 16€–40€; fixed-price menus 32€ lunch, 42€–105€ dinner. Thurs–Tues 12:15–1:30pm; Mon and Thurs–Sat 7:30–9:30pm. Closed Jan. From downtown Annecy, follow signs leading uphill to Le Semnoz.

WHERE TO EAT & STAY NEARBY

The original Maison de Marc Veyrat on Lac d'Annecy is now run by his former student Yoann Conte (**www.yoann-conte.com**).

La Maison de Bois Marc Veyrat ★★★ MODERN FRENCH   World famous Marc Veyrat is back on the scene, inviting true gastronomes into his chalet-home 45 minutes up the mountain from Annecy. In 2009, health problems forced him to throw in his apron and his six—six!—Michelin stars. He couldn't stay out of the kitchen for long, but this time he's left behind pompous etiquette and gone back to his roots. Veyrat actually lives at the cozy wooden chalet and throughout the meal he takes the time to interact with guests like a real host, offering an unparalleled culinary experience. After a morning of forest foraging, the evening menu might feature "virtual" foie gras yogurt with wild fool's-watercress, clay-cooked egg with wood sorrel, freshly caught frogs' legs with fern aroma or veal tendon baked for 12 hours.

For the complete experience stay in one of their classy yet rustic rooms or the chalet. Their four rooms start at 690€ and 900€ for the chalet.

Col de la Croix-Fry, 74230 Manigod. ✆ **04-50-60-00-00.** www.marcveyrat.fr. Fixed-price lunch and dinner 145€ and 345€. Some closures in mid-spring and fall.

SEEING THE SIGHTS

Built around the river Thiou, Annecy has been called the Venice of the Alps because of the canals that cut to the old part of town, **Vieil Annecy.** You can explore the arcaded streets where Jean-Jacques Rousseau arrived in 1728.

You can also take a cruise on the ice-blue lake for which the town is famous. Tours of **Lac d'Annecy,** conducted from February to December, last an hour and cost 14€ adults and 9.50€ children 5 to 15, free for children under 4. An English-speaking guide points out the sights. Tours depart between one and six times a day, depending on the season. Inquire at the Office de Tourisme (see above), or call the **Compagnie des Bateaux du Lac d'Annecy** (www.annecy-croisieres. com; ✆ **04-50-51-08-40**).

Château de Montrottier ★★ CASTLE   Within walking distance of the gorges, in the hamlet of Montrottier, is the 13th- and 14th-century Château de Montrottier. A one-time feudal citadel partially protected by the rugged geology around it, the château's tower offers a panoramic view of Mont Blanc. A small museum features items collected by a local dilettante, showcasing pottery, Asian and African costumes, armor, tapestries, and lace antiques, as well as some bronze bas-reliefs from the 16th century.

Lovagny 74330. ✆ **04-50-46-23-02.** www.chateaudemontrottier.com. Admission 8€ adults, 6.50€ students, 5€ children 7–15, free for children 6 and under. Mar 15–May 31 Wed–Mon 2–6pm; June–Aug daily 2–7pm; Sept Wed–Mon 2–6pm; Oct daily 2–6pm.

Musée Château d'Annecy ★ MUSEUM   You cannot miss spotting the Queen's Tower, a foreboding gray-stone 12th-century pinnacle dominating the town. It's home to a museum of regional artifacts such as Alpine furniture, religious art, oil paintings, and modern works. There is also a display on geology and marine life of the region's deep, cold lakes.

Place du Château. ✆ **04-50-33-87-30.** http://musees.agglo-annecy.fr. Admission 5.20€ adults, 3.70€ ages 12–25, free for children 11 and under. June–Sept daily 10:30am–6pm; Oct–May Wed–Mon 10am–noon and 2–5pm.

Le Palais de l'Ile ★ PALACE   This is the town's most potent and most frequently photographed visual symbol. Built before the 18th century and connected to the "mainland" of Annecy via a bridge, it resembles a miniature château, surrounded by water, despite its long-term use as a prison (and certainly a very cold one) for local malefactors.

3 passage de l'Ile. ✆ **04-50-33-87-30.** http://musees.agglo-annecy.fr. Admission 3.70€ adults, 2.60€ students and persons 12–25, free for children 11 and under. June–Sept daily 10:30am–6pm; Oct–May Wed–Mon 10am–noon and 2–5pm.

Alpine Resorts ★★★

Popularized in the 1920s, especially by the 1924 Winter Olympics, the resorts of the French Alps offer some of the best skiing in Europe. There are now dozens of resorts providing year-round activities in addition to the over 1,000 ski slopes. Snowshoeing, hiking, biking, rock climbing or visual thrills can be had by rising in the Chamonix cable car or by cruising along the Route des Grandes Alpes from Lake Geneva to the Riviera.

CHAMONIX–MONT BLANC ★★★

At an altitude of 1,027m (3,369 ft.), Chamonix is the historic capital of Alpine skiing. This is the resort to choose if you're not a millionaire. Site of the first Winter Olympic Games in 1924, Chamonix is in a valley almost at the junction of France, Italy, and Switzerland. Skiers the world over know its 20km (12-mile) **Vallée Blanche run,** one of the most rugged, and the longest, in Europe. With exceptional equipment—gondolas, cable cars, and chairlifts—Chamonix is among Europe's major sports resorts, attracting an international crowd with lots of English and Swedish skiers. An old-fashioned mountain town, Chamonix has

SEEING THE AREA by cable car

An alternative way to experience the mountains without zooming down the slopes is via the Chamonix cable car. It offers a series of heart-leaping journeys venturing higher and higher up the mountain peaks, reaching an altitude of 3,781m (12,402 ft.). It's well worth the harrowing trip for the incredible views of Mont Blanc, the aiguilles of Chamonix and Vallée Blanche, the largest glacier in Europe (15km/9¼ miles long and 6km/3¾ miles wide), and of the Jura and the French, Swiss, and Italian Alps. The Aiguille de Midi stop now offers a thrilling "Step into the Void" glassed-in lookout to truly feel encompassed by the mountains. The cable cars operate year-round: in summer daily 7am to 5pm, leaving at least every 10 minutes, and in winter daily 8:30am to 3:30pm, leaving every 10 minutes. The first stage, to Plan de L'Aiguille, costs 14€ round-trip. The complete round-trip from Chamonix to Aiguille du Midi goes for 55€. For information, contact **Compagnie du Mont-Blanc,** 35 place de la Mer de Glace (www.compagniedumontblanc.fr; ✆ **04-50-53-22-75**).

a breathtaking backdrop, **Mont Blanc ★★★**, Western Europe's highest mountain, at 4,734m (15,528 ft.).

Chamonix's **Office de Tourisme** is on place du Triangle-de-l'Amitié (www.chamonix.com; ✆ **04-50-53-00-24**).

COURCHEVEL 1850 ★★

Courchevel has been called a resort of "high taste, high fashion, and high profile," a chic spot where multimillion-dollar chalets sit on pristine pine-covered slopes. Skiers and geographers know it as part of Les Trois Vallées, sometimes called "the skiing supermarket of France."

The resort has 150km (93 miles) of ski runs in Courchevel and 604km (374 miles) of ski runs in the Trois Vallées. Courchevel consists of four planned ski towns, each designated by its elevation in meters. They are the less fashionable Courchevel 1300 (Le Prez), Courchevel 1550, Courchevel 1650, and crowning them all, Courchevel 1850. The latter has excellent resorts and hotels—with price tags to match—so it draws the super-rich. Travelers on average budgets should instead head for more reasonably priced resorts, especially Chamonix.

Information on the towns can be acquired at the **Office de Tourisme,** at La Croisette in the heart of town (www.courchevel.com; ✆ **04-79-08-00-29**).

MEGÈVE ★★

With its quaint medieval village and varied activities for non-skiers, the rather upscale resort of Megève is a good crowd pleaser and perfect for families. It's part of the Evasion Mont-Blanc range that includes 440km (273 miles) of ski slopes. Its days as resort date back to the 1920s when the Rothschilds sought to create a St. Moritz–style resort in France and it's attracted the European elite ever since. However, it retains its traditional Haute Savoyard character with cobbled streets, wooden chalets, and a 13th-century church. There are plenty of shops, award-winning restaurants, a casino, and other nighttime entertainment venues.

The Megève **Office de Tourisme** is at 70 Rue Monseigneur Conseil (www.megeve.com; ✆ **04-50-21-27-28**).

THE RHÔNE VALLEY

By Louise Simpson

W hen food and wine lovers go to heaven, they end up in the Rhône Valley. Many top French chefs make their names in this famous culinary region where restaurants on all levels vie for attention in competing culinary associations. Even small market towns and villages host chefs with three Michelin stars such as Pic in Valence, Troisgros in Roanne and Bocuse in Collonges-au-Mont-d'Or. The wealth of local produce is impressive: its chickens from Bresse and chestnuts from Ardèche have been given their own *appellation d'origine controlee* quality-control status.

Oenophiles head to the Northern Rhône where the double-dug vines of Côte-Rôtie and Hermitage date back to Roman times and to Beaujolais country where the light, fruity wines are drunk young. Whatever your agenda, you should fit in time for Roman ruins and summertime jazz festivals in Lyon and Vienne, canyons and limestone caves in the Ardèche, lovers' tombs in Bourg-en-Bresse and picture-perfect medieval houses in Pérouges.

LYON ★★★

431km (267 miles) SE of Paris; 311km (193 miles) N of Marseille

The forks of the River Saône and River Rhône meander through France's third city with its monumental Roman ruins, UNESCO-classified medieval lanes, and majestic Baroque squares. France's gastronomic capital inspires a culinary spirit that pervades its Michelin-starred restaurants and even its modest *bouchons*. Museums tell the tale of the city's contribution to cinema, silk production, printing and Guignol puppets. Only 2 hours by train from Paris, Lyon is the ultimate city break.

Essentials

ARRIVING If you're arriving from the north by **train,** don't get off at Lyon's first station, Gare de Lyon Part-Dieu; continue to Gare de Perrache, where you can begin sightseeing. The high-speed TGV takes only 2 hours from Paris; the one-way fare is 73€ to 130€. Lyon makes a good stopover en route to the Alps or the Riviera. For information, visit www.voyages-sncf.com or call ✆ **08-92-33-53-35.**

By **plane,** it's a 1-hour flight from Paris to Lyon-Saint Exupéry airport (www.lyonaeroports.com; ✆ **08-26-80-08-26**), 25km (16 miles) east of the city. The 30-minute **RhônExpress** tram link from the airport runs every quarter of an hour to central Lyon (100m/328 ft. from TGV train station Lyon Part-Dieu) for 14.50€. **Taxis** cost 40€-45€ by day and 55€–60€ by night and take the same amount of time.

If you're **driving** from Paris, head southeast on A6/E15 into Lyon. From Nice, head west on A8 toward Aix-en-Provence, continuing northwest toward Avignon on A7. Bypass the city and continue north along the same route into Lyon. From Grenoble or the French Alps, head northwest on A48 to A43, which will take you northwest into Lyon.

PREVIOUS PAGE: **Lyon viewed from the Saone River**

VISITOR INFORMATION   The **Office de Tourisme** is on place Bellecour (www.lyon-france.com; ✆ **04-72-77-69-69**).

CITY LAYOUT   Like Paris, Lyon is divided into *arrondissements* (districts). There are 9 in total—the main tourist areas are listed below.

VIEUX LYON, 5TH DISTRICT   The cheek-by-jowl cobbled lanes of the medieval town with its Renaissance *traboules* were awarded UNESCO status in 1998, helping this former slum area transform into a fashionable area for artisans and antiques dealers. Above the old town lies Fourvière Hill—home to Roman ruins and panoramic views towards the snowcapped Alps.

PLACE BELLECOUR, 2ND DISTRICT   With its 18th-century buildings and enormous Ferris wheel, place Bellecour is Lyon's finest square. Further north, you'll find designer shops and one of France's oldest shopping arcades, **Passage de l'Argue.** Spend an afternoon wandering around museums devoted to decorative arts and printing, as well checking out the new ethnology museum, **Musée de la Confluence.**

PLACE DES TERREAUX, 1ST DISTRICT   Locals hang out in *bouchons*—restaurants serving traditional Lyonnaise cuisine. You can glimpse Lyon's illustrious silken past at **L'Atelier de Soierie,** admire Matisse at the **Musée des Beaux Arts** and marvel at the ancient amphitheater in Lyon's oldest park, the Jardin des Plantes.

GETTING AROUND   A network of Métro lines, trams, and buses branches out to serve the city. A *plan de poche* (pocket map) is available at any office of **TCL** (www.tcl.fr; ✆ **04-26-10-12-12**), which handles all forms of mass transport. Tickets are valid on all forms of public transport, costing 1.70€ for the average ride or else 15.10€ for a *carnet* of 10 tickets. Most short-time visitors may want to purchase a **Ticket Liberté** day pass for 5.20€. Renting and then parking a car is an expensive waste of time as Lyon has one of the most efficient city taxi services we've ever discovered: call **Taxi Radio de Lyon** (www.taxilyon.com) on ✆ **04-72-10-86-86** and you'll be surprised at the speed with which a taxi is

Place des Terreaux, Lyon

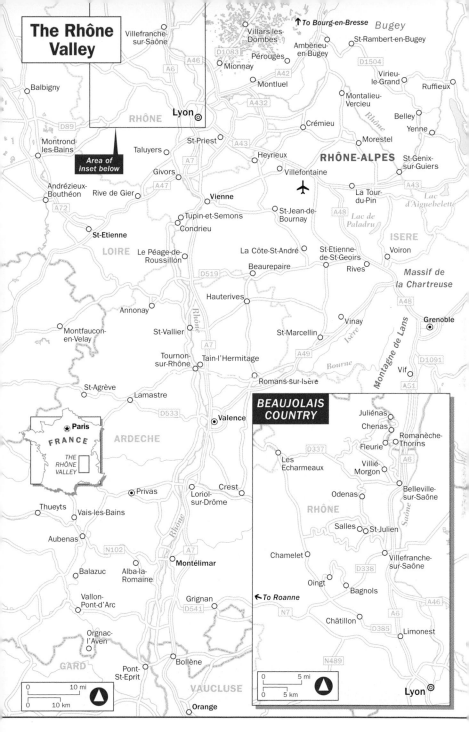

The Rhône Valley

Villefranche-sur-Saône

To Bourg-en-Bresse

Bugey

Villars-les-Dombes

Pérouges

Ambérieu-en-Bugey

St-Rambert-en-Bugey

D1083

Mionnay

D1504

Virieu-le-Grand

Ruffieux

Balbigny

A46

A6

Montluel

A42

Belley

Yenne

Lyon

A432

Montalieu-Vercieu

Morestel

RHÔNE

Crémieu

RHÔNE-ALPES

St-Genix-sur-Guiers

Montrond-les-Bains

D89

St-Priest

A43

Heyrieux

Lac d'Aiguebelette

Taluyers

A7

Villefontaine

La Tour-du-Pin

Andrézieux-Bouthéon

Givors

A47

Vienne

St-Jean-de-Bournay

A48

Lac de Paladru

A72

Rive de Gier

Tupin-et-Semons

Condrieu

St-Etienne

LOIRE

Le Péage-de-Roussillon

La Côte-St-André

St-Etienne-de-St-Geoirs

Voiron

ISERE

Rives

Massif de la Chartreuse

D519

Beaurepaire

Hauterives

A48

Annonay

Rhône

Vinay

Grenoble

Montfaucon-en-Velay

St-Vallier

St-Marcellin

Isère

A7

Tournon-sur-Rhône

Tain-l'Hermitage

A49

Bourne

Montagne de Lans

Vif

D1091

St-Agrève

Lamastre

Romans-sur-Isère

A51

D533

BEAUJOLAIS COUNTRY

Valence

Juliénas

Paris

Chenas

FRANCE

D337

Romanèche-Thorins

THE RHÔNE VALLEY

Fleurie

A6

Les Echarmeaux

Villié-Morgon

ARDECHE

Belleville-sur-Saône

Privas

Crest

Odenas

RHÔNE

Thueyts

Loriol-sur-Drôme

Vais-les-Bains

Salles

St-Julien

Saône

N102

Aubenas

Chamelet

Villefranche-sur-Saône

Balazuc

Alba-la-Romaine

A7

Montélimar

D338

Oingt

Vallon-Pont-d'Arc

Grignan

Bagnols

To Roanne

A46

D541

Châtillon

D385

Limonest

Orgnac-l'Aven

N7

A6

GARD

Bollène

N489

Pont-St-Eprit

VAUCLUSE

Lyon

0   10 mi

0   10 km

0   5 mi

0   5 km

Orange

335

winging its way to your door. That said, it's worth renting a car if you're planning on visiting the wine countries North and South of the city. You can rent cars at the train station Lyon Part Dieu including **Avis** (☎ **08-20-61-16-58**); **Hertz** (☎ **08-25-80-01-14**); **Europcar** ☎ **04-72-34-32-66**); **Sixt** ☎ **04-78-18-92-05**) and **Budget** ☎ **08-21-23-05-92**). The best way to get around the narrow streets of the old town is by foot, while the easiest way to reach Fourvière Hill is by **Funicular Railway** (see p. 342).

[Fast FACTS] LYON

ATMs/Banks   ATMs are widespread. There is also a branch of international bank **HSBC,** 1 place de la Bourse (☎ **04-78-52-25-48**).

Dentists   **Dr. Joseph Benamran,** 25 rue Bugeaud, (☎ **04-78-52-25-48**) or **Dr. Alexandre Baroud,** 74 rue Pierre Corneille (☎ **04-78-60-36-68**).

Doctors & Hospitals   For non-urgent medical attention, adults should try **Dr. Dominique Faysse,** 25 rue Garibaldi (☎ **04-78-93-13-25**), while families should contact **Dr. François Payot,** 143 rue de Sèze (☎ **04-78-24-85-09**). There is a central number for most hospitals in Greater Lyon: ☎ **08-20-08-20-69** including Hôpital Edouard Herriot, 5 place d'Arsonval and Hôpital de la Croix-Rousse, Centre Livet, 103 grande rue de la Croix-Rousse. For more information, go to **www.chu-lyon.fr**.

Embassies & Consulates   Lyon has an **American Presence Post** at 1 quai Jules Courmont (☎ **04-78-38-36-88**), Mon to Fri 10am to noon and 2 to 5pm.

Emergencies   For emergency medical assistance, your first call should be to SOS Doctors, 10 place Dumas de Loire (☎ **04-78-83-51-51**).

Internet Access   **Cyber Café BD en Bulles** has an English-keyboard computer at 14 rue Confort (☎ **04-78-37-41-46**).

Mail   There is a branch of La Poste near place Bellecour at 10 place Antonin Poncet (☎ **08-00-00-90-42**).

Pharmacies   Open 24/7, the Grande Pharmacie Lyonnais is on 22 rue de la République (☎ **04-72-56-44-00**).

SPECIAL EVENTS   Festivals take place practically every day, especially in summer. Music festivals reign supreme, with the most popular occurring on France's **Fête de la Musique,** which turns the streets of Lyon into performance spaces for local bands around June 21. For 4 days around December 8, the spectacular **Fête des Lumières** lights up Lyon's churches, monuments, and neighborhoods. In June and July, **Les Nuits de Fourvière** festival combines music, theater, dance, and cinema in the Gallo-Roman theaters on Fourvière hill and in Parc de Parilly in the suburb of Bron. Prices depend on the act and can be purchased by phone at ☎ **04-72-32-00-00** (info at www. nuitsdefourviere.com).

Hipster Hotel

Since opening in summer 2013, **Mama Shelter** at 13 rue Domer (☎ **04-78-02-58-00;** www.mamashelter.com; Métro: Jean Macé) has been a trendy place to stay for beautiful young things who don't mind the not-so-central location. Check out the hip furnishings by Philippe Starck. Rates start at 119€ per night.

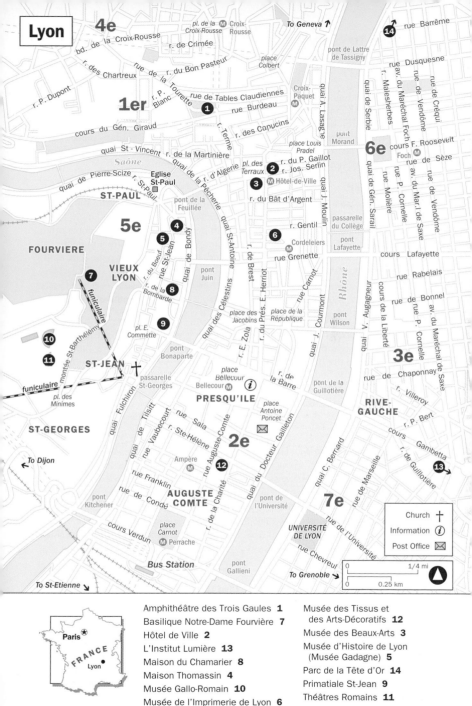

Lyon

4e

pl. de la Croix-Rousse ⓜ Croix-Rousse

To Geneva ↑

rue Barrême

⑭

bd. de la Croix-Rousse

r. de la Croix-Rousse

r. de Crimée

pont de Lattre de Tassigny

rue Duesquesne

r. des Chartreux

rue de la Tourette

r. du Bon Pasteur

place Colbert

quai A. Lasagne

quai de Serbie

av. du Maréchal Foch

rue de Vendôme

rue de Créqui

r. P. Dupont

r. P. Blanc

rue de Tables Claudiennes

Croix-Paquet ⓜ

rue Malesherbes

1er

①

rue Burdeau

6e

cours F. Roosevelt

cours du Gén. Giraud

r. Terme

r. des Capucins

place Louis Pradel

pont Morand

Foch ⓜ

rue de Sèze

quai St - Vincent

r. de la Martinière

r. du P. Gaillot

r. Jos. Serlin

quai de Gén. Sarail

av. du Mar.l de Saxe

rue de Vendôme

quai de Pierre-Scize

r. St-Paul

r. d'Algerie

pl. des Terraux

②

⑤

Hôtel-de-Ville ⓜ

rue P. Corneille

rue Molière

Saône

Eglise St-Paul

③

r. du Bât d'Argent

quai J. Moulin

FOURVIERE

ST-PAUL

pont de la Feuillée

quai de la Pêcherie

r. Gentil

passerelle du Collège

5e

④

r. de Bondy

⑥

Cordeliers ⓜ

pont Lafayette

cours Lafayette

⑤

quai St-Antoine

rue Grenette

r. du Bœuf

r. St-Jean

r. de Brest

rue Rabelais

VIEUX LYON

⑦

pont Juin

r. de la Bombarde

⑧

rue Carnot

cours de la Liberté

rue de Bonnel

rue P. Corneille

av. du Maréchal de Saxe

pl. E. Commette

⑨

quai des Célestins

place des Jacobins

r. du Prés. E. Herriot

place de la République

quai J. Courmont

pont Wilson

Rhône

⑩

montée St-Barthélémy

pont Bonaparte

r. E. Zola

3e

⑪

ST-JEAN

funiculaire

passarelle St-Georges

place Bellecour

Bellecour ⓜ ⓘ

r. de la Barre

pont de la Guillotière

rue de Chaponnay

r. Villeroy

pl. des Minimes

PRESQU'ILE

place Antoine Poncet

RIVE-GAUCHE

r. P. Bert

ST-GEORGES

quai Fulchiron

rue de Tilsitt

rue Sala

rue Auguste-Comte

✉

place Antoine Poncet

quai du Docteur Gailleton

cours Gambetta

r. de Guillotière

⑬

To Dijon ←

quai de Vaubecourt

r. Ste-Hélène

2e

Ampère ⓜ

⑫

rue Franklin

rue de Condé

AUGUSTE COMTE

r. de la Charité

quai C. Bernard

pont de l'Université

7e

pont Kitchener

cours Verdun

place Carnot

Perrache ⓜ

UNIVERSITÉ DE LYON

rue de l'Université

rue de Marseille

Bus Station

pont Gallieni

rue Chevreul

To Grenoble →

To St-Etienne ↓

Church ✝
Information ⓘ
Post Office ✉

0   1/4 mi
0   0.25 km

Where to Stay

Choosing where to stay in Lyon can be tricky if you don't know the city well. If you're planning a 1- or 2-night stopover, it's worth staying in the heart of Vieux Lyon where the UNESCO-certified medieval streets will be on your doorstep. However, you should be aware of high prices and narrow streets with some street noise—rooms facing internal courtyards are quietest. Hotels in the nearby 2nd district across the Bonaparte bridge from Vieux Lyon are more reasonably priced; the most sought after hotels overlook elegant, open squares such as place Belle-cour or place des Célestins. For the sake of older visitors or those with heavy suitcases, we've noted hotels that don't have an elevator.

EXPENSIVE

Cour des Loges ★★   This UNESCO-protected landmark is the most celebrated hotel in Lyon. It suits romantic couples who like breathtakingly lavish decor and don't mind low lighting and small bedrooms. Classic bedrooms often have an open-plan bathroom in the bedroom. Among its lures are a magnificent loggia-ringed courtyard, two restaurants, and a spa with indoor pool. The staff, Lyon's savviest, is courteous and efficient.

2–8 rue du Boeuf, Vieux Lyon 69005. ✆ **04-72-77-44-44.** www.courdesloges.com. 61 units. 190€–485€ double; 340€–870€ suite. Parking 35€. Métro: Vieux Lyon. **Amenities:** 2 restaurants; bar; room service; spa (with fitness room, indoor pool and sauna); free Wi-Fi.

Le Royal Lyon ★   Place Bellecour provides a suitably grand setting for this Haussmanian-style mansion that has welcomed numerous famous faces from Sophia Loren to the Beatles. Fine fabrics by Pierre Frey and Ralph Lauren adorn every corner of the hotel. Rooms vary enormously in size and quality. A smart new restaurant, **L'Institut** (see p. 341), opens in 2014.

20 place Bellecour, 69002 Lyon. ✆ **04-78-37-57-31.** www.lyonhotel-leroyal.com. 74 units. 145€–390€ double; 235€–500€ suite. Parking 19€. Métro: Bellecour. **Amenities:** Restaurant; bar; tea room; free Wi-Fi.

Villa Florentine ★★★   This 17th-century convent has been converted into a five-star, Relais & Châteaux hotel and our favorite place to stay in Lyon. Up on Fourvière Hill, the hotel's verdant landscaped terraces offer panoramic views over Vieux Lyon. The Italianate accommodations are spacious and comfortable. The annex offers modern and slightly larger rooms.

25 montée Saint Barthélémy, ✆ **04-72-56-56-56.** www.villaflorentine.com. 28 units. 290€–490€ double; 590€–960€ suite. Métro: Vieux Lyon, then funicular railway to Fourvière Hill. **Amenities:** Restaurant; bar; baby-sitting; exercise room; heated outdoor pool; room service; sauna; mini spa; free Wi-Fi.

MODERATE

Artelit ★   Housed in Lyon's original **Tour de la Rose** (not to be confused with the overpriced, shabby hotel next door) in Vieux Lyon, this exceptional B&B is like an art-museum-cum-antiques-shop. Charming owner Frédéric Jean is a renowned Lyonnais photographer. This place is for art

---

Japan Meets France

Chef Tsuyoshi Arai has taken Lyon by storm with his romantic Franco-Japanese dining concept. His first venue in Vieux Lyon (6 rue Morguet; ✆ **04-78-92-91-39;** www.au14 fevrier.com) won over diners with its Raymond Peynet romantic drawings and trompe-l'oeil French cuisine. In 2013, he set up another establishment in the aptly named **Saint-Amour Bellevue** (✆ **03-85-37-11-45**) in Beaujolais.

The best place for an authentic Lyonnais meal that won't break the bank is a *bouchon*. This low-price bistro concept was set up years ago by women such as Mère Brazier (see p. 340) and Mère Blanc, although nowadays men run the show. The meat-oriented fare favors such classics as sausages, duck pâté and roast pork. Such is the allure of the *bouchon* appellation that an official association has been set up to protect the 20 or so officially certified *authentique bouchon lyonnais* from the numerous fakes that parade around the old town. Our favorites include perennially popular **Les Adrets** (📞 **04-78-38-24-30**) at 30 rue du Boeuf; up-and-coming **Le Musée,** 2 rue des Forces (📞 **04-78-37-71-54**); long-established **Café des Fédérations** (www.lesfedeslyon.com; 📞 **04-78-28-26-00**) at 8-10 rue Major-Martin; and **Le Garet,** 7 rue du Garet (📞 **04-78-28-16-94**) famously frequented by Jean Moulin, hero of *La Résistance*.

lovers who don't mind the slightly rustic approach to hospitality such as ladders to reach the bed and occasional low ceilings. *Note:* There's no elevator.

16 rue du Boeuf. 📞 **04-78-42-84-83.** www.dormiralyon.com. 4 units. 100€–180€ double; 125€–250€ suite. Métro: Vieux Lyon. **Amenities:** Free Wi-Fi.

Hôtel Carlton ★★   Fresh from a renovation in 2013, this four-star hotel in the 2nd district is fast becoming the most popular place to stay in Lyon, as it combines 19th-century architecture with contemporary comfort and reliable service. Adults will appreciate the Cinq Mondes spa, while families will like connecting rooms and cartoon TV channels.

4 rue Jussieu, 📞 **04-78-42-56-51.** www.accorhotels.com. 80 units. 165€–315€ double. Métro: Cordeliers. **Amenities:** Bar; hammam; room service; free Wi-Fi.

Hôtel des Célestins ★   Seconds from the place des Célestins with its splendid 18th-century theatre, this discreet three-star hotel has quietly established itself as one of the best mid-range hotels in Lyon. The secret to their success lies in its homely atmosphere, with bedrooms containing bookshelves lined with well-worn books.

4 rue des Archers. 📞 **04-72-56-08-98.** www.hotelcelestins.com. 27 units. 87€–185€ double. 173€–258€ suite. Métro: Bellecour. **Amenities:** Breakfast room; free Wi-Fi.

INEXPENSIVE

Hôtel Bayard Bellecour ★   This 16th-century townhouse on elegant place Bellecour is one of the most reliable, inexpensive places to stay in Lyon. Beautifully outfitted rooms with wooden floors vary from contemporary to traditional. Most of the compact bathrooms have showers and tubs. Classic rooms are somewhat cramped. *Note:* There's no elevator.

23 place Bellecour. 📞 **04-78-37-39-64.** www.hotelbayard.fr. 22 units. 54€–209€ double. Parking 20€ (call ahead). Métro: Bellecour. **Amenities:** Free Wi-Fi.

Hôtel Saint-Paul   This friendly hotel is your best value option for staying in Vieux Lyon during peak season. Rooms are plainly furnished; more expensive rooms have bathtubs.

6 rue Lainerie,. 📞 **04-78-28-13-29.** www.hotelsaintpaul.eu. 20 units. 75€–82€ double. Métro: Vieux Lyon/Hôtel de Ville. **Amenities:** Free Wi-Fi.

Where to Eat

Gastronomic capital Lyon is the training ground for many of France's top chefs. Yet dining in Lyon isn't all about Michelin stars. You can try traditional Lyonnaise cuisine at a modest *bouchon* where you'll likely dine at a gingham-clothed table on dishes such as quenelles de brochet (creamed pike) and andouillettes Lyonnaise (course-grained pork sausages in an onion sauce).

EXPENSIVE

Mère Brazier ★★★ MODERN LYONNAISE   The only two-Michelin-starred restaurant in central Lyon, this legendary Lyon institution is run by the charismatic darling of French food critics, Mathieu Viannay. In a striking Art-Deco setting, you can taste Mère Brazier classics (such as Bresse chicken poached with truffles) that have been reworked by Viannay, as well as Renée Richard cheese accompanied by fine Rhône red wines.

12 rue Royale. ✆ **04-78-23-17-20.** www.lamerebrazier.fr. Main courses 55€–90€; fixed-price lunch menus 57€–70€; dinner menus 95€–140€. Mon–Fri noon–1:30pm, 7:45–9:15pm. Métro: Croix Paquet.

MODERATE

Brasserie Georges ★ TRADITIONAL FRENCH   Founded in 1836, this bustling Lyonnais institution serves up to 450 diners. You can ask for a table that is identified with a plaque for hosting Ernest Hemingway or Edith Piaf. Specialties include roast beef and snails in garlic butter.

30 cours de Verdun. ✆ **04-72-56-54-54.** www.brasseriegeorges.com. Main courses 15€–25€; fixed-price menus 19.50€–25€. Daily 11:30am–11:15pm (until 12:15am Fri–Sat). Closed May 1. Métro: Perrache.

Daniel et Denise ★★ LYONNAISE   If you dine at just one *bouchon* during your stay, make it this one. With its wood-paneled walls and gingham tablecloths, this old-fashioned restaurant is always filled with locals. Hearty meat-based Lyonnaise cuisine is king here: chef Joseph Viola won the Champion de Monde 2009

beaucoup DE BOCUSE

Paul Bocuse is the godfather of Lyonnaise cuisine and the only chef within the Lyon area to boast three Michelin stars. Gourmands flock from Paris and the world over to dine at his sumptuous culinary headquarters in **Collonges-au-Mont-d'Or** (✆ **04-72-42-90-90;** www.bocuse.fr; North of Lyon on the N433) where you'll have to book months in advance to secure a table to taste memorable dishes such as his black-truffle soup. If you're not that organized or that well-heeled, you can also grab a taste of Bocuse at one of his popular mass-market brasseries (www.nordsudbrasseries.com) that are open daily for lunch and dinner with main courses starting at 14€. Our favorites are **Le Sud,** 11 place Antonin Poncet (✆ **04-72-77-80-00**), an airy venue for Provençal and North-African flavors and **L'Est,** 14 place Jules-Ferry (✆ **04-37-24-25-26**), a bustling *brasserie de gare* that evokes faraway Paris and serves French and Italian cuisine. With its extravagant turn-of-the-century furnishings and traditional French cuisine, **Marguerite** (57 avenue des Frères Lumière next to the Lumière museum; ✆ **04-37-90-03-00**) is the latest to join the Paul Bocuse group.

award for his foie gras and sweetbread pâté en croute (pâté in a pastry case). Viola has been wise enough to add lighter salads and fish dishes too. There's another outlet at 36 rue Tramassac in Vieux Lyon.

156 rue de Créqui. www.daniel-et-denise.fr. 𝒞 **04-78-60-66-53.** Main courses 15€-26€; fixed-price lunch menu 21€; dinner menu 30€. Mon–Fri noon–2pm. Métro: Foch/Brotteaux.

L'Institut ★ MODERN FRENCH 2014 sees the opening of this hotly anticipated restaurant run by the well-reputed catering school **L'Institut Paul Bocuse.** You can marvel at the sight of head chef Cyril Bosviel guiding future celebrity chefs in the glassed-in kitchen—part of a lavish design by Pierre-Yves Rochon. Cooking classes in English are offered at the school upstairs.

29 place Bellecour. 𝒞 **04-78-37-23-02.** Fixed-price starters 12€; fixed-price main courses 20€. Tues–Sat noon–1pm and 7:30–9:30pm. Métro: Bellecour.

Pléthore et Balthazar ★ INTERNATIONAL In 2014, this lavish restaurant opened and has been frequented by a young Lyonnais crowd. New York–trained chef Brice Lambert is behind the stove to oversee a non-stop service from 8am to 1am, though the food is second to the hip ambience.

72 rue Mercière. 𝒞 **04-72-16-09-21.** www.plethoreetbalthazar.com. Main courses 10€–35€. Fixed-price lunch menu 17€. Daily 8am–1am. Metro: Cordeliers.

La Rémanence ★★ FRENCH Warm bare-stone walls and immaculate table linen set the scene for this striking restaurant that's perfect for a romantic dinner. Fabien Blanc's imaginative cuisine made this one of Lyon's best-kept secrets until its 2014 Michelin star bought diners flocking to its door.

31 rue du Bât d'Argent. 𝒞 **04-72-74-44-61.** http://laremanence.fr. Main courses 26€–31€; fixed-price lunch menu 27€; fixed-price menus 37€–71€. Tues–Sat noon–1:30pm and 8–9:30pm. Métro: Hôtel de Ville.

Exploring Lyon

IN VIEUX LYON ★★★

The UNESCO-certified cobbled streets of Vieux Lyon are a good place to start discovering the city. You'll find the entrance to Vieux Lyon around the corner from the neo-classical **Palais de Justice** (nicknamed the "Palace of 24 columns") on the left bank of the Saône River. Try to spot Gothic facades such as 15th-century **Maison Thomassin,** 2 place du Change, and the 16th-century **Maison du Chamarier,** 37 rue St-Jean, where Mme. de Sévigné lived. You can admire these buildings from the outside, but you are not allowed to enter.

Musée d'Histoire de Lyon (Musée Gadagne) ★ MUSEUM This museum is housed in the **Hôtel de Gardagne,** the 16th-century residence of an Italian banking family so famed for their wealth that the Lyonnais phrase "riche comme Gardagne" evolved. The Lyonnais collection ranges from Romanesque sculptures to numerous paintings and engravings. If you're short on time, skip this section and head straight to the **Musée des Marionnettes du Monde** where you'll see fun puppets by Laurent Mourguet, creator of Guignol, the best-known French marionette character.

1 place du Petit-Collège ✆ **04-78-42-03-61.** www.gadagne.musees.lyon.fr. Admission to both museums 8€ adults, free for 25 and under and children. Wed–Sun 11am–6:30pm.

Primatiale St-Jean ★★ CATHEDRAL   With ongoing renovations until 2017, this majestic Gothic cathedral remains only partly open to the public. The exteriors have already been restored to their original creamy glory, while new contemporary stained glass windows and nave seating are planned inside. Built over the foundations of at least five former churches, the current cathedral was built in the Middle Ages. Of particular note are the 14th-century rose window, the Romanesque apse and the 16th-century clock that announces the hour daily (at noon, 2, 3, and 4pm) with rooster crows, and angels heralding the event. Paintings around the cathedral belonged to Napoleon's uncle, Cardinal Fesch.

Place St-Jean. ✆ **04-78-92-82-29.** Free admission. Daily 7am–7:30pm (Sun closes at 5pm). The cathedral is closed to tourists for mass during the week and on Sun mornings.

Traboules ★ HISTORIC SITE   No visit to Vieux Lyon is complete without a tour of its unique *traboules,* a series of short covered passageways that connect longer streets running parallel to one another. Dirty brown doors open unexpectedly into flower-ringed courtyards with balconies perching atop medieval columns, or onto vaulted ceilings and spiral stairs.

Vieux Lyon. 2-hr. guided tour for 10€; call the tourist office in advance for times.

IN FOURVIERE HILL ★★★

From Vieux Lyon, take the 19th-century **funicular railway** up to the **Colline de Fourvière** (www.fourviere.org) where you can discover Gallo-Roman Lyon. The funicular railway ride is priced at 1.60€ each way; the cable-driven funiculars run every 10 minutes between 6am and 10pm.

Enthroned on the hill's summit is the monumental 19th-century **Basilique Notre-Dame de Fourvière,** 8 place de Fourvière (✆ **04-78-25-13-01**), rising fortress-like with four octagonal towers and crenellated walls. During 2013, the interior decorations were renovated and new lighting was added so visitors can enjoy the Byzantine mosaics and frescos in their brightly colored original glory. Lyonnais architect Bossan designed the basilica in eclectic styles that combine as a poem to the Virgin Mary. From the outside, spot the gold-leafed Virgin Mary that was inaugurated on 8 December 1852—a date now celebrated annually with the **Fête des Lumières.** Admission is free; open daily 8am to 7pm.

Nearby, an altar dedicated to a bull cult and a marble statue of a goddess are on display in the **Musée Gallo-Romain,** 17 rue Cléberg (✆ **04-72-38-49-30**). With a staircase that recalls the Guggenheim Museum, the museum houses a fine collection of Gallo-Roman artifacts. The site is open Tuesday through Sunday 10am to 6pm. Admission is 7€ adults, free for ages 17 and under and for everyone on Thursdays.

Rather than trekking all the way down to the **Théâtres Romains** (Roman theaters) at 6 rue de l'Antiquaille (✆ **04-72-32-00-00**), you'll have a bird's eye view over this impressive Roman theater-odeum complex from a viewing point on the left of the Musée Gallo-Romain. The theater is the most ancient in France,

Roman theater, Lyon

built by order of Augustus and expanded during the reign of Hadrian to seat up to 10,000 people. Reserved for elite society, the smaller odeum seated up to 3,000 people for musical, oratory and poetry performances. There are only two odeums like this in France—the other is in Vienne. Its orchestra floor still contains mosaics of marble and porphyry. The site is open from 7am until sunset, and entrance is free. If you come during June and July, try to book tickets for **Les Nuits de Fourvière** staged in this extraordinary setting (see "Special Events," p. 336).

2ND ARRONDISSEMENT

From Vieux Lyon, walk across Bonaparte bridge to the East bank of the River Saône. Begin your tour of the 2nd district at 18th-century **place Bellecour,** one of France's largest and most charming squares where you can take a ride on the huge Ferris wheel.

Musée de l'Imprimerie de Lyon ★ MUSEUM   Occupying a 15th-century mansion, this museum is devoted to Lyon's role in the world of printing. Exhibits include a page from a Gutenberg Bible, as well as *incunabula*, books printed before Easter 1500.

13 rue de la Poulaillerie. **☎ 04-78-37-65-98.** www.imprimerie.lyon.fr. Admission 5€ adults, 3€ students, free for 26 and under. Wed–Sun 10:30am–6pm. Métro: Cordeliers.

> ### Take the Scenic Route
>
> The most scenic way back to Vieux Lyon is by foot through the **Jardin du Rosaire,** a minute away from the **Musée Gallo-Romain** and next to the Conservatoire music school where you'll often hear music trickling from the windows. In late spring, you can enjoy roses and cherry trees in bloom as well as panoramic views over Lyon.

Musée des Tissus et des Arts Décoratifs ★★ MUSEUM The decorative arts are housed in the Lacroix-Laval mansion by Soufflot (architect of Paris' Panthéon). Among the furniture and *objets d'art*, there's a five-octave harpsichord by Donzelague, the 18th-century creator of musical instruments. The collection next door in the **l'Hôtel de Villeroy** takes you through 2000 years of priceless fabrics from around the world. Look for the partridge-motif brocade from Marie Antoinette's bedchamber and a 150-color brocaded satin woven for Queen Victoria.

34 rue de la Charité. ✆ **04-78-38-42-00.** www.musee-des-tissus.com. Admission 10€ adults, 8€ adults arriving after 4pm, free for children under 12. Tues–Sun 10am–5:30pm. Métro: Ampère.

1ST ARRONDISSEMENT

Further North, check out **place des Terreaux** dominated by one of Europe's most splendid city halls, the 17th-century **Hôtel de Ville** and by the elaborate **Fontaine Bartholdi.** Designed by Frédéric Auguste Bartholdi, who also sculpted the iconic **Statue of Liberty** in New York, this historic fountain depicts France as a female on a chariot controlling four wild horses representing the four great French rivers. Another interesting sight is the wall mural **Fresque des Lyonnais** with illustrations of famous Lyonnais residents such as Paul Bocuse and Antoine de Saint-Exupéry on rue de la Martinière (north-west of place des Terreaux).

Amphithéâtre des Trois-Gaules ★ RUINS   Constructed in 19 ad at the base of the Croix Rousse hill, this Roman amphitheater held up to 20,000 spectators. It became the site of gatherings for the 60 Gallic tribes, for gladiatorial combats and later for the Christian persecutions in 177. Classified as a historic monument in 1961, it is now integrated into Lyon's oldest park, the Jardin des Plantes.

Rue Lucien Sportisse. Free admission. Métro: Croix Paquet.

Musée des Beaux-Arts ★★ ART MUSEUM   Housed in a former Benedictine abbey, this museum has an outstanding collection of paintings and sculpture including Etruscan, Egyptian, Phoenician, Sumerian, and Persian art. The top floor holds one of France's richest 19th-century collections, with works by artists from Veronese, Tintoretto, and Rubens to Matisse, Monet, and Picasso. Be sure to see Joseph Chinard's bust of **Mme. Récamier,** the Lyon beauty who charmed Napoleonic Paris by merely reclining, and the Fantin-Latour masterpiece *La Lecture* (The Reading).

20 place des Terreaux. ✆ **04-72-10-17-40.** www.mba-lyon.fr. Admission 7€ adults; free for children under 18. Wed–Mon 10am–12:30pm, 2–6pm (Fri opens 10:30am). Métro: Hôtel de Ville.

ELSEWHERE AROUND THE CITY

L'Institut & Musée Lumière ★ HISTORIC HOME   Film buffs from all over the world head to this living museum of cinema dedicated to the famous Lumière family, who once lived in Lyon. They invented the Lumière process of color photography and produced films, including "La Sortie de L'Usine Lumière," released in 1895 and considered the first movie.

25 rue du Premier Film. ✆ **04-78-78-18-95.** www.institut-lumiere.org. Admission 6.50€ adults; 5.50€ adults over 60, students and children 7–18 (need proof of age); free for children 6 and under. Tues–Sun 10am–6:30pm. Métro: Monplaisir-Lumière.

Parc de la Tête d'Or ★★★ PARK/GARDEN   On the right bank of the Rhône, you can explore the largest public city park in France. This 117-hectare (289-acre) park has a magnificent lakeside setting. Deer wander freely around the grounds, while the **Zoological Park** (open daily 9am to 5pm; ✆ **04-72-82-35-00**) hosts some 1000 animals including rose-pink flamingos and Senegalese dwarf goats. The **Botanical Garden** (open daily 9am to 4:30pm; www.jardin-botanique-lyon.com; ✆ **04-72-69-47-60**) features 15,000 plants including carnivorous plants and orchids. Families will be kept busy with pony rides, carousels and pedal boats on the lake.

Entrances on boulevard des Belges, quai Général de Gaulle and avenue Verguin. www.loisirs-parcdelatetedor.com. Free admission. Daily 6am–9pm (until 11pm Apr–Sept). Métro: Masséna.

Shopping

Vieux Lyon has an array of art galleries and one-off boutiques. Shops in Vieux Lyon tend to be open on Sundays, while they are usually closed on Mondays (also Tues and even Wed in low season). A good day to go shopping in Vieux Lyon is on Sunday morning when the **Marché de la Création** takes place on nearby Quai Romain Rolland along the banks of the River Saône—more than 150 artists come to show their jewelry, ceramics and sculptures while poets and musicians give live performances.

With its dazzling array of *tartes au praline*, the best baker in the area is **Boulangerie du Palais** (8 rue du Palais; ✆ **04-78-37-09-43**) where you'll always find a queue of locals at weekends. **Antic Wine** is one of the best and most amusing wine shops in France, at 18 rue du Boeuf (www.anticwine.com; ✆ **04-78-37-08-96**).

The wide avenues of the 2nd district are home to designer and high-street brands. This district tends to have more traditional Monday to Saturday openings with lunchtime and Sunday closures, although some shops are also closed on Mondays too. The densest concentrations of retail shops lie in the streets leading north of place Bellecour. The Southern end of rue du Président Edouard Herriot is home to sought-after international brands from **Louis Vuitton** to **Mont Blanc.** Around the corner lies our favorite shopping street in Lyon: **rue des Archers.** Here you'll find chic Parisian clothes brands for adults and children, as well as two of Lyon's award-winning chocolate shops: **Bouillet** at no. 14 (www.chocolatier-bouillet.com; ✆ **04-78-42-98-40**) and **Bernard Dufoux** at no. 15 (www.chocolatsdufoux.com; ✆ **04-72-77-57-95**). Linking rue du Président Edouard Herriot with rue de la République, the historic **Passage de L'Argue,** designed by architect Farge in 1827, houses long-established merchants of hats, umbrellas, knives and shaving brushes.

South of place Bellcour, antiques dealers concentrate around rue Auguste-Comte. Also consider venturing to the **Cité des Antiquaires,** 117 bd. de Stalingrad (www.cite-antiquaires.fr; ✆ **04-72-69-00-00**) in the 6th district, with more than 100 dealers spread over two floors, and merchandise from the 18th century to the 1950s. It's open Thursdays and weekends from 10am to 7pm.

More than 235 shops and boutiques fill the largest shopping center in Lyon, the **Centre Commercial La Part-Dieu,** 17 rue du Dr. Bouchut in the 3rd district (www.centrecommercial-partdieu.com; ✆ **04-72-60-60-62**).

L'Atelier de Soierie ★   Although Lyon is not the major silk center that it once was, it is home to several silk manufacturers. This workshop is the perfect place to watch silk *carrés* being printed using traditional Lyonnais techniques, before browsing the scarves on display in the neighboring boutique. A new outlet opened in 2014 on rue du Boeuf in Vieux Lyon.

33 rue Romarin. ✆ **04-72-07-97-83.** www.atelierdesoierie.com. Mon–Fri 9am–noon, 2–7pm; Sat 9am–1pm, 2–6pm. Métro: Hôtel de Ville.

Les Halles Paul Bocuse ★★★ At weekends, local gourmands crowd this covered food market to stock up on high-quality Lyonnais specialties: sausage-filled brioche, *Cervelle de Canut* cream cheese and marzipan *coussins de Lyon* (cushions carried by the Aldermen during the 1643 Plague). There are numerous cafes offering a well-priced lunch.

102 cours Lafayette. ✆ **04-78-62-39-33.** www.hallespaulbocuse.lyon.fr. Free admission. Mon–Sat 7am–10:30pm; Sun 7am–2:30pm. Métro: Brotteaux/Part Dieu.

Lyon Nightlife

At any newsstand, pick up a copy of the weekly guide "Lyon-Poche," which lists happenings and venues around town, from bars to classical concerts.

In 2013, several hotly anticipated bar openings took Lyon by storm. **La Maison Mère** (21 place Gabriel Rambaud (http://mmlyon.com; ✆ **04-78-27-71-41;** Métro: Hôtel de Ville) near place des Terreaux is a bar and late-night club (open Tues to Sat) offering an eclectic musical program from soul to rock and hip-hop including live concerts. Live music and arts venue, **Sucre** (50 quai Rambaud; www.le-sucre.eu; Métro: Perrache) has been installed on the rooftop of a 1930s warehouse in the fashionable Confluence district. Finally, hip young Lyonnais have been flocking to the plush bar at **Mama Shelter** 13 rue Domer (✆ **04-78-02-58-00;** www.mamashelter.com; Métro: Jean Macé): the brain-child of the Trigano family (founders of Club Med) and Cyril Aouizerate along with Philippe Starck designs.

Lyonnais microbrewery chain **Ninkasi** (www.ninkasi.fr) continues from strength to strength. You'll find live music, fresh beer, and burgers at each of their nighttime venues around Lyon. Most live concerts are free, although there is sometimes a cover charge for well-known bands playing at the brewery headquarters, **Ninkasi Gerland.** To keep things simple, each venue is named after the nearest metro station. Our favorites are **Gerland,** at 267 rue Marcel Mérieux (✆ **04-72-76-89-00**); **Hôtel de Ville** at 27 rue de l'Arbre Sec (✆ **04-78-28-37-74**) and **Cordeliers** at 22 rue Ferrandière (✆ **04-72-77-91-47**).

A good place to start the evening over a glass or two of wine is **La Cave des Voyageurs** is 7 place Saint-Paul (http://lacavedesvoyageurs.free.fr; ✆ **04-78-28-92-28**) in Vieux Lyon. Around the corner is the Anglophone pub **Smoking Dog,** 16 rue Lainerie (✆ **04-78-28-38-27**), with its bookshelf-lined walls, billiard table, and eight beers on tap. It's a popular place to watch international sports matches on T.V. Open daily from 5pm to 1am (from 2pm on weekends).

In summertime, locals flock to the quays along the Rhône. The best of the former cargo boats parked on the Rhône is **Le Sirius,** Berges du Rhône, 4 quai Augagneur (www.lesirius.com; ✆ **04-78-71-78-71;** Métro: Guillotière). An under-35 crowd packs the ship for dancing to the sounds of Lyon's best DJs on the lower-level floor. It's open daily from 4pm to 3am.

One of Lyon's best and largest nightclubs is **First Révolution,** 13/14 place Jules Ferry (www.first-aperiklub.com; Métro: Brotteaux) whose house music and chic decor attract a young, kitten-heeled 20s to 30s crowd. Housed in the Brotteaux old railway station, the club has room for 500 people: even so, you should expect a strict door policy. It's open Thursday to Saturday from 11:45pm until

7am. The most popular gay bar and club is the long-standing **La Ruche,** 22 rue Gentil, 2e (© **04-78-37-42-26;** Métro: Cordeliers), that's open daily from 5pm to 4am. Meanwhile, **Le Domaine** has sadly closed down its permanent venue, but holds regular club nights at **Quai des Arts,** 8 bis Quai Saint Vincent (© **04-72-00-97-36;** www.restaurant-quaidesarts.com; Métro: Hôtel de Villa) attracting a young, vibrant lesbian crowd.

Opera buffs head to **Opéra,** place de la Comédie (© **04-69-85-54-54;** www.opera-lyon.com; Métro: Hôtel de Ville), while **La Halle Tony Garnier,** 20 place des Docteurs Charles et Christophe Mérieux (© **04-72-76-85-85;** www. halle-tony-garnier.fr; Métro: Debourg) is a popular venue for international pop concerts and dance shows.

DAY TRIPS FROM LYON

There is much to discover in the verdant countryside to the North and South of Lyon. Some places such as Vienne and the wine countries of the Northern Rhône and Beaujolais will fill several days, while Valence and the Ardèche are far enough to require an overnight stay. However, chicken-famed Bourg-en-Bresse and postcard-pretty Pérouges make ideal day trips.

BOURG-EN-BRESSE ★

37km (xx miles) E of Mâcon; 425km (264 miles) SE of Paris; 61km (38 miles) NE of Lyon

The ancient capital of Bresse, Bourg-en-Bresse is often overlooked by tourists. Yet it's worth a day trip from Lyon for two reasons alone—firstly to explore the intensely romantic national historic monument **Brou Monastery,** as well as arguably the best-preserved **apothecary** in France; secondly, to dine on the only free-range chickens in the world to have their own *appellation d'origine contrôlée* (certificate of origin).

Essentials

GETTING THERE   If you're driving down the A6 from Paris, you head east out of Mâcon on the A40 towards Bourg-en-Bresse. If **driving** from Lyon, take A42 North, before turning onto A40 for the 70-minute trip. Bourg-en-Bresse is accessible by **train** from Lyon Perrache (about 1 hr.); over 20 trains arrive per day. For information, visit www.voyages-sncf.com or call © **08-92-33-53-35.**

VISITOR INFORMATION   The **Office de Tourisme** is at 6 av. Alsace-Lorraine (www.bourgenbressetourisme.fr; © **04-74-22-49-40**).

Exploring Bourg-en-Bresse

Apothecary ★★ HISTORIC LANDMARK   This 18th-century pharmacy and laboratory is worth a detour. The laboratory has a wood-burning stove complete with 17th-century alembic distillers. In the adjoining storeroom and shop, you'll find china pots and boxes still filled with medicines such as licorice pills and even powdered deer antler. Visits to this hidden gem need to be organized in advance with the tourist office.

Hôtel de Dieu, 47 bd de Brou. Guided visits every Sat afternoon and during summertime every Tues as well; contact the tourist office for more information.

Royal Monastery of Brou ★★★ MONASTERY   Romantics and historians alike gasp at the extravagance of the royal tombs housed in this monastery's

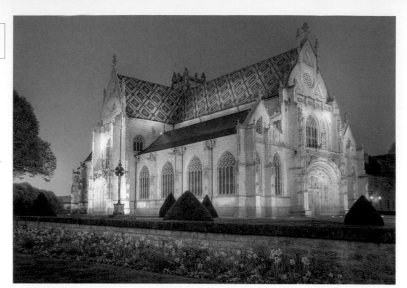

Royal Monastery of Brou, Bourg-en-Bresse

mausoleum. This flamboyant Gothic mausoleum was built by the ill-fated Margaret of Austria as a testament to her love for husband Philibert the Handsome, who died prematurely at the age of 24 after catching a cold on a hunting expedition. For the first time ever in 2014, you can visit the secret passageway designed for the mourning Margaret to access her chapel from her monastery residence without being seen by the public. The three cloisters of the adjacent medieval monastery and art museum are also worth a look.

63 bd. de Brou. ✆ **04-74-22-83-83.** Admission to church, cloisters, and museum 7.50€ adults, free for children 17 and under if accompanied by an adult. July–Sept daily 9am–6pm; Apr–June daily 9am–12:30pm and 2–6pm; Oct–Mar daily 9am–noon and 2–5pm. Closed Jan 1, May 1, Nov 1 and 11, and Christmas.

Where to Eat & Shop

No trip to Bourg-en-Bresse is complete without visiting the **covered food market** in avenue du Champ de Foire. Every Wednesday and Saturday, you'll be able to browse the myriad stalls for flowers, fruit, vegetables, cheese and even live chickens. Chocoholics are catered for with no less than seven chocolate shops: one of the best is **Chocolaterie Monet** (14 rue Bichat; ✆ **04-74-23-47-42**) where you'll find excellent truffles and seasonally themed chocolates.

Boutique Giraudet ★   Since 1910, Giraudet's quenelles à brochet (creamed pike) have been the gold standard of Rhône cuisine. It is one of the last manufacturers that still produce certain quenelles by hand. This smart boutique offers over 40 different quenelles with matching sauces as well as sweet and savory soups made from classical recipes. Even the Ministry of Agriculture has recognized Giraudet's contribution to French cuisine in awarding the prestigious *EPV* (Living Heritage Company) label.

21 rue Maréchal Joffre ✆ **04-74-22-45-85.** www.giraudet.fr. Tues–Sat 8:30am–noon, 2–7pm.

La Table Ronde ★ TRADITIONAL FRENCH Across the street from the Brou Monastery, this restaurant is a reasonably priced alternative to the celebrated, but expensive **Auberge de Bressane** along the same street. You'll find plenty of hearty French dishes to fill you up such as Bresse chicken with creamy dauphinoise potatoes, frogs' legs and foie gras. Summertime dining is on the terrace facing the Hôtel de Dieu park.

126 bd. de Brou. © **04-74-23-71-17.** Main courses 10eu]–24€; fixed-price menu 18€–29€. Mon–Fri noon–2pm; Mon–Sat 7:30–9pm.

PÉROUGES ★★

464km (288 miles) SE of Paris; 35km (22 miles) NE of Lyon

Pérouges is a medieval village that begs to be photographed. Saved from demolition by a courageous mayor in 1909 and preserved by the government, this thousand-person village of craftspeople has often attracted movie crews: "The Three Musketeers" (1961), "Monsieur Vincent" (1947) and "The Advocate" (1993) have all been filmed here. The town sits on what has been called an "isolated throne," atop a hill northeast of Lyon. Tourism has caused excessive prices in local restaurants so consider taking a picnic instead.

Essentials

GETTING THERE Trains serve **Mérimieux-Pérouges** from Lyon Part Dieu taking 30 minutes; for information, visit www.voyages-sncf.com or call © **08-92-33-53-35.** If you **drive** to Pérouges, beware that the signs for the town, especially at night, are confusing. From Lyon, take A42/E611 northeast and exit near Merimieux.

VISITOR INFORMATION The **Tourist Office** (Maison Saint Crépin, rue des Princes; www.perouges.org; © **04-74-46-70-84**) lies adjacent to the entrance of this very small village. It's closed in winter.

Exploring Pérouges

Wander down the rue des Princes to place des Tilleuls where you'll find the **Arbre de la Liberté** (Tree of Liberty) planted in 1792 to commemorate the Revolution. Nearby the 14th-century **Maison des Princes de Savoie,** houses the **Musée du Vieux-Pérouges** (© **04-74-61-00-88**) with its panoramic watchtower and perfectly tended 13th-century knot garden. The

Ancient house in Pérouges

museum is open June to August daily 10am to noon and 2 to 6pm; off season, weekends 10am to noon and 2 to 6pm. Admission is 4€ for adults, free for children ages 10 and under.

Where to Stay & Eat

Hostellerie du Vieux-Pérouges ★   Run by the town mayor Thibaut, this 13th-century timbered inn is chock-a-block with antiques, from iron lanterns to dressers lined with pewter plates. You can soak up the medieval atmosphere over an unashamedly old-fashioned lunch of Bresse chicken with creamed morels. With prices from 136€–257€ for a double, the bedrooms are rather overpriced. If you do decide to stay, go all out for a *lit à baldaquin* (four-poster bedroom) in **Le Manoir** or **St Georges,** as **Pavillion** rooms lack charm.

Place du Tilleul, Pérouges. 📞 **04-74-61-00-88.** www.hostelleriedeperouges.com. Main courses 23€–35€; menus from 39€–67€.

BEAUJOLAIS COUNTRY ★★★

Beaujolais is famous for its *vin en primeur*, fermented for just a few weeks before being released on sale during November. The craze for **Beaujolais Nouveau** table wine started in Paris three decades ago. Nowadays, Beaujolais Nouveau counts for just one third of the annual production of Beaujolais wine. Wine drinkers are gradually becoming aware of the potential of the Gamay grape to produce red wines of finesse, yet light enough to pair with white meat and even fish.

The narrow strip of Beaujolais vineyards start about 40km (25 miles) north of Lyon and finish just South of Mâcon. Though wine lovers tend to include this wine-producing region as part of Greater Burgundy, geographically speaking, Beaujolais belongs to the Rhône region. This small, hilly wine region punches above its size: producing around 190 million bottles of wine every year and boasting more castles than Bordeaux. While Northern Beaujolais is where the serious Cru appellation wines are grown, Southern Beaujolais is famed for its warm-hued stone houses that have earned it the name: "Land of the Golden Stones."

Beaujolais vineyards in the summer

Unlike Alsace, with its Route du Vin, Beaujolais country doesn't have a defined route. You can branch off in any direction from the A6 highway, stopping whenever you desire as there are clear road signs.

Southern Beaujolais

With its postcard-pretty villages, Southern Beaujolais is the most attractive place to stay for a couple of days in Beaujolais, as it's easy enough to organize day trips into Northern Beaujolais to explore the **Beaujolais Cru** wines. Capital of Beaujolais, Villefranche-sur-Saône is a businesslike base to start, but you'll probably want to stay in one of the 39 *villages dorés* (golden-stone villages).

ESSENTIALS

GETTING THERE **Villefranche-sur-Saône** is accessible by **trains** from Lyon. It's a 25-minute journey from Lyon Part Dieu station at 7.40€. For information, visit www.voyages-sncf.com or call ✆ **08-92-33-53-35.** However, the most practical way of exploring Southern Beaujolais is by car. If you're driving from Lyon, take the A6 North to Villefranche.

VISITOR INFORMATION The **Office de Tourisme** is at 96, rue de la Sous-Préfecture, Villefranche-sur-Saône (www.villefranche-beaujolais.fr; ✆ **04-74-07-27-40**).

EXPLORING SOUTHERN BEAUJOLAIS

Go to Villefranche-sur-Saône tourist office, not far from the marketplace for a booklet on Beaujolais country. It includes a map and itineraries, and lists the wine-tasting cellars open to the public. It also lists and details some 30 villages.

Any tour of Southern Beaujolais should include the pedestrianized, medieval village of Oingt—officially designated as one of the most beautiful villages in France. Only the tower remains of the medieval castle, but it's worth climbing for the panoramic views over Beaujolais. A good place to stock up on local Beaujolais wine is **Terroir des Pierres Dorées** (www.vignerons-pierres-dorees.fr; ✆ **04-78-15-91-07**) at place de Presberg on the edge of the pedestrianized center.

Another pretty village is **St-Julien-Sous-Montmelas,** 11km (6¾ miles) northwest of Villefranche (take D35). Claude Bernard, the father of physiology, was born here in 1813. His small stone house—the **Musée Claude-Bernard** (✆ **04-74-67-51-44**)—re-opened in 2013 after an extensive renovation and now exhibits the scholar's mementos, instruments, and books.

If you like fairy-tale castles, you should visit **Château de Montmelas** (www.chateau-montmelas.com; ✆ **04-74-67-32-94**). Known locally as Sleeping Beauty castle, it has been lived in by descendants of the same aristocratic family since the Middle Ages. From this hilltop castle, you'll find breathtaking views towards the distant Mont Blanc. The castle interiors are only open to the public one Saturday per month (unless you're willing to pay 175€ for a private visit), but you can telephone in advance for a wine tasting in the cellars with the charming Comtesse d'Harcourt, Delphine. Award-winning red and white table wines, and even sparkling wines are produced by the Comte himself. If you'd like to stay, there are even two four-bedroom gîtes available for weekend and week-long stays. From St Julien, take the D19 west and then the D44 towards the castle.

WHERE TO STAY & EAT

Château de Bagnols-en-Beaujolais ★★★ Europe's finest castle-hotel, now restored to its former glory, finally reopened in 2014. Knight in shining armor Jean-Claude Lavorel has spent 3 million euros transforming this historic building from an increasingly badly run hotel back into a sumptuous boutique hotel with six more bedrooms, a new spa, and a fabulous glassed-in courtyard extension. Prices are eye watering, but so are the antiques, paintings, and art that fill the mansion. Guest rooms have antique

beds, period velvets, embroidered linen sheets, and down pillows. New head chef Jean-Alexandre Quaratta has upped the culinary game with gastronomic French cuisine concentrating on local produce.

Place du Château, Bagnols. ☎ **04-74-71-40-00.** www.chateaudebagnols.fr. 21 units. 450€–960€ double; 600€–1,160€ suite. To reach Bagnols, head west out of Villefranche on D338. **Amenities:** Restaurant; heated outdoor pool; lounge; room service; spa; free Wi-Fi.

La Grande ★ TRADITIONAL FRENCH This homely address has been keeping local diners happy with traditional French dishes such as Burgundy snails, Quercy foie gras and Beaujolaise andouillettes (blood sausage) since 2002. There's also a market-fresh fish of the day. Cheerful owner Florence provides a swift service.

322 rue de Belleville, Villefranche. ☎ **04-74-60-65-81.** Main courses 13€–15€. Fixed-price menus 21€–31€. Tues–Fri 12:30–2pm, 7:30–9pm.

Northern Beaujolais

Serious wine connoisseurs head straight to Northern Beaujolais. Most of the 10 **Beaujolais Crus** (certified as the region's best wines that are more nuanced in flavor and capable of aging longer) are within a short drive of **Belleville-sur-Saône,** the largest town in Northern Rhône. From Lyon or Villefranche-sur-Saône, drive North on the A6.

ESSENTIALS

GETTING THERE **Belleville-sur-Saône** is accessible by **trains** from Lyon. It's a 35-minute journey from Lyon Part Dieu station at 9.70€. For information, visit www.voyages-sncf.com or call ☎ **08-92-33-53-35.** However, the most practical way of exploring Northern Beaujolais is by car. If you're driving from Lyon, take the A6 North to Belleville.

VISITOR INFORMATION The **Office de Tourisme** is at 27, rue du Moulin, Belleville-sur-Saône (www.beaujolaisvignoble.com; ☎ **04-74-66-44-67**).

EXPLORING NORTHERN BEAUJOLAIS

Caveau de Morgon ★ WINERY A good place to start exploring Northern Beaujolais is at this cellar in the basement of the 18th-century Château de Fontcrenne, next to the Hôtel de Ville. Here you can taste red wines from the well-regarded Beaujolais Cru **Morgon.** Caveau de Morgon produces and bottles wines under its own label, using grapes from local independent wine growers.

Château de Fontcrenne, Villié-Morgon. ☎ **04-74-04-20-99.** www.morgon.fr. From Belleville, head North on the A6, then west on the D9. Tastings 3€ for 3 glasses of wine. 10am–noon, 2:30–6pm in winter; 9:30am–noon, 2:30–7pm in summer. Closed first 3 weeks of Jan.

Château de la Chaize ★★ WINERY   This is a fairy-tale setting to taste the sought-after wines of Brouilly. Lived in by the Marquise de Roussy de Sales, this 17th-century castle produces some of the most prestigious Beaujolais Cru Brouilly wines. Grapes are picked by hand and seven wine-growing families living on the estate are given a portion of the crop according to the ancient custom of *métayage*. Wine tastings include a visit to the cellars as well as to the immaculate castle grounds with a formal topiary garden, rose garden, and star-formed vegetable garden. Telephone in advance to organize a tasting.

Odenas ✆ **04-74-03-41-05.** www.chateaudelachaize.com. From Belleville, head west on D337, then South on D43 to Odenas—the castle is well-signed from the village. Tasting 4€–5€. Tasting and visit of gardens: weekday 10€; weekend 15€. Closed Nov–Apr, Aug, and during grape harvest.

Hameau DuBoeuf ★ MUSEUM/WINERY/ADVENTURE PARK   Families and wine virgins will enjoy a trip to Europe's premier wine adventure park run by the godfather of Beaujolais wine, George Duboeuf. The wine museum takes you through 2,000 years of wine history, while the original town train station has been converted into a wine transport exhibition. Interactive games and holograms keep your kids amused as you take a video-animated wine tour through Beaujolais and onto the winery with its cutting-edge technology. The adventure golf and Beaujolais garden open from April to mid-October. There's also an excellent cafe.

796 route de la gare, Romanèche-Thorins. ✆ **03-85-35-22-22.** www.hameauduvin.com. From Belleville, head north on D906, then west on D32 to the Hameau Duboeuf. Admission to wine center, gardens and adventure golf: adult, including free pass for 1 child up to 15 yrs. old 19€; children 4–15 yrs. 10€; free admission under 3 yrs. Daily 10am–6pm.

WHERE TO EAT

Le Cêp ★★ GASTRONOMIC FRENCH   This Michelin-starred institution that has been a popular address for gastronomes since the 1970s finally reopened in 2013. Alain Souliac has taken the helm as the new chef with a little help from his friend Alain Ducasse. Come here for warm service combined with a taste of classic French dishes such as frog's legs, coq au vin and grain-fed pigeon.

Place de L'Eglise, Fleurie. ✆ **04-74-04-10-77.** Fixed-price lunch menu 27€; fixed-price dinner menus 48€–66€. Wed–Sun noon–2pm; Tues–Sat 7:30–9pm.

VIENNE ★★

489km (303 miles) SE of Paris; 31km (19 miles) S of Lyon

Vienne is famous for three things: Roman architecture, gastronomy and jazz. Historians flock to see no less than 41 classified historic monuments filling this small town, a testament to the importance of this Roman settlement. The good news for tourists is that you can visit some for free. Gastronomes know Vienne because it's the home of one of France's leading restaurants, La Pyramide. Jazz fans make their annual pilgrimage for the Jazz Festival that fills this small town with more than 35,000 spectators. As the festival director says, "Every Viennois has a history with this festival; it's in their blood." For train-travelling visitors, Vienne provides an easy twin city break with Lyon.

Essentials

GETTING THERE   Vienne is 20 minutes away from Lyon by **train** (at Jean Mace or Part Dieu train stations). For information, visit www.voyages-sncf.com or call

☎ **08-92-33-53-35.** The one-way train fare from Lyon is about 7€. If you're **driving** from Lyon, take the A7.

VISITOR INFORMATION The **Office de Tourisme** is at 14, cours Brillier (www.vienne-tourisme.com; ☎ **04-74-53-80-30**).

SPECIAL EVENTS Vienne is alive with summer festivals. In the first 2 weeks of July, Vienne attracts some of the biggest names in jazz for the annual **Festival du Jazz à Vienne.** Tickets are 36€. You can get tickets and information online (www.jazzavienne.com; ☎ **04-74-78-87-87**). There are also several historic festivals: a Gallo-Roman reconstruction weekend in June where everyone gets dressed up for mock battles; a medieval reconstruction weekend in late August and *Vinalia*, and a Gallo-Roman grape harvest in October. For more information on these festivals, go to www.vienne-tourisme.com or phone the tourist office.

Exploring Vienne

A good place to start your exploration of Gallo-Roman Vienne is at the **Musée Gallo-Roman Saint-Romain-en-Gal** (☎ **04-74-53-74-01**). This 7-hectare (17-acre) archaeological site merely scratches the surface of the myriad Roman remains that still exist beneath the foundations of modern Vienne. As you take a tour around the remains of Roman houses and public baths, you'll marvel at their sophistication. Inside the museum, you'll see mosaic floors, frescos and household items. The museum is open Tuesday to Sunday 10am to 6pm.

Back in central Vienne, you can wonder around some Roman sites for free. In place Charles de Gaulle, you'll find one of best preserved Roman remains in France: the **Temple d'Auguste et de Livie,** built on the orders of the Roman emperor Claudius and turned into a "temple of reason" during the French Revolution. Nearby, you'll find the **Jardin de Cybèle** where summer concerts are held for free during the June Jazz Festival. Another outstanding monument is **La Pyramide** (rue Fernand Point next to the Michelin-starred restaurant) part of the Roman circus. Rising 16m (52 ft.) and resting on a portico with four arches, it is sometimes called the tomb of Pilate.

Further east than the **Jardin de Cybèle** at the foot of Mont Pipet lies one of the most impressive remains: the **Roman Theater (Théâtre Romain)** ★, 7 rue du Cirque (☎ **04-74-85-39-23**) where concerts are still held for up to 7,500 people. You can visit November to March Tuesday to Friday 9:30am to 12:30pm and 2 to 5pm, weekends 1:30 to 5:30pm; September and October Tuesday to Sunday 9:30am to 1pm and 2 to 6pm; and April to August daily 9:30am to 1pm and 2 to 6pm. Admission is 2.80€.

As well as Roman remains, you'll find many religious buildings. If you have to choose just one during a busy itinerary, we'd recommend the **Cloître de Saint-André-Le-Bas** (☎ **04-74-78-71-06**) in Cour Saint-André-Le-Bas near the river. With its Romanesque stone carvings, columns and ornately carved capital stones, this church and cloister are all that remains of the 12th-century abbey. You can visit November to March Tuesday to Friday 9:30am to 12:30pm and 2 to 5pm, weekends 1:30 to 5:30pm; April to October Tuesday to Sunday 9:30am to 1pm and 2 to 6pm. Admission is 2.80€.

If you have a couple of hours for a side trip, you'll find one of the world's strangest pieces of architecture in Hauterives (south of Vienne). The **Palais Idéal du Facteur Cheval,** or **Palace of the Mailman Cheval** (www.facteurcheval.com; ☎ **04-75-68-81-19**) is the lifelong work of French postman Ferdinand Cheval. Built of stone and concrete and elaborately decorated with clamshells, it's a monumental tribute to one man's whimsical imagination. The work was finished in 1912, when Cheval was 76. Admission is 5.80€ for adults, 4.10€ for children 6 to 16. The palace is open in April to September daily 9:30am to 12:30pm and 1:30 to 6:30pm (until 7pm in July and Aug); November to March daily 9:30am to 12:30pm and 1:30 to 4:30pm.

Where to Shop

Every Saturday, the streets around central Vienne play host to one of the Rhône Valley's largest **food markets** so it's a great place to stock up on fresh fruit and vegetables as well as regional products such as pear-infused *Eau de Vie* (colorless fruit brandy). Check out **rue Testé du Bailler** for art galleries and **Yves Caire Créations** (7 rue Boson, ☎ **04-74-85-20-72**) for artisanal jewelry.

Where to Stay & Eat

Domaine de Clairefontaine ★★   Surrounded by a dreamy three-hectare park, this luxurious hotel is our favorite choice for Vienne and the Northern Rhône wine region. After wandering around the violet-carpeted forest and the peacock aviary, you can dine on trout from the freshwater pond in the Michelin-starred restaurant run by chef/owner Philippe Girardon. Well-priced accommodation is provided in the manor, the former stables and **Le Cottage,** a new complex for 2014 that also houses an informal bistro.

Chemin des Fontanettes, Chonas L'Amballan. ☎ 04-74-58-81-52. www.domaine-de-clairefontaine.fr. 35 units. 61€–250€ double. **Amenities:** Restaurant, bar, garden, tennis court, free Wi-Fi.

L'Estancot ★ FRENCH   With its bare-stone walls and bistro-style furnishings, this Bib Gourmand restaurant is famed for chef Bruno Ray's *criques*. Served with a simple green salad, these grated potato rostis come in all guises from Gourmandine (scallops and king prawns) to Strate de Boeuf (Charolais beef and spinach).

4 rue de la Table Ronde. ☎ **04-74-85-12-09.** Main courses 16.50€–25€. Fixed-price menus 17.50€–32€. Tues–Sat noon–2pm, 7:30–9:30pm.

La Pyramide ★★★ MODERN FRENCH   La Pyramide is one of the most famous restaurants in the Rhône Valley. It's where Parisians-in-the-know stop over on their annual pilgrimage to holiday in the Riviera. It was once home to the historic chef, Fernand Point, who died in 1955. Current owner and Chef Patrick Henriroux has preserved many of Point's secrets, especially his sauces. Gourmands should try the lobster prepared three ways or the Aubrac beef with foie gras cooked like a burger. The excellent, affordable bistro **Espace PH3** received an interior-designed makeover in 2012. Compared to the strikingly contemporary restaurants, the expensive bedrooms are rather old-fashioned. Doubles go for 200€ to 240€, suites for 390€ to 420€.

14 bd. Fernand Point, Vienne. ☎ **04-74-53-01-96.** www.lapyramide.com. Main courses 55€–95€; fixed-price weekday lunch with wine 64€; fixed-price dinner menu 112€–177€. Thurs–Mon 12–1:30pm and 7:30–9:30pm. Closed mid-Feb to mid-Mar and 1 week in mid-Aug.

NORTHERN RHÔNE WINE COUNTRY ★★★

A must-do side trip from Vienne is to explore the wine region of the Northern Rhône that stretches along the River Rhône from Vienne to Valence. Wines have been grown here since Gallo-Roman times: nowadays the region boasts sought-after red wines from **Côte-Rôtie** and **Hermitage,** as well as aromatic white wines from **Condrieu.** This photogenic wine region is characterized by steep hills terraced with golden-hued stone walls and horse-drawn ploughs, as some appellations are still cultivated by hand.

Tupin et Semons

Heading out of Vienne on the route national 86 (D386), you'll pass the mythical vineyards of Côte-Rôtie that cling to steep escarpments up to 60 percent gradient. The names of famous wine producers, such as Guigal and Chapoutier, are hewn into the hillside. The small village of Tupin et Semons lies at the heart of Côte-Rôtie. An undiscovered treasure of this appellation is **Le Domaine de Corps de Loup** (2 route de Lyon; ✆ 09-53-87-84-64; www.corpsdeloup.com) where energetic young vintner Tristan Daubrée has taken over the family domaine. You can call in advance for a tour around the vineyard and the 15th-century cellar before a tasting in the ancient chapel-turned-tasting-room. Nearby, you'll find the far grander **La Maison Vidal-Fleury** (RD 386, 48 route de Lyon; ✆ 04-74-56-10-18; www.vidal-fleury.com). Founded in 1781, Vidal-Fleury is the oldest continuously operating wine producer in the Rhône Valley. A long-standing US connection started with Thomas Jefferson dining there in 1787. The domaine is now owned by renowned wine producer Guigal and produces over one million bottles per year. After a tour of the bottling plant and the enormous vaulted cellars, you can enjoy tasting some of the 22 different wines.

WHERE TO STAY & EAT

Hôtel Le Beau Rivage ★   The best thing about this hotel in nearby Condrieu is its restaurant overlooking the majestic River Rhône. The fixed-price menus (from 39.50€ to 92€) are expensive, but the rich French fare served on Limoges porcelain plates comes complete with *amuses-bouches* and a tray of chocolates to end your meal. There's also a well-stocked wine list. This four-star hotel offers generously sized rooms complete with stylish fittings and a separate toilet and tub/shower.

2 rue Beau Rivage, Condrieu. ✆ **04-74-56-82-82.** www.hotel-beaurivage.com. 30 units. 160€–170€ double; 290€ suite. Parking free; garage 13€. On Southern outskirts of Condrieu, look for signs on the left. **Amenities:** Bar, restaurant; free Wi-Fi.

Tain-L'Hermitage

Drive south from Tupin et Semons along the D4 and then A7 towards Tain-L'Hermitage. A good way to start your exploration of the prestigious Hermitage appellation is with a *Balade Viticole:* a guided cycle ride around the vineyards accompanied by knowledgeable sommelier-turned-wine-merchant, **Fabien Louis** (✆ 04-75-08-40-56 / 06-70-11-09-18; www.ausommelier.com). The electric cycles make light work of the steep hillside as Fabien explains the geography and *terroir* of Hermitage and its neighbor Crozes-Hermitage. After the tour, you can check out more than 600 different Rhône Valley wines sold at vineyard prices at **Des Terrasses du Rhône** (22 rue des Bessards). Prices for vineyard cycle tours range from 25€ to 50€. Back in central Tain, you can turn up (groups over 5 people need to book in advance) for a free wine tasting at celebrated wine producer Michel Chapoutier's **wine school** (18 ave. Dr Paul Durand; ✆ 04-75-08-92-61; www.chapoutier.fr). It's a great way to learn about Côtes du Rhône wines as his expansive range covers appellations throughout the Northern and Southern Rhône Valley. Finally, gourmands of all ages will enjoy a visit to **La Cité du Chocolat (12 avenue du Président Franklin Roosevelt;**

C 04-75-09-27-27; www.citeduchocolat.com). This chocolate emporium is run by commercial chocolatier, Valrhona, who has been producing chocolate for the world's finest pastry chefs since 1922. More recently, they have developed a range of consumer chocolate bars. Rather than a fact-heavy history, you're taken on a sensorial experience through the stages of chocolate making from collecting pods to a live factory-line replica. There's also plentiful chocolate tasting along the way.

WHERE TO STAY & EAT

Hôtel Les Deux Côteaux ★   This tidy bed-and-breakfast is a convenient stopover for wine enthusiasts on the Rhône Valley trail. With views over the River Rhône, rooms have wooden floors and smart furnishings. Shower rooms are very small. No dinner is served, but **Brasserie Le Quai** (*C* 04-75-07-05-90) with its riverside terrace, is next door. Breakfast is copious with plentiful fresh fruit and homemade jams.

18 rue Joseph Peala. *C* **04-75-08-33-01.** www.hotel-les-2-coteaux.com. 67€–75€ double. **Amenities:** Free Wi-Fi.

Le Mangevins ★★★ FRENCH   The buzz of animated local diners fills this diminutive village restaurant with its wooden floors and simply stylish, contemporary decor. While owner Vincent welcomes diners, his Japanese wife Keiko is busy in the kitchen. For a chef with no formal training, Keiko shows a hint of genius, cooking dishes such as yellow tuna and Iberica Bellota pork to perfection. The small menu changes daily and is excellent value, while the extensive wine list includes wines by the glass.

6 ave. du Docteur Paul Durand, Tain-L'Hermitage. *C* **04-75-08-00-76.** Fixed-price dinner menu 31€. Mon–Fri noon–2pm, 8–9:30pm.

Umia ★ FUSION   It's surprising and yet refreshing that Tain's two best restaurants are both run by Japanese female chefs. Surrounded by Hermitage vineyards, Umia is a dreamy place for a summertime lunch. Chef Rika's Franco-Japanese fusion cuisine ranges from salmon teriyaki to foie gras. Her husband Frédéric Bau is Valrhona's creative director so you can be sure the chocolate desserts are good.

Domaine Gambert de Loche, 2 rue de la Petite Pierrelle, Route de Chantemerle les Blés. *C* **04-75-09-19-85.** www.umia.fr. Fixed price lunch menu 21€–26€; fixed-price dinner menu 63€–75€. Tues–Sat noon–2pm and 7:30–9pm.

VALENCE ★

671km (416 miles) SE of Paris; 100km (62 miles) S of Lyon

Follow the Rhône river south from Lyon and you'll reach this unassuming market town whose identity is now inextricably linked to its star attraction: Anne-Sophie Pic, France's only female three-star Michelin chef. A former Roman colony, it later became the capital of the Duchy of Valentinois, set up by Louis XII in 1493 for Cesare Borgia. Today Valence is a market town and distribution point for Rhône Valley fruit and vegetable producers. It's fitting that François Rabelais, who wrote of gargantuan appetites, spent time here as a student. Valence is a convenient day trip from Vienne or stopover on your way further South to Provence.

Essentials

GETTING THERE **Trains** take 1 hour from Lyon. For information, visit www.voyages-sncf.com or call ✆ **08-92-33-53-35.** If you're **driving** from Lyon, take A7 south.

VISITOR INFORMATION The **Office de Tourisme** is at 11 bd. Bancel (www.valencetourisme. com; ✆ **04-75-44-90-40**).

Exploring Valence

Gastronomy is the essential draw of Valence, but we'd recommend visiting the **Musée de Valence Art et Archaéologie** (place des Ormeaux, www.musee-valence.org; ✆ **04-75-79-20-80**), that re-opened in December 2013 fresh from an awe-inspiring renovation by architect Jean-Paul Philippon. A fusion of ancient and modern architecture, the museum focuses on landscapes, art collections spanning 16th-century to contemporary art. The new wing is topped by a 360-degree panorama over the Rhône valley towards the Vercors mountains. Open Tuesday to Sunday 10am-6pm (Tues from 2pm); entry fee is 5€.

Where to Stay, Eat & Shop

It's unusual for a small market town to have a Michelin-starred restaurant, but Valence has no less than three: the intimate **Flaveurs,** 32 Grande Rue (✆ **04-75-56-08-40**); the well-regarded **La Cachette,** 16 rue des Cévennes (✆ **04-75-55-24-13**) and the incomparable **Maison Pic** (see below). Check out Anne-Sophie Pic's **Scook,** (243 avenue Victor Hugo; ✆ **04-75-44-14-14;** www.scook.fr), a cooking school and shop selling kitchen utensils, cookbooks and aprons: ideal as souvenirs from this gastronomic hub.

Maison Pic ★★★ FRENCH   Anne-Sophie Pic is an unassuming culinary legend. When you meet her, she shakes your hand with a lop-sided grin as if to say that she really doesn't know what all the fuss is about. Whatever you choose, you'll be amazed by her imaginative flavors from ingredients sourced around the globe. As you sink into your plush upholstered chair, an army of staff serves you course after course for you to consume with specially commissioned cutlery. For those on more of a budget, we would recommend the on-site brasserie, **Le 7** (✆ **04-75-44-53-86**), where you'll dine like a king on a 30€-menu. Pic also rents 15 luxurious, contemporary guest rooms that are definitely worth a look. They cost 190€ to 400€ for a double, 410€ to 890€ for a suite.

285 av. Victor-Hugo. ✆ **04-75-44-15-32.** www.pic-valence.com. **Restaurant:** Fixed-price menus 95€–240€; Tues–Sat noon–1:30pm and 7:30–9:30pm. **Brasserie:** Fixed-price menu 30€; daily 12:30–2:30pm and 8–10pm. Closed Jan.

THE ARDÈCHE ★★

43km (27 miles) W of Montélimar; 138km (86 miles) SW of Lyon

The Ardèche is often dismissed as a tourist hub for campers visiting its spectacular gorges. Yet this verdant region offers much more for the discerning visitor: Troubadour castles, limestone caves and museums dedicated to the area's impressive prehistoric heritage. The world's largest replica cave is scheduled to reopen in 2015.

Essentials

GETTING THERE Vallon-Pont-d'Arc is accessible by **trains** from Lyon connecting in Valence. It's a 3-hr. journey from Lyon at about 40€ or 2 hr., 15 min. from Valence TGV station at about 20€. For information, visit www.voyages-sncf.com or call ✆ **08-92-33-53-35.** However, the Ardèche is best explored by car. If you're driving from Lyon, take the A7 south, then N7 at Montélimar Sud towards Pierrelatte. Head west on D13, then D59 and finally D4 to Vallon-Pont-d'Arc.

Vallon-Pont-d'Arc, a natural bridge in the Ardèche

VISITOR INFORMATION The **Office de Tourisme** is at 1 place de l'Ancienne Gare, Vallon-Pont-d'Arc (www.vallon-pont-darc.com; ✆ **04-75-88-04-01**).

Where to Stay & Eat

Château de Balazuc ★★★ With views over exquisite Balazuc and the Ardèche, the setting is exceptional. Home to courtly troubadours and writers since the Middle Ages, this bed-and-breakfast is now aptly owned by two Parisian ex-journalists. Since taking over in 2012, Luc and Florence have imbibed the castle with a convivial ambience greeting guests with evening cocktails and serving a communal dinner on Saturdays. The contemporary designed rooms show attention to details such as in-room Nespresso machines. The narrow outdoor pool is aptly described as a swimming corridor. Due to the number of stone steps, the castle is unsuitable for children or elderly guests.

Balazuc. ✆ **09-51-39-92-11.** www.chateaudebalazuc.com. 4 units. 130€–170€ double. **Amenities:** Jacuzzi; outdoor pool; free Wi-Fi.

Exploring the Ardèche

The Ardèche Gorges ★★ CANYON Hewn over centuries by the River Ardèche, a 60m (197-ft.) high natural limestone arch is the emblem of the Ardèche gorges. France's fastest-flowing river has carved a 30km (19-mile) path through limestone cliffs that ascend up to 300m high. Visitors have been able to canoe down the gorges since 1932. There are dozens of kayak rental companies, but one of the best is **Aventure Canoës,** 1 place Allende Neruda (www.aventure-canoes.fr; ✆ **04-75-37-18-14**). The best time for kayaking is April to late November when the waters are green and sluggish and safer than during winter months. Alternatively, you can drive around the

> ### Insider Tip
>
> The best place for a snack in tourist-swarmed Vallon-Pont-d'Arc is **Le Chelsea** (45 bd Peschaire Alizon, Vallon-Pont-d'Arc; ✆ **04-75-88-01-40**) whose motto, "Take It Easy," sums up its laid-back charm. In summer months, meals are served on the shaded terrace.

Grotte Chauvet

In 2015, the cavern near Vallon-Pont-d'Arc will reopen. This cavern depicts life in Upper Paleolithic times. With a surface area of 3000 sq. m, it is the world's largest replica cave. The original cavern, dating back 36,000 years, is awaiting UNESCO World Heritage status. Check with the tourist office for opening hours.

gorges on a well-marked route between Vallon-Pont-d'Arc and Pont St-Esprit. Watch out for careless drivers too busy taking snapshots to look where they are going.
Vallon-Pont-d'Arc to Pont St-Esprit.

Le Grand Site de L'Aven Orgnac ★★ MUSEUM/CAVE   This is the perfect wet-weather attraction as the limestone caves are most beautiful when it rains. Discovered in 1939, the *grotte* is one of the largest in France with a dazzling array of stalactites and stalagmites. After a top-to-bottom renovation, the adjacent archaeological museum, **Cité de la Préhistoire,** reopened in 2014. The dry ancient artifacts have been brought alive through child-friendly exhibits, 3D animations and drawings by artist-cum-archaeologist Benoit Clarys. This imaginatively developed archaeological experience leaves visitors of all ages with palpable ideas of how prehistoric men lived in Paleolithic to Iron Age times.
Orgnac-L'Aven. ✆ **04-75-39-65-10.** www.orgnac.com. Children over 14 and adults 10.30€; children 6–14 6.40€; free children 5 and under. Mid-Nov to Jan daily 2–4:45pm; Feb–Mar and Oct to mid-Nov daily 10am–noon, 2–4:45pm; Apr–June and Sept daily 9:30am–5:30pm; Jul–Aug daily 9:30am–6pm.

Néovinum ★ MUSEUM   This wine experience opened in 2013 to provide a showcase for the table wines of Ardèche. The exhibition is adapted for wine beginners and families with easy-to-understand explanations on the basics of *terroir*, wine production and tasting. Children are entertained with puzzles, games and interactive exhibits, while adults are given their own wine profile.
Boulevard de L'Europe Unie, Ruoms. ✆ **04-75-39-98-08.** www.neovinum.fr. Adults 6€; under 18 free. Oct–Mars Tues–Sat 9am–noon, 2–6pm; Apr–Sept Mon–Sun 9:30am–1pm and 3–7pm, Sun 9:30–1pm.

Grotto Orgnac

PROVENCE

By Kathryn Tomasetti

The ancient Greeks left their vines, the Romans their monuments, but it was the 19th-century Impressionists who most shaped the romance of Provence today. Cézanne, Gauguin, Chagall, and countless others were drawn to the unique light and vibrant spectrum brought forth by what van Gogh called "the transparency of the air." Modern-day visitors will delight in the region's culture, colors, and world-class museums. And they will certainly dine well, too.

Provence, perhaps more than any other part of France, blends past and present with an impassioned pride. It has its own language and customs, and some of its festivals go back to medieval times. The region is bounded on the north by the Dauphine River, on the west by the Rhône, on the east by the Alps, and on the south by the Mediterranean. In chapter 13, we focus on the part of Provence known as the Côte d'Azur, or the French Riviera.

AVIGNON ★★★

691km (428 miles) S of Paris; 83km (51 miles) NW of Aix-en-Provence; 98km (61 miles) NW of Marseille

In the 14th century, Avignon was the capital of Christendom. What started as a temporary stay by Pope Clement V in 1309, when Rome was deemed too dangerous even for clergymen, became a 67-year golden age. The cultural and architectural legacy left by the six popes who served during this period makes Avignon one of Europe's most alluring medieval destinations.

Today this walled city of some 95,000 residents is a major stop on the route from Paris to the Mediterranean. In recent years, it has become known as a cultural center, thanks to its annual international performing-arts festivals and wealth of experimental theaters and art galleries.

Essentials

ARRIVING Frequent TGV **trains** depart from Paris's Gare de Lyon. The ride takes 2 hours and 40 minutes and arrives at Avignon's modern TGV station 10 minutes from town by shuttle bus. The one-way fare is around 80€ depending on the date and time, although it can also be as cheap as 25€ if booked well in advance. Regular trains arrive from Marseille (trip time: 70 min.; 20.80€ oneway) and Arles (trip time: 20 min.; 7.50€ one-way), arriving at either the TGV or Avignon's central station. Hourly trains from Aix-en-Provence (trip time: 20 min.; 25€ one-way) shuttle exclusively between the two towns' TGV stations. For rail information, visit www.voyages-sncf.com or call ✆ **36-35.** The regional **bus** routes (www.info-ler.fr; ✆ **08-21-20-22-03**) go from Avignon to Arles (trip time: 1 hr., 10 min.; 7.10€ one-way) and Aix-en Provence (trip time: 1 hr., 15 min.; 17.40€ one-way). The bus station at Avignon is the **Gare Routière,** 5 av. Monclar (✆ **04-90-82-07-35**). If you're **driving** from Paris, take A6 south to Lyon, and then A7 south to Avignon.

Provence

VISITOR INFORMATION The **Office de Tourisme** is at 41 cours Jean-Jaurès (www.avignon-tourisme.com; ☎ 04-32-74-32-74).

CITY LAYOUT Avignon's picturesque Old Town is surrounded by 14th-century ramparts. Within the walls is a mix of winding roads, medieval townhouses, and pedestrianized streets. To the west of the city is the Rhône River, and beyond, Villeneuve les Avignon. Just south of the Old Town sits the Gare d'Avignon Centre train station.

SPECIAL EVENTS The international **Festival d'Avignon** (www.festival-avignon. com; ☎ **04-90-14-14-14**), held for 3 weeks in July, focuses on avant-garde theater, dance, and music. Tickets are 17€ to 40€. Prices for rooms skyrocket during this period, so book yours well in advance. An edgier alternative festival, the **Avignon OFF** (www.avignonleoff.com; ☎ **04-90-85-13-08**), takes place almost simultaneously in July, with theater performances in various improbable venues.

Getting Around

ON FOOT All of Avignon's major sights—as well as its infinitely enchanting back streets—are easily accessible on foot. The helpful tourist office's free maps are marked with four easy walking routes, ideal for getting a feel for the city.

BY BICYCLE & MOTOR SCOOTER The **Vélopop** bicycle-sharing scheme (www. velopop.fr, from 1€ per day) lets registered riders borrow any of the city's 200 bikes for up to 30 minutes at a time for free. To get out of town and explore the surrounding countryside, **Provence Bike,** 7 av. St-Ruf (www.provence-bike. com; ☎ **04-90-27-92-61**), rents different models for around 12€ to 40€ per day. It's possible to reserve a bike online.

BY CAR Traffic and a labyrinthine one-way system means it's best to park once you've arrived in Avignon's town center. Seven fee-paying parking lots and two free ones are dotted around the city.

BY TAXI Taxis **Avignon** (www.taxis-avignon.fr; ☎ 04-90-82-20-20).

BY PUBLIC TRANSPORT Eco-friendly **Baladine** vehicles (www.tcra.fr; Mon–Sat 10am–12:30pm and 2–6pm; during July and Aug daily 10am–8pm) zip around within the city walls for 0.50€ per ride.

[FastFACTS] AVIGNON

ATMs/Banks Avignon's town center is home to banks aplenty, including three along cours Jean-Jaurès.

Doctors & Hospitals **Hôpital Général Henri Default,** 305 rue Raoul Follereau (www. ch-avignon.fr; ☎ **04-32-75-33-33**).

Internet Access **Chez M@W,** 41 rue de Vieux Sextier (☎ **04-90-86-19-03**).

Mail & Postage **La Poste,** 4 cours Président Kennedy (☎ **36-31**).

Pharmacies **Pharmacie des Halles,** 48 rue Bonneterie (☎ **04-90-82-54-27**).

Where to Stay

For travelers on a budget, the friendly **Hôtel Le Colbert** (www.avignon-hotel-colbert.com) is an excellent town center option.

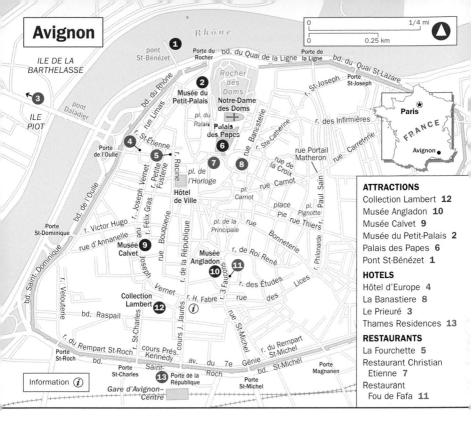

Avignon

ILE DE LA BARTHELASSE

ILE PIOT

Rhône

pont St-Bénézet **1**

pont Daladier **3**

Porte du Rocher

bd. du Quai de la Ligne

Porte de la Ligne

bd. du Quai St-Lazare

r. St-Joseph

Porte St-Joseph

Rocher des Doms

Musée du Petit-Palais **2**

Notre-Dame des Doms

pl. du Palais

Palais des Papes **6**

bd. du Rhône

r. Limas

r. St-Étienne **5**

Porte de l'Oulle **4**

r. Petite Fusterie

r. Racine

pl. de l'Horloge

Hôtel de Ville

7

8

r. Banasterie

r. Ste-Catherine

r. des Infirmières

rue Portail Matheron

rue Carreterie

rue de la Croix

rue Carnot

pl. Carnot

place Pie

pl. Pignotte

rue Thiers

r. Paul Sain

r. Philonarde

FRANCE

Paris ★

Avignon ●

bd. de l'Oulle

Porte St-Dominique

r. Victor Hugo

r. d'Annanelle

r. Félix Gras

r. Joseph Vernet

r. Bouquerie

r. de la République

Musée Calvet **9**

Musée Angladon **10**

r. de Roi René

r. des Études

Lices

11

bd. Saint-Dominique

r. Velouterie

bd. Raspail

Collection Lambert **12**

r. J. Jaurès

r. H. Fabre

(i)

r. des Faucons

rue St-Michel

r. du Rempart St-Roch

cours Prés. Kennedy

cours J. Jaurès

r. St-Charles

Porte St-Roch

bd.

Porte St-Charles

Saint-

Roch

av. du 7e Génie

r. du Rempart St-Michel

bd. St-Michel

Porte Magnanen

13 Porte de la République

Porte St-Michel

Gare d'Avignon–Centre

Information **(i)**

0 — 1/4 mi
0 — 0.25 km

ATTRACTIONS

Collection Lambert **12**
Musée Angladon **10**
Musée Calvet **9**
Musée du Petit-Palais **2**
Palais des Papes **6**
Pont St-Bénézet **1**

HOTELS

Hôtel d'Europe **4**
La Banastiere **8**
Le Prieuré **3**
Thames Residences **13**

RESTAURANTS

La Fourchette **5**
Restaurant Christian Etienne **7**
Restaurant Fou de Fafa **11**

La Banasterie ★ This oh-so-pretty B&B is situated in a 16th-century property just opposite the Palais des Papes. It's owned by gregarious chocolate lovers Françoise and Jean-Michel—and their candy-fueled passion permeates throughout. The traditionally decorated bedrooms (exposed stone walls, sumptuous fabrics) are named for varieties of chocolate, and decadent cups of cocoa are offered at bedtime. The indulgent breakfast alone (included in the rate) makes this spot unmissable. Note that there is no elevator.

11 rue de la Banasterie. ✆ **06-87-72-96-36.** www.labanasterie.com. 5 units. 90€–145€ double; 145€–190€ suite. Parking 10€. **Amenities:** Free Wi-Fi.

Le Prieuré ★ Those who perceive Provence as breakfast under an arbor, a set of tennis on a leaf-strewn court, a lazy lunch, then a doze by the pool—all topped off by chilled rosé at sunset—have found the right place. What could be calmer than staying in a former 14th-century convent ringed by lavender-scented gardens in the historic suburb of Villeneuve? Individually styled rooms and suites are casually arranged over three ancient buildings. Original floors, hardwood furniture, and locally purchased antiques blend with marble bathrooms, fine linens, and modernist Louis XIV chairs. Lunch (fixed-price menu 40€–50€) and dinner (fixed-price menus 78€–140€) in the herb-filled gardens are prepared by young head chef Fabien Fage from Arles. Luxurious locally sourced cuisine includes strawberries from Beaucaire, pigeon from Nimes, and rockfish from the Mediterranean near Marseille.

7 place du Chapitre. ✆ **04-90-15-90-15.** www.leprieure.com. 38 units. 200€–540€ double; 350€–900 suite. Free parking. Closed Nov–Mar. **Amenities:** Restaurant; bar; concierge; outdoor pool; room service; tennis; free Wi-Fi.

ALTERNATIVE ACCOMMODATIONS

Thames Résidences ★★ This handful of suites and superbly equipped apartments lies a short stroll from both the train station and Avignon's city center. Decor is Provençal-themed, and each one boasts either its own private balcony or panoramic views over the town's medieval ramparts. As well as free satellite TVs, speedy Wi-Fi, and unlimited free telephone calls abroad, some of the residences also possess kitchenettes and sleek Nespresso Pixie espresso machines. *Note:* Apartments may also be rented (at a discount) by the week.

36 bd. Saint Roch. ✆ **04-32-70-17-01.** www.thames-residences.com. 9 units. 169€–259€ 2-person apartments. Free parking. **Amenities:** Free Wi-Fi.

Where to Eat

La Fourchette ★★ PROVENÇAL Set a block back from the bustling place de l'Horloge, this upscale bistro has been a local favorite since it opened its doors in 1982. Philippe Hilly, the sixth generation in his family's long line of chefs, dishes up a cuisine that's sophisticated yet hearty: Think saffron-infused salt cod *brandied* served with crusty bread, or seared scallops atop fennel puree. Walls are adorned with an eclectic collection of antique cutlery (*la fourchette* translates as "the fork"), making the ambience as alluring as the food.

17 rue Racine. ✆ **04-90-85-20-93.** www.la-fourchette.net. Main courses 20€; fixed-price menu 33€. Mon–Fri 12:15–1:45pm and 7:15–9:45pm. Closed 3 weeks in Aug.

Restaurant Christian Etienne ★★★ PROVENÇAL This Michelin-starred temple of gastronomy is perched atop a 12th-century stone edifice—complete with 15th-century frescoes—just next door to the Palais des Papes. Avignon-born Chef Etienne is wildly innovative, and many of his dishes have more than a hint of molecular influence. Fixed-price menus are themed around single ingredients such as duck, lobster, truffles, or (summertime only) heavenly heirloom tomatoes.

10 rue de Mons. ✆ **04-90-86-16-50.** www.christian-etienne.fr. Main courses 30€–50€; fixed-price lunch 35€, dinner 80€–150€. Tues–Sat noon–1:15pm and 7:30–9:15pm. Closed 2 wks in Nov.

Restaurant Fou de Fafa ★★ FRENCH/PROVENÇAL It may be British-owned, but this cozy little restaurant dishes up authentic local cuisine—often with a contemporary twist—that truly hits its mark. Delicious combinations may include pork filet mignon served with a cider jus and mashed sweet potato, or sea bream in saffron cream paired with Camargue rice. *Note:* The menu is short and highly seasonal.

17 rue des Trois Falcons. ✆ **04-32-76-35-13.** Fixed-price menu 23€–28€. Tues–Sat noon–1:15pm and 7:30–9:15pm. Closed Dec–Jan.

Exploring Avignon

Avignon is undoubtedly one of the prettiest towns in France. From its impressively imposing skyline to the verdant Ile de la Barthelasse opposite, it's a delight to simply amble along aimlessly, perhaps stopping at a sidewalk cafe or two en route. Countless hidden gems crop up along the way, including the sun-dappled courtyard of the **Hôtel d'Europe** (www.heurope.com). This luxury hotel has

The Papal Palace dominates the Avignon skyline

been in operation since 1799, welcoming luminaries from Charles Dickens to Jacqueline Kennedy.

Poking westward from the grassy banks of the Rhône River, **Pont St-Bénézet** ★★ (www.avignon-pont.com; ✆ **04-32-74-32-74**) was constructed between 1177 and 1185. Once spanning the Rhône and connecting Avignon with Villeneuve-lèz-Avignon, it is now a ruin, with only 4 of its original 22 arches remaining (half of it fell into the river back in 1669). The remains of the bridge have the same opening hours as those of the Palais des Papes (see below). Admission is 4.50€ adults, 3.50€ seniors and students, and free children 7 and under.

Collection Lambert ★★ MUSEUM   This contemporary art space is housed within an 18th-century private home that once belonged to collector and gallery owner Yvonne Lambert. It stages three groundbreaking exhibitions each year. Works may range from video and photography to conceptual installations. Major artists such as Anselm Kiefer, Jenny Holier, and Cy Tomboy have all been featured. The museum reopens in July 2015 after a lengthy expansion project.

5 rue Violate. ✆ **04-90-16-56-20.** www.collectionlambert.fr. Admission changes according to exhibition, free for children 5 and under. July–Aug daily 11–7pm; Sept–June Tues–Sun 11–6pm.

Musée Angladon ★★ MUSEUM   Haute-couture designer Jacques Doucet (1853–1929) didn't limit himself to the appreciation of finely cut fabrics. His former home is now a showcase for the international artworks that he and his wife collected over their lifetimes—from 16th-century Buddhas and Louis XVI chairs to Degas's famous dancers and canvases by Cézanne, Sisley, and Modigliani. Temporary exhibitions may showcase works by Pierre Bonnard or Henri de Toulouse-Lautrec.

5 rue Laborer. ✆ **04-90-82-29-03.** www.angladon.com. Admission 6€ adults, 4€ students and children 13–17, 1.50€ children 7–12, free for children 6 and under. Tues–Sun 1–6pm. Closed Tues in winter.

Musée Calved ★ MUSEUM   Housed in what was formerly an 18th-century private home, the Musée Calved is Avignon's top fine art museum. Native son Esprit Calved bequeathed to the city upon his death a lifetime's worth of acquired art, including works by Verne, David, Corot, Manet, and Soutine, plus a collection of ancient silverware. Recent additions include a display dedicated to art and artifacts of ancient Egypt.

65 rue Joseph-Verne. ✆ **04-90-86-33-84.** www.musee-calvet-avignon.com. Admission 6€ adults, 3€ students, free for children 12 and under. Wed–Mon 10am–1pm and 2–6pm.

Musée du Petit-Palais ★ MUSEUM An ideal complement to the Palais des Papes' architectural austerity, this museum's artworks were originally part of a collection belonging to 19th-century art lover Giampietro Campania. Today the museum exhibits a myriad of paintings from the Italian and Provençal schools of the 13th to 16th centuries. Botticelli's "Madonna with Child" is a particular highlight.

Palais des Archevêques, place du Palais des Papes. ✆ **04-90-86-44-58.** www.petit-palais.org. Admission 6€ adults, 3€ students, free for children 11 and under. Wed–Mon 10am–1pm and 2–6pm.

Palais des Papes ★★★ PALACE Dominating Avignon from a hilltop is one of the most famous, or notorious, palaces in the Christian world. Headquarters of a schismatic group of cardinals who came close to destroying the authority of the popes in Rome, this fortress is the city's most popular monument. Because of its massive size, you may be tempted to opt for a guided tour—but these can be monotonous. The detailed audioguide, included in the price of admission will likely suffice.

A highlight is the **Chapelle St-Jean,** known for its frescoes of John the Baptist and John the Evangelist, attributed to the school of Matteo Giovanetti and painted between 1345 and 1348. The **Grand Tinsel (Banquet Hall)** is about 41m (134 ft.) long and 9m (30 ft.) wide; the pope's table stood on the south side. The walls of the **Pope's Bedroom,** on the first floor of the Tour des Anges, are painted with foliage, birds, and squirrels. The **Studium (Stag Room)**—the study of Clement VI—was frescoed in 1343 with hunting scenes. The **Grande Audience (Great Receiving Hall)** contains frescoes of the prophets, also attributed to Giovanetti and painted in 1352.

Palais des Papes

St-André Abbey Gardens

Note that the 12th-century **Cathédrale Notre-Dame des Doms cathedral,** just next door on the main square, contains the elaborate tombs of popes Jean XXII and Benoît XII.

Place du Palais des Papes. ℰ **04-32-74-32-74.** www.palais-des-papes.com. Admission (including audioguide) 11€ adults, 9€ seniors and students, free for children 7 and under. Daily Nov–Feb 9:30am–5:45pm; Mar 9am–6:30pm; Apr–June and Sept–Oct 9am–7pm; July 9am–8pm; Aug 9am–8:30pm.

Outlying Attractions in Villeneuve-Lez-Avignon ★

While the popes lived in exile, cardinals built palaces, or *livers,* just across the Rhône in sleepy Villenueve-lez-Avignon. Many visitors prefer to stay or dine here—it's quieter and less modernized, while still convenient to Avignon's major attractions. Take bus no. 5, which crosses the larger of the two relatively modern bridges, the **Pont Daladier.**

Avignon's **Office de Tourisme** can provide further information, as can the local branch in place Charles David (www.tourisme-villeneuvelezavignon.fr; ℰ **04-90-25-61-33**).

St-André Abbey Gardens ★★ GARDENS   Clustered around the 17th-century Benedictine Abbaye St-André (under new ownership as of 2013), these spectacular gardens include a rose-trellis colonnade, fountains flecked with lily pads, and an olive orchard. They also offer unbeatable views over the Rhône Valley and Avignon's skyline beyond. Fort St-André (separate entrance fee, 5.50€), founded in 1360 by Jean-le-Bon to serve as a symbol of might to the pontifical powers across the river, is adjacent to the monastery.

Fort Saint-André, rue Montée du Fort. ℰ **04-90-25-55-95.** www.abbayesaintandre.fr. Admission 5€ adults, 4.50€ students and ages 13–18, free for children 12 and under. Tues–Sun Mar and Oct 10am–1pm and 2–5pm, Apr 10am–1pm and 2–6pm, May–Sept 10am–6pm. Closed Nov–Feb.

Val de Bénédiction Chartreuse ★ MONASTERY   France's largest Carthusian monastery, built in 1352, comprises a church, three cloisters, cells that housed the medieval monks, and a 12th-century graveyard where Pope Innocent VI is entombed. Part of the complex houses the *Centre National d'Ecritures du Spectacle,* a residence for artists and playwrights who live rent-free for up to a year to deepen their crafts. Art exhibitions, concerts, and theater take place throughout the year.

58 rue de la République. © **04-90-15-24-24**. www.chartreuse.org. Admission 8€ adults, 5.50€ students and under 25, free for children 17 and under. Aug daily 9am–7:30pm; July and Sept daily 9am–6:30pm; Apr–June daily 9:30am–6:30pm; Oct–Mar Mon–Fri 9:30am–5pm, Sat–Sun 10am–5pm.

Shopping

The chain boutique **Souleiado,** 19 rue Joseph-Verne (© **04-90-86-32-05**), sells reproductions of 18th- and 19th-century Provençal fabrics by the meter or made into clothing and linens. There is also a large selection of housewares and gifts.

Hervey Baume, 19 rue Petite Fusterie (© **04-90-86-37-66**), is the place to buy a Provençal table—or something to put on it. A massive inventory includes French folk art and hand-blown hurricane lamps. **Jaffier-Parsi,** 42 rue des Four-bisseurs (© **04-90-86-08-85**), is known for copper saucepans from the Nor-man town of Villedieu-les-Poêles, which has been making them since the Middle Ages.

A covered market with 40 different merchants is **Les Halles,** place Pie, open Tuesday through Sunday (6am–1:30pm). The **flower market** is on place des Carmes on Saturday (8am–1pm), and the **flea market** occupies the same place each Sunday morning (6am–1pm).

Nightlife

Avignon's beautiful people frequent **Les Ambassadeurs,** 27 rue Braincase (www.clubesambassadeurs.fr; © **04-90-86-31-55**), an upscale dance club. The **Red Zone DJ bar,** 25 rue Carnot (www.redzonedjbar.com; © **04-90-27-02-44**), offers a different musical theme every night (salsa, electronic, and more). **83 Verne,** 83 rue Joseph Vernet (www.83vernet.com; © **04-90-85-99-04**), switches from restaurant into dance club mode around 10pm, under the high-ceilinged hallways and stone courtyards of a former 1363 Benedictine convent.

Behind the Hôtel d'Europe, disco-bar **L'Esclave,** 12 rue du Limas (www.esclavebar.com; © **04-90-85-14-91**), is a focal point of the city's gay scene.

DAY TRIPS FROM AVIGNON

Orange ★

31km (19 miles) N of Avignon

Antiquities-rich Orange was not named for citrus fruit, but as a dependency of the Dutch House of Orange-Nassau during the Middle Ages. It is home to two UNESCO World Heritage sites: Europe's third-largest **triumphal arch** and its best-preserved **Roman theater.** Louis XIV, who once considered moving the theater to Versailles, claimed: "It is the finest wall in my kingdom." The Théâtre Antique is now the site of **Les Choragi's d'Orange** (www.choregies.fr), a sum-mertime opera and classical music festival.

Just 10km (6 miles) south along the D68 is **Châteauneuf-du-Pape,** a prestigious appellation known for its bold red wines. Spend an afternoon visiting the village's numerous tasting rooms, winding your way up to the ruins of a castle that served as a summer residence for Pope John XXII.

Roman theater at Orange

ESSENTIALS

Frequent **trains** (trip time: 20 min.; 6.20€ one-way) and **buses** (www.sudest-mobilites.fr; ✆ **04-32-76-00-40;** trip time: 1 hr.; 2€ one-way) connect Avignon and Orange. If you're **driving** from Avignon, take A7 north to Orange. The **Office de Tourisme** is at 5 cours Aristide-Briand (www.otorange.fr; ✆ **04-90-34-70-88**).

EXPLORING ORANGE & AROUND

The carefully restored **Théâtre Antique ★★★**, rue Madeleine Roch (www.theatre-antique.com; ✆ **04-90-51-17-60**), dates from the days of Augustus. Built into the side of a hill, it once held 9,000 spectators in tiered seats. Nearly 105m (344 ft.) long and 37m (121 ft.) high, it's open daily November to February 9:30am to 4:30pm; March and October 9:30am to 5:30pm; April, May, and September 9am to 6pm; and June to August 9am to 7pm. Admission (which includes a free audioguide) is 9.50€ adults, 7.50€ students and children 8 to 17, and free children 7 and under.

The imposing **Arc de Triomphe ★**, avenue de lark-de-Triomphe, comprises a trio of arches held up by Corinthian columns embellished with military and maritime emblems. Also built during the reign of Augustus, it was once part of the original town's fortified walls.

WHERE TO EAT

At **Au Petit Patio,** 58 cours Aristide Briand (✆ **04-90-29-69-27**), contemporary Provençal cuisine is served on a petite outdoor terrace. Sample honey-glazed sea bass or summery strawberry tartare.

Vaison-la-Romaine ★★

50km (31 miles) NE of Avignon

Part medieval village, part Roman ruins, and all crowned by a 13th-century castle, Vaison-la-Romaine sits in the fertile northern reaches of Provence. Well off this region's traditional tourist trail, the combination of history and low-key allure makes for an exquisite escape. To the east of Vaison-la-Romaine towers Mont Venous, a monolith of a mountain (1,900m/6,300 ft.) famed for its bogeyman role in the annual Tour de France cycle race.

Cyclists climb Mont Venous in stage 15 of the 2013 Tour de France

ESSENTIALS

Frequent **trains** (trip time: 20 min.; 6.20€ one-way) connect Avignon and Orange. From Orange, hop aboard bus no. 4 (www.vaucluse.fr; trip time: 45 min.; 2€ one-way). If you're **driving** from Avignon, take A7 north, veering northeast onto D977. The **Office de Tourisme** is at place du Chanoine Sauté (www.vaison-ventoux-tourisme.com; ✆ **04-90-36-02-11**).

EXPLORING VAISON-LA-ROMAINE & AROUND

Ancient capital to the Voconce people, Vaison-la-Romaine is home to two important archaeological sites, **Payment** and **La Vilasse** (www.provenceromaine.com; ✆ **04-90-36-50-48**). Both are peppered with ancient Roman residences, the remains of thermal baths, statues, and mosaics. The sites are open daily November, December and February 10am to noon and 2 to 5pm; March and October 10am to 12:30pm and 2 to 5:30pm; April and May 9:30am to 6pm; and June to September 9:30am to 6:30pm. From January to early February both sites are closed. Admission (which includes a free audioguide and is valid for 24 hr.) is 8€ adults, 3€ students and children 12 to 18, and free children 11 and under.

For more detailed information about Vaison-la-Romaine's history, visit the **Musée Archéologique Théo Desplans,** located within Payment (entrance valid with same ticket, same opening hours), which focuses on local and regional discoveries.

The oldest part of Vaison-la-Romaine itself—the Cité Médiévale—is a medieval wonderland, crisscrossed by winding alleyways and splashed with pretty squares. To the south sits its **Roman bridge,** dating from the first century ad, which spans the Ouvèze River. If possible, time your visit to coincide with the town's superb regional market (Tues, 8am–1pm, held around town).

Every 3 years, Vaison-la-Romaine holds the 10-day **Chorales,** or Choral Festival, in August (www.choralies.fr, next edition 2016). Visitors also descend on the town annually for **Vaison Dances** (www.vaison-danses.com), a prestigious dance festival held every July.

SHOPPING FOR brocante IN PROVENCE

In France, there's a wide gap between true antiques and old knickknacks, and it's wise to know the difference. For serious purchases, stick to well-established *antiquaires*, found in almost every town and city. If you're looking for more affordable treasures and enjoy flea markets, what you really want is a *brocante*. These are usually held outside on specific days (the markets in Cannes are a good example; see chapter 13). Furniture and objects can also be found in warehouses known as *depot-ventes*.

A village that specializes in *brocante* is **Isle-sur-la-Sorgue,** situated 23km (14 miles) east of Avignon, 11km (6¾ miles) north of Cavaillon, and 42km (26 miles) south of Orange. The **Déballage Brocante** is held on Sundays; the activity starts at 9am and finishes around 6pm. From 8am to 2pm, there's also a Provençal food market. If you're driving, try for a parking space in the Parking Portalet or

Parking Allele des Muriers (both free). The *brocante* is concentrated in the southern part of town, where you'll find warehouses filled with dealers and loot—although there are plenty of small stalls dotted throughout the pedestrianized town center, too.

Isle-sur-la-Sorgue's **Office de Tourisme** is at place de la Liberté (www.oti-delasorgue.fr; ✆ **04-90-38-04-78**).

WHERE TO EAT

Head to **Restaurant le Bleater,** place Théodore Subpanel (www.le-bateleur.com; ✆ **04-90-36-28-04,** closed Mon) for one of their seasonal lunchtime menus (two courses for 19€, three courses for 23€). Cuisine makes the most of local ingredients, from wild mushrooms and Mediterranean bonito to free-range chicken from nearby Monteux and heirloom tomatoes.

GORDES ★★★

720km (446 miles) S of Paris; 38km (24 miles) E of Avignon; 77km (48 miles) N of Aix-en-Provence; 92km (57 miles) N of Marseille

Hilltop Gordes is a supremely chic rocky outcrop deep in Provence. From afar, this gorgeous *village perches* (perched village) is a pastiche of beiges, grays, and terra cotta that blushes golden at sunrise and sunset. The place also served as a backdrop for the love affair between Marion Cotillard and Russell Crowe in the movie "A Good Year."

Essentials

ARRIVING Gordes is difficult to reach via public transportation. The closest train station is Cavaillon, where trains arrive from Avignon's central station (trip time: 35 min.; 7€ one-way).

Gordes

From here, bus no. 15.3 departs three times daily for place du Château in Gordes (www.sudest-mobilites.fr; trip time: 35 min.; 2€ one-way). Another option is to take a 1-day coach tour from either Avignon or Aix-en-Provence. **Autocars Lieutaud** (www.excursionprovence.com; ✆ **04-90-86-36-75;** from 55€ per person) offers this service in Avignon, as does the Aix-en-Provence tourist office (www.aixenprovencetourism.com; ✆ **04-42-16-11-61;** from 60€ per person). By car, Gordes is a 38km (24-mile) drive east of Avignon via D900.

VISITOR INFORMATION   The **Office de Tourisme** is at Le Château (www.gordes-village.com; ✆ **04-90-72-02-75**).

[FastFACTS] GORDES

Mail & Postage   **La Poste,** place du Jehu de Boules (✆ **36-31**). Note that the post office also offers an ATM.

Pharmacies   **Pharmacie de Gordes,** 2 rue de l'Eglise (✆ **04-90-72-02-10**).

Where to Stay

La Ferme de la Hope ★★   This combination bed-and-breakfast, and its superb Provençal restaurant (also open to non-guests), spills over a pristinely renovated 18th-century farmhouse. Country-style guest rooms are named after their former functions, such as Hay Loft or Wine Cellar, and all boast cute modern bathrooms. An abundant buffet breakfast (croissants, fresh juices, local cheeses) is served on the poolside terrace. La Ferme's location, just down the road from Gordes itself, makes it perfectly positioned for exploring the wider Luberon region, including the gorgeous villages of Bonnie and Roussillon.

R.D. 156, Les Pourquiers. ✆ **04-90-72-12-25.** www.lafermedelahuppe.com. 10 units. 145€–225€ double, breakfast included. Half-board available. Free parking Closed Nov–Feb. **Amenities:** Restaurant, outdoor pool; free Wi-Fi.

Where to Eat

L'Artegal ★ PROVENÇAL   A standout venue among Gordes' handful of eateries, this family-run restaurant prides itself on its creative local cuisine. Well-conceived dishes include lentil and salmon tartare, rich lamb *nearing* stew, and the restaurant's own generous adaptation of duck-heavy *salade Landaise*. Tucked into the shadow of the Château de Gordes, L'Artegal is a romantic spot to dine, particularly in the evening when the town's day trippers have disappeared.

Place du Château. ✆ **04-90-72-02-54.** Main courses 16€–26€; fixed-price lunch 22€; fixed-price dinner 36€. Thurs–Tues noon–1:45pm; Thurs–Mon 7:15–8:45pm. Closed mid-Jan to mid-Mar.

Exploring Gordes

Gordes is best explored on foot. Its primarily pedestrianized streets unwind downhill from the Château de Gordes, the Renaissance rehabilitation of a 12th-century fortress. Its windows still bear grooves from bows and arrows used to protect Gordes during Gallo-Roman times, when it was a border town. Today Gordes is more likely to be invaded by easels. Its austere beauty has drawn many artists, including Marc Chagall and Hungarian painter Victor Vasarely, who spent summers here gathering inspiration for his geometric abstract art.

Caves du Palais St. Firming ★ RUINS Steep Gordes lacks an abundance of surface area, so early settlers burrowed into the rock itself, creating an underground network of crude rooms and stairways over seven levels. Over the centuries, these rooms have housed the village's production of olive oil and grain. Though the tunnels are adequately lit, children are provided with a small headlamp to let them feel like true explorers.

Rue du Belvédère. ✆ **04-90-72-02-75.** www.caves-saint-firmin.com. Admission 6€ adults, 4.50€ students. Free audioguide. May–Sept Wed–Mon 10am–6pm. Oct–Apr by reservation only.

Château de Gordes ★ HISTORIC HOME/ART MUSEUM Access to the ancient château is reserved for visitors of its small museum, dedicated to contemporary Flemish painter Pol Mara (1920–98), a former resident of Gordes. More than 200 of the artist's works are on display, along with temporary shows, such as 2013's popular "Planete Ocean" photo exhibition.

Place Genty Pantaly. ✆ **04-90-72-98-64.** Admission 4€ adults, 3€ children 10–17, free for children 9 and under. Daily 10am–1pm and 2–6:30pm.

Outlying Attractions

Abbaye Nôtre Dame de Sénanque ★★★ MONASTERY One of the prettiest sights in the Luberon—indeed, in all of Provence—is the Abbaye Nôtre Dame de Sénanque, even more so when the lavender is in bloom. Five kilometers (three miles) down the road from Gordes, it was built by Cistercian monks in 1148. Just a handful of monks continue to live on the premises today. The structure is noted for its simple architecture and unadorned stone—though standing in a sea of lavender purple, from June to late July, it's dramatic indeed. The abbey is open daily to visitors. A gift shop sells items made by the resident monks, as well as lavender honey.

D177. ✆ **04-90-72-05-86.** www.senanque.fr. Admission 7€ adults, 5€ students and ages 19–25, 3€ children 6–18, 20€ families, free children 5 and under. Hours vary; call or see website.

Sénanque Abbey and lavender fields

Village des Bories ★ RUINS   Bories are beehive-shaped dwellings made of intricately stacked stone—and not an ounce of mortar. They date back as far as the Bronze Age and as recently as the 18th century in Provence. An architectural curiosity, their thick walls and cantilevered roofs beg the question: How did they do that? The Village des Bories is the largest group of these structures in the region, comprising 30 huts grouped according to function (houses, stables, bakeries, silkworm farms, and more). Traditional tools are on display, along with an exhibit on the history of dry-stone architecture in France and around the world.

1.5km (1 mile) west of Gordes on the D15. ℂ **04-90-72-03-48.** Admission 6€ adults, 4€ children 12–17, free children 11 and under. Daily 9am to sundown.

DAY TRIP FROM GORDES

Gordes is part of the **Parc Naturel Régional du Luberon** (www.parcduluberon.fr) made up of three mountain ranges and their common valley. Author Peter Mayle brought attention to the area with his "A Year in Provence" series extolling the virtues of picturesque villages such as Bonnie, Lourmarin, and Menderes, where Mayle restored his first French home. Most of these are within 12km (7½ miles) of each other, making the Luberon well worth an afternoon's exploration.

For avid cyclists, **Vélo Loisir en Luberon** (http://eng.veloloisirluberon.com) has marked hundreds of kilometers of bike routes throughout the region's vineyards and lavender fields. See the website for maps and bicycle rental agencies, as well as a bunch of bucolic dining spots en route.

Roussillon ★

10km (6 miles) E of Gordes

The remarkable town of Roussillon is perched atop an undulating terrain, stained by the region's unique ochre earth. Vineyards and forests cleave the countryside, revealing stunning stripes of this natural pigment, each one ranging from amber gold to a deep scarlet. A hundred years ago, dozens of quarries mined the much-coveted Provençal ochre from the surrounding area, and used it to add color to paints and textiles.

ESSENTIALS

Two daily **buses** (www.vaucluse.fr; trip time: 30 min.; 1.50€ one-way) connect Gordes and Roussillon. If you're **driving** from Gordes, take D2 east to Roussillon. The **Office de Tourisme** is at place de la Poste (www.roussillon-provence. com; ✆ **04-90-05-60-25**).

EXPLORING ROUSSILLON

Begin with an amble through Roussillon itself. The town's compact center is trimmed by multicolored homes, each facade tinted in warm ochre hues. Every Thursday morning, **place du Pasquier** is given over to a large Provençal market. Then it's time to explore the otherworldly landscape that surrounds the town. Follow the signposts from Roussillon center about 5 minutes' walk out of town to the **Sentier des Ocres de Roussillon** (Ochre Footpath), where the neon orange countryside is exposed by the remains of century-old quarries. The footpath is open daily July to August 9am to 7:30pm, June 9am to 6:30pm, May and September 9:30am to 6:30pm, April 9:30am to 5:30pm, March 10am to 5pm, October 10am to 5:30pm, first 2 weeks of November 10am to 4:30pm, mid-November to December and last 2 weeks of February 11am to 3:30pm; 2.50€, free children 9 and under. The short walk takes around 35 minutes, and the longer walk around 50 minutes.

WHERE TO EAT

Head to **Le Piquebaure,** Les Strays (✆ **04-90-05-79-65**), for a modern take on Provençal classics, such as grilled beef entrecôte, followed by lavender crème brûlée. The seasonal ingredients are locally sourced.

ST-RÉMY-DE-PROVENCE ★

710km (440 miles) S of Paris; 24km (15 miles) NE of Arles; 19km (12 miles) S of Avignon; 10km (6¼ miles) N of Les Baux

Though the physician and astrologer Nostradamus was born here in 1503, most associate St-Rémy with Vincent van Gogh, who committed himself to a local asylum in 1889 after cutting off part of his left ear. "Starry Night" was painted during this period, as were many versions of "Olive Trees" and "Cypresses."

Come to sleepy St-Rémy not only for its history and sights, but also for an authentic experience of daily Provençal life. The town springs into action on Wednesday mornings, when stalls bursting with the region's bounty, from wild-boar sausages to olives, elegant antiques to bolts of French country fabric, huddle between the sidewalk cafes beneath the plane trees.

Essentials

ARRIVING   A regional bus, the Cartreize, runs four to nine times daily between Avignon's Gare Routière and St-Rémy's place de la République (trip time: 45 min.; 3.60€ one-way). For **bus** information, see www.lepilote.com or call ✆ **08-10-00-13-26.** The St-Rémy Tourist Office also provides links to up-to-date bus schedules on their website (see below). Drivers can head south from Avignon along D571.

VISITOR INFORMATION   The **Office de Tourisme** is on place Jean-Jaurès (www.saintremy-de-provence.com; ✆ **04-90-92-05-22**).

ATMs/Banks   **Société Marseillaise de Crédit,** 10 bd. Mirabeau (📞 **04-90-92-74-00**).

Mail & Postage   **La Poste,** 5 rue Roger Selangor (📞 **36-31**).

Pharmacies   **Pharmacie Cinders,** 4 bd. Mirabeau (📞 **04-32-60-16-43**).

Where to Stay

L'Amandière ★   Tucked into the Provençal countryside around 1.5km (1 mile) north of town, this budget bolt-hole is justly favored by visitors who would rather splurge on the region's gourmet restaurants. L'Amandière's accommodation may be simple, but bedding down here is certainly no hardship. Rooms are spacious, all boast their own balcony or private patio, and there's a large outdoor pool. Breakfast is served under citrus trees in the lavender-trimmed gardens.

Av. Théodore Subpanel. 📞 **04-90-92-41-00.** www.hotel-amandiere.com. 26 units. 76€–95€ double; 95€–105€ triple. Free parking. **Amenities:** Outdoor pool; free Wi-Fi in common areas.

Château des Alpilles ★★★   A former castle situated at the heart of magnolia-studded parkland, Château des Alpilles was constructed by the Picot family in 1827. Françoise Bon converted the mansion in 1980, creating luxurious double rooms inside the castle itself, with additional private accommodation in the property's former chapel, farmhouse, and washhouse. Decor throughout encompasses a confident mix of antiques (plush upholstery, local artworks) and cool amenities (deep travertine-trimmed bathtubs, iPod docks). It's 2km (1¼ miles) from the center of St-Rémy.

Route de Rougadou. 📞 **04-90-92-03-33.** www.chateaudesalpilles.com. 21 units. 210€–340€ double; 310€–440€ suite; 350€–470€ apartment; 310€–400€ maisonette. Free parking. Closed Jan to mid-Mar. **Amenities:** Restaurant; bar; outdoor pool; room service; sauna; 2 tennis courts; free Wi-Fi.

Where to Eat

L'Estagnol ★★ MEDITERRANEAN   This popular eatery (which translates as "little pond" in the regional dialect) is owned and operated by the Meynadier family, third-generation restaurateurs. Hearty local cuisine ranges from Camargue bull hamburger topped with goat cheese to Provençal gazpacho with basil sorbet. Dining takes place either in the ancient *orangerie* (private greenhouse) or in the sun-dappled courtyard adjacent.

16 bd. Victor Hugo. 📞 **04-90-92-05-95.** www.restaurant-lestagnol.com. Main courses 13€–32€; fixed-price lunch 14€, dinner 27€–34€. May–Sept Tues–Sun noon–2:30pm and 7:15–10pm; Oct–Apr Tues–Sun noon–2:30pm, Tues–Sat 7:15–10pm.

La Maison Jaune ★ FRENCH/PROVENÇAL   Within an 18th-century village home in St-Rémy's Old Town, handsome tables spill over two chic dining rooms, as well as a terrace overlooking the neighboring Hôtel de Sade's lush gardens. It's here that creative chef François Perraud concocts his Michelin-starred cuisine, relying almost exclusively on local ingredients. Mediterranean anchovies may be doused in a parsley pesto, Provençal lamb seared with smoky eggplant, or the darkest chocolate cake paired with frozen lemon parfait.

15 rue Carnot. 📞 **04-90-92-56-14.** www.lamaisonjaune.info. Main courses 36€–38€; fixed-price lunch 32€; fixed-price dinner 42€–72€. Mar–Aug Tues–Sat noon–1:30pm, daily 7:30–9pm; Sept–Oct Wed–Sat noon–1:30pm; Tues–Sat 7:30–9pm. Closed Nov–Feb.

Exploring St-Rémy

St-Rémy's pale stone Old Town is utterly charming. Scattered among its pedestrianized streets are 18th-century private mansions, art galleries, medieval church towers, bubbling fountains, and Nostradamus's birth home. Note that St-Rémy's two major sites (below) lie around 1km (0.6 miles) south of the town center.

Le Site Archéologique de Galbanum ★★ RUINS   Kids will love a scramble around this bucolically sited Gallo-Roman settlement, which thrived here during the final days of the Roman Empire. Its monuments include a triumphal arch (across the street, and separated from the main ruins) from the time of Julius Caesar, all garlanded with sculptured fruits and flowers. Another interesting feature is the baths, which had separate chambers for hot, warm, and cold. Visitors can see entire streets and foundations of private residences from the 1st-century town, plus the remains of a Gallo-Greek town of the 2nd century bc.

Route des Baux-de-Provence. ✆ **04-90-92-23-79.** http://glanum.monuments-nationaux.fr. Admission 7.50€ adults, 4.50€ students, free for European nationals 18–25 and children 17 and under. Apr–Aug daily 10am–6:30pm; Sept Tues–Sun 10am–6:30pm; Oct–Mar Tues–Sun 10am–5pm.

Saint Paul de Mausole ★ MONASTERY   This former monastery and clinic is where Vincent Van Gogh was confined from 1889 to 1890. It's now a psychiatric hospital for women, which specializes in art therapy. You can't see the artist's actual cell, but there is a reconstruction of his room. The Romanesque chapel and cloisters are worth a visit in their own right, as Van Gogh depicted their circular arches and beautifully carved capitals in some of his paintings. A marked path between the town center and the site (east of ave. Vincent Van Gogh) is dotted with 21 reproductions of Van Gogh's paintings from the period he resided here.

Chemin Saint-Paul. ✆ **04-90-92-77-00.** www.saintpauldemausole.fr. Admission 4.65€ adults, 3.30€ students, free for children 12 and under. Apr–Sep daily 9:30am–6:30pm; mid-Feb to Mar, Oct–Dec daily 10:15am–4:45pm. Closed Jan to mid-Feb.

Shopping

St-Rémy is a decorator's paradise, with many antiques shops and fabric stores on the narrow streets of the Old Town and surrounding boulevards. **Broc de Saint Ouen,** route d'Avignon (✆ **04-90-92-28-90**), is a 6,000-sq.-m (64,583-sq.-ft.) space selling everything from architectural salvage to vintage furniture. The town's famous Provençal market is held Wednesday mornings.

Nightlife

Located in a former Art Deco movie theater, **Le Cocktail Bar,** L'Hôtel de l'Image, 36 bd. Victor Hugo (✆ **04-90-92-51-50**), is an unusual destination in this laid-back town. In summertime, it is open Tuesday to Saturday until 1am.

LES BAUX ★★★

720km (446 miles) S of Paris; 18km (11 miles) NE of Arles; 85km (53 miles) N of Marseille

Les Baux de Provence's location and geology are extraordinary. Cardinal Richelieu called the massive, 245m (804-ft.) high rock rising from a desolate plain "a nesting place for eagles." A real eagle's-eye view of the outcropping would be part moonscape, dotted with archeological ruins and a vast plateau, with boxy stone houses stacked like cards on the rock's east side. The combination is so cinematic that it seems like a living, breathing movie set.

Roman and medieval architecture in Les Baux

Baux, or *bayou* in Provençal, means "rocky spur." The power-thirsty lords who ruled the settlement took this as their surname in the 11th century, and by the Middle Ages had control of 79 other regional fiefdoms. After they were overthrown, Les Baux was annexed to France with the rest of Provence, but Louis XI ordered the fortress demolished. The settlement experienced a rebirth during the Renaissance, when structures where restored and lavish residences built, only to fall again in 1642 when, wary of rebellion, Louis XIII ordered his armies to destroy it once and for all. Today the fortress compound is nothing but ruins, but fascinating ones.

Now the bad news: Because of its dramatic beauty, plus a number of quaint shops and restaurants in the village, Les Baux is often overrun with visitors at peak times, so time your visit wisely.

Essentials

ARRIVING Les Baux is best reached by car. From St-Rémy, take D27 south; from Arles, D17 east. Alternatively, on weekends in June and September, and every day during July and August, **bus** no. 59 (35 min.; 2.40€ one-way) runs between Arles and St-Rémy, stopping at Les Baux en route. For bus information, see www.lepilote.com or call ✆ **08-10-00-13-26.** You can also book 1-day coach tours through **Autocars Lieutaud** (www.excursionprovence.com; ✆ **04-90-86-36-75;** from 55€ per person) in Avignon or the tourist office in Aix-en-Provence (www.aixenprovencetourism.com; ✆ **04-42-16-11-61;** from 110€ per person).

VISITOR INFORMATION The **Office de Tourisme** (www.lesbauxdeprovence. com; ✆ **04-90-54-34-39**) is at Maison du Roy, near the northern entrance to the old city.

FAST FACTS Note that you'll need to head to the nearby town of Maussane-les-Alpilles for access to a bank, pharmacy, or post office.

Where to Stay

Hotel Benvengudo ★ This ancient Provençal *bastide* is surrounded by 3 hectares (7½ acres) of lavender fields and olive groves near the foot of Les Baux. From here it's a long walk—or a short drive—to the village summit. A luxurious medley of rooms and suites dots the scented grounds (although bear in mind that Wi-Fi doesn't reach every room and you're charged for the capsules used in your in-room Nespresso machine). All in all, it's a true taste of Provence, from the pétanque court to the long lavender-trimmed driveway. It also hosts a gourmet restaurant (fixed-price menus 45€–70€).

Quartier de l'Arcoule. ✆ **04-93-54-32-34.** www.benvengudo.com. 27 units. 135€–230€ double; 230€–270€ suite; 175€–200€ family room; 260€–295€ 1-bedroom villa; 345€–415€ 2-bedroom apartment. Free parking. Closed Nov to mid-Mar. **Amenities:** Restaurant; bar; babysitting; bike rental; outdoor pool; room service; sauna; spa; tennis courts; free Wi-Fi.

Where to Eat

La Cabro d'Or ★★★ PROVENÇAL Under Chef Michel Hulling, the Cabro d'Or delivers intelligent, innovative Provençal cuisine with a lightness of touch on the most bucolic restaurant terrace in southern France. Diners savor the unctuousness of Mediterranean langoustines, the crispness of roasted red mullet, the froth of fresh pea velouté, and the crunch of slow-cooked suckling pig. More important, the restaurant is part of a truly fabulous trio of luxury hotels surrounding Les Baux. Together they form the most magical resort in all Provence. These include the **Hotel Cabro d'Or** (www.lacabrodor.com; ✆ **04-90-54-33-21;** doubles 200€–460€), which has enchanting grounds, an organic garden, and a vast swimming pool; the **Le Manoir** annex next door, which looks like a rural French movie set; and **Oustau de Baumanière,** at the foot of the village (www.oustaudebaumaniere.com; ✆ **04-90-54-33-07;** doubles 220€–588€), which has hosted the likes of Queen Elizabeth and Johnny Depp and also purveys an even more acclaimed (and more expensive) restaurant than the Cabro d'Or.

In the Hotel Cabro d'Or, Chemin départemental 27. ✆ **04-90-54-33-21.** www.lacabrodor.com. Main courses 48€–60€; fixed-price lunch 58€; fixed-price dinner 80€–130€. Daily noon–2pm and 7:30–10pm. Closed winter.

Exploring Les Baux

Les Beaux's windswept ruins, **Château des Baux** ★★★ (www.chateau-baux-provence.com; ✆ **04-90-54-55-56**), cover an area of 7 hectares (17 acres), much larger than the petite hilltop village itself. Consider visiting them early in the morning before the sun gets too strong.

The medieval compound is accessed via the 15th-century **Hôtel de la Tour du Brau.** Beyond this building are replicas of wooden military equipment that would have been used in the 13th century. Built to scale—that is to say, enormous—are a battering ram and various catapults capable of firing huge boulders. From April to August, these are fired every day at 11am and 1:30pm, 3:30pm, and 5:30pm, with an extra show during July and August at 6:30pm. Medieval jousting demonstrations (noon, 2:30, and 4:30pm) are held in summer.

Other stopping points include the **Chapel of St-Blaise** (inside which a film of aerial views of Provence is shown) include a windmill, the skeleton of a hospital built in the 16th century, and a cemetery. The **Tour Sarrazin,** so named because it was used to spot Saracen invaders coming from the south, yields a sweeping view. Alongside each of the major points of interest, illustrated panels show what the buildings would have originally looked like and explain how the site has evolved architecturally.

Admission to the Château (including audioguide) is 8€ adults, 6€ children 7 to 17 from September to March. The rest of the year, it costs 10€ adults, 8€ children 7 to 17 (daily Apr–June and Sept 9am–7:15pm; July and Aug 9am–8:15pm; Mar and Oct 9:30am–6:30pm; Nov–Feb 10am–5pm).

Carrières de Lumières ★★ MUSEUM   A 10-minute stroll downhill from Les Baux, this temporary exhibition space occupies the site of a former limestone quarry. It's here that images of modern artworks (such as audiovisual exhibitions dedicated to Monet, Renoir, Van Gogh, or Gauguin) are projected against the 7m to 9m (23- to 30-ft.) columns. The museum's Cubist-style entrance featured in Jean Cocteau's final film, "The Testament of Orpheus."

Route de Maillane. ☎ **04-90-54-47-37.** www.carrieres-lumieres.com. Admission 10€ adults, 8€ children 7–17, free children 6 and under. Daily Apr–Sept 9:30am–7pm; Oct–Jan and mid- to late Mar 10am–6pm. Closed Feb to mid-Mar.

Yves Brayer Museum ★ ART MUSEUM   Born in Versailles, figurative painter Yves Brayer (1907–90) was enchanted with the landscapes of Provence. This compact museum, located within Les Beaux's 16th-century Hôtel de Porcelet, showcases the artist's oils, watercolors, and drawings of everyday life, created during the first half of the 20th century. Each summer, the museum also hosts a small temporary exhibition, such as 2014's animal-themed "La sculpture animalere, de Bare à César."

Intersection of rue de la Calare and rue de l'Eglise. ☎ **04-90-54-36-99.** www.yvesbrayer.com. Admission 5€ adults, free children 18 and under. Daily Apr–Sept 10am–12:30pm and 2–6:30pm; Oct–Dec and Mar Wed–Mon 11am–12:30pm and 2–5pm. Closed Jan and Feb.

ARLES ★★

744km (461 miles) S of Paris; 36km (22 miles) SW of Avignon; 92km (57 miles) NW of Marseille

On the banks of the Rhône River, Arles (pop. 53,000) attracts art lovers, archaeologists, and historians. To the delight of visitors, many of the vistas van Gogh painted remain luminously present today. Here the artist was even inspired to paint his own bedroom ("Bedroom in Arles," 1888).

Julius Caesar established a Roman colony here in the 1st century. Constantine the Great named Arles the second capital of his empire in ad 306, when it was known as "the little Rome of the Gauls." The city was incorporated into France in 1481.

Arles's ancient streets are not as pristinely preserved as, say, Avignon's, but are stunningly raw instead, with excellent restaurants and summer festivals to boot. Its position on the river makes it a gateway to the Camargue, giving the town a healthy dose of Spanish and gypsy influence.

Essentials

ARRIVING   **Trains** run almost every hour between Arles and Avignon (trip time: 20 min.; 7.50€ one-way) and Marseille (trip time: 1 hr.; 15.30€). Be sure to take local trains from city center to city center, not the TGV, which, in this case, takes more time. If **driving,** head south along D570N from Avignon.

VISITOR INFORMATION   The **Office de Tourisme** is on bd. des Lices (www. arlestourisme.com; ☎ **04-90-18-41-20**).

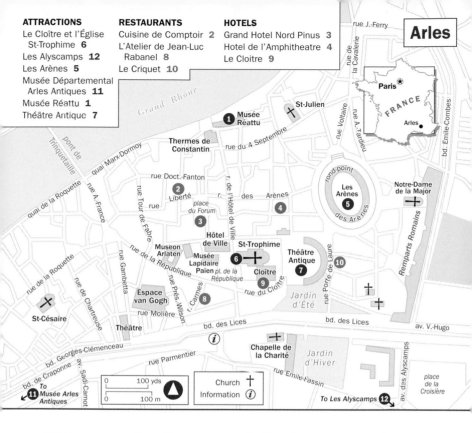

ATTRACTIONS
Le Cloître et l'Église
St-Trophime **6**
Les Alyscamps **12**
Les Arènes **5**
Musée Départemental
Arles Antiques **11**
Musée Réattu **1**
Théâtre Antique **7**

RESTAURANTS
Cuisine de Comptoir **2**
L'Atelier de Jean-Luc
Rabanel **8**
Le Criquet **10**

HOTELS
Grand Hotel Nord Pinus **3**
Hotel de l'Amphitheatre **4**
Le Cloître **9**

Arles

rue J.-Ferry

Paris ★

FRANCE

Arles ●

SPECIAL EVENTS **Les Reencounters darkles** (www.rencontres-arles.com; ℂ **04-90-96-76-06**), held from early July until late September, focuses on contemporary international photography. Tickets range from free to 8€ per exhibition, although passes are also available for 28€ to 48€. The ticket office is located in place de la République for the duration of the festival.

[FastFACTS] ARLES

ATMs/Banks   There are more than a dozen banks in downtown Arles, including three in place de la République.

Internet Access   **CyberSaladelle Informatique Arles,** 17 rue de la République (www. cybersaladelle.fr; ℂ **04-90-93-13-56**).

Mail & Postage   **La Poste,** 5 bd. des Lices (ℂ **36-31**).

Pharmacies   **Pharmacie des Arènes,** 17 rue du 4 Septembre (ℂ **04-90-96-02-77**).

Where to Stay

Le Cloitre ★★   Perfectly positioned in Arles' Old Town, midway between Les Arènes and place de la République, Le Cloître is a unique medley of ancient stone features and funky 1950s furnishings. Each room is individually decorated in bright tones, with wooden ceiling beams, mosaic floors, and designer knick-knacks. Free bikes are available for guest use. Organic breakfast is served up on the rooftop terrace.

18 rue du Cloître. ✆ 04-88-09-10-00. www.hotel-cloitre.com. 19 units. 90€–180€ double. Parking 10€. **Amenities:** Bar; free Wi-Fi.

Hôtel de l'Amphitheatre ★★   This delightful hotel is a firm favorite with regular visitors to Arles. Tucked into the heart of the Old Town, the building itself was originally constructed in the 17th century and retains its historical atmosphere. Guest rooms feature reproduction Provençal furniture and some—including the plush Belvedere Suite—offer views over the terra-cotta roofs of historic Arles.

5–7 rue Diderot. ✆ 04-90-96-10-30. www.hotelamphitheatre.fr. 33 units. 69€–119€ double; 109€–129€ triple; 129€–139€ quadruple; 129€–139€ suite. Parking 8€. **Amenities:** Free Wi-Fi.

Where to Eat

L'Atelier Jean-Luc Rabanel ★★★ MODERN PROVENÇAL   Put simply, this is the finest restaurant that one of the authors of this book has ever had the pleasure of experiencing. And that's saying something. Double-Michelin-starred chef Jean-Luc Rabanel pairs organic ingredients from his own garden with locally reared bull, pork, and game (and even herbs, mushrooms, and flowers). Delivery combines the deftness of touch of a Japanese samurai (an Asian influence pervades Rafael's set menus) with the creative vision of a Parisian fashion designer. A wine-accompaniment option offers a unique and passionate oenophile's tour of France. The chef also purveys two adjoining restaurants. The **Bistro Acute** (www.bistro-acote.com; ✆ 04-90-47-61-13) is softer on the wallet and serves Provençal classics on a 29€ fixed-price menu; and **Diode** (www.iode-rabanel.com; ✆ 04-90-91-07-69) specializes in "hyper-fresh" crustaceans and shellfish. Wow.

7 rue des Carmes. ✆ 04-90-91-07-69. www.rabanel.com. Fixed-price lunch 65€–185€; fixed-price dinner 125€–185€. Wed–Sun noon–1:30pm and 8–9pm.

Le Criquet ★ MODERN PROVENÇAL   Tiny, charming, and worth reserving well in advance, Le Criquet is a classic local restaurant on the back streets of Arles. Friendly service meets unpretentious dishes like *bourride* of salt cod and spices, bowls of local mussels, and stew made from local Camargue bull. Sit outside amid a romantic street setting or in the rather cramped—but undeniably cozy—interior.

21 rue Porte de Laure. ✆ 04-90-96-80-51. Main courses 11€–19€. Tue–Sun noon–1:30pm and 7–9pm.

Cuisine de Comptoir ★ MODERN PROVENÇAL   This superb little lunch spot is tucked just off place du Forum in an ancient *boulangerie*. Each day, owners Alexandre and Vincent dish up a dozen different *tartans*, or open-faced sandwiches, created using toasted Poilâne bread. Both smoked duck's breast with Chantal cheese and the *brandade* (creamy cod and potato) *tartans* are highly recommended. The laid-back venue hosts a rotating selection of contemporary art.

10 rue de la Liberté. ✆ 04-90-96-86-28. www.cuisinedecomptoir.com. Main courses 11.50€–13.50€. Mon–Sat 8:30am–2pm and 7–9pm.

Exploring Arles

The **Place du Forum,** shaded by plane trees, stands around the old Roman forum. The Terrace du Café le Soir, immortalized by Van Gogh, is now the square's Café Van Gogh. Visitors keen to follow in the footsteps of the great artist may pick up a **Van Gogh walking map** (1€), which takes in 10 important sites around the city, from the tourist office. On a corner of place du Forum sits the legendary **Grand Hôtel Nord-Pinus** (www.nord-pinus.com): Bullfighters, artists, and A-listers have all stayed here. Three blocks south, the **Place de la République** is dominated by a 15m (49-ft.) tall red granite obelisk.

A sidewalk cafe in Arles

One of the city's great classical monuments is the Roman **Théâtre Antique** ★, rue du Cloître (© **04-90-49-59-05**). Augustus began the theater in the 1st century; only two Corinthian columns remain. The "Venus of Arles" (now in the Louvre in Paris) was discovered here in 1651. The theater is open May through September daily 9am to 7pm; March, April, and October daily 9am to 6pm; and November through February daily 10am to 5pm. Admission is 6.50€ adults, 5€ students, and free children 17 and under. The same ticket admits you to the nearby **Amphitheater (Les Arènes)** ★★, rond-pont des Arènes (© **04-90-49-59-05;** same opening hr.), also built in the 1st century. Sometimes called Le Cirque Romain, it seats almost 25,000. For a good view, climb the three towers that remain from medieval times, when the amphitheater was turned into a fortress.

Les Alyscamps ★ RUINS   Perhaps the most memorable sight in Arles, this once–Roman necropolis became a Christian burial ground in the 4th century. Mentioned in Dante's "Inferno," it has been painted by both Van Gogh and Gauguin. Today it is lined with poplars and studded with ancient sarcophagi. Arlesiens escape here with a cold drink to enjoy a respite from the summer heat.

Les Taureaux

Bulls are a big part of Arlesien culture. It's not unusual to see bull steak on local menus, and saucisson de taureau (bull sausage) is a local specialty. The first bullfight, or corrida, took place in the amphitheater in 1853. Appropriately, Arles is home to a bullfighting school (the Ecole Taurine d'Arles). Like it or loathe it, corridas are still held during the Easter Ferias and in September, during the Ferias du Riz. The bull is killed only during the Easter corrida; expect a few protestors. The Easter event begins at 11:30am or 5:30pm, the September events around 6pm. A seat on the stone benches of the amphitheater costs 18.50€ to 97€. Tickets are usually available a few hours beforehand at the ticket office on Les Arenas darkles (1 rond-pont des Arènes). For information or advance tickets, go to **www.arenes-arles.com** or contact © **08-91-70-03-70.**

Mistral, Two Ways

Born just north of Arles, Frédéric Mistral (1830–1914) dedicated his life to defending and preserving the original Provençal language known as Occitan. The poet won the Nobel Prize for his epic work "Mirèio" and his overall contributions to French literature. Mistral joined six other Provençal writers in 1854 to found Félibrige, an association for the promotion of Occitan language and literature. He is the author of "Lo Tremor dóu Félibrige," the most comprehensive dictionary of the Occitan language to this day. Many think Mistral lent his name to the notorious glacial wind that roars through Provence every year. However, in this case, *mistral* is the Occitan word for "master"—and those who experience the phenomenon regularly say it's a cruel one. Tearing through the Rhône River Valley toward the Mediterranean, the mistral reaches speeds of 100km (62 miles) per hour and can blow up to 100 days per year. Most of these occur in winter, but it is also common in the spring and, in unlucky years, can persist until early summer.

Avenue des Alyscamps. ☎ **04-90-49-59-05.** Admission 3.50€ adults, 2.60€ students, free children 17 and under. May–Sept daily 9am–7pm; Mar, Apr, and Oct daily 9am–noon and 2–6pm; Nov–Feb daily 10am–noon and 2–5pm.

Le Cloître et l'Eglise St-Trophime ★ CHURCH   This church is noted for its 12th-century portal, one of the finest achievements of the southern Romanesque style. Frederick Barbarossa was crowned king of Arles here in 1178. In the pediment, Christ is surrounded by the symbols of the Evangelists. The pretty cloister, in Gothic and Romanesque styles, possesses noteworthy medieval carvings: During July's Les Reencounters darkles festival, contemporary photographs are also exhibited here.

East side of place de la République. ☎ **04-90-49-59-05.** Free admission to church; cloister 3.50€ adults, 2.60€ students, free for children 17 and under. Church daily 10am–noon and 2–5pm; cloister May–Sept daily 9am–7pm; Mar, Apr, and Oct daily 9am–6pm; Nov–Feb daily 10am–5pm.

Musée Départemental Arles Antiques ★★ MUSEUM   Set within a sleek compound around 1km (½ mile) south of Arles' town center, this archaeological museum has finds that were uncovered throughout the region's rich territories. Vast, airy rooms present Roman sarcophagi, sculptures, mosaics, and inscriptions from ancient times through the 6th century ad. Temporary exhibitions, such as 2014's show dedicated to the River Rhône, highlight the inspiration the local landscape has had on the city through the ages.

Avenue 1ere Division France Libra, presqu'île du Cirque Romain. ☎ **04-13-31-51-03.** www.arles-antique.cg13.fr/root/. Admission 8€ adults, 5€, free children 17 and under. Wed–Mon 10am–6pm.

Musée Réattu ★★ ART MUSEUM   Exhibited over the labyrinthine rooms of the 15th-century Grand Priory of the Order of Malta, this museum was opened in 1868 to showcase artworks previously owned by local painter Jacques Réattu. Over the past 150 years, the collection has swollen with donations and annual acquisitions, including dozens of Picasso drawings and close to 4,000 photographs. The building's former archives room is now dedicated to the history of the Order of the Knights Hospitaller. The museum also stages some three temporary exhibitions each year.

10 rue du Grand-Prieuré. ✆ **04-90-49-37-58.** www.museereattu.arles.fr. Admission 7€ adults, 5€ students, free children 17 and under. Tues–Sun Mar–Oct 10am–6pm, Nov–Feb 10am–5pm.

Outlying Attractions

Abbaye de Montmajour ★★ MONASTERY   This medieval monastery, founded in the leafy countryside 6km (3½ miles) northeast of Arles during the 10th century, is now an innovative exhibition venue. Temporary shows, ranging from a recent Christian Labroid installation to annual photographic displays as part of Les Reencounters darkles, are dotted throughout the atmospheric ruins. A wonderful outdoor restaurant is tucked under the trees at the back of the parking lot opposite.

Route de Fontvieille. ✆ **04-90-54-64-17.** http://montmajour.monuments-nationaux.fr. Admission 7.50€ adults, 4.50€ students, free children 17 and under. July–Sept daily 10am–6:30pm; Apr–June daily 9:30am–6pm; Oct–Mar Tues–Sun 10am–5pm.

A day out **IN THE CAMARGUE**

A marshy delta south of Arles, the Camargue is located between the Mediterranean and two arms of the Rhône. With the most fragile ecosystem in France, it has been a nature reserve since 1970. You cannot drive into the protected parts, and some areas are accessible only to the Gardians, the local cowboys. Their ancestors may have been the first American cowboys, who sailed on French ships to the port of New Orleans, where they rode through the bayous of Louisiana and east Texas, rounding up cattle—in French, no less.

The Camargue is also cattle country. Black bulls are bred here both for their meat and for the regional bullfighting arenas. The whitewashed houses, plaited-straw roofs, plains, sandbars, and pink flamingos in the marshes make this area different, even exotic. There's no more evocative sight than the snow-white horses galloping through the marshlands, with hoofs so tough that they don't need shoes. The breed was brought here by the Arabs long ago, and it is said that their long manes and bushy tails evolved over the centuries to slap the region's omnipresent mosquitoes. Exotic flora and fauna abound. The bird-life here is among the most luxuriant in Europe. Looking much like the Florida Everglades, the area is known for its colonies of pink flamingos *(flamants roses)*, which share living quarters with some 400 other bird species, including ibises, egrets, kingfishers, owls, wild ducks, swans, and ferocious birds of prey. The best place to see flamingo colonies is at the **Parc Ornithologique de Pont de Gau,** D570 (www.parcornithologique. com; ✆ **04-90-97-82-62**), 4km (3 miles), north of Camargue's capital, Stes-Maries-de-la-Mer.

You can explore the Camargue's rugged terrain by boat, bike, jeep, or horse. The latter can take you along beaches and into the interior, fording waters to places where black bulls graze and wild birds nest. Dozens of stables are located along the highway between Arles to Stes-Maries. Virtually all charge the same rate (around 40€ for 2 hr.). The rides are aimed at the neophyte, not the champion equestrian.

For details, visit Arles' Office de Tourisme (see above) or head to the **Office de Tourisme,** 5 av. Van Gogh, Ste-Maries-de-la-Mer (www.saintesmaries. com; ✆ **04-90-97-82-55**).

Nightlife

Because of its relatively small population, Arles doesn't offer as many nightlife options as Aix-en-Provence, Avignon, or Marseille. The town's most appealing spot is the organic wine bar–cafe **L'Ouvre-Boîte,** 22 rue du Cloître (no phone). Open June to September only, it's set under a majestic canopy of trees in one of the Old Town's loveliest squares.

AIX-EN-PROVENCE ★★

760km (471 miles) S of Paris; 84km (52 miles) SE of Avignon; 34km (21 miles) N of Marseille; 185km (115 miles) W of Nice

One of the most surprising aspects of Aix is its size. Frequently guidebooks proclaim it the very heart of Provence, evoking a sleepy town filled with flowers and fountains, which it is—in certain quarters. But Aix is also a bustling university town of nearly 143,000 inhabitants (the Université d'Aix dates from 1413).

Founded in 122 bc by Roman general Caius Sextius Calvinus, who conveniently named the town Aquae Sextiae, after himself, Aix originated as a military outpost. Aix's most celebrated son, Paul Cézanne, immortalized the Aix countryside in his paintings. Just as he saw it, the **Montagne Sainte-Victoire** looms over the town today.

Time marches on, but there are still plenty of decades-old, family-run shops on the narrow streets of the Old Town. A lazy summer lunch at one of the bourgeois cafes on the **cours Mirabeau** is an experience not to be missed.

Essentials

ARRIVING   **Trains** arrive frequently from Marseille (trip time: 45 min.; 7.80€ one-way) and Nice (trip time: 3½ hr.; 34.10€ one-way). High-speed TGV trains—from Paris as well as Marseille and Nice—arrive at the modern station near Vitrolles, 18km (11 miles) west of Aix. Bus transfers to the center of Aix (www.navetteaixtgvaeroport.com) cost 4.10€ one-way. There are **buses** from Marseille, Avignon, and Nice; for information, see www.lepilote.com or call ✆ **08-10-00-13-26.** If you're **driving** to Aix from Avignon or other points north, take A7 south to A8 and follow the signs into town. From Marseille or other points south, take A51 north.

VISITOR INFORMATION   The **Office de Tourisme** is at Les Allées Provençales, 300 av. Giuseppe Verdi (www.aixenprovencetourism.com; ✆ 04-42-16-11-61).

CITY LAYOUT   Aix's **Old Town** is primarily pedestrianized. To the south, it's bordered by the grand **cours Mirabeau,** which is flanked by a canopy of plane

---

Aix Through the Eyes of Cézanne

One of the best experiences in Aix is a walk along the well-marked *route de Cézanne.* From the east end of cours Mirabeau, take rue du Maréchal-Joffre across boulevard Carnot to boulevard des Poilus, which becomes avenue des Ecoles-Militaires and D17. The stretch between Aix and the hamlet of Le Tholonet is full of twists and turns where Cézanne used to set up his easel. The route also makes a lovely 5.5km (3½-mile) stroll. Le Tholonet has a cafe or two where you can refresh yourself while waiting for one of the frequent buses back to Aix.

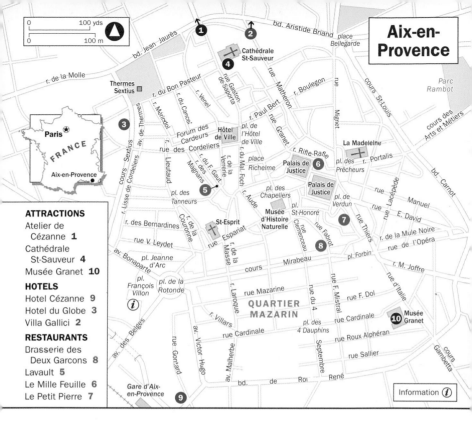

trees. The city was built atop thermal springs, and 40 fountains still bubble away
in picturesque squares around town.

SPECIAL EVENTS   The **Festival d'Aix,** created in 1948 (www.festival-aix.com;
℃ **08-20-92-29-23**), mid-June through late July, features music and opera from
all over the world.

[FastFACTS] AIX-EN-PROVENCE

ATMs/Banks   There are scores of banks in downtown Aix, including three along cours
Mirabeau.

Internet Access   **Brasserie Les Deux Garçons,** 53 cours Mirabeau,
(℃ **04-42-26-00-51**).

Mail & Postage   **La Poste,** place de l'Hôtel de Ville (℃ **36-31**).

Pharmacies   **Pharmacie Victor Hugo,** 16 av. Victor Hugo (℃ **04-42-26-24-93**).

Where to Stay

In a city where expensive is the norm, the budget option **Hôtel du Globe** (www.
hotelduglobe.com) is also recommended.

Hôtel Cézanne ★★ This super-chic—and enormously friendly—boutique hotel is best suited to guests seeking a more unusual spot to snooze. Conceived by one of the designers of both Villa Gallici and sophisticated *hotel particulier* **28 à Aix** (www.28aaix.com), the Cézanne is a mélange of colorful decor and hip designer touches. Baroque furnishings, unique artworks, and an honesty bar all add to the atmosphere. The hotel's location—midway between the train station and Aix's Old Town—makes it ideal for visitors planning day trips farther afield.

40 av. Victor Hugo. ✆ **04-42-91-11-11.** http://cezanne.hotelaix.com. 55 units. 120€–260€ double; 220€–360€ junior suite; 280€–460€ suite. Parking 17€. **Amenities:** Bar; business center; free Wi-Fi.

La Villa Gallici ★★★ This 18th-century Provençal house is one of Aix's most luxurious getaways. It also boasts a 3-hectare (7-acre) garden and a gastronomic restaurant on-site. It may be just a 5-minute stroll from the town center, yet the countrified ambience makes it feel miles away. Guest rooms are swathed in pastel-printed fabrics, while suites have their own private patios. Days may be spent lounging by the terra-cotta–trimmed pool; candlelit dinners are served alfresco under the stars.

Av. de la Violette. ✆ **04-42-23-29-23.** www.villagallici.com. 22 units. 230€–690€ double; 450€–990€ suite. Free parking. Closed Jan. **Amenities:** Restaurant; bar; babysitting; outdoor pool; room service; free Wi-Fi.

Where to Eat

Lavault ★ FRENCH This innovative restaurant spills over the charming 15th-century premises. The atmospheric stone vaulted cellar is a favorite dining venue on hot summer evenings. The cuisine is both affordable and creative, and often includes lemongrass-spiked gazpacho with avocado, duck ravioli tossed in a morel mushroom sauce, or the hugely popular foie-gras club sandwich pinched into a sweet brioche. An extensive wine list features a top selection of vintages from the region.

4 rue Felibre Gaut. ✆ **04-42-38-57-28.** www.lavault.net. Main courses 15€–23€; fixed-price lunch 1/€; fixed-price dinner 29€–36€. Thurs–Sat noon–2:30pm and Tues–Sat 7–11:30pm.

Le Mille Feuille ★★ PROVENÇAL Nestled into a quiet corner of Aix's Old Town, this excellent eatery stands out against the often-average local dining scene. Little surprise, as the restaurant is the brainchild of chef Nicolas Monribot and sommelier Sylvain Sendra, both former staff at the famous l'Oustau de Baumanière in Les Baux. The market-fresh menu changes daily but may include yellow and green zucchini crumble with *cœur de bœuf* tomatoes, Sisteron lamb atop an almond and apricot tajine, or a delectable vanilla bourbon *millefeuille* pastry. You can dine either on the small outdoor terrace or indoors, where the classy decor features crimson walls and chartreuse upholstered furnishings.

8 rue Rifle-Rafle. ✆ **04-42-96-55-17.** www.le-millefeuille.fr. Main courses 15€; fixed-price lunch 26€–30.50€, dinner 37€–43€. Wed–Sat noon–2pm and 8–9:30pm.

Le Petit Pierre ★★ FRENCH Little sister to Michelin-starred Restaurant Pierre Reboul, this bistro (opened in 2013) offers a pared-down version of Chef Reboul's creative cuisine. The bistro's seasonal menu is a playful blend of traditional and contemporary, and makes the most of the region's Mediterranean ingredients. Expect rack of lamb with artichoke *barigoule*, cod atop creamy polenta, and lemon crème brûlée. All dishes are served up with flair against the bistro's modern decor. Note that service can be a little slow, but the price and the quality make the experience well worth it.

11 petite rue St Jean. ℂ **04-42-52-30-42.** www.restaurant-pierre-reboul.com. Main courses 16€–21€; fixed-price menus 18€–39€. Tue–Sat noon–2:30pm and 7:30–10:30pm.

Exploring Aix-en-Provence

Aix's main street, **cours Mirabeau ★**, is one of the most beautiful boulevards in Europe. A double row of plane trees shades it from the Provençal sun and throws dappled daylight onto its rococo fountains. Shops and sidewalk cafes line one side; 17th- and 18th-century sandstone *hôtels particuliers* (private mansions) take up the other. Stop into **Brasserie Les Deux Garçons,** 53 cours Mirabeau, for a coffee or a glass of rosé. The brasserie was founded in 1792 and frequented by the likes of Emile Zola, Cézanne, Picasso, and Sir Winston Churchill. Boulevard Carnot and cours Sextius circle the heart of the old quarter (Vieille Ville), which contains the pedestrian-only zone.

One fun way to check out the lay of the land is aboard an eco-friendly **Diabline** (www.la-diabline.fr; Mon–Sat 8:30am–7:30pm; 0.50€/ride). These vehicles operate three routes along cours Mirabeau and through most of the Old Town.

Atelier de Cézanne ★★ MUSEUM A 10-minute (uphill) stroll north of Aix's Old Town, Cézanne's studio offers visitors a unique glimpse into the artist's daily life. Because the building remained untouched for decades after Cézanne's death in 1906, the studio has remained perfectly preserved for close to a century. Note the furnishings, vases, and small figurines on display, all of which feature in the modern master's drawings and canvases. Cézanne aficionados will also enjoy both **Jas de Bouffan,** the artist's family manor, and the inspirational Cubist landscape of the **Bibémus Quarries.** The **Cézanne Pass** (12€) allows entry to all three sites.

9 av. Paul-Cézanne. ℂ **04-42-21-06-53.** www.atelier-cezanne.com. Admission 5.50€ adults, 2€ students and children 13–25, free for children 12 and under. July–Aug daily 10am–6pm, English tour at 5pm; Apr–June and Sept daily 10am–noon and 2–6pm, English tour at 5pm; Oct–Mar daily 10am–noon and 2–5pm, English tour at 4pm. Closed Sun Dec–Feb.

Cours Mirabeau, Aix-en-Provence

To the Markets We Will Go

Aix offers the best markets in the region. Place Richelme holds a **fruit and vegetable market** every morning from 8:30am to 12:30pm. Come here to buy exquisite products such as olives, lavender honey, and local cheeses. There's a **flower market** every day, with the same hours, at either place de l'Hôtel de Ville or place des Prêcheurs (the former on Tues, Thurs, and Sat; the latter on Mon, Wed, Fri, and Sun). The **fish market** takes place every morning on the south side of place Richelme.

Flowers and produce at an Aix open-air market

Cathédrale St-Sauveur ★ CATHEDRAL   The cathedral of Aix is dedicated to Christ under the title St-Sauveur (Holy Savior or Redeemer) and dates from the 4th and 5th centuries. Its pièce de résistance is a 15th-century Nicolas Froment triptych, *The Burning Bush.* One side depicts the Virgin and Child; the other, Good King René and his second wife, Jeanne de Laval.

34 place des Martyrs de la Résistance. ✆ **04-42-23-45-65.** www.cathedrale-aixenprovence-monument.fr. Free admission. Daily 8am–noon and 2–6pm. Mass Sun 10:30am and 7pm.

Musée Granet ★★ MUSEUM   One of the South of France's top art venues, this popular museum displays a permanent collection of paintings and sculpture ranging from 15th-century French canvases to 20th-century Giacometti sculptures. However, it's the large-scale temporary exhibitions that truly impress, such as 2014's "Cézanne and Modernity."

Place Saint Jean de Malte. ✆ **04-42-52-88-32.** www.museegranet-aixenprovence.fr. Permanent collection: admission 5€ adults, 4€ students and children 13–25, free children 12 and under. Additional fee for temporary exhibitions. Tues–Sun June–Sept 10am–7pm; Oct–May noon–6pm.

Shopping

Opened more than a century ago, **Béchard,** 12 cours Mirabeau (✆ **04-42-26-06-78**), is the most famous bakery in town. It specializes in the famous *Calissons* *d'Aix,* a candy made from ground almonds, preserved melon, and fruit syrup. **Chocolaterie de Puyricard,** 7 rue Rifle-Rafle (www.puyricard.fr; ✆ 04-42-21-13-26), creates sensational chocolates filled with candied figs, walnuts, or local lavender honey.

Founded in 1934 on a busy boulevard just east of the center of town, **Santons Fouque,** 65 cours Gambetta (www.santons-fouque.com; ✆ 04-42-26-33-38), stocks close to 2,000 traditional *santons* (crèche figurines).

For a range of truly useful souvenirs, including copper pots and pocket knives by famous French forgers such as Laguiole, try **Quincaillerie Centrale,** 21 rue de Monclar (✆ 04-42-23-33-18), a hardware/housewares store that's been offering a little bit of everything since 1959.

Nightlife

Open daily from 8am until 2am, **La Rotonde,** 2A place Jeanne d'Arc (www.larotonde-aix.com; ✆ 04-42-91-61-70), is a bar, cafe, and historic hangout.

Under-30s who like thumping beats should head for **Le Mistral,** 3 rue Frédéric Mistral (www.mistralclub.fr; ✆ 04-42-38-16-49), where techno and house pumps long and loud for a cover charge of around 10€ to 20€.

For jazz produced by a changing roster of visiting musicians, head for the **Scat Club,** 11 rue de la Verrerie (✆ 04-42-23-00-23), a preferred venue for more mature local patrons.

Last but certainly not least is the **Joïa Glam Club** ✆ 06-80-35-32-94), chemin de l'Enfant, in the hamlet of Les Milles, 8km (5 miles) south of Aix (follow the signs to Marseille). There is also a shuttle bus from La Rotonde in Aix proper –probably a safer bet. On site is a restaurant, several bars, an outdoor swimming pool, and indoor/outdoor dance floor. Be forewarned that there are long lines on Fridays (when females get in free) and Saturdays. Entrance usually costs around 16€, unless you're a star or self-confident enough to schmooze the doorman.

MARSEILLE ★★

776km (481 miles) S of Paris; 203km (126 miles) SW of Nice; 32km (20 miles) S of Aix-en-Provence

Marseille, with nearly 1.5 million inhabitants, is the second-largest city in France. It's also the country's oldest metropolis, founded as a port by the Greeks in the 6th century bc.

Author Alexandre Dumas called teeming Marseille "the meeting place of the entire world." It's a working city with many faces, both figuratively and literally. A view from high up reveals the colorful Vieux Port, with its elegant old buildings, boat-filled harbor, and the Mediterranean beyond. The city is sprawling and can be down at heel in parts, but it's also a cosmopolitan nexus of vibrant sounds, smells, and sights—unlike any other place in France.

Marseille's age-old problems may include unemployment, the Mafia, and racial tension (around a quarter of the population is of North African descent, with significant Armenian, Jewish, and Asian communities, too), but civic pride is strong, and the city is firmly focused on the future, evidenced by the ongoing **Euroméditerranée urban regeneration project** (www.euromediterranee.fr). Marseille proudly held the title of **European Capital of Culture 2013** (www.mp2013.fr), sparking the construction of a flurry of new cultural venues, the creation of landmark museums, and the completion of long-term architectural

Fort Saint-Jean, on the Marseille waterfront

projects, particularly in the old docklands neighborhood west of the Vieux Port. France's second city has finally come of age.

Essentials

ARRIVING **Marseille-Provence Airport** (www.marseille-airport.com; ✆ 04-42-14-14-14), 27km (17 miles) northwest of the city center, receives international flights from all over Europe. From the airport, shuttle buses (*navettes;* www.navettemarseilleaeroport.com; ✆ 08-92-70-08-40) make the trip to Marseille's St-Charles rail station, near the Vieux-Port, for 8.20€, 5.80€ passengers 12 to 26, and 4.10€ children under 12. The shuttle buses run daily every 20 minutes from 5am until midnight; the trip takes 25 minutes.

Marseille has **train** connections from all over Europe, particularly to and from Nice, and on to Italy. It's also linked to Paris via the TGV bullet train, which departs almost every hour from the Gare de Lyon (trip time: 3 hr., 20 min.; 30€–113€ one-way). **Buses** serve the **Gare Routière,** rue Honnorat (✆ 04-91-08-16-40), adjacent to the St-Charles railway station. Several buses run daily between Aix-en-Provence and Marseille (www.navetteaixmarseille.com; trip time: 40 min.; 5.70€ one-way). If you're **driving** from Paris, follow A6 south to Lyon, and then continue south along A7 to Marseille. The drive takes about 8 hours. From Provence, take A7 south to Marseille.

VISITOR INFORMATION The **Office de Tourisme** is at 11 la Canebière (www.marseille-tourisme.com; ✆ 08-26-50-05-00; Métro: Vieux-Port).

CITY LAYOUT Marseille is a large, sprawling metropolis. Unlike any of the other towns mentioned in this chapter, if you're keen to explore different parts of the city, you'll probably need to take advantage of its comprehensive public transport.

NEIGHBORHOODS IN BRIEF The major arteries divide Marseille into 16 *arrondissements*. Like Paris, the last two digits of a postal code tell you within which *arrondissement* an address is located. Visitors tend to spend most of their time in four main neighborhoods. The first is the **Vieux Port,** the atmospheric natural harbor that's a focal point for the city center. From here, the wide La

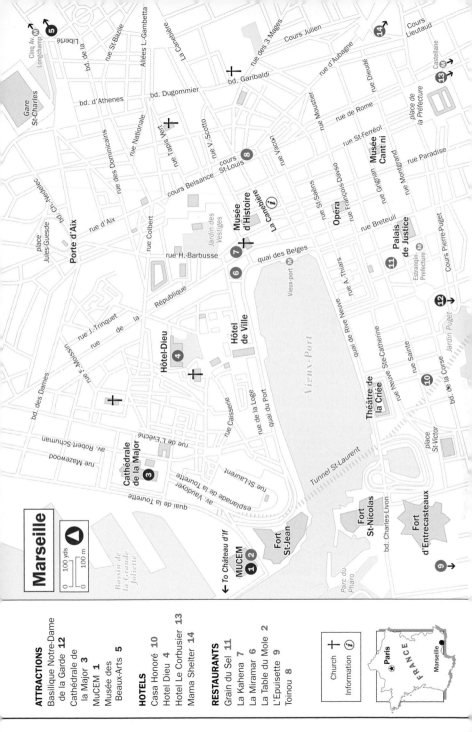

Marseille

0 100 yds
0 100 m

ATTRACTIONS

Basilique Notre-Dame de la Garde **12**
Cathédrale de la Major **3**
MuCEM **1**
Musée des Beaux-Arts **5**

HOTELS

Casa Honoré **10**
Hotel Dieu **4**
Hotel Le Corbusier **13**
Mama Shelter **14**

RESTAURANTS

Grain du Sel **11**
La Kahena **7**
La Miramar **6**
La Table du Mole **2**
L'Epuisette **9**
Toinou **8**

Church
Information

FRANCE
Paris
Marseille

Canebière boulevard runs eastwards, bisected by Marseille's most popular shopping avenues. To the north lies **Le Panier,** the original Old Town, crisscrossed by a pastel network of undulating alleyways. This neighborhood's western edge is trimmed by former docklands, which have been completely redeveloped over the past few years. Southeast of the Vieux Port, the alternative neighborhood around **cours Julien** is home to convivial restaurants and one-off boutiques aplenty. And come summertime, action shifts to the **Plages du Prado,** a strip of beaches due south of the city center.

Getting Around

ON FOOT   Each of Marseille's neighborhoods is easily navigable on foot. However, unless you're an avid walker, you may want to rely on either the Métro or the tramway (see below) to zip around town.

BY CAR   Parking and car safety are so problematic that your best bet is to park in a garage and rely on public transport. The website **www.parking-public.fr** lists Marseille's public parking lots and hourly fees.

BY TAXI   Taxis Radio Marseille (www.taximarseille.com; ✆ **04-91-02-20-20**).

BY PUBLIC TRANSPORT   **Métro** lines 1 and 2 both stop at the main train station, Gare St-Charles, place Victor Hugo. Line 1 makes a U-shaped circuit from the suburbs into the city and back again; Line 2 runs north and south in the downtown area. Also with two lines, the **tramway** services the Canabière and the refurbished Joliette Docks district, as well as continuing out to the suburbs. Individual tickets are 1.50€; they're valid on Métro, tram, and bus lines for up to 60 minutes after purchase. If you plan to take public transport several times during your stay, buy a **pass journée,** valid for 1 day for 5€ or 3 days for 10.50€. Public transit maps are downloadable from the Régie des Transport de Marseille (www.rtm.fr; ✆ **04-91-91-92-10**).

Alternatively, it's also possible to purchase a 1-day (24€), 2-day (31€), or 3-day (39€) **City Pass** from the Marseille Tourist Office. The pass covers all public transport, including the round-trip ferry trip to **Château d'If** (p. 401), as well as entrance to more than a dozen of the city's museums and a ride on the *petit-train* (p. 401) up to the **Basilique Notre-Dame-de-la-Garde** (p. 399).

[Fast FACTS] MARSEILLE

ATMs/Banks   Marseille's banks are plentiful, including three along La Canebière.

Doctors & Hospitals   **Hopital Saint Joseph,** 26 bd. de Louvain (www.hopital-saint-joseph.fr; ✆ **04-91-80-65-00**).

Embassies & Consulates   **British Consulate Marseille,** 24 av. du Prado (www.gov.uk; ✆ **04-91-15-72-10**); **Consulate General of the United States Marseille,** place Varian Fry (http://marseille.usconsulate.gov; ✆ **04-91-54-92-00**).

Internet Access   In 2013, Marseille's municipality installed 50 free Wi-Fi hotspots around the city. Central locations (including Jardin du Pharo, the square outside the Hôtel de Ville, and La Vieille Charité) are indicated on the free maps distributed by the tourist office.

Mail & Postage   **La Poste,** 1 cours Jean Ballard (✆ **36-31**).

Newspapers & Magazines   Bilingual **"COTE Magazine"** (www.cotemagazine.com) offers a good selection of tried-and-true Marseille tips, as well as local interviews and recent openings.

Pharmacies   **Leader Santé,** 37 la Canebière (📞 **04-91-91-32-06**).

Safety   As in any big city, it's wise to keep a close eye on your belongings and avoid poorly lit areas at night.

Where to Stay

Although slightly removed from the city center, the iconic **Hôtel le Corbusier** (www.gerardin-corbusier.com) is a must for architecture aficionados. In 2013, local French designers transformed the hotel's rooftop gym into a hip contemporary art space, **MAMO** (www.mamo.fr).

Casa Honoré ★   Interior designer Annick Lestrohan, creator of the Honoré brand of housewares, has transformed this former print shop into an ultra-stylish bed-and-breakfast. Unsurprisingly, guest rooms are decorated with Lestrohan's exquisite creations, from sleek designer furnishings to quality linens (and all are for sale, too). An oasis of tranquility just south of Marseille's Vieux Port, the B&B's four rooms all center around a courtyard splashed with tropical foliage and a small swimming pool. Book as far in advance as you dare.

123 rue Sainte. 📞 **04-96-11-01-62.** www.casahonore.com. 4 units. 150€–200€ double. Minimum 2-night stay. No credit cards. Métro: Vieux-Port. **Amenities:** Breakfast room; outdoor pool; free Wi-Fi.

Hôtel-Dieu ★★   Opened in 2013, the luxurious Hôtel-Dieu is perched just behind Marseille's Hôtel de Ville, overlooking the Vieux Port from Le Panier. This five-star hotel occupies what was once an 18th-century hospital. It's now managed by the InterContinental Group with aplomb. As well as modern, minimalist guest rooms with superb views, guest may enjoy the indoor pool, the Clarins Spa, brasserie **Les Fenêtres,** and gastronomic restaurant **Alcyone** onsite.

1 place Daviel. 📞 **04-13-42-42-42.** www.ihg.com. 194 units. 220€–440€ double; 500€–1,500€ suite. Parking 25€. Métro: Vieux-Port. **Amenities:** Restaurant; bar; business center; fitness center; indoor pool; room service; spa; free Wi-Fi.

Mama Shelter ★★   Tucked into the hipster cours Julien district, this unique hotel is the brainchild of designer Philippe Starck. Rooms are bright and cool, from the modular furnishings to the wall-mounted iMacs offering dozens of free on-demand movies. Downstairs, Egyptian graffiti artist Tarek has tagged the industrial-chic restaurant's ceiling. And outdoors, Mama Shelter's yellow-striped courtyard hosts a pastis bar where guests can sip their way through more than four dozen variants of the city's beloved anise-flavored tipple. An excellent bet for a contemporary taste of France's second city.

64 rue de la Loubière. 📞 **04-84-35-20-00.** www.mamashelter.com. 127 units. 69€–109€ double; 129€ family room; 199€ suite. Parking 19€. Métro: Notre Dame du Mont. **Amenities:** Restaurant; bar; free Wi-Fi.

Where to Eat

For diners interested in re-creating Marseille's famous *bouillabaisse* fish stew at home, **Miramar Restaurant** (www.lemiramar.fr) offers cooking classes (120€/ 5-hr. lesson including lunch). Contact the tourist office for details.

L'Epuisette ★★ SEAFOOD/MEDITERRANEAN This Michelin-starred option is undoubtedly the premier place in Marseille to sample **bouillabaisse** stew. Pack your appetite: Fresh fish is poached in saffron-infused soup; the final product is served as two separate courses, accompanied by *rouille,* a mayonnaise-like sauce flavored with garlic, cayenne pepper, and saffron. L'Epuisette's setting is as sublime as the cuisine: The seaside dining room overlooks Château d'If from the picturesque fishing port of Vallon des Auffes, 2.5km (1½ miles) south of Marseille's Vieux Port. Vallon des Auffes. ℂ **04-91-52-17-82.** www.l-epuisette.fr. Main courses 18€–65€; fixed-price dinner 70€–125€. Tues–Sat noon–1:30pm and 7:30–9:30pm. Closed Aug. Bus: 83.

Le Grain du Sel ★★ MODERN MEDITERRANEAN Marseille-born chef Pierre Giannetti concocts what many locals consider to be the city's most creative bistro cuisine. Dishes are infinitely innovative, often taking inspiration from Giannetti's years of cooking in Barcelona. Following morning market finds, the daily menu may include Sardinian gnocchi with clams, mussel *escabèche,* or Spanish rice with shellfish harvested from the Camargue seaside town of Saintes-Maries-de-la-Mer. The wine list is carefully considered, and you can dine outside on sunny days in the petite courtyard. 39 rue de la Paix Marcel Paul. ℂ **04-91-54-47-30.** Main courses 16€–35€; fixed-price lunch 16€–19€. Tues–Sat noon–2pm, Fri–Sat 8–10pm. Closed Aug. Métro: Vieux-Port.

La Kahena ★ TUNISIAN Among Marseille's many Tunisian restaurants, this 35-year-old eatery stands out from the crowd. Named for a 6th-century-bc Tunisian princess, La Kahena's specialty is couscous: Among the 10 varieties are versions with lamb, *merguez* spicy sausages, and cod. Other Tunisian classics such as *mechoua* salad (spicy grilled vegetables), tajines, and crispy *brick* pastry stuffed with shrimp are also served up in the ornate blue-tiled dining room. A solid budget choice. 2 rue de la République. ℂ **04-91-90-61-93.** Main courses 10€–18€. Daily noon–2pm and 7–10:30pm. Métro: Vieux-Port.

La Table du Môle ★★★ MODERN MEDITERRANEAN Triple Michelin-starred-chef Gérard Passédat's newest restaurant, this "chic bistro" opened atop the MuCEM (p. 400) in 2013. Much like the MuCEM itself, stellar dishes herald from across the Mediterranean, including seafood tart served with a creamy ginger jus, crab paired with spicy harissa, or grilled turbot with truffled potatoes. All served against a sweeping backdrop of Marseille's port and the Mediterranean Sea. Note that it's also possible to dine at Le Môle's lower-key (and cheaper) sister restaurant, **La Cuisine** (lunch only), also located at the MuCEM. Almost all vegetables used are sourced from the organic Les Olivades d'Ollioules farm. MuCEM, 1 esplanade du J4. www.passedat.fr. Reservations via internet only. Main courses 18€–65€; fixed-price lunch 43€; fixed-price dinner 73€. Wed–Mon 12:30–2:30pm; Wed–Sat and Mon 7:30–10:30pm. Métro: Vieux-Port. Bus: 49, 60, or 82.

Toinou ★★ SEAFOOD For the veritable seafood aficionado, there is no better place to dine in Marseille than this landmark restaurant. Platters are piled high with dozens of varieties of mussels, oysters, clams, and this region's famous sea urchins, as well as sea snails of all shapes and sizes. Doing a bustling local business for close to 50 years, Toinou's format changed from table service to a slightly more chaotic variation on self-service in late 2013. No matter: the seafood dished up here is just as sublime. Want your fish with a sea view? Choose your own selection of shellfish from the restaurant's kiosk out front, then head down to the coast for a beachside picnic.

3 cours St-Louis. ✆ **08-11-45-45-45.** www.toinou.com. Shellfish by the half dozen 2.10€–9€; fixed-price platters 15.70€–88.90€. Daily 11:30am–11:30pm. Métro: Vieux-Port or Noailles.

Exploring Marseille

Immerse yourself in local life with a wander through Marseille's busy streets, including along the famous **La Canebière.** Lined with hotels, shops, and restaurants, it used to be a very seedy street indeed, saturated with sailors from every nation. With Marseille's ongoing urban regeneration, however, it has become the heart and soul of the city.

La Canebière joins the **Vieux Port ★★**, dominated at its western end by the massive neoclassical forts of St-Jean and St-Nicolas. The harbor is filled with fishing craft and yachts and ringed by seafood restaurants. For a panoramic view, head to the **Jardin du Pharo,** a promontory facing the entrance to the Vieux-Port. From the terrace of the Château du Pharo, built by Napoleon III, you can clearly see the city's old and new cathedrals, as well as the recently redeveloped docklands, now the **Cité de la Méditerranée,** which includes **Fort Saint-Jean** and the architectural wonder that is **MuCEM** (Museum of European and Mediterranean Civilizations).

North of the old port is **Le Panier,** Marseille's Old Town. Small boutiques and designer ateliers now populate these once-sketchy streets. To the south, the **corniche Président-J.-F.-Kennedy** is a 4km (2½-mile) promenade. You'll pass villas and gardens facing the Mediterranean, before reaching the popular **Plages du Prado.** Patrolled by lifeguards in the summer, these spacious sandy beaches have children's playgrounds, sun loungers, and waterside cafes. Serious hikers can continue south of here into the **Parc Nationale des Calanques** (www. calanques-parcnational.fr), France's newest national park (see box, p. 406). This series of stunning limestone cliffs, fjords, and rocky promontories stretches along the coast for 20km (12 miles) southeast of Marseille.

Basilique Notre-Dame-de-la-Garde ★ CHURCH   This landmark church crowns a limestone rock overlooking the southern side of the Vieux-Port. It was built in the Romanesque-Byzantine style popular in the 19th century and topped

Museum of European and Mediterranean Civilizations (MuCEM), Marseille

by a 9.7m (32-ft.) gilded statue of the Virgin. Visitors come for the views (best at sunset) from its terrace. Spread out before you are the city, the islands, and the shimmering sea.

Rue Fort-du-Sanctuaire. © **04-91-13-40-80.** www.notredamedelagarde.com. Free admission. Daily Apr–Sept 7am–7:15pm, Oct–Mar 7am–6.15pm. Métro: Estrangin-Préfecture. Bus: 60.

Cathédrale de la Major ★ CATHEDRAL   One of the largest cathedrals (some 135m/443 ft. long) built in Europe during the 19th century, this massive structure has almost swallowed its 12th-century predecessor, built on the ruins of a temple of Diana. Its striped exterior is a bastardized Romanesque-Byzantine style with domes and cupolas; the intricate interiors include mosaic floors and red-and-white marble banners. The cathedral's architecture is particularly arresting now that it overlooks Marseille's redeveloped port and dockland areas. It also provides shady respite from sightseeing on a summer's day.

Esplanade de la Major. © **04-91-90-53-57.** Free admission. Hours vary. Head west of Le Panier district. Métro: Vieux-Port. Bus: 49, 60, or 82.

MuCEM (Museum of European and Mediterranean Civilizations) ★★ MUSEUM   Opened in 2013, the long-anticipated MuCEM is the first national gallery in France to be located outside of Paris. More than 250,000 objects have been collected from throughout the Mediterranean region and are exhibited here, along with local prints, photographs, and historical postcards. Architect Rudy Ricciotti designed the museum's contemporary form, which is encased in unique concrete lace. The premises encompass the 12th-century **Fort Saint-Jean,** its suspended gardens, and Michelin-starred-chef Gérard Passédat's primarily organic restaurant, **La Table du Môle** (p. 398).

1 esplanade du J4. © **04-84-35-13-13.** www.mucem.org. Admission 5€ adults, 3€ seniors and students, 9€ family ticket, free children 17 and under. Additional fee for temporary exhibitions. May–Oct Wed–Thurs and Sat–Mon 11am–7pm, Fri 11am–10pm; Nov–Apr Wed–Thurs and Sat–Mon 11am–6pm, Fri 11am–10pm. Métro: Vieux-Port. Bus: 49, 60, or 82.

Musée des Beaux-Arts ★ MUSEUM   The 150-year-old Museum of Fine Arts is Marseille's oldest exhibition venue. Following 2013's blockbuster show "Le Grand Atelier du Midi: Van Gogh a Bonnard," held in tandem with the **Musée Granet** in Aix (p. 392), the museum reopened its permanent collection to the public in 2014, after an incredible nine years of renovations. Exhibits range from 16th-century Italian works to 19th-century French masterpieces, including Rodin's sculpture "La Voix Intérieure" ("The Inner Voice").

Palais Longchamp. © **04-91-14-59-30.** http://musee-des-beaux-arts.marseille.fr. Admission 5€ adults, 3€ students and seniors, free for children 17 and under. Additional fee for temporary exhibitions. Tues–Sun 10am–6pm. Métro: Longchamp. Tram: Longchamp.

Musée Cantini ★ ART MUSEUM   Fully renovated for Marseille's European Capital of Culture 2013 festivities, this 17th-century *hôtel particulier* (private mansion) organizes outstanding modern art exhibitions. Recent shows have been dedicated to Chilean surrealist Roberto Matta and native Marseillaise sculptor César. The museum also houses a permanent collection, particularly strong on masterpieces (by Picasso, Dufy, de Staël, Ernst, and others) created during the first half of the 20th century.

19 rue Grignan. © **04-91-54-77-75.** http://musee-cantini.marseille.fr. Admission 5€ adults, 3€ students and seniors, free for children 17 and under. Tues–Sun 10am–6pm. Métro: Estrangin/Préfecture.

Few know that France's national anthem was actually composed in Strasbourg. Originally titled "War Song of the Army of the Rhine," it was written in 1 night by army captain Claude-Joseph Rouget de Lisle in 1792. That same year, revolutionaries from Marseille (who had been given printed copies) marched into Paris singing it. In their honor, the song became known as "La Marseillaise" and was quickly adopted as the rallying cry of the French Revolution. It was officially declared the national anthem of France in 1795, only to be banned by Napoleon during the Empire, Louis XVIII in 1815, and Napoleon III in 1830. The anthem was reinstated for good in 1879.

Outlying Attractions

You can take a 25-minute ferry ride to the **Château d'If** (http://if.monuments-nationaux.fr), a national monument built by François I as a fortress to defend Marseille. Alexandre Dumas used it as a setting for the fictional adventures of "The Count of Monte Cristo." The château is open daily May 16 to September 16 9:30am to 6:10pm; September 17 to March 31 Tuesday to Sunday 9:30am to 4:45pm; and April 1 to May 15 daily 9:30am to 4:45pm. Entrance to the island is 5.50€ adults, free children 17 and under. Boats leave approximately every 45 to 60 minutes, depending on the season; the round-trip transfer is 10.10€. For information, contact the **Frioul If Express** (www.frioul-if-express.com; ⏰ **04-96-11-03-50;** Métro: Vieux-Port).

Organized Tours

One of the easiest ways to see Marseille's centrally located monuments is aboard the fleet of open-top **Le Grand Tour Buses** (www.marseillelegrandtour.com; Métro: Vieux-Port). You can hop off at any of 13 different stops en route and back on to the next bus in the day's sequence, usually arriving between 1 and 2 hours later, depending on the season. The buses run four to eight times a day during each month except January. A 1-day pass costs 18€ adults and 16€ seniors and students with ID; the fare for children ages 4 to 11 is 8€. Two-day passes are also available for just a few euros more.

The motorized **Trains Touristiques de Marseille** (www.petit-train-marseille.com; ⏰ **04-91-25-24-69;** Métro: Vieux-Port), or *petit-trains,* make circuits around town, too. Year-round, train no. 1 drives a 75-minute round-trip to Basilique Notre-Dame-de-la-Garde and Basilique St-Victor. From April to mid-November, train no. 2 makes a 65-minute round-trip of old Marseille by way of the cathedral, Vieille Charité, and the Quartier du Panier. Both trains make a 30-minute stop for sightseeing en route. The trains depart from the quay just west of the Hôtel de Ville. The fare for train no. 1 is 8€ adults and 4€ children; train no. 2 is 1€ less for both.

Boat tours to the **Parc National des Calanques** are popular. Many tour operators with different prices and formulas (for example, three Calanques in 2 hr./22€, or eight in 3 hr./28€) can be found on the quai des Belges at the Vieux-Port. For more information about visiting the Calanques from nearby Cassis, see p. 405.

Shopping

Only Paris and the French Riviera can compete with Marseille for its breadth and diversity of merchandise. Your best bet is a trip to the streets just southeast of the **Vieux-Port,** crowded with stores of all kinds.

Rue Paradis and **rue Saint Ferréol** have many of the same upscale fashion boutiques found in Paris, as well as a Galeries Lafayette, France's largest chain department store. For more bohemian wear, try **cours Julien** and **rue de la Tour** for richly brocaded and beaded items on offer in North African boutiques. **Le Panier** is now home to a vibrant range of unique boutiques. Try **5.7.2,** 23 rue du Panier (www.5-7-2.com; ✆ **06-07-14-62-92**) for 1950s to 1970s housewares, or **Les Baigneuses,** 3 rue de l'Eveche (www.lesbaigneuses. com; ✆ **09-52-68-67-64**), which sells a gorgeous range of retro-styled swimwear.

For unique souvenirs, head to **Ateliers Marcel Carbonel,** 49 rue Neuve-Ste-Catherine (www.santonsmarcelcarbonel.com; ✆ **04-91-13-61-36**). This 80-year-old business specializes in *santons,* clay figurines meant for Christmas nativities. In addition to personalities you may already know, the carefully crafted pieces depict Provençal common folk such as bakers, blacksmiths, and milkmaids. The figurines sell for around 12.60€ and up.

Navettes, small cookies that resemble boats, are a Marseillaise specialty. Flavored with secret ingredients that include orange zest and orange flower water, they were invented in 1791 and are still sold at **Le Four des Navettes,** 136 rue Sainte (www.fourdesnavettes.com; ✆ **04-91-33-32-12**), for around 9.60€ per dozen.

One of the region's most authentic fish markets at **Quai des Belges** (daily 8am–1pm), on the old port, is partially sheltered under the new Norman Foster–designed Ombrière mirrored canopy. On **cours Julien,** you'll find a market with fruits, vegetables, and other foods (Tues, Thurs, and Sat 8am–1pm); exclusively organic produce (Wed 8am–1pm); stamps (Sun 8am–1pm); and secondhand goods (3rd Sun of the month 8am–1pm).

Nightlife

For an amusing and relatively harmless exposure to the town's saltiness, walk around the **Vieux-Port,** where cafes and restaurants angle their sightlines for the best view of the harbor.

L'Escale Borély, avenue Pierre Mendès France, is 20 minutes south of the town center (take bus no. 83). With a dozen animated bars and cafes, plus restaurants of every possible ethnicity, you'll be spoiled for choice.

Marseille's dance clubs are habitually packed out, especially **Trolley Bus,** 24 quai de Rive-Neuve (www.letrolley.com; ✆ **04-91-54-30-45;** Métro: Vieux-Port), known for techno, house, hip-hop, jazz, and salsa. Equally buzzing is **l'Exit,** 12 quai de Rive-Neuve (✆ **06-42-59-96-24;** Métro: Vieux-Port), a bar/disco with a terrace that profits from Marseille's sultry nights and two floors of seething nocturnal energy (happy hour starts at 5pm, and runs all night on Thursdays). The **New Can Can,** 3–7 rue Sénac (www.newcancan.com; ✆ **04-91-48-59-76;** Métro: Noailles), is a lively, sprawling bar and disco that identifies itself as a gay venue but attracts many straight folks too. It's open Friday through Sunday midnight until 7am. Brand-new sister bar **Le Petit Cancan,** 10 rue Beauvau (www.lepetitcancan.com; ✆ **06-52-26-90-75;** Métro: Vieux-Port) is open daily from 6pm for cocktails and tapas.

For jazz right on the port, head to **La Caravelle,** 34 quai du Port (www. lacaravelle-marseille.com; ✆ **04-91-90-36-64;** Métro: Vieux-Port), an aperitif bar and dinner club that serves a different flavor almost every night, including *manouche,* the French gypsy style most associated with guitarist Django Reinhardt.

CASSIS ★★

806km (501 miles) S of Paris; 128km (80 miles) SE of Avignon; 50km (31 miles) S of Aix-en-Provence; 32km (20 miles) E of Marseille

Cassis is unarguably the prettiest coastal town in Provence. The settlement dates from Ancient Greek times—that's as far back as both Marseille and Nice—but its fame rose in the early 20th century, when famous personalities like Virginia Woolf and Sir Winston Churchill guzzled its crisp white wines. The resort recently found a new outdoor-oriented audience as the capital of France's first mainland National Park since 1979.

Essentials

ARRIVING   Cassis Station is a cinch to reach by rail. Half-hourly **trains** arrive from Marseille (trip time: 25 min.; 6€ one-way). Sound easy? It's not, as Cassis Station is then a 3km (1¾ miles) downhill walk from Cassis town center. Walk down, grab one of the waiting taxis (10€), or catch the Marcouline city bus (.80€) every 30 minutes.

VISITOR INFORMATION   The helpful **Office de Tourisme** is on the beachfront quai des Moulins (www.ot-cassis.com; ✆ **08-92-39-01-03**).

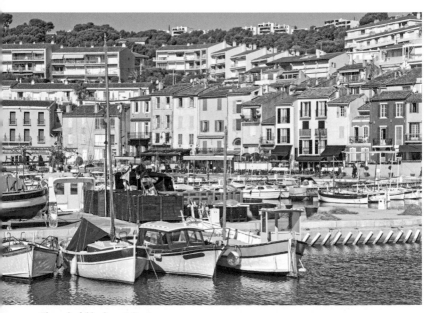

The colorful harbor at Cassis

[FastFACTS] CASSIS

Mail & Postage   **La Poste,** 3 rue Arène (📞 **36-31**). Note that the post office also offers an ATM.

Pharmacies   **Pharmacie Trossero,** 11 av Victor Hugo (📞 **04-42-01-70-03**).

Where to Stay

Hotel La Rade ★   The pick of Cassis's mid-range hotels, La Rade gazes out over the ocean, a 3-minute walk from the pedestrian only quays. Its enviably tranquil position is also convenient for strolls west to plage du Bestouan and into the Calanques National Park beyond. In summer, the hotel's locally sourced breakfast—think Cassis jams and Provençal *saucisson*—is served by the swimming pool, the only sea view *piscine* in town. The hotel terrace is justly popular with artists. Indeed, Sir Winston Churchill honed his painting skills at the Camargo Foundation (www.camargofoundation.org) artist residency just across the street.

1 avenue des Dardanelles. 📞 **04-42-01-02-97.** www.bestwestern-cassis.com. 28 units. 90€–215€ double. Breakfast 16€ per person. **Amenities:** Restaurant, outdoor pool; free Wi-Fi.

Where to Eat

Bar de la Marine ★ BISTRO   This harborside eatery won't feature in the Michelin guide or any other French foodie bible. And thank heavens for that. This no-nonsense bar and bistro has been dishing up *steak-frites*, *salade Niçoise*, and seafood salad to tired fisherman since time began. In season, its proximity to Cassis's working port makes it a prime spot to try sea urchins, the local delicacy. Simply order a platter from the septuagenarian street vendor to be delivered to your table. Like almost every other restaurant in Cassis, Bar de la Marine boasts rustic service and age-old tableware.

5 quai des Baux. 📞 **04-42-01-76-09.** Main courses 10€–17€. Daily noon–2:30pm and 7–10:30pm.

La Poissonnerie ★★ SEAFOOD   The Giannettini family have been serving harbor-fresh seafood at this portside emplacement since 1940. They've had 75 years to perfect their simple recipes. My goodness they're good. Grilled sardines, octopus salad, and the special house spicy aïoli share the menu with local urchins (in season) and oysters from near Marseille. Bouillabaisse, the famed seafood stew from the latter city, may be ordered in advance.

5 quai Barthélémy. 📞 **04-42-01-71-56.** Main courses 11€–24€. Tues–Sun noon–1:30p; Jun-Sept Tues–Sat 7:30–10pm. Closed Jan.

Exploring Cassis

The deliciously beautiful center of Cassis is best explored on foot. The coastal path winds from the wide expanse of Grande Plage beach past restaurant terraces and boutiques all the way to Plage du Bestouan and the start of the Parc Nationale des Calanques. Each August the entire town comes alive for a series of literary festivals, fireworks shows, and sea jousting tournaments (yes, involving lances and motor boats).

Cassis Snorkeling Tour ★ TOUR   As you might expect from a town that borders a massive marine and land National Park, Cassis is awash with diving schools. These include **Cassis-Plongée** (www.cassis-calanques-plongee.com) and **Narval Plongée** (www.narval-plongee.com). Novice divers may also scuba or snorkel along the **Sentier Sous-Marin de Cassis,** or underwater trail. This self-guided 30-minute swim route begins on the Promenade des Lombards. Four buoys mark marine life discovery spots along the way. Be aware that a mineral water source (as in thousands of bottles of chilled Evian) seeps from the limestone cliffs into Cassis harbor, so sea temperatures are often chilly!

Cassis Wine Tour ★ WALKING TOUR   White wines from Cassis (www.vinsdecassis.fr) are so superb that they were protected as an AOC region in 1936 (along with Châteauneuf-du-Pape, see p. 370, outside of Avignon). Most vintages are infused with flowery Marsanne from the Rhône Valley, and herby Clairette from Provence. Just a dozen small, mostly organic producers tend their ocean-facing vineyards that are planted from the port up to the Cassis train station. All can be toured (with free tasting sessions to those who wish to purchase a bottle or three) by foot or by bicycle using the free Vineyard Tour map from the Cassis Tourist Office. Cheers.

Cassis environs. www.vinsdecassis.com.

Outlying Attractions

In 2012 Cassis was declared the capital of the new **Parc Nationale des Calanques** (see box, below). The calanques are towering cliffs created 120 million years ago. They were then split apart by rising sea levels and bleached white by the Provençal sun. Each calanque crashes into the azure sea from heights of up to 565m (nearly 2,000 ft.). Like Norway's fjords, they surround a series of boat-only bays that stretch for 32km (20 miles) from Cassis to Marseille. So sturdy is the snow-white stone from Calanque Port-Miou, a creek within walking distance of Cassis, that it was used to build the base of the Statue of Liberty in New York.

The main public pathway through the park is the GR51, a long-distance hiking trail known as the "Balconies of the Mediterranean." This *grande randonnée* route links Marseille with Monaco. Those visitors without Ironman thighs (or

Boaters and swimmers explore Parc Nationale des Calanques

without a spare 3 weeks of vacation) may hike along a score of shorter marked paths instead, passing lonely islands, rocky passes, secret beaches, and gaping creeks. Park maps are available from Cassis's ever-helpful Tourist Office.

A more relaxed way to tour the park is by sea. From Cassis harbor regular **boat trips** take in three calanques (45 min., adults 16 €, children under 10 9.50€), five calanques (65 min., adults 19€, children 13€,) or nine calanques (2 hr., adults 27€, children 16€). A particular favorite is Calanque de Sugiton, which crumbles into an island-strewn bay. The postcard-perfect **Calanque d'En Vau** is also well worth seeking out. As non-official motorboats are banned from the National Park, try paddling under the calanques by kayak or SUP instead. For equipment, contact **Cassis Sport Loisirs Nautiques** (www.cassis-kayak.com).

ILES D'HYÈRES ★★

39km (24 miles) SE of Toulon; 119km (74 miles) SW of Cannes

Bobbing off the French Riviera in the Mediterranean Sea, a small group of islands encloses the eastern boundary of Provence. During the Renaissance, they were coined the Iles d'Or (Golden Islands), named for the glow the rocks give off in sunlight. As might be expected, their location only half an hour from the French coast means the islands are often packed with tourists in summer—but there is still space on its breathtaking beaches for everyone.

If you have time for only one island, choose the beautiful, lively **Ile de Porquerolles.** The **Ile de Port-Cros** is quieter—and perhaps better for an overnight stay in order to take advantage of the great hiking, exploring, and snorkeling that would be too rushed for a 6-hour day trip. As for the **Ile du Levant,** 80 percent belongs to the French army and is used for missile testing; the remainder is a nudist colony.

Essentials

GETTING TO ILE DE PORQUEROLLES Ferries leave from several points along the Côte d'Azur. The most frequent, cheapest, and shortest trip is from the harbor of La Tour Fondue on the peninsula of Giens, a 32km (20-mile) drive east of Toulon. Depending on the season, there are 5 to 19 departures per day. The round-trip fare for the 15-minute crossing is 19.50€ adults and 17.30€ children 4 to 10. For information, contact **TLV-TVM,** La Tour Fondue, Giens 83400 (www.tlv-tvm.com; ✆ **04-94-58-21-81**). **Bateliers de la Côte d'Azur** (www.bateliersdelacotedazur.com; ✆ **04-94-05-21-14**) and **Les Vedettes Ile d'Or & Le Corsaire** (www.vedettesilesdor.fr; ✆ **04-94-71-01-02**) also offer services from La Londe-les-Maures and Le Lavandou respectively.

GETTING TO ILE DE PORT-CROS The most popular ferry route to the island is the 35-minute crossing that departs from Le Lavandou 3 to 7 times daily, depending on the season (28.10€ adults, 24.90€ children 4–12 round-trip). For information, contact **Les Vedettes Ile d'Or & Le Corsaire** (see above). The **TLV-TVM** and **Bateliers de la Côte d'Azur** (see above) also service Ile de Port-Cros. Some of the former's services travel onwards to Ile de Levant.

VISITOR INFORMATION Other than temporary, summer-only kiosks that distribute brochures and advice near the ferry docks in Porquerolles and Port-Cros, there are no tourist bureaus on the islands. For further information, contact the **Office de Tourisme de Hyères, Bureau de Porquerolles,** Rotonde du Park Hôtel, av. de Belgique, Hyères (www.hyeres-tourisme.com; ✆ **04-94-01-84-50**). Information can also be found at www.porquerolles.com and www.port-crosparcnational.fr.

MAIL/POSTAGE & MONEY The post office, **La Poste,** place d'Armes, Porquerolles (✆ **36-31**), also has an ATM, but it's best to bring petty cash. Most establishments accept credit cards.

Exploring Ile de Porquerolles ★★

Ile de Porquerolles is the largest and westernmost of the Iles d'Hyères. It has a rugged south coast, but the northern strand, facing the mainland, boasts a handful of pristine white-sand beaches. The island is about 8km (5 miles) long and 2km (1¼ miles) wide, and is 4.8km (3 miles) from the mainland. The permanent population is only 400.

The island is said to receive 275 days of sunshine annually. The landscape is one of rocky capes, pine forests twisted by the mistral, sun-drenched vineyards, and pale ochre houses. It's best explored on foot or by bike (look for plenty of bike-rental agencies just behind the harbor). The **place d'Armes,** former site of the garrison, is home to several quaint cafes—your best bet for lunch if you're here for a day trip.

The island has a history of raids, attacks, and occupation by everyone from the Dutch and the English to the Turks and the Spaniards. Ten forts, some in ruins, testify to its fierce past. The most ancient is **Fort Ste-Agathe,** built in 1531 by François I. In time, it was a penal colony and a retirement center for soldiers of the colonial wars.

In 1971, the French government purchased a large part of the island and turned it into a national park. Indigenous trees such as fig, mulberry, and olive are protected, as well as plants that attract butterflies.

WHERE TO EAT & STAY

Hotel et Residence Les Medes (www.hotel-les-medes.fr) also offers good-value guest rooms and apartments.

Mas du Langoustier ★★ This Provençal-style hotel is far and away Porquerolles' most luxurious accommodation. Located on the island's western tip, it's set in a 40-hectare (99-acre) park shaded by eucalyptus and Aleppo pines, and overlooks a lovely pine-ringed bay. Elegant rooms are decorated with classic local textiles; many have their own private patio. And come evening time, there's no need to leave paradise. The onsite **Restaurant L'Olivier** (open to non-guests) is Michelin-starred: Prepare for unique pairings like steamed crayfish and fig ravioli or foie gras with hibiscus jelly.

C **04-94-58-30-09.** www.langoustier.com. 50 units. 300€–660€ double; 690€–760€ suite; 920€–1,200€ family room. Rates include half-board. Closed Oct to late Apr. **Amenities:** 2 restaurants; bar; babysitting; outdoor pool; tennis court; free Wi-Fi.

Exploring Ile de Port-Cros ★★

The most mountainous island of the archipelago, Port-Cros has been France's smallest national park since 1963. It's just 5km (3 miles) long and 2km (1¼ miles) wide. It's blanketed with beautiful beaches, pine forests, and subtropical vegetation (birders flock here to observe nearly 100 different species). A hiker's paradise, it also has a number of well-marked trails. The most popular and scenic is the easy, 1-hour *sentier des plantes.* The more adventurous and athletic take the 10km (6¼-mile) *circuit de Port-Man* (and pack their lunch). There is even a 274m (899-ft.) "underwater trail" along the coast where you can snorkel past laminated signs identifying the plants and fish you'll see.

WHERE TO EAT & STAY

Le Manoir de Port-Cros ★   Port-Cros's only hotel sits within an 18th-century whitewashed building. Accommodation may be simple—crisp white sheets, oversized copper vases, terra-cotta tiled floors—but guests stay here to truly switch off. Paddle in the pool, head out for a hike, or simply amble the surrounding palm and eucalyptus-studded gardens. Rates are half-board, although plenty of day trippers visit for the restaurant's hearty three-course lunch (58€).

C **04-94-05-90-52.** www.hotel-lemanoirportcros.com. 21 units. 165€–265€ double; 210€–240€ family room; 230€–265€ bungalows for 4. Closed Nov–Mar. **Amenities:** Restaurant; bar; outdoor pool; room service; free Wi-Fi in common areas.

THE FRENCH RIVIERA

By Tristan Rutherford

13

The fabled real estate known as the French Riviera, also called the Côte d'Azur (Azure Coast), ribbons for 200km (125 miles) along the sun-kissed Mediterranean. The region has long attracted artists and jetsetters alike with its clear skies, blue waters, and carefree cafe culture. Chic, sassy, and incredibly sexy, the Riviera can be explored by bus, train, boat, bikes, Segway, electric car, or in a dozen novel ways.

A trail of modern artists captivated by the region's light and setting has left a rich heritage: Matisse at Vence, Cocteau at Villefranche, Léger at Biot, Renoir at Cagnes, and Picasso at Antibes and seemingly everywhere in between. The finest collection of modern artworks is at the Foundation Maeght in St-Paul-de-Vence. New museums dedicated to Jean Cocteau in Menton and Pierre Bonnard near Cannes offer a vivid introduction to the Riviera's storied art scene.

A century ago, winter and spring were considered high season on the Riviera. In recent decades, July and August have become the most crowded months, and reservations are imperative. The region basks in more than 300 days of sun per year, and even December and January are often pleasant and sunny.

The ribbonlike corniche roads stretch across the western Riviera from Nice to Menton, and are scenic stars in scores of films including Cary Grant's "To Catch a Thief" and Robert de Niro's "Ronin." The lower road, the 32km (20-mile) Corniche Inférieure, takes in the resorts of Villefranche, Cap-Ferrat, Beaulieu, Monaco, and Cap-Martin. The 31km (19-mile) Moyenne Corniche (Middle Road) winds in and out of mountain tunnels and takes in the picture-perfect village of Eze. Napoleon built the Grande Corniche—the most panoramic roadway—in 1806. La Turbie is the principal town along the 32km (20-mile) stretch, which reaches more than 480m (1,574 ft.) high at Col d'Eze.

ST-TROPEZ ★★★

874km (542 miles) S of Paris; 76km (47 miles) SW of Cannes

While this sun-kissed town has a well-known air of hedonism, Tropezian style is blissfully understated—it's not in-your-face. St-Tropez attracts artists, musicians, models, writers, and an A-lister movie colony each summer, with a flamboyant parade of humanity trailing behind. In winter it morphs back into a boho fishing village, albeit one with modern art galleries and some of the best restaurants along the coast.

The 1956 Brigitte Bardot movie "And God Created Woman" put St-Tropez on the tourist map. Droves of decadent tourists baring almost all on the peninsula's white-sand beaches trailed in her wake. Two decades ago, Bardot pronounced St-Tropez dead, "squatted by a lot of no-goods, drugheads, and villains." But even she returned, followed in recent years by celebrity A-listers including David Beckham, Paris Hilton, Jay-Z, and Beyoncé.

PREVIOUS PAGE: **Beach near promenade des Anglais, Nice**

Sunset over St-Tropez

Essentials

ARRIVING   The nearest rail station is in St-Raphaël, a neighboring coastal resort. **Boats** depart (www.bateauxsaintraphael.com; ✆ **04-94-95-17-46**) from its Vieux Port for St-Tropez (trip time: 1 hr.) five times a day in high summer, reducing to once- or twice-daily sailings in winter. The one-way fare is 15€. Year-round, 10 to 15 Varlib **buses** per day leave from the Gare Routière in St-Raphaël (www.varlib.fr; ✆ **04-94-24-60-00**) for St-Tropez. The trip takes 1½ to 2 hours, depending on the bus and the traffic, which during midsummer is usually horrendous. A one-way ticket is 3€. Buses also run from Toulon train station, 56km (35 miles) away.

If you **drive,** note that parking in St-Tropez is tricky, especially in summer. For parking, follow the signs for **Parking des Lices** (✆ **04-94-97-34-46**), beneath place des Lices, or **Parking du Nouveau Port,** on waterfront avenue Charles de Gaulle (✆ **04-94-97-74-99**). To get here from **Cannes,** drive southwest along the coastal highway (D559), turning east when you see signs to St-Tropez.

VISITOR INFORMATION   The **Office de Tourisme** is on quai Jean-Jaurès (www.ot-saint-tropez.com; ✆ **08-92-68-48-28**). Note that they charge 2€ for a town map. Meanies.

[FastFACTS] ST-TROPEZ

ATMs/Banks   **Crédit Agricole,** 17 place des Lices (✆ **32-25**).

Internet Access   There's free WiFi—as well as a handy table and stools—at the **Casino Supermarket,** av. Genéral Leclerc.

Mail & Postage   **La Poste,** rue de la Poste (✆ **36-31**).

Pharmacies   **Pharmacie du Port,** 9 quai Suffren (✆ **04-94-97-00-06**).

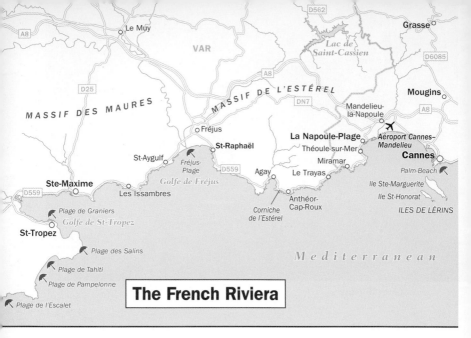

The French Riviera

Where to Stay

Hôtel Byblos ★★★   Opened in 1967 on a hill above the harbor, this hamlet of pastel-hued, Provençal-style houses is opulence personified. Inspired by the legendary Phoenician city of the same name, Byblos is favored by visiting celebrities, rock stars, aristocrats, and the über-rich. Its patios and private spaces are splashed with antiques, rare objects, bubbling fountains, and ancient olive trees. Rooms range in size from medium to mega; some units have such special features as four-posters with furry spreads or sunken whirlpool tubs. The breakfast is to die for. Served around the deep swimming pool, we're talking chocolate fountains, hand-baked pastries, their own organic granola, and unique teas from across the globe.

20 av. Paul Signac. © **04-94-56-68-00.** www.byblos.com. 96 units. 420€–1,180€ double; 840€–2,960€ suite. Parking 35€. Closed Nov to mid-Apr. **Amenities:** 2 restaurants; 1 bar; nightclub; babysitting; concierge; exercise room; massage; outdoor pool; room service; sauna; spa; free Wi-Fi.

Hôtel Les Palmiers ★   In a town packed with pricey accommodation options, this friendly, family-run hotel is a real find. Apart from its fantastic location—directly astride place des Lices in the center of St-Tropez—Les Palmiers boasts compact Provençal-style rooms and a sun-dappled courtyard garden. Part of the hotel dates from the late 18th century and gives the place a cozy, vintage feel.

24–26 bd. Vasserot (place des Lices). © **04-94-97-01-61.** www.hotel-les-palmiers.com. 25 units. 85€–275€ double. **Amenities:** Bar; free Wi-Fi.

Pastis Hôtel-St-Tropez ★★   This portside Provençal house feels more like a sophisticated, eclectic home than a hotel—albeit one decorated with a phenomenal eye for design. British owners John and Pauline Larkin have arranged their private collection of Matisse prints, vintage photographs, 1970s framed album artwork, and Provençal antiques in and around the guest-only lounge and inspired guestrooms surrounding the courtyard swimming pool. Each unique unit is spacious yet intimate and possesses its own balcony or breakfast terrace. Highly recommended.

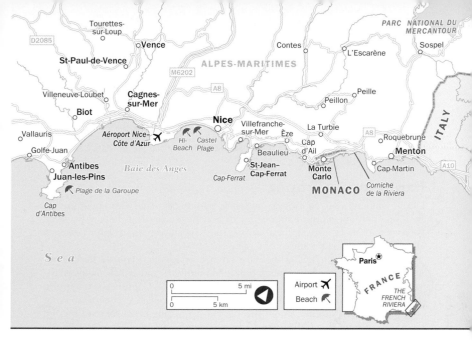

75 av. du Général Leclerc. ✆ **04-98-12-56-50.** www.pastis-st-tropez.com. 10 units. 225€–750€ double. Free parking. Closed Nov to Jan **Amenities:** Bar; outdoor pool; free Wi-Fi.

Where to Eat

St-Tropez's dining scene is both expensive and exclusive, particularly during the summer season. Reserve well in advance or be prepared to dine very early or very late. In addition to the suggestions below, the long-established Moroccan restaurant **Salama,** 1 rue Tisserands (✆ **04-94-97-59-62**), cooks up a fine selection of couscous, pastilla, and tajines; **Chez Madeleine,** 4 place aux Herbes (✆ **04-94-96-59-81**), behind the fish market, serves stellar seafood platters; and **Barbarac,** 2 rue Allard (www.barbarac.fr; ✆ **04-94-97-67-83**), scoops up the finest ice cream in town.

L'Aventure ★ MODERN PROVENÇAL   A backstreet St-Tropez eatery beloved of locals and visitors alike, L'Aventure serves globally inspired market-fresh cuisine: think snails, Provençal lamb, and harbor-fresh fish alternately laced with pesto, honey, and ginger. Blessedly unpretentious, right down to the authentically battered tables on the petite terrace.

4 rue du Portail-Neuf. ✆ **04-94-97-44-01.** Main courses 21€–34€. Tue-Sun 7:30–10pm.

Pizzeria Bruno ★ ITALIAN   Proving that not all good meals in St-Tropez have to break the bank, this casual joint has been turning out thin, crispy, wood-fired pizzas since 1959. Even Bardot was a regular. The menu includes a handful of creative salads, pasta dishes, and grilled meats. Note that the restaurant's copious wood-paneled and overly snug seating isn't the comfiest, but the atmosphere is among the liveliest in town.

2 rue de l'Eglise. ✆ **04-94-97-05-18.** Main courses 12€–20€. Daily noon–2pm and 7–11pm. Closed Oct–Apr.

Rivea ★★ MODERN PROVENÇAL   In 2013, French restaurateur Alain Ducasse's latest offering opened downstairs from the Hotel Byblos. Set across a palm-shaded posing terrace, it has wow-factor in spades. Head chef Vincent Maillard uses ingredients sourced exclusively from the French and Italian Rivieras to create tapas-style sharing dishes, including *vitello tonnato* marinated tuna, sardines *confit*, and perfect mini portions of *spaghetti alle vongole*. Rivea is also the best place to sample Brad and Angelina's exclusive Château Miraval wine, which is produced a few miles inland.

27 avenue Maréchal Foch 56 68 20. ℭ **04-94-56-68-20.** Main courses 25€–44€. Daily 7pm–12.30am. Closed Oct to mid-Apr.

Exploring St-Tropez

During summertime, St-Tropez's pleasure port is trimmed with super-yachts, each one berthing stern-to after a day of hedonistic excess at nearby Plage de Pampelonne. Yacht owners, their lucky guests, spectators, and celebrity-seekers all intermingle along the town's chic quays.

In the Old Town, one of the most interesting streets is **rue de la Miséricorde.** It's lined with stone houses that hold boutiques and evokes medieval St-Tropez better than any other in town. At the corner of rue Gambetta is **Chapelle de la Miséricorde,** with a blue, green, and gold tile roof. Locals come to swim on **Plage de la Ponche,** an old fishing boat launching beach beyond the old town, or at **Plage des Graniers,** a longer beach 5 minutes farther east underneath the Citadelle.

Citadelle de St-Tropez & Maritime Museum ★★ MUSEUM & CASTLE
Towering above town is the Citadelle, a fortified castle complete with drawbridges and stunning views across the Bay of St-Tropez. It's also the best place in town for escaping the crowds, soaking up the sun, and exhausting tiny travelers bored by too many cafes. In 2013, a brand-new Maritime Museum opened within the Citadelle. It charts local historical figures and their travels around the world including Admiral Suffren, who whupped the British several times during the War of American Independence.

Above St-Tropez. ℭ **04-94-54-84-14.** Admission 3€ adults, free for children 8 and under. Apr–Sept daily 10am–6:30pm; Oct–Mar daily 10am–12:30pm and 1:30-5:30pm. Closed Nov.

A beach at St-Tropez

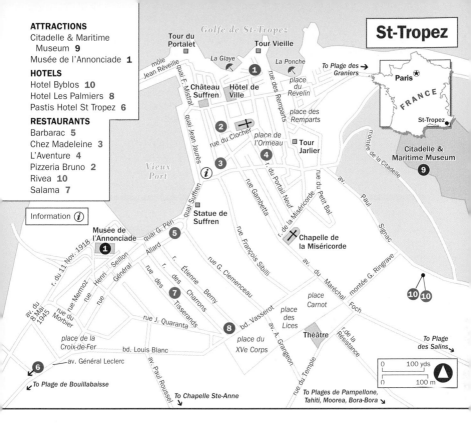

ATTRACTIONS
Citadelle & Maritime
  Museum **9**
Musée de l'Annonciade **1**

HOTELS
Hotel Byblos **10**
Hotel Les Palmiers **8**
Pastis Hotel St Tropez **6**

RESTAURANTS
Barbarac **5**
Chez Madeleine **3**
L'Aventure **4**
Pizzeria Bruno **2**
Rivea **10**
Salama **7**

St-Tropez

Musée de l'Annonciade (Musée St-Tropez) ★★★ MUSEUM   If you leave town without seeing this spellbinding museum, you've missed a colorful part of St-Tropez's past. Set inside a 16th-century chapel just off the harbor, it showcases a collection of superb post-Impressionist paintings (1890–1950). Many of the artists, including St-Tropez's adopted son, Paul Signac, painted the port of St-Tropez, a backdrop that lies right outside the building. The museum includes such masterpieces as Bonnard's "Nu devant la Cheminée" as well as artworks by Matisse, Braque, Dufy, Marquet, and Derain. Temporary shows are held on the ground floor.
Place Grammont. ✆ **04-94-17-84-10.** Admission 6€ adults, 4€ children 11 and under. Wed–Mon 10am–1pm and 2–6pm. Closed Nov.

Outdoor Activities

BEACHES   The hottest Riviera beaches are at St-Tropez. The best for families are closest to the center, including **Plage de la Bouillabaisse** and **Plage des Salins.** More daring and infinitely more famous is the 5km (3-mile) crescent of **Plage de Pampelonne,** about 10km (6¼ miles) from town. Here, around 35 hedonistic beach clubs dot the sand. Overtly decadent is **Club 55** (www.club55. fr; ✆ **04-94-55-55-55**), a former Bardot hangout, while the American-run **Nikki Beach** (www.nikkibeach.com; ✆ **04-94-79-82-04**) is younger and more understated, if painfully chic. Gay-friendly **Aqua Club** (✆ **04-94-79-84-35**) and bare-all **Plage de Tahiti** (www.tahiti-beach.com; ✆ **04-94-97-18-02**) are extremely welcoming.

FRENCH boules

A game of *pétanque*, or French boules, is seriously cool for kids. Hop to **Le Café** (www.lecafe.fr; ✆ **04-94-97-44-69**), one of many alfresco bars in place des Lices, and request a handful of *pétanque* boules to toss around the tree-dappled square. The game was created down the coast and is about as Provençal as it gets. Pick up some tips by watching the locals. Games begin with a toss of the jack, or *bouchon*. Teams then take turns to throw. Whoever is farthest away keeps trying to get closest to the *bouchon*, with any remaining balls tossed in at the end. A point is awarded for each steel ball that's closer to the jack than any balls from the opposing team.

You'll need a car, bike, or scooter to get from town to Plage de Pampelonne. Parking is around 10€ for the day. More than anywhere else on the Riviera, topless bathing is the norm.

BOATING   In St-Tropez port, **Octopussy** (www.octopussy.fr; ✆ **04-94-56-53-10**) rents boats 5 to 16m (16–52 ft.) long. Larger ones come with a captain at the helm. Prices begin at 320€ per day.

DIVING   Multilingual scuba training and equipment rental is available from the **European Diving School** (www.europeandiving.com; ✆ **04-94-79-90-37**), on Plage de Pampelonne. Regular dives, including all equipment, cost 38€.

Shopping

St-Tropez is awash in stylish shops. The merchandise is Mediterranean, breezy, and sophisticated. Dotted throughout the town's *triangle d'or,* the rough triangle formed by place de la Garonne, rue François Sibilli and place des Lices, chic labels include Hermès, Sonia Rykiel, and Louis Vuitton. For the past 5 years, a summer pop-up shop has occupied the old Hotel la Mistralée at 1 av. du Général

St-Tropez Harbor

Leclerc, while nearby, Michelin-starred chef Yannick Alléno dishes up delights at **Dior des Lices,** 13 rue François Sibilli, the fashion house's own summertime pop-up eatery. There are also scores of unique boutiques around the Vieille Ville (Old Town), including **Chichou 88,** 27 rue Georges Clémenceau (📞 04-94-96-48-93), which stocks Indian-inspired housewares and neon handbags; **Truffaux Chapelier,** 44 rue de la Citadelle (📞 04-94-45-33-14), packed with Panama hats; and **K. Jacques,** 25 rue Allard (www.lestropeziennes.com; 📞 04-94-97-41-50), with its iconic *tropéziennes* sandals. Place des Lices hosts an excellent **outdoor market,** Marché Provençal, with food, clothes, and *brocante,* on Tuesday and Saturday mornings.

Nightlife

On a lower level of the Hôtel Byblos' grounds, **Les Caves du Roy,** 20 avenue Paul-Signac (www.lescavesduroy.com; 📞 04-94-56-68-00), is the most self-consciously chic nightclub in St-Tropez. Entrance is free, but drink prices are eye-wateringly high. It's open nightly from Easter to early October from 11:30pm until dawn. Brand-new for 2013 was **White 1921,** place des Lices (www.white1921.com; 📞 04-94-45-50-50), a champagne and cocktail bar set within a jasmine-cloaked courtyard garden. **Le Papagayo,** port de St-Tropez (www.papagayo-st-tropez.com; 📞 04-94-97-95-95), is one of the largest nightclubs in town. The decor is inspired by the psychedelic 1960s. Entrance is around 20€ and includes one drink, although those dining at the attached restaurant can routinely sneak in for free. Adjacent to Le Papagayo is **Le VIP Room,** in the Résidence du Nouveau-Port (www.st-tropez.viproom.fr; 📞 06-38-83-83-83), a younger yet similarly chic version of Les Caves du Roy. Paris Hilton and Snoop Dogg have been known to drop by. Cocktails hover around the 20€ mark.

Le Pigeonnier, 19 rue de la Ponche (📞 06-33-58-92-45), rocks, rolls, and welcomes a mostly gay and lesbian crowd between 20 and 50. **L'Esquinade,** 2 rue de Four (📞 04-94-56-26-31), equally gay-friendly, is the habitual sweaty follow-up club.

Below the Hôtel Sube in the port, **Café de Paris** (www.cafedeparis.fr; 📞 04-94-97-00-56), is one of the most popular—and friendly—hangouts in town. It has 1900s-style globe lights, masses of artificial flowers, and a long zinc bar. **Café Sénéquier,** quai Jean Jaurès (www.senequier.com; 📞 04-94-97-20-20), is historic, venerable, snobbish by day, and off-puttingly stylish by night.

HEAD TO THE hills

Unfurling along the shores between St-Tropez and Cannes is a scarlet stretch of coastline known as the Esterel. It's both regional nature reserve and a cluster of mountains (the Massif de l'Esterel), the latter renowned for their ethereal crimson hue. The area is criss-crossed with hiking trails and splashed by tiny turquoise beaches, perfect for private picnics. Best of all, the Esterel receives just a fraction of the tourists that congregate along the Riviera's more popular seaside resorts. Regular trains run from Cannes to Théoule-sur-Mer, a village in the centre of the park. One-way tickets cost 2.50€, and journey time is around 10 minutes. The **Théoule-sur-Mer Tourist Office,** 2 bd. de la Corniche d'Or (www.theoule-sur-mer.org; 📞 04-93-49-28-28) distributes walking and cycling maps of the region.

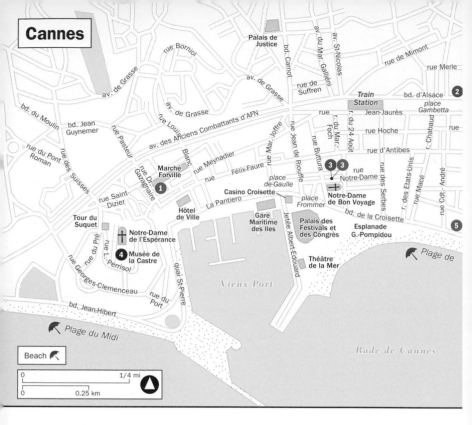

CANNES ★★★

905km (561 miles) S of Paris; 163km (101 miles) E of Marseille; 26km (16 miles) SW of Nice

When Coco Chanel came here and got a suntan, returning to Paris bronzed, she shocked the milk-white society ladies—who quickly began to copy her. Today the bronzed bodies, clad in nearly nonexistent swimsuits, line the beaches of this chic resort and continue the late fashion designer's example. A block back from the famed promenade de la Croisette are the boutiques, bars, and bistros that make Cannes the Riviera's capital of cool.

Essentials

ARRIVING By **train,** Cannes is 10 minutes from Antibes, 30 minutes from Nice, and 45 minutes from Monaco. The TGV from Paris reaches Cannes in an incredibly scenic 5 hours. The one-way fare from Paris is 45€ to 129€, although advance purchase bargains can be had for as low as 26€. For rail information and schedules, visit www.voyages-sncf.com or call ✆ **36-35. Lignes d'Azur** (www.lignesdazur.com; ✆ **08-10-06-10-06**) provides bus service from Cannes' Gare Routière (place Bernard Cornut Gentille) to Antibes every 20 minutes during the day (trip time: 25 min.). The one-way fare is 1.50€.

The **Nice International Airport** (www.nice.aeroport.fr; ✆ **08-20-42-33-33**) is a 30-minute drive east. **Bus no. 210** picks up passengers at the airport

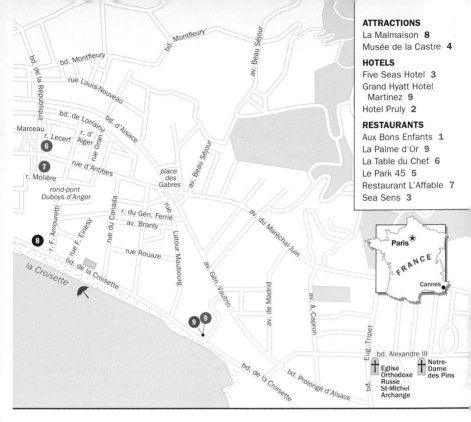

ATTRACTIONS
La Malmaison **8**
Musée de la Castre **4**

HOTELS
Five Seas Hotel **3**
Grand Hyatt Hotel
   Martinez **9**
Hotel Pruly **2**

RESTAURANTS
Aux Bons Enfants **1**
La Palme d'Or **9**
La Table du Chef **6**
Le Park 45 **5**
Restaurant L'Affable **7**
Sea Sens **3**

every 30 minutes during the day (hourly at other times) and drop them at Cannes' Gare Routière. The one-way fare is 20€, round-trip is 30€.

By **car** from Marseille, take A51 north to Aix-en-Provence, continuing along A8 east to Cannes. From Nice, follow A8 or the coastal D6007 southwest to Cannes.

VISITOR INFORMATION   The **Office de Tourisme** is at 1 bd. de la Croisette (www.cannes-destination.fr; ✆ **04-92-99-84-22**).

SPECIAL EVENTS   Cannes is at its most frenzied in mid-May during the **International Film Festival** (www.festival-cannes.com) at the Palais des Festivals, on promenade de la Croisette. It attracts not only film stars (you can palm the cement molds of their handprints outside the Palais des Festivals), but also seemingly every photographer in the world. You have a better chance of being named prime minister of France than you do attending one of the major screenings, although if you're lucky, you may be able to swing tickets to screenings of one of the lesser films. (Hotel rooms and tables at restaurants are equally scarce during the festival.) But the people-watching is absolutely fabulous!

Getting Around

ON FOOT   Cannes' small town center is a labyrinth of one-ways and serious traffic—which makes it best explored on foot.

Promenade de la Croisette and beach, Cannes

BY BICYCLE & MOTOR SCOOTER   Despite the summertime commotion, the flat landscapes between Cannes and satellite resorts such as La Napoule and Juan-les-Pins are well suited for bikes and motor scooters. At **Daniel Location,** 7 rue de Suffren (www.daniel-location-2roues.com; ☎ **04-93-99-90-30**), *vélos tout terrain,* or VTT (mountain bikes) cost 16€ a day. Motorized bikes and scooters cost from 30€ per day. For larger motorbikes, you must present a valid driver's license. Another bike shop is **Mistral Location,** 4 rue Georges Clémenceau (www.mistral-location.com; ☎ **04-93-39-33-60**), which also charges 16€ per day for bike rentals.

BY CAR   The Cannes Tourist Office website (see above) offers a downloadable document (under "Cannes Practical," then "Useful Information") listing all of the town's **public parking lots** and their hourly fees.

BY TAXI   Allô Taxi Cannes (www.allo-taxis-cannes.com; ☎ 08-90-71-22-27).

BY PUBLIC TRANSPORT   Bus Azur (www.busazur.info; ☎ **08-25-82-55-99**) operates all public transport in and around Cannes. There's little need for public transport in the city center—although the open-top nr. 8, which runs along the seafront from the port in the west to the Palm Beach peninsula in the east, makes for a fun and scenic ride. Tickets cost 1.50€ and can be purchased directly aboard any bus.

[FastFACTS] CANNES

ATMs/Banks   Banks are dotted throughout the city, including more than a dozen along the central rue d'Antibes.

Dentists   For emergency dental services, contact **SOS Dentaire** (☎ **04-93-68-28-00**).

Doctors & Hospitals   **Hopital de Cannes,** 15 av. Broussailles (www.ch-cannes.fr; ☎ **04-93-69-70-00**).

Internet Access   Cannes is in the process of blanketing the city with free Wi-Fi. The first area with coverage is the Jardins de l'Hotel de Ville, just behind the port; the network is "Cannes sans fil."

Mail & Postage   **La Poste,** 22 rue Bivouac Napoléon (✆ **36-31**).

Pharmacies   **Pharmacie du Casino,** 9 bis square Mérimée (✆ **04-93-39-25-48**).

Where to Stay

Five Seas Hôtel ★★   The newest, coolest hotel in Cannes harks back to a Gatsby era of Art Deco furnishings and no-limits lavishness. The style is Louis Vuitton meets vintage ocean liner. The furniture design is based on classic traveling cases, albeit with Apple computers and Nespresso machines thrown into the mix. Popular with both guests and non-residents is the hotel's **Cinq Mondes & Carita Spa.** The top-floor terrace features a small infinity pool, a cocktail bar, and linen-shaded sun loungers. It's also the location of the acclaimed **Sea Sens** modern Mediterranean restaurant (fixed-price dinner 39€–95€ Tues–Sat) under the direction of head chef Arnaud Tabarec. And boy, what a view it has. Desserts come courtesy of 29-year-old World Pastry Champion Jérôme de Oliveira, who also maintains **Intuitions by J** (see p. 426), a tea and pastry shop on the ground floor.

1 rue Notre Dame. ✆ **04-63-36-05-05.** www.five-seas-hotel-cannes.com. 45 units. 295€–805€ double; from 595€ suite. **Amenities:** Restaurant; bar; concierge; outdoor pool; room service; spa; free Wi-Fi.

Grand Hyatt Hotel Martinez ★★★   The Martinez has been the socialite hub of the South of France for a century. The great and good have marched through its revolving doors including recent guests Eva Longoria, Nicole Kidman, and Steven Spielberg. This Art Deco masterpiece is more than just an ultra-luxe hotel. Non-guests can mingle with celebrities in the **l'Amiral** cocktail bar, bathe next to A-listers in the **ZPlage** beach club, or dine alongside minor royalty in one of the finest restaurants in the South of France, **La Palme d'Or** (p. 422). Hotel management was taken over by Hyatt in 2013, which ushered in a sleek refurbishment and a popular bicycle-sharing scheme—and what deliciously cool bikes they are.

73 bd. de la Croisette. ✆ **04-93-90-12-34.** http://cannesmartinez.grand.hyatt.com. 409 units. 750€–990€ double; from 3,300€ suite. Parking 40€. **Amenities:** 3 summer restaurants, 2 winter restaurants; bar; babysitting; private beach; free bikes; children's center; concierge; exercise room; outdoor pool; room service; sauna; spa; free Wi-Fi.

Hôtel Pruly ★★   Relatively new on the local scene, this delightful hotel spills from a renovated century-old townhouse. Charming rooms are decorated in bright colors and Provençal textiles; some boast traditional terra-cotta *tomette* floors or private balconies. An afternoon nap on a sun lounger in the hotel's palm-splashed private garden is a welcome respite from Cannes' summertime crowds. It's located just behind the train station.

32 bd. d'Alsace. ✆ **04-93-38-41-28.** www.hotel-pruly.com. 12 units. 65€–270€ double; 110€–320€ triple. **Amenities:** Garden; free Wi-Fi.

Where to Eat

Cannes' dining scene is all-encompassing: expect to stumble across everything from Michelin-starred gastronomy to traditional Provençal peasant cuisine. Restaurants are scattered across the city center, with a particularly heavy concentration around Le Suquet, Cannes' Old Town.

EXPENSIVE

La Palme d'Or ★★★ MODERN FRENCH   Double-Michelin-starred chef Christian Sinicropi has presided over this theater of fine dining for more than a decade. His level of innovation knows no bounds. Think algae lollipops, flavored smoke, and herb perfume. Guests are greeted at the table by the man himself, then taken on an intensely seasonal 5- to 10-course gastronomic journey in a dining room so rococo that even Liberace would feel at home. Sinicropi also serves the Cannes Film Festival jury a special set dinner each spring. Spellbinding dishes created for recent festival presidents, like Tim Burton and Woody Allen, can be sampled from the menu. Unforgettable.

In the Grand Hyatt Hotel Martinez, 73 bd. de la Croisette. ✆ **04-92-98-74-14.** http://cannes martinez.grand.hyatt.com. Jacket and tie recommended. Main courses 68€–84€; fixed-price menu 90€–205€. Wed–Sat 12:30–2pm and 8–10pm. Closed Jan–Feb.

Le Park 45 ★★★ MEDITERRANEAN   One of the most inventive—and least expensive—Michelin-starred restaurants on the Riviera is run by one of the coast's youngest chefs, baby-faced Sébastien Broda. Nicknamed the "Petit Prince de la Croisette," Broda scooped up his first Michelin star before the age of 30, after a career at La Palme d'Or in Cannes and L'Amandier in Mougins, two dens of fine Riviera dining. Locally grown vegetables and Atlantic seafood sparkle with additions of yuzu condiment, ponzu cream, Parmesan bouillon, and zingy Granny Smith apple *jus*. Surrounding Le Park 45 is the modernist splendor of **Le Grand Hotel** (www.grand-hotel-cannes.com; ✆ **04-93-38-15-15**). Originally the first hotel on the Croisette, this current 1960s incarnation boasts the best sea views in Cannes and perfectly preserved period features—from funky plastic telephones to Art Deco lampshades. Prices run 140€ to 500€ for a double and from 450€ for a suite, including free Wi-Fi.

In Le Grand Hotel, 45 bd. de la Croisette. ✆ **04-93-38-15-15.** www.grand-hotel-cannes.com. Main courses 32€–44€; fixed-price lunch 55€, dinner 55€–120€. Daily noon–2pm and 7:30–10pm.

MODERATE

Restaurant L'Affable ★★ MEDITERRANEAN   Chef Jean-Paul Battaglia's menu may be petite. But his creations are as innovative and as contemporary as can be. The frequently changing selection of dishes may include pumpkin soup with foie gras foam, ceviche "Grenoble-style" drizzled with capers and lime, or tartare of scallops and oysters served with lemon Chantilly cream. Be sure to save space for Battaglia's signature *soufflé au Grand-Marnier*. Note the ambiance is decidedly formal and the service is superb—making L'Affable a good choice for a special occasion.

5 rue Lafontaine. ✆ **04-93-68-02-09.** www.restaurant-laffable.fr. Main courses 36€–40€; fixed-price lunch 24€–28€; fixed-price dinner 43€. Mon–Fri 12:30–2pm, Mon–Sat 7–10pm. Closed Aug.

La Table du Chef ★ FRENCH/PROVENÇAL   Just off Cannes' premier shopping street, rue d'Antibes, this unassuming little bistro serves up some of the city's tastiest cuisine. Chef Bruno Gensdarme (who spent almost 20 years working alongside superchef Guy Savoy in Paris) puts his own spin on traditional French dishes, such as Muscadet-infused rabbit terrine, or eggplant *millefeuilles* drizzled in goat's cheese cream and olives. Picky eaters beware: Menus are either fixed or offer very limited choices.

5 rue Jean Daumas. ✆ **04-93-68-27-40.** Fixed-price menu 24€–41€. Tues–Sat noon–2pm; Thurs–Sat 7–10pm.

INEXPENSIVE

Aux Bons Enfants ★ PROVENÇAL   You could easily miss this old-fashioned eatery, tucked among a crowd of mediocre tourist-targeted restaurants. But what an oversight that would be. Family-run for three generations, the authentic Aux Bons Enfants today is headed up by Chef Luc Giorsetti. Dishes are traditional: *daube de canard,* slow-cooked *duck à la niçoise;* zucchini flower fritters; or house-cured salmon gravlax. Seasonal ingredients are sourced each morning from Marché Forville. **Note:** The restaurant has no telephone and does not accept reservations or credit cards.

80 rue Meynadier. www.aux-bons-enfants.com. No telephone; no reservations. Main courses 16€–23€; fixed-price menus 27€–34€. No credit cards. Tues–Sat noon–2pm and 7–10pm.

Exploring Cannes

Far and away, Cannes' most famous street is the **promenade de la Croisette**— or simply La Croisette—which curves along the coast. It's lined by grand hotels (some dating from the 19th c.), boutiques, and exclusive beach clubs. It's also home to temporary exhibition space **La Malmaison,** 47 La Croisette (© **04-97-06-44-90**), which holds three major modern art shows each year. It's open daily July to August 11am to 8pm (Friday until 9pm), September 10am to 7pm, and October to April Tuesday to Sunday 10am to 1pm and 2 to 6pm. Admission is 3.50€ for adults, 2.50€ for ages 18 to 25, and free for children under 17. Above the harbor, the Old Town of Cannes sits on Suquet Hill, where visitors can climb the 14th-century **Tour de Suquet.**

Musée Bonnard ★★ ART MUSEUM   The only museum in the world dedicated to the Impressionist painter Pierre Bonnard is located 3km (1¾ miles) north of Cannes, in the suburb of Le Cannet. Portraits, sculptures, and sketches on display in this petite museum were created primarily between 1922 and 1947, the period during which the artist was a local resident. The museum's audio guide comes courtesy of an iPod Touch.

La Croisette

16 bd. Sadi Carnot, Le Cannet. ℂ **04-93-94-06-06.** www.museebonnard.fr. Admission 5€–7€ adults, 3.50€–5€ ages 12–18, free for children 11 and under. June–Sept Tues–Sun 10am–8pm (Thurs until 9pm); Oct–May Tues–Sun 10am–6pm (Thurs until 8pm). Closed 3 weeks in Jan. Bus no. 1 and 4 from Cannes city center.

Musée de la Castre ★ MUSEUM   Perched above Cannes' Old Town within the medieval Château de la Castre, this museum focuses primarily on ethnographic finds from around the world. Spears from the South Seas and Tibetan masks are interspersed with Sumerian cuneiform tablets and 19th-century paintings of the Riviera. Many visitors, however, will be most impressed by the astounding views from the museum's viewing tower—accessed via 109 steep steps. The shady Mediterranean gardens, just outside the museum's entrance, are a welcome respite for tired sightseers.

Le Suquet. ℂ **04-93-38-55-26.** Admission 6€ adults, 3€ ages 18–25, free for children under 17. July–Aug daily 10am–7pm (Wed until 9pm); Sept and Apr–June Tues–Sun 10am–1pm and 2–6pm (June and Sept Wed until 9pm); Oct–Mar Tues–Sun 10am–1pm and 2–5pm.

Organized Tours

One of the best ways to get your bearings in Cannes is to climb aboard the **Petit Train touristique de Cannes** (www.cannes-petit-train.com; ℂ **06-22-61-25-76**). The vehicles operate every day from 9 or 10am to between 7 and 11pm, depending on the season. Three itineraries are offered: Modern Cannes, with a ride along La Croisette and its side streets (35 min.); Historical Cannes, which weaves through the narrow streets of Le Suquet (35 min.); or the Big Tour, a combination of the two (1 hr.). All trains depart from outside the Palais des Festivals every 30 to 60 minutes. Shorter tours cost 7€ for adults and 3€ for children aged 3 to 10; the Big Tour costs 10€ for adults and 5€ for children aged 3 to 10.

Outdoor Activities

BEACHES   Beachgoing in Cannes has more to do with exhibitionism than actual swimming. **Plage de la Croisette** extends between the Vieux Port and the Port Canto. The beaches along this billion-dollar stretch of sand are *payante,* meaning entrance costs between 15€ to 30€. You don't need to be a guest of the Martinez, say, to use the beaches associated with a high-end hotel (see "Where to Stay," above), and Cannes has heaps of buzzing beach clubs dotted around, including sassy **3.14 Beach** (www.314cannes.com; ℂ **04-93-94-25-43**). Why should you pay an entry fee at all? Well, the fee includes a full day's use of a mattress, a chaise lounge (the seafront is more pebbly than sandy), and a parasol, as well as easy access to freshwater showers. There are also outdoor restaurants and bars (some with organic menus, others with gourmet burgers and sushi) where no one minds if you dine in your swimsuit. Every beach allows topless bathing. Looking for a free public beach without chaises or parasols? Head for **Plage du Midi,** just west of the Vieux Port, or **Plage Gazagnaire,** just east of the Port Canto. Here you'll find families with children and lots of RV-type vehicles parked nearby.

BOATING   Several companies around Cannes's Vieux Port rent boats of any size, with or without a crew, for a day, a week, or even longer. An outfit known for short-term rentals of small motorcraft is **Boat Evasion,** 110 boulevard du Midi (www.boatevasion.com; ℂ **06-26-59-10-77**). For kayak rental and guided tours of the coastline by canoe, try **SeaFirst,** place Franklin Roosevelt (www.seafirst.fr).

GOLF   Cannes is ringed by 10 golf courses, almost all within a 20-minute drive of the city. The **Old Course,** 265 route de Golf, Mandelieu (www.golfoldcourse.com;

Sailboats at harbor, Cannes

C 04-92-97-32-00), is a leafy gem dating from 1891. Greens fees start at 90€, with big reductions for lunch deals and afternoon tee-offs. The prestigious **Royal Mougins Golf Club,** 424 av. du Roi, Mougins (www.royalmougins.fr; *C* 04-92-92-49-69), also boasts a gourmet restaurant and spa. Greens fees start at 180€, including cart hire; it's half-price for 9 holes.

PADDLEBOARDING Cannes is nothing if not cutting edge. And like the rest of the world, this city has fallen in love with stand-up paddleboarding (SUP). Rent your own from **Cannes Standup Paddle Location,** Plage du Mouré Rouge, bd. Gazagnaire, Palm Beach (www.cannesstanduppaddle.fr; *C* 06-82-17-08-77). Fees start at 12€ per hour.

TENNIS Some resorts have their own courts. The city of Cannes also maintains 16 synthetic courts and 6 clay-topped ones at the **Garden Tennis Club,** 99 av. Maurice Chevalier (*C* 04-93-47-29-33). You'll pay from 13€ to 17€ per hour, plus 3.70€ per hour for floodlights.

Shopping

Cannes achieves a blend of resort-style leisure, glamour, and media glitz more successfully than many of its neighbors. You'll see every big-name designer you can think of, plus a legion of one-off designer boutiques and shoe stores. There are also real-people shops; resale shops for star-studded castoffs; flea markets for funky junk; and a fruit, flower, and vegetable market.

BOOKS **Ciné-Folie,** 14 rue des Frères-Pradignac (*C* 04-93-39-22-99), is devoted entirely to film. Called "La Boutique du Cinema," it is the finest film bookstore in the south of France; vintage film stills and movie posters are also for sale. **Cannes English Bookshop,** 11 rue Bivouac Napoleon (www.cannes englishbookshop.com; *C* 04-93-99-40-08), stocks locally based classics from Peter Mayle and Carol Drinkwater, plus bestselling novels, travel guides, and maps.

DESIGNER SHOPS Most of the big names in fashion line promenade de la Croisette, the main drag running along the sea. Among the most prestigious are **Dior,** 38 La Croisette (✆ 04-92-98-98-00), and **Hermès,** 17 La Croisette (✆ 04-93-39-08-90). The stores stretch from the Hôtel Carlton almost to the Palais des Festivals, with the top names closest to the **Gray-d'Albion,** 38 rue des Serbes (www.lucienbarriere.com; ✆ 04-92-99-79-79), both a mall and a hotel (how convenient). Near the train station, department store **Galeries Lafayette** has all the big-name labels crammed into one smallish space at 6 rue du Maréchal-Foch (www.galerieslafayette.com, ✆ 04-97-06-25-00).

Young hipsters should try **Bathroom Graffiti,** 52 rue d'Antibes (✆ 04-93-39-02-32), for sexy luggage, bikinis, and designer houseware. The rue d'Antibes is also brilliant for big-brand bargains (Zara and MaxMara), as well as one-off boutiques.

FOOD The Marché Forville (see below) and the surrounding streets are unsurprisingly the best places to search for picnic supplies. For bottles of Côtes de Provence, try **Cave du Marché,** 5 place Marché Forville (✆ 04-93-99-60-98). It also serves up glasses of local rosé and olive crostini on tables outside. **La Compagnie des Saumons,** 12 place Marché Forville (✆ 04-93-68-33-20), brims with caviar, bottles of fish soup, and slabs of smoked salmon. Local cheese shop **Le Fromage Gourmet,** 8 rue des Halles (✆ 04-93-99-96-41), is a favorite of celebrated chef Alain Ducasse. Closer to the seafront, World Pastry Champion Jérôme Oliveira creates fairy-tale desserts in bite sizes—from flower-topped tarts to a pastel rainbow of *macarons*—at **Intuitions by J,** 22 rue Bivouac Napoléon (www.patisserie-intuitions.com; ✆ 04-63-36-05-07).

MARKETS The **Marché Forville,** in place Marché Forville just north of the Vieux Port, is a covered stucco structure with a few arches but no walls. From Tuesday to Sunday, 7am to 1pm, it's the fruit, vegetable, and flower market that supplies the dozens of restaurants in the area. Monday (8am–6pm) is *brocante* day, when the market fills with dealers selling everything from Grandmère's dishes and bone-handled carving knives to castaways from estate sales. Tuesdays to Sundays, 8am to 12:30pm, the small **Marché aux Fleurs** (Flower Market) takes place outdoors along the edges of the allée de la Liberté, across from the Palais des Festivals.

Nightlife

BARS & CLUBS A strip of sundowner bars stretches along rue Félix Faure. Most are chic, some have happy-hour cocktails, and several have DJs after dinner. Tapas bar **Le Bivi,** 7 rue des Gabres (www.lebivi-cannes.com; ✆ 04-93-39-97-90), is a convivial spot to sample more unusual South of France wines. For an aperitif with history, the **Bar l'Amiral,** in the Hôtel Martinez, 73 La Croisette (✆ 04-93-90-12-34), is where deals have always gone down during the film festival. The bar comes complete with the nameplates of stars that once propped it up, Humphrey Bogart among them. Alternatively, head to **Le 360,** Radisson Blu 1835 Hotel & Thalasso, 2 bd. Jean Hibert (www.radissonblu.com; ✆ 04-92-99-73-20), a panoramic rooftop terrace overlooking the port that's idyllic for a cocktail as the sun sets. Continue the party at **B.Pub,** 22 rue Macé (✆ 04-93-38-17-30), with live pop, international DJs, and the resident bartenders' favorite trick, a flaming ring of alcohol-fuelled fire round the bar. At **Le Bâoli,** Port Pierre Canto, La Croisette (www.lebaoli.com; ✆ 04-93-43-03-43), Europe's partying elite, from Prince Albert of Monaco to Jude Law, dance until dawn. Dress to the nines to slip past the über-tight security and into this Asian-inspired wonderland.

CASINOS   Cannes is invariably associated with easygoing permissiveness, film-making glitterati, and gambling. If the latter is your thing, Cannes has world-class casinos loaded with high rollers, voyeurs, and everyone in between. The better established is the **Casino Croisette,** in the Palais des Festivals, 1 espace Lucien Barrière (www.lucienbarriere.com; © **04-92-98-78-00**). A well-respected fixture in town since the 1950s, a collection of noisy slot machines it is most certainly not. Its main competitor is the newer **Palm Beach Casino,** place F-D-Roosevelt, Pointe Croisette (www.casinolepalmbeach.com; © **04-97-06-36-90**), on the southeast edge of La Croisette. It attracts a younger crowd with a summer-only beachside poker room, a beach club with pool, a restaurant, and a disco that runs until dawn. Both casinos maintain slots that operate daily from lunchtime to around 4am. Smarter dress is expected for the *salles des grands jeux* (blackjack, roulette, craps, poker, and chemin de fer), which open nightly 8pm to 4am. The casino also pulls in daytime visitors with tasty inexpensive lunches and Sunday brunches, both of which come with free gaming chips.

DAY TRIPS FROM CANNES
Iles de Lérins ★★
Short boat ride from Cannes

Floating in the Mediterranean just south of Cannes' southern horizon, the Lérins Islands are an idyllic place to escape the Riviera's summertime commotion. Head for Cannes port's western quai Laubeuf, where ferryboats operated by **Trans-Côte d'Azur** (www.trans-cote-azur.com; © **04-92-98-71-30**) offer access to Ile Ste-Marguerite. To visit Ile St-Honorat, head for the same quay, to the **Transports Planaria** (www.cannes-ilesdelerins.com; © **04-92-98-71-38**) ferryboats. Both companies offer frequent service to the islands at intervals of between 30 and 90 minutes depending on the season, and operate daily and year-round. Round-trip transport to Ile Ste-Marguerite costs 13€ per adult and 8€ for children 5 to 10; round-trip transport to Ile St-Honorat costs 15.50€ per adult and 7.50€ for children 5 to 10 (although discount tickets of 13€ per adult and 6.50€ for children 5 to 10 are often available if you book in advance online). Travel to both islands is free for children 4 and under. As dining options on the islands are limited, pack up a picnic lunch from Cannes' Marché Forville before you set off.

EXPLORING ILE STE-MARGUERITE
Ile Ste-Marguerite is one big botanical garden—cars, cigarettes, and all other pollutants are banned—ringed by crystal-clear sea. From the dock, you can stroll along the island to Fort Royal, built by Spanish troops in 1637 and used as a military barracks and parade ground until World War II. The infamous "Man in the Iron Mask" was allegedly imprisoned here, and you can follow the legend back to his horribly spooky cell.

   Musée de la Mer, Fort Royal (© **04-93-38-55-26**), traces the history of the island, displaying artifacts of Ligurian, Roman, and Arab civilizations, plus the remains discovered by excavations, including paintings, mosaics, and ancient pottery. The museum is open June to September daily from 10am to 5:45pm, and Tuesday to Sunday October to May 10:30am to 1:15pm and 2:15 to 4:45pm (closing at 5:45pm Apr–May). Admission is 6€ for adults, 3€ for visitors 25 and under, and free for children 17 and under.

EXPLORING ILE ST-HONORAT ★★

Only 1.6km (1 mile) long, the Ile St-Honorat is much quieter than neighboring Ste-Marguerite. But in historical terms, it's much richer than its island sibling and is the site of a monastery whose origins date from the 5th century. The **Abbaye de St-Honorat ★** (www.abbayedelerins.com; ✆ **04-92-99-54-00**) is a combination of medieval ruins and early-20th-century ecclesiastical buildings, and is home to a community of about 25 Cistercian monks. Most visitors content themselves with a wander through the pine forests on the island's western side, a clamber around the ruined monastery on the island's southern edge, and a bathe on its seaweed-strewn beaches.

The monks also transform the island's herbs, vines, and honey into a wealth of organic products, including lavender oil and wine. All can be purchased in the monastery shop. There is also an excellent lunch-only seafood restaurant, **La Tonnelle** (www.tonnelle-abbayedelerins.com; ✆ **04-92-99-54-08**). It's closed from November to mid-December. And no, it's not the monks who cook, but they can organize a wine-tasting or small island tour if arranged in advance.

Grasse ★

18km (11 miles) N of Cannes

Grasse, a 20-minute drive from Cannes, has been renowned as the capital of the world's perfume industry since the Renaissance. It was once a famous resort, attracting such royals as Queen Victoria and Princess Pauline Borghese, Napoleon's lascivious sister.

Today some three-quarters of the world's essences are produced here from thousands of tons of petals, including violets, daffodils, wild lavender, and jasmine. The quaint medieval town, which formed the backdrop for the 2006 movie "Perfume," has several free perfume museums where visitors can enroll in workshops to create their own scent.

ESSENTIALS

Trains run to Grasse from Cannes, depositing passengers a 10-minute walk south of town. From here, a walking trail or shuttle bus leads visitors into the center. One-way train tickets cost 4.30€ from Cannes, and journey time is around 30 minutes. For further train information, visit www.voyages-sncf.com or call ✆ **36-35. Buses** pull into town every 10 to 60 minutes daily from Cannes (trip time: 50 min.), arriving at the Gare Routière, place de la Buanderie (✆ **04-93-36-37-37**), a 5-minute walk north of the town center. The one-way fare is 1.50€. Visitors arriving by **car** may follow RN85 from Cannes. The **Office de Tourisme** is at place du cours Honoré Cresp (www.grasse.fr; ✆ **04-93-36-66-66**).

EXPLORING GRASSE

Musée International de la Parfumerie ★ MUSEUM   This comprehensive museum chronicles both Grasse's fragrant history, as well as worldwide perfume development over the past 4,000 years. Wander among raw materials, ancient flasks (including Marie Antoinette's 18th-c. toiletry set) and scented soaps, all set against a backdrop of temporary exhibitions and contemporary artworks. Kids age 7 and older have their own dedicated pathway, lined with interactive exhibits to touch—and, of course, smell.

2 bd. du Jeu-de-Ballon. ✆ **04-97-05-58-00.** www.museesdegrasse.com. Admission (depending on exhibition) 4€–6€ adults, 2€–3€ students, free for children under 18. Apr–Sept daily 10am–7pm; Oct–Mar Wed–Mon 10:30am–5:30pm. Closed Nov.

WHERE TO EAT & SHOP

For light lunch or an afternoon snack, pop into **Le Péché Gourmand,** 8 rue de l'Oratoire (✆ **06-62-69-61-57**), a combination mini-restaurant, tearoom, and ice cream parlor. Try the goat's cheese and candied tomato crumble, or order up a bowl of the decadent chocolate sorbet.

Both **Parfumerie Molinard,** 60 bd. Victor Hugo (www.molinard.com; ✆ **04-93-36-01-62**), and **Parfumerie Fragonard,** 20 bd. Fragonard (www.fragonard.com; ✆ **04-93-36-44-65**), offer factory tours, where you'll get a first-hand peek into scent extraction and perfume and essential oil production. You can also purchase their products on-site.

Vallauris ★

7km (4½ miles) NE of Cannes

Once simply a stopover along the Riviera, Vallauris's ceramics industry was in terminal decline until it was "discovered" by Picasso just after World War II. The artist's legacy lives on both in snapshots of the master in local galleries and in his awesome "La Paix et La Guerre" fresco.

ESSENTIALS

Envibus **bus** (www.envibus.fr; ✆ **04-89-87-72-00**) connects Cannes' train station with Vallauris every 30 minutes (journey time 20 min.). Tickets cost 1€ each way. There's an **Office de Tourisme** (www.vallauris-golfe-juan.fr) on square du 8 Mai 1945 (✆ **04-93-63-82-58**).

EXPLORING VALLAURIS

In Vallauris, Picasso's **"l'Homme au Mouton"** ("Man and Sheep") is the outdoor statue at place Paul Isnard in front of which Prince Aly Kahn and screen goddess Rita Hayworth were married. The local council had intended to enclose this statue in a museum, but Picasso insisted that it remain on the square, "where the children could climb over it and dogs piss against it."

Musée Magnelli, Musée de la Céramique & Musée National Picasso La Guerre et La Paix ★★ ART MUSEUM Three museums in one, this petite cultural center developed from a 12th-century chapel where Picasso painted "La Paix" ("Peace") and "La Guerre" ("War") in 1952. Visitors can physically immerse themselves in this tribute to pacifism. Images of love and peace adorn one wall; scenes of violence and conflict the other. Also on site is a permanent exposition of works by Florentine-born abstract artist Alberto Magnelli, as well as a floor dedicated to traditional and innovative ceramics from potters throughout the region.

Place de la Libération. ✆ **04-93-64-71-83.** www.musees-nationaux-alpesmaritimes.fr. Admission 4€ adults, 2€ for visitors 25 and under, free for children 15 and under. July–Aug daily 10am–7pm; June 16–30 and Sept 1–15 Wed–Mon 10am–12:15pm and 2–6pm; Sept 16–June 15 Wed–Mon 10am–12:15pm and 2–5pm.

WHERE TO EAT & SHOP

Join the locals for lunch at **Le Cafe du Coin,** 16 place Jules Lisnard (www.cafe-du-coin.com; ✆ **04-92-90-27-79**), where a small selection of market-fresh specials are scribbled on the chalkboard daily. For souvenirs, head around the corner to avenue Georges-Clemenceau, lined with small shops selling brightly glazed, locally made ceramics. In early 2014, Vallauris's Tourist Office began offering free tours of the newly renovated **Galerie Madoura,** rue Georges et Suzanne

Ramié, Picasso's former ceramics studio. Tours take place Monday to Friday at 10:30am in French only; be sure to book in advance.

Mougins ★★

7km (4½ miles) N of Cannes

A fortified hill town, Mougins preserves the quiet life in a postcard-perfect manner. The town's artsy legacy—Picasso, Jean Cocteau, Paul Eluard, Fernand Léger, Isadora Duncan, and Christian Dior were all previous residents—has blessed the town with must-see galleries. Real estate prices are among the highest on the Riviera, and the wealthy residents support a dining scene that also punches well above its weight. The **Etoile des Mougins food festival** (www.lesetoilesdemougins.com), held each September, is a highbrow gastronomic love-in featuring Michelin-starred chefs from across the globe.

ESSENTIALS

From Cannes, the best way to get to Mougins is to **drive** north of the city along D6285. By bus, **Société Tam** (www.cg06.fr; ✆ 08-00-06-01-06) runs bus no. 600 from Cannes to Val-de-Mougins, a 10-minute walk from the center of Mougins. One-way fares cost 1.50€. The **Office de Tourisme** is at 18 bd. Courteline (www.mougins.fr; ✆ 04-93-75-87-67).

WHERE TO EAT

Le Moulin de Mougins, Notre Dame de Vie (www.moulindemougins.com; ✆ 04-93-75-78-24; menus 60€–120€), is a place of foodie pilgrimage. Inside an enchanting 16th-century mill, talented chef Erwan Louaisil follows in the footsteps of founder Roger Vergé and previous head chef Alain Llorca with modern twists on culinary traditions from both Provence and his native Brittany. The restaurant is open from Wednesday to Sunday for lunch and dinner. It also rents six double rooms (200€–250€) and three suites (250€–300€) on site.

Etoile des Mougins food festival

RIDING THE Riviera Rails

Summer visitors to the French Riviera have their transport taken care of. From June 1 until September 30, consider a **ZOU! Pass** (www.ter-sncf.com, 15€ at any SNCF station). This allows unlimited hop-on hop-off train travel from Grasse to Italy (taking in Cannes, Monaco, and Nice among other stations en-route) from 7am until midnight. Families may also purchase the **Isabelle Famille Pass.** Valid for two adults travelling with two children aged 16 and under, it costs just 35€ per day.

On a budget? Try the traditional bistro **Le Resto des Arts,** 2 rue Maréchal Foch (✆ **04-93-75-60-03**), which dishes up hearty specials like basil-spiked *soupe au pistou,* red mullet doused in tomato sauce, or seared steak with morel mushrooms.

EXPLORING MOUGINS

Picasso discovered Mougins' tranquil maze of flower-filled lanes in the company of his muse, Dora Marr, and photographer Man Ray, in 1935. The Vieux Village's pedestrianized cobblestone streets—each corner prettier than the last—have changed little over the decades since. The setting is so romantic that, according to locals, French President François Hollande wined and dined his former first lady, Valérie Trierweiler, in one of the restaurants listed below. He then proceeded to indulge his mistress, Julie Gayet, in the same establishment. Classy guy.

Chapelle Notre-Dame de Vie ★ RELIGIOUS SITE   The most romantic site in Mougins—unless you are the President of France—is surely this medieval chapel. It lies 1.5km (1 mile) southeast of Mougins. It was built in the 12th century and reconstructed in 1646. Its tree-dappled grounds were once painted by Sir Winston Churchill. More importantly, the priory next door was once Picasso's studio and private residence for the last 12 years of his life. It's still a private home occupied intermittently by the Picasso heirs.

Chemin de la Chapelle. Admission free.

Musée d'Art Classique de Mougins ★★ MUSEUM   The newest addition to Mougins' art scene is wonderfully quirky: Egyptian, Greek, and Roman artifacts are juxtaposed alongside similarly themed modern artworks, including sculptures, drawings, and canvases from Matisse, Dufy, Cézanne, Dali, and Damien Hirst. A personal favorite pairing matches an ancient statue of Venus with Yves Klein's neon-blue "Venus" sculpture.

32 rue Commandeur. ✆ **04-93-75-18-65.** www.mouginsmusee.com. Admission 12€ adults, 7€ students and seniors, 5€ children 10–17, free for children 9 and under. Daily 10am–6pm.

Musée de la Photographie André Villers ★ ART MUSEUM   Picasso's close friend, photographer André Villers, chronicled the artist's Mougins years in black-and-white photos. Images line the walls of an ancient medieval home: Some are hilarious, such as the photo showing Picasso sitting down for breakfast in his trademark Breton shirt, pretending he has croissants for fingers. Additional portraits by Villars—including snaps of Dali, Catherine Deneuve, and Edith Piaf—are frequently on display, along with three major temporary exhibitions each year.

Porte Sarrazine. ✆ **04-93-75-85-67.** Free admission. Daily 10am–12:30pm and 2–6pm (until 7pm from June–Sept). Closed Jan.

JUAN-LES-PINS ★★

913km (566 miles) S of Paris; 9.5km (6 miles) S of Cannes

Just west of the Cap d'Antibes, this Art Deco resort burst onto the South of France scene during the 1920s, under the auspices of American property developer Frank Jay Gould. A decade later, Juan-les-Pins was already drawing a chic summer crowd, as the Riviera "season" flipped from winter respites to the hedonistic pursuit of summer sun, sea, and sensuality. It has been attracting the young and the young-at-heart from across Europe and the U.S. ever since. F. Scott Fitzgerald decried Juan-les-Pins as a "constant carnival." His words ring true each and every summer's day.

Essentials

ARRIVING   Juan-les-Pins is connected by **rail** to most nearby coastal resorts, including Nice (trip time: 30 min.; 3.90€ one-way), Antibes, and Cannes. For further train information, visit www.voyages-sncf.com or call ☎ **36-35.** A **bus** (www.envibus.fr; ☎ **04-89-87-72-00**) leaves for Juan-les-Pins from Antibes' Gare Routière (bus station) daily every 20 minutes and costs 1€ one-way (trip time: 10 min.). To **drive** to Juan-les-Pins from Nice, travel along coastal D6007 south; from Cannes, follow the D6007 north.

VISITOR INFORMATION   The **Office de Tourisme** is at 51 bd. Charles-Guillaumont (www.antibes-juanlespins.co.uk; ☎ **04-97-23-11-10**).

SPECIAL EVENTS   The town offers some of the best nightlife on the Riviera. The action reaches its peak during the annual 10-day **Festival International de Jazz** (www.jazzajuan.com) in mid-July. It attracts jazz, blues, reggae, and world music artists who play nightly on the beachfront Parc de la Pinède. Recent performers have included George Benson, Maceo Parker, Norah Jones, and B. B. King. Tickets cost 25€ to 75€ and can be purchased at the Office de Tourisme in both Antibes and Juan-les-Pins, as well as online.

[FastFACTS] JUAN-LES-PINS

ATMs/Banks   **BNP Paribas,** 14 av. Maréchal Joffre (☎ **08-20-82-00-01**).

Internet Access   **Mediterr@net-phone.com,** av. du Dr Fabre (☎ **04-93-61-04-03**).

Mail & Postage   **La Poste,** 1 av. Maréchal Joffre (☎ **36-31**).

Pharmacies   **Pharmacie Provençale,** 144 bd. Président Wilson (☎ **04-93-61-09-23**).

Where to Stay

Le Grand Pavois ★   Nestled in an unbeatable location between the base of the Cap d'Antibes and Juan-les-Pins' center, this Art Deco edifice is literally a 2-minute walk to the beach. The elegant period lobby has been perfectly restored, and a live pianist often graces the ground-floor **La Rotonde** bar with jazzy tunes. Guestrooms are simply decorated with Provençal furnishings; many possess private balconies and sea views. Breakfast is served in the palm-fringed garden outside.

5 av. Saramartel. ☎ **04-92-93-54-54.** www.bestwestern-legrandpavois.com. 60 units. 78€–195€ double; 117€–278€ suite. Parking 8€. **Amenities:** Bar; restaurant; room service; free Wi-Fi.

Hôtel Belles-Rives ★★★   This luxurious hotel is one of the Riviera's most fabled addresses. It started life in 1925 as a holiday villa rented by Zelda and F. Scott Fitzgerald (as depicted in Fitzgerald's semi-autobiographical novel "Tender Is the Night"). Today, 85 years after her grandparents first opened the Belles-Rives' doors, the elegant Madame Estène-Chauvin owns and oversees this waterside gem. Guestrooms are sumptuous yet eclectic—each one its own unique size and shape. The lower terraces hold garden dining rooms, an elegant bar and lounge, as well as a private jetty. Also on site is the superb **La Passagère** restaurant and a private beach. If you're daring, you can even try waterskiing at the waterside aquatic club where, almost a century ago, the sport was invented.

33 bd. Edouard Baudoin. ✆ **04-93-61-02-79.** www.bellesrives.com. 43 units. 180€–960€ double; 750€–2,000€ suite. Parking 30€. Closed Jan–Feb. **Amenities:** 2 summer restaurants; 1 winter restaurant; 2 bars; private beach; room service; free Wi-Fi.

Where to Eat

Cap Riviera ★★ FRENCH   One of Juan-les-Pins' most appealing attributes is its endless ripple of beachside restaurants, all peering out over the picturesque Iles de Lérins. And Cap Riviera is undoubtedly one of this resort's finest. Cuisine is classically French. Think shrimp flambéed in pastis, lemon-infused sardine *rillettes*, or *sole meunière*; staff are charming and attentive. It's well worth popping by in advance to select your own special sea-facing table.

13 bd. Edouard Baudoin. ✆ **04-93-61-22-30.** www.cap-riviera.fr. Reservations recommended. Main courses 23€, fixed-price menu 39€. Daily noon–3pm, Mon–Sat 8–10pm. Closed Nov to mid–Dec and Jan.

Le Perroquet ★ PROVENÇAL   One of the best restaurants in Juan-les-Pins, Le Perroquet attracts both casual visitors and longtime locals. The *assortiment de poissons grillés*—grilled sea bream, John Dory, giant prawns, and red mullet—is an excellent introduction to the best of the Mediterranean. The pretty sidewalk seating looks out over La Pinède's Aleppo pines, and a good-value fixed-price lunch menu changes daily.

Av. Georges-Gallice. ✆ **04-93-61-02-20.** www.restaurantleperroquet.fr. Reservations recommended. Main courses 16€–32€; fixed-price lunch 18€; fixed-price dinner 30€–39€. Daily noon–2pm and 7–10pm. Closed Nov–Dec.

Les Pirates ★ ITALIAN/MEDITERRANEAN   For casual toes-in-the-sand dining, head to this family-friendly seaside restaurant. Within its palm-trimmed oasis, Les Pirates' summery menu is perfect for punctuating lazy afternoons on the beach. There's a very good range of salads, including La Jazz (local baby-leafed mesclun, violet artichokes, Parma ham, and avocado), as well as more extravagant offerings, such as seared scallops or *fritto misto* (Italian-style fried fish). *Tiramisu della Mamma* is whipped up in the kitchen by true Italian mamma Anna.

23 bd. Edouard Baudoin. ✆ **04-93-61-00-41.** www.plage-les-pirates.fr. Main courses 17€–45€. Daily noon–3pm and 8–10pm. Closed Nov–Jan.

Exploring Juan-les-Pins

Spilling over from Antibes' more residential quarter, Juan-les-Pins is petite—which makes the resort town best navigated on foot. Be sure to swing by the shady square known as **La Pinède** (square Frank Jay Gould) to check out the legions of local *pétanque* players. Nearby, the town's long-awaited **Palais des Congrès,** or Convention Center (www.antibesjuanlespins-congres.com) opened to much fanfare in fall of 2013. With the perennial success of year-round conferences in nearby Cannes, Juan-les-Pins' local municipality is hoping to shift some of the business action here.

Most of us, however, would rather stroll the long, beachside promenade to Golfe-Juan where Napoleon kicked off his march to Paris and famous Hundred Days in power in 1815. Alternatively, pick a beach bar, order a glass of rosé, and watch the sun drop over the Iles de Lérins (see p. 427).

Outdoor Activities

BEACHES   Part of the reason people flock to Juan-les-Pins is for the town's wealth of sandy beaches, all lapped by calm waters. The town also basks in a unique microclimate, making it one of the warmest places on the Riviera to soak up the sun, even in winter. **Plage de Juan-les-Pins** is the most central beach, although quieter stretches of sand wrap around the Cap d'Antibes and include family-friendly **Plage de la Salis** and chic **Plage de la Garoupe.** If you do want to stretch out on a sun lounger, go to any of the beach-bar concessions that line the bay, where you can rent a mattress for around 12€ to 20€. Topless sunbathing and overt shows of cosmetic surgery are the norm.

WATERSPORTS   If you're interested in scuba diving, try **Easy Dive,** bd. Edouard Baudouin (www.easydive.fr; ✆ 04-93-61-26-07). A one-tank dive costs 30€ to 55€, including all equipment. **Sea kayaking, pedalos, parasailing,** and **donuts** are available at virtually every beach in Juan-les-Pins. **Waterskiing** was invented at the Hôtel Belles-Rives in the 1920s, and it's still a great place to try out the sport.

Nightlife

For a faux-tropical-island experience, head to **Le Pam Pam,** 137 bd. Wilson (www.pampam.fr; ✆ 04-93-61-11-05), a time-honored "rhumerie" where guests sip rum and people-watch while reggae beats drift around the bar. More modern is **La Réserve,** av. Georges Gallice (✆ 04-93-61-20-06), where a younger crowd sips rosé on leopard-print seats.

If you prefer high-energy partying, you're in the right place. The entire Riviera descends upon Juan-les-Pins' discos every night in summer, and it's best to follow the crowds to the latest hotspot. **Le Village,** 1 bd. de la Pinède (✆ 04-92-93-90-00), is one of the more established clubs and boasts an action-packed dance floor with DJs spinning summer sounds from salsa to soul. The cover charge is usually 16€ including one drink; more for themed evenings. For top jazz, head to **Le New Orleans,** 9 av. Georges Gallice (✆ 04-93-67-41-71), a relatively new addition to the local live music scene.

FRENCH RIVIERA pass

The new **French Riviera Pass** lets visitors explore the coast for 26€ for 24 hours, 38€ for 48 hours, or 56€ for 72 hours. Over 60 choice sights are completely free including the **Villa Kerylos** on Cap-Ferrat, the **Musée Chagall** in Nice, and the **Oceanographic Museum** in Monaco. City tours like **Nice–Le Grand open-top bus** route, the **Mobilboard Segway** tour, and the **Train Touristique de Nice** are also free. Holders of the 72-hour pass are granted free entry into the normally wallet-busting **Marineland** in Antibes. Passes are available to purchase on the Nice Tourism website (www.nicetourisme.com).

ANTIBES & CAP D'ANTIBES ★★

913km (566 miles) S of Paris; 21km (13 miles) SW of Nice; 11km (6¾ miles) NE of Cannes

Antibes has a quiet charm unique to the Côte d'Azur. Its harbor is filled with fishing boats and pleasure yachts. The likes of Picasso and Monet painted its oh-so-pretty streets, today thronged with promenading locals and well-dressed visitors. A pedestrianized town center makes it a family-friendly destination as well, and a perfect place for an evening stroll. An excellent covered market is also located near the harbor, open every morning except Mondays.

Spiritually, Antibes is totally divorced from Cap d'Antibes, a peninsula studded with the villas of the super-rich. But the less affluent are welcome to peek at paradise, and a lovely 6km (3¾ miles) coastal path rings the headland, passing picnic and diving spots en route.

Essentials

ARRIVING   **Trains** from Cannes arrive at the rail station, place Pierre-Semard, every 20 minutes (trip time: 15 min.); the one-way fare is 2.90€. Around 25 trains arrive from Nice daily (trip time: 20 min.); the one-way fare is 3.60€. For further train information, visit www.voyages-sncf.com or call ✆ **36-35.** The **bus** station, or Gare Routière, place Guynemer (www.cg06.fr or www.envibus.fr; ✆ **04-89-87-72-00**), offers bus service throughout Provence. Bus fares to Nice, Cannes, or anywhere en route cost 1.50€ one-way.

To **drive** to Antibes from Nice, travel along coastal D6007 south; from Cannes, follow the D6007 north. The Cap d'Antibes is clearly visible from most parts of the Riviera. To drive here from Antibes, follow the coastal road south—you can't miss it.

VISITOR INFORMATION   The **Office de Tourisme** is at 11 place du Général de Gaulle (www.antibes-juanlespins.co.uk; ✆ **04-97-23-11-11**).

Fishing boats, yachts, and sailboats at Antibes' harbor

[FastFACTS] ANTIBES

ATMs/Banks   Among others, there are half a dozen banks dotted along av. Robert Soleau.

Internet Access   **Wilson.net,** 74 bd. Wilson (☏ **04-92-90-25-34**).

Mail & Postage   **La Poste,** 2 av. Paul Doumer (☏ **36-31**).

Pharmacies   **Grande Pharmacie d'Antibes,** 2 place Guynemer (☏ **04-93-34-16-12**).

Where to Stay

Hôtel du Cap–Eden-Roc ★★★
This legendary hotel was first launched in 1887, serving as a Mediterranean getaway for visitors seeking winter sunshine. Over the intervening years, it's played host to the world's most famous clientele, from the Duke and Duchess of Windsor (who escaped here after the former king's abdication) to the Hollywood superstars who cavort at the "Vanity Fair" Cannes Film Festival party. Surrounded by a maze of manicured gardens, accommodation is among the most sumptuous on the Riviera. Guest rooms benefitted from a 2013 renovation that outfitted every one with sleek modern fittings, iPod docks, and LED screens. Guests lounge by the seawater swimming pool, carved from natural basalt rock, while evenings are spent at the panoramic **Restaurant Eden-Roc** or the **Bellini Bar.** Looking to splurge? Pick up an exclusive Eden-Roc-label beach sarong. Alternatively, signature treatments at the onsite spa come courtesy of luxury Swiss brand La Prairie.

The Old Town, Antibes

Bd. J.F. Kennedy. ☏ **04-93-61-39-01.** www.hotel-du-cap-eden-roc.com. 118 units. 830€–1,400€ double; 1,700€–2,250€ suite; villa rates available upon request. Closed mid-Oct to mid-Apr. **Amenities:** 2 restaurants; 2 bars; babysitting; exercise room; massage; outdoor pool; room service; spa; tennis; free Wi-Fi.

La Jabotte ★★   Just a 5-minute stroll from one of Antibes' sandy beaches, this cozy little bed-and-breakfast is a favorite with regular visitors. Eight rooms, each with its own small terrace, cluster around a jasmine-splashed courtyard garden, and a suite and another double are upstairs. Guestrooms may be petite, but rooms are brightly decorated and beds are all brand-new. Owners Nathalie and Pierre make warm and welcoming hosts.

13 av. Max Maurey, Cap d'Antibes. ☏ **04-93-61-45-89.** www.jabotte.com. 10 units. 80€–209€ double; 139€–239€ triple; 129€–249€ suite (sleeps up to 4). Parking 10€. **Amenities:** Garden; bar; free Wi-Fi.

Where to Eat

The Zelda and Scott Fitzgeralds of today head for the **Restaurant Eden-Roc** at the Hôtel du Cap-Eden-Roc for grand service and grand cuisine. Alternatively, the excellent **Restaurant de Bacon,** bd. de Bacon (www.restaurantdebacon. com; ✆ **04-93-61-50-02**), has served the best seafood around for more than 6 decades. For light bites and unusual local wines, stop into **Entre 2 Vins,** 2 rue James Close (✆ **04-93-34-46-93**).

L'Armoise ★★ PROVENÇAL   Talented chef Laurent Parrinello, who honed his skills at Eze's Chèvre d'Or à Eze and the nearby Hôtel du Cap–Eden-Roc, crafts modern adaptations of traditional dishes, such as pestro-drizzled asparagus, fennel, and goat-cheese salad, or sea bream served with curry-infused red cabbage. Fresh ingredients come from Antibes' daily market; cheeses and wines are sourced from local producers. Note that advance reservations at this tiny restaurant are strongly recommended.

2 rue de la Tourraque. ✆ **04-92-94-96-13.** Main courses 22€–24€; fixed-price menu 48€–80€. Tues–Sun 7:30–9:30pm, Sat–Sun 12:30–2pm. Closed 2 weeks in July & 2 weeks in Dec.

Bistro Le Rustic ★ FRENCH/PIZZA   For hearty local dishes on a budget, it's hard to beat family-run Le Rustic. The menu here focuses on wood-fired pizzas and rich pots of fondue, with plenty of Riviera classics (fish soup, a fresh shrimp platter, slow-roasted duck) thrown in, too. The restaurant is located at the heart of Antibes' Old Town, with spacious (and kid-friendly) outdoor seating in the square.

33 place Nationale. ✆ **04-93-34-10-81.** Main courses 10€–18€; fixed-price menu 14€–19€. Daily noon–3pm and 7–11pm.

Chez Helen ★ VEGETARIAN   Whether you're a vegetarian on the road or simply seeking a little bit of lighter fare—despite the fact that Southern French food tends to eschew butter, cream, and heavier meats—this petite restaurant is a delight. All ingredients are organic and locally sourced. Expect subtle dishes like roasted tomato salad with basil *pistou* and mustard leaves, or spinach and feta stuffed Tunisian-style *brik*. Lunch only, or try Chez Helen for afternoon tea and a homemade pastry (8.50€).

35 rue des Revennes. ✆ **04-92-93-88-52.** www.chezhelen.fr. Main courses 12€; fixed-price menu 12€–15€. Mon–Sat 11am–5pm.

Exploring Antibes

Antibes' largely pedestrianized Old Town—all pale stone homes, weaving lanes, and window boxes of colorful flowers—is easily explored on foot. A dip into Picasso's former home, now a museum, and a stroll along the bling-tastic pleasure port, where artist Jaume Plensa's giant "Nomad" sculpture shimmers against the night sky, are undoubtedly its highlights.

The town is also skirted by wonderful walking trails. It's an easy stroll around the ancient walls of the 16th-century **Fort Carré,** just north of Antibes's port. Alternatively, like all of the prominent peninsulas on the French Riviera, the Cap d'Antibes boasts a scenic hiking trail around its perimeter. Highlights include the rustic coastal path south of Plage de la Garoupe, as well as a stop—if you can time it correctly—at the **Villa Eilenroc Gardens,** 460 av. L.D. Beaumont (✆ **04-93-67-74-33**). The latter is open July to September Wednesday, Saturday, and Sunday 3 to 7pm; April to June Wednesday and Saturday 10am to 5pm; and October to March Wednesday and Saturday 1 to 4pm. Admission is 2€, free

Beach at Antibes

for children 11 and under. There's a rose garden, sun-dappled olive groves, and a small eco-museum on-site.

Espace du Littoral et du Milieu Marin ★★ MARITIME CENTER Located within this stone-sided fort and tower on the Cap d'Antibes, built in stages in the 17th and 18th centuries, is a child-friendly space showcasing a permanent Jacques Cousteau exhibition. Prominent displays range from models of Costeau's research vessel, the Calypso, as well as the explorer's intimidating shark cage. Visitors keen to escape the crowds will revel in the center's seaside park (which overlooks the grounds of the ultra-exclusive Hôtel du Cap–Eden-Roc!). The view of the coastline here is worth the admission price alone.

Boulevard J.F. Kennedy. ✆ **04-93-61-45-32.** Admission 3€ adults, free for children 18 and under. Tues–Sat 10am–4:40pm.

Musée Picasso ★★ ART MUSEUM   Perched on the Old Town's ramparts, the 14th-century Château Grimaldi was home to Picasso in 1946, when the Spanish artist lived and worked here at the invitation of the municipality. Upon his departure, he gifted all the work he'd completed to the château museum: 44 drawings and 23 paintings, including the famous "La Joie de Vivre." In addition to this permanent collection, contemporary artworks by Nicolas de Staël, Arman and Modigliani, among many others, are also on display.

Château Grimaldi, Place Mariejol. ✆ **04-92-90-54-28.** Admission 6€ adults, 3€ students and seniors, free for children 17 and under. Mid-June to mid-Sept Tues–Sun 10am–6pm (July–Aug Wed and Fri until 8pm); mid-Sept to mid-June Tues–Sun 10am–noon and 2–6pm.

DAY TRIP FROM ANTIBES
Biot ★

6.5km (4 miles) NW of Antibes

Biot has been famous for its pottery since merchants began to ship earthenware jars to Phoenicia and throughout the Mediterranean. It's also where Fernand Léger painted until the day he died, leaving a magnificent collection of his work on display just outside town.

ESSENTIALS

Bus line no. 10 from Antibes's Gare Routière, place Guynemer (www.envibus.fr; ✆ **04-89-87-72-00**), runs to Biot's town center. Tickets cost 1€. To **drive** to Biot from Antibes, follow D6007 east, then head west on the D4. Biot's **Office de Tourisme** is at 46 rue St-Sébastien (www.biot-tourisme.com; ✆ **04-93-65-78-00**).

EXPLORING BIOT

Exploration of Biot's small historic center begins at **place des Arcades,** where you can see the 16th-century gates and the remains of the town's ramparts. The **Musée d'Histoire et Céramique Biotoise,** 8 rue St-Sebastien (www.musee-de-biot.fr; ✆ **04-93-65-54-54**), has assembled the best works from local artists, potters, ceramists, painters, and silver- and goldsmiths. Hours are mid-June to mid-September Tuesday to Sunday 10am to 6pm, and mid-September to mid-June Wednesday to Sunday 2 to 6pm. Admission is 4€, 2€ for seniors and students, and free for children 16 and under.

Outside of town, the excellent **Musée National Fernand Léger,** 316 chemin du Val de Pôme (www.musees-nationaux-alpesmaritimes.fr/fleger; ✆ **04-92-91-50-20**), displays a comprehensive collection of the artist's colorful creations, from 1930s Cubist ladies to circus scenes of the 1950s. Hours are Wednesday to Monday May to October 10am to 6pm, November to April 10am to 5pm. Admission is 5.50€, 4€ for students and seniors, and free for ages 25 and under. There are temporary exhibitions and a cafe garden on site.

The very zen **Musee du Bonsaï,** 299 chemin du Val de Pôme (www.museedubonsai-biot.fr, ✆ **04-93-65-63-99**), is located just around the corner. Cultivated by father and son team Jean and Karol Okonek, more than 1,000 sq. m (1,076 sq. ft.) of Japanese-style gardens are dedicated to bonsai trees collected from as far afield as Australia and China. It's open Wednesday to Monday from 10am to noon and from 2 to 6pm. Admission is 4€, 2€ for students and seniors. Note that the museum is closed from early January until the third week of February.

WHERE TO EAT & SHOP

For a Provençal take on crêpes—such as summery tomato, olive tapenade with basil or the house speciality, crêpe-pizza—stop in to **Crêperie Auberge du Village,** 29 rue Saint Sébastien (www.creperie-aubergeduvieuxvillage.com; ✆ **04-93-65-72-73**). This low-key lunch spot sits at the northern end of Biot's main shopping street. In the late 1940s, local glassmakers created a bubble-flecked glass known as *verre rustique*. In brilliant cobalts and emeralds, it's purveyed in the many store windows here.

ESPECIALLY FOR KIDS

Just south of Biot sits a kid-tastic complex of theme parks. **Marineland** (www.marineland.fr) offers the chance to get personal with penguins, polar bears, and sharks. **Aqualand** (www.aqualand.fr) boasts more than 2km (1¼ miles) of waterslides, including toboggan-style Le Draguéro and the Rainbow Cannon. **Adventure Golf** is criss-crossed by two dinosaur-dotted miniature golf courses. And, new for 2014, **Kid's Island** caters to animal-loving little ones, with pony rides and a petting zoo, plus plenty of jungle gyms and a Magic River. Admission is as follows: Marineland 39€, 31€ children between 3 and 12; Aqualand 27€, 21€ children between 3 and 12; Adventure Golf 11€, 9€ children between 3 and 12; and Kid's Island 13.50€, 10.50€ children between 3 and 12. All are free for children 2 and under; combination entrance tickets are also available. Marineland is open daily July and August 10am to 11pm, mid-April to June and September 10am to 7pm, and mid-March to mid-April 10am to 6pm. Aqualand, Adventure Golf, and Kid's Island all have varying opening hours. See the Marineland website for further details.

ST-PAUL-DE-VENCE ★★

926km (574 miles) S of Paris; 23km (14 miles) E of Grasse; 28km (17 miles) E of Cannes; 31km (19 miles) N of Nice

Of all the hilltop villages of the Riviera, St-Paul-de-Vence is by far the most famous. It gained popularity in the 1940s and '50s, when artists including Picasso, Chagall, and Matisse frequented the town, trading their paintings for hospitality at the Colombe d'Or inn. Art is now the town's principal attraction, and the winding streets are studded with contemporary galleries and museums. Circling the town are magnificent old ramparts (allow about 30 min. to walk the full loop) that overlook flowers and olive and orange trees.

Essentials

ARRIVING   The nearest **rail** station is in Cagnes-sur-Mer. Some 20 **buses** per day (no. 400) leave from central Nice, dropping passengers off in St-Paul-de-Vence (1.50€ one-way, trip time: 1 hr.), then in Vence 10 minutes later. For information, contact **Lignes d'Azur** (www.lignesdazur.com; ✆ **08-10-06-10-06**). If you're **driving** from Nice, take either the A8 highway or the coastal route du Bord du Mer west, turn inland at Cagnes-sur-Mer, and follow signs north to St-Paul-de-Vence.

VISITOR INFORMATION   The **Office de Tourisme** is at 2 rue Grande (www.saint-pauldevence.com; ✆ **04-93-32-86-95**).

Art galleries in St-Paul-de-Vence

Getting Around

St-Paul's Old Town is entirely pedestrianized, and most of the narrow streets are paved in cobblestones. Note that driving a car here is prohibited, except to drop off luggage at an Old Town hotel, and by prior arrangement only. The Fondation Maeght is around half a mile out of town.

[FastFACTS] ST-PAUL-DE-VENCE

ATMs/Banks   **BNP Paribas,** rd-pt Sainte Claire (📞 **08-20-82-00-01**).

Mail & Postage   **La Poste,** rd-pt Sainte Claire (📞 **36-31**).

Pharmacies   **Pharmacie Saint Paul,** rd-pt Sainte Claire (📞 **04-93-32-80-78**).

Where to Stay

La Colombe d'Or rents deluxe rooms (see "Where to Eat," below). Note that Vence's hotels make an accessible base for exploring St-Paul-de-Vence, too.

La Vague de Saint-Paul ★★★   La Vague opened in 2013 to fill a glaring gap in the St-Paul accommodations market: an affordable hotel for art lovers seeking country tranquility and wow-factor design. It delivers with aplomb. The wavelike main hotel building was originally conceived by far-out architect André Minangoy in the 1960s. Color-coded guestrooms now look out onto a vast garden complete with *pétanque* run, tennis court, bar, and pool. The attached (almost 100 percent organic) restaurant delivers five daily starters and mains on 22€ and 29€ set menus. The complex sits a short walk from the Fondation Maeght contemporary art museum—and a longer stroll through the forest to St-Paul-de-Vence village via a secret trail. Highly recommended.

Chemin des Salettes. 📞 **04-920-11-20-00.** www.vaguesaintpaul.com. 37 units. 96€–240€ double; from 253€ suite. Free parking. **Amenities:** Restaurant; bar; concierge; outdoor pool; room service; spa; tennis; free Wi-Fi.

Where to Eat

St-Paul's petite size means that dining options are limited and may also be pricey. That said, the views and the ambience of pretty much any local eatery often make up for these shortcomings.

La Colombe d'Or ★★ PROVENÇAL   This celebrated restaurant opened its doors in 1920. At the time it was little more than a scattering of tables overlooking an overgrown artichoke patch. It was Paul Roux, the restaurant's art-adoring owner, who encouraged the era's struggling artists, such as Raoul Dufy, Paul Signac, and Chaime Soutine, to swap a canvas or two for generous room and board. Picasso, Braque, and Miró followed—and today La Colombe d'Or's art collection is one of the finest in the world. For a peek at these masterpieces, you'll need to dine here, either indoors beneath works by the likes of Signac, Matisse, and Braque or outdoors on the fig-trimmed terrace. The house specials include a selection of fresh hors-d'oeuvres (such as *crudités* and *anchoïade,* a traditional anchovy dip), and crispy roast chicken. It also offers 25 luxurious doubles and suites sprawling over the original 16th-century stone house and the two 1950s wings. Prices are 250€ for a double, 430€ for a suite.

1 place du Général-de-Gaulle. ✆ **04-93-32-80-02.** www.la-colombe-dor.com. Main courses 17€–35€. Daily noon–2pm and 7:30–10pm. Closed late Oct to 3rd week of Dec and 10 days in Jan.

Les Terrasses ★ PROVENÇAL   A few minutes' stroll downhill from the Fondation Maeght, this laidback eatery offers classic regional cuisine and superb views over St-Paul's Old Town. Opt for *aïoli,* steamed vegetables and cod served with a garlic-spiked mayonnaise dip; *secca d' Entrevaux,* a locally cured beef dished up with grilled goat cheese; or one of a dozen different pizzas. Prices are the best in the area, and the atmosphere is convivial—do note, however, that the restaurant is a favorite with large groups.

20 chemin des Trious. ✆ **04-93-32-85-60.** www.laterrassesursaintpaul.com. Main courses 11€–29.50€; fixed-price menu 29€. Thurs–Tue 9am–10pm. Closed 2 weeks in Nov.

Exploring St-Paul

Perched at the top of the village, the **Collégiale de la Conversion de St-Paul** ★ was constructed in the 12th and 13th centuries and has been much altered over the years. The Romanesque choir is the oldest part, containing some remarkable stalls carved in walnut in the 17th century. Look to the left as you enter: You'll see the painting "Ste-Cathérine d'Alexandrine," which has been attributed to Tintoretto. The **Trésor de l'Eglise** is one of the most beautiful in the Alpes-Maritimes, with a spectacular ciborium. Look also for a low relief of the "Martyrdom of St-Clément" on the last altar on the right. It's open daily 9am to 6pm (to 7pm July–Aug). Admission is free.

Just around the corner is the light-flooded **Chapelle des Pénitents Blanc** (✆ **04-93-32-41-13**). The artist Jean-Michel Folon, who worked on this unmissable masterpiece until his death in 2005, decorated the church with stained-glass windows, shimmering mosaics, and rainbow-hued frescos. It's open April to September daily 11am to 1pm and 3 to 6pm, and October to March daily from 2 to 5pm. Admission is 3€ adults, 2€ students and children 6 to 18, and free for children 5 and under.

Fondation Maeght ★★★ ART MUSEUM   Established by Parisian art dealers Aimé and Marguerite Maeght in 1964, this avant-garde building houses one of the most impressive modern art collections in Europe. It was Spanish architect José Luis Sert who designed the pagoda-like exhibition space, ensuring the artwork it displays sits in perfect harmony with the surrounding pine-studded woods. In the gardens, colorful Alexander Calder installations are clustered with skinny bronze sculptures by Alberto Giacometti. A rotating selection of artworks is displayed over the various levels inside, showcasing key pieces by artists like Matisse, Chagall, Bonnard, and Léger. Each summer the museum stages a large seasonal show. There's also a library, a cinema, a cafeteria, and a magnificent museum store on-site.

623 chemin des Gardettes, outside the town walls. ✆ **04-93-32-81-63.** www.fondation-maeght. com. Admission 15€ adults, 10€ students and ages 10–18, free for children 9 and under, 5€ fee for photographs. July–Sept daily 10am–7pm; Oct–June daily 10am–6pm.

Organized Tours

With advance booking, the local tourist office offers 10 different walking tours of the town's historic core and outskirts. **Themed tours** (5€, free for children under 12) last around 1½ hours. They include following in the footsteps of former resident Marc Chagall, trying your hand at the beloved Provençal pastime of *pétanque* (also known as *boules*) under the instruction of accomplished locals, or guided tours of the Fondation Maeght. Almost all tours are given in both English and French.

In nearby La Colle sur Loup, culinary legends Alain and Jean-Michel Llorca offer cooking workshops for adults and children at their **Ecole de Cuisine** (www.alainllorca.com; 60€–170€ per person). Lessons are in French and English and are often followed by an informal dinner.

Shopping

The pedestrian-only **rue Grande** is St-Paul's most evocative street, running the length of the town. Most of the stone houses along it are from the 16th and 17th centuries, and several still bear the coats of arms placed there by the original builders. Today many of the houses are antiques shops, arts-and-crafts galleries, and souvenir and gift shops; some are still artists' studios.

Galerie du Vieux Saint-Paul, 16–18 rue Grande (www.galeries-bartoux.com; ✆ **04-93-32-74-50**), is the place to pick up serious art, from sculptures by local artist Arman to bronze works by Salvador Dali. Just down the road, **Galerie Capricorne,** 64 rue Grande (www.galeriecapricorne.com; ✆ **04-93-58-34-42**), offers a colorful array of prints, including a selection by Marc Chagall. **Galerie Paul Rafferty,** 67 rue Grande (www.raffertyart.com; ✆ **04-93-58-78-31**), purveys paintings inspired by the local village life. Stock up on olive oils, fruit vinegars, and olive-wood chopping boards at **Premier Pression Provence,** 68 rue Grande (www.ppp-olive.com; ✆ **04-93-58-07-69**). It's worth plunging into the town's winding streets, too: **Saint Georges Editions,** 5 montée de l'Eglise (✆ **09-71-57-68-21**), stocks superb, unique handbags, each one created from lengths of unusual antique textiles. Nearby **Atelier Silvia B**, 11 place de la Mairie (www.silviabertini.com; ✆ **04-93-32-18-13**) is packed with bright collages of St-Paul.

VENCE ★

926km (574 miles) S of Paris; 31km (19 miles) N of Cannes; 24km (15 miles) NW of Nice

Often bypassed in favor of nearby St-Paul-de-Vence, the pretty village of Vence is well worth a detour. Its pale stone Old Town is atmospheric yet untouristy, splashed with shady squares and pavement cafes. The highlight is undoubtedly Matisse's Chapelle du Rosaire, set among a countryside studded with cypresses, olive trees, and oleanders.

Essentials

ARRIVING   Frequent **buses** (no. 94 or 400) originating in Nice take 65–80 minutes to reach Vence, passing the nearest **rail** station in Cagnes-sur-Mer, about 10km (6¼ miles) southwest from Vence, en route. The one-way fare is 1.50€. For bus information, contact **Lignes d'Azur** (www.lignesdazur.com; ✆ **08-10-06-10-06**). For train information, visit www.voyages-sncf.com or call ✆ **36-35.** To **drive** to Vence from Nice, take D6007 west to Cagnes-sur-Mer, and then D36 north to Vence.

VISITOR INFORMATION   The **Office de Tourisme** is on place due Grand-Jardin (www.ville-vence.fr; ✆ **04-93-58-06-38**).

[FastFACTS] VENCE

ATMs/Banks   Many banks are dotted around Vence, including **BNP Paribas,** 28 place du Grand-Jardin (📞 **08-20-82-00-01**).

Internet Access   **SIMS,** 165 av. des Poilus (www.secretariat-services-vence.weebly. com; 📞 **04-93-58-23-27**), offers high-speed Internet access, but no Wi-Fi.

Mail & Postage   **La Poste,** place Clemenceau (📞 **36-31**).

Pharmacies   **Pharmacie du Grand-Jardin,** 30 place du Grand-Jardin (📞 **04-93-24-04-07**).

Where to Stay

Note that St-Paul-de-Vence's hotels also make an excellent base for exploring Vence.

Cantermerle Hotel ★   Just south of Vence's Old Town, this hotel, restaurant, and spa is set within 3 acres of lush gardens. Spacious guestrooms feature terra-cotta tile floors and Provençal fabrics; many also boast their own private terrace. At the gourmet restaurant **La Table du Cantemerle,** chef Jérôme Héraud dishes up grilled Aveyron lamb in a parsley crust and lobster ravioli in the elegant dining room or outdoors alongside the pool. Use of the spa's heated indoor pool, mosaic Turkish baths, and fitness area is complimentary for guests.

258 chemin Cantemerle. 📞 **04-93-58-08-18.** www.cantemerle-hotel-vence.com. 27 units. 180€–298€ double; 537€–587€ suite. Closed Nov–Mar. **Amenities:** Restaurant; 2 bars; outdoor pool; spa; free Wi-Fi.

Château Saint-Martin & Spa ★★★   Just 20 minutes from the Nice airport, amid 14 hectares (35 acres) of enchanting gardens, lies one of the most sumptuous hotels in the world. Take, for example, the Château Saint-Martin's spa. In addition to massages, it offers La Prairie and Bamford signature treatments, yoga lessons, color chromotherapy, and a wellness shower than can emulate the misting breeze of a tropical rainstorm. Moreover, the hotel complex is shared by a mere handful of guests, who revel in the vast infinity pool, the outdoor **Oliveraie** grill restaurant set in an ancient olive grove, and mammoth château suites that overlook the shimmering sea below. Six independent villas are larger and more luxurious still. The Michelin-starred restaurant is under the accomplished command of Franck Ferigutti, new head chef in 2014. The cuisine switches from modern French fare to infused foam creations and desserts chilled with nitrogen steam. And it sits atop a wine cellar worth far more than the average Riviera mansion.

2490 av. des Templiers. 📞 **04-93-58-02-02.** www.chateau-st-martin.com. 39 units, 6 villas. 250€–640€ double; 660€–1,500€ suite; 1,470€–3,800€ villa. Rates include breakfast. Closed Oct to mid-Apr. **Amenities:** 3 restaurants; bar; babysitting; outdoor pool; room service; sauna; spa; tennis; free Wi-Fi.

Where to Eat

Vence's unpretentious attitude is also evident in the local cuisine. It tends to be traditional and tasty, occasionally Michelin-starred, and often dished up in a sublime setting. For homemade hot chocolate or artisanal sweets, **Entre Mes Chocolats,** 12 av. Marcellin Maurel (www.entre-mes-chocolats.com; 📞 **09-81-82-34-59**), is highly recommended.

Les Bacchanales ★★ PROVENÇAL   A short stroll from the Chapelle du Rosaire, Les Bacchanales is located inside a century-old villa, overlooking chef Christophe Dufau's enchanting kitchen garden. The creative menu uses almost exclusively local ingredients, transforming them into strikingly innovative versions of traditional Provençal cuisine. Mediterranean bream may be paired with apricots and Italian Taggiasche olives; sweet cantaloupe melon is grilled and served with fresh almonds and Corsican *brousse* cheese. Note that the market-fresh weekly menu is limited: Diners may simply select their preferred number of courses (two to five at lunch, four to seven at dinner). The restaurant holds one Michelin star.

247 av. de Provence. ✆ **04-93-24-19-19.** www.lesbacchanales.com. Fixed-price menus 28€–85€. July–Aug Wed–Fri & Mon 7:30–9:30pm, Sat–Sun 12:30–2pm and 7:30–9:30pm; Sept–June Thurs–Mon 12:30–2pm and 7:30–9:30pm. Closed last 2 weeks of Dec, 3 weeks in Jan.

Le Pigeonnier ★ PROVENÇAL   One of the Old Town's most welcoming eateries, Le Pigeonnier spills across the dining rooms of a 14th-century building and a sunny square, the latter perfect for people-watching. The restaurant menu is traditional. Linger over slow-cooked *daube* (a classic Niçois beef stew), a generous steak, or fish soup served with garlic croutons and *rouille,* saffron mayonnaise.

5-7 place du Peyra. ✆ **04-93-58-03-00.** Main courses 11€–19€; fixed-price menu 23€. July–Aug daily noon–2:30pm and 7:30–10pm; Sept–June Tues–Sat noon–2:30pm and 7:30–10pm, Sun noon–2:30pm.

Exploring Vence

Vence's medieval **Vieille Ville (Old Town)** is compact, making it easy to explore on foot. A poke around its picturesque squares reveals place du Peyra's bubbling **Vieille Fontaine (Old Fountain),** while nearby the **Château de Villeneuve/ Fondation Emile Hugues,** 2 place du Frêne (www.museedevence.com; ✆ **04-93-58-15-78**), is a temporary exhibition space dedicated to 20th-century art. Recent exhibits have showcased works by Matisse, Cézanne, and Jean-Michel Basquiat. Hours are Tuesday to Sunday 10am to 12:30pm and 2 to 6pm. Admission is 7€ for adults, 5€ for students, and free for children under 12. Also in the Old Town is **place Godeau,** where the **mosaic** "Moses Saved from the Nile" by Marc Chagall adorns the 11th-century **cathedral**'s baptistery (free).

Vence's main draw, however, lies just outside the fortified main town. The Chapelle du Rosaire represents one of Matisse's most remarkable achievements.

Chapelle du Rosaire ★★ RELIGIOUS SITE   From the age of 47, Henri Matisse made Nice his home. But Vence held a special place in the artist's heart: It was his place of residence during World War II, as well as home to Dominican nun Sister Jacques-Marie, Matisse's former nurse and muse. So in 1947, when Matisse discovered that the sisters were planning the construction of a new chapel, he offered not only to design it, but fund the project as well. Matisse was 77 at the time.

The Chapelle du Rosaire was completed in 1951. A beautifully bright space, it offers the exceptional possibility of stepping into a three-dimensional artwork. Matisse described his creation: "What I have done in the chapel is to create a religious space . . . in an enclosed area of very reduced proportions and to give it, solely by the play of colors and lines, the dimensions of infinity."

From the front of the chapel, you may find the structure unremarkable and pass it by—until you spot a 12m (39-ft.) crescent-adorned cross rising from a blue-tile roof. Within, dozens of stained-glass windows shimmer cobalt blue (symbolizing the sea), sapphire green (the landscape), and golden yellow (the sun). Most remarkable are the 14 black-and-white-tile Stations of the Cross, featuring Matisse's self-styled "tormented and passionate" figures.

The bishop of Nice came to bless the chapel in the late spring of 1951; Matisse died 3 years later.

466 av. Henri-Matisse. ✆ **04-93-58-03-26.** Admission 6€ adults; contributions to maintain the chapel are welcome. Mon, Wed, and Sat 2–5:30pm; Tues and Thurs 10–11:30am and 2–5:30pm. Closed mid-Nov to mid-Dec.

NICE ★★★

929km (576 miles) S of Paris; 32km (20 miles) NE of Cannes

The largest city on this fabled stretch of coast, Nice is known as the "Queen of the Riviera." It's also one of the most ancient, founded by the Greeks, who called it Nike (Victory). By the 19th century, Russian aristocrats and the British upper class—led by Queen Victoria herself—were sojourning here. These days, however, Nice is not as chi-chi as Cannes or St-Tropez. In fact, of all the major French resorts, Nice is the most down-to-earth, with an emphasis on fine dining and high culture. Indeed, it has more museums than any other French city outside Paris. In late 2013 it inaugurated a new city center urban park, one of the largest public spaces in the South of France.

Nice is also the best place to base yourself on the Riviera, especially if you're dependent on public transportation. You can go to San Remo, a glamorous town over the Italian border, for lunch and return to Nice by nightfall. From Nice airport, the second busiest in France, you can travel by train or bus along the entire coast to resorts such as Antibes, Juan-les-Pins, and Monaco.

Beachfront promenade des Anglais, Nice

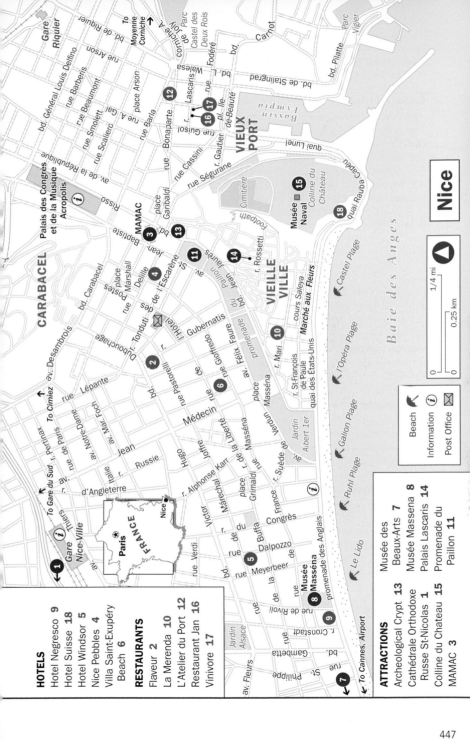

Nice

HOTELS
Hotel Negresco **9**
Hotel Suisse **18**
Hotel Windsor **5**
Nice Pebbles **4**
Villa Saint-Exupéry Beach **6**

RESTAURANTS
Flaveur **2**
La Merenda **10**
L'Atelier du Port **12**
Restaurant Jan **16**
Vinivore **17**

ATTRACTIONS
Archeological Crypt **13**
Cathédrale Orthodoxe Russe St-Nicolas **1**
Colline du Chateau **15**
MAMAC **3**
Musée des Beaux-Arts **7**
Musée Massena **8**
Palais Lascaris **14**
Promenade du Paillon **11**

Beach
Information
Post Office

Baie des Anges

VIEUX PORT

VIELLE VILLE

CARABACEL

0   1/4 mi
0   0.25 km

Because of its brilliant sunshine and liberal attitude, Nice has long attracted artists and writers, among them Dumas, Nietzsche, Flaubert, Hugo, Sand, and Stendhal. Henri Matisse, who made his home in Nice, said, "Though the light is intense, it's also soft and tender." The city averages 300 sunny days a year.

Essentials

ARRIVING **Trains** arrive at the city's main station, Gare Nice-Ville, avenue Thiers. From here you can take trains to Cannes for 6.80€, Monaco for 3.80€, and Antibes for 4.50€, with easy connections to Paris, Marseille, and anywhere else along the Mediterranean coast.

Buses (www.lignesdazur.com; ✆ **08-10-06-10-06**) to towns east, including Monaco (no. 100) depart from place Garibaldi; to towns west, including Cannes (no. 200) from Jardin Albert I.

Transatlantic and intercontinental flights land at **Aéroport Nice–Côte d'Azur** (www.nice.aeroport.fr; ✆ **08-20-42-33-33**). From there, municipal bus nos. 98 and 99 depart at 20-minute intervals for the Port and Gare Nice-Ville, respectively; the one-way fare is 6€. **Taxis** are not cheap. A ride from the airport to the city center costs between 35€ and 40€ each way. Trip time is about 20 minutes.

Ferryboats operated by **Trans-Côte d'Azur** (www.trans-cote-azur.com; ✆ **04-92-00-42-30**), on quai Lunel on Nice's port, link the city with Ile Ste-Marguerite (see p. 427) from June to September and St-Tropez from June through August.

VISITOR INFORMATION Nice maintains three **tourist offices.** The largest is at 5 promenade des Anglais, near place Masséna (www.nicetourisme.com; ✆ **08-92-70-74-07**). Additional offices are in the arrivals hall of the Aéroport Nice–Côte d'Azur and outside the railway station on avenue Thiers.

CITY LAYOUT The city is divided into five main neighborhoods: the Italianate Old Town; the vintage port; the commercial city center between place Masséna and the main train station; the affluent residential quarter known as the Carre d'Or, just inland from the promenade des Anglais; and hilltop Cimiez. All are easy to navigate on foot, with the exception of Cimiez. For more, see "Exploring Nice," p. 452.

SPECIAL EVENTS The **Nice Carnaval** (www.nicecarnaval.com), known as the "Mardi Gras of the Riviera," runs from mid-February to early March, celebrating the return of spring with 3 weeks of parades, *corsi* (floats), *veglioni* (masked balls), confetti, and battles in which young women toss flowers at the audience.

The **Nice Festival du Jazz** (www.nicejazzfestival.fr) runs for a week in mid-July, when jazz, funk, and reggae artists perform in the Jardins Albert I near the seafront. Recent performers have included Herbie Hancock and George Benson.

Getting Around

ON FOOT Nice is very walkable, and no point of interest downtown is more than a 10-minute walk from place Massena, including the seafront promenade des Anglais, Old Town, and harbor.

BY BICYCLE & MOTOR SCOOTER Like many French cities, Nice has its own bike-sharing scheme, **Vélo Bleu** (www.velobleu.org). You can register directly at one of Nice's 175 bike stands (difficult) or online (much easier); fees range from 1€ for 1 day to 5€ for a week. Alternatively, you can rent bikes (from 12€ per day) and scooters (from 26€ per day; driver's license and deposit required) from **Holiday Bikes,** 23 rue de Belgique (www.holiday-bikes.com; © 04-93-16-01-62).

BY CAR A novel addition to the Nice transport scene is **Auto Bleue** (www.auto-bleue.org; © **09-77-40-64-06**). The scheme allows visitors to rent an electric Peugeot car from one of 50 vehicle stands around Nice for 45€ per day, inclusive of electricity, parking, and insurance. Sign-up online in advance. Cooler cats may rent an E Type Jaguar or Ford Mustang from **Rent A Classic Car** (www.rentaclassiccar.com; © **09-54-00-29-33**) from 189 € per day.

BY TAXI **Taxis Niçois Indépendants** (www.taxis-nicois-independants.fr; © **04-93-88-25-82**) will pick up within 5 minutes across town. Alternatively, call a **Cyclopolitain** (nice.cyclopolitain.com; © **04-93-81-76-15**) electronic tricycle for a ride around town (until 7pm, maximum two passengers, from 5€ per ride).

BY PUBLIC TRANSPORT Most local buses leave from the streets around place Masséna. Municipal **buses** charge 1.50€ for rides within the entire Alpes-Maritime province, even as far as Monaco or Cannes. The same ticket can also be used on Nice's **tramway,** which connects the Old Town with Gare Nice-Ville and northern Nice. Tickets, day passes (5€), and week passes (15€) can be bought directly onboard buses (although not trams) or at electronic kiosks around the city. For further information, see www.lignesdazur.com.

[Fast FACTS] NICE

ATMs/Banks Nice is home to dozens of banks; **LCL Banque,** 15 av. Jean Médecin (© **04-93-82-84-61**), is one of the most central.

Dentists **SOS Dentaire** (© **04-93-01-14-14**).

Doctors & Hospitals **Hôpital Saint-Roch,** 5 rue Pierre Dévoluy (www.chu-nice.fr; © **04-92-03-33-33**).

Embassies & Consulates **U.S. Consular Agency Nice,** 7 av. Gustave V (© **04-93-88-89-55**); **Consulate of Canada,** 2 place Franklin (© **04-93-92-93-22**).

Internet Access As of 2013, various public squares and streets (such as the cours Saleya) throughout Nice offer free Wi-Fi. Look for the network "NiceGOWEXFREEWiFi."

Local Information The **"Riviera Times"** (www.rivieratimes.com) and the **"Riviera Reporter"** (www.rivierareporter.com) both cover news, art, culture, and events in and around Nice. Alternatively, **"Angloinfo French Riviera"** (http://riviera.angloinfo.com) is an invaluable resource.

Mail & Postage **La Poste,** 6 rue Louis Gassin (© **36-31**).

Pharmacies **Pharmacie Masséna,** 7 rue Masséna (© **04-93-87-78-94**).

Safety Nice is generally a very safe place. However, as in any big city, it's important to keep an eye on your valuables, in particular anywhere that's crowded. Avoid poorly lit streets at night, including in Nice's Old Town.

Where to Stay

EXPENSIVE

Hôtel Negresco ★★   For more than a century, the Negresco has been Nice's most iconic hotel. Its flamingo-pink dome crowns the promenade des Anglais, its Belle Epoque facade turned towards the sea. Guestrooms—a mix of Louis XIV antiques and state-of-the-art bathrooms—have hosted each era's most noted celebrities, from the Beatles and Salvador Dali to Michael Jackson. Public areas are decorated with works from an exceptional collection of private art, including the shimmering Nikki de St-Phalle sculpture welcoming guests at the hotel's entrance. Dining ranges from the exquisite (the double-Michelin-starred **Chantecler** and its 15,000-bottle wine cellar) to the playful (the kooky merry-go-round-style brasserie, **La Rotonde**).

37 promenade des Anglais. ✆ **04-93-16-64-00.** www.hotel-negresco-nice.com. 117 units. 165€–600€ double; 620€–2,500€ suite. Parking 28€. **Amenities:** 2 restaurants; bar; babysitting; exercise room; massage; room service; free Wi-Fi.

MODERATE

Hôtel Suisse ★★   A score of artists have set up their easels on the promenade in front of the Hôtel Suisse. As if to prove it, a reproduction canvas of a sea view scene by Raoul Dufy is surrounded by a bevy of amateur iPhone photographers, all hoping to snap the same panorama. The view from the recently renovated hotel rooms above is stupendous, and arguably the best in town. Deferential service in the lobby-cum-breakfast room is all very well, but for more color (and less cash) guests are advised to source their croissants and coffee on the nearby cours Saleya instead. Look online for the Suisse's heavily discounted winter and advance booking rates.

15 quai Rauba Capeu. ✆ **04-92-17-39-00.** www.hotel-nice-suisse.com. 38 units. 114€–337€ double. Public parking nearby. **Amenities:** Bar; babysitting; room service; free Wi-Fi.

Hôtel Windsor ★★★   The coolest, funkiest, and most friendly hotel in Nice is also one of its best-value lodgings. This *maison bourgeoise* was built by disciples of Gustav Eiffel in the 1890s and has remained a family-run hotel for three generations. Current owner Mme Payen-Redolfi has ushered in an artsy era where a different acclaimed artist decorates another guest room each year. The hotel currently has 31 contemporary-art rooms, including one painted entirely in gold leaf by Claudio Parmigiani. Art and color stream outside into the bamboo garden— **WiJungle**—where alfresco breakfasts are also served. Back indoors, **WiLounge** serves dinner and chilled rosé. **WiZen** is the fifth-floor health club, hammam, sauna, and meditation zone.

11 rue Dalpozzo. ✆ **04-93-88-59-35.** www.hotelwindsornice.com. 57 units. 89€–225€ double. Parking 15€. **Amenities:** Restaurant; bar; babysitting; health club; outdoor pool; room service; sauna; free Wi-Fi.

INEXPENSIVE

Villa Saint Exupéry Beach ★   Just outside Nice's Old Town, this upscale hostel makes an ideal base for budget travelers of all ages. Accommodation ranges from dormitory-style beds to private twin rooms, and includes an abundant free buffet breakfast. Also onsite is a communal kitchen, gym with sauna, daily happy hour, and quality meals at backpacker prices. Its award-winning sister hostel, **Villa Saint Exupéry Gardens,** 22 ave Gravier (✆ **04-93-84-42-83**), is located in a converted monastery just north of the city center. A former chapel with stained-glass windows now serves as its buzzing bar.

6 rue Sacha Guitry. ✆ **04-93-16-13-45.** www.villahostels.com. 60 units. 25€–80€ per person in a single or twin-bedded room; 16€–40€ per person for dormitory bed. Rates include continental breakfast, sheets, and towels. **Amenities:** Bar; cooking facilities; computers; luggage room; TV lounge; free WiFi.

ALTERNATE ACCOMMODATIONS

Nice Pebbles ★★★   A short-term rental of one of these holiday apartments allows you time to truly immerse yourself in local life, from cooking up morning-market bounty to sipping sunset aperitifs on your private terrace. More than 150 carefully selected properties (from studios to 10-bed homes) are dotted throughout the city's central neighborhoods, including the Old Town and harbor and along the promenade des Anglais. Apartments boast first-class amenities (iPod docks, high-def TVs, and designer bathrooms are common), yet weigh in at just a fraction of the price of a hotel room. Demand is high, so book well in advance. Sister agency **Riviera Pebbles** (www.rivierapebbles.com) manages additional properties along the coast.

20 rue Gioffredo. ✆ **04-97-20-27-30.** www.nicepebbles.com. 90€–350€ per apartment per night. **Amenities:** Babysitting; free Wi-Fi.

Where to Eat

The Riviera boasts more Michelin commendations (45 stars over 36 establishments as of 2014) than almost anywhere else on the planet. The regional capital of Nice teems with exquisite restaurants, from the high end to the downright local. Excellent eateries are scattered across the city—although beware of many of the Old Town's careless offerings, keen to lure in tourists for a single night only. In addition to the suggestions below, the portside **Le Bistrot du Port,** 28 quai Lunel (www.lebistrotduportdenice.fr; ✆ **04-93-55-21-70**), is where the Orsini family has been dishing up top-quality fish and creative seafood concoctions for over 30 years.

EXPENSIVE

Flaveur ★★ MODERN FRENCH   Brothers Gaël and Mickaël Tourteaux (whose last name, almost unbelievably, translates as "cake") are a pair of very talented chefs. They may be relatively young—39 and 35 respectively—yet they've already spent decades in the kitchens of the Riviera's top restaurants. Little surprise, then, that in 2011 their contemporary bistro, Flaveur, earned its first Michelin star. A childhood growing up on the tropical islands of Réunion and Guadeloupe means their modern French cuisine is laced with exotic flavors: Plump scallops are seasoned with Japanese *gomasio;* artistically displayed lemongrass and bubbles of lemon caviar sit atop risotto. Meals are variations on fixed-price menus only; there's no ordering à la carte, although lunchtime menus allow for gourmet bites on a relative budget.

25 rue Gubernatis. ✆ **04-93-62-53-95.** www.flaveur.net. Fixed-price lunch 40€–68€; fixed-price dinner 52€–85€. Tues–Fri noon–2pm and 7:30–11pm; Sat 7:30–11pm. Closed early Jan.

MODERATE

L'Atelier du Port ★★ NIÇOIS   A design-heavy restaurant that mixes sleek contemporary furniture with an open kitchen and indoor citrus garden . . . and gets it completely right. Two of this guidebook's authors live around the corner from this new establishment and are devoted regulars. Chalkboard menus chart locally sourced daily delights including squid from the Italian border, lemons (for various desserts) from Menton, and stuffed ricotta tortelli from Nice Old Town's finest pasta store, **Barale** (7 rue Saint Réparate). Home-made terrines, pâtés, and tarts are also a joy, as are the fairly priced Provençal wines by the *pichet*.

45 rue Bonaparte. ✆ **09-83-03-88-44.** Main courses 14€–21€. Daily noon–3:30pm, 7–11pm.

La Merenda ★★ NIÇOIS   Top chef Dominique Le Stanc left the world of *haute cuisine* far behind to take over this tiny, traditional, family-run bistro. And how lucky we all are. La Merenda is now one of the most authentic and unpretentious eateries along the French Riviera. Market-fresh specials are scribbled on a small chalkboard; depending on the season, they may include stuffed sardines, tagliatelle drenched in delicious basil pesto, or a delectable *tarte au citron*. **Note:** The restaurant has no phone, so you'll need to make reservations in person.

4 rue Raoul Bosio. No phone. www.lamerenda.net. Main courses 14€–29€. No credit cards. Mon–Fri noon–2pm and 7:30–10pm.

Restaurant Jan ★★★ MODERN MEDITERRANEAN   This new Franco–South African gourmet restaurant is 2014's hottest meal ticket. Situated in the city's new dining district a block behind Nice Port, both décor and service (under the watchful eye of Maître d' Philippe Foucault, formerly of the Negresco and Grand Hotel du Cap-Ferrat) are akin to being a guest in a French Presidential retreat. The inventive cuisine of South African chef Jan Hendrik van der Westhuizen blends regional ingredients (line-caught seabass, Charolais beef) with African spice (Madagascar vanilla, rooibos jelly) and Italian style (Parmesan shavings, prosciutto chips). Dishes may include slow-roasted pork belly with scallops and sweet potato puree, and soya tuna with capers and crispy onion rings.

12 rue Lascaris. ✆ **04-97-19-32-23.** www.restaurantjan.com. Main courses 20€–32€; fixed-price lunch 22€. Wed–Fri noon–3pm, Tues–Sat 7:30–10:30pm.

INEXPENSIVE

Vinivore ★★ MODERN FRENCH   This vibrant eatery, located just behind the port, mixes fresh Provençal ingredients with Cantonese flair. Each day, Hong Kong–born chef Chun Wong's changing menu features just four appetizers, four main courses, and four desserts. Recent highlights include beef *tataki* with garlic flowers, wild rice risotto with grilled scallops, and vanilla-infused candied pineapple. Québécois sommelier Bonaventure Blankstein has handpicked some 200 vintages—carefully noted on the large chalkboards—from mostly organic wineries across southern France. In 2013 the small **Vinivore wine bar** opened next door to the main restaurant. And finally, note that Chun's Chinese parents and younger sister own an authentic bargain Cantonese restaurant, **Les Secrets de Lili,** 8 rue de Suisse (✆ **04-93-88-11-48**), near Nice-Ville train station—also well worth a visit.

10 rue Lascaris. ✆ **04-93-14-68-09.** www.vinivore.fr. Main courses 11€–18€; fixed-price lunch 18€; fixed-price dinner 45€. Tues–Fri noon–2pm, Tues–Sat 7:30–10:30pm.

Exploring Nice

In 1822, Nice's orange crop had an awful year. The workers faced a lean time, so the English residents employed them to build the **promenade des Anglais** ★★, today a wide boulevard fronting the bay that stretches for 7km (4¼ miles), all the way to the airport. Along the beach are rows of grand cafes, the Musée Masséna, and the city's most glamorous hotels.

Crossing this boulevard in the tiniest bikinis are some of the world's most attractive bronzed bodies. They're all heading for the **beach.** Tough on tender feet, *le plage* is made not of sand, but of pebbles (and not small ones, either).

Rising sharply on a rock at the eastern end of the promenade is the **Colline du Château.** Once a fortified bastion, the hill has since been turned into a wonderful public park complete with a waterfall, cafes, and a giant children's play area, as well as an incredibly ornate cemetery. Head up aboard an elevator from the quai des Etats-Unis; more athletic visitors can walk up one of five sets of steep steps. The park is open daily from 8am to dusk.

Continuing east of the Colline, you reach the **Vieux Port,** or harbor, where the restaurants are filled with locals. While lingering over a drink at a sidewalk cafe, you can watch the ferries depart for Corsica and the yachts for St-Tropez. Just inland, the neighborhood around rue Bonaparte and place Garibaldi has become one of the hippest in town: head here for authentic eateries, hip bars, and the superb **MAMAC Museum of Contemporary Art,** place Yves Klein (www.mamac-nice.org; ✆ **04-97-13-42-01;** free admission; closed Mon).

The **Vieille Ville ★★**, or Old Town, begins at the foot of the Colline and stretches to place Masséna. Sheltered by red-tiled roofs, many of the Italianate facades suggest 17th-century Genoese palaces, including the free museum **Palais Lascaris,** 15 rue Droite (✆ **04-93-62-72-40**). The Old Town is a maze of narrow streets teeming with local life, flower-strewn squares, and traditional *boulangeries:* sample a Niçois-style onion pizza *(pissaladière)* here. Many of the buildings are painted a faded Roman gold, and their banners are laundry flapping in the sea breeze.

Marché aux Fleurs (flower market) at cours Saleya

From Tuesday through Sunday (8am–1pm), the Old Town's main pedestrianized thoroughfare, the **cours Saleya,** is crowded with local producers selling seasonal fruits and vegetables, cured meats, and artisanal cheeses. At the market's western end is the **Marché aux Fleurs.** A rainbow of violets, lilies and roses, the market operates Tuesday to Sunday from 8am to around 6pm. On Monday (8am–6pm) the cours Saleya is occupied by a superb **antiques market,** with vendors carting wares in from across France and Italy.

Nice's centerpiece is **place Masséna,** with rococo buildings and bubbling fountains, as well as the new **Promenade du Paillon** parkway that stretches from the MAMAC down to the **Jardin Albert-1er.** With palms and exotic flowers, this pedestrian-only zone is one of the prettiest places in town. During renovations, the city authorities discovered an **Archeological Crypt** near place Garibaldi, place Jacques Toja (nice.fr/culture; ✆ **04-92-00-41-90;** 5€ adults, 2.50€ children under 16; closed Tues). The site can

453

now be visited on a 60-minute guided tour daily except Tuesdays at 10am, 11am, 2pm, 3pm and 4pm.

Cathédrale Orthodoxe Russe St-Nicolas à Nice ★ CATHEDRAL Ordered built by none other than Tsar Nicholas II, this recently renovated cathedral is the most beautiful religious edifice of the Orthodoxy outside Russia. It dates from the Belle Epoque, when some of the Romanovs and entourage turned the Riviera into their stomping ground. Everyone from grand dukes to ballerinas arrived on the recently reinstated direct train from Moscow, then paraded their tiaras on the promenade. The cathedral is richly ornamented and decorated with icons. You'll spot the building from afar because of its collection of ornate onion-shaped domes.

Av. Nicolas II (off bd. Tzaréwitch). ✆ **04-93-83-94-08.** www.cathedrale-russe-nice.fr. Free admission. Tues–Sun 9am–noon and 2–6pm. From the central rail station, bus no. 71, or head west along av. Thiers to bd. Gambetta, and then go north to av. Nicolas-II.

Musée des Beaux-Arts ★★ ART MUSEUM Housed in the fabulous former residence of the Ukrainian Princess Kotchubey, this fine collection of 19th- and 20th-century art includes works by Rodin and Dufy, as well as works by a dynasty of painters, the Dutch Vanloo family. One of its best-known members, Carle Vanloo, born in Nice in 1705, was Louis XV's premier *peintre*. High drama hit the museum in 2007, when armed robbers broke into the museum on a quiet summer Sunday, stealing priceless canvases by Monet and Sisley. The artworks were recovered less than a year later in Marseille.

33 av. des Baumettes. ✆ **04-92-15-28-28.** www.musee-beaux-arts-nice.org. Free admission. Tues–Sun 10am–6pm. Bus: 3, 9, 10, 22, or 38.

Musée Masséna ★★★ MUSEUM Riviera aficionados will adore this astounding history museum. Located within an imposing Belle Epoque villa, it exhibits a quirky range of objects charting local life in Nice and its surrounds, from the first Victorian visitors through the roaring 1920s. Elegantly printed menus, train tickets from London to Nice, period maps, and snapshots of the promenading rich on vacation bring the past to life. Of additional note are the paintings and *objets d'art* donated by the Masséna family, a noble set of locals who constructed the villa. Botanist Edouard Ardre, who also designed the verdant greenery in front of the Casino de Monte-Carlo, landscaped the museum's neatly manicured gardens.

65 rue de France or 35 promenade des Anglais. ✆ **04-93-91-19-10.** Free admission. Wed–Mon 9am–6pm.

Outlying Attractions in Cimiez

In the once-aristocratic hilltop quarter of Cimiez, 5km (3 miles) north of Nice, Queen Victoria wintered at the Hôtel Excelsior. Half the English court traveled down from Calais with her on a luxurious private train. Be sure to stroll over to the adjacent **Monastère de Cimiez** (Cimiez Convent), which offers panoramic views over Nice and the Baie des Anges; artists Matisse and Dufy are buried in the cemetery nearby. To reach this suburb and its attractions, take bus no. 15 from bd. Dubouchage.

Musée Matisse ★★ ART MUSEUM In 1963, this beautiful old Italian villa was transformed into a museum honoring Henri Matisse, one of the 20th century's greatest painters. Matisse came to Nice for the light and made the city his home, living in the Hotel Beau Rivage and on the cours Saleya, and dying in

Cimiez in 1954. Most of the pieces in the museum's permanent collection—including "Nude in an Armchair with a Green Plant" (1937) and "Blue Nude IV" (1952)—were created in Nice. Artworks are interspersed with Matisse's personal possessions, such as ceramic vases and antique furniture, as well as scale models of his architectural masterpiece, Vence's **Chapelle du Rosaire** (p. 445).

164 av. des Arènes de Cimiez. ✆ **04-93-81-08-08.** www.musee-matisse.nice.org. Free admission. Wed–Mon 10am–6pm.

Musée National Message Biblique Marc Chagall ★★ ART MUSEUM

Surrounded by pools and a garden, this handsome museum is devoted to Marc Chagall's treatment of biblical themes. Born in Russia in 1887, Chagall became a French citizen in 1937 and painted with astonishing light and color until his death in St-Paul-de-Vence in 1985. This museum's focal set of artworks—12 large paintings, illustrating the first two books of the Old Testament—was originally created to adorn the central cathedral in Vence. The church's high humidity nixed the artist's original plans, and Chagall assisted in planning this purpose-built space instead. The 200 additional artworks include gouaches, a mosaic, sculptures, and prints.

Av. du Dr. Ménard. ✆ **04-93-53-87-20.** www.musee-chagall.fr. Admission 8€ adults, 6€ students, free for children 17 and under. May–Oct Wed–Mon 10am–6pm; Nov–Apr Wed–Mon 10am–5pm.

Organized Tours

One of the most enjoyable ways to quickly gain an overview of Nice is aboard a **Nice–Le Grand Tour** (www.nicelegrandtour.com; ✆ **04-92-29-17-00**) double-decker bus. Between 10am and 6pm year-round, one of a flotilla of this company's buses departs from a position adjacent to the Jardin Albert I. The panoramic 90-minute tour takes in the harbor, the museums of Cimiez, the Russian church, and the promenade. Per-person rates for the experience are 21€ adults, 18€ students, and 5€ children 4 to 11. Participants can get off at any of 11 stops en route and re-board any other buses, which follow at 30- to 60-minute intervals, depending on the season. Advance reservations aren't necessary, and commentary is piped through to headsets in seven different languages. Tickets are valid the entire day of purchase.

Another easy way to see the city is by the small **Train Touristique de Nice** (www.trainstouristiquesdenice.com; ✆ **06-08-55-08-30**), which also departs from the promenade des Anglais, opposite Jardin Albert I. The 45-minute ride passes many of Nice's most-heralded sites, including place Masséna, the Old Town, and the Colline du Château. Departing every 30 minutes, the train operates daily 10am to 5pm (until 6pm Apr–May and Sept, until 7pm June–Aug). The round-trip price is 8€ adults and 4€ children 4 to 12.

Possibly the coolest way to get around Nice is by Segway, the two-wheeled electronic scooters. Tours are run by **Mobilboard**, 2 rue Halévy (www.mobilboard.com; ✆ **04-93-80-21-27**). Children 14 (minimum age) to 17 must be accompanied by an adult. An hour-long tour of Nice costs 30€ per person. More energetic guests may join **Nice Cycle Tours** (www.nicecycletours.com; ✆ **06-19-99-95-22**), 3-hour bike voyages around the city. Tours cost 30€ per person, and the friendly team also run food tours and cycle expeditions. Alternatively, **2CV Escapade,** 7 place Ile de Beauté (www.2cv-escapade.com; ✆ **06-52-01-30-40**), in Nice Port, offers multilingual city tours in a classic Citroën convertible from 60€ per group of 2 or 3 persons.

Outdoor Activities

BEACHES   Along Nice's seafront, beaches extend uninterrupted for more than 7km (4¼ miles), going from the edge of Vieux-Port (the old port, or harbor) to the international airport. Tucked between the public areas are several rather chic private beaches. Many of these beach bars provide mattresses and parasols for 12€ to 22€. The coolest clubs include **Hi-Beach** (www.hi-beach.net; ✆ **04-97-14-00-83**), which has a sushi bar, blanket Wi-Fi, and family-friendly playpens; and **Castel Plage** (www.castelplage.com; ✆ **04-93-85-22-66**), a celebrity hangout in summer.

SCUBA DIVING   Of the many diving outfits in Nice harbor, **Nice Diving,** 13 quai des Deux Emmanuel (www.nicediving.com; ✆ **06-14-46-04-06**), offers bilingual instruction and *baptêmes* (dives for first-timers) around Nice and Cap-Ferrat. A dive for experienced divers, equipment included, costs around 50€; appropriate diver's certification is required.

Shopping

CLOTHES   Nice's densest concentrations of fashionable French labels are clustered around **rue Masséna** and **avenue Jean-Médecin.** For more high-end couture, the streets around **place Magenta,** including **rue de Verdun, rue Paradis,** and **rue Alphonse Karr** are a credit card's worst nightmare. A shop of note is **Cotelac,** 12 rue Alphonse Karr (✆ **04-93-87-31-59**), which sells chic women's clothing. Men should try **Façonnable,** 7–9 rue Paradis (www.faconnable.com; ✆ **04-93-88-06-97**). This boutique is the original site of a chain with several hundred branches worldwide; the look is conservatively stylish. For more unusual apparel, **Lucien Chasseur,** 2 rue Bonaparte (✆ **04-93-55-52-14**), is the city's coolest spot for Italian-designed shoes, scarves, and soft leather satchels.

FOOD   The winding streets of Nice's Old Town are the best place to find local crafts, ceramics, gifts, and foodie purchases. If you're thinking of indulging in a Provençale *pique-nique,* **Nicola Alziari,** 14 rue St François de Paule (www.alziari.com.fr; ✆ **04-93-62-94-03**), will provide everything from olives, anchovies, and pistous to aiolis and tapenades. For an olive-oil tasting session—and the opportunity to buy the goods afterward—check out **Oliviera,** 2 rue Benoit Bunico (www.oliviera.com; ✆ **04-93-11-06-45**), run by the amiable Nadim Beyrouti. In the port, **Confiserie Florian,** 14 quai Papacino (www.confiserie florian.com; ✆ **04-93-55-43-50**), has been candying fruit, chocolate-dipping roasted nuts, and crystallizing edible flowers since 1949.

SOUVENIRS   The best selection of Provençal fabrics is at **Le Chandelier,** 7 rue de la Boucherie (✆ **04-93-85-85-19**), where you'll see designs by two of the region's best-known producers of cloth, Les Olivades and Valdrôme. For antiquarian books, contemporary art, kitsch, and comic books, wander north of place Garibaldi to **rue Delille and rue Defly,** just past the MAMAC modern art gallery. Hairdresser-cum-clothes atelier **My Cut Concept,** 11 rue Delfy (✆ **04-93-01-53-19**) is a typical local store. For further offbeat gifts, **Chambre Cinquante-Sept,** 16 rue Emmanuel Philibert (✆ **04-92-04-02-81**), stocks beautifully unique Art Deco *objets d'art.* More vintage is for sale at **Deux Pièces,** 2 rue Antoine Gautier (✆ **06-68-86-23-00**),

Cours Saleya, a daytime and nighttime hotspot in Nice

Nightlife

Nice has some of the most active nightlife and cultural offerings along the Riviera. Big evenings out usually begin at a cafe or bar, take in a restaurant, opera, or film, and finish in a club. The website **riviera.angloinfo.com** lists all the week's English-language movies in VO, or *version originale.*

The major cultural center on the Riviera is the **Opéra de Nice,** 4 rue St-François-de-Paule (www.opera-nicc.org; ✆ **04-92-17-40-00**), built in 1885 by Charles Garnier, fabled architect of the Paris Opéra. It presents a full repertoire, with emphasis on serious, often large-scale operas, such as "Tristan and Isolde" and "La Boheme," as well as a *saison symphonique* dominated by the Orchestre Philharmonique de Nice. The opera hall is also the major venue for concerts and recitals. Tickets are available right up until the day of performance. You can show up at the box office (Mon–Thurs 9am–5:30pm; Fri until 7:45pm; Sat until 4:30pm) or buy tickets in advance online. Tickets run from 10€ to 80€.

A chic gaming spot is the **Casino in the Palais de Mediterranée,** 15 promenade des Anglais (www.casinomediterranee.com; ✆ **04-92-14-68-00**), which offers a similar experience daily from 10am for slot machines, 8pm for gaming tables.

The Old Town's most happening spot is **Villa,** 7 rue Raoul Bosio (✆ **04-93-87-99-45**), whose house aperitif is the wickedly named Putain de le Palais: crushed strawberries topped with Champagne. Within the cool-kitsch decor of a former garage in the port area, talented staff serves up fruity cocktails and organic local wines at **Rosalina,** 16 rue Lascaris (✆ **04-93-89-34-96**). Around the corner, gay-friendly **Comptoir Central Electrique,** 10 rue Bonaparte (✆ **04-93-14-09-62**), has been the place Garibaldi neighborhood's epicenter of cool since opening in 2013. Also on the same street, **Deli Bo,** 5 rue Bonaparte (✆ **04-93-56-33-04**), is a hip dining spot for ladies who lunch.

The party spirit is best lapped up in the alfresco bars on the **cours Saleya.** Otherwise, head 1 block inland to **Wayne's Bar,** 15 rue de la Préfecture (www.waynes.fr; ✆ **04-93-13-46-99**), where dancing on the tables to raucous cover bands is the norm. For excellent house tunes, nonstop dancing, and heaps of understated cool, head to **Bliss,** 12 rue de l'Abbaye (✆ **04-93-16-82-38**).

DAY TRIP FROM NICE

Cagnes-sur-Mer ★

7km (4 1/2 miles) W of Nice

Cagnes-sur-Mer encompasses **Haut-de-Cagnes,** a 17th-century hilltop village with panoramic views over the coast, and the old fishing port and beach resort of **Cros-de-Cagnes,** known for its 4km (2½ miles) of pebbly beach.

For years Cagnes-sur-Mer attracted the French literati, such as Simone de Beauvoir. Great Impressionist painter Renoir said the village was "the place where I want to paint until the last day of my life." His former residence, the **Musée Renoir**, chemin des Collettes (✆ **04-93-20-61-07**), is the highlight of any visit to the area. Reopened in 2013 after 18 months of renovation, Renoir's home, gardens, and citrus groves have been restored to their original layout. There are 17 new sculptures and two new paintings on display, too. Hours are June to September Wednesday to Monday 10am to 1pm and 2 to 6pm (gardens open 10am to 6pm); October to March Wednesday to Monday 10am to noon and 2 to 5pm; and April to May Wednesday to Monday 10am to noon and 2 to 6pm. Admission is 6€ for adults and free for visitors under 26.

Frequent no. 200 buses (1.50€) and trains (1.90€) zip along the coast between Nice and Cagnes-sur-Mer. The climb to hilltop Haut-de-Cagnes is strenuous; a free minibus runs daily about every 15 minutes year-round from place du Général-de-Gaulle in the center of Cagnes-sur-Mer to Haut-de-Cagnes. Cagnes' **Office de Tourisme** is at 6 bd. Maréchal Juin, Cagnes-sur-Mer (www.cagnes-tourisme.com; ✆ **04-93-20-61-64**).

ROYA VALLEY & THE MERCANTOUR
national park

The timeless Roya Valley and the Mercantour forests (one of only seven National Parks in mainland France) are a train hop away from Nice. The entire area was once the private hunting ground of Italy's Turin-based kings. It only became part of France in 1947, and the Italianate train stations and tumbling hill villages remain. Thankfully, there's a lot of wildlife left, too, in the form of wolves, marmots, ibex, eagles, and deer.

The **Train de Merveilles** (tendemerveilles.com), climbs up into the Roya Valley from Nice-Ville station up to six times daily. A stunning stop is **Sospel,** 45 minutes from Nice. This age-old village is sliced in two by a raging river, and is a center for mountain biking, horseback riding, and alpine hikes.

Further north up the valley, the village of **Breil-sur-Roya** has stolen a few hearts, too. It lies at the nexus of several hiking paths, one of them leading downhill to Sospel.

The large ex-Italian town of **Tende,** 2 hours from Nice, is the train's final stop.

The names above its stores, on its churches, and in its rococo graveyard are distinctly non-French. It's also the gateway to the **Mercantour National Park** (www.parc-mercantour.eu). Before partaking in the park's 100 hiking routes, make a visit to Tende's **Musée des Merveilles** (www.museedesmerveilles.com; ✆ **04-93-04-32-50**), which highlight's the area's prehistory, cave paintings, and fairytale geography.

Lovers of *la bella italia* may continue on to Cuneo in Italy using a locals-only train that runs from Tende towards Turin several times each day.

WHERE TO EAT

In Haut-de-Cagnes, the ever-popular **Josy-Jo,** 2 rue du Planastel (www.restaurant-josyjo.com; ✆ **04-93-20-68-76**), was the home and studio of painters Modigliani and Soutine during their hungriest years. The menu features Niçois speciality *petits farcis* (tiny stuffed vegetables), grilled lamb from the Hautes-Alpes, and a variety of homemade desserts. In Cros-de-Cagnes, chef Jacques Maximin dishes up fresh fish and superb seafood at the seafront **Bistrot de la Marine,** 96 promenade de la Plage (www.bistrotdelamarine.com; ✆ **04-93-26-43-46**).

VILLEFRANCHE-SUR-MER ★★

935km (580 miles) S of Paris; 6.5km (4 miles) E of Nice

Just east of Nice, the coastal Lower Corniche sweeps inland to reveal Villefranche, its medieval Old Town tumbling downhill into the shimmering sea. Paired with a dazzling sheltered bay set against picturesque Cap-Ferrat beyond, it's little wonder than countless artists made this beachy getaway their home—or that it's served as the cinematic backdrop for numerous movies.

Essentials

ARRIVING Trains arrive from all the Côte d'Azur's coastal resorts from Cannes to Monaco every 30 minutes or so. For rail schedules, visit www.voyages-sncf.com or call ✆ **36-35. Lignes d'Azur** (www.lignesdazur.com; ✆ **08-10-06-10-06**) maintains a **bus** service at 5- to 15-minute intervals aboard line no. 100 from Nice to Monte Carlo via Villefranche. One-way fares cost 1.50€. Buses deposit passengers just above the Old Town, almost directly opposite the tourist information office. Many visitors **drive** via the Basse Corniche (Lower Corniche).

VISITOR INFORMATION The **Office de Tourisme** is on Jardin François-Binon (www.villefranche-sur-mer.com; ✆ **04-93-01-73-68**).

[FastFACTS] VILLEFRANCHE

ATMs/Banks **LCL Banque,** 6 av. du Maréchal Foch (✆ **04-93-76-24-01**).

Internet Access **Chez Net,** 5 place du Marché (www.cheznet.com; ✆ **04-89-08-19-43**).

Mail & Postage **La Poste,** 6 av. Albert 1er (✆ **36-31**).

Pharmacies **Pharmacie Laurent,** 2 av. du Maréchal Foch (✆ **04-93-01-70-10**).

Where to Stay

Hotel Villa Patricia ★ This petite seaside hotel really does offer some of the Riviera's cheapest double rooms during the height of summer. A 5-minute stroll from the water, it also boasts a shared garden sheltered by lemon trees. As one might expect for the price, some rooms are small, while others are oddly shaped, but all are stylish, smart, and exceptionally clean, and share a large lounge area complete with book swap, outdoor sofas, and a piano. It's a gentle 10-minute stroll from Villefranche, Beaulieu, and Cap-Ferrat.

310 Avenue de l'Ange Gardien. ✆ **04-93-01-06-70.** www.hotel-patricia.riviera.fr. 10 units. 65€–89€ double; 89€–119€ triple; 80€–119€ suite. Free parking. Closed Dec–Jan. **Amenities:** Free Wi-Fi.

Hôtel Welcome ★ Villefranche's most prestigious hotel, the Welcome sits in the center of town and has been home to Riviera artists since the 1920s, including author and filmmaker Jean Cocteau (in room 22). Every one of the modern hotel's midsize-to-spacious rooms possesses a balcony and sea views. The on-site **wine bar** spills out onto the quay in warm weather. The hotel also rents out *Orphée,* its eight-person private sailboat, for daily cruises; prices from 650€ per half-day with crew.

3 quai Amiral Courbet. **☎ 04-93-76-27-62.** www.welcomehotel.com. 35 units. 145€–358€ double; 220€–525€ suite. Parking 45€. **Amenities:** Bar; babysitting; room service; free Wi-Fi.

Where to Eat

Le Cosmo ★★ MEDITERRANEAN This friendly sidewalk cafe has been pulling in punters for a decade—and with good reason. Prices are reasonable, the creative menu is perfectly executed, and the setting is sublime: The restaurant's terraced seating overlooks Cocteau's Chapelle St-Pierre and the seafront beyond. Sample sautéed scallops with aubergine caviar, or *salade Cosmo,* topped with avocado, shrimp, grapefruit, and hearts of palm. Dozens of fantastical ice cream creations (think yogurt ice cream piled high with strawberries and raspberry puree, or a tower of praline ice cream, whipped cream, and chocolate sauce) are also on offer.

11 pl. Amélie Pollonais. **☎ 04-93-01-84-05.** www.restaurant-lecosmo.fr. Main courses 14€–25€. Daily 7:45am–2am.

Exploring Villefranche

Villefranche's long arc of golden sand, **plage des Marinières,** is the principal attraction for most visitors. From here, **quai Courbet** runs along the sea to the colorful Old Town past scores of bobbing boats; it's lined with waterside restaurants.

Old-town action revolves around **place Amélie Pollonnais,** a delightful square shaded by palms and spread with the tables of six easygoing restaurants. It's also the site of a Sunday antiques market, where people from across the Riviera come to root through vintage tourism posters, silverware, 1930s jewelry, and ex-hotel linens.

The painter, writer, filmmaker, and well-respected dilettante Jean Cocteau left a fine memorial to the town's inhabitants. He spent a year (1956–57) painting frescoes on the 14th-century walls of the Romanesque **Chapelle St-Pierre,** quai Courbet (**☎ 04-93-76-90-70**). He presented it to "the fishermen of Villefranche in homage to the Prince of Apostles, the patron of fishermen." In the apse is a depiction of the miracle of St. Peter walking on the water, not knowing that an angel supports him. Villefranche's busty local women, in their regional costumes, are honored on the left side of the narthex. Admission is 3€ for adults, free for children under 15. In spring and summer, it is open Wednesday to Monday 10am to noon and 3 to 7pm; fall and winter hours are Wednesday to Monday 10am to noon and 2 to 6pm. It's closed from mid-November to mid-December.

A short coastal path leads from the car park below place Amélie Pollonnais to the **16th-century citadelle.** This castle dominates the bay, and its ramparts can be wandered around at leisure. Inside the citadel sits a cluster of small, locally focused **museums** (**☎ 04-93-76-33-27**), including the **Fondation Musée-Volti,** a collection of voluptuous female sculptures by Villefranche artist Volti (Antoniucci Voltigero) and **Le Musée Goetz-Boumeester,** featuring around 50 artworks by Dutch artist Christine Boumeester. Opening hours are

Alfresco dining at Villefranche-sur-Mer

July to August, Monday and Wednesday to Saturday 10am to noon, Wednesday to Monday 3 to 7pm; June to September, Monday and Wednesday to Saturday 9am to noon, Wednesday to Monday 3 to 6pm; and October and December to May, Monday and Wednesday to Saturday 10am to noon, Wednesday to Monday 2 to 5pm. Admission is free.

ST-JEAN-CAP-FERRAT ★★

942km (584 miles) S of Paris; 9.5km (6 miles) E of Nice

Of all the oases along the Côte d'Azur, no other place has the snob appeal of Cap-Ferrat. It's a 15km (9¼-mile) promontory sprinkled with luxurious villas and out-lined by sheltered bays, beaches, and sun-kissed coves. In the charming port of St-Jean, the harbor accommodates yachts, fishing boats, and a dozen low-key eateries.

It's worth mentioning that Cap-Ferrat is seriously wealthy. As in seriously, seriously rich. Stars like David Niven and Gregory Peck called "Le Cap" home before a new generation of Russian oligarchs and Hollywood A-listers moved in. The world's most expensive property, Villa Leopolda, went on sale here a few years back for a cool half-billion dollars. In 2012, the BBC confirmed that the peninsula is the second most expensive location in the world (since you ask, Monaco came first). A wonderful coastal path loops past many of the world's richest residents' private homes.

St-Jean-Cap-Ferrat

Essentials

ARRIVING   **Trains** connect Beaulieu with Nice, Monaco, and the rest of the Côte d'Azur every 30 minutes. Many visitors then take a **taxi** to St-Jean from Beaulieu's rail station; alternatively, it's a 30-minute walk along Cap-Ferrat's promenade Maurice Rouvier to St-Jean village. For **rail** information, visit www.voyages-sncf.com or call © **36-35**. **Bus** line no. 81 connects Nice with St-Jean every hour. One-way fares costs 1.50€. For bus information and schedules, contact **Lignes d'Azur** (www.lignesdazur.com; © **08-10-06-10-06**). By **car** from Nice, take D6098 (the *basse corniche*) east.

VISITOR INFORMATION   St-Jean's **Office de Tourisme** is on 59 av. Denis-Séméria (www.saintjeancapferrat.fr; © **04-93-76-08-90**).

[FastFACTS] ST-JEAN

ATMs/Banks   **Banque Populaire Côte d'Azur,** 5 av. Claude Vignon, St-Jean 06230 (© **04-89-81-11-42**).

Mail & Postage   **La Poste,** 51 av. Denis Séméria, St-Jean 06230 (© **36-31**).

Pharmacies   **Pharmacie Pont Saint Jean,** 57 bd. Dominique Durandy, St-Jean 06230 (© **04-93-01-62-50**).

Where to Stay

Grand Hôtel du Cap-Ferrat ★★★   Put simply, this grande dame of a hotel is the greatest building on Europe's richest peninsula. It's sumptuous, stylish, and incredibly sexy. Set on 17 acres of tropical trees and manicured lawns, it's been the exclusive retreat of the international elite since 1908. The **Le Spa** wellness centre spills outside into curtained cabanas, where massages and other treatments can be indulged in. Aside from the modernist guestrooms, the coolest place to hang out is the seaside **Club Dauphin** beach club (non-guests can gain access for 90€ per day). It's reached by a funicular rail pod that descends from the hotel. The children of many visiting celebrities, including the Kennedys and Paul McCartney, have learned to swim in the Olympic-size infinity pool.

71 bd. du Général-de-Gaulle. © **04-93-76-50-50.** www.ghcf.fr. 73 units. 285€–1,120€ double; 700€–5,100€ suite. Closed Jan and Feb. **Amenities:** 3 restaurants; bar; babysitting; beach club; bikes; Olympic-size heated outdoor pool; room service; spa; tennis; free Wi-Fi.

Hôtel Brise Marine ★   An Italianate villa constructed in 1878, the Brise Marine is tucked into a quiet residential neighborhood south of St-Jean. Rooms are simply furnished and sunny, with enchanting sea views. Breakfast on the rose-twined terrace, and you can almost imagine you're aboard one of the luxury super-yachts bobbing off nearby Paloma Plage.

58 av. Jean-Mermoz. © **04-93-76-04-36.** www.hotel-brisemarine.com. 16 units. 160€–203€ double; 190€–233€ triple. Parking 15€. Closed Nov–Feb. **Amenities:** Bar; room service; free Wi-Fi.

Where to Eat

Le Cap ★★ FRENCH/INTERNATIONAL   The Grand Hôtel du Cap-Ferrat's acclaimed gourmet restaurant is overseen by head chef Didier Aniès. His Michelin-starred cuisine is heavy on caviar, oysters, and luxurious French

CAP-FERRAT'S HOMES OF THE
rich & famous

The global aristocratic, business, and cultural elite have long favored Cap-Ferrat. As you wander around keep your eyes out for these four key villas. **Lo Scoglietto** is a rococo pink edifice looking out towards Monaco from the promenade Maurice Rouvier coastal path. Once owned by Charlie Chaplin, it later passed to fellow British actor David Niven. More famous still is **Villa Mauresque** at the Cap's southern tip. In 1928 it was aquired by British author Somerset Maugham. The writer took up residence again after World War II to find that the liberating Allies had bombed his ornamental garden and the occupying Italians had raided his wine cellar. More modernist is **Villa La Voile.** This yacht-shaped mansion has 'sails' that draw across the property each day to diffuse the Riviera sun. To lend an idea of Cap-Ferrat's worth, that particular project was overseen by Lord Norman Foster, the architect responsible for the world's biggest airport (in Beijing). Peek over the fence between Villefranche and Cap-Ferrat at the **Villa Nelcotte.** Once owned by Count Ernst de Brulatour, a secretary of the American embassy in France, then by Samuel Goldenberg, a wealthy American survivor of the Titanic, it was rented in 1971 by reprobate rocker Keith Richards. That summer the Rolling Stones recorded the album *Exile on Main Street* in the villa's sweaty basement. John Lennon and Eric Clapton dropped by, as did half the personalities of the Riviera underworld.

classics, while the wine list includes every vintage of the esteemed Château d'Yquem label since the 1890s. Some Michelin-starred restaurants listed in this guidebook welcome guests wearing Birkenstocks, shorts, and an eager smile. Le Cap is not one of them. Expect stiff formality as bow-tied waiters open silver cloches to reveal Wagyu beef with oysters and grapefruit, and slow-baked John Dory with citron confit.

71 bd. du Général-de-Gaulle. ✆ **04-93-76-50-26.** www.ghcf.fr. Main courses 86€–108€; fixed-price menu 158€–198€. Daily 7:45–9:45pm. Closed Oct–Mar.

Capitaine Cook ★ PROVENÇAL/SEAFOOD   Perhaps the peninsula's most beloved eatery, Capitaine Cook is run by husband-and-wife team Lionel and Nelly Pelletier. Dine outdoors on the leafy terrace or indoors within the ruggedly maritime dining room. The menu is particularly strong on hearty yet imaginative fish dishes, from stuffed sardines to salmon ravioli.

11 av. Jean-Mermoz. ✆ **04-93-76-02-66.** Main courses 18€–30€; fixed-price menu 27€–32€. Fri–Tues 12:30–2pm; Thurs–Tues 7:30–10:30pm. Closed mid-Nov to Dec.

Exploring St-Jean

One way to enjoy the area's beautiful backdrop is to stroll the public pathway that loops around Cap-Ferrat from Beaulieu all the way to Villefranche. The most scenic section runs from chic **plage de Paloma,** near Cap-Ferrat's southernmost tip, to **pointe St-Hospice,** where a panoramic view of the Riviera landscape unfolds. Allow around 3 hours to hike from St-Jean to family-friendly **plage Passable,** on the northwestern "neck" of the peninsula.

Villa Ephrussi de Rothschild ★★ HISTORIC HOME/MUSEUM   The winter residence of Baronne Béatrice Ephrussi de Rothschild, this Italianate villa was completed in 1912 according to the finicky specifications of its ultra-rich owner. Today the pink edifice preserves an eclectic collection, gathered over her lifetime: 18th-century furniture, Tiepolo ceilings, tapestries from Gobelin, a games table gifted from Marie-Antoinette (Ephrussi's hero) to a friend, and tiny seats for her beloved poodles. The nine themed gardens, from Florentine to Japanese, are a particular delight. An attractive tea salon overlooks the Bay of Villefranche.

1 av. Ephrussi de Rothschild. ✆ **04-93-01-33-09.** www.villa-ephrussi.com. Admission 13.50€ adults, 9.50€ students and children 7–17, free for children 6 and under. July–Aug daily 10am–7pm; Mar–June and Sept–Oct daily 10am–6pm; Nov–Feb Mon–Fri 2–6pm, Sat–Sun 10am–6pm.

BEAULIEU-SUR-MER ★

941km (583 miles) S of Paris; 9.5km (6 miles) E of Nice

Cradled on the mainland just east of Cap-Ferrat, the Belle Epoque resort of Beaulieu-sur-Mer has long attracted *bons vivants* with its casino and fine restaurants. Its genteel environs once sheltered Sir Winston Churchill. Its palm-backed beaches and alfresco restaurants now welcome visiting celebrities from Bono to Sylvester Stallone.

Essentials

ARRIVING   **Trains** connect Beaulieu with Nice, Monaco, and the rest of the Côte d'Azur every 30 minutes. For **rail** information, visit www.voyages-sncf.com or call ✆ **36-35. Bus** line no. 100 from Nice to Monte Carlo passes through Beaulieu. One-way fares costs 1.50€. For bus information and schedules, contact **Lignes d'Azur** (www.lignesdazur.com; ✆ **08-10-06-10-06**). By **car** from Nice, take D6098 (the *basse corniche*) east.

VISITOR INFORMATION   Beaulieu's **Office de Tourisme** is on place Georges Clémenceau (www.beaulieusurmer.fr; ✆ **04-93-01-02-21**) adjacent to the Train Station.

[FastFACTS] BEAULIEU

ATMs/Banks   **Banque Populaire Côte d'Azur,** 40 boulevard Marinoni (✆ **04-89-81-10-56**).

Mail & Postage   **La Poste,** place Georges Clemenceau (✆ **36-31**).

Pharmacies   **Pharmacie Internationale,** 38 boulevard Marinoni (✆ **04-93-01-01-39**).

Where to Stay

Le Havre Bleu ★   You could easily spend a fortune on a luxury hotel. Or you could check into this Riviera stalwart that underwent a design overhaul in 2013 and blow your money in boutiques and beach clubs instead. Le Havre Bleu has a variety of rooms, some with terraces and patios, that never rise above 100€ per night year-round. Breakfast (10€) is served on the sunny communal terrace, where guests may sip a rosé or a café au lait any time of the day. The establishment also offers what vies to be the least expensive parking in the South of France.

29 bl Maréchal Joffre. ✆ **04-93-01-01-40.** www.lehavrebleu.com. 19 units. 70€–95€ double. Parking 8€. **Amenities:** Bar; free Wi-Fi.

Royal Riviera ★ At last, a bona-fide Riviera luxury hotel with all the trappings, yet none of the pretention. The palatial splendor of the Royal Riviera's interior is paired with contemporary elegance inside the light, airy guestrooms. Rooms and suites inside the ancient Orangerie annex are even cooler, calmer, and quieter. Two factors mark the Royal Riviera out from other hotels in the area: location and facilities. Guests may take a short stroll into Beaulieu, Villefranche, or St-Jean-Cap-Ferrat, or simply wander along the private beach and through the flower-filled gardens. The hotel's low-key friendliness extends to kids, too, who may enjoy treasure hunts, waterskiing lessons, and pottery workshops while grown-ups lounge at the gigantic pool.

3 av Jean Monnet. ✆ **04-93-76-31-00.** www.royal-riviera.com. 94 units. 170€–850€ double; from 630€ suite. Parking 15€. **Amenities:** 2 restaurants; bar; babysitting; concierge; exercise room; indoor pool; outdoor pool; private beach; room service; spa; free Wi-Fi.

Where to Eat

The African Queen ★ FRENCH/INTERNATIONAL A lively mix of yachties, celebrity patrons, and excellent cuisine makes this portside restaurant perennially popular. Wood-fired pizzas are superb; the finely chopped *salade Niçoise* is dressed at your table; the sole *meunière* is a buttery classic. Service can be erratic, but both the menu and the atmosphere are a delight. Celebrity-spotting opportunities abound all summer long.

Port de Plaisance. ✆ **04-93-01-10-85.** www.africanqueen.fr. Pizzas 12€–28€; main courses 12€–80€. Daily noon–midnight. Closed some holidays.

Pignatelle ★ FRENCH A neighborhood favorite that spills out from a rustic dining room onto a simple, sunny terrace. La Pignatelle's à la carte selection and bargain fixed-price menus don't do pretention. Solid yet sublime starters include smoked salmon crêpes, frog's legs with parsley sauce, and garlic-laced escargot. Mains won't earn a Michelin star but have already won the hearts of local French diners: think roast rabbit with Dijon mustard, and cod with aïoli Provençal.

10 rue de Quincenet. ✆ **04-93-01-03-37.** www.lapignatelle.fr. Main courses 17€–28€; fixed-price lunch 15.50€; fixed-price dinner menu 24€–36€. Thurs–Tue noon–2pm and 7–10pm (Nov–Mar closed Wed & Thurs).

Exploring Beaulieu

All of Beaulieu's (admittedly low-key) action takes place between two almost entirely public beaches: Plage des Fourmis near Cap-Ferrat and La Petite Afrique to the east of town. The rococo resort's ancient casino, age-old cafes, and daily market lie in between. Beaulieu's luxury marina is a fine place for a stroll. Its long line of alfresco harbor restaurants get progressively cheaper as you wander eastwards towards the sands of La Petite Afrique.

Villa Kérylos ★★ HISTORIC HOME/MUSEUM This replica ancient Greek residence, constructed between 1902 and 1908, was painstakingly designed by archaeologist and devoted Hellenophile Theodore Reinach. Both indoors and out, the villa is a fastidiously flawless copy of a second-century Greek home. All period furniture was re-created using traditional Greek methods, while various rooms incorporated 20th-century conveniences, such as running water in the villa's *balaneion,* or thermal baths. The bucolic waterside gardens are dotted with olive and pomegranate trees and offer sweeping vistas over nearby Cap-Ferrat.

Impasse Gustave Eiffel. © **04-93-01-01-44.** www.villa-kerylos.com. Admission 11.50€ adults, 9€ students and children 7–17, free for children 6 and under. July–Aug daily 10am–7pm; Mar–June and Sept–Oct daily 10am–6pm; Nov–Feb Mon–Fri 2–6pm, Sat–Sun 10am–6pm.

EZE & LA TURBIE ★★

942km (584 miles) S of Paris; 11km (6¾ miles) NE of Nice

The hamlets of Eze and La Turbie, 6.5km (4 miles) apart, are picture-perfect hill villages that literally cling to the mountains. Both have fortified medieval cores overlooking the coast, and both were built during the early Middle Ages to stave off raids from Saracen pirates. In Eze's case, it's now tour buses that make daily invasions into town. Impossibly cute streets contain galleries, boutiques, and artisans' shops. La Turbie is much quieter, offering a welcome respite from the coast's summertime heat.

Essentials

ARRIVING **Trains** connect Eze-sur-Mer with Nice, Monaco, and the rest of the Côte d'Azur every 30 minutes. You may take a taxi from here up 427m (1,400 ft.) to Eze; alternatively, bus no. 83 connects the rail station with the hilltop village. For rail information, visit www.voyages-sncf.com or call © **36-35. Bus** line no. 82 runs between Nice and Eze around every 90 minutes, while five to seven daily buses (no. 116) connect Nice and La Turbie. Both journeys take 40 minutes. One-way fares cost 1.50€. For all bus information and schedules, contact **Lignes d'Azur** (www.lignesdazur.com; © **08-10-06-10-06**). By **car** from Nice, take the spellbindingly pretty D6007 (the *moyenne corniche*) east.

VISITOR INFORMATION Eze's **Office de Tourisme** is on place du Général-de-Gaulle, Eze-Village (www.eze-tourisme.com; © **04-93-41-26-00**). La Turbie's small **tourist information point** is at 2 place Detras, La Turbie (www.ville-la-turbie.fr; © **04-93-41-21-15**).

[FastFACTS] EZE & LA TURBIE

ATMs/Banks **Société Générale,** place de la Colette, Eze 06360 (© **04-92-41-51-10**); **BNP Paribas,** 6 av Général de Gaulle, La Turbie 06360 (© **08-20-82-00-01**).

Mail & Postage **La Poste,** av. du Jardin Exotique, Eze 06360; **La Poste,** place Neuve, La Turbie 06360; both © **36-31.**

Pharmacies **Pharmacie Lecoq,** place Colette, Eze 06360 (© **04-93-41-06-17**); **Pharmacie de La Turbie,** 6 av Général de Gaulle, La Turbie 06360 (© **04-93-41-16-50**).

Where to Stay

Château de la Chèvre d'Or ★★★ No hotel better sums up the glamour and grace of the French Riviera than La Chèvre d'Or. This resort hotel is built into and around the elegant hilltop town of Eze. Each sumptuously decorated suite is a grand apartment with a panoramic view of the coastline. It's a habitual favorite of royalty and A-listers, and recent makeovers have made it popular with vacationing families and young hipsters as well. The 38 terraced gardens drip down the hill towards the Mediterranean to ensure absolute privacy—indeed there's a ratio of one garden and three staff members to each room or suite. The best thing about La Chèvre d'Or? That would be the eponymous double-Michelin-starred **restaurant** overseen by top chef Ronan Kervaree (fixed-price menus 80€–230€). Experimental dishes include a vegan square decorated with an edible garden of herbs and flowers; San Remo shrimp wrapped in oyster-infused gossamer-thin pasta; and baby lamb shot through with parsley and violet.

Rue du Barri. ✆ **04-92-10-66-66.** www.chevredor.com. 37 units. 300€–610€ double; suites from 740€–2,600€ suite. Parking 15€. Closed Dec–Feb. **Amenities:** 4 restaurants; bar; babysitting; exercise room; outdoor pool; room service; sauna; free Wi-Fi.

Where to Eat

Gascogne Café ★ FRENCH/ITALIAN On the main road just outside of Eze's fortified Old Town, this bustling eatery is a friendly spot to sample authentic local fare. The menu ranges from traditional flavors (homemade lasagna, sea bass on a bed of ratatouille) to more creative offerings (Asian-style rolls stuffed with snails and garlic cream). Tasty pizzas are also available. Ambience is decidedly casual.

151 av. de Verdun, place de la Collette, Eze 06360. ✆ **04-93-41-18-50.** www.gascogne-hotel-restaurant.fr. Main courses 10€–24€; fixed-price menus 17€–29€. Daily 12:30–3pm and 7:30–10pm.

Exploring Eze & La Turbie

Aside from its pretty lanes, the leading attraction in Eze is the **Jardin d'Eze** ★, 20 rue du Château (✆ **04-93-41-10-30**). Here exotic plants are interspersed with feminine sculptures by Jean Philippe Richard, all perched atop the town at 427m (1,400 feet. Admission is 6€ adults, 2.50€ students and ages 12 to 25, and free children 11 and under. In July and August, it's open daily 9am to 7:30pm; the rest of the year it opens daily at 9am and closes between 4 and 7pm, depending on the time of sunset.

La Turbie boasts an impressive monument erected by Roman emperor Augustus in 6 bc, the **Trophée des Alps (Trophy of the Alps)** ★. Still partially intact today, it was created to celebrate the subjugation of the French Alpine tribes by the Roman armies. The nearby **Musée du Trophée d'Auguste,** cours Albert-1er de Monaco (✆ **04-93-41-20-84**), is an interactive mini-museum containing finds from digs nearby, a historical 3D film, and details about the monument's restoration. Both the ruins and the museum are open Tuesday to Sunday mid-May to mid-September 9:30am to 1pm and 2:30 to 6:30pm, and mid-September to mid-May 10am to 1:30pm and 2:30 to 5pm. Admission to both sites is 5.50€ adults, free children 17 and under.

MONACO ★★

939km (582 miles) S of Paris; 18km (11 miles) E of Nice

This sunny stretch of coast became the property of the Grimaldi clan in 1297, when one Francesco Grimaldi tricked his way into the fortress protecting the harbor. The dynasty has maintained something resembling independence ever since. In recent decades the clan has turned Monaco into the world's chicest

The Principality of Monaco

city-state with its own mini-airport (with direct helicopter links to Nice and St-Tropez, no less).

Hemmed in by France on three sides and the Mediterranean on the fourth, this feudal anomaly harbors the world's greatest number of billionaires per capita. And as almost everybody knows, the Monégasques do not pay taxes. Celebrity exiles—including tennis player Rafael Nadal and racing driver Lewis Hamilton—are attracted by the tax regime, too. Nearly all of Monaco's revenue comes from banking, tourism, and gambling. Better still, in an astute feat of cunning, local residents aren't allowed to gamble away their inheritance, so visitors must bring a passport to play on the Principality's famed poker, roulette, and blackjack tables.

Monaco, or, more precisely, its capital of Monte Carlo, has for a century been a symbol of glamour. The 1956 marriage of Prince Rainier III to actress Grace Kelly enhanced its status. She met the prince when she was in Cannes to promote "To Catch a Thief." Their daughter, Caroline, was born in 1957; a son, Albert, in 1958; and a second daughter, Stephanie, in 1965. The actress's life and times were recently relived on the silver screen in "Grace of Monaco." Starring Nicole Kidman as Grace Kelly, the movie opened at the 2014 Cannes Film Festival.

Prince Rainier was nicknamed the "Builder Prince" as he expanded Monaco by building into the Mediterranean. Prince Albert took over from his late father in 2005 and burnishes his "Eco-Prince" credentials with pride. Newer, more environmentally conscious land-reclamation schemes near the Fairmont Hotel were announced in 2014, and work starts on this man-made yacht-lined

ATTRACTIONS
Grimaldi Forum **10**
Monte-Carlo Casino & Opera **7**
Musée du Palais du Prince/
  Les Grands Appartements
  du Palais **3**
Musée Océanographique **4**
Nouveau Musée National
  de Monaco **1** & **11**

HOTELS
Fairmont
  Monte-Carlo **8**
Hotel Ambassador **2**
Hotel de Paris **6**

RESTAURANTS
Le Café de Paris **9**
Le Loga **12**
Le Louis XV **6**
Le Saint Benoit **5**

Monaco

Church †
Information *(i)*
Post Office ✉

peninsula soon. The Principality also has its own green car manufacturer, Venturi—although this marquee specializes in a typically Monégasque market for all-electric supercars.

Fortunately for the Grimaldi line, Albert married his girlfriend, South African swimmer Charlene Wittstock, in July 2011, now Her Serene Highness The Princess of Monaco. Despite rumors of a pre-wedding fallout, the couple are idolized in the Principality. Following a hasty course in both Monégasque dialect and European court protocol, Princess Charlene is now a familiar sight at society events. The royal couple's official portrait has pride of place in every bar, hotel, and bakery in the land.

469

Essentials

ARRIVING Monaco has rail, bus, highway—and helicopter—connections from other coastal cities, particularly Nice. There are no border formalities when entering Monaco from France. The 19km (12-mile) **drive** from Nice takes around 30 minutes and runs along the N7 Moyenne Corniche. The pretty D6098 coast road takes a little longer. **Lignes d'Azur** (www.lignesdazur.com; ☎ 08-10-06-10-06) runs a **bus** service at 15-minute intervals aboard line no. 100 from Nice to Monte Carlo. One-way bus transit from Nice costs 1.50€. **Trains** arrive every 30 minutes from Cannes, Nice, Menton, and Antibes. Monaco's underground railway station (*gare*) is on place St. Devote. A system of pedestrian tunnels, escalators, and elevators riddle the Principality, and such an underground walkway links the train station to Monte Carlo. The scheduled **chopper** service to Nice Airport costs 120€ via **Heli Air Monaco** (www.heliairmonaco.com; ☎ 92-05-00-50). By **bus** it's just 20€ (www.niceairportxpress.com; ☎ 04-97-00-07-00).

VISITOR INFORMATION The **Direction du Tourisme et des Congrés** tourist office is at 2A bd. des Moulins (www.visitmonaco.com; ☎ 92-16-61-16).

CITY LAYOUT The second-smallest state in Europe (Vatican City is the tiniest), Monaco consists of four parts. The Old Town, **Monaco-Ville,** on a rocky promontory 60m (197 ft.) high. It's the seat of the Prince's Palace and the government building, as well as the Oceanographic Museum. To the west, **La Condamine** is at the foot of the Old Town, forming its ritzy harbor and port sector. This area also has an open-air daily market. Up from the port (Monaco is seriously steep) is **Monte Carlo,** the playground of royalty and celebrity, and the setting for the casino, the Tourist Office, and various luxurious hotels. The fourth part, **Fontvieille,** is a neat industrial suburb housing the Monaco Football club, which was purchased by Russian billionaire Dmitry Rybolovlev. Thanks to the Russian's financial backing, the club was promoted to the French premier league in 2013, and topped the table several times in 2014.

SPECIAL EVENTS Two of the most-watched **car-racing events** in the world take place here in January (**Le Rallye**) and May (the **Grand Prix**); see www.acm.mc and www.formula1monaco.com. The **Monte-Carlo Masters** ATP tennis tournament (www.monte-carlorolexmasters.com) takes place in April. The **Monte-Carlo International Fireworks Festival** lasts all summer long. The skies above the harbor are lit up several times a week as millions of euros go up in smoke, courtesy of those who can assuredly afford it.

[Fast FACTS] MONACO

ATMs/Banks Among many others, there are several banks along boulevard Albert 1er behind the Port of Monaco.

Internet Access **Bilig Café,** 11 rue Princesse Caroline (☎ 97-98-20-43).

Mail & Postage **La Poste,** place de la Mairie in Monte-Carlo (☎ 36-31).

Pharmacies **Pharmacie Internationale,** 22 rue Grimaldi (☎ 04-93-50-35-99).

Getting Around

BY FOOT   Aside from two very steep hills, the world's second-smallest country is **pedestrian-friendly.** Hardy local Jean-Marc Ferrie at **Monaco Rando** (www.monaco-rando.com; ✆ **06-30-12-57-03**) organizes **guided hikes** around his hometown from 10€ per person with an interpreter in-tow.

BY TAXI   Taxis wait outside Monaco train station, or call ✆ **08-20-20-98-98.**

BY PUBLIC TRANSPORT   CAM (www.cam.mc; ✆ **97-70-22-22**) runs buses inside the Principality. Line nos. 1 and 2 link Monaco-Ville with the casino area. CAM's **solar-powered shuttle boat** hops between the banks of Monaco's port every 20 minutes. The ride is great for kids and connects the casino area with the foot of Monaco-Ville. All CAM tickets cost 2€.

BY OPEN-TOP BUS   Monaco–Le Grand Tour (www.monacolegrandtour.com; ✆ **97-70-26-36**) open-top minibuses allow visitors to hop on and hop off at the Principality's 12 main sights. Day passes cost 18€ adults; 7€ children between 4 and 11; free children under 4.

BY ELECTRIC CAR   It may be the land of the gas-guzzling Grand Prix, but Monaco is a global pioneer in green technology and is justly proud of its eco-credentials. Join the club with a rented two-person **Renault Twizy** (a super-tiny electric car; 50€ for 4 hr.) or an **Estrimo Brio** (an even cuter electric buggy; same rates) from **MC Eco Rental** (www.mc-eco-rental.com; ✆ **06-80-86-54-09**). These electric cars enjoy complimentary parking anywhere in Monaco. Guests renting either vehicle for more than 2 hours may have them delivered to their hotel for free.

BY LUXURY CAR   Of course, nothing shouts Monaco more than a rented **Ferrari California** (1,500€ per day) or a **Porsche 911** (790€ per day). Reserve your ride with **Elite Rentacar** (www.eliterent.com; ✆ **97-77-17-37**).

> ## Earth Calling Monaco
>
> To call Monaco from within France, dial 00 (the access code for all international long-distance calls from France); followed by the **country code, 377;** and then the eight-digit local phone number. (Don't dial 33; that's the country code for France.)

Where to Stay

Fairmont Monte Carlo ★★   This five-star hotel is easily Monaco's most fun. It combines fine-dining restaurants, a spa, and a rooftop pool with an unstuffy attitude; albeit one backed by a legion of ever-smiling, mostly Italian, staff. Of course, this vision of modern opulence is also one of the most valuable pieces of real estate on the Côte d'Azur. It dips into the Mediterranean from behind the Casino de Monte-Carlo—indeed, a private passageway runs to the casino's rear entrance—and guests may combine the endless breakfast with the best sea views in the Principality. Formula 1 fans should also note that the fastest part of the Monaco Grand Prix zips right beneath the basement. The Fairmont also has a partnership with four local beach clubs, where families are dropped off with towels, mineral water, and sun spray, then picked up on demand. Diners are in for a treat, too. Choose between bistro **Saphir**, Japanese atelier **Nobu** (opened in 2013), and rooftop Italian restaurant **Horizonte** (newly opened in 2014).

12 av. des Spélugues. ✆ **93-50-65-00.** www.fairmont.com/montecarlo. 602 units. 279€–879€ double; from 889€ suite. Parking 50€. **Amenities:** 3 restaurants; 2 bars; babysitting; concierge;

health club; 1 outdoor pool; room service; spa; Wi-Fi (20€/day or free if you enroll in the Fairmont President Club at no charge at check-in).

Hôtel Ambassador ★   A 5-minute stroll from the main Monaco action, the Ambassador makes a bargain base from which to explore the Principality. Elegant guestrooms benefit from a recent style overhaul. Dimensions are tiny, however (but heh, the entire country occupies less than 1 sq. mile, so little wonder). A buffet breakfast (included in the price) is offered next door in the cheap and tasty **P&P** restaurant and pizzeria.

10 avenue Prince Pierre, Monaco 98000. ✆ **97-97-96-96.** www.ambassadormonaco.com. 35 units. 110€–225€ double. Parking 18€. **Amenities:** Bar; free WiFi.

Hôtel de Paris ★★★   Never has so much history and glamour been suffused into 182 effortlessly chic guest rooms. La Prairie products and free access to the **Thermes Marins spa** (p. 476) come as standard in all of them. Accommodation culminates in two splendid super-suites, one of which, the "Churchill," overlooks the harbor and features Sir Winston's furniture. The former British Prime Minister used to sneak along a secret rooftop passageway to **Le Grill,** one of three award-winning restaurants in the hotel (see also the Louis XV, below). If that isn't enough, the Hôtel de Paris boasts several sister hotels, including the five-star family friendly **Monte-Carlo Beach Hotel** (www.monte-carlo-beach. com; ✆ **93-28-66-66**)—whose **Restaurant Elsa** received the region's first 100 percent organic certificate in 2013—and the imposingly elegant **Hôtel Hermitage** (www.hotelhermitagemontecarlo.com; ✆ **98-06-40-00**), just around the corner.

Place du Casino, Monaco 98007. ✆ **98-06-30-00.** www.montecarloresort.com. 182 units. 475€–1,400€ double; from 775€ suite. Valet parking 40€. **Amenities:** 3 restaurants (see Le Louis XV under "Where to Eat," below); bar; babysitting; concierge; exercise room; large indoor pool; room service; sauna; Thermes Marins spa offering thalassotherapy; Wi-Fi (free in lobby, or 20€/day).

Where to Eat

Pinch yourself. This postcard-sized Principality boasts a total of seven Michelin stars, and includes the most highly rated eatery on the entire Mediterranean, Le Louis XV.

Le Café de Paris ★ MODERN FRENCH   Pricey, pretentious, and ever-popular, this Parisian-style restaurant-cafe on place du Casino has a location to die for. The menu has taken on an even more classic edge under head chef Jean-Claude Brugel, who trained alongside several top Riviera chefs including Roger Vergé and Joël Garault. Simple starters like garlic escargot and *croque-monsieur* share the menu with more innovative mains like filet of plaice (a North Sea fish) with pumpkin purée or steak tartare. From October to March, a special seafood stall dispenses Oléron oysters, sea urchins, and platters of chilled crab to passersby.

Place du Casino. ✆ **98-06-76-23.** Main courses 15€–49€; fixed-price menu 35€. Daily 8am–2am.

Le Loga ★ MEDITERRANEAN   This locals-only find is one of the best—not to mention cheapest—places to find *barbajuans*, the Monégasque national dish of ravioli stuffed with ricotta and chard. A tea room-cum-bistro, it's ever popular with ladies who lunch (and shop) on the boulevard des Moulins. Le Loga's Italian chef busts out home-made saffron gnocchi, brésaola pressed beef, and classic

Milanese schnitzel. Dine inside the hipster tearoom interior or outside on the south-facing street terrace.

25 boulevard des Moulins. ☎ **93-30-87-72.** Main courses 11€–21€; fixed-price lunch 22€; fixed-price menu 38€. Mon, Tue, Thu–Sat noon–2:30pm and 7–11pm, Wed noon–2:30pm. Closed middle 2 weeks Aug.

Le Louis XV ★★★ MEDITERRANEAN   In the Hôtel de Paris, the Louis XV offers one of the finest dining experiences on the Riviera, and thus the world. Superstar chef Alain Ducasse oversees the refined but not overly adorned cuisine. The restaurant's head chef, Franck Cerutti, can be seen in Nice's market buying local cheeses or wandering through the corridors of the Hôtel de Paris carrying white truffles purchased from Italy. Everything is light and attuned to the seasons, with intelligent, modern interpretations of Provençal and northern Italian dishes. You'll find chargrilled breast of baby pigeon with sautéed duck liver, and a specialty known as Provençal vegetables with crushed truffles, all served under a magnificent frescoed ceiling, which includes the portraits of Louis XV's six mistresses. The restaurant celebrated 25 years as the Principality's top eatery in 2013.

In the Hôtel de Paris, place du Casino. ☎ **98-06-88-64.** Jacket and tie recommended for men. Main courses 80€–160€; fixed-price lunch 145€, dinner 230€–310€. Thurs–Mon 12:15–1:45pm and 8–9:45pm. Closed first 2 weeks Mar.

Le Saint Benoit ★ MEDITERRANEAN   This restaurant is a seafood specialist with an esteemed reputation and panoramic view over Monaco Port, the rock of Monte-Ville, and the Mediterranean, albeit one with charming staff and extremely honest prices. The two-course lunch—which may include foie gras ravioli in a cep sauce followed by roast turbot—must rank as one of Monaco's best bargains. *Sole meunière* and platters of oysters grace the more traditional à la carte menu. Come spring, Le Saint Benoit's canvas roof and glass walls are taken away to reveal a sun-kissed dining terrace. The only tricky thing is finding the place: follow our map and the restaurant's knee-height street signs, or ride the elevator up from avenue d'Ostende.

10 avenue de la Costa. ☎ **93-25-02-34.** Main courses 19€–38€; fixed-price lunch 22€; fixed-price dinner menus 31€-42€. Tue–Sat 10am–2pm and 7:30–10:30pm, Sun noon–3pm.

Exploring Monaco

Monaco's main sights—including its glamorous port, casino, and hotels—are clustered around the pedestrianized Place du Casino Square. Its principal museums, including the Prince's Palace and Oceanographic Museum, are situated on the history-laden rock of Monaco-Ville.

Les Grands Appartements du Palais ★ PALACE   The home of Monaco's royal family, the Palais du Prince dominates the Principality from the Rock. A tour of the Grands Appartements—with audio tour recorded by none other than Prince Albert himself—allows visitors to glimpse the Throne Room and artworks by Bruegel and Holbein. The palace was built in the 13th century, and some of it dates from the Renaissance. The ideal time to arrive is 11:55am, so you can watch the 10-minute **Relève de la Garde (Changing of the Guard).** Summer concerts by the **Monte-Carlo Philharmonic Orchestra** are held outside in the courtyard.

Place du Palais. ☎ **93-25-18-31.** www.palais.mc. Admission 8€ adults, 4€ children 8–14, free for children 7 and under. Daily Apr–Oct 10am–6pm. Closed Nov–Mar.

Place du Casino Square

Musée Océanographique de Monaco ★ AQUARIUM   This mammoth oceanfront museum was founded by Albert I, great-grandfather of the present prince, in 1910. It's now a living, breathing science lesson covering the world's oceans by way of a Mediterranean aquarium, tropical tanks, and a shark reserve. A delight for budding marine scientists is the 18m-long (60-ft.) whale skeleton that washed up on a local beach a century ago. Equally as compelling are the scientific specimens brought up from the ocean depths over the past 100 years.

Av. St-Martin. ☎ **93-15-36-00.** www.oceano.mc. Admission 14€ adults, 7€ children 4–18, free for children 3 and under. Apr–June and Sept daily 10am–7pm; July–Aug daily 10am–8:30pm; Oct–Mar daily 10am–6pm.

Nouveau Musée National de Monaco ★★ ART MUSEUM   Over the past decade Monaco has touted its cultural credentials to attract a savvier, younger, and more artistically aware crowd. The new Villa Sauber and Villa Paloma museums are two stunning art spaces set in palatial former homes across the city from one another. Both bring in global culture vultures by the score by way of contemporary-art exhibitions and shows covering sculpture, architecture, photography, and the glamorous history of the French Riviera.

Villa Sauber, 17 av. Princess Grace; Villa Paloma, 56 bd. du Jardin Exotique. ☎ **98-98-16-82.** www.nmnm.mc. Admission to both 6€ adults, free entrance for visitors 26 and under. June–Sept daily 11am–7pm; Oct–May daily 8am–6pm.

Opéra de Monte-Carlo ★ OPERA HOUSE   Monaco takes music seriously. In 2014 Robbie Williams played live to sell-out crowds. The Principality's lavish Opera House sits next to the casino, where its Salle Garnier hosts rock, pop, classical, and opera events—and even hosted the wedding reception of Prince Albert and Charlene Wittstock in 2011. For big-hitting pop and DJ events, try the **Grimaldi Forum,** 10 av. Princesse-Grace (www.grimaldiforum.com; ☎ **99-99-20-00**).

Place du Casino. ☏ **98-06-28-28.** www.opera.mc. Year-round admission prices 20€–120€ adults, reduced entrance for visitors 26 and under.

Outdoor Activities

BEACHES Just outside the border on French soil, the **Monte-Carlo Beach Club** adjoins the **Monte-Carlo Beach Hotel,** 22 av. Princesse-Grace (www.monte-carlo-beach.com; ☏ **93-28-66-66**), a five-star sister establishment of the ultra-elegant Hôtel de Paris. Princess Grace used to frolic on the beach here, and today it's an integral part of Monaco social life. It now has an Olympic-size swimming pool, a La Prairie spa, cabanas, a poolside fine dining restaurant called Le Deck, and a low-key Mediterranean restaurant called La Vigie. Sea Lounge is an afternoon and late-evening club featuring live DJs and *nargile* hubble-bubble pipes. Beach activities include donuts, jet skis, and parachute rides. As the temperature drops in late October, the beach closes for the winter. The admission charge of 60€ to 150€, depending on the season, grants you access to changing rooms, toilets, restaurants, and bar, along with use of a mattress for sunbathing.

More low-key swimming and sunbathing is also available at **Plage du Larvotto,** off avenue Princesse-Grace. Part of this popular man-made strip of sand is public. The other part contains private beach clubs with bars, snacks, and showers, plus a kids' club. A jogging track runs behind the beach.

All-Night Glamour

Museums are all well and good, but to survey the soul of Monaco you need a credit card, a suntan, and a late-morning wake-up call. Early-evening glamour revolves around the bars that surround the historic port. Here, locally based luxury yacht agencies like **Y.CO** (www.ycoyacht.com; ☏ **93-50-12-12**) charter 50m-long (262 ft.) sailing craft for around $200,000 per week. At sundown the action moves uphill to Casino Square, where **Buddha Bar** (☏ **98-06-19-19**) is bedecked with chinoiserie, Asian statues, and a raised DJ booth. For sheer class, the **Crystal Bar** (☏ **98-06-98-99**) inside the Hôtel Hermitage pulls out all the stops. Elegant dress, vintage champagne, and the odd feather boa set the scene until 1am. **Le Bar Américain** (☏ **98-06-38-38**), in the Hôtel de Paris, is far more raucous, with chillingly expensive cocktails and nightly jazz. Across place du Casino, the timeless superclub **Jimmy'z** (☏ **98-06-36-36**), open nightly

11pm to 5am, has attracted stars from Farrah Fawcett to George Clooney. But it's the mythical **Casino de Monte-Carlo** (www.montecarlocasinos.com; ☏ **98-06-21-21**) that lends the square its name. Since 2012, the casino's marble-floored Atrium has been open—for free—to all comers from 2pm who wish to shoot slots or play blackjack in the hallowed Salle des Amériques or try their luck at roulette in the Salle Europe. For roulette, *trente et quarante,* and Texas Hold'em in the private areas of rococo Salon Touzet and Salon Médecin, gamers must pay a 10€ fee. Entrance to Les Salons Supers Privés is by invitation only (heh, they've got our number!) and requires smart dress and nerves of steel. Another great summer addition is the Casino de Monte-Carlo **alfresco** terrace. Here visitors may play roulette and poker overlooking the moonlit Mediterranean. Now *that's* glamorous.

Attacking the Plastic

If you insist on the likes of Hermès, Gucci, and Lanvin, you'll find them cheek by jowl near the Hôtel de Paris and the Casino de Monte-Carlo. But the prize for Monaco's hippest store goes to **Lull,** 29 rue de Millo (☎ **97-77-54-54**), awash in labels like Dries Van Noten and Raf Simons. Almost next door, **Une Femme à Suivre** (☎ **97-77-10-52**) sells French classics from the likes of Tara Jarman and Mariona Gen. Just west of Casino Square, **Pretty You,** 5 place Saint James (☎ **97-70-48-08**), vends Oscar de la Renta and Elie Saab. Just east of this piazza, **Galeries du Métropole** is packed with high fashion and specialty stores. As well as Dunhill and Gant, try **McMarket** (☎ **97-77-12-12**). Serious labels in this fashion emporium include Balenciaga, Louboutin, and Jimmy Choo. **FNAC** (☎ **08-25-02-00-20**) is recommended for English-language novels, Monaco history books, and the latest electronics. Heading east from Casino Square, **boulevard de Moulins** sells "everyday" Monaco labels. We're talking **Baby Dior,** no. 31 (☎ **97-25-72-12**) and swimwear-to-the-stars brand **Erès,** also at no. 31 (☎ **97-70-76-50**). For Repetto ballet slippers and Michael Kors satchels try **La Botterie,** no. 15 (☎ **97-25-80-55**). For real-people shopping, stroll **rue Grimaldi,** the Principality's most commercial street, near the fruit, flower, and food market at **place des Armes,** which is open daily from 7:30am until noon.

SPA TREATMENTS The century-old **Thermes Marins,** 2 av. de Monte-Carlo (www.thermesmarinsmontecarlo.com; ☎ **98-06-69-00**), reopened in summer 2014. It embodies wellness at its most chic. Spread over four floors is a pool, Turkish *hammam* (steam bath), healthy restaurant, juice bar, tanning booths, fitness center, beauty center, and private treatment rooms. A day pass, giving access to the sauna, steam rooms, fitness facilities, and pools is 90€. Therapies include an hour-long Dead Sea salt peel for 150€.

SWIMMING Overlooking the yacht-studded harbor, the **Stade Nautique Rainier-III,** quai Albert-1er, at La Condamine (☎ **93-30-64-83**), a pool frequented by the Monégasques, was a gift from Prince Rainier to his subjects. It's open May to October daily 9am to 6pm (until 8pm June–Aug). Admission costs 5.30€ per person. Between November and March, it's an ice-skating rink.

TENNIS & SQUASH The **Monte Carlo Country Club,** 155 av. Princesse-Grace, Roquebrune-Cap Martin, France (www.mccc.mc; ☎ **04-93-41-30-15**), has 21 clay and 2 concrete tennis courts. The 43€ fee provides access to a restaurant, health club with Jacuzzi and sauna, putting green, beach, squash courts, and well-maintained tennis courts. Guests of the hotels administered by the Société des Bains de Mer (Hôtel de Paris, Hermitage, Monte Carlo Bay, and Monte Carlo Beach Club) pay half-price. It's open daily 8am to 8 or 9pm, depending on the season.

MENTON ★★

963km (559 miles) S of Paris; 30km (19 miles) E of Nice

Pack your shades. For the Belle Époque resort of Menton is the sunniest place in all France. It's no surprise that this balmy locale hosts both a winter lemon

THE SENTIER LE CORBUSIER coastal trail

Cap-Martin is the fabulously rich spit of land between Monaco and Menton. Not as glitzy as Cap-Ferrat nor as fabled as Cap d'Antibes, its beauty lies in a 2-hour-long coastal trail that loops past the gardens of countless billionaires. This seaside path is as historical as it is beautiful. It was named after Le Corbusier, the zany French architect who built an urban utopia in Marseille before constructing a coastal retreat here.

The **Sentier le Corbusier** path extends between Pointe du Cap-Martin to the eastern frontier of Monaco. If you have a car, you can park it in the lot at avenue Winston-Churchill, and begin your stroll. A sign labeled PROMENADE LE CORBUSIER marks the path. As you hike along, you'll take in a view of Monaco set in a natural amphitheater. In the distance, you'll see Cap-Ferrat and, high above, Roquebrune village.

The final stages of the path run past Corbusier's **Cabanon** log cabin, which was created by the architect to showcase his love of low-impact prefabricated living spaces. Guided visits can be arranged with the Roquebrune Tourist Office (www.roquebrune-cap-martin.com;

✆ **04-93-35-62-87;** admission 10€ adults, 6€ children aged 12–18, free for children aged 12 and under). Almost next door is the **Villa E-1027.** This modernist beach home was designed in 1924 by the famed Irish architect Eileen Gray and is due to reopen to the public in 2015.

The scenic path ends at Monte-Carlo Beach and passes several secret sandy coves en-route. Walkers may then take the line no. 100 bus back to their rough starting point. An alternative is to return on foot from either Monte-Carlo Beach or Roquebrune-Cap-Martin train station, following the walking signs back through the Parc des Oliviers, which occupies the central spine of Cap-Martin.

festival and the finest botanical gardens in the country. Liberal sprinklings of sun, sand, and citrus also attracted artists by the dozens, among them Picasso, Matisse, and Jean Cocteau. The brand-new Musée Cocteau dedicated to the latter artist makes the town worth visiting alone.

The aptly named Promenade du Soleil runs in front of Menton's Old City, port and casino. Game guests may follow this seaside boulevard all the way into Monaco—provided they have a spare 90 minutes and a sturdy set of legs.

Essentials

ARRIVING **Trains** run to Menton from Nice, Monaco, the rest of the Côte d'Azur en route, and right into Italy every 30 minutes. For **rail** information, visit www.voyages-sncf.com or call ✆ **36-35. Bus** line no. 100 to Nice runs every 15 minutes until 8pm. One-way fares costs 1.50€. For bus information and schedules, contact **Lignes d'Azur** (www.lignesdazur.com; ✆ **08-10-06-10-06**). By **car** from Nice, take D6098 (the *basse corniche*) east.

VISITOR INFORMATION The **Office de Tourisme** occupies a magnificent Belle Époque building near the Train Station at 8 avenue Boyer (www.tourisme-menton.fr; ✆ **04-92-41-76-76**).

[FastFACTS] MENTON

ATMs/Banks   **Crédit Mutuel,** 24 rue de la République (© **32-25**).

Internet Access   For free WiFi, hit **Menton Tourist Office,** which maintains its own wireless hotspot.

Mail & Postage   **La Poste,** 2 cours George V (© **36-31**).

Pharmacies   **Pharmacie Otto,** place St Roch (© **04-93-35-70-16**).

Where to Stay

Hôtel Palm Garavan ★   The prize for the friendliest hotel in Menton goes to the Palm Garavan. Superior rooms boast cracking views over the resort's botanical gardens, while guests may also gaze at Italy in their bathrobes. The spotless modern accommodation boasts touch-sensitive lights and ice-white decor. A top touch is the 3.50€ express breakfast, offering early-bird guests a croissant and cappuccino before they hit the resort's gardens, art museums, and beach.

3 porte de France. © **04-93-78-80-67.** www.hotel-menton-garavan.fr. 19 units. 75€–160€ double. Parking 10€. **Amenities:** Bar; free Wi-Fi.

Hôtel Royal Westminster ★   A grand hotel without the grand prices, the venerable Westminster has a plum emplacement, facing due south towards the shimmering Mediterranean in the epicenter of town. Attracting an older clientele, guests may relax in the genteel front gardens or in the various lobby bars. The hotel boasts a library and billiards room, too.

28 avenue Félix Faure. © **04-93-28-69-69.** www.hotel-royal-westminster.com. 92 units. 80€–215€ double. Parking 12€. **Amenities:** Bar; concierge; library; restaurant; free Wi-Fi.

Where to Eat

A mere mile from the Italian border, Menton does pizza and pasta with aplomb. For more exotic fare laced with Menton lemons and offerings from the Ligurian fishing fleet, sail in to one of the eateries below.

La Pergola ★ MEDITERRANEAN   Open since 1902, it's doubtful as to whether La Pergola has changed its menu over the last century. And that's no bad thing. Vast platters of *fritto misto* seafood, grilled fish, salt-baked sea bream, and *paella de la mer* are heaved from the kitchen to the sand-in-the-toes tables. Local wines by the jug and a hotlist of ten daily specials make for a beach blowout that won't break the bank—a rarity on the French Riviera. This beach bar also possesses a line of sun loungers, which can be rented for a post-prandial siesta year-round.

4 promenade de la Mer. © **04-93-35-44-72.** Main courses 12€–26€. Fixed-price menus 40€. Daily noon–3pm and 6–11:30pm.

Restaurant Mirazur ★★ MODERN MEDITERRANEAN   The awards have rolled in for Mirazur's young Argentine chef Mauro Colagreco. Two Michelin stars. A place on San Pellegrino's World's 50 Best Restaurants list. The watchword on his multiple fixed-price menus (which range from a moderately priced lunchtime "Déjeuner" to the wallet-crunching "Carte Blanche") is élan, not experimentation. This is sleepy Menton after all. Expect tuna carpaccio with raspberries and almonds, langoustine decorated with edible flowers, and a heady volley of desserts topped with homemade marshmallows. Graceful service and a panoramic sea view over Menton Port complete this priceless picture.

30 avenue Aristide Briand. ✆ **04-92-41-86-86.** www.mirazur.fr. Main courses 39€–58€; fixed-price menus 49€–135€. Wed–Sun noon–2pm and 7:30–10pm. Closed mid-Nov to mid-Feb.

Al Vecchio Forno ★ ITALIAN   As authentic as a Neapolitan scooter, this established eatery serves Menton's Italian neighbors from just across the border. If the dress and dialect of its patrons shouts "Godfather," the pizza is just as genuine. Seasonal artichokes and *funghi* come from Italy, as does the mozzarella and sea bream. The latter is seared crisp alongside the pizzas in the wood-fired oven.
39 quai Bonaparte. ✆ **04-92-10-04-78.** Main courses 6€–19€. Daily noon–2pm and 7–11pm.

Exploring Menton

Mentonnaise are lucky devils. They can choose to hang out in the historic Old Town, on a very long beach, or on the seaside boulevard (the Promenade du Soleil). The resort's world-famous gardens all lie just behind this ocean walk. Meanwhile, Jean Cocteau's artist legacy is spread out along the seafront.

Jardin Val Rahmeh ★★★ GARDEN   Even if you loathe botanical gardens, and even if you only visit one in Menton (although the resort boasts five), we beg you to come here. Menton's microclimate has reared a leafy wonderland within its protective walls. Fragrant paths weave past giant Amazon water lillies, Buddha's Hand citruses from Thailand, and flowering *toromiro* trees from Easter Island. The scene is most magical within the black bamboo plantation, where sunlight dapples a babbling brook.
Route St Jacques. ✆ **04-93-35-86-72.** www.jardins-menton.fr. Admission 6€ adults, 4.50€ for children 16 and under. Apr–Sep Wed–Mon 10am–12:30pm and 3:30–6:30pm; Oct–Mar Wed–Mon 10am–12:30pm and 2–5pm.

Musée Jean Cocteau ★★★ MUSEUM   When not judging the Cannes Film Festival or chasing ballet dancers from the Monaco stage, *bon viveur* Jean Cocteau turned his artistic hand to painting on a grand scale. In 2011, many of his finest works were displayed in this oceanfront museum. Most of the 1,8000 exhibits were donated by Belgian-American collector Séverin Wunderman. These include canvases by Cocteau's friends Picasso, Modigliani, and Miró, plus movies shot by the Frenchman at the Villa Santo Sospir on Cap-Ferrat. Architect fans may note that the curvy, light-filled building that houses the Musée Jean Cocteau was designed by Rudy Ricciotti, who also styled the new MuCEM European and Mediterranean Museum in Marseille (see p. 400). A few blocks away, Cocteau's life-size love scenes inside Menton's **Salle des Marriages** (marriage office, Place Ardoïno; adults 2€, free to children under 18; open Mon–Fri 8:30am–noon and 2–4:30pm) earned him honorary citizenship of the town in 1958. Three years after Cocteau's death in 1963, the **Musée du Bastion** (Tue–Sun 10am–noon and 2–6pm) opened on Menton's seafront to showcase his final period of work.
2 quai de Monléon. ✆ **04-89-81-52-50.** www.museecocteaumenton.fr. Admission 8€ adults, free for children 18 and under. Wed–Mon 10am–6pm.

Outdoor Activities

BEACHES   The all-public Plage du Soleil pans west from Menton to Cap Martin. Private beach clubs are found on Plage du Garavan just east of town. All-day sun loungers at **Terenga Plage** (✆ **04-93-28-27-56**) and **Napoléon Plage** (✆ **04-92-10-92-60**) cost around 12€ per day.

BIKING The verdant hills around Menton are the training ground for several Tour de France cyclists. Lesser mortals may still peddle along the seafront from Italy to Monaco on a rented mountain bike (from 14€ per day) or electric bike (from 35€ per day) from **Bike Trip,** 1 avenue Carnot (www.rent-bike.fr, ✆ **04-94-96-48-93**), which also offers self-guided tour maps of the Menton Riviera.

SAILING From the end of April until October visitors may bob around the Bay of Menton on a paddleboard, kayak, or sailing dinghy available for rent from the **Centre Nautique de Menton** (www.voile-menton.fr, ✆ **04-93-35-49-70**), located beside beach bar La Pergola.

Shopping

Menton has an Italian heart, with the taste buds to match. The best place to start is the pedestrian-only **rue Saint Michel.** Try **Maison Larnicol** at no. 28 (✆ **04-93-97-80-92**) for chocolates; **Famille Mary** at no. 10 (✆ **04-92-09-19-43**) for flowery honey; or Menton-based **Oliviers & Co** at no. 5 (✆ **04-89-74-19-76**) for olive oil tastings. The town's most venerated product, its home-grown lemons, are served by two rival stores at no. 22 and no. 27. From the former, **Au Pays du Citron** (✆ **04-92-09-22-85**), purchase lemon soap and citrus liqueur. From the latter, **Coté Citron** (✆ **04-89-74-19-76**), find limoncello and marmalade. One of Menton's most charming stores is **Maison Herbin,** 2 rue Vieux Collège (www.confitures-herbin.com, ✆ **04-93-57-20-29**). Visitors can see local citrus turned into jams, chutneys, and candies in their adjoining sweet factory.

Nightlife

Sunny Menton hosts the highest number of retirees in France, so the resort doesn't exactly dance until dawn. However, the town buzzes all August during the **Menton Music Festival** (www.festival-musique-menton.fr), where evening classical concerts occupy over almost every Old Town square. Gamblers may also test their luck at the **Menton Casino,** at 2 avenue Félix Faure (www.lucien barriere.com; ✆ **04-92-10-16-16**). It boasts a traditional poker room as well as a vast seaview gaming terrace.

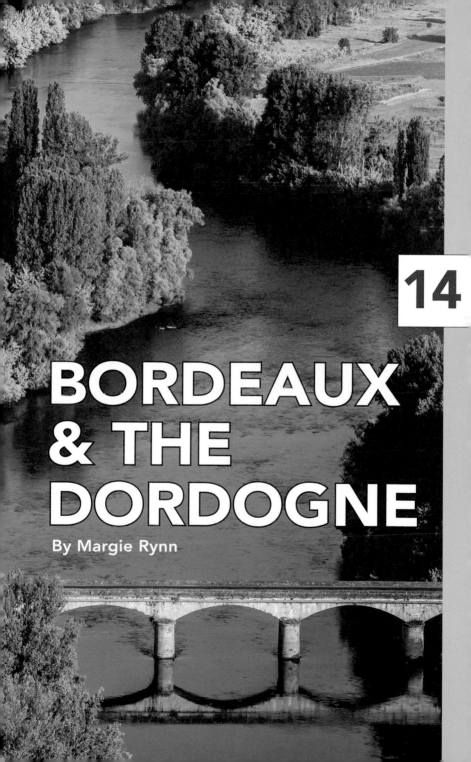

14

BORDEAUX & THE DORDOGNE

By Margie Rynn

The French southwest is famed for its food, its wine and its *joie de vivre*, but also for its sumptuous landscapes and cultural treasures. Bordeaux's 18th-century architecture, the vine-covered expanse of the wine country, and the lovely villages and castles that line the Dordogne River are all great reasons to visit the region, as are the enigmatic wall paintings left behind by Cro-Magnon ancestors in the caves at Lascaux and other prehistoric sites.

Aquitaine, as this southwestern chunk of France was dubbed by the Romans, has a long and torrid history. After an extended stay by Caesar and his minions, the region was invaded by Vandals, Visigoths, and even Arabs from nearby Al-Andalus. After a couple of centuries of relative calm, things got hot in the 12th century when Eleanor of Aquitaine went and married Henry Plantagenet, setting the stage for the Hundred Years' War, an endless struggle between the English and the French for domination of the region.

That turbulent period had a profound effect on the area's economy and architecture: tidily organized *bastides*, or fortified towns, still dot the countryside (like Montpazier and Sauveterre-de-Guyenne), and the English love of claret laid the foundation of the mighty wine trade that eventually built the sumptuous limestone mansions of Bordeaux. This is a lovely and accessible area to explore, though once you leave Bordeaux you'll probably want to rent a car to make the most of the countryside. That said, if you are *sans* wheels, you can also get around by train or bus, or if you are up for it, by bicycle or even by canoe (see box "Biking & Canoeing Down the Dordogne," below).

BORDEAUX ★★★

578km (358 miles) SW of Paris; 549km (340 miles) W of Lyon

Long called *La Belle Endormie* ("Sleeping Beauty"), over the last decade Bordeaux has at last woken up and is currently stretching its legs and fluffing its finery. First the **historic city center** was cleaned up, revealing the splendors of its harmonious 18th-century architecture. Then a nifty tramway (streetcar) system was installed, and cars were banished from most of the historic center. Finally, the **quays of the Garonne River** were given an extensive overhaul and are now lined with public gardens, fountains, and playgrounds. The city has reconnected with the river, as best symbolized by the stunning 18th-century **Place de la Bourse,** which opens directly on the banks and is now scrubbed down and bedecked with a "water mirror," a long, shallow fountain that you can walk and splash around in on sunny days.

As you move away from the center, elegant streets give way to narrow cobbled streets, ancient churches, and a more youthful, funky Bordeaux. Home to 70,000 students, one-third of the population is under 25, fueling a lively nightlife scene. The recent urban overhaul has bled into working-class neighborhoods like **Chartrons,** where you can find galleries, bars and restaurants.

PREVIOUS PAGE: **Medieval bridge over the Dordogne River**

Bordeaux, of course, is also a wine capital. Not only does it makes a great base for exploring a few of the **thousands of nearby wine estates,** but you can also taste not a few of the region's wares right here, particularly if you stop in at the **Maison du Vin** (see box "Buying Bordeaux in Bordeaux," below).

Essentials

ARRIVING   Bordeaux–Mérignac **airport** (www.bordeaux.aeroport.fr; ✆ **05-56-34-50-50** for flight information) is 15km (9¼ miles) west of the city in Mérignac. A **shuttle bus** (Jet'Bus) runs from the airport to the train station every 45 minutes (trip time: 55 min.). The one-way trip is 7€ adults, 6€ 25 and under, free children under 5. A **taxi** (✆ **05-56-96-00-34**) from the airport to the train station costs about 45€.

Some 15 to 30 high-speed TGV **trains** arrive from Paris each day; the trip takes 3½ hours and one-way fare is 77€–94€. Other rail connections include Toulouse, Avignon, Biarritz, and destinations in Spain. For train information, visit www.voyages-sncf.com or call ✆ **36-35.**

While Bordeaux is easy to reach by **car** (about a 6-hr. drive on the A10 autoroute from Paris; 2 hr. via the A62 from Toulouse; 2¼ hr. on the A63 from the Spanish border), you won't use it much once you get here as most of the historic center is closed to motorized traffic.

VISITOR INFORMATION   The **Office de Tourisme** is at 12 cours du 30-Juillet (www.bordeaux-tourisme.com; ✆ **05-56-00-66-00**), with a branch office in the Gare St-Jean (✆ **05-56-91-64-70**).

CITY LAYOUT   Bordeaux lays almost entirely on the western bank of the **Garonne River,** though there is a small up-and-coming neighborhood on the eastern bank, which can be accessed by the **Pont de Pierre** or the ferry. The historic center is rather compact and clusters near the river. Most hotels offer city maps to guests; you can also pick up a map at the tourist office.

Modern tram on the Place de la Comedie, Bordeaux

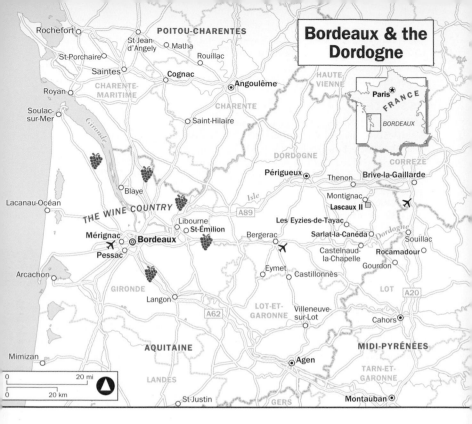

Getting Around

ON FOOT   With a good pair of comfortable shoes, you should be able to visit most sites on foot. If you want to explore more far-flung neighborhoods, or are just plain tired, you can easily get around town on the sleek new tram system (see below).

BY PUBLIC TRANSPORTATION   The new **tram** (streetcar) makes it a snap to get around the city. There are three lines (A, B, and C) that crisscross the town. The tram runs daily from 5am to 1am. Tickets (called "Tickarte") are good on the tram, the **city bus,** and the **ferry** that crosses the river, and cost 1.40€, transfers included during a 1-hour period. You can get a 5-ticket card for 5.90€, a 10-ticket card for 11.30€, as well as one-day pass for 4.30€ and a seven-day pass for 11.30€. Don't forget to validate your ticket once you are on board. For information, maps, and a phone app, visit www.infotbc.com or call ✆ **05-57-57-88-88.**

BY TAXI   As mentioned above, most of the city center is car-free, so taxis are only practical for longer distances. You must hail a taxi from a taxi stand, which can be found at the Place Gambetta, the Grand Théâtre, the Hôtel de Ville, and the Place de la Victoire. Or call Taxi-Tele at ✆ **05-56-96-00-34.**

[FastFACTS] BORDEAUX

ATMs/Banks There are plenty of banks in the historic center, including several ATMs on the cours de l'Intendance.

Doctors & Hospitals **Groupe Hospitalier Pellegrin,** Place Amélie Raba-Léon, (www.chu-bordeaux.fr; ✆ **05-56-79-56-79**).

Embassies & Consulates **American Presence Post,** 89 quai des Chartrons (http://bordeaux.usconsulate.gov; ✆ **05-56-48-63-85**), **British Consulate Bordeaux,** 353 bd. du President Wilson, (www.gov.uk; ✆ **05-57-22-21-10**).

Mail & Postage **La Poste,** 6 place Saint-Projet (✆ **36-31**).

Pharmacies **Pharmacie des Grands Hommes,** 1 place des Grands Hommes (✆ **05-56-81-70-90**). Pharmacy open 24/7: **Pharmacie des Capucins,** 30 place des Capucins (✆ **05-56-91-62-66**).

Safety The area around the Gare Saint Jean train station and Place des Victoires can get a little seedy at night.

Where to Stay

EXPENSIVE

Grand Hôtel de Bordeaux & Spa ★★★ After decades of neglect, the majestic Grand Hôtel was reborn in 2007, with an exquisite interior makeover by decor-maestro Jacques Garcia. Taking inspiration from its splendiferous neighbor, the Grand Théâtre, the lush decoration hints at 19th century theater trimmings, and the unusual color schemes gracefully blend the old and the new. The spa on the top floor goes even farther into the past—ancient Rome, to be exact, with red columns, black trim, and a mosaic pool with a ceiling that opens to the sky. There's a rooftop terrace with terrific view; in the warmer months it is a popular nightspot. There is a bistro as well as a gourmet restaurant, Le Pressoir d'Argent (see below).

2–5 place de la Comédie. ✆ **05-57-30-44-44.** www.ghbordeaux.com. 130 units. 320€–550€ double; 640€–3,000€ suite. Parking 35€. **Amenities:** 2 restaurants; 2 bars; business center, concierge; room service; tea room; spa; free Wi-Fi.

La Maison Bord'eaux ★★ In a quiet, residential area slightly out of the center, lies this chic hideaway, just across the street from a chunk of a 2nd-century Gallo-Roman arena, (the Palais Gallien). Back in the 18th century these buildings made up a postal relay; today the golden limestone facade hides a collection of comfortable, modern rooms with polished wood floors, contemporary furniture, and luscious colors on the walls. The "deluxe" rooms are particularly spacious; families can indulge in the "Apolline" suite on the top floor, which has a beautiful view and oodles of exposed beams. There are several plush salons on the ground level for reading, lounging, or participating in a wine tasting. **Note:** Only three rooms have elevator access.

111/113 rue Docteur Albert Barraud. ✆ **05-56-44-00-45.** www.lamaisonbord-eaux.com. 14 units. 180€–260€ double; 360€ family suite. Parking 15€. **Amenities:** Massage (by appointment); wine tastings; winery tours; free Wi-Fi.

MODERATE

Hôtel La Tour Intendance ★★★ On a quiet side street just a few steps away from the chic shops of the Cours de l'Intendance, this delightful hotel is an

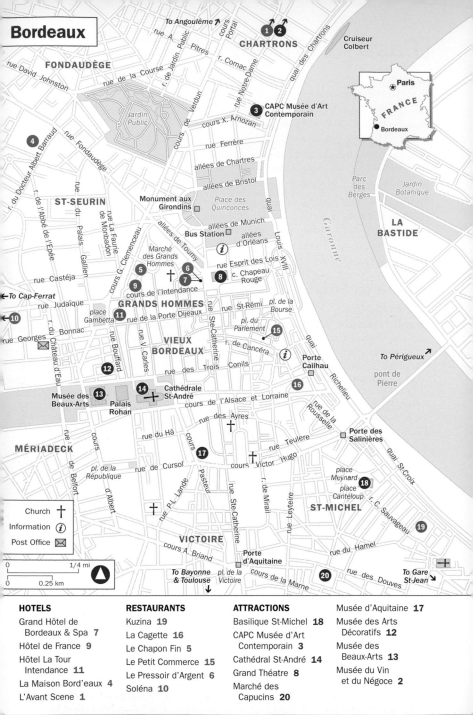

Bordeaux

FONDAUDÈGE

CHARTRONS

Cruiseur Colbert

To Angoulême ↗

CAPC Musée d'Art Contemporain

FRANCE

★ Paris

Bordeaux

Jardin Public

cours Portal

rue A.
Pitres
r. Cornac
r. Notre-Dame
cours de Verdun
rue de Jardin Public

quai des Chartrons

cours X. Arnozan

rue Ferrère

allées de Chartres

allées de Bristol

Place des Quinconces

Parc des Berges

Jardin Botanique

LA BASTIDE

ST-SEURIN

Monument aux Girondins

allées de Munich

Bus Station

allées d'Orléans

allées de Tourny

Marché des Grands Hommes

rue Esprit des Lois

c. Chapeau Rouge

Garonne

Louis XVIII

quai

GRANDS HOMMES

cours de l'Intendance

place Gambetta

rue de la Porte Dijeaux

rue St-Rémi

pl. de la Bourse

pl. du Parlement

r. de Cancéra

Porte Cailhau

To Périgueux ↗

pont de Pierre

VIEUX BORDEAUX

rue des Trois Conils

quai Richelieu

Musée des Beaux-Arts

Palais Rohan

Cathédrale St-André

cours de l'Alsace et Lorraine

rue de la Rousselle

Porte des Salinières

quai St-Croix

MÉRIADECK

rue des Ayres

rue du Hâ

rue Teulere

cours Victor Hugo

place Meynard

place Canteloup

pl. de la République

rue de Cursol

ST-MICHEL

To Cap-Ferrat ←

To Gare St-Jean ↗

VICTOIRE

Porte d'Aquitaine

cours A. Briand

pl. de la Victoire

cours de la Marne

rue des Douves

rue du Hamel

To Bayonne & Toulouse ↓

Church ✝
Information ⓘ
Post Office ✉

0   1/4 mi
0   0.25 km

HOTELS

Grand Hôtel de Bordeaux & Spa **7**

Hôtel de France **9**

Hôtel La Tour Intendance **11**

La Maison Bord'eaux **4**

L'Avant Scene **1**

RESTAURANTS

Kuzina **19**

La Cagette **16**

Le Chapon Fin **5**

Le Petit Commerce **15**

Le Pressoir d'Argent **6**

Soléna **10**

ATTRACTIONS

Basilique St-Michel **18**

CAPC Musée d'Art Contemporain **3**

Cathédral St-André **14**

Grand Théatre **8**

Marché des Capucins **20**

Musée d'Aquitaine **17**

Musée des Arts Décoratifs **12**

Musée des Beaux-Arts **13**

Musée du Vin et du Négoce **2**

affordable find. Not only are the rooms light-filled and airy, with lots of exposed stone walls and blonde wood, but the beds are comfortable, the toiletries are top class, and the service is impeccable. Doubles range from the smallish "Comfort" to the roomy "Personalisée." There are also four nifty duplexes that sleep four in an annex with huge windows and mezzanines. It's best to reserve directly by calling the hotel; they often have promotional rates that are not advertised on the website.

14–16 rue de la Vielle Tour. ✆ **05-56-44-56-56.** www.hotel-tour-indendance.com. 36 units. 115€–165€ double. 165€ family suite. **Amenities:** Concierge service; baby-sitting; dry-cleaning; free Wi-Fi.

L'Avant Scene ★★ Just across the street from the wine museum (the Musée du Vin, see p. 492) in the thick of the gentrifying Chartrons neighborhood, this atmospheric hotel was once the home of a wealthy 18th-century merchant, and the ground floor was at various times a wine broker's office and a cabaret. The current decor combines stark modernism with lots of authentic architectural details, including some that are left "as is," like the peeling paint on the mantelpiece in #4. Don't worry; the rest of the decor is impeccably contemporary, complete with high-tech furniture and stereos. Several of the rooms have balconies fitted with cafe tables that face a small but leafy interior courtyard.

36 rue Borie. ✆ **05-57-29-25-39.** www.lavantscene.fr. 9 units. 110€–160€ double. Parking 15€. **Amenities:** Free Wi-Fi.

INEXPENSIVE

Hôtel de France ★★ Right around the corner from the elegant Cours de l'Intendance, these cozy lodgings offer simple comforts and excellent service smack in the middle of town. The friendly owners keep their rooms clean and comfy, with white walls and modern bedsteads; for the most part, the quiet side street ensures peace and tranquility at night, though you may have to cope with an occasional early morning garbage truck.

7 rue Franklin. ✆ **05-56-48-24-11.** www.hotel-france-bordeaux.fr. 20 units. 79€ double, 91€ triple. **Amenities:** Free Wi-Fi.

Where to Eat

Eating is serious business in Bordeaux, where tantalizing restaurants seem to line every street. If you aren't ready for a full meal, fear not. Tapas are currently all the rage; you can even tapas-hop from bar to bar on rue du Parlement-Saint-Pierre. Keep an eye out for tearooms, too—a great option for breakfast or a quick snack. My favorite: **La Pâtisserie Essentielle** (2 place Saint Pierre, ✆ **09-81-28-83-40**), exquisite pastries and quiches by a young and highly-trained couple of pastry chefs.

EXPENSIVE

Le Chapon Fin ★★ MODERN FRENCH   Founded in 1825, this famous restaurant is known almost as much for its unusual decor as for its food. Dramatic man-made rocks deck the walls of this gourmet grotto, soaring almost 7.5m (25 ft.) to a skylight that floods the interior with light. A delicate Belle-Epoque trellis offsets the restaurant's cave-like contours, creating an exotic background for the offbeat ingredients that spice up the classics on the menu. Venison can be found in a cacao crust, sweetbreads like to snuggle up to roast eggplant, and sea bass might be doused in licorice butter. Reserve well in advance for a meal to remember.

5 rue Montesquieu. ☎ **05-56-79-10-10.** www.chapon-fin.com. Main courses 34€–40€; fixed-price lunch 29€–39€; fixed-price dinner 68€–190€. Tues–Sat noon–1:30pm and 7:45–9:30pm. Closed last week of July through first 2 weeks of Aug.

Le Pressoir d'Argent ★★★ CLASSIC FRENCH/SEAFOOD   Decked out in warm colors and lush fabrics like the rest of the Grand Hôtel (see above), this renowned eatery draws the high and mighty of Bordeaux society, as well as regular lovers of terrific food. Named after its rare silver lobster press, this gastronomic palace honors seafood in all its many forms. You could start with some local caviar (yes, they raise caviar in Aquitaine), move on to a delectable sole *meunière*, or watch your lobster get the squeeze in the famous press right at your table. If you are not a seafood fan, there are usually veal and lamb options. Reservations are a must here.

5 cours de l'Intendance. ☎ **05-57-30-43-04.** www.ghbordeaux.com. Main courses 36€–59€; fixed-price menus 90€–150€. Tues–Sat 7:30–10pm. Closed last 2 weeks of Feb, first week of Nov.

MODERATE

Le Petit Commerce ★★ TRADITIONAL FRENCH/SEAFOOD   This unassuming restaurant is so successful it had to open a second dining room across the narrow street. Fish, fish and more fish is the motto here, though a steak or veal roast can be found on the menu as well. You can do the tapas thing here, too: order up a platter of oysters, prawns, grilled sardines, or other fishy fun to share with your friends. And don't forget the wine: There are many quality bottles on the list and your waiter will help you choose. They have a great two-course lunch deal during the week for 13€.

22 rue du Parlement-Saint-Pierre. ☎ **05-56-79-76-58.** Main courses 17€–38€, fixed-price lunch 13€, tapas 7€–14€, oysters 18€–26€. Daily noon to midnight.

Soléna ★★★ MODERN FRENCH   A Bordeaux native meets a San Francisco expat and the next thing you know, a restaurant is born. Chef Aurelien Crosato helms the kitchen, Serena Lee runs the dining room, and you enjoy delicious dishes based on farm-fresh, seasonal ingredients. Mesquite-smoked local sturgeon might share the menu limelight with French venison raviolis in Madeira or today's catch, which could be dressed in coconut and kaffir lime. In order to keep things fresh, the brief menu changes frequently; there's no à la carte ordering, just a choice of fixed-price menus. This dynamic duo is getting smash reviews, so be sure to reserve.

5 rue Chauffour. ☎ **05-57-53-28-06.** www.solena-restaurant.com. 3- to 5-course fixed-price menus 39€–62€. Wed–Sat 8–9:30pm; Sun noon–2pm and 7:30–9:30pm. Closed 2 weeks in Feb and 2 weeks in Aug.

INEXPENSIVE

La Cagette ★ FRENCH   A *cagette* is a crate, usually full of fresh produce—which is the main ingredient at this low-key restaurant. High ceilings and wide windows set the tone: lots of light in both the menu and the ambiance. At lunch there is a quiche, a seasonal soup, a sandwich *du jour*, and a couple of main dishes to choose from, like a shrimp risotto with spinach, or a steak *tartare*. At dinner, you create your own combo, choosing 4, 6 or 8 small portions from a list of 20 or so delightful possibilities.

8 place du Palais. ☎ **09-80-53-84-35.** www.lacagette.com. Main courses lunch 6€–14€; fixed-price dinner 12€–22€; Sunday brunch 18€. Tues–Sat noon–3pm and 7:30–10:30pm, Sun brunch 11:30am–3:30pm. Closed first 2 weeks of Jan.

MARCHÉ DES CAPUCINS—A terrific taste OF ANOTHER BORDEAUX

Out in a working-class quarter just east of the Place de la Victoire lies Bordeaux's best and largest **covered market.** Food fans will go nuts when they see the vast selection of goodies before them: fresh vegetables, fruits, meats, fish, cheese, bread, charcuterie—not to mention all the delicious prepared foods waiting for you to pounce. You can buy dried sausage, pastries, olives, and salads to take away, or you can treat yourself to one of the dozen or so food stands that serve from their bars or seating areas. On Saturdays, there are tapas everywhere: everyone seems to be selling them, from the charcutier to the cheese guy. Other stands serve their treats on a daily basis. Crepes, couscous, and steamed mussels are all on hand, but there are two standouts. **La Maison de Pata Negra** (www.maisondupatanegra.com; ✆ 05-56-88-59-92) specializes in the famous Spanish ham but also terrific tapas (1.50€–4€, technically, pintxos, served on slices of bread) made with various smoked meat combos as well as grilled bonito, or even sautéed foie gras. The other favorite is **Chez Jean-Mi** (www.facebook.com/chez.jean.mi; ✆ 06-81-20-24-49) where if you stand too close to the bar, you'll suddenly find yourself savoring a plate of six sparkling fresh oysters with a cold glass of white wine (7€).

Place des Capucins. Tues–Fri 6am–1pm; Sat–Sun 5:30am–1:30pm. Tram B: Place de la Victoire; Tram C: Sainte Croix.

Kuzina ★★ FRENCH/CRETAN   Part of Jean-Pierre Xiradakis' gourmet empire (the chef of the famed Tupina restaurant has five, count 'em, five restaurants on this same street), this cozy cafe is a homage to the chef's Greek roots. There's a Mediterranean feel to the decor and the menu, which highlights simple, fresh fish (and a few meat) dishes, like they do it in Crete. A savory roast mackerel or generous chunk of poached hake is accompanied by a choice of flavorful vegetables, like pumpkin baked with capers. In short, it's healthy and delicious. Attention vegetarians: There's a veggie fixed-price menu—a rare find in this meat-eating region.

22 rue Porte de la Monnaie. ✆ 05-56-74-32-92. www.latupina.com. Main courses 10€–17€; fixed-price lunch 18€–27€, fixed-price dinner 21€–27€. Wed–Sat noon–2pm; Tues–Sat 7–11pm.

Exploring Bordeaux
THE HISTORIC CENTER ★★★

At first sight, the 18th-century grandeur of Bordeaux is almost overwhelming. At the very center is the supremely sophisticated "**Golden Triangle**," defined by three boulevards: Cours Georges Clemenceau, **Cours de l'Intendance,** perhaps the grandest street in the city, and Allées de Tourny. This last leads down the **Place de la Comédie,** the unofficial heart of the city, a large square that is dominated by the **Grand Théâtre,** a colonnaded masterpiece by 18th-century architect Victor Louis, who also designed the Comédie Française.

A quick walk east towards the river brings you to the splendid **Place de la Bourse,** a creation of Ange-Jacques Gabriel, King Louis XV's architect. Considered the nec plus ultra of French 18th-century architecture, the two wings of the plaza open onto the Garonne River like a giant bird. On warm days, Bordelais

Place de la Bourse, Bordeaux

(particularly the youngest ones) come here to splash through the huge 1-inch deep fountain, known as the **Miroir d'Eau** (Water Mirror) that lies between the square and the river.

Those suffering from elegance overload will be relived to find a younger, more accessible version of Bordeaux hiding just behind the grandiose plaza. A warren of small streets and pretty squares extends from **Place du Parlement** south-ish to **Place Saint Pierre, Place du Palais,** and **Place Camille-Jullien.** The farther you get from Place du Parlement, the less touristy it is, and the better the restaurants get. That amazingly turreted gateway at Place du Palais is the **Porte Caihau,** left over from the days when the city was surrounded by ramparts.

Heading back westward, you will doubtless cross **rue Saint Catherine,** which is hyped as the longest pedestrian street in Europe. Further on are the spires of the imposing **Cathedral Saint André** and its separated bell tower, the **Tour Pey-Berland.** Just behind the cathedral are two of the city's best-known museums: the **Musée des Beaux Arts** and the **Musée des Arts Decoratifs.** A little farther to the south lies the **Musée d'Aquitaine,** a regional history museum.

Grand Théâtre ★ THEATER   As soon as it was inaugurated in 1780, everybody who was anybody in the performing arts wanted to perform in this gorgeous theater. Then as now, top names in opera, classical music, and dance grace the stage here. If you don't have time for a show, you can still take a tour on Wed and Sat afternoons at 2:30, 4, and 5:30pm (3€ adults, 2€ 11 and under), or at least pop in and check out the magnificent staircase.

Place de la Comédie. ✆ **05-56-00-85-95.** www.opera-bordeaux.com. Tram B: Grand Théâtre.

Cathédrale Saint-André de Bordeaux ★★ CHURCH   This towering edifice, originally built in the early 12th century, was where Eleanor of Aquitaine celebrated her first (and ill-fated) marriage to Louis VII. While there have been additions and subtractions over the centuries (during the French Revolution it was used for storing animal feed), the main attraction is the soaring heights of the nave, with its 12th century Plantagenet Gothic arches that reach as high as 29m (95 ft). The church is also known for its stunning organ, whose sculpted wood case has been declared a historic monument. Outside, there are two beautifully sculpted portals: The North Portal, dating from 1250, shows the Judgment of

Christ, while the Royal Portal (c. 1330) details the Ascension. Next to the church is the 15th-century **Tour Pey-Berland,** the cathedral's belfry, which is separate because the vibrations from the huge bells could have damaged the cathedral if the tower had been attached. If you can handle climbing the 232 stairs, there is a terrific view from the top.

Place Pey Berland. ✆ **05-56-52-68-10.** www.cathedrale-bordeaux.fr. Free admission to the cathedral. Admission to the Tour Pey-Berland: adults 5.50€, free 17 and under. **Church hours:** Mon 2–6pm, Tues–Sat 10am–noon and 2–6pm, Sun 9:30am–noon, 2–6pm. **Tower hours:** Jun–Sept daily 10am–1:15pm and 2–6pm; Oct–May Tues–Sun 10am–12:30pm and 2–5:30pm. Tram A or B: Hôtel de Ville.

Musée d'Aquitaine ★ HISTORY MUSEUM   Any questions you had about the history of the region should be answered at this museum, which charts Aquitaine's saga from prehistory to modern times. Cro-Magnon jewelry, Gallo-Roman sculptures, model ships, and portraits of the masters of the wine trade are on display, as well as souvenirs from another, much less glorious Bordeaux business—the slave trade.

20 cours Pasteur. ✆ **05-56-01-51-00.** www.musee-aquitaine-bordeaux.fr. Free admission to the permanent collections. Tues–Sun 11am–6pm. Tram B: Musée d'Aquitaine.

Musée des Arts Décoratifs ★★ MUSEUM   Housed in the Hôtel de Lalande, a stunning mansion built in 1779, this decorative-arts museum has an excellent collection of sculptures, paintings, furniture, ceramics, and other art objects dating primarily from the 18th and 19th centuries. What makes it all hang together is the way the objects are arranged as they might have been in the good old days, including several period rooms that approximate the world of the rich aristocracy in the 18th century. Recently, the collection has been expanded to include objects from the 20th century, including Art Nouveau, Art Deco and periodic samplings of contemporary design.

39 rue Bouffard. ✆ **05-56-10-14-00.** www.bordeaux.fr. Free admission to the permanent collection. Wed–Mon 2–6pm. Tram B: Gambetta.

Musée des Beaux Arts ★★ MUSEUM   Recently renovated with improved lighting and a large dose of digital tablets, this fine arts museum has an impressive collection of works from the 16th to the 20th centuries. While paintings by Perugina, Titian, Rubens, and Veronese grace the walls, the main emphasis here is on the 19th century. Examples from that century's various movements (Romantic, Barbizon School, Impressionism, and so on), include paintings by Delacroix, Corot, Boudin, and Bordeaux local Rosa Bonheur. The collection eventually spills into the early 20th century, with works by Picasso, Braque, and Zadkine, among others.

20 cours d'Albret, Jardin du Palais-Rohan. ✆ **05-56-10-20-56.** www.musba-bordeaux.fr. Free admission to the permanent collections. Wed–Mon 11am–6pm. Tram B: Hôtel de Ville.

THE QUAYS ★★★

In the 18th century, the banks of the Garonne were just as elegant as the rest of the city, and wealthy wine merchants lived in limestone mansions on the edge of the river. However, time was not kind to the quays, which became known as a messy array of warehouses, gritty bars, and traffic jams. Fortunately, the city came to the rescue, and after a multi-year overhaul, the banks of the Garonne River have been given a superb makeover. Today, a **stroll along the quays** is Bordeaux's favorite weekend activity. You can start your walk at the vast

Esplanade des Quinconces, just north of the Place de la Bourse. Laid out in the early 1800s, this gargantuan esplanade covers 12 hectares (30 acres). Be sure to admire the huge **Monument to the Girondins.** During the French Revolution, this relatively moderate local faction tried to put the brakes on a revolution that was getting out of hand. They butted heads with the radical Montagnards, who came out on top, resulting in the mass execution of the Girondins and the beginning of the Reign of Terror.

Now stroll northwards along the river, and enjoy the new gardens, skateboard park, and playgrounds that line the **quai Louis XVIII** and the **quai des Chartrons.** At the **quai de Bacalan,** just before the new space-age **Pont Jacques-Chaban-Delmas** bridge, a few old warehouses were left intact and transformed into a giant outlet center, but one where you can both shop and relax. Among the bargains, there are spiffy cafes, restaurants and bars with terraces overlooking the water, as well as plenty of benches to plunk yourself down on.

THE CHARTRONS QUARTER ★★

Once the beating heart of the Bordeaux wine trade, where every wine broker worth a cork set up shop, today Chartrons is the hot spot for young and enterprising creative types, especially those with some money to throw around. The neighborhood's hub is the refurbished **Halle des Chartrons,** an erstwhile covered market that is now a cultural center. A block east is **rue Notre Dame,** which is lined with antiques stores and high-end boutiques. The neighborhood is also home to two good museums: on the southern end, the enormous **CAPC Musée d'Art Contemporain;** and up near the skateboard park, the small, but fascinating **Musée du Vin et du Négoce.**

CAPC Musée d'Art Contemporain ★★ CONTEMPORARY ART MUSEUM   Back in the 19th century, this vast building was a customs depot, where goods from the French colonies were held before being sold off in Northern Europe. Those crusty civil servants would probably faint at the sight of today's wacky holdings, a compendium of avant-garde art from the 1950s up until today. Stripe-y Daniel Buren pieces, enigmatic Sol Lewitt "wall drawings," John Baldessari videos, and Nan Goldin photos are just some of the mind-bending artworks on display here. If you are hungry, stop in at the museum's chic cafe, designed by design maven Andrée Putman.

7 rue Ferère. ✆ **05-56-00-81-50.** www.capc-bordeaux.fr. 5€ adults, 2.50€ students, free 17 and under. Thurs–Sun and Tues 11am–6pm, Wed 11am–8pm. Tram B: CAPC station.

Musée du Vin et du Négoce de Bordeaux ★ WINE MUSEUM   Everywhere you turn in Bordeaux, someone is talking about wine—its history, how it's made, or where you can go to drink some. Here is the place to learn the basics of all three. This small museum is set, appropriately, in the erstwhile wine cellar of a 19th century *négociant* or wine trader. Wine still is big business, and the displays show how it all works, from the fabrication of barrels to labeling bottles, through photos, films, posters, and historical documents, as well as some impressive mechanics. All of the written explanations are in French, so be sure to ask for a paper guide in English. Don't miss out on the **wine tasting** at the end of your visit.

41 rue Borie. ✆ **05-56-90-19-13.** www.mvnb.fr. With wine tasting: 7€ adults, 5€ students; without wine tasting: 5€ adults, 3.50€ students; 3.50€ children 11 and under. Mon–Sun 10am–6pm. Tram B: Chartrons.

SAINT MICHEL QUARTER ★

This neighborhood revolves around its church, the **Basilica of Saint Michel.** This lively, working-class quarter is home to Arab, Portuguese, and African immigrants, as well as a good sprinkling of the city's artists and *bobos* (bourgeois bohemians). The main draw here is the wide plaza (**Place Duburg**) surrounding the church where there is an **open-air food market** on Mondays and Saturdays (7am–2pm). The market also invades the nearby quai des Salinières. On Sunday it's a **flea market** (7am–4pm). A drink at one of the cafes on the edge of the square is a post-shopping must. At press time, the plaza was undergoing a major renovation, which should be finished by the summer of 2014.

Basilique Saint Michel ★★ CHURCH   The most stunning thing about this church is it's bell tower, which is not even attached to the building. Like the Cathedral of Saint André (see above), the vibrations of the bells and the weight of the tower were deemed too much for a church built on marshy land. At 114m (374 ft.), "la fleche" (the arrow), can be seen for miles around. The church itself is nothing to sniff at either. Built between the 14th and 16th centuries, it is lauded for its architectural harmony, its Flamboyant Gothic style, and its organ, which was recently restored. There is a fantastic view from the top of the tower (open from May to Oct), if you are up for climbing the 230 stairs to get there.

Place Canteloup et Meynard. ✆ **05-56-00-66-00.** www.bordeaux-tourisme.com. Free admission to church. Tower: 5€ adults, 3.50€ seniors and students, free 11 and under. Church open daily 3–6pm. Tower open May–Oct 10am–noon and 1–6pm. Tram C: Saint-Michel.

Organized Tours & Boat Rides

The Bordeaux Tourist Office (see above) organizes a variety of guided tours in both French and English. The most popular is the 2-hour bilingual **walking tour** of the city center, which leaves the tourist office at 10am, Thurs to Tues (9€ adults, 6€ ages 13–17, free ages 12 and under). For an extra 3€, they'll throw in a wine tasting at the classy Bar à Vins (see box "Buying Bordeaux in Bordeaux," below).

A tour boat passes under the Saint Pierre bridge on the Garonne River, Bordeaux

Not surprisingly, there are wine stores on just about every corner of the city, many staffed with knowing initiates of the mysteries of the vine. If you want to sigh over rare bottles and legendary vintages, take a spin at **Badie,** 62 allées de Tourny (www.badie.com, (© **05-56-52-23-72**), or **La Vinothèque,** 8 cours du 30-Juillet (www.vinotheque-bordeaux.com; © **05-56-52-32-05**). For a more educational approach, in July and August you can take a **2-hour class in English** at the **Ecole du Vin** (Wine School), which is housed at the Conseil Interprofessionnel du Vin de Bordeaux (**CIVB**), an industry association that represents some 10,000 Bordeaux wine producers and growers (1 cours du 30-Juillet, www.bordeaux.com, © **05-56-00-22-66**). Their English-language website is a goldmine of information; be sure to check out their "Wine 101" page for a quick overview. Finally, the CIVB is home to the **Bar à Vin,** a chic wine-tasting bar where you can sample the local wares.

They also offer several **day trips to nearby wineries.** For a complete list of tours, visit the website.

You can also get a riverside view of Bordeaux on a **boat cruise** on the Garonne. You can taste wine, eat, or just gaze at the view, depending on the cruise and your budget. The two best cruise companies are **Crosières Burdigala** (quai Richelieu, www.evolutiongaronne.fr, © **05-56-49-36-88**) which offers a 1¹/₂-hour cruise of Bordeaux for 15€, and **Bordeaux River Cruise** (quai des Chartrons, www.croisiere-bordeaux.com, © **05-56-39-27-66**) which has a 2-hour Bordeaux cruise with a winemaker and onboard tasting for 18€. Both also offer much more elaborate tours of Bordeaux and the wine country.

Shopping

For classy clothing and designer shops, go to the couture quarter around **place des Grands Hommes** and **cours de l'Intendance.** More high-end goodies, including wine and chocolates, can be found on the **Allées de Tourny.** For shopping that is easier on the budget, stroll down **rue Ste-Catherine,** which claims to be the longest pedestrian street in France. Another good budget option is the pleasant riverside **outlet shops** at the Hangars (also known as the **Quai des Marques,** quai des Chartrons, www.quaidesmarques.com).

Antiques hunters will want to head to **rue Notre-Dame** in the Chartrons quarter, which harbors the **Village Notre-Dame** (www.antiquitesbordeaux.com; © **05-56-52-66-13**), an indoor antiques market with dozens of stands.

Food hounds can find lots of yummy things at the **Marché des Capucins** (see box, above), as well as **Le Comptoir Bordelais** (1 bis rue des Piliers de Tutelle, © **05-56-79-22-61**), a terrific *epicerie fine,* or gourmet grocery. Chocoholics will feel compelled to pay their respects at **Cadiot-Badie,** (26 Allées de Tourny, www.cadiot-badie.com, © **05-56-44-24-22**), considered the best in the city.

Bordeaux Nightlife

Starting at **place du Parlement,** the tiny streets are filled with night spots and tapas bars, particularly as you approach **place St-Pierre** and **place Camille-Jullian. Place Gambetta** and **place de la Victoire** swarm with students. Night owls in Bordeaux gravitate toward **quai du Paludate,** where restaurants, bars, and discos remain open until the wee hours.

The hottest drinking spot in Bordeaux is **Le Calle Ocho,** (24 rue des Piliers de Tutelle, www.calle-ocho.eu, ✆ **05-56-48-08-68**), a red-and-black enclave of Cuban music, photographs, and mojitos. Just up the street is **Wato-Sita** (8 rue des Piliers de Tutelle, ✆ **05-56-52-61-85**), another happening bar with an Afro-Latin vibe and a bar that serves 50 different types of rums. For a more laidback night on the town, **Café Populaire** (1 rue Kléber, www.cafepop. fr, ✆ **05-56-94-39-06**) is a fun place to have a drink and mix with the natives.

For dancing, try **La Plage** (40 quai de Paludate, www.laplage-leclub.fr, ✆ **05-56-84-89-23**), with its 1970s decor and just as classic 25- to 45-year-old crowd. **La Dame de Shanghai** (Quai A. Lalande, www.damedeshanghai.com, ✆ **05-57-10-20-50**), a restaurant-bar-club in a moored boat in the Bassins a Flot, is another good bet for a late night.

Day Trip from Bordeaux
ST-EMILION ★★
40km (25 miles) E of Bordeaux

Surrounded by vineyards, the village of St-Emilion sits on a ridge overlooking the Dordogne Valley. Aside from its famous wine, the town is a treasure in itself: Ancient alleyways lined with centuries-old limestone buildings, half-timbered homes from the Renaissance era, and pleasant cobblestoned plazas draw visitors from all over the world. Sometimes too many—the town can get clogged with tourists in the summer months. Since most come for the day, the best time to visit is in the late afternoon when they are all leaving, and you can enjoy an early evening glass of red in relative peace.

Essentials
Trains from Bordeaux make the 35-minute trip to St-Emilion 10 to 15 times per day; the one-way fare is 9.20€. Trains from elsewhere in France require transfers in either Bordeaux or Libourne, a 10-minute train ride from St-Emilion. For train schedules visit www.voyages-sncf.com or call ✆ **36-35.**

The **Office de Tourisme** is on place des Créneaux (www.saint-emilion-tourisme.com; ✆ **05-57-55-28-28**).

Exploring St-Emilion
At the heart of the town is the medieval **place de l'Eglise Monolithe,** which is brimming with outdoor cafes. From here, a knot of cobbled streets and stone houses beckon with gift shops, wine-tasting rooms, and boutiques.

The **Eglise Monolithe ★★**, place de l'Eglise Monolithe (✆ **05-57-55-28-28**), was carved into the limestone side of a small hill sometime around the beginning of the 12th century. The largest underground church in Europe, it is dedicated to a saintly hermit named Emilion who frequented the neighborhood in the 8th century. To get in, you'll have to take a tour, which also gets you into the **catacombs,** the 13th-century Chapelle de la Trinité, and its underground grotto—where St-Emilion sequestered himself during the latter part of his life. The 45-minute tour costs 7.50€ for adults, 5.25€ for students, and is free for children 11 and under. English-language tours are regularly scheduled between April and October.

For a splendid view of the town and its vine-covered environs, climb the 196 steps to the top of the **bell tower** (*clocher*) of the Eglise Monolithe (see above). To get in, you'll need a key, which you pick up from the tourist office for a fee of 1.50€ per person (leave your ID as a deposit). More views can be had from the top of the **Tour du Roi** (✆ **05-57-55-28-28**), a 13th-century castle keep. Open from April through September, this moody tower offers views of the surrounding countryside—on a clear day you can see the Dordogne River. For more medieval thrills, take a stroll around the crenellated **ramparts.**

Where to Stay & Eat

Hotels are few and pricey in St-Emilion, but **Hôtel du Palais Cardinal,** place du 11 Novembre 1918 (www.palais-cardinal.com, ✆ **05-57-24-72-39**) is a solid choice, with a lovely pool and garden. Doubles start at 100€. There are a few bed-and-breakfasts in town; see the tourist office website for listings. For modern cuisine and terrific bottles, try **L'Envers du Décor,** 11 rue du Clocher (www.envers-dudecor.com; ✆ **05-57-74-48-31**; daily noon–2pm and 7–10pm; main courses 21€–23€, fixed-price menus 25.50€–35€), a popular restaurant and wine bar with a courtyard terrace.

THE WINE COUNTRY ★★

There are so many wonderful vineyards all over France that the entire country could be considered "the wine country." Still, when it comes to mystique, nothing says wine like the **Bordelais,** the most famous wine-growing region in the world. **Pomerol, St-Emilion, Margaux, St-Estèphe**—this is where you'll find the wine world's greatest stars, a sort of oenological Beverly Hills. However, not all of the wine estates are grandiose affairs with names like Mouton-Rothschild and Château d'Yquem. There are literally thousands of wineries in this region, and many are relatively approachable family affairs where if you call ahead, you can drop in for a *dégustation* (wine tasting). But there's the rub: Your hard-working vintners are not always available to show off their estate to tourists. In fact, you'll have to reserve far in advance to visit the famous châteaux (in the wine country, a château is a wine estate, not a castle, though some of them appear to be). So what's a wine lover to do?

Wine tasting in wine country

There are several ways to enjoy this beautiful region, whether you are a wine fanatic or just someone who likes wine and would like to learn (and taste) more. The five major areas of the Bordelais are the Médoc, Haute-Gironde, Entre-Deux-Mers, Grand Libournais, and Graves et Sauternes. The **Médoc** and the **Blaye** are both fairly flat, stretching out towards either side of the Gironde estuary. Both are pretty, but you don't come here to sightsee: these are some of the most high-rent vineyards in the country. **Graves et Sauternes** is more scenic, but for rolling hills, adorable villages and photo opportunities, **Entre-Deux-Mers** and the **Grand Libournais** are where it's at. The latter is home to the beautiful town of **St-Emilion** (see below), while the former harbors *bastides* (neatly ordered towns around a central square—strategic urban planning left over from the Hundred Years' War) like **Sauveterre-de-Guyenne** and **Cadillac.**

Visiting the Grand Crus

If you are a serious wine fan, you will no doubt be aching to visit the famous château. You can visit these estates, but in general, you must reserve a visit well in advance. Below are a few of the *grand crus*; for a more complete listing visit the tourist websites of the individual areas, or visit the official **Grand Crus of 1855 website:** www.crus-classes.com.

Château Lynch Bages ★ WINE ESTATE   This is one of the more user-friendly *grand crus* (most superior wines), located in a village decked with boutiques and cafes, and is right near the luxurious hotel-restaurant Château Cordeillan-Bages (www.cordeillanbages.com).

Pauillac 33250. ✆ **05-56-73-24-00.** www.lynchbages.com. Daily tours by appointment 9.30am–1pm, 2–6:30pm. 1 hr. tour and tasting 2 wines. 9€ adult; 1½-hr. tour and tasting 5 wines: 35€ adult; 2½-hr. tour including class and tastings: 75€. Tours in English on request.

Château Margaux ★ WINE ESTATE   Known as the Versailles of the Médoc, this stately Empire-style château was built in the 19th century. The visit includes a tasting, but you can't buy bottles onsite.

On D2, Margaux 33460. ✆ **05-57-88-83-83.** www.chateau-margaux.com. By appointment only, Mon–Fri. Closed Aug. Free admission. Tours in English on request.

Château Pichon-Longueville ★ WINE ESTATE   This 19th-century wonder includes turrets and a reflecting pool.

Pauillac 33250. ✆ **05-56-73-17-17.** www.pichonlongueville.com. 10€ with tasting. Daily 9am–12:30pm, 2–6:30pm, by appointment only. Tours in English on request.

Visiting Smaller Estates

As noted above, there are thousands of wine estates in the Bordelais, and the smaller, less-hyped wineries are becoming increasingly visitor-friendly. Some have joined up with labels or listings publications. One of the most comprehensive is a booklet entitled "**Itineraires Dans Les Bordeaux,**" which also has a terrific website (where you can download the booklet): www.itineraires-vignobles.fr. They have a huge list of wine estates, including many smaller operations where you can actually drop in (though even they prefer that you call ahead to let them know you are coming). The listings include hours, websites, if they speak English,

---

Bed & Breakfasting in Wine Country

While you can easily fit your wine country excursion into a day trip from Bordeaux, you could also use it as an excuse to get away from it all. There aren't a lot of hotels to choose from, but there are loads of adorable *gîtes* (vacation cottages) and bed-and-breakfasts. Even more intriguing, **many wine producers have onsite bed-and-breakfasts,** and offer their overnight guests tours and tastings. Your best bet is to visit the **Gîtes de France** website: www.gites-de-france.com. This vast network has been around for decades and has very strict standards about cleanliness and comfort. If you want to stay at a vineyard, just search for "Oenology" under the "themed stays" heading on the site's English version. If you can surf in French, go to the **Gîtes de France Gironde** site (www.gites-de-france-gironde, look under "vacances à thèmes), which will give you plenty of options in the Bordeaux region. Aside from vineyards, both sites list restored dovecotes, ancient outbuildings, and country castles, as well as humbler farms and homes. Rates for a double with breakfast run 50€–120€ per night, depending on comfort levels. Many bed-and-breakfasts offer a *table d'hôte*, a dinner with other guests for 20€–30€.

whether or not you need to reserve—in short, everything you need to know to plan your own wine trip.

Another good strategy is to contact the area's wine association (see box above).

Going on a Wine Tour

If you'd like to know more about wine, but are not sure where to begin, or are strapped for time and not up for adventure, an organized tour is a good option.

Bordeaux Tourist Office Tours ★ TOURS   Led by guides with ample wine expertise, these tours start with half-day outings including a tasting or two at a top-grade château and perhaps a short walking tour of St-Emilion (70€-85€ per person, reductions for children) and move on to more elaborate full-day tours (120€-160€ per person), which might include a tour of Château d'Yquem and lunch at a Michelin-starred restaurant. For a complete list, click on "departing from Bordeaux" under the Wine Tours heading on the website.

12 cours du 30-Juillet, Bordeaux. ✆ **05-56-00-66-00.** www.bordeaux-tourisme.com.

Bordeaux Wine Trip ★ APP   For do-it-yourselfers who could use a little help, this free application (Android and iOS) helps you navigate the wine country, with maps and listings for wineries, restaurants, accommodations, and so on.

www.bordeauxwinetrip.com

Bordovino ★ TOURS   Specializing in wine tours, this well-established company works to open up the sometimes intimidating Bordeaux wine world to non-expert wine fans. A wide variety of tour configurations range from a day-long "wine and bike" tour of St-Emilion and two château (145€ per person), to a 3-day/2-night tour of wine estates with a side trip to Arcachon, a seaside resort on the Atlantic, to taste fresh oysters with white wine (from 475€ per person).

3 rue Enghien, Bordeaux. ✆ **05-57-30-04-27.** www.bordovino.com.

THE DORDOGNE ★★★

It's hard not to wax ecstatic about this beautiful region. Writer Henry Miller went so far as to say that the Dordogne "gives me hope for the future of the race, for the future of the earth itself." From the time of the Cro-Magnons, humans have been setting up camp in this gorgeous valley, where the river loops around soft limestone cliffs, where troglodyte dwellings still exist, and prehistoric cave-paintings abound. Today, humans come here to visit the castles that loom over the cliffs, to paddle down the river in canoes, to enjoy the delightful villages carved into the limestone, and to admire the magnificent cave paintings in places like **Lascaux** and **Font de Gaume.**

About 2 hours east of Bordeaux by *autoroute* (express highway), the most delightful part of the valley starts somewhere around the tiny village of Saint Cyprien and ends near Souillac. If you are coming from other parts of France, the principal gateways to the area are the pretty, but sleepy towns of Bergerac, Brive-la-Gaillarde, and Périgueux. Of the three, Périgueux is the most interesting (see below). The low-cost airlines Ryanair, Flybe, Twinjet, and Transavia fly into Bergerac airport; another handful of low-cost airlines fly to Brive-la-Gaillarde. Périgueux can be reached by train from Paris, Bordeaux, and Limoges. Centrally located, Sarlat-la-Canéda is a logical base for visiting the area, but it gets quite crowded; in fact, you can make any of the villages your base, as the distances between sites are relatively short, if you've got wheels.

Be advised that during high season this area is very popular with European tourists. Between mid-July and mid-August, the narrow road that follows the river can get jammed; on the other hand, the period between October and April is so slow that most hotels and restaurants close. ***Note:*** Many hotels in the area have restaurants and offer half-board (that is, breakfast and dinner); this can be a good option in small villages where restaurants are few and far between.

For extra help in planning your trip, visit the **Comité Départemental du Tourisme de la Dordogne (Dordogne Regional Tourist Office),** 25 rue Wilson, Périgueux (www.dordogne-perigord-tourisme.fr, © **05-53-35-50-24**). Local tourist offices are listed throughout this section.

Périgueux ★

485km (301 miles) SW of Paris; 85km (53 miles) SE of Angoulême; 130km (81 miles) NE of Bordeaux; 101km (63 miles) SW of Limoges

Capital of the Dordogne *département* (or sub-region), Périgueux is known for its food (foie gras and truffles reign supreme here), its medieval and Renaissance architecture, and its Gallo-Roman ruins. Though pretty and historic, Périgueux (pop. 31,300) is a quiet place and probably won't hold your interest for more than a day. It makes a pleasant jumping-off point for your trip through the Dordogne if you are arriving by train.

ESSENTIALS

ARRIVING   At least a dozen **trains** per day arrive from Paris from either Montparnasse or Gare d'Austerlitz (trip time: 4½–5½ hr.; 75€–105€ one-way), another dozen direct trains from Bordeaux (trip time: 1½ hr.; 21.90€ one-way), and about 1 train per hour from Limoges (trip time: 1¼ hr.; 17.20€ one-way). For train information, visit www.voyages-sncf.com or call © **36-35.** If you're **driving** from Paris, take A10 to Orléans, the A20 to Limoges, and pick up the N21 to Périgueux.

VISITOR INFORMATION   The **Office du Tourisme** is at 26 place Francheville (www.tourisme-perigueux.fr; © **05-53-53-10-63**).

WHERE TO STAY

Château des Reynats ★★★   If you've ever dreamed of staying in a turreted castle in the French countryside, here's your chance. Built by a wealthy 19th-century notary, these splendid lodgings include 13 rooms in the main château with a classic decor, and another 37 more modern ones in the adjacent Orangerie. Many come for the restaurant, which has a Michelin star and fabulous food. The château is 6.5km (4 miles) outside of Périgueux.

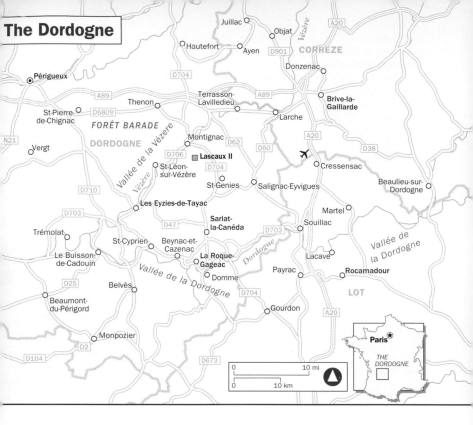

15 Avenue des Reynats, Chancelade 24650. ☏ **05-53-03-53-59.** www.chateau-hotel-perigord.com. 50 units. 95€–121€ doubles in the Orangerie; 137€–225€ doubles in the chateau; 208€–295€ suites. **Amenities:** Restaurant, bistro, free Wi-Fi.

Hôtel des Barris ★★   Located on the east bank of the Isle River, right across the bridge from the Puy St-Front quarter, most of the rooms in this humble hotel have a terrific view of the cathedral. Rooms are clean and tidy, with dark 1930s-style wood furniture, light colors on the walls, and big windows. Even if you don't get a room with a view, you can enjoy the riverside terrace, where you can sip a drink from the hotel's bar. The hotel's restaurant, La Cantina, serves good pizzas and local dishes in the evenings.

2 rue Pierre Magne, Périgueux. ☏ **05-53-53-04-05.** www.hoteldesbarris.com. 14 units. 53€–55€ doubles, 60€–62€ triples, 74€–76€ quad, 80€–82€ quint. **Amenities:** Bar, restaurant, free Wi-Fi.

WHERE TO EAT

Eating is a major occupation in Périgueux, which is known for gourmet goodies like smooth, melt-in-your-mouth foie gras. Stores that sell this delicacy abound. One of the best is **La Maison Léon,** 9 place de la Clautre (☏ **05-53-53-29-96**). Truffles are another local specialty, and fans of this extremely expensive and delectable fungus come from far and wide, especially during the **Truffle Festival** (Fête de la Truffe) in mid-December.

Au Bien Bon ★★ TRADITIONAL FRENCH   The name means "at the place that is really good" and this homey restaurant doesn't disappoint. Hearty portions of *magret de canard* (duck breast in wine sauce), *andouillette* sausage, duck *confit*, and other delicious regional specialties are on the menu here, which changes according to what's good at the market that day. Wash it all down with a glass of Bordeaux and you've had a true southwestern experience.

15 rue des Places, Périgueux. © **05-53-09-69-91.** Main courses 10€–14€, fixed-price lunch 11€–15€, fixed-price dinner 23€. Sept–June Tues–Fri noon–1:30pm, Fri–Sat noon–1:30pm and 7:30–9:30pm; July–Aug Tues–Sat noon–1:30pm and 7:30–9:30pm. Closed first 2 weeks of Nov.

Le Clos Saint Front ★★ MODERN FRENCH   A local institution, this gourmet gathering spot is known for its innovative, and even tropical takes on French cuisine, like lobster and shrimp in banana leaves, or beef sliced and grilled before your very eyes, served with exotic condiments. It has a lovely garden for summer months, but this is a year-round destination.

5-7 rue de la Vertu, Perigueux. © **05-53-46-78-58.** www.leclossaintfront.com. Main courses 21.50€; fixed-price menus 30€–65€. Tues–Sat noon–1:45pm and 7:15–9:45pm, Sun noon–1:45pm.

EXPLORING PÉRIGUEUX

The first thing you see when you approach the river is the neo-Byzantine cupolas of the imposing **Cathédral St-Front ★** (see below). Radiating up and away from the cathedral is a warren of incredibly narrow medieval streets known as the **Puy St-Front ★★** quarter. Give yourself some time to amble around and admire the medieval and Renaissance facades of the buildings here. Then continue up the hill to the lovely **place de Coderc ★**, once a literal pigsty, and later the administrative center of the medieval town. Today there is a **covered market** here (open every day 8am to 1pm, on Wed and Sat it spills out onto nearby by streets) and the square has outdoor cafes and food stores. Two other pretty squares to explore are **place St-Louis ★**, with its turreted 16th-century **Maison Tenant,** and shady **place St-Silan.**

Périgueux was once an important Gallo-Roman city complete with temples, arenas, and forums, and there are still some impressive ruins to be seen in the **Cité** quarter. The most visible is the **Tour de Vésone ★**, the last remains of temple dedicated to the goddess Vesunna, which stands in a public garden. In 1959, the vestiges of a large 1st-century Gallo-Roman villa were discovered next to the temple, and in 2003, a sleek new museum was opened, **Musée Gallo-Romain Vesunna ★★** (see below). Nearby is the **Jardin des Arènes,** a public garden that holds a few remains of an amphitheater that held as many as 22,000 spectators back in the 2nd century.

Cathédrale St-Front ★ CATHEDRAL   This 12th-century cathedral is one of the rare Byzantine-style churches to be found in France. Left in ruins after the Wars of Religion, it was restored with more than a few 19th-century flourishes by Paul Abadie, who, thus inspired, went on to design the Sacre-Coeur in Paris. With its five white domes and colonnaded turrets, St-Front evokes Constantinople. The cloisters, which date from the 9th century, are being restored and should be open to the public by early 2014.

Place de la Clautre. © **05-53-53-23-62.** www.amiscathedralesaintfront.fr. Free admission. Daily 8am–7pm (closes at 6pm in winter).

Musée Gallo-Romain Vesunna ★★ MUSEUM   This sleek museum displays the ruins of a massive Roman villa, which are protected under a mostly glass shell designed by the renowned architect Jean Nouvel. The shell is positioned directly above excavations, creating a vast 3,000 sq. m (32,300 sq. ft.)

Biking & Canoeing Down the Dordogne

To truly enjoy the beauty of the Dordogne Valley, you have to get out of the car. Hiking is always a possibility, and the local tourist offices are well stocked in trail maps. But you'll see a lot more if you get on a bike and head down one of the country roads and ramble across the landscape. It's easy to transport a bike on the French railways, but if you prefer, you can rent a bike when you get here (see rental options in this chapter's sections on Sarlat and Les Eyzies-de-Tayac). Away from the tourist attractions, the area is lightly populated and very rural. If you're ever in doubt about where your handlebars should lead you, know that you'll rarely go wrong if your route parallels the riverbanks of the Vézère, the Dordogne, or any of their tributaries.

Exploring the rivers by canoe or kayak is another option. Every summer, a flotilla of bathing-suited visitors can be seen paddling down the Dordogne; the Vézère gets less traffic and is also beautiful. The rivers tend to be shallow and lazy, perfect for a family outing.

For information on where to find equipment and outfitters for biking, hiking, kayaking, and canoe trips, visit the **regional tourist office** (see Visitor Information, above). Two of the best outdoor outfitters are **Canoë Loisir,** Vitrac (www.canoes-loisirs.com; ✆ **05-53-28-23-42**), and **Adventure Plein Air,** St-Léon sur Vézère, (www.canoevezere.com; ✆ **05-53-50-67-71**).

Kayaking on the Dordogne River at Beynac-et-Cazenac

space where you can walk through the ruins and see displays of artifacts found therein. Traces of frescoes in vibrant colors, similar to the paintings seen at Pompeii, still cover the lower couple of feet of what remains of the villa's walls. Artifacts give a sense of what life was like back in the day; there are tools and textiles, but also dice, marbles, and even a child's terracotta dinette. Most of the documentation is in French, so be sure to take a free audioguide in English.

Rue du 26e Régiment d'Infanterie. ✆ **05-53-53-00-92.** www.vesunna.fr. Admission 6€ adults, 4€ students and children ages 6–25, free for children 5 and under. Oct–Mar Tues–Fri 9:30am–12:30pm and 1:30–5pm, Sat–Sun 10am–12:30pm and 2:30–6pm; Apr–June and Sept Tues–Fri 9:30am–5:30pm, Sat–Sun 10am–12:30pm and 2:30–6pm; July–Aug daily 10am–7pm. Closed 1st and 2nd week of Jan.

Les Eyzies-De-Tayac ★★★

533km (330 miles) SW of Paris; 45km (28 miles) SE of Périgueux

Les Eyzies is a bustling little town that sells itself as a sort of Prehistory Central, and indeed, it is an ideal base for visiting the **prehistoric sites** in the area, a dozen or so of which are minutes away. When five 30,000-year-old skeletons were unearthed on the nearby hill of Cro-Magnon in 1868, archaeologists rejoiced—these were the earliest modern humans (that is, *homo sapiens*) found in Europe. Explorations continued and this area proved to be a bonanza in ancient sites and deposits, and most famously, **prehistoric artwork.** Several nearby caves (including **Lascaux**) are veritable Paleolithic art galleries, with beautiful paintings and engravings of animals and symbols. So far, no one has figured out why they were painted or what they mean, but one thing is certain: those Cro-Magnons had a killer sense of aesthetics.

The village itself is tiny but cute—many of its buildings are partially carved into the limestone cliff that hovers above. There is an excellent **museum of prehistory** here (see below). Les Eyzies is also a good base for exploring the lush **Vézère Valley** and its many hiking, biking, and canoeing possibilities.

ESSENTIALS

ARRIVING   There are a 8 to 10 direct **trains** from Agen and Périgueux per day. For information, visit www.voyages-sncf.com or call ✆ **36-35.** To **drive** from Périgueux, start along D710 southeast the D47 then follow the signs to Les Eyzies-de-Tayac.

VISITOR INFORMATION   The **Office de Tourisme** (www.tourisme-vezere.com; ✆ **05-53-06-97-05**) is open year-round at 19 rue de la Préhistoire (place de la Mairie). The tourist office **rents bicycles.** Prices begin at 15€ per half-day, 20€ per full day. A photo ID or 20€ cash is required as a deposit.

WHERE TO STAY & EAT

Hôtel Les Glycines ★★★   A former postal relay, this 19th-century building is now a classy, yet relaxed inn with an assortment of inviting, impeccable rooms decorated in a soothing palate of creams, taupes, and beiges. Rooms with a view cost more, but for the extra euros you'll be able to contemplate the splendid garden, pool, and Perigord landscape first thing in the morning. At press time, the hotel was upgrading, with construction of three "eco-lodges" (private bungalows with a garden view), and a spa with an indoor pool. There is also a lovely on-site restaurant; ingredients for the meals come from the kitchen garden, or *potager,* on the premises. The gourmet dinner menu features modernized classics (fixed-price menus 65€–105€; lunch is a more casual affair (fixed-price menus 17€).

Rte. de Périgueux (D47), Les Eyzies-Tayac 24620. ℭ **05-53-06-97-07.** www.les-glycines-dordogne.com. 23 units. 125€–195€ double; 250€–265€ junior suite, 260€–365€ eco-lodges. Closed mid-Nov to Dec; Jan–Mar closed Sun–Tues. **Amenities:** Restaurant; bar; babysitting; outdoor pool; spa; free Wi-Fi.

Hôtel Le Moulin de la Beune ★★

Just off the main road, this vine-covered mill (complete with waterwheel), has been transformed into a cozy and afford-able hotel. Hemp was once ground in these 17th-century buildings (for textile use); today the larger one features simple, but comfortable rooms, while the smaller one is a restaurant. Rooms facing the stream feature a view of lush green-ery and if you prop the window open, the calming sound of swooshing water. A bit of traffic noise filters through from the nearby road during high season, but all is calm after 7pm. The restaurant, Au Vieux Moulin, features gourmet regional classics, which are served with a flourish under domed silver plate covers (fixed-price menus start at 19€). There's a garden where you can sprawl in a lounge chair and listen to the brook babble.

2 rue du Moulin Bas, Les Eyzies-de-Tayac 24620. ℭ **05-53-06-94-33.** www.moulindelabeune.com. 20 units. 66€–80€ double. Closed Nov–Apr. **Amenities:** Restaurant; free Wi–Fi in common areas only.

EXPLORING THE PREHISTORIC SITES

Grotte des Combarelles ★ PREHISTORIC ENGRAVINGS

Officially discovered at the turn of the 20th century (it had been used by local farmers as a stable for years before), this 300m (980 ft.) cave on the southeast edge of town has over 600 etchings of animals and symbols, including musk oxen, horses, bison, and aurochs (prehistoric oxen) from the Magdalenian period (17,000–12,000 years ago). While the etchings are harder to see than the paintings in other caves, there are lots of them to admire. The tunnels are long and quite nar-row so claustrophobics should be prepared. Advance reservations are vital—only 60 visitors per day are admitted. The reservation system and ticket office is the same as Font-de-Gaume (see below), so pick up your tickets there.

2.5km (1.5 mi) from Les Eyzies. ℭ **05-53-06-86-00.** http://eyzies.monuments-nationaux.fr/en. Admission 7.50€ adults, 4.50€ 18–25, free for ages 17 and under. May 15–Sept 15 Sun–Fri 9:30am–5:30pm; Sept 16–May 14 Sun–Fri 9:30am–12:30pm and 2–5:30pm.

Grotte de Font-de-Gaume ★★★ CAVE PAINTINGS

This is the last cave with multicolored prehistoric paintings that is still open to the public. Only 80 visi-tors are allowed per day, so be sure to reserve a month or two ahead of time. There are tours all day, but only two time-slots can be reserved (3:15 and 4pm); you can buy same-day tickets for the other slots (but you'll need to line up at opening time). You will be on a 45-minute guided tour (make sure to request one in English) through a rather narrow cave (claustrophobics beware). Discovered in 1901, the paintings and etchings in the cave date from the Magdalenian period (17,000–9,000 BC). While the paintings are not as spectacular as those at Lascaux, here you are seeing the real thing, including depictions of bison, mammoths, horses, and other animals. The knowledgeable guides will point out how prehistoric artists used the shape of the caves walls to make their paintings more lifelike. If you are lucky, your guide will point out prehistoric handprints—seeing actual proof of the people who painted here creates an eerie connection to the distant past.

On D47, 1.5km (1 mile) outside Les Eyzies. ℭ **05-53-06-86-00.** http://eyzies.monuments-nationaux.fr/en. Admission 7.50€ adults, 4.50€ 18–25, free for ages 17 and under. May 15–Sept 15 Sun–Fri 9:30am–5:30pm; Sept 16–May 14 Sun–Fri 9:30am–12:30pm and 2–5:30pm.

Grotte de Rouffignac ★★ CAVE PAINTINGS   This is one of the largest cave networks in the area—the site includes 8km (5 miles) worth of tunnels. Though the paintings here are fewer than at Font-de-Gaume or Lascaux, and monochromatic, the visit is still exciting because of how you see them. A small electric train brings groups deep into the cave. The guide lights up the dark cavern with his flashlight, first on the claw scratches and beds of ancient cave bears that once lived here, and then suddenly, on a painting of two wooly mammoths. Mammoths make up the majority of the images to come, but there are also rhinoceros, horses, bison, and billy goats painted on walls and ceilings, in spots that did not lend themselves to easy access. Why did these cave painters decide to go so deep into the tunnels to paint images that few would ever see? It's just one of the many unanswered questions that make these caves so fascinating.

Since this cave is not as famous as the others, it is usually easier to get tickets, but you can't buy them in advance. In July and August, you can buy tickets for any hour of the day starting at 9am; the rest of the year you buy a morning ticket in the morning and an afternoon ticket after 2pm. The tour is in French, but an iPod audioguide in English is available for 1.50€.

18km (11 miles) from Les Eyzies, take the D47 to the D32. ☎ **05-53-05-41-71.** www.grottede rouffignac.fr. Admission 7€ adults, 4.60€ children 6–12, free ages 5 and under. Mid-Apr to June and Sept–Oct daily 10–11:30am and 2–5pm; Jul–Aug daily 9–11:30am and 2–6pm. Closed Nov to mid-Apr.

Lascaux II ★★★ CAVE PAINTINGS   A half-hour drive (19km/12 miles) northeast on the D65 from Les Eyzies will bring you to this most famous of caves, discovered by four boys looking for their dog in 1940. Unfortunately, you can't go into the actual cave, which was closed to the public to prevent it from being ruined forever. What you will see is "Lascaux II," **a precise replica** that is extremely faithful to the original.

Why can't you see the real one? When the cave opened to the public in 1948, it quickly became one of France's major attractions, drawing 125,000 visitors annually. However, the hordes of tourists caused atmospheric changes in the caves, endangering the paintings. Scientists went to work to halt the destructive fungus plaguing the paintings, known as "the green sickness," and the cave was closed to the public in 1963.

A short walk away from the real cave is the replica that you can visit. Years of painstaking artistic and scientific labor went into its creation, including the use of prehistoric painting techniques and natural colorants. While some of the magic is lost, what you see is virtually identical to the real thing. Molded in concrete to look and feel like the original stone, the 39m-long (128-ft.) tunnel faithfully reproduces the section of the cave harboring 90 percent of the famous paintings. You'll see majestic bulls, wild boars, stags, horses, and deer, the originals of which were painted by Cro-Magnon peoples 15,000 to 20,000 years ago.

If you are coming in high season, try to show up as close to opening time as possible—tickets usually sell out by 2pm. From April to October, you must purchase tickets in Montignac (the closest village) from a kiosk adjacent to tourist office, place Bertran-de-Born. Off season, you can buy tickets directly on site (remember, it's closed Mon in the off season).

2km (1¼ miles) from Montignac, off D706. ☎ **05-53-51-95-03.** www.semitour.com/lascaux-ii. Admission 9.90€ adults, 6.40€ children 5–12, free for children 4 and under. Apr–June daily 9:30am–6pm, July–Aug daily 9am–7pm; Sept–Oct daily 9:30am–noon and 2–6pm; Nov–Dec Tues–Sun 10am–noon and 2–5:30pm; mid-Feb to Mar Tues–Sun 10am–12:30pm and 2–5:30pm. Closed Jan to mid-Feb.

Musée National de la Préhistoire

★★ MUSEUM   In the shadow of the limestone cliff that hovers above the village, this museum is set in a modern limestone building next to a fortress-castle from the 16th century. One of the largest collections of prehistoric artifacts in Europe ("only" 18,000 of its 5 million objects are on display), this museum traces 400,000 years of human history, from the origins to the end of the Ice Age (around 10,000 BC). Highlights include an exquisite 15,000-year-old **etching of a bison ★** carved on a bone, showing its head licking its flank; a 40,000-year-old skeleton of a newborn; Neanderthal jewelry; and

Musée National de la Préhistoire

stone tools dating back 150,000 years. Also on display are the first replicas of the first-known human footprints, dating from around 3.6 million years ago.

1 rue du Musée, Les Eyzies 24640. ✆ **05-53-06-45-45.** www.musee-prehistoire-eyzies.fr. Admission 6€ adults, free 17 and under. July–Aug daily 9:30am–6:30pm; June and Sept Wed–Mon 9:30am–6pm; Oct–May Wed–Mon 9:30am–12:30pm and 2–5:30pm.

The Dordogne River Valley ★★★

The Dordogne River loops through some of France's most beautiful scenery. Limestone cliffs alternate with lush green landscapes; ancient villages and castles are either perched high above or literally carved into the cliffs below. You can see most of it by car, but you'll appreciate it even more if you get out and walk or climb around, or better yet, rent a canoe and get out into the river itself (see box, "Biking & Canoeing Down the Dordogne," above).

ESSENTIALS

ARRIVING   It is difficult to access this area without your own vehicle, be it a car or a bicycle. The D53 follows the river on the south bank; the D703 partially follows it on the north.

VISITOR INFORMATION   **Office de Tourisme:** www.dordogne-perigord-tourisme. fr, ✆ **05-53-35-50-24.**

WHERE TO STAY & EAT

La Belle Etoile ★★   Hovering over the banks of the Dordogne, this ancient *auberge* (country inn) offers waterside views, comfortable, spacious rooms and a superb restaurant. In fact, the chef, Régis Ongaro, runs the place. There is a distinctly relaxed ambiance here, which contrasts nicely with the buzz outside in high season. Rooms are simply decorated with gold-toned fabrics and regional antiques; for more quiet you can read a book in the atmospheric salon, which resembles an antique hunting-lodge. The restaurant, which serves elegant versions of the local cuisine (fixed-price menus start at 29€), has a reputation; reserve a couple days in advance if you are planning on eating in, or opt for half-pension (for stays of at least three nights).

On the riverfront, La Roque-Gageac, 24250. ✆ **05-53-29-51-44.** www.hotel-belle-etoile-dordogne. fr. 55€–75€ doubles; 130€ suite. Closed Nov to Apr. **Amenities:** Restaurant; free Wi-Fi.

EXPLORING THE AREA

Château de Beynac ★★ CASTLE   Remarkably intact, this 12th-century fortress peers out over the Dordogne Valley from a rocky crag that overshadows the tiny town of Beynac-et-Cazenac. The castle played an important role in the Hundred Years' War and at one point was seized by Richard the Lion-hearted. The Grosso family, who live on-site, have been renovating the monument for almost 40 years, and they've done an amazing job; the castle has served as a backdrop in several movies, including Luc Besson's *Jean d'Arc*. The view alone is worth the hike up the hill; fans of knights in shining armor will surely appreciate the visit.

Beynac-et-Cazenac 24220. ✆ **05-53-29-50-40.** 8€ adults, 4.50€ ages 12–16, 3.50€ ages 5–11. Apr–Sept daily 10am–6:30pm; Oct–Mar daily 10am–dusk.

Château de Castelnaud ★ CASTLE   Looming over the valley from the other side of the river is this magnificent castle, which is particularly well suited to the kids in your party. Originally built in the 12th century, the château played a role in the Albigensian Crusades, as well as the Hundred Years' War, making it an appropriate setting for a museum dedicated to the military campaigns of the Middle Ages. Armor, swords, and other weapons are on display inside; various war machines (catapults, trebuchets, and so on) can be found outside, as well as medieval activities like a smithy working at his forge.

Castelnaud-la-Chapelle 24250. ✆ **05-53-31-30-00.** www.castelnaud.com. 8.60€ adult, 4.30€ ages 10–17, free ages 9 and under. Feb–Mar and Oct to mid-Nov daily 10am–6pm; mid-Nov to Jan daily 2–5pm; Apr–May and Jun–Sept daily 10am–7pm; July–Aug daily 9am–8pm.

Château des Millandes ★ CASTLE   This splendid Renaissance castle once belonged to Josephine Baker. Yes, the legendary singer and dancer, most famously known for her dances wearing bananas and little else, bought the château in 1947, at the height of her fame and lived here until 1968. What is most interesting here is to learn about this amazing woman, who was so much more than a bunch of bananas. Born into abject poverty, she began dancing at 14 and eventually moved to Paris where she became a star. During World War II, she was a secret agent for the Resistance, for which she was later awarded the Legion of Honor. An active supporter of civil rights, she adopted a "Rainbow Tribe" of 12 children of all colors and creeds, who lived with her in the château. She was generous to a fault and not good with money; eventually, she went bankrupt and had to sell the castle for a pittance.

Castelnaud-la-Chapelle 24250. ✆ **05-53-59-31-21.** www.milandes.com. 9.20€ adults, 5.80€ children 5 to 16, free 4 and under. Apr–May and Oct–Nov daily 10am–6:30pm; Jun to mid-Jul and Sept daily 10am–7pm; mid-Jul to Aug daily 9:30am–7:30pm. Closed mid-Nov to Apr.

La Roque Gageac ★★ HISTORIC VILLAGE   Literally carved into the limestone cliff behind it, this extraordinary village is a delight to stroll around, as well as being a jumping-off point for a trip on a *gabarre*, a traditional flat-bottomed boat. **Gabarres Norbert** (www.gabarres.com, ✆ **05-53-29-40-44;** 9€ adults, 7€ children under 13) offers hour-long guided tours every day from April to November. The commentary is in French, but English-language audioguides are available. Due to the town's southern exposure, it has its own microclimate, making it possible to grow cactus and banana trees in the **tropical garden** (next to the church).

La Roque Gageac 24250. Tourist office ✆ **05-53-29-17-01.** www.sarlat-tourisme.com.

La Roque Gageac

Sarlat-La-Canéda ★★★

21km (13 miles) E of Les Eyzies-de-Tayac; 51km (32 miles) SW of Brive-la-Gaillarde; 67km (42 miles) SE of Périgueux

If Sarlat looks like it could be a movie set, that's because it is so picture perfect that it actually has starred in a dozen or so films, including Luc Besson's *Jean d'Arc*, and Peter Hyams' *D'Artagnan*. A pristine collection of medieval architecture and delightful squares, you can't come to the Dordogne and not at least take a quick stroll through its narrow streets. Unfortunately, you won't be alone, especially if you come in high season. Traffic can snarl as you enter the town, so try to plan your arrival for early morning, or better yet, late afternoon, when everyone is leaving.

Sarlat grew up around a Benedictine abbey back in the 8th century, but its glory days were in the 14th, when it bustled with artisans, painters, and students. Many of the buildings from that era survived, along with other jewels from the Renaissance and subsequent periods, and the town's beauty was such that it was the first to be officially preserved by French law in the 1960s. The **Old Town (Vieille Ville) ★★★**, which has been carefully restored, is as romantic and historic as ever—if anything, it's been overly cleaned up, giving it a slightly Disney-esque feel. If you ignore the tourist traps and wander off down the tiny medieval streets, you will still fall under the spell of this beautiful place.

ESSENTIALS

ARRIVING   There are 6 to 8 direct **trains** per day from Bordeaux (trip time: 2¾ hr., 27.50€). Trains from Paris (trip time: around 6 hours, 80€–120€) include a change at Libourne or Bordeaux. For train information, visit www.voyages-sncf. com or call ✆ **36-35.** To **drive** from Les Eyzies, take the D27 southwest; from Brive-la-Gaillarde take the A20 to Souillac and then the D704 to Sarlat. *Note:* You will have to park your car in one of the parking lots outside of the old town, which is a pedestrian zone.

VISITOR INFORMATION   **Office de Tourisme,** 3 rue Tourny (www.sarlat-tour-isme-com, ✆ **05-53-31-45-45**). **Bicycle rental:** Liberty Cycle, 24 rue Jean Jaurès (www.liberty-cycle.com, ✆ **07-81-24-78-79**) or Cycles Sarladais, 18 av A. Briand (www.cycles-sarladais.com, ✆ **05-53-28-51-87**).

WHERE TO STAY

La Maison des Peyrat ★★   This long one-story stone building dates back to the middle ages and at various times was used as a hospital for plague victims, a residence for nuns, and a farm. Rooms are decked out in light colors and rattan furniture, and there's a lovely lobby-salon where you can relax in front of the fireplace. Outside, nature takes over—an enormous chestnut tree shades the terrace and a wealth of greenery surrounds the building and the pool, where lounge chairs await. One more plus: if you are willing to walk down the hill (10 min.) to the center of Sarlat, you can avoid the ordeal of trying to park in town.

Le Lac de la Plane, Sarlat 24200. ☎ **05-53-59-00-32.** www.maisondespeyrat.com. 10 units. 69€–109€ double. Closed Nov 15–Apr 1. **Amenities:** Outdoor pool; free Wi-Fi.

WHERE TO EAT

Le Grand Bleu ★★   If you've taken the train to Sarlat, you can tumble out of the station and right into this Michelin-starred restaurant. The low-key decor is a decoy to an exciting menu that includes dishes like goose breast with a sauce infused with coffee and tobacco leaf, and cod with fresh foie gras and smoked salt. If you want to go all out, there's a truffle menu that will knock your socks off.

43 av. de la Gare, Sarlat 24200. ☎ **05-53-31-08-48**. www.legrandbleu.eu. Fixed-price lunch 36€–50€, fixed-price dinner 54€–70€, truffle menu 100€–125€. Tues–Wed 7:30–9pm, Thurs–Sat 12:30–1:30pm and 7:30–9pm, Sun 12:30–1:30pm. Closed in Jan.

WHERE TO STAY & EAT NEARBY

Domaine de la Rhonie ★★   Located halfway between Les Eyzies and Sarlat in a verdant country setting, this family-run establishment is half working farm, half country inn and restaurant, with a wide variety of activities on offer. This means that in addition to pretty rooms in a beautifully restored stone farmhouse, you can enjoy meals made with ingredients that come straight from the farm (half- and full-board available, fixed-price menus from 21€–36€); go on a guided hike; or sign your kids up for a nature workshop (with an English-speaking

Old Town, Sarlat

leader). There's an on-site store where you can buy the owner's foie gras, cassoulet, and other products, as well as a heated pool, a game room, and a nearby stable for the horse-inclined. This is a unique opportunity to taste the good life and meet the locals.

14km (9 miles) from Sarlat on the D47, Meyrals, 24220. ✆ **05-53-29-29-07.** www.domainede larhonie.com. 14 units. 97€–115€ doubles, 109€–127€ triple, 156€–200€ communicating family rooms. Closed Nov–Mar. **Amenities:** Restaurant; bar; concierge service; hiking trails; laundry service; outdoor pool; playground; free Wi-Fi.

EXPLORING THE TOWN

Start from **place du Peyrou ★**, which is dominated by the **Cathédral de Saint Sacerdos.** Founded in the 14th century, what you see today dates mostly from the 16th and 17th centuries. The interior is mostly late Gothic style.

Opposite the cathedral is the **Maison de la Boétie ★**, one of Sarlat's prettiest Renaissance houses. Built in 1525, this gabled delight is the birthplace of writer and humanist Etienne de la Boétie, a buddy of philosopher Michel de Montaigne.

Now wander down rue Cahuet to **rue des Consuls ★★**, a street lined with magnificent stone mansions, including **Hôtel Plamon** (at No. 8) with its Gothic windows. At the entry to **place du Marché-aux-Oies** (where there used to be a goose market) is the turreted **Hôtel de Gisson,** which has recently opened to the public; (www.manoirdegisson.com, ✆ **05-53-28-70-55,** 7€ adults, 6€ students, 3.50€ children 6 to 15, free under 6); you can visit the private apartments of the Gisson family and ogle a cabinet of curiosities in the basement.

Roam around the back streets and you'll invariably wind up back at **place de la Liberté,** in the center of town, where in the mornings there is an outdoor market on Wednesday and Saturday, and a covered market Friday to Wednesday. The square is full of outdoor cafes where you can rest and recover with a nice cool drink.

Rocamadour ★★★

530m (329 miles) SW of Paris; 51km (32 miles) SE of Sarlat-la-Canéda; 55km (34 miles) S of Brive-la-Gaillarde

Rocamadour reached the zenith of its fame and prosperity in the 13th century, when it was one of the most famous pilgrimage sites in Christendom. Countless miracles were said to have taken place there, thanks to the sacred aura of the Chapel of Notre Dame and, specifically, the statue of the Black Madonna. Pilgrims still come here (in significantly smaller numbers), but most visitors are secular tourists who come to admire this spectacular village that seems to be carved into sheer rock. It's definitely worth a detour, even if it's out of your way. The setting is one of the most unusual in Europe: Towers, churches, and

Rocamadour

oratories rise in stages up the side of a cliff on the slope of the usually dry gorge of Alzou.

Only around 600 people live in the village year-round, but in the summer that numbers skyrockets during the day, when crowds of tourists arrive. For obvious logistical reasons, vehicles are prohibited in the town and there is a lot of stair climbing to do. The faint of heart or the mobility-impaired can take an elevator from the village at the base of the cliff up to the religious sanctuary, and from the religious sanctuary to the castle (see below). It's a short walk from the parking lot to the village.

ESSENTIALS

ARRIVING   The best way to reach Rocamadour is by **car.** From Brive-la-Gaillarde, take the A20 and the D840. From Sarlat, take the D703 to the N20 and then the winding but beautiful D673.

Rocamadour and neighboring Padirac share a **train** station, **Gare de Rocamadour-Padirac,** that isn't really convenient to either—it's 4km (2½ miles) east of Rocamadour. Trains arrive about five or six times a day from Brive; you'll have to call a **taxi** (phone numbers posted at the station) to get to the village. For train information, visit www.voyages-sncf.com or call ✆ **36-35.**

VISITOR INFORMATION   There are two **tourist offices:** one in l'Hospitalet, a small village in the heights facing Rocamadour; and the other in the Cité itself, on the main street (www.rocamadour.com; ✆ **05-65-33-22-00**).

EXPLORING THE TOWN

The **site ★★★** of this gravity-defying village rises abruptly across the landscape. Its single street, lined with souvenir shops, runs along the side of a steep hill. The main event is getting from the lower town (Basse Ville) to the town's **Cité Réligieuse,** a cluster of chapels and churches halfway up the cliff. The main way of getting there is a narrow street/staircase that loops and twists its way upward, called the **Chemin de la Croix** (Stations of the Cross). This was the route medieval penitents used to make their way to the sacred chapel—the most penitent did it on their knees.

For the unrepentant, and others who are loath to negotiate the town's steep inclines, the town maintains two elevators. One goes from Basse Ville to Cité Réligieuse, midway up the rocky heights of Rocamadour. The ride costs 2€ one-way, 3€ round-trip. The other goes from Cité Réligieuse to the panoramic medieval ramparts near the hill's summit; it costs 2.50€ one-way, 4€ round-trip. A tourist train also trundles up and down at regular intervals from April to September, for 2.50€ one-way, 3.50€ round-trip.

For a superb **view,** climb or ride up to the **Château de Rocamadour,** which perches on a rock spur high above the town center. It was built in the 14th century and restored by the local bishops in the 19th century. Its interior is off-limits, but you can walk along its panoramic **ramparts ★★** (admission: 2€), which open at 8am daily year-round and stay open until dusk. *Note:* You must buy your entrance ticket at a machine; be sure to have exact change, or you will have made the trip up for nothing.

Basilique St-Sauveur ★   Set against the cliff, this small basilica was built in the Romanesque-Gothic style from the 11th to the 13th centuries. It's decorated with paintings and inscriptions recalling visits of celebrated persons, including Philippe the Handsome.

Chapelle Notre-Dame ★★ This is the "chapelle miraculeuse," the holy of holies, where St. Amadour is said to have carved out an oratory in the rock (who exactly St. Amadour was, however, is subject of debate). It shelters the venerated **Black Madonna,** a small sculpture carved out of wood that dates from the 12th century, depicting the Virgin seated with a small Jesus on her knee. Hanging from the roof is a 9th-century **bell** that was rung when a miracle occurred. Outside, above the door leading to the chapel, is an iron sword stuck in the rock that is said to be **Durandal,** the sword of Roland, the legendary 8th-century knight.

Chapelle St-Michel ★ Sheltered by an overhanging rock on the outside of this Romanesque chapel are two impressive **12th-century frescoes** representing the Annunciation and the Visitation. There are more frescoes inside, though many are damaged.

Free admission; donations appreciated. Daily 9am–11pm.

Cité Réligieuse ★★★ RELIGIOUS SITE This cluster of chapels and churches is the town's religious centerpiece, visited by both casual tourists and devoted pilgrims. Site of many conversions, with mystical connotations that date to the Middle Ages, it's accessible from the town by climbing the **Grand Escalier,** up to the **parvis des Eglises,** place St-Amadour, with its seven chapels.

WHERE TO STAY & EAT

Grand Hôtel Beau-Site ★★ This 15th-century building has atmosphere galore, starting with exposed beams and a massive stone fireplace in the lobby. Owned by the same family for generations, this venerable building was once the home of Commander Jehan de Valon, Knight of Malta. Today modern guest rooms range from classic comfort to spiffy suites with Jacuzzis; several have terrific views. Even if you don't get the view, you can enjoy looking out over Rocamadour from the terrace. Guests have access to an outdoor pool at their sister hotel, 1km (½ mile) away.

The restaurant has a view that may make you forget what you are eating, but that would be a shame, because the menu features regional specialties like duck *magret*, roast Quercy lamb, and Rocamadour, the famed goat cheese. Fixed-price menus run from 26€- 62€.

Cité Médiévale, Rocamadour 46500. ✆ **05-65-33-63-08.** www.bw-beausite.com. 37 units. 87€– 165€ double. Free parking. Closed mid-Nov to mid-Feb. **Amenities:** Restaurant; bar; outdoor pool; free Wi-Fi.

WHERE TO STAY NEARBY

Domaine de La Rhue ★★ After raising sheep for 15 years, Eric Jooris picked up his toolbox and virtually single-handedly transformed the 19th-century stables on the family property into a beautiful country inn. The beams that used to separate the horse stalls have been incorporated into the spacious lobby, and the lattice-like ceiling support is exposed on the upper floor. The rooms are spotless and fresh, with an uncluttered, elegant look. The view adds to the effect; aside from the enormous manor house out back (where Jooris' parents live), all you see is vast fields and open countryside. There are hiking trails that take you to Rocamadour, or if you are feeling lazy, you could take a hot-air balloon tour (ask when you reserve).

5km (3 miles) from Rocamadour on the D673, then N140. Rocamadour 46500. ✆ **05-65-33-71-50.** www.domainedelarhue.com. 14 units. 95€–135€ double. Studio La Forge 525€ per week. Closed Nov–Easter. **Amenities:** Outdoor pool; free Wi-Fi.

PLANNING YOUR TRIP & USEFUL PHRASES

By Tristan Rutherford and Kathryn Tomasetti

15

O f almost any destination in the world, flying into France is one of the most effortless undertakings in global travel. There are no shots to get and no particular safety precautions, and more and more French people now speak English. With your passport, airline or train ticket, and enough money, you just go. In the pages that follow, you'll find everything you need to know to plan your trip: finding the best airfare, deciding when to go, getting around the country, and much, much more.

GETTING THERE
By Plane

The two Paris airports—**Orly** (airport code: ORY) and **Charles de Gaulle** (airport code: CDG)—are about even in terms of convenience to the city's center. Orly, the older of the two, is 13km (8 miles) south of the center; Charles de Gaulle is 22km (14 miles) northeast. Air France serves Charles de Gaulle (Terminal 2E) from North America. U.S. carriers land at both airports. Flight status and transport information for both airports can be found online (www.aeroportsdeparis.fr). If you're heading to the South of France, **Nice Côte d'Azur** (airport code: NCE; www.nice.aeroport.fr) is served by direct flights from New York.

Most airlines charge their lowest fares between November and mid-March. The shoulder season (Oct and mid-Mar to mid-June) is a bit more expensive, but we think it's the ideal time to visit France.

By Train

Paris is one of Europe's busiest rail junctions, with trains departing from its seven major stations every few minutes. If you are in the U.K., Germany, Holland, Italy, or Spain, our recommendation is to travel to the country by train.

Eurostar (www.eurostar.com; ✆ 800/387-6782 in the U.S.) links London directly with Paris Gare du Nord station from as little as $66 one-way; trip time just over 2 hours. It also runs direct seasonal routes to Disneyland Paris, Avignon, and Aix-en-Provence. Better still, trips from London can be booked online to any major station in France. For the best deals, book as tickets become available exactly three months in advance (although tickets between London and Paris are available up to six months in advance). Highly recommended is train and accommodation specialist **Railbookers** (www.railbookers.com; ✆ 888/829-3040 in the U.S.). Their specialized teams can plan rail journeys throughout France.

By Bus

Paris is a major arrival and departure point for Europe's largest bus operator, **Eurolines** (www.eurolines.fr; ✆ 08-92-89-90-91). Its rather nasty bus terminal, Gallieni, is a 35-minute Métro ride from central Paris, at the terminus of line no. 3 (Métro: Gallieni). Despite the inconvenience, tickets are cheap, cheap, cheap. Standard singles to London are $29; trip time is around 7 hours.

Long-haul buses are equipped with toilets, and they stop at mealtimes for rest and refreshment. Tickets must be purchased online before you travel.

PREVIOUS PAGE: **Gare du Nord train station, Paris**

By Car

The major highways into Paris are A1 from the north (Great Britain and Benelux); A13 from Rouen, Normandy, and northwest France; A11 from Nantes and the Loire valley; and the A6 from Lyon, Provence, the Riviera, and Italy.

By Boat from England

Ferries and hydrofoils operate day and night from the English Channel ports to Normandy. The major routes include at least 12 trips a day between Dover or Folkestone and Calais or Boulogne. Ferries often drop passengers off by the rail junction of each port.

There are various operators of ferries across the channel depending on your destination. **P&O Ferries** (www.poferries.com; ✆ **0871/664-2121** in the U.K.) operate car and passenger ferries between Dover, England and Calais, France. **Brittany Ferries** (www.brittanyferries.com; ✆ **0871/244-0744**) operates ferry services from Portsmouth to Cherbourg, Caen, Le Havre or St. Malo, France; from Poole, England to Cherbourg, France; and from Plymouth, England to Roscoff, France. **DFDS Seaways** (www.dfds.co.uk; ✆ **0844/576-8836** in the U.K.) operates between Portsmouth and Le Havre. It also sails twice daily between Newhaven and Dieppe; and between Dover and Calais and Dover and Dunkirk.

SPECIAL-INTEREST TRIPS & TOURS

Academic Trips & Language Classes

The **Alliance Française,** 101 bd. Raspail, Paris 75006 (www.alliancefr.org; ✆ **01-42-84-90-00**), is a nonprofit French-language teaching organization with a network of 1,040 establishments in 136 countries. The school in Paris is open all year; three-week courses range from 100€ to 314€.

Just outside Nice, the **Institut de Francais,** 23 av. Général-Leclerc, Ville-franche-sur-Mer 06230 (www.institutdefrancais.com; ✆ **04-93-01-88-44**), offers highly acclaimed month-long French immersion courses. Each day includes 8 hours of lessons, plus breakfast and lunch taken together with professors. Prices range from 2,910€ to 3,520€.

A clearinghouse for information on French-language schools is **Lingua Service Worldwide** (www.linguaserviceworldwide.com; ✆ **800/394-5327**). Its programs are available in many cities throughout France. Cost ranges from around $200 to close to $6,000 per week, depending on the city, the school, and accommodation.

Adventure Trips

ACTIVE VACATIONS Bourgogne Escapades (www.bourgogne-escapades. com; ✆ **06-26-97-01-70**) offers a variety of activity holidays in Burgundy including walking (occasionally accompanied by donkeys), cycling, sailing, wine tours, and golf breaks. In the Beaune area, **Dilivoyage** (www.dilivoyage.com; ✆ **03-80-24-24-82**) specializes in short breaks on the themes of wine tourism, local heritage, and family fun.

BARGE CRUISES Before the advent of rail, many crops, building supplies, raw materials, and finished products were barged through France on a series of rivers, canals, and estuaries. Many of these waterways retain their old-fashioned locks and pumps, allowing shallow-draft boats easy access through idyllic countryside.

Go Barging (www.gobarging.com; ✆ 800/394-8630) operates 6-night river cruises departing from Paris along the River Seine, as well as trips through Burgundy, the Canal du Midi, Alsace-Lorraine, the Loire Valley, Gascony, Bordeaux, Champagne and Provence. Fares range from 3,360€ to 5,500€ per person (double occupancy) including all meals and drinks.

Viking River Cruises (www.vikingrivercruises.com; ✆ 800/304-9616) leads 1-week tours from Paris through Normandy, with stops in Rouen and at the D-Day beaches, through the wine country of Bordeaux and Saint-Emilion, and along the Rhône, taking in Arles and Avignon en route. For double occupancy, prices start at $1,356.

Wellness Trips

The luxury hotel **La Cueillette** (www.lacueillette.com; ✆ 03-80-20-62-80), located in Meursault, Burgundy, offers well-being stays of 3 to 5 nights which include bike rides through the vineyards and spa treatments using products from their own grape-based Fruitithérapie range.

For serious Provençal pampering just outside of Gordes, the five-star **Les Bories Hotel & Spa** (www.hotellesbories.com, ✆ 04-90-72-00-51) offers 2- to 5-day treatment programs at their on-site spa, La Maison d'Ennea. Facials, massages, and wraps use locally sourced essential oils, such as lavender and sweet orange.

There are plenty of excellent **yoga** and **meditation** retreats dotted around the country. A few popular places include **Les Passesroses** (www.passesroses. com) northeast of Bordeaux; **Dévi Yoga Retreats** (www.deviyogaretreats.com) across the South of France; **Kaliyoga/France** (www.kaliyoga.com) in Provence's Luberon; and **LuxYoga** (www.luxyoga.com) on the French Riviera.

Food & Wine Trips

The famous/infamous Georges Auguste Escoffier (1846–1935) taught the Edwardians how to eat. Today the Hôtel Ritz maintains the **Ecole Ritz Escoffier,** 15 place Vendôme, Paris 75001 (www.ritzescoffier.com; ✆ 01-43-16-30-50), with culinary, cocktail, and pastry workshops, as well as professional-level courses and lessons for kids. The school reopened in 2014 after 2 years of renovations; further details can be found online.

Established in 1895, **Le Cordon Bleu,** 8 rue Léon Delhomme, 75015 Paris (www.cordonbleu.edu; ✆ 01-53-68-22-50), is the most famous French cooking school, where Julia Child learned to perfect her *pâté brisée* and *mousse au chocolat.* The best-known courses last 10 weeks and cost 8,950€, after which you are awarded a certificate. While you could spend up to a year here and earn a prestigious diploma, many enthusiasts prefer a less intense immersion, opting for a 4-day workshop (from 940€) or a 1- to 2-hour demonstration class (from 45€).

Less formal but equally enjoyable are the cooking classes offered by **La Cuisine Paris,** 80 quai de l'Hôtel de Ville, 75004 (www.lacuisineparis.com; ✆ 01-40-51-78-18), a friendly school set up by a Franco-American team. It offers small classes by professional chefs in both French and English, including the popular French Macaron Class. Prices range from 65€ for 2 hours to 150€ for 4 hours.

At Home with Patricia Wells (www.patriciawells.com) is a Paris- and Provence-based cooking school taught by Patricia Wells, cookbook author and famed former restaurant critic for the "International Herald Tribune." The extremely popular 5-day classes are limited to either 7 students (in Paris) or 10 students (in Provence) and cost $5,500 (accommodation not included).

Les Petits Farcis (www.petitsfarcis.com), run by Cordon Bleu–trained Canadian chef Rosa Jackson, offers tours of Nice's colorful produce market, followed by daylong gourmet cooking sessions. Prices begin at 195€ per person and include a four-course lunch with wine.

In Burgundy, **L'Ecole des Vins de Bourgogne** (www.ecoledesvins-bourgogne.com; ✆ 03-80-26-35-10) in Beaune has courses ranging from 2 hours to 12 days for both novices and experts to learn about the region's wines. Or explore the market in Beaune on Wednesday or Saturday morning with American chef Marjorie Taylor and **The Cook's Atelier** (www.thecooksatelier.com; ✆ 06-84-83-16-18), before preparing and eating your lunch in her chic 16th-century kitchen. **La Cuisine de Madeleine** (www.lacuisinedemadeleine.fr; ✆ 03-80-31-72-75) in Dijon offers a wide range of short cookery courses in English including how to make mustard and pain d'épice.

Bordovino (www.bordovino.com) is a specialist in wine tourism in the Bordeaux area, offering everything from 2-hour intensive tasting classes (45€), to an all-day bike trip to St-Emilion and nearby vineyards (145€), to 2- and 3-day all-inclusive trip packages (starting from 250€ per person).

Guided Tours

BIKE TOURS   Some of the best cycling tours of France are offered by **VBT** (www.vbt.com; ✆ 800/245-3868), which offers trips in six of the most scenic parts of France. Rides range from a gentle peddle among the Loire's châteaux or skirting Burgundy's legendary vineyards, to a more challenging exploration of the D-Day beaches. Prices start at $2,495 per person, with airfare packages also available.

Cycling for Softies (www.cycling-for-softies.co.uk; ✆ 44/161-248-8282) is ideal for easygoing travelers with little cycling experience. Tours cover most of France. Prices vary according to type of tour (both self-guided and small groups are available); buffet breakfasts and gourmet dinners are included.

Fat Tire Bike Tours (http://paris.fattirebiketours.com; ✆ 01-56-58-10-54) offers a 4-hour day or night tour of Paris by bike in English; adult tickets cost 30€. It also organizes cycling tours of Versailles and Giverny.

BUS TOURS   Most larger cities in France offer hop-on, hop-off bus tours, ideal for scoping out the lay of the land. See specific chapters for details.

CHAUFFEURED TOURS   **4 Roues Sous 1 Parapluie** (www.4roues-sous-1parapluie.com; ✆ 08-00-80-06-31) offers chauffeur-driven themed rides around Paris in its colorful fleet of Citroën 2CV. Tours for three start at 10€ per person for 15 minutes and 60€ per person for a 1½-hour tour. The fewer people in the car, the more expensive the tour.

SHOPPING TOURS   Paris is a dream come true for shopaholics. **Chic Shopping Paris** (www.chicshoppingparis.com; ✆ 06-77-65-08-01) offers tours designed to give visitors a behind-the-scenes shopping experience. Themed tours include Chic and Cheap and Arts and Antiques. All of the standard tours are 4 to 4½ hours and start at 100€ per person.

GETTING AROUND

Within most major cities—including Paris, Lyon, and Marseille—public transportation is efficient, comprehensive, and cheap. In smaller towns, such as Rouen, Arles, or Antibes, it's easy to navigate the city center on foot. See each chapter for specific details.

By Plane

Air France (www.airfrance.com; ✆ **800/237-2747** in the U.S.) is the country's primary carrier, serving around 30 cities in France and 30 more destinations throughout Europe. Air travel time from Paris to almost anywhere in France is about 1 hour. **British Airways** (www.ba.com) links London with Paris, Bordeaux, Grenoble, Lyon, Marseille, Montpellier, Nantes, Strasbourg, Toulouse, and Nice. Low-cost airline **EasyJet** (www.easyjet.com) also links London with Paris, Bordeaux, Grenoble, La Rochelle, Montpellier, Nantes, Strasbourg, Toulouse, Marseille, and Nice. The budget airline offers additional internal French flights between Paris, Bordeaux, Lyon, Nantes, Toulouse, and Nice, and connects both cities to dozens of other European destinations.

By Car

The most charming châteaux and country hotels always seem to lie away from the main cities and train stations. Renting a car is a good way to travel around the French countryside, especially along the Normandy beaches, the Loire Valley, the vineyards of Bordeaux, and in rural Provence. Day car hire is inexpensive, so visitors may want to rent a vehicle just for a day en-route if they wish.

Driving schedules in Europe are largely a matter of conjecture, urgency, and how much sightseeing you do along the way. Driving time is 2½ hours from Paris to Rouen, 3½ hours to Nantes, and 7 hours to anywhere in Provence.

RENTALS   To rent a car, you'll need to present a passport, a driver's license, and a credit card. You will also have to meet the company's minimum-age requirement: 21 or above at most rental agents. The biggest agencies have pickup spots all over France, including **Budget** (www.budget.com; ✆ **800/472-3325**); **Hertz** (www.hertz.com; ✆ **800/654-3001**); and **Europcar** (www.europcar.com; ✆ **877/940-6900** in the U.S. and Canada).

Note: The best deals are always booked online, in advance. Though the rental company won't usually mind if you drive your car into, say, Germany, Switzerland, Italy, or Spain, it's often forbidden to transport your car by ferry, including across the Channel to England.

In France, **collision damage waiver (CDW)** is usually factored into the overall rate quoted, but you should always verify this before taking a car on the road. At most companies, the CDW provision won't protect you against theft, so if this is the case, ask about purchasing extra theft protection. Automatic transmission is a luxury in Europe. If you prefer it to stick-shift, you must specifically request it—and you'll pay a little extra for it.

GASOLINE   Known in France as *essence,* gas is expensive for those accustomed to North American prices, although the smaller cars common in Europe use far less gas. Depending on your car, you'll need either leaded (*avec plomb*) or unleaded (*sans plomb*).

Note: Sometimes you can drive for miles in rural France without encountering a gas station; don't let your tank get dangerously low.

DRIVING RULES   Everyone in the car, in both the front and the back seats, must wear seat belts. Children 10 and under must ride in the back seat.

In France, you drive on the right. Drivers are supposed to yield to the car on their right (*priorité a droite*), except where signs indicate otherwise, as at traffic circles. If you violate the speed limit, expect a big fine. Limits are 130kmph (80 mph) on expressways, 110kmph (68 mph) on major national highways, and 90kmph (55 mph) on country roads. In towns, don't exceed 50kmph (31 mph).

Note: It's illegal to use a cellphone while you're driving in France; you will be ticketed if you're stopped.

MAPS   While most French drivers are happy with Google Maps, traditional motorists opt for the large **Michelin maps** of the country and regions (www. viamichelin.com) on sale at all gas stations. Big travel-book stores in North America carry these maps as well. GPS navigation devices can be rented at most car-hire stations.

BREAKDOWNS/ASSISTANCE   A breakdown is called *une panne* in France. Call the police at ✆ **17** (if calling from a landline) or ✆ **112** (if calling from a mobile phone) anywhere in France to be put in touch with the nearest garage. Most local garages offer towing.

By Train

The world's fastest trains—known as *Train à Grande Vitesse,* or TGVs—link some 50 French cities, allowing you to travel from Paris to just about anywhere else in the country within hours. With 32,000km (20,000 miles) of track and 3,000 stations, **SNCF** (French National Railroads; www.voyages-sncf.com, or call ✆ **36-35** in France) is fabled for its on-time performance and comfy trains. You can travel in first or second class by day and couchette by night. Most trains have light dining facilities.

For information or reservations, go online (www.voyages-sncf.com). You can also visit any local travel agency. If you have a chip credit card and know your PIN, you can use your card to buy your ticket at the easy-to-use *billetteries* (ticket machines with an English-menu option) in every train station.

RAIL PASSES   Rail passes as well as individual rail tickets are available from **Rail Europe** (www.raileurope.com; ✆ **800/622-8600** in the U.S.). Options include a 5-day rail pass usable for a 1-month period for $322. **Eurail** (www.eurail.com) offers regional rail passes throughout Europe, including a France-and-Italy combined pass for $540, allowing 6 days of first-class travel within a 2-month period.

[Fast FACTS] FRANCE

Business Hours   Business hours in France can be erratic. Most banks are open Monday through Friday from 9:30am to 4:30pm. Many, particularly in small towns, take a long lunch break. Hours are usually posted on the door. Most museums close 1 day a week (often Tues), and they're generally closed on national holidays. Usual hours are from 9:30am to 5pm. In Paris or other big French cities, stores are open from around 10am to 6 or 7pm, with or without a lunch break (up to 2 hr.). Some shops, delis, cafes, and newsstands open at 8am and close at 8 or 9pm.

Disabled Travelers   Facilities for travelers in France, and nearly all new or modern hotels, provide disabled access. The TGVs (high-speed trains) are wheelchair accessible; older trains have compartments for wheelchair boarding. If you visit the Paris tourist office website (www.parisinfo.com) and click on "Practical Paris," the section "Practical Information for Disabled Visitors" includes links to a number of websites dedicated to travelers with disabilities. For disabled-access to Paris public transport, see www.infomobi.com.

Doctors   Doctors are listed in Pages Jaunes (Yellow Pages; www.pagesjaunes.fr) under "Médecins: Médecins généralistes." The minimum fee for a consultation is about 23€—for this rate, look for a doctor who is described as "secteur 1." The higher the "secteur," the higher the fee. **SOS Médecins** (www.sosmedecins.fr; ✆ **36-24**) can make house calls. See also "Emergencies" and "Health," later in this section.

Drinking Laws   As well as bars and restaurants, supermarkets and cafes sell alcoholic beverages. The legal drinking age is 18, but persons under that age can be served alcohol if accompanied by a parent or guardian. Drinking and driving is illegal, and incurs a heavy fine.

Drugstores   Spot French *pharmacies* by the green neon cross above the door. If your local pharmacy is closed, there should be a sign on the door indicating the nearest one open. Alternatively, **Pharmacies de Garde** (www.pharmaciesdegarde.com or www.3237.fr; ✆ **32-37**) can direct you to the nearest open pharmacy.

Electricity   Electricity in France runs on 220 volts AC (60 cycles). Adapters or transformers are needed to fit sockets, which you can buy in branches of Darty or FNAC.

Embassies & Consulates   If you have a passport, immigration, legal, or other problem, contact your consulate. Many are open Monday to Friday, approximately 10am to 5pm. However, call or check online before you visit to confirm.

Australian Embassy: 4 rue Jean-Rey, 15e (www.france.embassy.gov.au; ✆ **01-40-59-33-00;** Métro: Bir Hakeim).

Canadian Embassy: 35 av. Montaigne, 8e (www.amb-canada.fr; ✆ **01-44-43-29-00;** Métro: Franklin-D-Roosevelt or Alma-Marceau).

Irish Embassy: 4 rue Rude, 16e (www.embassyofireland.fr; ✆ **01-44-17-67-00;** Métro: Argentine).

New Zealand Embassy: 7ter rue Léonard de Vinci, 16e (www.nzembassy.com/france; ✆ **01-45-01-43-43;** Métro: Victor Hugo).

UK/British Embassy: 35 rue du Faubourg St-Honoré, 8e (http://ukinfrance.fco.gov.uk; ✆ **01-44-51-34-00;** Métro: Concorde or Madeleine).

United States Embassy: 2 av. Gabriel, 8e (http://france.usembassy.gov; ✆ **01-43-12-22-22;** Métro: Concorde).

Emergencies   In an emergency while at a hotel, contact the front desk. If the emergency involves theft, go to the police station in person. Otherwise, call ✆ **112** from a cellphone. The fire brigade can be reached at ✆ **18.** For an ambulance, call ✆ **15.** For the police, call ✆ **17.**

Etiquette & Customs   French value pleasantries and take manners seriously: Say "Bonjour, Madame/Monsieur" when entering an establishment and "Au revoir" when you depart. Always say "Pardon" when you accidentally bump into someone. With strangers, people who are older than you and professional contacts use *vous* rather than *tu* (*vous* is the polite form of the pronoun *you*).

Health   For travel abroad, non–E.U. nationals should consider buying medical travel insurance. For U.S. citizens, Medicare and Medicaid do not provide coverage for medical costs incurred abroad; check your health insurance before leaving home. U.K. nationals need a **European Health Insurance Card** (**EHIC;** www.ehic.org.uk) to receive free or reduced-cost medical care during a visit to France.

If you take regular medication, pack it in its original pharmacy containers, along with a copy of your prescription.

Holidays   Major holidays are New Year's Day (Jan 1), Easter Sunday and Monday (late Mar/Apr), Labor Day (May 1), VE Day (May 8), Ascension Thursday (40 days after Easter), Pentecost/Whit Sunday and Whit Monday (seventh Sun/Mon after Easter), Bastille Day (July 14), Assumption Day (Aug 15), All Saints' Day (Nov 1), Armistice Day (Nov 11), and Christmas Day (Dec 25).

Hospitals   Dial ✆ **15** for medical emergencies. In Paris, the **American Hospital,** 63 bd. Victor-Hugo, in the suburb of Neuilly-sur-Seine (www.american-hospital.org; ✆ **01-46-41-25-25;** Métro: Pont-de-Levallois), operates a 24-hour, bilingual emergency service. For hospitals in other major French cities, see individual chapters.

Hotlines   SOS Help is a hotline for English-speaking callers in crisis ✆ **01-46-21-46-46** (www.soshelpline.org). Open 3 to 11pm daily.

LGBT Travelers   France is one of the world's most tolerant countries toward gays and lesbians. Paris boasts a large gay population, with many clubs, restaurants, organizations, and services. For books, DVDs, and local information, visit Paris's best-stocked gay bookstore, **Les Mots à la Bouche,** 6 rue Ste-Croix-de-la-Bretonnerie, 4e (www.motsbouche. com; ✆ **01-42-78-88-30;** Métro: Hôtel-de-Ville). Both www.paris-gay.com and www.gay vox.fr have updated listings about the gay and lesbian scene.

Mail   Most post offices in France are open Monday to Friday from 8am to 5pm and every Saturday from 8am to noon. A 24-hour post office is located in Paris at 52 rue du Louvre 1e (✆ **36-31**). Allow 5 to 8 days to send or receive mail from home. Stamps are also sold in *tabacs* (tobacconists). For more information, see www.laposte.fr.

Mobile Phones   You can use your mobile phone in France, provided it is **GSM** (Global System for Mobile Communications) and triband or quad-band; just confirm with your operator before you leave.

Using your phone abroad can be expensive, so it's a good idea to get it "unlocked" before you leave. This means you can buy a French SIM card from one of the three main French providers, **Bouygues Télécom** (www.bouyguestelecom.fr), **Orange** (www.orange.fr), or **SFR** (www.sfr.fr). Or do like the locals do and use **Skype** (www.skype.com) for long-distance calls.

Money & Costs   Frommer's lists exact prices in the local currency. The currency conversions quoted above were correct at press time. However, rates fluctuate, so before departing, consult a currency exchange website such as www.oanda.com to check current rates. It's always advisable to bring a mix of cash and credit cards on vacation. Before you leave home, exchange enough petty cash to cover airport incidentals, tipping, and transportation to your hotel. Alternatively, withdraw money upon arrival at an airport ATM. In many international destinations, ATMs offer the best exchange rates. Avoid exchanging money at commercial exchange bureaus and hotels, which often have the highest transaction fees and terrible exchange rates. ATMs are widely available in France.

Newspapers   The most popular French newspapers are **"Le Monde"** (www.lemonde. fr), **"Le Figaro"** (www.lefigaro.fr), and left-leaning **"Libération"** (www.liberation.fr).

The English-language **"International Herald-Tribune"** (www.iht.com), based in Paris and published Monday to Saturday, is distributed all over France.

Passports   Citizens of the U.K., New Zealand, Australia, Canada, and the United States need a valid passport to enter France. The passport is valid for a stay of 90 days.

Police   In an emergency, call ✆ **17** or **112** from a land-line or mobile phone anywhere in France.

THE VALUE OF THE EURO VS. OTHER POPULAR CURRENCIES

Euro (€)	US$	C$	UK£	A$	NZ$
1	1.36	1.49	0.82	1.53	1.63

Safety   The most common menace, especially in large cities, is the plague of *pickpockets*. Take precautions and be vigilant at all times: Don't take more money with you than necessary, keep your passport in a concealed pouch or leave it at your hotel, and ensure that your bag is firmly closed at all times. In cafes, bars, and restaurants, it's best not to leave your bag under the table, on the back of your chair, or on an empty chair beside you. Keep it between your legs or on your lap. Never leave valuables or luggage in a car, and never travel with your car unlocked.

In general, Paris is a safe city and it is safe to use the Métro late at night, though it is always best to not drawn attention to the fact you are foreign by speaking loudly in English. Use common sense when taking public transport at night.

Although there is a significant level of discrimination against West and North African immigrants, there has been almost no harassment of African-American tourists to Paris or France itself in recent decades. However. **S.O.S. Racisme,** 51 av. de Flandre, 19e (www.sos-racisme.org; ✆ **01-40-35-36-55**), offers legal advice to victims of prejudice and will even intervene to help with the police.

Female travelers should not expect any more hassle than in other major cities, and the same precautions apply. Avoid walking alone at night and never get into an unmarked taxi. If you are approached in the street or on public transportation, it's best to avoid entering into conversation, and walk into a well-lit, populated area.

Senior Travel   Many discounts are available to men and women over 60. Senior citizens do not get a discount for traveling on public transport in Paris, but national trains have senior discounts. Check out www.voyages-sncf.com for more information. Frommers.com offers more information and resources on travel for seniors.

Smoking   Smoking is banned in all public places in France, including cafes, restaurants, and nightclubs. It's permitted on outdoor and semi-enclosed terraces.

Student Travel   Student discounts are less common in France than in other countries, simply because young people under 26 are usually offered reduced rates. Be on the lookout for the **Ticket Jeunes Week-end** when using the Métro in Paris. It can be used on a Saturday, Sunday, or bank holiday, and provides unlimited travel in zones 1 to 3 for 3.75€. SNCF also offer discounts for under-26-year-olds traveling on national trains (www.voyages-sncf.com).

Taxes   As a member of the European Union, France routinely imposes a value-added tax (VAT in English; TVA in French) on most goods. The standard VAT is 20 percent, and prices that include it are often marked TTC (*toutes taxes comprises,* "all taxes included"). If you're not an E.U. resident, you can get a VAT refund if you're spending less than 6 months in France, you purchase goods worth at least 175€ at a single shop on the same day, the goods fit into your luggage, and the shop offers *vente en détaxe* (duty-free sales or tax-free shopping). Give them your passport and ask for a *bordereau de détaxe* (export sales invoice). When you leave the country, you need to get all three pages of this invoice validated by France's Customs officials. They'll keep one sheet, and you must post the pink one back to the shop. Once the shop receives its stamped copy, it will send you a *virement* (fund transfer) using the payment method you requested. It may take several months. You can also opt to receive your VAT refund in cash at some airports for an additional fee.

Telephones   Public phones can still be found in France. All require a phone card (known as a *télécarte*), which can be purchased at post offices or *tabacs.*

The country code for France is 33. To make a local or long-distance call within France, dial the person or place's 10-digit number. If you're calling from outside of France, drop the initial 0 (zero).

Mobile numbers begin with 06 or 07. Numbers beginning with 0-800, 0-804, 0-805, and 0-809 are free in France; other numbers beginning with 8 are not. Most four-digit numbers starting with 10, 30, and 31 are free of charge.

Time France is on Central European Time, which is 1 hour ahead of Greenwich Mean Time. French daylight saving time lasts from the last Sunday in March to the last Sunday in October, when clocks are set 1 hour ahead of the standard time. France uses the 24-hour clock (so 13h is 1pm, 14h15 is 2:15pm, and so on).

Tipping By law, all bills in **cafes, bars, and restaurants** say *service compris,* which means the service charge is included. However, it is customary to leave 1€ or 2€, depending on the quality of the service; in more upscale restaurants leave 5€ to 10€. **Taxi drivers** usually expect a 5 percent to 10 percent tip, or for the fare to be rounded up to the next euro. The French tip **hairdressers** around 15 percent, and if you go to the theater, you're expected to tip the **usher** about 2€.

Toilets If you're in dire need, duck into a cafe or brasserie to use the lavatory. It's customary to make a small purchase if you do so. Paris is full of gray-colored automatic street toilets, some of which are free to use, and are washed and disinfected after each use. France still has some hole-in-the-ground squat toilets. Try not to lose your change down the pan!

Visas E.U. nationals don't need a visa to enter France. Nor do U.S., Canadian, Australian, New Zealand, or South African citizens for trips of up to 3 months. Nationals of other countries should make inquiries or look online at the nearest French embassy or consulate.

Visitor Information Before you go, your best source of information is the **French Government Tourist Office** (www.francetourism.com).

Water Drinking water is generally safe. If you ask for water in a restaurant, it'll be served bottled (for which you'll pay), unless you specifically request *une carafe d'eau or l'eau du robinet* (tap water). Your waiter may ask if you'd like your water *avec gas* (carbonated) or *sans gas* (without bubbles).

GLOSSARY OF FRENCH-LANGUAGE TERMS

A word or two of halting French will often change your hosts' dispositions in their home country. Try to learn at least a few numbers, basic greetings, and—above all—the life raft, *"Parlez-vous anglais?"* Many French speak passable English and will use it liberally if you demonstrate the basic courtesy of greeting them in their language. Go on, try our glossary, and don't be bashful. *Bonne chance!*

BASICS

English	French	Pronunciation
Yes/No	Oui/Non	**wee/nohn**
Okay	D'accord	**dah-*core***
Please	S'il vous plaît	**seel voo *play***
Thank you	Merci	**mair-*see***
You're welcome	De rien	**duh ree-*ehn***
Hello (during daylight hours)	Bonjour	**bohn-*jhoor***
Good evening	Bonsoir	**bohn-*swahr***
Goodbye	Au revoir	**o ruh-*vwahr***
What's your name?	Comment vous appellez-vous?	**ko-*mahn* voo za-pell-ay-*voo?***
My name is . . .	Je m'appelle . . .	**jhuh ma-*pell* . . .**
Happy to meet you	Enchanté(e)	**ohn-shahn-*tay***
Miss	Mademoiselle	**mad-mwa-*zel***
Mr.	Monsieur	**muh-*syuh***

English	French	Pronunciation
Mrs.	Madame	**ma-*dam***
How are you?	Comment allez-vous?	**ko-mahn tahl-ay-*voo*?**
Fine, thank you, and you?	Très bien, merci, et vous?	**tray bee-*ehn*, mair-*see*, ay voo?**
Very well, thank you	Très bien, merci	**tray bee-ehn, mair-*see***
So-so	Comme ci, comme ça	**kum-*see*, kum-*sah***
I'm sorry/excuse me	Pardon	**pahr-*dohn***
I'm so very sorry	Désolé(e)	**day-zoh-*lay***
That's all right	Il n'y a pas de quoi	**eel nee ah pah duh kwah**

GETTING AROUND/STREET SMARTS

English	French	Pronunciation
Do you speak English?	Parlez-vous anglais?	**par-lay-voo ahn-*glay*?**
I don't speak French	Je ne parle pas français	**jhuh ne parl pah frahn-*say***
I don't understand	Je ne comprends pas	**jhuh ne kohm-*prahn* pas**
Could you speak more loudly/ more slowly?	Pouvez-vous parler un peu plus fort/plus lentement?	**poo-vay-voo par-lay un puh ploo for/ploo lan-te-*ment*?**
Could you repeat that?	Répétez, s'il vous plaît?	**ray-pay-*tay*, seel voo *play***
What is it?	Qu'est-ce que c'est?	**kess kuh *say*?**
What time is it?	Qu'elle heure est-il?	**kel uhr eh-*teel*?**
What?	Quoi?	**kwah?**
How? or What did you say?	Comment?	**ko-*mahn*?**
When?	Quand?	**kahn?**
Where is . . . ?	Où est . . . ?	**ooh eh . . . ?**
Who?	Qui?	**kee?**
Why?	Pourquoi?	**poor-*kwah*?**
Here/there	ici/là	**ee-*see*/lah**
Left/right	à gauche/à droite	**a goash/a drwaht**
Straight ahead	tout droit	**too drwah**
I'm American/Canadian/British	Je suis américain(e)/canadien(e)/ anglais(e)	**jhe sweez a-may-ree-*kehn*/ can-ah-dee-*en*/ahn-glay (*glaise*)**
Fill the tank (of a car), please	Le plein, s'il vous plait	**luh plan, seel voo *play***
I'm going to . . .	Je vais à . . .	**jhe vay ah . . .**
I want to get off at . . .	Je voudrais descendre à . . .	**jhe voo-*dray* day-son-drah ah**
I'm sick	Je suis malade	**jhuh swee mal-*ahd***
airport	l'aéroport	**lair-o-*por***
bank	la banque	**lah bahnk**
bridge	pont	**pohn**
bus station	la gare routière	**lah gar roo-tee-*air***
bus stop	l'arrêt de bus	**lah-ray duh boohss**
by means of a bicycle	en vélo/par bicyclette	**ahn vay-low/par bee-see-*clet***
by means of a car	en voiture	**ahn vwa-*toor***
cashier	la caisse	**lah *kess***
cathedral	cathédral	**ka-tay-*dral***
church	église	**ay-*gleez***
dead end	une impasse	**ewn am-*pass***
driver's license	permis de conduire	**per-mee duh con-*dweer***

English	French	Pronunciation
elevator	l'ascenseur	**lah-sahn-*seuhr***
stairs	l'escalier	**les-kal-*yay***
entrance (to a building or a city)	une porte	**ewn port**
exit (from a building or a freeway)	une sortie	**ewn sor-*tee***
fortified castle or palace	château	**sha-*tow***
garden	jardin	**jhar-dehn**
gasoline	du pétrol/de l'essence	**duh pay-*trol*/de lay-*sahns***
highway to . . .	la route pour	**la root por**
hospital	l'hôpital	**low-pee-*tahl***
museum	le musée	**luh mew-*zay***
no entry	sens interdit	**sehns ahn-ter-*dee***
no smoking	défense de fumer	**day-*fahns* de fu-may**
on foot	à pied	**ah pee-*ay***
one-day pass	ticket journalier	**tee-kay jhoor-nall-ee-*ay***
one-way ticket	aller simple	**ah-*lay* sam-pluh**
police	la police	**lah po-*lees***
rented car	voiture de location	**vwa-*toor* de low-ka-see-on**
round-trip ticket	aller-retour	**ah-*lay*-re-*toor***
slow down	ralentir	**rah-lahn-*teer***
store	le magasin	**luh ma-ga-*zehn***
street	rue	**roo**
subway	le Métro	**le *may*-tro**
telephone	le téléphone	**luh tay-lay-*phone***
ticket	un billet	**uh *bee*-yay**
ticket office	vente de billets	**vahnt duh bee-*yay***
toilets	les toilettes/les WC	**lay twa-*lets*/lay vay-*say***

NECESSITIES

English	French	Pronunciation
I'd like . . .	Je voudrais . . .	**jhe voo-*dray* . . .**
a room	une chambre	**ewn *shahm*-bruh**
the key	la clé (la clef)	**la *clay***
I'd like to buy . . .	Je voudrais acheter . . .	**jhe voo-dray ahsh-tay . . .**
aspirin	des aspirines/des aspros	**deyz ahs-peer-*eens*/deyz ahs-*prohs***
condoms	des préservatifs	**day pray-ser-va-*teefs***
dictionary	un dictionnaire	**uh deek-see-oh-*nare***
dress	une robe	**ewn robe**
envelopes	des envelopes	**days ahn-veh-*lope***
gift (for someone)	un cadeau	**uh kah-*doe***
handbag	un sac	**uh sahk**
hat	un chapeau	**uh shah-*poh***
magazine	une revue	**ewn reh-*vu***
map of the city	un plan de ville	**unh plahn de *veel***
matches	des allumettes	**dayz a-loo-*met***

English	French	Pronunciation
necktie	une cravate	eun cra-*vaht*
newspaper	un journal	uh jhoor-*nahl*
phone card	une carte téléphonique	ewncart tay-lay-fone-*eek*
postcard	une carte postale	ewn carte pos-*tahl*
road map	une carte routière	ewn cart roo-tee-*air*
shirt	une chemise	ewn che-*meez*
shoes	des chaussures	day show-*suhr*
skirt	une jupe	ewn jhoop
soap	du savon	dew sah-*vohn*
socks	des chaussettes	day show-*set*
stamp	un timbre	uh *tam*-bruh
trousers	un pantalon	uh pan-tah-*lohn*
writing paper	du papier à lettres	dew pap-pee-ay a *let*-ruh
How much does it cost?	C'est combien? / Ça coûte combien?	say comb-bee-*ehn*?/sah coot comb-bee-*ehn*?
Do you take credit cards?	Est-ce que vous acceptez les cartes de credit?	es-kuh voo zaksep-*tay* lay kart duh creh-*dee*?

NUMBERS & ORDINALS

English	French	Pronunciation
zero	zéro	zare-*oh*
one	un	uh
two	deux	duh
three	trois	twah
four	quatre	*kaht*-ruh
five	cinq	sank
six	six	seess
seven	sept	set
eight	huit	wheat
nine	neuf	nuf
ten	dix	deess
eleven	onze	ohnz
twelve	douze	dooz
thirteen	treize	trehz
fourteen	quatorze	kah-*torz*
fifteen	quinze	kanz
sixteen	seize	sez
seventeen	dix-sept	deez-*set*
eighteen	dix-huit	deez-*wheat*
nineteen	dix-neuf	deez-*nuf*
twenty	vingt	vehn
twenty-one	vingt-et-un	vehnt-ay-*uh*
twenty-two	vingt-deux	vehnt-*duh*
thirty	trente	trahnt
forty	quarante	ka-*rahnt*
fifty	cinquante	sang-*kahnt*
sixty	soixante	swa-*sahnt*

English	French	Pronunciation
sixty-one	soixante-et-un	**swa-*sahnt*-et-*uh***
seventy	soixante-dix	**swa-sahnt-*deess***
seventy-one	soixante-et-onze	**swa-sahnt-et-*ohnze***
eighty	quatre-vingts	**kaht-ruh-*vehn***
eighty-one	quatre-vingt-un	**kaht-ruh-vehn-*uh***
ninety	quatre-vingt-dix	**kaht-ruh-venh-*deess***
ninety-one	quatre-vingt-onze	**kaht-ruh-venh-*ohnze***
one hundred	cent	**sahn**
one thousand	mille	**meel**
one hundred thousand	cent mille	**sahn meel**
first	premier	***preh*-mee-ay**
second	deuxième	***duhz*-zee-em**
third	troisième	***twa*-zee-em**
tenth	dixième	***dees*-ee-em**
twentieth	vingtième	***vehnt*-ee-em**
thirtieth	trentième	***trahnt*-ee-em**
one-hundredth	centième	***sant*-ee-em**

THE CALENDAR

English	French	Pronunciation
Sunday	dimanche	**dee-*mahnsh***
Monday	lundi	***luhn*-dee**
Tuesday	mardi	***mahr*-dee**
Wednesday	mercredi	***mair*-kruh-dee**
Thursday	jeudi	***jheu*-dee**
Friday	vendredi	***vawn*-druh-dee**
Saturday	samedi	***sahm*-dee**
yesterday	hier	**ee-*air***
today	aujourd'hui	**o-jhord-*dwee***
this morning/this afternoon	ce matin/cet après-midi	**suh ma-*tan*/set ah-preh-mee-*dee***
tonight	ce soir	**suh *swahr***
tomorrow	demain	**de-*man***

GLOSSARY OF BASIC MENU TERMS

Note: To order any of these items from a waiter, simply preface the French-language name with the phrase *"Je voudrais"* (jhe voo-*dray*), which means "I would like . . ." *Bon appétit!*

MEATS

English	French	Pronunciation
beef stew	du pot au feu	**dew poht o *fhe***
beef braised with red wine	du boeuf à la mode	**dew bewf ah lah *mhowd***
chicken	du poulet	**dew poo-*lay***

English	French	Pronunciation
chicken, veal, or fish rolls	des quenelles	day ke-*nelle*
chicken with mushrooms and wine	du coq au vin	dew cock o vhin
frogs' legs	des cuisses de grenouilles	day cweess duh gre-*noo*-yuh
ham	du jambon	dew jham-bohn
kidneys	des rognons	day *row*-nyon
lamb	de l'agneau	duh lahn-*nyo*
rabbit	du lapin	dew lah-pan
sirloin	de l'aloyau	duh lahl-why-*yo*
steak	du bifteck	dew beef-*tek*
pepper steak	un steak au poivre	uh stake o *pwah*-vruh
beef tenderloin	du chateaubriand	dew *sha*-tow-bree-ahn
sweetbreads	des ris de veau	day *ree* duh voh
veal	du veau	dew *voh*

FRUITS/VEGETABLES

English	French	Pronunciation
cabbage	du choux	dew *shoe*
eggplant	de l'aubergine	duh loh-ber-*jheen*
grapefruit	un pamplemousse	uh *pahm*-pluh-moose
grapes	du raisin	dew ray-*zhan*
green beans	des haricots verts	day ahr-ee-coh *vaire*
green peas	des petits pois	day puh-tee *pwah*
lemon/lime	du citron/du citron vert	dew cee-*tron*/dew cee-tron *vaire*
orange	une orange	ewn o-*rahnj*
pineapple	de l'ananas	duh lah-na-*nas*
potatoes	des pommes de terre	day puhm duh *tehr*
french fried potatoes	des pommes frites	day puhm *freet*
spinach	des épinards	dayz ay-pin-*ards*
strawberries	des fraises	day *frez*

BEVERAGES

English	French	Pronunciation
beer	de la bière	duh lah bee-*aire*
milk	du lait	dew *lay*
orange juice	du jus d'orange	dew joo d'or-*ahn*-jhe
water	de l'eau	duh lo
red wine	du vin rouge	dew vhin *rooj*
white wine	du vin blanc	dew vhin *blahn*
coffee	un café	uh ka-*fay*
coffee (black)	un café noir	uh ka-fay *nwahr*
coffee (with cream)	un café crème	uh ka-fay *krem*
coffee (with milk)	un café au lait	uh ka-fay o *lay*
coffee (decaf)	un café décaféiné (slang: un déca)	un ka-fay day-kah-fay-*nay* (uh *day*-kah)
coffee (espresso)	un café espresso (un express)	uh ka-fay e-*sprehss*-o (un ek-*sprehss*)
tea	du thé	dew *tay*

INDEX

Restaurants & Cafes

LIST OF MAPS

PHOTO CREDITS